# Sales Management:
## Analysis and Decision Making

*6th Edition*

**Thomas N. Ingram**
*Colorado State University*

**Raymond W. LaForge**
*University of Louisville*

**Ramon A. Avila**
*Ball State University*

**Charles H. Schwepker Jr.**
*Central Missouri State University*

**Michael R. Williams**
*Illinois State University*

THOMSON
™
SOUTH-WESTERN

Australia · Canada · Mexico · Singapore · Spain · United Kingdom · United States

**THOMSON**

**SOUTH-WESTERN**

TM

### Sales Management: Analysis and Decision Making, Sixth Edition
Thomas N. Ingram, Raymond W. LaForge, Ramon A. Avila, Charles H. Schwepker, Jr., Michael R. Williams

**VP/Editorial Director:**
Jack W. Calhoun

**VP/Editor-in-Chief:**
Dave Shaut

**Acquisitions Editor:**
Neil Marquardt

**Developmental Editor:**
Rebecca von Gillern

**Marketing Manager:**
Nicole Moore

**Production Editor:**
Stephanie Schempp

**Manager of Technology, Editorial:**
Vicky True

**Technology Project Editor:**
Pam Wallace

**Web Coordinator:**
Karen Schaffer

**Manufacturing Coordinator:**
Diane Lohman

**Production House:**
Stratford Publishing Services, Inc.

**Printer:**
Edwards Brothers
Ann Arbor, MI

**Art Director:**
Stacy Jenkins Shirley

**Internal Designer:**
Bethany Casey and Lou Ann Thesing

**Cover Designer:**
Bethany Casey and Lou Ann Thesing

**Cover Illustration:**
Ted Knapke

Library of Congress Control Number:
2005920275

For more information about our
products, contact us at:

Thomson Learning Academic Resource
Center

1-800-423-0563

**Thomson Higher Education**
5191 Natorp Boulevard
Mason, OH 45040
USA

**Asia (including India)**
Thomson Learning
5 Shenton Way
#01-01 UIC Building
Singapore 068808

**Australia/New Zealand**
Thomson Learning Australia
102 Dodds Street
Southbank, Victoria 3006
Australia

**Canada**
Thomson Nelson
1120 Birchmount Road
Toronto, Ontario
M1K 5G4
Canada

**Latin America**
Thomson Learning
Seneca, 53
Colonia Polanco
11560 Mexico
D.F.Mexico

**UK/Europe/Middle East/Africa**
Thomson Learning
High Holborn House
50/51 Bedford Row
London WC1R 4LR
United Kingdom

**Spain (including Portugal)**
Thomson Paraninfo
Calle Magallanes, 25
28015 Madrid, Spain

*To Jacque*
*—Thomas N. Ingram*

*To Susan, Alexandra, Kelly, and*
*in memory of my Mom and Dad*
*—Raymond W. LaForge*

*To Terry, Sarah, Anne, Ryan,*
*Laura, Kate, and my parents*
*—Ramon A. Avila*

*To Laura, Charlie III, Anthony, Lauren, my Mom,*
*and in memory of my Dad, "Big C"*
*—Charles H. Schwepker Jr.*

*To Marilyn, Aimee and Rodney, Kerri and Bart,*
*my Mom, and in memory of my Dad*
*—Michael R. Williams*

Our objective in writing the sixth edition of *Sales Management: Analysis and Decision Making* was to continue to present comprehensive and rigorous coverage of contemporary sales management in a readable, interesting, and challenging manner. Findings from recent sales management research are blended with examples of current sales management practice into an effective pedagogical format. Topics are covered from the perspective of a sales management decision maker. This decision-making perspective is accomplished through a modular format that typically consists of discussing basic concepts, identifying critical decision areas, and presenting analytical approaches for improved sales management decision making. Company examples from the contemporary business world are used throughout the text to supplement module discussion.

## STRENGTHS OF THIS EDITION

The sixth edition of *Sales Management: Analysis and Decision Making* has several important strengths. The authors teach sales management courses and interact with sales managers and sales management professors on a regular basis. These interactions with practicing professionals and students ensure that the text covers the appropriate sales management topics and employs effective pedagogy. This new edition continues what has been effective in previous editions, but contains changes that improve content and pedagogy. The key strengths of the sixth edition include:

- The 10 modules and paperback format from the previous edition are maintained. This makes it easy for professors to cover the text in a semester or quarter, and still have sufficient time to use active learning exercises throughout the course. All of the important sales management topics are addressed and students can purchase the text for much less than a typical hardcover sales management book.

- All new Opening Vignettes are used to introduce each module. These vignettes generate student interest by presenting examples of current sales management practice in leading firms.

- Revised "Sales Management in the 21st Century" boxes and new sales executives have been added in our Sales Executive Panel.

- The introduction of an important trend—the move from an administrative to an entrepreneurial perspective—has been introduced in Module 1. The turbulent environment facing most sales organizations requires that sales managers act more as entrepreneurs and less as administrators to be successful.

- New or expanded coverage of important topics such as customer relationship management (CRM); outsourcing the salesforce; and key differences among sales leadership, management, and supervisory activities can be found throughout the text.

- Role-play exercises for Ethical Dilemmas and the short cases are included at the end of each module. These role plays give professors the opportunity to involve students actively in exploring complex ethical and sales management situations.

- New or updated exercises in the Building Sales Management Skills section can now be found at the end of each module. Many of these exercises require the use of the Internet, but all involve students actively in the learning process.

v

## LEVEL AND ORGANIZATION

This text was written for the undergraduate student enrolled in a one-semester or one-quarter sales management class. However, it is sufficiently rigorous to be used at the MBA level.

A sales management model is used to present coverage in a logical sequence. The text is organized into five parts to correspond with the five stages in the sales management model.

Part One, "Describing the Personal Selling Function," is designed to provide students with an understanding of personal selling prior to addressing specific sales management areas. We devote one module at the beginning of the text to this topic.

Part Two, "Defining the Strategic Role of the Sales Function," consists of two modules; one discusses important relationships between personal selling and organizational strategies at the corporate, business, marketing, and sales levels. This module focuses on how strategic decisions at different organizational levels affect sales management decisions and personal selling practices.

The second module in this part investigates alternative sales organization structures and examines analytical methods for determining salesforce size, territory design, and the allocation of selling effort.

Part Three, "Developing the Salesforce," changes the focus from organizational topics to people topics. The two modules in this part cover the critical decision areas in the recruitment and selection of salespeople and in training salespeople once they have been hired.

Part Four, "Directing the Salesforce" continues the people orientation by discussing the leadership, management, and supervisory activities necessary for successful sales management and examining important areas of salesforce motivation and reward systems.

Part Five, "Determining Salesforce Effectiveness and Performance," concludes the sales management process by addressing evaluation and control procedures. Differences in evaluating the effectiveness of the sales organization and the performance of salespeople are highlighted and covered in separate modules.

## PEDAGOGY

The following pedagogical format is used for each module to facilitate the learning process.

**Learning Objectives.**   Specific learning objectives for the module are stated in behavioral terms so that students will know what they should be able to do after the module has been covered.

**Opening Vignettes.**   All modules are introduced by an opening vignette that typically consists of a recent, real-world company example addressing many of the key points to be discussed in the module. These opening vignettes are intended to generate student interest in the topics to be covered and to illustrate the practicality of the module coverage.

**Key Words.**   Key words are highlighted in bold type throughout each module and summarized in list form at the end of the module to alert students to their importance.

**Boxed Inserts.**   Each module contains two boxed inserts titled "Sales Management in the 21st Century." The comments in these boxes are provided by members of our Sales Executive Panel and were made specifically for our text.

**Figure Captions.**   Most figures in the text include a summarizing caption designed to make the figure understandable without reference to the module discussion.

**Module Summaries.** A module summary recaps the key points covered in the module by restating and answering questions presented in the learning objectives at the beginning of the module.

**Developing Sales Management Knowledge.** Ten discussion questions are presented at the end of each module to review key concepts covered in the module. Some of the questions require students to summarize what has been covered, while others are designed to be more thought-provoking and extend beyond module coverage.

**Building Sales Management Skills.** Application exercises are supplied for each module, requiring students to apply what has been learned in the module to a specific sales management situation. Many of the application exercises require data analysis. Many modules also have an Internet exercise to get students involved with the latest technology. Role plays are also included in most modules.

**Making Sales Management Decisions.** Each module concludes with two short cases. Most of these cases represent realistic and interesting sales management situations. Several require data analysis. Most are designed so that students can role play their solutions.

## CASES

The book contains a mixture of short, medium, and long cases. The 18 short cases at the end of modules can be used as a basis for class discussion, short written assignments, or role plays. The longer cases are more appropriate for detailed analysis and class discussions or presentations by individuals or student groups. The longer cases are located at the end of the book.

## SUPPLEMENTS

### Instructor's Resource CD (IRCD)

The Instructor's Resource CD delivers all the traditional instructor support materials in one handy place: a CD. Electronic files are included on the CD for the complete Instructor's Manual, Test Bank, computerized Test Bank and computerized Test Bank software (ExamView), and chapter-by-chapter PowerPoint presentation files that can be used to enhance in-class lectures.

- **Instructor's Manual**
  The Instructor's Manual for the sixth edition of *Sales Management: Analysis and Decision Making* contains many helpful teaching suggestions and solutions to text exercises to help instructors successfully integrate all the materials offered with this text into their class. Each module includes the following materials designed to meet the instructor's needs.

  - Learning objectives
  - Module outline and summary
  - Ideas for student involvement
  - Possible answers to review sections in the text, Developing Sales Management Knowledge and Building Sales Management Skills
  - Ideas for how to incorporate the role play exercises found in the text into the classroom setting, as well as suggestions for conducting the Role Plays

  The Instructor's Manual files are located on the IRCD in Microsoft Word 2000 format.

- **Test Bank**
  The revised and updated Test Bank includes a variety of multiple choice and true/false questions, which emphasize the important concepts presented in each

chapter. The Test Bank questions vary in levels of difficulty so that each instructor can tailor his/her testing to meet his/her specific needs. The Test Bank files are located on the IRCD in Microsoft Word 2000 format.

- **ExamView (Computerized) Test Bank**
  The Test Bank is also available on the IRCD in computerized format (ExamView), allowing instructors to select problems at random by level of difficulty or type, customize or add test questions, and scramble questions to create up to 99 versions of the same test. This software is available in DOS, Mac, or Windows formats.

- **PowerPoint Presentation Slides**
  Created by an expert in the field of sales, Scott Inks of Ball State University, this package brings classroom lectures and discussions to life with the Microsoft PowerPoint 2000 presentation tool. Extremely professor-friendly and organized by chapter, these chapter-by-chapter presentations outline chapter content. The eye-appealing and easy-to-read slides are, in this new edition, tailored specifically to the *Sales Management* text from the Ingram author team. The PowerPoint presentation slides are available on the IRCD in Microsoft 2000 format and as downloadable files on the text support site (http://ingram-sales.swlearning.com).

## Web site

Visit the text web site at http://ingram-sales.swlearning.com to find instructor's support materials as well as study resources that will help students practice and apply the concepts they have learned in class.

- **Student Resources**
  - Online quizzes for each chapter are available on the web site for those students who would like additional study materials. After each quiz is submitted, automatic feedback tells the students how they scored and what the correct answers are to the questions they missed. Students are then able to email their results directly to the their instructor if desired.
  - Crossword quizzing of glossary terms and definitions arranged by chapter is also available for extra review of key terms found in the text.
  - Students can download the PowerPoint presentation slides from the web site.

- **Instructor Resources**
  - Downloadable Instructor's Manual files are available in Microsoft Word 2000 format and Adobe Acrobat format.
  - Downloadable PowerPoint presentation files are available in Microsoft PowerPoint 2000 format.

## Brand-New Videos!

A brand-new video package has been professionally filmed and produced specifically for this text. The authors and a team of experienced selling educators have developed a series of videos illustrating the concepts and skills of professional selling and management aspects of professional selling including coaching, sales training, motivation, and evaluating performance. Each video has been carefully developed to *accurately* and *effectively* demonstrate and teach specific concepts. Experienced actors provide clear examples and an off-camera spokesperson provides narrative explanation and reinforcement and asks a variety of teaching-related questions for students to consider and answer.

## ACKNOWLEDGMENTS

The writing of a book is a long and arduous task that requires the dedicated efforts of many individuals. The contributions of these individuals are greatly appreciated and deserve specific recognition. We are especially grateful to those who provided valuable insight and to the following reviewers who provided useful suggestions for revising the fifth edition of this text.

Anne L. Balazs, Ph.D., *Mississippi University for Women*

Duane Davis, *University of Central Florida*

Mark Johlke, *University of North Carolina—Wilmington*

Michael J. Swenson, *Brigham Young University*

Scott A. Inks, *Ball State University*

We sincerely appreciate the willingness of many individuals to allow us to include their cases in the book. These cases have substantially enhanced the effectiveness and interest of the text.

A great deal of credit for this book should go to all of the wonderful people at South-Western. Their expertise, support, and constant encouragement turned an extremely difficult task into a very enjoyable one. We would like to recognize specifically the tremendous efforts of the following professionals and friends: Neil Marquardt, Nicole Moore, Rebecca von Gillern, and Stephanie Schempp. Without their efforts this edition would not have seen the light of day. However, we also want to thank the many individuals with whom we did not have direct contact but who assisted in the development and production of this book.

We are also very appreciative of the support provided by our colleagues at Colorado State University, the University of Louisville, Central Missouri State University, Ball State University, and Illinois State University.

Thomas A. Ingram
Raymond W. LaForge
Ramon A. Avila
Charles H. Schwepker Jr.
Michael R. Williams

March 2005

**Thomas N. Ingram** (Ph.D., Georgia State University) is professor of marketing at Colorado State University. Before commencing his academic career, he worked in sales, product management, and sales management with Exxon and Mobil. Tom is a recipient of the Marketing Educator of the Year award given by Sales and Marketing Executives International (SMEI). He was honored as the first recipient of the Mu Kappa Tau National Marketing Honor Society recognition award for Outstanding Scholarly Contributions to the Sales Discipline. On several occasions, he has been recognized at the university and college level for outstanding teaching. Tom has served as the editor of *Journal of Personal Selling & Sales Management*, chair of the SMEI Accreditation Institute, and as a member of the Board of Directors of SMEI. He is the former editor of *Journal of Marketing Theory & Practice*. Tom's primary research is in personal selling and sales management. His work has appeared in the *Journal of Marketing*, *Journal of Marketing Research*, *Journal of Personal Selling & Sales Management*, and *Journal of the Academy of Marketing Science*, among others. He is the co-author of one of the "Ten Most Influential Articles of the 20th Century" as designated by the Sales and Sales Management Special Interest Group of the American Marketing Association.

**Raymond W. (Buddy) LaForge** is the Brown-Forman Professor of Marketing at the University of Louisville. He is the founding executive editor of the *Marketing Education Review*, founding executive editor of the Sales Educator Network, has served as associate editor, Sales Education and Training section of the *Journal of Personal Selling & Sales Management*, has co-authored *Marketing: Principles & Perspectives*, *Sales Management: Analysis and Decision Making*, *Professional Selling: A Trust-Based Approach*, *The Professional Selling Skills Workbook*, and co-edited *Emerging Trends in Sales Thought and Practice*. His research is published in many journals including the *Journal of Marketing*, *Journal of Marketing Research*, *Decision Sciences*, *Journal of the Academy of Marketing Science*, and *Journal of Personal Selling & Sales Management*. Buddy has served as vice president/marketing for the Academy of Business Education, vice president of marketing, teaching, and conferences for the American Marketing Association Academic Council, chair of the American Marketing Association Sales Interest Group, and on the Direct Selling Education Foundation Board of Directors and Academic Program Committee, DuPont Corporate Marketing Faculty Advisory Team for the Sales Enhancement Process, Family Business Center Advisory board, and Strategic Planning Committee for the National Conference on Sales Management. He currently serves as vice chair for awards and recognition for the AMA Sales SIG and administers the AMA Sales SIG/DSEF Sales Dissertation Grants.

**Charles H. Schwepker Jr.** (Ph.D., University of Memphis) is professor of marketing at Central Missouri State University. He has experience in wholesale and retail sales. His primary research interests are in sales management, personal selling, and marketing ethics. His articles have appeared in the *Journal of the Academy of Marketing Science*, *Journal of Business Research*, *Journal of Public Policy and Marketing*, *Journal of Personal Selling & Sales Management*, and *Journal of Business Ethics*, among other journals, various national and regional proceedings, and books including *Marketing Communications Classics* and *Environmental Marketing*. He has received both teaching and research awards. He is on the editorial review boards of the *Journal of Personal Selling & Sales Management*, *Journal of Marketing Theory & Practice*, *Journal of Business & Industrial Marketing*, *Journal of Relationship Marketing*, and *Southern Business Review*, and has won awards for outstanding reviewer. He is a co-author of *Professional Selling: A Trust-Based Approach.*

**Ramon A. Avila** (Ph.D., Virginia Tech University) is the George and Frances Ball Distinguished Professor of Marketing at Ball State University. Before coming to Ball State, he worked in sales with the Burroughs Corporation. He has held two visiting professorships at the University of Hawaii and another at the Kelley School of Business at Indiana University. In April 2002, Ramon received a Leavey Award. This award was given for innovation in the classroom with his advanced selling class. Ramon was presented the 1999 Mu Kappa Tau's Outstanding Contributor to the Sales Profession. He is only the third recipient of this award. Ramon has also received the University's Outstanding Service award, the University's Outstanding Junior Faculty award, the College of Business Professor of the Year, and the Dean's Teaching award every year since its inception in 1987. Ramon also sits on four editorial review boards. Ramon's primary research is in personal selling and sales management. His work has appeared in the *Journal of Marketing Research*, *Journal of Personal Selling & Sales Management*, *The Journal of Management*, *Industrial Marketing Management*, *The Marketing Management Journal*, and the *Journal of Marketing Theory & Practice*, among others. He is the co-author of *The Professional Selling Skills Workbook.*

**Michael R. Williams** (Ph.D., Oklahoma State University) is professor of marketing and director of the Professional Sales Institute at Illinois State University. Prior to his academic career, Mike established a successful 30-plus year career in industrial sales, market research, and sales management and continues to consult and work with a wide range of business organizations. He has co-authored *The Professional Selling Skills Workbook*, *Professional Selling: A Trust-Based Approach*, and a variety of executive monographs and white-paper on sales performance topics. Mike's research has been published in many different national and international journals including *Journal of Personal Selling & Sales Management*, *International Journal of Purchasing and Materials Management*, *Journal of Business and Industrial Marketing*, *Quality Management Journal*, and *Journal of Industrial Technology*. His work has also received numerous honors, including Outstanding Article for the Year in *Journal of Business and Industrial Marketing*, the AACSB's Leadership in Innovative Business Education Award, and the Marketing Science Institute's Alden G. Clayton Competition. Mike has also been honored with numerous university, college, and corporate teaching and research awards including Old Republic Research Scholar, the presentation of a seminar at Oxford's Braesnose College, Who's Who in American Education, and Who's Who in America. Mike has and continues to serve in leadership roles as an advisor and board member for sales and sales management associations and organizations including the University Sales Center Alliance, National Conference in Sales and Sales Management, and Vector Marketing.

# BRIEF CONTENTS

# CONTENTS

**xv**

# CHANGING WORLD OF SALES MANAGEMENT

Jason Karem is sales manager for Automatic Data Processing (ADP) Emerging Business Services Division. He manages nine sales associates who sell payroll, tax filing, time-and-attendance, and human resource–related services to business customers. Although each day is different and challenging, Jason describes a "typical day" for him.

*A majority of my time is spent out in the field with the sales associates, helping them master all of the business calls they make in a given day.*

*7:45 A.M.—Arrive at the office to revisit training topic for the morning, review sales calls for the afternoon, and handle administrative tasks such as e-mail and voice-mail. This is when I touch base with my boss to brainstorm any focus items for the week.*

*8:30 A.M.—Group training with the sales associates. This is a 45-minute training topic focused around either improving selling skills or building relationships with key business partners. We review the material for 15 minutes and break into groups for 30 minutes of role playing. The role playing is the most important part of any training, because it really helps the associates feel comfortable with what they will say when they get out in the field. It is the practice before game time.*

*9:30 A.M.–12:00 noon—Planning sessions with various salespeople on the team. The purpose of these sessions is to go over certain accounts or specific sales presentation items and to develop each person while assisting him or her close any outstanding quotes.*

*During this time I typically make thank-you calls to partners that referred business to us in the past week and make executive thank-you calls to prospects that sales associates met with during the past week. The goal is to build that partner relationship even more and let the prospects know that we appreciate the opportunity to earn their business.*

*12–4 P.M.—Sales calls. During a field ride with my sales associates I have one goal: Help them improve. The way I do this is with a sales call feedback form, which outlines the whole sales call, from building rapport to closing the sale. We review the calls together and develop action items to talk about at our planning session at 4 P.M.*

*4–5 P.M.—Planning session with the sales associate. This is when we really focus on the items the associate wants to improve. Using a coaching and counseling model, I assist the salesperson in creating a game plan to take what he or she learned today and incorporate into tomorrow's calls. This is primarily done through doing a mock sales call. First, I model the call to the associate and then the associate role plays the call back to me. If my associates can each get better at one item and closer to their goals, whether that item is a certain selling skill or strategizing on closing a deal, I feel I have done my job. That feeling is what energizes me into getting up the next morning and doing it all over again.*

What an interesting day! Jason is a field sales manager. He works directly with the sales associates assigned to him. He conducts some of this work in the office, but much of his time is spent in the field making calls with sales associates, then coaching them to help them improve.

Most of our focus is on field sales managers such as Jason. However, some of our discussion is more relevant to sales managers at various levels within a sales organization. These sales managers have different titles and may not have direct responsibility for specific salespeople, but they all perform sales management activities that affect all or most of the salespeople in a sales organization. Consider the following examples:

- Clint Geffert is national account division manager for Respironics. His division sells respiratory equipment to home-care providers. There are 110 salespeople in this division. He travels about 95 percent of the time and has many sales management responsibilities.[1]

- Tony Bridge is regional sales manager with World Savings. He manages the mortgage origination department, which has three sales managers and 15 sales reps. Most of his time is spent on personnel issues, daily activity reports, and handling fires throughout the department.[2]

- Paul Gerrard is vice president of the central region for Hewlett-Packard's enterprise and commercial sales division. He spends a large portion of his time communicating with the 340 sales managers and salespeople in his region. Much of this communication is through conference calls and e-mail. However, he is often in a different city each day and always starts the day with an informal coffee talk with sales managers and salespeople.[3]

- Brad Graver is western regional sales manager for Professional Office Services. He works directly with 30 sales reps to provide marketing services for healthcare firms. His reps are organized into protected geographical territories to serve mid-sized doctor's offices.[4]

- Mary Kay Nedrich is director of sales training and development for Convergys. The training programs she develops for the company's 100 salespeople include online sessions that salespeople can access as their schedule allows, as well as traditional seminars.[5]

- Randy Lofland is sales manager for Lanx Fabric. He is the one-person sales and marketing department for the company. Instead of having salespeople, he works with six to eight distributors to reach customers. Sometimes he goes on sales calls with these distributors and sometimes he calls on customers by himself.[6]

These examples illustrate some of sales managers' possible titles and activities. Depending on the company and position, sales managers may perform some or all of the sales management functions.

Our objective in this module is to introduce the exciting world of sales management. We begin by presenting a general sales management model and discussing each stage in the sales management process. Then we examine some of the emerging trends in sales management, discuss the key characteristics of effective sales managers, and describe the basic format of each module. The goal is to "set the stage" for your journey into the dynamic and challenging world of sales management.

## SALES MANAGEMENT PROCESS

The marketing communications tools available to any firm are typically classified as personal selling, advertising, sales promotion, and publicity. *Personal selling* is defined as personal communication with an audience through paid personnel of an organization or its agents in such a way that the audience perceives the communicator's organization as being the source of the message. This definition differentiates personal selling as personal communication, whereas advertising and sales promotion are nonpersonal. Second, in personal selling the audience perceives the message as being delivered by the organization, whereas in publicity, even when it is in the form of personal communication, the audience typically perceives the medium, not the organization, as being the source of the message.

*Sales management* is simply management of an organization's personal selling function. Sales managers are involved in both the strategy (planning) and people (implementation) aspects of personal selling, as well as in evaluating and controlling personal selling activities. They must be able to deal effectively with people in the personal selling function, with people in other functional areas in the organization, and with people outside the organization, especially customers. The sales management model presented in Figure 1.1 illustrates the major stages in the sales management process.

## Describing the Personal Selling Function

Because sales managers are responsible for managing the personal selling function, they must thoroughly understand it. This text therefore devotes a module to that subject before discussing sales management activities. Module 2 (Overview of Personal Selling) presents the historical evolution of selling, a look at the contributions of personal selling to our economic and social systems, an examination of various personal selling approaches, and a comprehensive review of the sales process. The appendix discusses different sales jobs and career paths.

## Defining the Strategic Role of the Sales Function

Many firms in the contemporary business world consist of collections of relatively autonomous business units that market multiple products to diverse customer groups. These multiple-business, multiple-product firms must develop and integrate strategic decisions at different organizational levels. Module 3 (Organizational Strategies and the Sales Function) discusses the key strategic decisions at the corporate, business, marketing, and sales levels and the basic relationships between these decisions and the personal selling and sales management functions. Corporate- and business-level strategic decisions typically provide guidelines within which sales managers and salespeople

| Sales Management Model | FIGURE 1.1 |
|---|---|

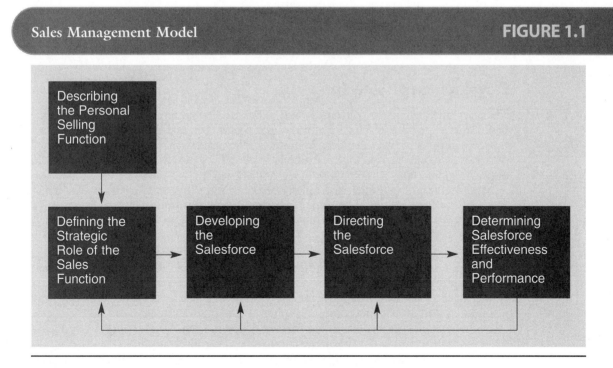

The four major stages of the sales management process and an understanding of personal selling are the focus of this book.

must operate. This is especially true for firms focusing on a customer relationship management (CRM) strategy. By contrast, personal selling is an important component of marketing strategies in specific product market situations. The role of personal selling in a given marketing strategy has direct and important implications for sales managers.

Strategic decisions at the corporate, business, and marketing levels must be translated into strategies for individual accounts. We discuss the major elements of a sales strategy: account targeting strategy, relationship strategy, selling strategy, and sales channel strategy. Because personal selling is typically important in organizational marketing situations, we provide an explanation of organizational buyer behavior as a foundation for the development of sales strategies.

Sales strategies are designed for individual accounts or groups of similar accounts. Therefore, an account targeting strategy is needed to identify and classify accounts into useful categories. Then, the type of relationship, the desired selling approach, and the most productive mix of sales channels are determined for each account category. These decisions result in an integrated sales strategy for each targeted account and account group.

The development and integration of corporate, business, marketing, and sales strategies establishes the basic strategic direction for personal selling and sales management activities. However, an effective sales organization is necessary to implement these strategies successfully. Module 4 (Sales Organization Structure and Salesforce Deployment) presents the basic concepts in designing an effective sales organization structure: specialization, centralization, span of control versus management levels, and line versus staff positions. Different decisions in any of these areas produce different sales organization structures. The appropriate structure for a firm depends on the specific characteristics of a given selling situation. If major account selling programs are used, specific attention must be directed toward determining the best organizational structure for serving these major accounts.

Closely related to sales organization decisions are decisions on the amount and allocation of selling effort. We present specific methods for making salesforce deployment decisions. Because the decisions on selling effort allocation, salesforce size, and territory design are interrelated, they should be addressed in an integrative manner. A number of different analytical approaches can assist in this endeavor, but "people" issues must also be considered.

## Developing the Salesforce

The sales strategy, sales organization, and salesforce deployment decisions produce the basic structure for personal selling efforts and can be considered similar to the "machine" decisions in a production operation. Sales managers must also make a number of "people" decisions to ensure that the right types of salespeople are available and have the skills to operate the "machine" structure effectively and efficiently.

Module 5 (Staffing the Salesforce: Recruitment and Selection) discusses the key activities involved in planning and carrying out salesforce recruitment and selection programs. These activities include determining the type of salespeople desired, identifying prospective salesperson candidates, and evaluating candidates to ensure that the best are hired. Legal and ethical issues are important considerations in the recruitment and selection process. The ramifications of this process for salespeople's subsequent adjustment to a new job (socialization) are also examined.

Module 6 (Continual Development of the Salesforce: Sales Training) emphasizes the need for continuous training of salespeople and the important role that sales managers play in this activity. The sales training process consists of assessing training needs, developing objectives, evaluating alternatives, designing the training program, carrying it out, and evaluating it. Sales managers face difficult decisions at each stage of the sales training process, because it is not only extremely important but also expensive, and there are many sales training alternatives available.

## Directing the Salesforce

Hiring the best salespeople and providing them with the skills required for success is one thing; directing their efforts to meet sales organization goals and objectives is another. Sales managers spend a great deal of their time in motivating, supervising, and leading members of the salesforce.

Module 7 (Sales Leadership, Management, and Supervision) distinguishes between the leadership, management, and supervisory activities of a sales manager. *Leadership activities* focus on influencing salespeople through communication processes to attain specific goals and objectives. *Management activities* include all aspects of the sales management process, such as recruiting, selecting, and training salespeople. *Supervisory activities* are concerned with day-to-day control of the salesforce under routine operating conditions. Key issues and problems in sales leadership, management, and supervision are discussed.

Module 8 (Motivation and Reward System Management) presents several content and process theories of motivation that attempt to explain how individuals decide to spend effort on specific activities over extended periods of time. Sales managers can use these theories as a foundation for determining the best ways to get salespeople to spend the appropriate amount of time on the right activities over a period of time. These theories provide the basis for specific salesforce reward systems. Both compensation and noncompensation rewards are examined. The advantages and disadvantages of different compensation programs are investigated, as well as methods for sales expense reimbursement. Specific guidelines for developing and managing a salesforce reward system are suggested.

## Determining Salesforce Effectiveness and Performance

Sales managers must continually monitor the progress of the salesforce to determine current effectiveness and performance. This is a difficult task, because these evaluations should address both the effectiveness of units within the sales organization and the performance of individual salespeople.

Module 9 (Evaluating the Effectiveness of the Organization) focuses on evaluating the effectiveness of sales organization units, such as territories, districts, regions, and zones. The *sales organization audit* is the most comprehensive approach for evaluating the effectiveness of the sales organization as a whole. Specific methods are presented for assessing the effectiveness of different sales organization units with regard to sales, costs, profitability, and productivity. Skill in using these analyses helps a sales manager to diagnose specific problems and develop solutions to them.

Module 10 (Evaluating the Performance of Salespeople) changes the focus to evaluating the performance of people, both as individuals and in groups. These performance evaluations are used for a variety of purposes by sales managers. Specific criteria to be evaluated and methods for providing the evaluative information are examined, and the use of this information in a diagnostic and problem-solving manner is described. A method for measuring salesperson job satisfaction, which is closely related to salesperson performance, is presented as well.

## SALES MANAGEMENT TRENDS

The turbulent business environment presents a variety of challenges. Many sales organizations face fierce global competition in both home and international markets. The purchasing function is increasingly viewed as an important way for organizations to lower costs and increase profits. Therefore, buyers are more demanding, better prepared, and highly skilled. The costs of maintaining salespeople in the field are escalating at the same time that sales organizations are being pressured to increase sales but decrease the costs of doing business. Thus, sales organizations are being challenged by competitors, customers, and even their own firms.

Many sales organizations are responding to these challenges by making dramatic changes in sales operations. Consider what some companies are doing.

- The Bose Corporation's sales organization is involved in hundreds of activities ranging from direct-to-consumer promotions to nationwide reseller programs. Since the sales organization is organized into regional groups, it is difficult to ensure that selling efforts are coordinated effectively. The company implemented a customized customer relationship management (CRM) program to address this problem. The CRM program standardized the process for planning and managing sales activities, tracking leads, and monitoring reseller programs. The system also automates tracking inventory records and submitting expense reports.[7]

- Marriott salespeople represent hotel brands such as Ritz-Carlton, Courtyard, and Fairfield Inns. Because customers differ in purchasing preferences, Marriott employs several sales channels. Customers who already know what they want can make bookings directly through the Internet or by calling one of Marriott's event-booking centers staffed by inside salespeople. Customers who need help in making an appropriate choice are serviced by the field salesforce. These salespeople try to identify the specific Marriott brand that will best meet a customer's needs.[8]

- Salespeople at Johnson Control's Automotive Systems Group (ASG) try to create long-term relationships with customers. To this end cross-functional sales teams work closely together, even going on joint sales calls. The marketing department does extensive consumer research on automobile buyers. Salespeople give this research to automobile manufacturers to add value to their relationship. Sometimes, salespeople set up offices at customer sites to service these customers more quickly.[9]

These situations illustrate some of the ways sales organizations are responding to the challenges facing them. Some of the changes are relatively minor, whereas others represent radical departures from past operating methods. Even though many firms are making significant changes in sales management, the framework presented in Figure 1.1 is still relevant. All sales organizations must somehow address each stage of the sales management process. What is changing, however, are the types of decisions made at each stage and how these decisions affect other stages in the sales management process.

We think that the challenges facing sales organizations will continue to increase. Therefore, successful sales organizations will be those that are willing to change and meet these challenges. Several of the most important sales management trends are presented in Figure 1.2.

Many of these trends are the result of a more strategic perspective toward sales organizations. As companies adopt a market orientation, the role of sales managers and salespeople becomes strategically more important. Market-oriented firms typically develop customer-centric cultures and establish organizational structures around customers rather than products. Market segmentation and prioritizing customers within target markets becomes increasingly important. Selling is viewed more as a core business process rather than a tactical activity. This strategic perspective considers the sales organization as critical in delivering value to customers and generating profits for the firm. Sales managers and salespeople need to change many of their activities to be successful in a more strategic role.[10]

## From Transactions to Relationships

The traditional transaction selling model is increasingly being replaced by more relationship-oriented selling approaches. Instead of an emphasis on selling products in the short run, salespeople are being required to develop long-term relationships by solving customer problems, providing opportunities, and adding value to customer businesses over an extended period of time. Sometimes, the shift to a relationship approach is demanded by specific customers. For example, companies such as Ford, Xerox, and General Electric have drastically reduced the number of their suppliers. Instead of working with many suppliers for a particular product or service, these firms want to deal with only one supplier or a few suppliers. Because these buyers desire

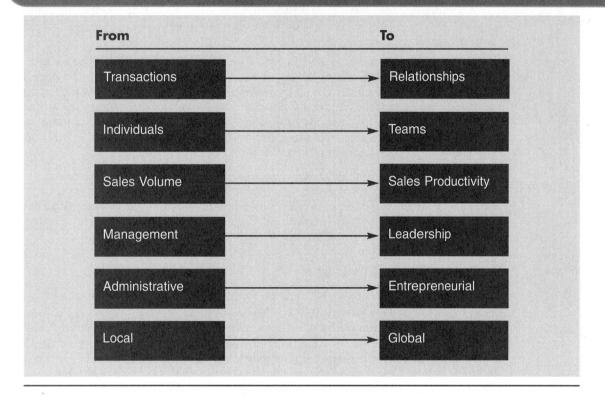

**Sales Management Trends**     FIGURE 1.2

| From | To |
| --- | --- |
| Transactions | → Relationships |
| Individuals | → Teams |
| Sales Volume | → Sales Productivity |
| Management | → Leadership |
| Administrative | → Entrepreneurial |
| Local | → Global |

Many sales organizations are responding to the challenges facing them by making changes in their sales operations.

long-term relationships with fewer suppliers, suppliers have no choice but to adopt a relationship approach if they want to sell to them.

In other cases, sales organizations have been more proactive in establishing a relationship strategy. These sellers realize that their long-term success depends on having long-term customers. Helping customers improve their business operations is the best way to develop the long-term customer relationships that will lead to long-term success.

The key sales management task is determining the appropriate type of relationship to pursue with specific customers. Some customers want and can best be served with a transaction approach. Others require some type of relationship strategy. There are, however, different types of relationships that might be established between buyers and sellers. These are difficult but critical decisions for sales organizations, because the type of relationship affects all other aspects of sales management.

The relationship selling trend is exhibited in the following examples:

- Texas Nameplate Company (TNC), with $4 million in annual sales, is the smallest company to win the Malcolm Baldrige National Quality Award. TNC focuses on retaining customers by being viewed as a trusted and valuable supplier. The company uses customer visits and response cards to generate feedback from customers and to take corrective action when problems are identified. Twice a year salespeople get a printout of customers who have not made a purchase during the past 12 months. The salespeople visit these customers, and one year they recovered 78 inactive accounts. This relationship orientation is working, as more than 62 percent of customers have been doing business with TNC for more than 10 years.[11]

- DXI sells software and services to companies that use ocean transportation. The company's online database with ocean transportation rates can help customers solve a variety of problems, but many customers viewed the company as just another vendor. Ed Ryan, vice president of sales and marketing, decided to change this.

He initiated a sales training program to help salespeople develop different types of relationships with different customers. Strategic resource relationships were established with the best customers. In these relationships, DXI is regarded as a consultant helping the customer improve its business by reducing transportation and other costs. DXI benefits from these relationships by generating higher margins and having more control over the sales process.[12]

- Salespeople from General Motors Service Parts Operation (GMSPO) used to focus entirely on selling car parts to dealers. Now, the emphasis is on helping the dealers improve business operations. The salespeople present detailed, easy-to-read reports on a dealer's business in the form of a Dealer Business Profile and Dealer Dashboard. The salesperson and dealer discuss this information to identify problem areas and to devise solutions to these problems. This consultative service is valued by the dealer and helps to strengthen the relationship with GMSPO.[13]

We examine the move from transactions to relationships throughout the remainder of the text. However, particular attention to relationship selling approaches is provided in the personal selling module (Module 2). In addition, an important element of a sales strategy is determining the type of relationship desired with each account. This strategic decision is examined in detail in Module 3.

## From Individuals to Teams

The importance of the "lone-wolf, superstar" salesperson is diminishing in many sales organizations, especially when the focus changes from just selling products to solving customer problems. In many situations, no one person possesses the knowledge and skills needed to identify and solve customer problems. Typically, some type of teamwork is required. This teamwork may be among individuals in the sales organization, between the sales and marketing departments, or among the functions within the business. Although there are many possible teamwork approaches, the trend from individuals to teams is becoming increasingly prevalent.

One way to view teamwork approaches is presented in Exhibit 1.1.[14] At one extreme is a core selling team—a formal sales team assigned to a specific customer. Team members can come from all business functional areas. Normally, a core selling team is headed by a sales manager. An example is the national account program employed by Nalco. When Nalco wins a national account, employees from Nalco and its customer form an

---

**EXHIBIT 1.1    Sales Teamwork Approaches**

| Core Selling Team | ← → | Selling Team |
|---|---|---|
| Relatively permanent, customer-focused group | ← → | Relatively temporary, transaction-focused group |
| Membership determined by job assignment to a specific buying organization | ← → | Membership determined by involvement in sales transaction for a particular good or service |
| One team per buying unit | ← → | One selling center per sales opportunity |
| Membership relatively stable | ← → | Membership very fluid |
| Characteristics of team depend on characteristics of buying organization | ← → | Characteristics of team depend on characteristics of sales opportunity |
| Mission is strategic with respect to the buying organization | ← → | Mission is tactical with respect to the sales opportunity |

Different teamwork approaches that sales organizations can use are represented by this continuum.

account team. The team includes a Nalco senior executive who is paired with a senior executive from the customer company. The remainder of the team consists of people from sales and other functions at Nalco matched by the customer's counterparts. As expressed by Jim Scott, Nalco's vice president of corporate sales: "To be successful, you have to have people matched up from both the customer and supplier sides, from the executive level on down."[15]

In the middle of this continuum is a formal sales team designed to close a transaction with a specific customer. For example, Lockheed Martin Information Technology put together a team of sales, management, technical, pricing, contracts, and executive leadership to try to win a contract with the Centers for Medicare and Medicaid Services. The team set up a command center near the customer, followed the Win Plan sales process, and created the slogan "One Company, One Team." All members of the team worked together to devise responses to the customer's negotiating points. This team process was expensive and took one and a half years to complete, but the result was a $401 million contract.[16]

At the other extreme is a selling center where individuals are involved in a particular sales transaction in an informal teamwork approach. Individuals can come from any business function and can participate at any stage of the sales process. Often, it is the responsibility of the salesperson to orchestrate the resources of the selling organization to meet the needs of the buying organization. The Holophane Corporation implemented a sales automation system to facilitate teamwork among the business functions. All orders are entered directly into a database that is accessible to all departments involved in manufacturing and executing the order. As engineering and manufacturing work on the order, its status is continuously updated. Customer service personnel can easily respond to customer inquiries about the order or make changes in the order requested by customers. The sales automation system provides the information the business functions need to work as a team to meet customer needs.[17]

Between these two extremes is a variety of approaches that differ in degree of formality, composition of team members, number of teams, and other characteristics. The important point is that the need for teamwork and the development of various types of selling teams is likely to increase in the future. And, as sales organizations move from a focus on individuals to an emphasis on teamwork, many aspects of sales management must change. Therefore, we examine the teamwork trend throughout the text.

## From Sales Volume to Sales Productivity

The basic role of a sales organization has been to sell. Salespeople and sales managers are normally evaluated and rewarded according to total sales volume generated over some time period. Although sales volume is important, many companies are finding that all sales are not equal. Some sales are more profitable than others. Therefore, more sales organizations are focusing not just on "sales for the sake of sales," but on the profitability of sales. This changes the focus from sales volume only to sales productivity. Sales productivity includes the costs associated with generating sales and serving customers. A sales productivity orientation emphasizes producing more sales for a given level of costs by doing things more effectively or more efficiently.

Increasing sales productivity usually requires a sales organization to do some things differently. Consider the following examples:

- Many companies use travel incentives to motivate salespeople. Because of tight budgets and tough economic times, companies are keenly interested in making sure the benefits from these incentive programs exceed program costs. TRAVEL' round designs, administers, and fulfills the awards for sales organization travel incentive programs. The company spent $1.5 million on Web technology to put these programs online. The cost savings from going online are tremendous. According to Bob Ryan, president of TRAVEL'round: "We can administer an incentive program online for 5,000 people for the same cost as for 50 people."[18]

- Intel's Business Conferencing Group uses what it makes to increase sales productivity. The company used a multipoint videoconference to communicate the launch of its new Team-Station 4.0 videoconferencing system to about 40 sales reps in North America and Europe. The full-day program linked 20 sales offices and some reps in their homes. The videoconference was interactive as all participants could ask questions at any time. The participants rated the program as very effective, and the cost savings in relation to bringing everyone to the same location were substantial.[19]

- Fisher Scientific International's salespeople often show up for training programs in their pajamas. That is because the training programs are on the Web. The salespeople can receive training programs in their homes, cars, hotel rooms, or wherever they bring their laptop computers. Using a Web-based product called Performance Learning System, salespeople receive product training, take an exam, or post messages to product experts wherever and whenever they want. The company saves money on travel costs and the salespeople save valuable selling time.[20]

The common element in all these situations is that some changes were made to increase sales productivity. Some things were done differently to get "more bang for the sales buck." This pressure to increase sales productivity is likely to intensify in the future for most sales organizations.

In one sense, all sales management decisions can be viewed from a sales productivity perspective. Sales managers should continuously be trying to "do more with less." Therefore, we address sales productivity throughout the sales management process. However, sales productivity is especially relevant when developing sales strategies (Module 3), organizing selling activities and deploying selling effort (Module 4), and evaluating sales organization effectiveness (Module 9).

## From Management to Leadership

Many sales organizations use a hierarchical, bureaucratic structure. Sales managers operate at different levels with direct supervisory responsibility for the level below and direct accountability to the management level above. Thus, field sales managers operate as the "boss" for the salespeople who report to them. They are responsible for the performance of these salespeople and exercise various types of control to get salespeople to produce desired results.

Although this approach might work well in very stable environments, many sales organizations realize that this approach makes it difficult for them to be responsive in a rapidly changing environment. These sales organizations are "flattening" the hierarchy and empowering salespeople to make more decisions in the field. This changes the role of sales managers and their relationship with salespeople. The basic trend is for a sales manager to lead more and manage less. One study found that sales managers are playing more of a leadership role by emphasizing:

- collaboration rather than control
- coaching instead of criticism
- salesperson empowerment rather than domination
- sharing information rather than withholding it
- adapting to individual salespeople rather than treating everyone the same.[21]

This emphasis on leadership means that a sales manager's job is more to help salespeople perform better and less to control and evaluate salespeople. This change in orientation is illustrated in Exhibit 1.2.[22]

Several studies reinforce the importance of leadership skills for sales managers. One study of 900 salespeople found that the skills salespeople most desired from their sales managers were good communication skills, the ability to motivate, and training and coaching.[23] Another study indicated that the major reason salespeople leave their firms is because of dissatisfaction with their sales manager.[24] Similar results were found in another study in which salespeople suggested less loyalty to their firm because of concerns about their sales manager's ability to lead them.[25] Finally, a study of 130 global firms reported that leadership was the most important quality of sales executives.[26]

| Leadership Trends   **EXHIBIT 1.2** | |
| --- | --- |
| **Yesterday** | **Today** |
| Natural resources defined power. | Knowledge is power. |
| Leaders commanded and controlled. | Leaders empower and coach. |
| Leaders were warriors. | Leaders are facilitators. |
| Managers directed. | Managers delegate. |

Several important changes in effective leadership have occurred over the years.

Debbie Smith, North American sales manager for Extended Systems, agrees with the results of these studies:

> Salespeople want to know that you're there for them. Managers need to show their reps that they're prepared to listen and work with them. Managers who just hand out leads, sit in their office doing budgets, and talk to salespeople only when necessary are going to be hated by their people.[27]

The trend toward a leadership orientation by sales managers is examined throughout the text. However, Module 7 (Sales Leadership, Management, and Supervision) is devoted entirely to discussing the important leadership versus management and supervision issues.

## From Administrative to Entrepreneurial

Consistent with the move from less management to more leadership, there is a trend from less emphasis on administrative activities to more of an entrepreneurial orientation throughout a sales organization. One study found that sales managers wanted to spend less of their time on administrative tasks and internal, nonsales functions and much more time with customers in selling and market development activities.[28] This shift requires sales managers to be more entrepreneurial in their sales management and marketplace activities.

An entrepreneurial orientation consists of three basic dimensions: proactiveness, risk-taking, and innovation. Sales managers exhibiting an entrepreneurial orientation do not just respond to whatever happens, they make things happen. These sales managers are willing to take calculated risks and to perform activities in new ways. They look for and pursue opportunities and leverage resources in unique ways. An entrepreneurial orientation is much different from the administrative orientation of the past.[29]

W. L. Gore & Associates provides an interesting example of an entrepreneurial orientation as well as several other sales management trends. No one in the company holds a title other than associate and technically no one is anyone else's boss. All work gets done by small teams. Sales leaders emerge by earning followers. These sales leaders function more like coaches than bosses, and spend most of their time guiding, directing, and encouraging salespeople through face-to-face communication. Sales associates develop their own territories and sales forecasts, and then discuss them with their sales leaders. The teams within each division are encouraged to generate their own ideas and strategies with a focus on customer retention and long-term success. This unusual but very entrepreneurial orientation has helped Gore grow to over $1 billion in annual sales.[30]

## From Local to Global

The marketplace is now global. Products and services are produced and marketed throughout the world. Most companies are involved in the international marketplace in some way now and are likely to become more involved internationally in the future. This trend toward a global orientation includes operating in international markets but goes well beyond just this geographic dimension. Even companies that do business only in the domestic market, such as the United States or a region of the United States, might compete against firms from other countries, use international suppliers, work with international partners, be affected by international events, serve customers from other countries regardless of where the customers are currently located, and/or have employees from other countries and cultures. Any of these situations requires a sales organization to expand from a local to a more global focus.

The most obvious need for a global orientation occurs when a company moves into unfamiliar international markets. More and more companies are having to do this to achieve growth objectives, because many local markets are not growing. Operating in international markets presents difficult challenges for sales managers. United Parcel Service (UPS) is a good example of a company facing these challenges. UPS delivers more than 1 million packages each day to over 200 countries. The company has invested $11 billion in technology to connect buyers and sellers around the world through e-commerce. Ted Gandolf, vice president of worldwide sales, thinks the technology infrastructure "helps us build credibility" to sell UPS services internationally.[31]

Less obvious, but of increasing importance, are the many situations in which a global orientation is needed to be effective in a sales organization's domestic market. Competing against international competitors, serving customers from other countries and cultures, and managing a diverse salesforce are of particular relevance to sales managers. Few markets or sales organizations are homogeneous. Most are becoming more and more heterogeneous and diverse.

Take the situation in the United States. One study projected that 75 percent of the population growth in the United States will come from Asian, Hispanic, and African-American groups.[32] Thus, in the years to come, an increasing proportion of the labor pool for sales organizations and customers for consumer marketers in the United States will come from these cultural groups. Jerry DiMonti, Century 21 People Services Realty, has taken advantage of this situation. His company operates in an area outside New York City with 89 nationalities. To sell effectively in this marketplace, his 33 sales agents include individuals with Italian, French, African-American, Guatemalan, Puerto Rican, Jamaican, Nigerian, Jewish, Indian, and South African backgrounds. This diverse sales organization selling to diverse customers has increased company sales dramatically in the past two years.[33]

The pharmaceutical industry provides another example of the importance of cultural issues in sales situations. Cultural issues are often relevant in the relationship between a pharmaceutical sales rep and physicians, and between physicians and patients from different cultures. CPRi Communications has developed online training that allows pharmaceutical sales reps to role play interactions in cultural situations and to receive feedback from trainers.[34]

## EFFECTIVE SALES MANAGERS

Sales managers face many challenges in today's business environment. They must be able to implement all stages of the sales management model (see Figure 1.1) and implement the sales management trends throughout this process. So, what does it take to be an effective sales manager? Several studies and evaluations of leading sales organizations suggest that effective sales managers employ a strategic perspective that focuses on customers; are able to attract, keep, and develop sales talent; and leverage technology throughout the sales organization.[35]

### A Strategic Perspective Focused on Customers

As emphasized earlier in this chapter, effective sales managers need to be more strategically oriented. This requires bringing a customer focus to the development of organizational strategies and creating sales strategies to meet the needs of different customers in a profitable manner.

PeopleSoft represents a good example of a customer-focused strategic perspective. All of the company's organizational strategies are built around customer satisfaction. Sales organization compensation is not only tied to sales quotas, but also to measures of customer satisfaction and the service customers receive from the PeopleSoft sales organization. Sales strategies emphasize a dedicated account executive for each major client. These clients have one point of contact with PeopleSoft. So, each customer can contact their account executive, and the account executive's job is to do whatever is necessary to meet the customer's needs.[36]

## Attract, Keep, and Develop Sales Talent

A critical part of sales management is related to people issues. Hiring the best salespeople, making sure they stay with the sales organization, and helping them perform at their highest levels are some of the most important accomplishments of effective sales managers. One study found that "sales is essentially a talent-driven occupation." World-class sales organizations hire the best people and engage them.[37]

General Electric does an especially good job with sales talent. It spends a great deal of time trying to hire the best salespeople; then its sales managers focus their attention on supporting and developing these salespeople. Sales managers help each salesperson develop a performance management plan and then meet with them three to four times a year to assess progress. Extensive product and selling skills training is also provided. These efforts have helped General Electric to attract and retain a talented salesforce.[38]

## Leverage Technology

The proper use of information and communication technologies can help salespeople and sales managers perform their jobs more effectively and efficiently. The key task is to select the right technology and ensure that it is used in the appropriate manner. Effective sales managers leverage technology to increase productivity throughout their sales organization.

Charles Schwab integrates technology into its sales strategy so that customers can choose any sales channel they want to use for any interaction. A customer could use the Internet one day, visit a salesperson the next day, and use the phone on another day. Oracle has taken a different approach by shifting to an online sales model. Routine activities are performed electronically so that salespeople can spend more time building relationships with customers and less time with mundane paperwork.[39] The most effective sales managers are those who find the proper blend of people and technology to meet the needs of customers and salespeople.

In addition to these general perspectives, the best sales managers focus on a number of specific activities in their interactions with salespeople:[40]

- Prepare their sales team for constant change by being a role model and mentoring salespeople.
- Earn the trust of salespeople by being dependable and competent, and exhibiting integrity.
- Give salespeople continuous feedback in a positive manner.
- Build enthusiasm throughout the sales team.
- Get involved by being accessible to salespeople and visible to customers.
- Grow and develop salespeople by emphasizing continuous job improvement and career development.

As you can see, sales management is a complex, constantly evolving field. Each module in the text is designed to address key sales management issues and to illustrate the important changes being implemented by leading sales organizations.

## MODULE FORMAT

*Sales Management: Analysis and Decision Making* was written for students. Therefore, its aim is to provide comprehensive coverage of sales management in a manner that students will find interesting and readable. Each module blends recent research results with current sales management practice in a format designed to facilitate learning.

At the beginning of each module, "Objectives" highlight the basic material that the student should expect to learn. These learning objectives are helpful in reviewing modules for future study. An opening vignette then illustrates many of the important ideas to be covered in the module, using examples of companies in various industries to illustrate the diversity and complexity of sales management. Most of the companies described in the vignettes are well known, and most of the situations represent real actions by these firms.

Key words in the body of each module are printed in bold letters, and figures and exhibits are used liberally to illustrate and amplify the discussion in the text. Every figure contains an explanation so that it can be understood without reference to the text.

Each module contains two boxed inserts entitled **Sales Management in the 21st Century**. The examples in both boxes have been provided specifically for this textbook by sales executives from various companies whom we recruited to serve as a **Sales Executive Panel**. To ensure that the textbook includes the latest practices from leading sales organizations, each executive was asked to provide specific examples of "best practices" in their company. Backgrounds of each executive are provided at the end of this module.

Sales managers are confronted with various ethical issues when performing their job activities. Many of these ethical issues are addressed in the **Ethical Dilemma** boxes that appear in the remaining modules. You will be presented with realistic ethical situations faced by sales managers and asked to recommend appropriate courses of action.

A module summary is geared to the learning objectives presented at the beginning of the module. **Understanding Sales Management Terms** lists the key words that appear in bold throughout the module. **Developing Sales Management Knowledge** presents 10 questions to help you develop an understanding of important sales management issues and relationships. **Building Sales Management Skills** consists of exercises in which you can apply the sales management knowledge learned in the module. **Making Sales Management Decisions** includes two interesting case situations that allow you to make important sales management decisions. If you understand sales management terms, develop sales management knowledge, and build sales management skills, you will be prepared to make successful sales management decisions.

## CONCLUDING STATEMENT

This brief overview of contemporary sales management and summary of the contents and format of *Sales Management: Analysis and Decision Making* set the stage for your journey into the dynamic and exciting world of sales management. This should be a valuable learning experience as well as an interesting journey. All the information contained in this textbook should prove very relevant to those of you who begin your career in personal selling and progress through the ranks of sales management.

## SALES EXECUTIVE PANEL

**Jane Hrehocik Clampitt** is marketing process manager for DuPont Consulting Solutions. Jane has spent most of her time at DuPont in sales and marketing roles with her current position aimed at raising the competency of sales and marketing professionals at DuPont. She has a B.S. in chemical engineering from Pennsylvania State University.

**Doug Clopton** is director of retail operations for Catholic Charities of Kansas, where he oversees the retail sales of stores generating revenue, which is returned to help those in need. Prior to this, Doug spent 22 years with Hershey Chocolate, in a variety of sales positions in the Kansas City, Chicago, Dallas, and Seattle markets, responsible for directing his team's selling efforts. Doug has a B.S.B.A. in marketing and an M.B.A. from Central Missouri State University.

**Jerry Heffel** started with The Southwestern Company as a college student salesperson in 1965, and has been president of the company since 1980. He is responsible for current profitability and setting the future direction for the company. Jerry has a B.A. in history from Oklahoma State University, and an M.B.A. from the University of Oklahoma.

**Jason Karem** is sales manager for Automatic Data Processing (ADP) Emerging Business Services Division. He manages nine associates who sell payroll, tax filing, time-and-attendance, and human resource–related services to business customers. Jason has a B.A. in marketing from Murray State University.

**Bob LaMontagne** is director of sales excellence for the Brown-Forman Corporation. He works with all operating groups to ensure the effectiveness of their sales professionals. This includes position descriptions, competency development, and training. Bob has a B.S. in business administration from Western New England College.

**L. A. Mitchell** is sales planner, business management, for Lucent Technologies. She works with the sales team as a strategic financial partner with the sales directors, which involves financial analysis, forecasting, and the identification of sales opportunities. She has a B.S.B.A. in marketing and an M.S. in marketing from Colorado State University.

**Steve Randazzo** is vice president of sales for KV Pharmaceutical, Inc. (ETHEX Division). He is responsible for all accounts in the United States. His primary customer base includes drug wholesalers, retail chains, managed care facilities, and hospitals. Steve has a B.S. in advertising from Southeast Missouri State University.

**Sabrina Rogers** is a district marketing manager for Federated Mutual Insurance. She manages eight sales representatives who sell property and causality, group health, and life and disability insurance to small and medium-sized businesses. Sabrina has a B.S.B.A. with a major in marketing from Central Missouri State University.

**André R. Wickham** is corporate regional sales manager southeast region and corporate national accounts sales manager for Hormel Foods' Foodservice Group. He is responsible for providing leadership of all sales activities in the southeast region of the United States. As national account manager, André directly manages the company's sales activities with many national foodservice chains throughout the United States. He has a B.S. degree in business administration from Morgan State University in Baltimore.

**Marty Zucker** is vice president/general manager for Allied Office Products. Allied Office Products is the largest independent office supply company in the United States. He is responsible for increasing revenues and margins at their Long Island, New York, Division. Marty has been in the office products industry for 32 years. He has held such positions as regional vice president National Accounts, Midwest Region; Vice president/general manager Chicago as well as director of operations for the Long Island, NY Division in the 1970s and 1980s. Marty studied marketing and business administration at the State University New York, Delhi.

# Describing the Personal Selling Function

The module and appendix in Part One describe the personal selling function. A clear understanding of personal selling is essential to gain a proper perspective on the issues facing sales managers. Module 2 presents the historical evolution of selling, along with a contemporary look at the contributions of personal selling to our economic and social systems. In addition, classifications of the various approaches to personal selling and the sales process are discussed.

Appendix 2 covers the characteristics of sales careers, classification of sales jobs, and the qualifications and skills required for salesperson success.

## OVERVIEW OF PERSONAL SELLING

## UPS BUILDS TRUST AND LONG-TERM CUSTOMER RELATIONSHIPS

When most people think of United Parcel Service (UPS), they probably think of the distinct brown-and-gold trucks that deliver small packages to homes and businesses. But UPS does a lot more than deliver packages. Using a highly customer-oriented approach, approximately 4,000 UPS salespeople in the United States function as value-building consultants to their business clients. Using this approach has paid off in sales growth, with UPS now in the top 50 of the *Fortune 500*.

Carl Strenger, a UPS vice president, describes the sales approach as a "consultative discussion across the supply chain. . . . We go in and we learn about the business. We talk to the functional people—information technology, finance, and so on. Once we decide what's important to this customer, we come up with a bundle of solutions to grow their top-line or reduce their bottom-line costs." To make its sales presentations effective, UPS conducts extensive training to focus on solutions for specific customers.

UPS salespeople from the package delivery side also frequently team up with UPS Capital sales personnel to offer customers integrated delivery and cash-flow management systems, and business process improvement programs. The overall sales strategy focuses on building long-term, trust-based relationships with customers. After almost a hundred years in business, UPS clearly is demonstrating that it understands how to implement a customer-focused strategy.

**Source:** From "UPS Builds Billions in Sales," by Robert McGarvey in *Selling Power* (June 2004): 56–62.

## EVOLUTION OF PERSONAL SELLING

The successful professional salesperson of today and the future is likely a better listener than a talker, is more oriented toward developing long-term relationships with customers than placing an emphasis on high-pressure, short-term sales techniques, and has the skills and patience to endure lengthy, complex sales processes. Like the UPS salespeople in the opening vignette, they strive to deliver relevant presentations based on unique customer needs. Teamwork between salespeople and others in the organization, also illustrated in the UPS example, is increasingly important for sales success. For more on teamwork, see "Sales Management in the 21st Century: The Importance of Teamwork in Sales."

**Personal selling** is defined as personal communication with an audience through paid personnel of an organization or its agents in such a way that the audience perceives the communicator's organization as being the source of the message. The audience may be an individual or a group representing another organization or a household. An audience may also be an individual acting solely on his or her behalf. In this book, we typically describe personal selling in a business-to-business context, in which a salesperson or sales team interacts with one or more individuals from another organization.

Personal selling has evolved into a different activity than it was just a decade ago. Throughout this course, you learn about new technologies and techniques that have contributed to this evolution. This module provides an overview of

## Objectives

After completing this module, you should be able to

1 Describe the evolution of personal selling from ancient times to the modern era.

2 Explain the contributions of personal selling to society, business firms, and customers.

3 Distinguish between transaction-focused traditional selling and trust-based relationship selling.

4 Discuss five alternative approaches to personal selling.

5 Describe the three primary roles fulfilled by consultative salespeople.

6 Understand the sales process as a series of interrelated steps.

### The Importance of Teamwork in Sales

Jerry Heffel, president of the Southwestern Company, offers his perspective on teamwork:

*Sometimes the salesperson is referred to as the lead car in the business train. But just having a lead car doesn't make a train. For this reason, a salesperson who is effective long term is also an effective team player—he or she realizes they need coordinated involvement from many different parts of the organization in order to serve the* *customer. At the same time, whenever they see themselves as part of the customer's team, and that they are both striving for the same outcome, they become an indispensable part of the value chain for that customer. Southwestern's sales training philosophy stresses this team aspect: we tell our salespeople that they are the gas and oil of the free enterprise system, but they also need the tires, the car body, the drive train, and what's in the trunk to get anywhere significant.*

personal selling, affording insight into the operating rationale of today's salespeople and sales managers. It also describes approaches to personal selling and presents the sales process as a series of interrelated steps. The appendix at the end of the module discusses several important aspects of sales careers, including types of selling jobs and characteristics and skills needed for sales success. In the highly competitive, complex environment of the world business community, personal selling and sales management have never played more critical roles.

## Origins of Personal Selling

Ancient Greek history documents selling as an exchange activity, and the term *salesman* appears in the writings of Plato.[1] However, true salespeople, those who earned a living only by selling, did not exist in any sizable number until the Industrial Revolution in England, from the mid-eighteenth century to the mid-nineteenth century. Prior to this time, traders, merchants, and artisans filled the selling function. These predecessors of contemporary marketers were generally viewed with contempt because deception was often used in the sale of goods.[2]

In the latter phase of the Middle Ages, the first door-to-door salesperson appeared in the form of the peddler. Peddlers collected produce from local farmers, sold it to townspeople, and, in turn, bought manufactured goods in town for subsequent sale in rural areas.[3] Like many other early salespeople, they performed other important marketing functions—in this case, purchasing, assembling, sorting, and redistributing of goods.

## Industrial Revolution Era

As the Industrial Revolution began to blossom in the middle of the eighteenth century, the economic justification for salespeople gained momentum. Local economies were no longer self-sufficient, and as intercity and international trade began to flourish, economies of scale in production spurred the growth of mass markets in geographically dispersed areas. The continual need to reach new customers in these dispersed markets called for an increasing number of salespeople.

It is interesting to note the job activities of the first wave of salespeople in the era of the Industrial Revolution. The following quotation describes a salesperson who served the customer in conjunction with a producer:

> Thus, a salesman representing the producing firm, armed with samples of the firm's products, could bring the latter to the attention of a large number of potential customers—whether buying for sale to others or for their

own production requirements—who might not, without the salesman's visit, have learnt of the product's existence, and give them the opportunity of examining and discussing it without having to go out of their way to do so. . . . Even if the salesman did not succeed in obtaining an order, he frequently picked up valuable information on the state of the market, sometimes the very reasons for refusal. . . . This information could be very useful to the producer.[4]

## Post–Industrial Revolution Era

By the early 1800s, personal selling was well established in England but just beginning to develop in the United States.[5] This situation changed noticeably after 1850, and by the latter part of the century, salespeople were a well-established part of business practice in the United States. For example, one wholesaler in the Detroit area reported sending out 400 traveling salespeople in the 1880s.[6]

At the dawning of the twentieth century, an exciting time in the economic history of the United States, it became apparent that marketing, especially advertising and personal selling, would play a crucial role in the rapid transition of the economy from an agrarian base to one of mass production and efficient transportation.

Glimpses of the lives of salespeople in the early 1900s, gained from literature of that period, reveal an adventuresome, aggressive, and valuable group of employees often working on the frontier of new markets. Already, however, the independent maverick salespeople who had blazed the early trails to new markets were beginning to disappear. One clear indication that selling was becoming a more structured activity was the development of a **canned sales presentation** by John H. Patterson of the National Cash Register Company (NCR). This presentation, a virtual script to guide NCR salespeople on how to sell cash registers, was based on the premise that salespeople are not "born, but rather they are made."[7]

Sales historians noted the changes occurring in personal selling in the early twentieth century. Charles W. Hoyt, author of one of the first textbooks on sales management, chronicled this transition in 1912, noting two types of salespeople:

> The old kind of salesman is the "big me" species. . . . He works for himself and, so far as possible, according to his own ideas. . . . There is another type of salesman. He is the new kind. At present he is in the minority, but he works for the fastest growing and most successful houses of the day. He works for the house, and the house works for him. He welcomes and uses every bit of help the house sends to him.[8]

Hoyt's observations about the "old" and the "new" salesperson summed up the changing role of personal selling. The managements of firms in the United States were beginning to understand the tremendous potential of personal selling and, simultaneously, the need to shape the growth of the sales function. In particular, a widespread interest arose in how to reduce the cost of sales. According to Hoyt, this did not mean hiring lower-cost salespeople, but instead called for "distributing much larger quantities of goods with less motion."[9]

## War and Depression Era

The 30-year span from 1915 to 1945 was marked by three overwhelming events—two world wars and the Great Depression in the United States. Because economic activity concentrated on the war efforts, new sales methods did not develop quickly during those periods. During the Great Depression, however, business firms, starved for sales volume, often employed aggressive salespeople to produce badly needed revenue. Then, with renewed prosperity in the post–World War II era, salespeople emerged as important employees for an increasing number of firms that were beginning to realize the benefits of research-based integrated marketing programs.

## Professionalism: The Modern Era

In the middle 1940s personal selling became more professional. Not only did buyers begin to demand more from salespeople, but they also grew intolerant of high-pressure, fast-talking salespeople, preferring instead a well-informed, customer-oriented salesperson. In 1947, the *Harvard Business Review* published "Low-Pressure Selling,"[10] a classic article followed by many others that called for salespeople to increase the effectiveness of their sales efforts by improving their professional demeanor.

An emphasis on **sales professionalism** is the keynote of the current era. The term has varied meanings, but in this context we use it to mean a customer-oriented approach that uses truthful, nonmanipulative tactics to satisfy the long-term needs of both the customer and the selling firm. The effective salesperson of today is no longer a mere presenter of information but now must stand equipped to respond to a variety of customer needs before, during, and after the sale. In addition, salespeople must be able to work effectively with others in their organizations to meet or exceed customer expectations.

In examining the status of sales as a true profession, one study found that sales meets four of the six criteria that define professions, and that progress is still needed on the other two dimensions.[11] This study concluded that sales meets the criterion of operating from a substantial knowledge base that has been developed by academics, corporate trainers and executives, and professional organizations. Sales also meets the criterion of making a significant contribution to society, which is discussed in the next section of this module. Third, through professional organizations such as the Strategic Account Management Association (SAMA) and through a common sales vocabulary such as that found in textbooks and training materials, sales meets the professional criterion of having a defined culture and organization of colleagues. Fourth, sales does have a unique set of professional skills, though these skills vary depending on the specific nature of a given sales position.

Two areas in the study indicated that sales needs additional progress to be viewed as a profession on a par with law, medicine, and other long-recognized professions. The first area has to do with how much autonomy salespeople have to make decisions and the amount of public trust granted to salespeople. While many business-to-business salespeople have considerable decision-making autonomy, others have very little. Public trust could be improved by a widely accepted certification program such as the CPA designation for accountants. At present, however, very few salespeople have professional certification credentials. While many salespeople do have considerable autonomy, public trust in certification programs is modest; thus the results are mixed as to whether the sales profession meets this professional criterion.

The final area where sales needs to improve is to adhere to a uniform ethical code. While many companies have ethical codes and some professional organizations have ethical codes for salespeople, there is no universal code of ethics with a mechanism for dealing with violators. Until such a code is developed and widely accepted in business, some members of society will not view sales as a true profession.

Whether or not sales is viewed as a true profession, comparable to law and medicine, salespeople can benefit tremendously by embracing high ethical standards, participating in professional organizations, and working from a continually evolving knowledge base. In so doing, they will not only be more effective, they will also help advance sales as a true profession.

Future evolution is inevitable as tomorrow's professional salesperson responds to a more complex, dynamic environment. Also, increased sophistication of buyers and of new technologies will demand more from the next generation of salespeople. Exhibit 2.1 summarizes some of the likely events of the future.[12]

| Continued Evolution of Personal Selling | **EXHIBIT 2.1** |

| Change | Salesforce Response |
| --- | --- |
| Intensified competition | More emphasis on developing and maintaining trust-based, long-term customer relationships |
| More emphasis on improving sales productivity | Increased use of technology (e.g., laptop computers, electronic mail, databases, customer relationship management software) <br> Increased use of lower-cost-per-contact methods (e.g., telemarketing for some customers) <br> More emphasis on profitability (e.g., gross margin) objectives |
| Fragmentation of traditional customer bases | Sales specialists for specific customer types <br> Multiple sales channels (e.g., major accounts programs, telemarketing, electronic networks) <br> Globalization of sales efforts |
| Customers dictating quality standards and inventory/ shipping procedures to be met by vendors | Team selling <br> Salesforce compensation sometimes based on customer satisfaction and team performance |
| Demand for in-depth, specialized knowledge as an input to purchase decisions | Team selling <br> More emphasis on customer-oriented sales training |

## CONTRIBUTIONS OF PERSONAL SELLING

Although advertising has traditionally captured most of the attention of students and researchers, personal selling is actually the most important part of marketing communications for most business firms. This is particularly true in firms that engage in business-to-business marketing. More money is spent on personal selling than on any other form of marketing communications, whether it be advertising, sales promotion, publicity, or public relations. We now take a look at how this investment is justified by reviewing the contributions of personal selling to society in general, to the employing firm, and to customers.

### Salespeople and Society

Salespeople contribute to their nations' economic growth in two basic ways. They act as stimuli for economic transactions, and they further the diffusion of innovation.

#### Salespeople as Economic Stimuli

Salespeople are expected to stimulate action in the business world—hence the term **economic stimuli**. In a fluctuating economy, salespeople make invaluable contributions by assisting in recovery cycles and by helping to sustain periods of relative prosperity. As the world economic system deals with issues such as increased globalization of business, more emphasis on customer satisfaction, and building competitiveness through quality improvement programs, it is expected that salespeople will be recognized as a key force in executing the appropriate strategies and tactics necessary for survival and growth.

#### Salespeople and Diffusion of Innovation

Salespeople play a critical role in the **diffusion of innovation**, the process whereby new products, services, and ideas are distributed to the members of society. Consumers who are likely to be early adopters of an innovation often rely on salespeople as a primary source of information. Frequently, well-informed, specialized salespeople provide useful information to potential consumers who then purchase from a lower-cost outlet.

The role of salespeople in the diffusion of industrial products and services is particularly crucial. Imagine trying to purchase a companywide computer system without the assistance of a competent salesperson or sales team!

While acting as an agent of innovation, the salesperson invariably encounters a strong resistance to change in the latter stages of the diffusion process. The status quo seems to be extremely satisfactory to many parties, even though, in the long run, change is necessary for continued progress or survival. By encouraging the adoption of innovative products and services, salespeople may indeed be making a positive contribution to society.

## Salespeople and the Employing Firm

Because salespeople are in direct contact with the all-important customer, they can make valuable contributions to their employers. Salespeople contribute to their firms as revenue producers, as sources of market research and feedback, and as candidates for management positions.

### Salespeople as Revenue Producers

Salespeople occupy the somewhat unique role of **revenue producers** in their firms. Consequently, they usually feel the brunt of that pressure along with the management of the firm. Although accountants and financial staff are concerned with profitability in bottom-line terms, salespeople are constantly reminded of their responsibility to achieve a healthy "top line" on the profit and loss statement. This should not suggest that salespeople are concerned only with sales revenue and not with overall profitability. Indeed, salespeople are increasingly responsible for improving profitability, not only by producing sales revenues, but also by improving the productivity of their actions.

### Market Research and Feedback

Because salespeople spend so much time in direct contact with their customers, it is only logical that they would play an important role in market research and in providing feedback to their firms. For example, entertainment and home products retailer Best Buy relies heavily on feedback from its sales associates in what it calls a customer-centricity initiative, which places the customer at the center of its marketing strategy. Feedback from sales associates helps Best Buy offer tailored products to specific customer segments, design appealing in-store merchandising formats, increase sales volume for in-home services, and improve the effectiveness of customer-support call centers. Results of the customer-centricity program have been so positive that Best Buy is rapidly increasing the number of participating stores as it tries to fend off Wal-Mart and other major competitors.[13]

Some would argue that salespeople are not trained as market researchers, or that salespeople's time could be better used than in research and feedback activities. Many firms, however, refute this argument by finding numerous ways to capitalize on the salesforce as a reservoir of ideas. It is not an exaggeration to say that many firms have concluded that they cannot afford to operate in the absence of salesforce feedback and research.

### Salespeople as Future Managers

In recent years, marketing and sales personnel have been in strong demand for upper management positions. Recognizing the need for a top management trained in sales, many firms use the sales job as an entry-level position that provides a foundation for future assignments. As progressive firms continue to emphasize customer orientation as a basic operating concept, it is only natural that salespeople who have learned how to meet customer needs will be good candidates for management jobs.

## Salespeople and the Customer

Given the increasing importance of building trust with customers and an emphasis on establishing and maintaining long-term relationships, it is imperative that salespeople be honest and candid with customers. Salespeople must also be able to demonstrate knowledge of their products and services, especially as they compare competitive offerings. Customers also expect salespeople to be knowledgeable about market opportunities and relevant business trends that may affect a customer's business. There has been a long-standing expectation that salespeople need to be the key contact for the buyer, who expects that they will coordinate activities within the selling firm to deliver maximum value to the customer.

The overall conclusion is that buyers expect salespeople to contribute to the success of the buyer's firm. Buyers value the information furnished by salespeople, and more than ever before, they value the problem-solving skills of salespeople.[14] See "An Ethical Dilemma" for a scenario in which the salesperson must think about where to draw the line in sharing information with customers.

As salespeople serve their customers, they simultaneously serve their employers and society. When the interests of these parties conflict, the salesperson can be caught in the middle. By learning to resolve these conflicts as a routine part of their jobs, salespeople further contribute to developing a business system based on progress through problem solving.

---

### AN ETHICAL DILEMMA

Terry Kelly, sales representative for EFAX, a computer software company, has just concluded a sales call with Landnet, one of his distributors. During the call, purchasing agent Linda Meyer mentioned that Ron Hawkins, Landnet's top salesperson, had suddenly resigned and moved out of the state. Ms. Meyer said that this unexpected resignation could not have come at a worse time, as several key customer contracts were pending renewal, and Landnet had no candidates to replace Hawkins. On his way to his next sales call with Netserve, his largest distributor, Terry debated whether or not he should share the news of Hawkins' resignation. After all, the buyer at Netserve viewed Terry as a great source of market information, and Terry figured that the Netserve buyer would hear the news anyway before the day was over. What should Terry do?

---

## CLASSIFICATION OF PERSONAL SELLING APPROACHES

In this section, we take a closer look at alternative approaches to personal selling that professionals may choose from to best interact with their customers. Some of these approaches are simple. Other approaches are more sophisticated and require that the salesperson play a strategic role to use them successfully. More than three decades ago, four basic approaches to personal selling were identified: stimulus response, mental states, need satisfaction, and problem solving.[15] Since that time, another approach to personal selling, termed *consultative selling*, has gained popularity. All five approaches to selling are practiced today. Furthermore, many salespeople use elements of more than one approach in their own hybrids of personal selling.

As a prelude to our discussion of approaches to personal selling, an expansion of two key points is in order. Recall that personal selling differs from other forms of marketing communications because it is a personal communication delivered by employees or agents of the sales organization. Because the personal element is present, salespeople have the opportunity to alter their sales messages and behaviors during a sales presentation or as they encounter unique sales situations and customers. This is referred to as **adaptive selling**. Because salespeople often encounter buyers with different personalities, communications styles, needs and goals, adaptive selling is an important concept.

A second point is that personal selling is moving from transaction-based methods to relationship-based methods. Rather than trying to maximize sales in the short run, relationship-based selling approaches focus on solving customer problems, providing opportunities, and adding value to the customer's business over an extended period. Exhibit 2.2[16] illustrates how transaction-based selling differs from relationship-based selling. We now explore one element of Exhibit 2.2 in detail—personal selling approaches.

## EXHIBIT 2.2    Comparison of Transaction-Focused Traditional Selling with Trust-Based Relationship Selling

| | Transaction-Focused Traditional Selling | Trust-Based Relationship Selling |
|---|---|---|
| Primary perspective | The salesperson and the selling firm | The customer and the customer's customers |
| Personal selling approaches | Stimulus response, mental states | Need satisfaction, problem solving, consultative |
| Desired outcome | Closed sales, order volume | Trust, joint planning, mutual benefits, enhance profits |
| Role of salesperson | Make calls and close sales | Business consultant and long-term ally Key player in the customer's business |
| Nature of communication | One-way, from salesperson to customer | Two-way and collaborative |
| Degree of salesperson's involvement in customer's decision-making process | Isolated from customer's decision-making process | Actively involved in customer's decision-making process |
| Knowledge required | Own company's products Competition Applications Account strategies Costs Opportunities | Own company's products and resources Competition Applications Account strategies Costs Opportunities General business and industry knowledge and insight Customer's products, competition, and customers |
| Typical skills required | Selling skills | Selling skills Information gathering Listening and questioning Strategic problem solving Creating and demonstrating unique, value-added solutions Teambuilding and teamwork |
| Post-sale follow-up | Little or none; move on to conquer next customer | Continued follow-through to: • Ensure customer satisfaction • Keep customer informed • Add customer value • Manage opportunities |

## Stimulus Response Selling

Of the five views of personal selling, **stimulus response selling** is the simplest. The theoretical background for this approach originated in early experiments with animal behavior. The key idea is that various stimuli can elicit predictable responses. Salespeople furnish the stimuli from a repertoire of words and actions designed to produce the desired response. This approach to selling is illustrated in Figure 2.1.

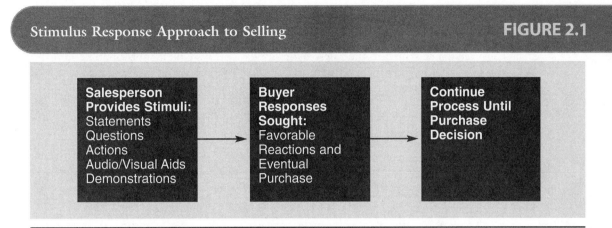

**Stimulus Response Approach to Selling**    FIGURE 2.1

The salesperson attempts to gain favorable responses from the customer by providing stimuli, or cues, to influence the buyer. After the customer has been properly conditioned, the salesperson tries to secure a positive purchase decision.

An example of the stimulus response view of selling would be **continued affirmation**, a method in which a series of questions or statements furnished by the salesperson is designed to condition the prospective buyer to answering "yes" time after time, until, it is hoped, he or she will be inclined to say "yes" to the entire sales proposition. This method is often used by telemarketing personnel, who rely on comprehensive sales scripts read or delivered from memory.

Stimulus response sales strategies, particularly when implemented with a canned sales presentation, have some advantages for the seller. The sales message can be structured in a logical order. Questions and objections from the buyer can usually be anticipated and addressed before they are magnified during buyer–seller interaction. Inexperienced salespeople can rely on stimulus response sales methods in some settings, and this may eventually contribute to sales expertise.

The limitations of stimulus response methods, however, can be severe, especially if the salesperson is dealing with a professional buyer. Most buyers like to take an active role in sales dialogue, and the stimulus response approach calls for the salesperson to dominate the flow of conversation. The lack of flexibility in this approach is also a disadvantage, as buyer responses and unforeseen interruptions may neutralize or damage the effectiveness of the stimuli.

Considering the net effects of this method's advantages and disadvantages, it appears most suitable for relatively unimportant purchase decisions, when time is severely constrained and when professional buyers are not the prospects. As consumers in general become more sophisticated, this approach will become more problematic.

## Mental States Selling

**Mental states selling**, or the *formula approach* to personal selling, assumes that the buying process for most buyers is essentially identical and that buyers can be led through certain mental states, or steps, in the buying process. These mental states are typically referred to as **AIDA** (attention, interest, desire, and action). Appropriate sales messages provide a transition from one mental state to the next.

Like stimulus response selling, the mental states approach relies on a highly structured sales presentation. The salesperson does most of the talking, as feedback from the prospect could be disruptive to the flow of the presentation.

A positive feature of this method is that it forces the salesperson to plan the sales presentation prior to calling on the customer. It also helps the salesperson recognize that timing is an important element in the purchase decision process and that careful listening is necessary to determine which stage the buyer is in at any given point.

A problem with the mental states method is that it is difficult to determine which state a prospect is in. Sometimes a prospect is spanning two mental states or moving back and forth between two states during the sales presentation. Consequently, the heavy guidance structure the salesperson implements may be inappropriate, confusing, and even counterproductive to sales effectiveness. We should also note that this method is not customer oriented. Although the salesperson tailors the presentation to each customer somewhat, this is done by noting customer mental states rather than needs. See "An Ethical Dilemma" for a situation in which the salesperson is contemplating the movement of the prospect into the "action" stage.

### AN ETHICAL DILEMMA

Rachel Duke sells advertising for her college newspaper. One of her potential clients is contemplating buying an ad for an upcoming special issue featuring bars and restaurants. Over the past two weeks, Rachel has tried unsuccessfully to get a commitment from the restaurant owner to place an ad. Her sales manager has suggested that Rachel call the prospect and tell him that there is only one remaining ad space in the special issue, and that she must have an immediate answer to ensure that the prospect's ad will appear in the special issue. The sales manager said, "Rachel, this guy is stalling. You've got to move him to action, and this technique will do the trick." Rachel was troubled by her manager's advice, since the special issue had plenty of ad space remaining. If you were Rachel, would you follow her sales manager's advice? Why or why not?

The mental states method is illustrated in Exhibit 2.3.[17] Note that this version includes "conviction" as an intermediate stage between interest and desire. Such minor variations are commonplace in different renditions of this approach to selling.

## Need Satisfaction Selling

**Need satisfaction selling** is based on the notion that the customer is buying to satisfy a particular need or set of needs. This approach is shown in Figure 2.2. It is the salesperson's task to identify the need to be met, then to help the buyer meet the need. Unlike the mental states and stimulus response methods, this method focuses on the

### EXHIBIT 2.3     Mental States View of Selling

| Mental State | Sales Step | Critical Sales Task |
|---|---|---|
| Curiosity | Attention | Get prospects excited, then you get them to like you. |
| Interest | Interest | Interview: needs and wants |
| Conviction | Conviction | "What's in it for me?"<br>Product—"Will it do what I want it to do?"<br>Price—"Is it worth it?" "The hassle of change" "Cheaper elsewhere"<br>Peers—"What will others think of it?"<br>Priority—"Do I need it now?" (sense of urgency) |
| Desire | Desire | Overcome their stall. |
| Action | Close | Alternate choice close: which, not if! |

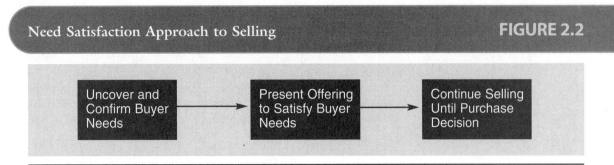

**Need Satisfaction Approach to Selling**    **FIGURE 2.2**

The salesperson attempts to uncover customer needs that are related to the product or service offering. This may require extensive questioning in the early stages of the sales process. After confirming the buyer's needs, the salesperson proceeds with a presentation based on how the offering can meet those needs.

customer rather than on the salesperson. The salesperson uses a questioning, probing tactic to uncover important buyer needs. Customer responses dominate the early portion of the sales interaction, and only after relevant needs have been established does the salesperson begin to relate how his or her offering can satisfy these needs.

Customers seem to appreciate this selling method and are often willing to spend considerable time in preliminary meetings to define needs prior to a sales presentation or written sales proposal. Also, this method avoids the defensiveness that arises in some prospects when a salesperson rushes to the persuasive part of the sales message without adequate attention to the buyer's needs.

## Problem-Solving Selling

**Problem-solving selling** is an extension of need satisfaction selling. It goes beyond identifying needs to developing alternative solutions for satisfying these needs. The problem-solving approach to selling is depicted in Figure 2.3. Sometimes even competitors' offerings are included as alternatives in the purchase decision.

The problem-solving approach typically requires educating the customer about the full impact of the existing problem and clearly communicating how the solution delivers significant customer value. This is true even in cases where the solution seems to be an obviously beneficial course of action for the buyer. For example, SoftSwitching Technologies' Dynamic Sag Corrector (DySC) practically eliminates expensive power-related downtime in manufacturing processes. Competitive products are expensive and hard to maintain. Yet the company found that DySC did not sell itself because buyers were used to having downtime in manufacturing and were not sure DySC would be a solution.[18] To be successful in

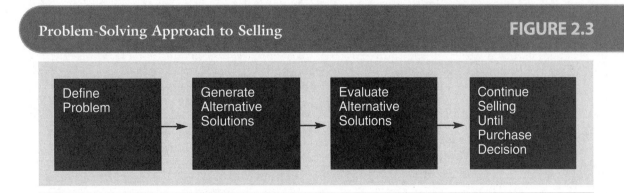

**Problem-Solving Approach to Selling**    **FIGURE 2.3**

The salesperson defines a customer problem that may be solved by various alternatives. Then an offering is made that represents at least one of these alternatives. All alternatives are carefully evaluated before a purchase decision is made.

problem-solution selling, salespeople must be able to get the buyer to agree that a problem exists and that solving it is worth the time and effort required.

The problem-solving approach to selling can take a lot of time. In some cases, the selling company cannot afford this much time with each prospective customer. In other cases, the customers may be unwilling to spend the time. Insurance salespeople, for example, report this customer response. The problem-solving approach appears to be most successful in technical industrial sales situations, in which the parties involved are usually oriented toward scientific reasoning and processes and thus find this approach to sales amenable.

## Consultative Selling

**Consultative selling** is the process of helping customers reach their strategic goals by using the products, services, and expertise of the sales organization.[19] Notice that this method focuses on achieving strategic goals of customers, not just meeting needs or solving problems. Salespeople confirm their customers' strategic goals, then work collaboratively with customers to achieve those goals.

In consultative selling, salespeople fulfill three primary roles: strategic orchestrator, business consultant, and long-term ally. As a **strategic orchestrator**, the salesperson arranges the use of the sales organization's resources in an effort to satisfy the customer. This usually calls for involving other individuals in the sales organization. For example, the salesperson may need expert advice from production or logistics personnel to fully address a customer problem or opportunity. In the **business consultant** role, the salesperson uses internal and external (outside the sales organization) sources to become an expert on the customer's business. This role also includes an educational element—that is, salespeople educate their customers on products they offer and how these products compare with competitive offerings. As a **long-term ally**, the salesperson supports the customer, even when an immediate sale is not expected.

Chester Sykes, a new business account executive for Information Handling Services (IHS) in Chandler, Arizona, suggests that salespeople should "use consultative selling to begin building a relationship based on identifying and satisfying your potential client's needs."[20] He advocates that salespeople do a detailed customer needs analysis to learn the customer's business, including their present and future goals. Sykes also says it is important to become "become your customer's coordinator/advocate to represent their ongoing needs. This builds trust, loyalty, and future sales."[21] For more on consultative selling, see "Sales Management in the 21st Century: Consultative Selling."

**Consultative Selling**

L. A. Mitchell, sales planner for Lucent Technologies, comments on the increasing use of consultative selling.

*Professional selling is becoming much more of a consultative process than in years past. The pace of business has accelerated, and it is hard for individual buyers to be experts on everything they buy. That's where consultative selling comes in. When buyers know they have a problem, but don't know how to solve it, our salespeople can offer a tailored solution. The solution must fit within the buyer's allotted budget, and it must be consistent with the goals and strategies within the buying organization. Consultative salespeople must also be on the scene after the sale to be sure that any necessary training and service issues are handled to the client's satisfaction. With consultative selling, making the sale is important, but the real focus is on providing expertise which enables clients to improve company operations and productivity.*

## SALES PROCESS

The nonselling activities on which most salespeople spend a majority of their time are essential for the successful execution of the most important part of the salesperson's job, the **sales process**. The sales process has traditionally been described as a series of inter-related steps beginning with locating qualified prospective customers. From there, the salesperson plans the sales presentation, makes an appointment to see the customer, completes the sale, and performs post-sale activities.

As you should recall from the earlier discussion of the continued evolution of personal selling (refer to Exhibit 2.1), the sales process is increasingly being viewed as a relationship management process, as depicted in Figure 2.4. In this conceptualization of the sales process, salespeople strive to attain lasting relationships with their customers. The basis for such relationships may vary, but the element of trust between the customer and the salesperson is an essential part of enduring relationships. To earn the trust of customers, salespeople should be customer oriented, honest, dependable, competent, and likable.[22] These attributes are reflected by Blake Conrad, who sells medical supplies for Centurion Specialty Care. Conrad, based in Denver, says:

> You simply cannot have productive relationships with your customers unless they trust you. I work really hard to show customers that I care about their bottom line, and I would never sell them something they don't really need. If I don't have an answer for them on the spot, I make every effort to get the answer and get back to them the same day. Customers appreciate the fact that I do what I say and follow up on all the details. To me, being customer oriented and dependable is just part of my job. It makes selling a lot more fun when your customers trust you, and—guess what—I sell more to customers who trust me.[23]

Another important element of achieving sound relationships with customers is to recognize that individual customers and their particular needs must be addressed with appropriate selling strategies and tactics. In selling, we discuss strategy at four levels: corporate,

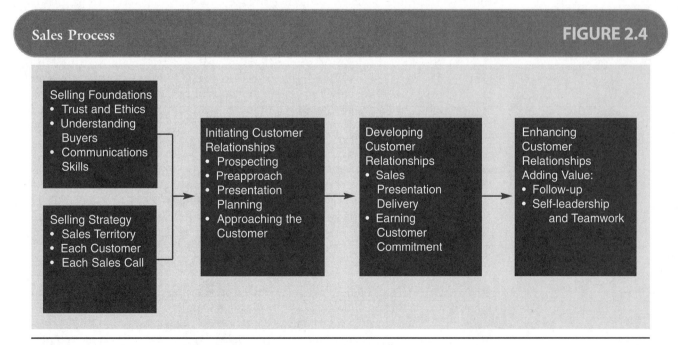

**Sales Process**                                                                **FIGURE 2.4**

**Selling Foundations**
- Trust and Ethics
- Understanding Buyers
- Communications Skills

**Selling Strategy**
- Sales Territory
- Each Customer
- Each Sales Call

**Initiating Customer Relationships**
- Prospecting
- Preapproach
- Presentation Planning
- Approaching the Customer

**Developing Customer Relationships**
- Sales Presentation Delivery
- Earning Customer Commitment

**Enhancing Customer Relationships Adding Value:**
- Follow-up
- Self-leadership and Teamwork

Salespeople must possess certain attributes to inspire trust in their customers and to be able to adapt their selling strategy to different situations. One or more selling approaches are used in the sales process. The three major phases of the sales process are initiating, developing, and enhancing customer relationships.

business unit, marketing department, and the overall sales function. An individual salesperson is strongly guided by strategy at these higher levels in the organization but must also develop selling strategies and tactics to fit the sales territory, each customer, and ultimately, each sales call.

When studying the sales process, we should note that there are countless versions of the process in terms of number of steps and the names of the steps. If, however, you were to examine popular trade books on selling and training manuals used by corporations, you would find that the various depictions of the sales process are actually more alike than truly unique. The sales process shown in Figure 2.4 is comparable to most versions of the sales process, with the exception of those versions that advocate high-pressure methods centering on how to get the customer to "say yes" rather than focusing on meeting the customer's true needs. This version of the sales process suggests that salespeople must have certain attributes to inspire trust in their customers and that salespeople should adapt their selling strategy to fit the situation. The three phases of the sales process are initiating, developing, and enhancing customer relationships. For discussion purposes, the first two phases have been subdivided into a total of five steps. The sixth and final step in the sales process is that of enhancing customer relationships, which, in many cases, extends over a prolonged period.

Another point that should be stressed is that the sales process is broken into steps to facilitate discussion and sales training, not to suggest discrete lines between the steps. The steps are actually highly interrelated and, in some instances, may overlap. Further, the stepwise flow of Figure 2.4 does not imply a strict sequence of events. Salespeople may move back and forth in the process with a given customer, sometimes shifting from step to step several times in the same sales encounter. Finally, completion of the sales process typically will require multiple sales calls.

## SUMMARY

1. **Describe the evolution of personal selling from ancient times to the modern era**. The history of personal selling can be traced as far back as ancient Greece. The Industrial Revolution enhanced the importance of salespeople, and personal selling as we know it today had its roots in the early twentieth century. The current era of sales professionalism represents a further evolution.

2. **Explain the contributions of personal selling to society, business firms, and customers**. Salespeople contribute to society by acting as stimuli in the economic process and by assisting in the diffusion of innovation. They contribute to their employers by producing revenue, performing research and feedback activities, and comprising a pool of future managers. They contribute to customers by providing timely knowledge to assist in solving problems.

3. **Distinguish between transaction-focused traditional selling and trust-based relationship selling**. As summarized in Exhibit 2.2, trust-based selling focuses more on the customer than does transaction-focused selling. The salesperson will act as a consultant to the customer in trust-based selling, whereas transaction-based selling concentrates more on making sales calls and on closing sales. There is far more emphasis on post-sales follow-up with relationship selling than with transaction selling, and salespeople must have a broader range of skills to practice relationship selling.

4. **Discuss five alternative approaches to personal selling**. Alternative approaches to personal selling include stimulus response, mental states, need satisfaction, problem solving, and the consultative approach. Stimulus response selling often uses the same sales presentation for all customers. The mental states approach prescribes that the salesperson lead the buyer through stages in the buying process. Need satisfaction selling focuses on relating benefits of the seller's products or services to the buyer's particular situation. Problem-solving selling extends need

satisfaction by concentrating on various alternatives available to the buyer. Consultative selling focuses on helping customers achieve strategic goals, not just meeting needs or solving problems. In consultative selling, salespersons fulfill three primary roles: strategic orchestrator, business consultant, and long-term ally to the customer.

5. **Describe the three primary roles fulfilled by consultative salespeople**. The three roles are strategic orchestrator, business consultant, and long-term ally. As a strategic orchestrator, salespeople coordinate the use of the sales organization's resources to satisfy the customer. As a business consultant, the salesperson becomes an expert on the customer's business and educates the customer on how his or her products can benefit the customer. The consultative salesperson acts as a long-term ally to the customer, acting in the customer's best interest even when an immediate sale is not expected.

6. **Discuss the sales process as a series of interrelated steps**. As presented in Figure 2.4, the sales process involves initiating, developing, and enhancing customer relationships. Salespeople initiate customer relationships through prospecting and preapproach activities, presentation planning, and approaching the customer. Customer relationships are developed when salespeople make sales presentations and earn a commitment from their customers. Salespeople enhance customer relationships by following up after the sale, taking a leadership role, and sometimes working as part of a team to constantly increase the value received by the customer.

## UNDERSTANDING SALES MANAGEMENT TERMS

| | |
|---|---|
| personal selling | mental states selling |
| canned sales presentation | AIDA |
| sales professionalism | need satisfaction selling |
| economic stimuli | problem-solving selling |
| diffusion of innovation | consultative selling |
| revenue producers | strategic orchestrator |
| adaptive selling | business consultant |
| stimulus response selling | long-term ally |
| continued affirmation | sales process |

## DEVELOPING SALES MANAGEMENT KNOWLEDGE

1. What factors will influence the continued evolution of personal selling?

2. How do salespeople contribute to our society? Are there negative aspects of personal selling from a societal perspective?

3. What are the primary contributions made by salespeople to their employers?

4. Most businesses would have a difficult time surviving without the benefits of the salespeople who call on them. Do you agree?

5. How are need satisfaction and problem-solving selling related? How do they differ?

6. How does the consultative selling approach differ from problem-solving and need satisfaction selling? Explain the three key roles of consultative salespersons.

7. When do you think stimulus response selling would be most effective?

8. How important is teamwork between the customer and the sales organization in practicing consultative selling? How does teamwork within the sales organization factor into consultative selling?

9. Is adaptive selling as important in domestic markets as it is in international markets?

10. Discuss the final step of the sales process (enhancing customer relationships) as related to the continuing evolution of personal selling.

## BUILDING SALES MANAGEMENT SKILLS

**ROLE PLAY**

1. **Situation:** Assume you are a salesperson for a packaging manufacturing company that supplies retail stores with custom-imprinted shopping bags. The company has manufacturing facilities in Texas, Georgia, New York, and California. There are five functional areas in the company: marketing (includes sales), production, finance and accounting, customer service and shipping, and human resources. You work out of the California plant, which serves the United States west of the Rocky Mountains. Within the marketing department, your key contact is the product manager who routinely interacts with individuals from production, customer service, and shipping to coordinate production runs with promised delivery dates. The product manager has no direct authority over any of the personnel in production or customer service and shipping. For the following situations, explain how you would try to gain the cooperation of the right people to meet customer needs. It is important that you achieve customer satisfaction but not at the expense of profitability.

   **Scenario A:** A large customer unexpectedly runs out of shopping bags and is requesting a shipment within 72 hours. Normal lead time for existing customers is 10 working days. Production is fully booked, that is, there is no idle capacity in the California plant.

   **Scenario B:** A long-time customer buys three sizes of shopping bags, all shipped in identical corrugated boxes. The smallest bags are packed 500 to a box, the medium-sized bags 250 to a box, and the largest 100 to a box. Black-and-white labels on one end of the corrugated boxes denote bag sizes. The customer wants labels in three different colors to denote bag size. According to the customer, store employees could then tell at a glance if stock for a particular size was running low and thus place prompt requests for reorders. Currently, the black-and-white labels are applied by a machine as part of the manufacturing process. The color labels would have to be custom produced and hand-fed into the labeling machine, whereas existing labels are printed inexpensively in large quantities and fed automatically into the labeling machine.

2. Your knowledge of selling can help you get started in a sales career. Landing a job is like making a major sale in that your knowledge, skills, and attitudes must meet the needs of the employer. One way to match up with employer needs is to use the feature-advantage-benefit (FAB) approach to assess yourself relative to employer needs. In selling, a feature is a factual statement about the product or service, for example, "at 10 pounds, it is the lightest electrical motor in its performance category." An advantage describes how the product can be used or help the customer, for example, "it is light enough to be used in portable applications." The benefit is the favorable outcome the customer will experience from the advantage, for example, "your customers no longer will have to come to the repair center for assistance, as service reps will be able to use portable repair kits in the field." To translate this method to the job search, think of yourself as the "product." Select an appropriate company and discover what they are looking for in sales job applicants. You can use classified ads, the college placement center, personal contacts, or other sources to find a sales position that you are interested in. Using the following example as a starting point, complete a FAB worksheet that shows how you are qualified for the job. In a real job search, this information could be translated to your résumé or cover letter requesting an interview.

## The FAB Job-Search Matrix (Example)

| A<br>Need | B<br>Feature | C<br>Advantage | D<br>Benefit |
|---|---|---|---|
| Employer or Problem<br>"This job requires . . ." | Student<br>"I have . . ." | "This means . . ." | Employer<br>"You will . . ." |
| frequent sales presentations to individuals and groups | taken 10 classes that required presentations | I require limited or no training in making presentations | save on the cost of training; you have ability and confidence to be productive early |

(List additional needs, features, advantages, and benefits.)

3. Many industry observers believe that entrepreneurs must have strong selling skills to succeed. At a minimum, entrepreneurs should understand the sales process well enough to direct the sales efforts of others. To better understand the linkages between entrepreneurship and selling, visit the *Inc* magazine Web site at **http://www.inc.com.** From the home page, click on the "Sales" link under the "How To" menu. What suggestions can you find that relate to material in this module?

## MAKING SALES MANAGEMENT DECISIONS

### Case 2.1: Biomod, Inc.
#### Background

Biomod, Inc., a California-based manufacturer of educational models of the human body, has been in business since the mid-1960s. The company's products, sold primarily to middle schools in the United States, are available in plastic or as computer images. Accompanying products include lesson plans for teachers, and workbooks and computer programs for students. Biomod has enjoyed healthy sales increases in recent years, as schools increasingly integrated computer-assisted instruction into their curricula. Five years ago, Biomod began selling consumer versions of its models through selected specialty educational toy stores and recently began selling on its own Web site. In addition, Biomod is also selling on the Web through Hypermart.com and Ed-Toys. Further, Biomod has had discussions with Toys "Я" Us, and the giant retailer seems eager to stock Biomod products.

#### Current Situation

Biomod has employed Zack Wilson, a recent graduate of San Diego State University, for the past six months. He has become familiar with all aspects of marketing the Biomod product line and is now the sales representative for electronic retailing accounts. Zack is truly excited about his job, as he sees the explosive growth potential for selling Biomod products on the Internet. His first big success came when he convinced Hypermart.com to sell Biomod products. After all, Hypermart has the reputation in most circles as the premier electronic retailer. Thirty days after his initial sales to Hypermart, Zack was thrilled to land Ed-Toys as his second electronic retailer.

No doubt about it, Zack Wilson was on a roll. Securing commitments from Hypermart and Ed-Toys within a month was almost too good to be true. In fact, there was only one problem facing Zack Wilson. Hypermart had begun discounting the Biomod product line as much as 20 percent off suggested retail, and Ed-Toys was unhappy with the intense price competition. The following conversation had just taken place between Zack and Ed-Toys buyer Andrea Haughton:

*Andrea*: Zack, your line looked really promising to us at suggested retail prices, but meeting Hypermart's pricing sucks the profit right out of the equation. Are you selling Hypermart at a lower price than us?

*Zack*: Absolutely not! Hypermart just decided to promote our line with the discounts.

*Andrea*: So the discounts are just a temporary promotion? When will Hypermart stop discounting?

*Zack*: Well, I don't really know. What I mean by that is that Hypermart often discounts, but in the case of the Biomod line, I've got to believe it's just a temporary thing.

*Andrea*: Why do you think so?

*Zack*: Because they haven't asked me for a lower price. Like you, they can't be making much of a profit after the discounts.

*Andrea*: Well, Zack, we need to stop the bleeding! I can't go on meeting their prices. If they're not making money either, maybe it's time you get them to stop the discounting. Can you talk with them about getting up to suggested retail?

*Zack*: Andrea, you know I can't dictate retail selling prices to them any more than I could to you.

*Andrea*: Nor am I suggesting you try to dictate prices. I am simply suggesting that you let them know that if they choose to go back to suggested retail, we will surely follow. If we can't sell at suggested retail, we will have little choice but to stop selling the Biomod line. I'm sure you can appreciate the fact that we have profit expectations for every line we sell. At 20 percent off, Zack, the Biomod line just doesn't cut it for us.

*Zack*: O.K., I will see what I can do.

Later in the day, Zack checked his e-mail and found a disturbing message from Barbara Moore, a Biomod sales representative for the retail store division. Barbara's message informed Zack that one of her key retailers had visited the Hypermart Web site and was extremely upset to see the heavy discounting on the Biomod line. Barbara claimed that she was in danger of losing her account and that she feared a widespread outcry from other specialty stores as word of the Hypermart discounting would quickly spread. Barbara strongly urged Zack to do what he could to get Hypermart back to suggested retail. Zack noted that Barbara had copied both her sales manager and Rebecca Stanley, Zack's sales manager, with her e-mail message.

The following day, Zack called on Warren Bryant, Hypermart's buyer for the Biomod line. He conveyed to Warren that Ed-Toys and some of the store retailers were upset with the discounting. Warren shrugged off the news, commenting only that "it's a dog-eat-dog" world and that price competition was part of the game. Zack asked Warren if he was happy with the profit margins on the Biomod line, and Warren responded that he was more concerned with growing Hypermart's market share than with profit margins. He told Zack, "Our game plan is grab a dominant share, then worry about margins." At this point, Warren gave Zack something else to think about:

*Warren*: Hey, Zack, I noticed you guys are selling the same products on your own Web site as the ones we're selling on ours.

*Zack*: True, what's the problem?

*Warren*: Well, I just read in the trade press where Home Depot told their vendors that they don't buy from their (Home Depot's) competitors and that they view vendor Web sites as competitors to their retail business. Maybe we feel the same way. We sell on the Web, and if you do too, then you're really a competitor for us.

*Zack*: Warren, you know that we only do a little volume on the Web. Our site is really more of an information site.

*Warren*: But you do offer an alternative to other electronic retailers and us by selling on your own site. And by the way, don't your store retailers oppose your selling on the Web?

*Zack*: At this point, most of them are small retailers, and frankly speaking, they view you as more of a threat than us selling on our own site. Besides, our store division salesforce is working on a software package that will enable our store retailers to easily set up their own Web sites over the next six months or so.

*Warren*: Unbelievable! What you're saying is that another division in your company is creating even more Web-based competition for me! I thought we had a real future together, but I've got to do some heavy-duty thinking on that. Thanks, Zack, but I'm really busy and need to move on to some other priorities this afternoon. Call me if you have any new thoughts on where we go from here.

Zack left Hypermart and began the hour-long drive back to the office. "Good thing I've a little time to think about this situation," he thought as he drove along. "I need to talk with Rebecca Stanley just as soon as I get to the office."

## Questions

1. How do you think Zack got into this dilemma?
2. If you were Rebecca Stanley, Zack's sales manager, what would you advise Zack to do?

**Situation:**   Read Case 2.1.

**ROLE PLAY**

**Characters:**   Zack Wilson, Biomod sales representative; Rebecca Stanley, Biomod sales manager.

**Scene 1:**   *Location*—Rebecca's office. *Action*—Zack explains to Rebecca what has occurred with the Ed-Toys and Hypermart accounts. Rather than telling Zack how to deal with Hypermart and Ed-Toys from this point forward, Rebecca directs Zack to devise his own strategy. Rebecca then tells Zack that she would like to visit both accounts with him within a week, and that she should like to review his strategy for Hypermart and Ed-Toys within 48 hours.

*Upon completion of the role play, address the following questions:*

1. Is Rebecca justified in telling Zack to devise his own strategy rather than giving him specific direction at this time? What are the advantages and disadvantages of her approach?
2. How could this situation have been prevented?

**Scene 2:**   *Location*—Rebecca's office. *Action*—Zack presents his strategy to Rebecca.

*Upon completion of the role play, address the following questions:*

1. What are the strengths and weaknesses of Zack's interaction with Ed-Toys and Hypermart?
2. What further suggestions can you make for dealing with Hypermart and Ed-Toys?

## Case 2.2: Plastico, Inc.

### Background

Plastico, Inc., located in New York, is a manufacturer of plastic components. The company is noted for producing high-quality products. Its sales-force calls on large accounts, such as refrigerator manufacturers who might need large quantities of custom-made products, such as door liners. Recent increases in new-home sales over the past several years have fueled refrigerator sales and, subsequently, sales at Plastico. Moreover, federal regulations requiring that dishwasher liners be made of plastic, rather than porcelain, have enhanced Plastico's sales.

### Current Situation

Sharon Stone had recently been assigned to the central Michigan territory. Although this was her first sales job, she felt confident and was eager to begin. She had taken a sales course in college and had just completed the company's training program. The company stressed the use of an organized sales presentation in which the salesperson organizes the key points into a planned sequence that allows for adaptive behavior by the salesperson as the presentation progresses. She was familiar with this approach because she had studied it in her college sales course.

Sharon's first call was at a small refrigerator manufacturer in Ann Arbor. She had called the day before to set up an appointment with materials purchasing manager David Kline at 9:00 A.M. On the morning of her meeting, Sharon was running behind schedule because of an alarm clock malfunction. As a result, she ended up in traffic she did not anticipate and did not arrive for her appointment until 9:10 A.M. When she informed the receptionist she had an appointment with David Kline, she was told he was in another meeting. He did agree, however, to see Sharon when his meeting was finished, which would be about 9:45 A.M. Sharon was upset Kline would not wait 10 minutes for her and let the receptionist know it.

At 9:50 A.M. Sharon was introducing herself to Kline. She noticed his office was filled with University of Michigan memorabilia. She remembered from her training that the first thing to do was build rapport with the prospect. Thus she asked Kline if he went to the University of Michigan. This got the ball rolling quickly. Kline had graduated from Michigan and was a big fan of the basketball and football teams. He was more than happy to talk about them. Sharon was excited; she knew this would help her build rapport. After about 25 minutes of football and basketball chitchat, Sharon figured it was time to get down to business.

After finally getting Kline off the subject of sports, Sharon began to discuss the benefits of her product. She figured if she did not control the conversation Kline would revert to discussing sports. She went on and on about the material compounds comprising Plastico plastics, as well as the processes used to develop plastic liners. She explained the customizing process, the product's durability, Plastico's ability to provide door liners in any color, and her company's return and credit policies. After nearly 25 minutes, she finally asked Kline if he had any questions.

Kline asked her if she had any product samples with her. Sharon had to apologize—in all the confusion this morning she ran off and left the samples at home. Then Kline asked her about the company's turnaround time from order to delivery. Knowing quick turnaround was important to Kline, and feeling this prospect may be slipping away, she told him it was about four weeks, although she knew it was really closer to five. However, she thought, if Kline ordered from them and it took a little longer, she could always blame it on production. When the issue of price emerged, Sharon was not able to clearly justify in Kline's mind why Plastico was slightly higher than the competition. She thought that she had clearly explained the benefits of the product and that it should be obvious that Plastico is a better choice.

Finally, Kline told Sharon he would have to excuse himself. He had a meeting to attend on the other side of town. He thanked her for coming by and told her he would consider her offer. Sharon thanked Kline for his time and departed. As she reflected on her first call she wondered where she went wrong. She thought she would jot down some notes about her call to discuss with her sales manager later.

## Questions

1. What problems do you see with Sharon's first sales call?
2. If you were Sharon's sales manager, what would you recommend she do to improve her chances of succeeding?

---

**ROLE PLAY**

**Situation:** Read Case 2.2.

**Characters:** Sharon Stone, Plastico sales representative

**Scene:** *Location*—Plastico's Michigan office during a weekly sales meeting shortly after her sales call with David Kline. *Action*—Sharon reviews her sales call with David Kilne with other Plastico sales representatives and their sales manager. This is a regular feature of the weekly meetings, with the idea being that all sales representatives can learn from the experiences of others. Sharon has decided to compare her call with David Kline to some of the material from her sales training with Plastico. This material, which contrasts transaction-focused selling with trust-based relationship selling, is shown in Exhibit 1.2. Her review will analyze whether she did or did not practice trust-based relationship selling during her call with David Kline.

*Upon completion of the role play, address the following questions:*

1. Is Sharon's review of her sales call accurate?
2. What steps should Sharon take to begin to develop a strong relationship with David Kline?

This appendix is designed to give an in-depth look at sales careers. We first discuss characteristics of sales careers, then describe several different types of personal selling jobs. The appendix concludes with a discussion of the skills and qualifications necessary for success in sales careers.

## CHARACTERISTICS OF SALES CAREERS

Although individual opinions will vary, the ideal career for most individuals offers a bright future, including good opportunities for financial rewards and job advancement. As you read the following sections on the characteristics of sales careers, you might think about what you expect from a career and whether your expectations could be met in a sales career. The characteristics to be discussed are:

- job security
- advancement opportunities
- immediate feedback
- prestige
- job variety
- independence
- compensation.

### Job Security

Salespeople are revenue producers and thus enjoy relatively good job security compared with other occupational groups. Certainly, individual job security depends on individual performance, but in general, salespeople are usually the last group to be negatively affected by personnel cutbacks.

Competent salespeople also have some degree of job security based on the universality of their basic sales skills. In many cases, salespeople are able to successfully move to another employer, maybe even change industries, because sales skills are largely transferable. For salespeople working in declining or stagnant industries, this is heartening news.

Furthermore, projections by the U.S. Department of Labor indicate enduring demand for salespeople in all categories in the future (see Exhibit 2A.1.)[1] And growth in the number of salespeople should bring a corresponding growth in the number of sales management positions. According to Exhibit 2A.1, there are particularly good opportunities in manufacturing and wholesaling companies.

### Advancement Opportunities

As the business world continues to become more competitive, the advancement opportunities for salespeople will continue to be an attractive dimension of sales careers. In highly competitive markets, individuals and companies that are successful in determining and meeting customer needs will be rewarded. A case in point is Carly Fiorina, CEO of Hewlett-Packard, who began her career as a sales representative for AT&T. She later led the spinoff of Lucent Technologies from AT&T and used her sales skills to raise $3 billion on Wall Street to fund the largest public offering in U.S. history. According to Jo Weiss of Catalyst, Inc., a company that

**EXHIBIT 2A.1**    Occupational Outlook for Salespeople

| Job Type | 2002 Employment | Projected Growth 2002–2012 Percentage |
|---|---|---|
| Manufacturers and Wholesale | 1,857,000 | 19.2 |
| Advertising Sales Representative | 157,000 | 13.4 |
| Real Estate | 407,000 | 4.9 |
| Securities/Financial Services | 300,000 | 13.0 |
| Insurance Agents | 381,000 | 8.4 |
| Retail | 4,706,000 | 14.6 |

tracks women in business, a sales background was key to Fiorina's ascent to the top at Hewlett-Packard. Joel Ronning, CEO of Digital River, an e-commerce company in Minneapolis, adds, "Any good CEO has to understand sales. You're constantly selling in all aspects of your life. In my early sales experience, I learned persistence and not to take rejection personally, which made all the difference in the world."[2]

## Immediate Feedback

Salespeople receive constant, immediate feedback on their job performance. Usually, the results of their efforts can be plainly observed by both salespeople and their sales managers—a source of motivation and job satisfaction. On a daily basis, salespeople receive direct feedback from their customers, and this can be stimulating, challenging, and productive. The opportunity to react immediately to customer feedback during sales presentations is a strong benefit of adaptive selling, and distinguishes selling from other forms of marketing communications such as advertising and public relations. The spontaneity and creativity involved in reacting to immediate feedback is one dimension of selling that makes it such an interesting job.

## Prestige

Traditionally, sales has not been a prestigious occupation in the eyes of the general public. There is some evidence that as the general public learns more about the activities and qualifications of professional salespeople, the image of salespeople, and thus the prestige of selling, is improving. An analysis of the popular press (excluding business publications) reveals that there are more positive than negative mentions of news-making salespeople. In a positive light, salespeople are frequently seen as knowledgeable, well trained, educated, and capable of solving customer problems. The negative aspects of salespeople's image often center on deception and high-pressure techniques.[3]

The struggling, down-and-out huckster as depicted by Willy Loman in Arthur Miller's 1949 classic *Death of a Salesman* is hardly typical of the professional salesperson of today and the future. Professional salespeople destroy such unfavorable stereotypes, and they would not jeopardize customer relationships by using high-pressure sales techniques to force a premature sale.[4] These perceptions are especially true in the business world, where encounters with professional salespeople are commonplace.

## Job Variety

Salespeople rarely vegetate due to boredom. Their jobs are multifaceted and dynamic. For a person seeking the comfort of a well-established routine, sales might not be a good career choice. In sales, day-to-day variation on the job is the norm. Customers change, new products and services are developed, and competition introduces new elements at a rapid pace.

The opportunity to become immersed in the job and bring creativity to bear is demonstrated by General Mills, whose salesforce has been named one of the best in America. According to John Maschuzik, vice president of sales in the western United States, salespeople's customization of promotional efforts for their customers is crucial to the company's success. Maschuzik says that General Mills gives their salespeople a lot of latitude and the opportunity to be creative in spending retail promotion money.[5]

## Independence

Sales jobs often allow independence of action. This independence is frequently a by-product of decentralized sales operations in which salespeople live and work away from headquarters, therefore working from their homes and making their own plans for extensive travel.

Independence of action and freedom to make decisions are usually presented as advantages that sales positions have over tightly supervised jobs. College students who prefer sales careers rate freedom to make decisions second only to salary as an important job consideration.[6] Despite its appeal, however, independence does present some problems. New recruits working from their homes may find the lack of a company office somewhat disorienting. They may need an office environment to relate to, especially if their past work experience provided regular contact in an office environment.

The independence of action traditionally enjoyed by salespeople is being scrutinized by sales managers more heavily now than in the past. The emphasis on sales productivity, accomplished in part through cost containment, is encouraging sales managers to take a more active role in dictating travel plans and sales call schedules.

## Compensation

Compensation is generally thought to be a strong advantage of sales careers. Pay is closely tied to performance, especially if commissions and bonuses are part of the pay package.

Starting salaries for inexperienced salespersons with a college degree typically average $40,000. Between the extremes of the highly experienced salesperson and the inexperienced recruit, an average salesperson earns approximately $50,000–$70,000 per year. More experienced salespersons, including those who deal with large customers, often earn in the $85,000–$135,000 range. Top salespeople can earn hundreds of thousands of dollars annually, with some exceeding a million dollars in annual earnings.

## CLASSIFICATION OF PERSONAL SELLING JOBS

Because there are so many unique sales jobs, the term *salesperson* is not by itself very descriptive. A salesperson could be a flower vendor at a busy downtown intersection or the sales executive negotiating the sale of Boeing aircraft to the People's Republic of China.

We briefly discuss six types of personal selling jobs:

- sales support
- new business
- existing business
- inside sales (nonretail)
- direct-to-consumer sales
- combination sales jobs

## Sales Support

**Sales support personnel** are not usually involved in the direct solicitation of purchase orders. Rather, their primary responsibility is dissemination of information and performance of other activities designed to stimulate sales. They might concentrate at the end-user level or another level in the channel of distribution to support the overall sales effort. They may report to another salesperson, who is responsible for direct handling of purchase orders, or to the sales manager. There are two well-known categories of support salespeople: missionary or detail salespeople and technical support salespeople.

**Missionary salespeople** usually work for a manufacturer but may also be found working for brokers and manufacturing representatives, especially in the grocery industry. There are strong similarities between sales missionaries and religious missionaries. Like their counterparts, sales missionaries are expected to "spread the word" with the purpose of conversion—to customer status. Once converted, the customer receives reinforcing messages, new information, and the benefit of the missionary's activities to strengthen the relationship between buyer and seller.

In the pharmaceutical industry, the **detailer** is a fixture. Detailers working at the physician level furnish valuable information regarding the capabilities and limitations of medications in an attempt to get the physician to prescribe their product. Another sales representative from the same pharmaceutical company will sell the medication to the wholesaler or pharmacist, but it is the detailer's job to support the direct sales effort by calling on physicians.

Technical specialists are sometimes considered to be sales support personnel. These **technical support salespeople** may assist in design and specification processes, installation of equipment, training of the customer's employees, and follow-up service of a technical nature. They are sometimes part of a sales team that includes another salesperson who specializes in identifying and satisfying customer needs by recommending the appropriate product or service.

## New Business

New business is generated for the selling firm by adding new customers or introducing new products to the marketplace. Two types of new-business salespeople are pioneers and order-getters.

**Pioneers**, as the term suggests, are constantly involved with either new products, new customers, or both. Their task requires creative selling and the ability to counter the resistance to change that will likely be present in prospective customers. Pioneers are well represented in the sale of business franchises, in which the sales representatives travel from city to city seeking new franchisees.

**Order-getters** are salespeople who actively seek orders, usually in a highly competitive environment. Although all pioneers are also order-getters, the reverse is not true. An order-getter may serve existing customers on an ongoing basis, whereas the pioneer moves on to new customers as soon as possible. Order-getters may seek new business by selling an existing customer additional items from the product line. A well-known tactic is to establish a relationship with a customer by selling a single product from the line, then to follow up with subsequent sales calls for other items from the product line.

Most corporations emphasize sales growth, and salespeople operating as pioneers and order-getters are at the heart of sales growth objectives. The pressure to perform in these roles is fairly intense; the results are highly visible. For these reasons, the new-business salesperson is often among the elite in any company's salesforce.

## Existing Business

In direct contrast to new-business salespeople, other salespeople's primary responsibility is to maintain relationships with existing customers. Salespeople who specialize in maintaining existing business include **order-takers**. These salespeople frequently work for wholesalers and, as the term *order-taker* implies, they are not too involved in creative selling. Route salespeople who work an established customer base, taking routine reorders of stock items, are order-takers. They sometimes follow a pioneer salesperson and take over the account after the pioneer has made the initial sale.

These salespeople are no less valuable to their firms than the new-business salespeople, but creative selling skills are less important to this category of sales personnel. Their strengths tend to be reliability and competence in assuring customer convenience. Customers grow to depend on the services provided by this type of salesperson. As most markets are becoming more competitive, the role of existing-business salespeople is sometimes critical to prevent erosion of the customer base.

Many firms, believing that it is easier to protect and maintain profitable customers than it is to find replacement customers, are reinforcing sales efforts to existing customers. For example, Frito-Lay uses 18,000 route service salespeople to call on retail customers at least three times weekly. Larger customers see their Frito-Lay representative on a daily basis. These salespeople spend a lot of their time educating customers about the profitability of Frito-Lay's snack foods, which leads to increased sales for both the retailer and for Frito-Lay.

## Inside Sales

In this text, **inside sales** refers to nonretail salespeople who remain in their employer's place of business while dealing with customers. The inside-sales operation has received considerable attention in recent years, not only as a supplementary sales tactic, but also as an alternative to field selling.

Inside sales can be conducted on an active or passive sales basis. Active inside sales include the solicitation of entire orders, either as part of a telemarketing operation or when customers walk into the seller's facilities. Passive inside sales imply the acceptance, rather than solicitation, of customer orders, although it is common practice for these transactions to include add-on sales attempts. We should note that customer service personnel sometimes function as inside-sales personnel as an ongoing part of their jobs.

## Direct-to-Consumer Sales

Direct-to-consumer salespeople are the most numerous type. There are more than 4.5 million retail salespeople in this country and perhaps another million selling real estate, insurance, and securities. Add to this figure another several million selling direct to the consumer for such companies as Tupperware, Mary Kay, and Avon.

This diverse category of salespeople ranges from the part-time, often temporary salesperson in a retail store to the highly educated, professionally trained stockbroker on Wall Street. As a general statement, the more challenging direct-to-consumer sales positions are those involving the sale of intangible services such as insurance and financial services.

## Combination Sales Jobs

Now that we have reviewed some of the basic types of sales jobs, let us consider the salesperson who performs multiple types of sales jobs within the framework of a single position. We use the case of the territory manager's position with GlaxoSmithKline Consumer Healthcare (GSK) to illustrate the **combination sales job** concept. GSK, whose products include Aqua-Fresh toothpaste, markets a wide range of consumer healthcare goods to food, drug, variety, and mass merchandisers. The territory manager's job blends responsibilities for developing new business, maintaining and stimulating existing business, and performing sales support activities.

During a typical day in the field, the GSK territory manager is involved in sales support activities such as merchandising and in-store promotion at the individual retail store level. Maintaining contact and goodwill with store personnel is another routine sales support activity. The territory manager also makes sales calls on chain headquarters personnel to handle existing business and to seek new business. And it is the territory manager who introduces new GSK products in the marketplace.

# QUALIFICATIONS AND SKILLS REQUIRED FOR SUCCESS BY SALESPERSONS

Because there are so many different types of jobs in sales, it is rather difficult to generalize about the qualifications and skills needed for success. This list would have to vary according to the details of a given job. Even then, it is reasonable to believe that for any given job, different persons with different skills could be successful. These conclusions have been reached after decades of research that has tried to correlate sales performance with physical traits, mental abilities, personality characteristics, and the experience and background of the salesperson.

Many of the skills and characteristics leading to success in sales would do the same in practically any professional business occupation. For example, the *Occupational Outlook Handbook* published by the U.S. Department of Labor points out the importance of various personal attributes for success in sales, including the following: communications and problem-solving skills, the ability to work independently and as part of a team, being goal-driven, having a pleasant personality and appearance, and perseverance.[7] Who could dispute the value of such traits for any occupation?

Success in sales is increasingly being thought of in terms of a strategic team effort, rather than the characteristics of individual salespersons. For example, three studies of more than 200 companies that employ 25,000 salespersons in the United States and Australia found that being customer-oriented and cooperating as a team player were critical to salespersons' success.[8]

Being careful not to suggest that sales success is solely a function of individual traits, let us consider some of the skills and qualifications that are thought to be especially critical for success in most sales jobs. Five factors that seem to be particularly important for success in sales are empathy, ego drive, ego strength, verbal communication skills, and enthusiasm. These factors have been selected after reviewing three primary sources of information:

- a study of more than 750,000 salespeople in 15,000 companies (Greenberg and Greenberg)[9]
- two reviews of four decades of research on factors related to sales success (Comer and Dubinsky; and Brown, Leigh, and Haygood)[10]
- surveys of sales executives[11]

## Empathy

In a sales context, **empathy** (the ability to see things as others would see them) includes being able to read cues furnished by the customer to better determine the customer's viewpoint. According to Spiro and Weitz, empathy is crucial for successful interaction between a buyer and a seller.[12] An empathetic salesperson is presumably in a better position to tailor the sales presentation to the customer during the planning stages. More important, empathetic salespeople can adjust to feedback during the presentation.

The research of Greenberg and Greenberg found empathy to be a significant predictor of sales success. This finding was partially supported in the review by Comer and Dubinsky, who found empathy to be an important factor in consumer and insurance sales but not in retail or industrial sales. Supporting the importance of empathy in sales success is a multi-industry study of 215 sales managers by Marshall, Goebel, and Moncrief.[13] These researchers found empathy to be among the top 25 percent of skills and personal attributes thought to be important determinants of sales success. Even though some studies do not find direct links between salesperson empathy and success, empathy is generally accepted as an important trait for successful salespeople. As relationship selling grows in importance, empathy logically will become even more important for sales success.

## Ego Drive

In a sales context, **ego drive** (an indication of the degree of determination a person has to achieve goals and overcome obstacles in striving for success) is manifested as an inner need to persuade others in order to achieve personal gratification. Greenberg and Greenberg point out the complementary relationship between empathy and ego drive that is necessary for sales success. The salesperson who is extremely empathetic but lacks ego drive may have problems in taking active steps to confirm a sale. However, a salesperson with more ego drive than empathy may ignore the customer's viewpoint in an ill-advised, overly anxious attempt to gain commitment from the customer.

## Ego Strength

The degree to which a person is able to achieve an approximation of inner drives is **ego strength**. Salespeople with high levels of ego strength are likely to be self-assured and self-accepting. Salespeople with healthy egos are better equipped to deal with the possibility of rejection throughout the sales process. They are probably less likely to experience sales call reluctance and are resilient enough to overcome the disappointment of inevitable lost sales.

Salespeople with strong ego drives who are well equipped to do their job will likely be high in **self-efficacy**; that is, they will strongly believe that they can be successful on the job. In situations in which their initial efforts meet resistance, rejection, or failure, salespeople high in self-efficacy are likely to persist in pursuing their goals. In complex sales involving large dollar amounts and a long sales cycle (the time from first customer contact to eventual sale), it is crucial to continue working toward a distant goal despite the very real possibility of setbacks along the way. For example, airplane manufacturers hoping to land contracts with the airlines typically pursue such contracts for several years before a buying decision is made. For those who persevere, however, the payoff can be well worth the extended effort.

## Interpersonal Communication Skills

**Interpersonal communication skills**, including listening and questioning, are essential for sales success. An in-depth study of 300 sales executives, salespeople, and customers of 24 major sales companies in North America, Europe, and Japan found that effective salespeople are constantly seeking ways to improve communication skills that enable them to develop, explain, and implement customer solutions. The companies in the study are some of the best in the world at professional selling: Sony, Xerox, American Airlines, Fuji, and Scott paper.[14]

Another major study across several industries found that three communications skills in particular were among the top 10 percent of success factors for professional salespeople.[15] The highest-rated success factor in this study was listening skills, with ability to adapt presentations according to the situation and verbal communications skills following close behind.

To meet customer needs, salespeople must be able to solicit opinions, listen effectively, and confirm customer needs and concerns. They must be capable of probing customer expectations with open- and closed-end questions and responding in a flexible manner to individual personalities and different business cultures in ways that demonstrate respect for differences.[16] This requires adaptable, socially intelligent salespeople, especially when dealing with multicultural customers.[17]

The importance of communication skills has been recognized by sales managers, recruiters, and sales researchers. These skills can be continually refined throughout a sales career, a positive factor from both a personal and a career development perspective.

## Enthusiasm

When sales executives and recruiters discuss qualifications for sales positions, they invariably include **enthusiasm**. They are usually referring to dual dimensions of enthusiasm—an enthusiastic attitude in a general sense and a special enthusiasm for selling. On-campus recruiters have mentioned that they seek students who are well beyond "interested in sales" to the point of truly being enthusiastic about career opportunities in sales. Recruiters are somewhat weary of "selling sales" as a viable career, and they welcome the job applicant who displays genuine enthusiasm for the field.

## Comments on Qualifications and Skills

The qualifications and skills needed for sales success are different today from those required for success two decades ago. As the popularity of relationship selling grows, the skills necessary for sales success will evolve to meet the needs of the marketplace. For example, Greenberg and Greenberg's research has identified what they call an "emerging factor" for sales success, a strong motivation to provide service to the customer. They contrast this **service motivation** with ego drive by noting that, although ego drive relates to persuading others, service motivation comes from desiring the approval of others. For example, a salesperson may be extremely gratified to please a customer through superior postsale service. Greenberg and Greenberg conclude that most salespeople will need both service motivation and ego drive to succeed, although they note that extremely high levels of both attributes are not likely to exist in the same individual. A survey of 28,000 people in 59 major companies by the Forum Corporation reports that a service motivation, along with understanding and respect for customers, is far more effective than aggressive selling tactics in terms of generating sales.[18]

Our discussion of factors related to sales success is necessarily brief, as a fully descriptive treatment of the topic must be tied to a given sales position. Veteran sales managers and recruiters can often specify with amazing precision what qualifications and skills are needed to succeed in a given sales job. These assessments are usually based on a mixture of objective and subjective judgments.

Professional selling offers virtually unlimited career opportunities for the right person. Many of the skills and qualifications necessary for success in selling are also important for success as an entrepreneur or as a leader in a corporate setting. For those interested in learning more about sales careers, consult these sources: *Sales & Marketing Management* magazine at http://salesandmarketing.com; *Selling Power* magazine at http://selling-power.com; and Sales & Marketing Executives-International, a professional organization, at http://www.smei.org.

## UNDERSTANDING SALES MANAGEMENT TERMS

| | |
|---|---|
| sales support personnel | combination sales job |
| missionary salespeople | empathy |
| detailer | ego drive |
| technical support salespeople | ego strength |
| pioneers | self-efficacy |
| order-getters | interpersonal communication skills |
| order-takers | enthusiasm |
| inside sales | service motivation |

# Defining the Strategic Role of the Sales Function

The two modules in Part Two discuss the sales function from a strategic perspective. Module 3 investigates strategic decisions at different levels in multi-business multiproduct firms. The key elements of corporate strategy, business strategy, marketing strategy, and sales strategy are described, and important relationships between each strategy level and the sales function are identified. Special attention is directed toward the role of personal selling in a marketing strategy and sales strategy development. Account targeting strategy, relationship strategy, selling strategy, and sales channel strategy are the key elements of a sales strategy.

Module 4 emphasizes the importance of sales organization design and salesforce deployment in successfully executing organizational strategies. The concepts of specialization, centralization, span of control, management levels, and line/staff positions are critical considerations in sales organization design. Special attention is directed toward the use of different sales organization structures in different selling environments. Salesforce deployment decisions include allocating selling effort to accounts, determining the appropriate salesforce size, and designing sales territories. The key considerations and analytical approaches for each of these decisions are discussed.

## CUSTOMER RELATIONSHIP MANAGEMENT (CRM) AND THE SALES FUNCTION: DEERE & COMPANY

Deere & Company was started as a one-person operation in 1868 by John Deere. Today, the heavy-equipment company has over 43,000 employees operating in about 160 countries. The company consists of three divisions: Agriculture, Commercial and Consumer Equipment, and Construction and Forestry. Deere equipment is sold through a 1,000-plus dealer/owner network. Most of these dealers started as mom-and-pop operations, but many have grown to be mid-sized businesses with 10 to 65 dealer locations.

The Agriculture Division has faced a tough business climate in recent years. Farmers have experienced rising operating costs but low prices for their products. This has led to consolidation within the agriculture industry. Although Deere dealers still serve many types and sizes of farms, there is a clear trend toward fewer, but larger accounts.

Deere is responding to the changes in its customer base by implementing a customer relationship management (CRM) strategy. Its dealers are developing stronger relationships with the largest accounts using a consultative selling process. They are using different types of relationships and selling processes to serve the smaller accounts. Many dealers are using the latest technology to implement their CRM strategy effectively.

For example, one dealer with 10 locations has created a database to keep track of its 90,000 customers. This database includes everything from basic contact information to complete purchase and service histories and is available to anyone in the dealership who might have contact with a customer. It is also integrated with the Deere quoting system. The data are used by management as a basis for developing sales strategies and deploying the selling effort to different accounts, and for tracking deals in process. Several interactive reporting capabilities provide valuable information to management as needed.

Salespeople also find the technology useful. All of the information a salesperson needs to plan sales calls, create quotes, and schedule customer follow-up contact is readily available. As one agricultural salesperson said, "It's improved my selling process." The dealers benefit from the increased productivity of their salespeople. For example, one dealer grew annual sales by 20 percent in a flat industry after implementing the CRM strategy and technology.

**Sources:** Julia Chang, "CRM at Any Size," *Sales & Marketing Mananagement* (August 2004): 33–34; "John Deere Would Have Been Proud," *Sales & Marketing Strategies and News* (May 2004): 22–23.

The Deere & Company example illustrates the close relationship between changes in organizational strategies at different levels and buyer behavior. Of particular importance in this example is the development of a customer relationship management (CRM) business strategy that is translated into specific sales strategies implemented effectively by salespeople. It is also critical to note that the process at Deere was driven by strategy with the latest technology used to implement the CRM and sales strategies effectively.

Many firms consist of multiple business units that market multiple products to different customer groups. Strategy development in these multibusiness, multiproduct

### Objectives

After completing this module, you should be able to

1 Define the strategy levels for multibusiness, multi-product firms.

2 Discuss how corporate and business strategy decisions affect the sales function.

3 List the advantages and disadvantages of personal selling as a marketing communications tool.

4 Specify the situations in which personal selling is typically emphasized in a marketing strategy.

5 Describe ways that personal selling, advertising, and other tools can be blended into effective integrated marketing communications programs.

6 Discuss the important concepts behind organizational buyer behavior.

7 Define an account targeting strategy.

8 Explain the different types of relationship strategies.

9 Discuss the importance of different selling strategies.

10 Describe the sales channel strategies.

firms is extremely complex. Strategy decisions must be made at many levels of the organization. However, the strategies must be consistent with each other and integrated for the firm to perform successfully. We now examine the key strategic decisions at each organizational level and highlight the impact of these strategic decisions on the sales organization.

## ORGANIZATIONAL STRATEGY LEVELS

The key strategy levels for multibusiness, multiproduct firms are presented in Exhibit 3.1. **Corporate strategy** consists of decisions that determine the mission, business portfolio, and future growth directions for the entire corporate entity. A separate **business strategy** must be developed for each **strategic business unit (SBU)** (discussed later in this module) in the corporate family, defining how that SBU plans to compete effectively within its industry. Because an SBU typically consists of multiple products serving different markets, each product/market combination requires a specific **marketing strategy**. Each marketing strategy includes the selection of target market segments and the development of a marketing mix to serve each target market. A key consideration is the role that personal selling will play in the marketing communications mix for a particular marketing strategy.

The corporate, business, and marketing strategies represent strategy development from the perspective of different levels within an organization. Although sales management may have some influence on the decisions made at each level, the key decision makers are typically from higher management levels outside the sales function. Sales management does, however, play the key role in sales strategy development. An example of one approach for strategy development at different organizational levels is presented in "Sales Management in the 21st Century: Integrating Organizational Strategies."

## CORPORATE STRATEGY AND THE SALES FUNCTION

Strategic decisions at the topmost level of multibusiness multiproduct firms determine the corporate strategy for a given firm, which is what provides direction and guidance for activities at all organizational levels. Developing a corporate strategy requires the following steps:[1]

1. Analyzing corporate performance and identifying future opportunities and threats
2. Determining corporate mission and objectives
3. Defining business units
4. Setting objectives for each business unit

---

**EXHIBIT 3.1**  Organizational Strategy Levels

| Strategy Level | Key Decision Areas | Key Decision Makers |
|---|---|---|
| Corporate strategy | Corporate mission<br>Strategic business unit definition<br>Strategic business unit objectives | Corporate management |
| Business strategy | Strategy types<br>Strategy execution | Business unit management |
| Marketing strategy | Target market selection<br>Marketing mix development<br>Integrated marketing communications | Marketing management |
| Sales strategy | Account targeting strategy<br>Relationship strategy<br>Selling strategy<br>Sales channel strategy | Sales management |

### Integrating Organizational Strategies

Jane Hrehocik Clampitt, marketing process manager at DuPont, discusses the importance of integrating strategies at different levels in a company:

*It is extremely important for large companies to develop effective strategies at different organizational levels. We focus a lot of attention on this process at DuPont. The corporate strategy defines business units and determines strategic objectives and basic resource allocations for each business unit. Then, each business unit follows a detailed process to create a business strategy that will achieve its objectives. Next, another rigorous process is used to develop specific marketing strategies for the business unit's product/markets. Finally, strategies for selling to specific customer groups within each product/market are determined. This type of sequential process is intended to develop effective and consistent strategies at each organizational level.*

Once the corporate strategy has been developed, management is concerned with implementation, evaluation, and control of the corporate strategic plan. Although the corporate strategy has the most direct impact on business-level operations, each element does affect the sales function.

## Corporate Mission

The development of a **corporate mission statement** is an important first step in the strategy formulation process. This mission statement provides direction for strategy development and execution throughout the organization. Sales managers and salespeople must operate within the guidelines presented in the corporate mission statement. Furthermore, they can use these corporate guidelines as a basis for establishing specific policies for the entire sales organization. Thus, in this way, the corporate mission statement has a direct effect on sales management activities.

Despite its importance, it has been estimated that only about 20 percent of companies have a clear mission statement that is articulated to salespeople by sales managers. The most successful corporate mission statements are simple, complete, and communicated directly to salespeople. Siebel Systems used this approach. It changed its mission statement to "Make one hundred percent customer satisfaction Siebel's overriding priority." This simplified version expressed the company's values succinctly and was easy for the salespeople to understand and adopt.[2]

## Definition of Strategic Business Units

Defining business units, often called SBUs, is an important and difficult aspect of corporate strategy development. The basic purpose is to divide the corporation into parts to facilitate strategic analysis and planning. Cravens defines an SBU as "a single product or brand, a line of products, or a mix of related products that meets a common market need or a group of related needs, and the unit's management is responsible for all (or most) of the basic business functions."[3]

The definition of SBUs is an important element of corporate strategy. Changes in SBU definition may increase or decrease the number of SBUs, and these changes typically affect the sales function in many ways. Salesforces may have to be merged, new salesforces may have to be established, or existing salesforces may have to be reorganized to perform different activities. These changes may affect all sales management activities from the type of salespeople to be hired to how they should be trained, motivated, compensated, and supervised.

Restructuring at General Electric (GE) provides a typical example. GE had considered lighting and appliances to be separate SBUs. The company, however, decided it could cut costs and better focus sales resources by combining lighting and appliances into a new business unit called GE Consumer Products. Except for some financial services at GE Capital Corp., all of the products GE sells to consumers are now included in GE Consumer Products. This change gives the GE sales organization more leverage in the consumer marketplace and increases the productivity of selling resources.[4] For example, Home Depot carries GE appliances, but not GE light bulbs. Wal-Mart sells many GE light bulbs, but few GE appliances. Because the same salesperson now sells both appliances and light bulbs, selling costs are reduced and the opportunity to get Home Depot to carry GE light bulbs and Wal-Mart to sell more GE appliances is increased.[5]

## Objectives for Strategic Business Units

Once SBUs have been defined, corporate management must determine appropriate strategic objectives for each. Many firms view their SBUs collectively as a portfolio of business units. Each business unit faces a different competitive situation and plays a different role in the **business unit portfolio**. Therefore, specific strategic objectives should be determined for each SBU. Corporate management has ultimate responsibility for establishing strategic objectives for each SBU. As illustrated in Exhibit 3.2,[6] the strategic objective assigned to a business unit has a direct effect on personal selling and sales management activities.

Determining strategic objectives for each SBU is an important aspect of corporate strategy. These strategic objectives affect the development of the sales organization's objectives, the selling tasks performed by salespeople, and the activities of sales managers. All sales organization policies are designed to help salespeople achieve the business unit strategic objective. However, too much emphasis on business unit objectives can place salespeople in uncomfortable situations as illustrated in "An Ethical Dilemma."

---

**EXHIBIT 3.2**  SBU Objectives and the Sales Organization

| Market Share Objectives System | Sales Organization Objectives | Primary Sales Tasks | Recommended Compensation |
|---|---|---|---|
| Build | Build sales volume<br>Secure distribution | Call on prospective and new accounts<br>Provide high service levels, particularly presale service<br>Product/market feedback | Salary plus incentive |
| Hold | Maintain sales volume<br>Consolidate market positions through concentration on targeted segments<br>Secure additional outlets | Call on targeted current accounts<br>Increase service levels to current accounts<br>Call on new accounts | Salary plus commission or bonus |
| Harvest | Reduce selling costs<br>Target profitable accounts | Call on and service most profitable accounts only and eliminate unprofitable accounts<br>Reduce service levels<br>Reduce inventories | Salary plus bonus |
| Divest/Liquidate | Minimize selling costs and clear out inventory | Dump inventory<br>Eliminate service | Salary |

AN ETHICAL DILEMMA

The personal computer business unit of Modern Technologies is reaching the end of its fiscal year and is very close to meeting its sales growth objective. Herb Smith, your sales manager, is rallying the troops to "get over the top" so everyone can earn a substantial performance bonus. You are motivated to do your share. Your first call today is to ABC Enterprises. ABC Enterprises purchased a number of computers from you last year. Mary Faulds, purchasing manager at ABC Enterprises, indicates that her information technology people want to upgrade these computers. You know this sale could be critical to meeting your quota and the business unit's sales growth objective. However, you also know that a new, more powerful personal computer will be available in three months. This new personal computer is exactly what ABC Enterprises needs, but the sale cannot be made until after the fiscal year ends. What would you do? Why?

## Corporate Strategy Summary

Strategic decisions at the topmost levels of multibusiness corporations provide guidance for strategy development at all lower organizational levels. Even though the sales function is often far removed from the corporate level, corporate strategy has direct and indirect impacts on personal selling and sales management. The corporate mission, definition of SBUs, and determination of SBU objectives all affect sales organization operations. However, corporate strategy decisions have their most immediate impact on business unit strategies.

## BUSINESS STRATEGY AND THE SALES FUNCTION

Whereas corporate strategy addresses decisions across business units, a separate strategy must be designed for each SBU. The essence of business strategy is competitive advantage: How can each SBU compete successfully against competitive products and services? What differential advantage will each SBU try to exploit in the marketplace? What can each SBU do better than competitors? Answers to these questions provide the basis for business strategies.

## Business Strategy Types

Although creating a business unit strategy is a complex task, several classification schemes have been developed to aid in this endeavor. One of the most popular is Porter's **generic business strategies**,[7] presented in Exhibit 3.3.[8] Each of these generic strategies—**low cost, differentiation**, or **niche**—emphasizes a different type of competitive advantage and has different implications for a sales organization. The sales function plays an important role in executing a generic business strategy.[9] As indicated in Exhibit 3.3, the activities of sales managers and salespeople differ depending on whether the business unit is using a low-cost, differentiation, or niche business strategy. The sales function can often provide the basis for differentiation.

As indicated by the Deere & Company example in the opening vignette, many companies are adopting **customer relationship management (CRM)** as a business strategy:

> Customer relationship management (CRM) is a business strategy to select and manage the most valuable customer relationships. CRM requires a customer-centric business philosophy and culture to support effective marketing, sales, and service processes. CRM applications can enable effective customer relationship management, provided that an enterprise has the right leadership, strategy, and culture.[10]

| EXHIBIT 3.3 | Generic Business Strategies and Salesforce Activities |
| --- | --- |
| **Strategy Type** | **Role of the Salesforce** |
| **Low-cost supplier**<br>Aggressive construction of efficient-scale facilities, vigorous pursuit of cost reductions from experience, tight cost, and overhead control, usually associated with high relative market share. | Servicing large current customers, pursuing large prospects, minimizing costs, selling on the basis of price, and usually assuming significant order-taking responsibilities |
| **Differentiation**<br>Creation of something perceived industrywide as being unique. Provides insulation against competitive rivalry because of brand loyalty and resulting lower sensitivity to price. | Selling nonprice benefits, generating orders, providing high quality of customer service and responsiveness, possibly significant amount of prospecting if high-growth industry, selecting customers based on low price sensitivity; usually requires a high-quality salesforce |
| **Niche**<br>Service of a particular target market, with each functional policy developed with this target market in mind. Although market share in the industry might be low, the firm dominates a segment within the industry. | To become experts in the operations and opportunities associated with the target market; Focusing customer attention on nonprice benefits and allocating selling time to the target market |

A critical aspect of this definition is that CRM is a business strategy. However, the effective implementation of a CRM strategy requires integrated, cross-functional business processes, specific organizational capabilities, an appropriate business philosophy, and the right technology to make everything work.[11] Successful firms address the strategy, philosophy, process, and capability issues first, and then find the best technology for implementation. Unsuccessful firms tend to focus on the technology first and then try to adapt their strategy, philosophy, process, and capability to fit the technology.[12] The Deere & Company example illustrates the correct approach. Deere developed a CRM strategy and addressed the other relevant areas first, and then spent a great deal of time finding the technology that best met its specific needs.

## Business Strategy Summary

Business strategies determine how each SBU plans to compete in the marketplace. Several strategic approaches are available, each placing its own demands on the sales function. The role of the sales function depends on how an SBU plans to compete in the marketplace, with the activities of sales managers and salespeople being important in executing a business strategy successfully.

## MARKETING STRATEGY AND THE SALES FUNCTION

Because SBUs typically market multiple products to multiple customer groups, separate marketing strategies are often developed for each of an SBU's target markets. These marketing strategies must be consistent with the business strategy. For example, marketers operating in an SBU with a differentiation business strategy would probably not develop marketing strategies that emphasize low price. The marketing strategies for each target market should reinforce the differentiation competitive advantage sought by the SBU.

Figure 3.1 illustrates the major components of a marketing strategy and highlights the position of personal selling within the marketing communications portion of a marketing strategy. The key components of any marketing strategy are the selection of a **target market** and the development of a **marketing mix**. Target market selection requires a definition of the specific market segment to be served. The marketing mix then consists of a marketing offer designed to appeal to the defined target market. This marketing offer contains a mixture of product, price, distribution, and marketing communications strategies. The critical task for the marketing strategist is to develop a marketing mix that satisfies the needs of the target market better than competitive offerings.

Personal selling may be an important element in the marketing communications portion of the marketing mix. The marketing communications strategy consists of a mixture

**Marketing Strategy and Personal Selling**                    **FIGURE 3.1**

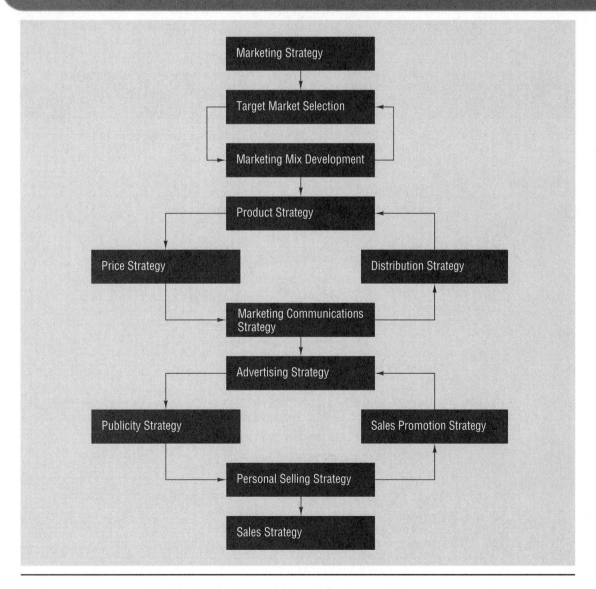

Personal selling is an important element of a marketing communications strategy. The marketing communications strategy is one element of a marketing mix designed to appeal to a defined target market. A marketing strategy can be defined in terms of target market and marketing mix components.

of personal selling, advertising, sales promotion, and publicity, with most strategies emphasizing either personal selling or advertising as the main tool. Sales promotion and publicity are typically viewed as supplemental tools. Thus, a key strategic decision is to determine when marketing communications strategies should be driven by personal selling or advertising. This decision should capitalize on the relative advantages of personal selling and advertising for different target markets and different marketing mixes.

## Advantages and Disadvantages of Personal Selling

Personal selling is the only promotional tool that consists of personal communication between seller and buyer, and the advantages and disadvantages of personal selling thus accrue from this personal communication. The personal communication between buyer and seller is typically viewed as more credible and has more of an impact (or impression) than messages delivered through advertising media. Personal selling also allows for better timing of message delivery, and it affords the flexibility of communicating different messages to different customers or changing a message during a sales call based on customer feedback. Finally, personal selling has the advantage of allowing a sale to be closed. These characteristics make personal selling a powerful tool in situations in which the benefits of personal communication are important (see Figure 3.2).

| FIGURE 3.2 | Personal Selling–Driven versus Advertising–Driven Marketing Communications Strategies |

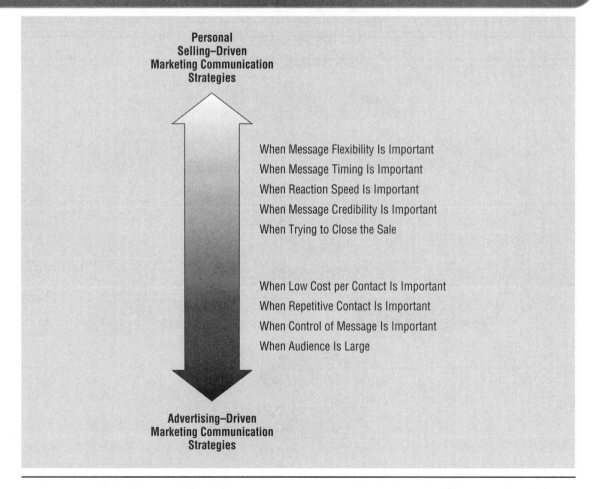

Personal selling–driven marketing communications strategies are most appropriate in situations in which the benefits of personal communication are important.

The major disadvantage of personal selling is the high cost to reach each member of the audience. Contrast this with the pennies that it costs to reach an audience member through mass advertising. The benefits of personal selling do not come cheap. They may, however, outweigh its costs for certain types of target market situations and for specific marketing mixes.

## Target Market Situations and Personal Selling

The characteristics of personal selling are most advantageous in specific target market situations. Personal selling–driven strategies are appropriate when (1) the market consists of only a few buyers that tend to be concentrated in location, (2) the buyer needs a great deal of information, (3) the purchase is important, (4) the product is complex, and (5) service after the sale is important. The target market characteristics that favor personal selling are similar to those found in most business purchasing situations. Thus, personal selling is typically the preferred tool in **business marketing**, whereas advertising is normally emphasized in consumer marketing situations (see Figure 3.3).

An effective marketing communications mix capitalizes on the advantages of each promotional tool. Moreover, characteristics of the target market must be considered, and the promotional mix must also be consistent with the other elements of the marketing mix to ensure a coordinated marketing offer.

## Marketing Mix Elements and Personal Selling

One of the most difficult challenges facing the marketing strategist is making sure that decisions concerning the product, distribution, price, and marketing communications areas result in an effective marketing mix. There are any number of ways that these elements can be combined to form a marketing mix. However, some combinations tend to represent logical fits. Exhibit 3.4[13] shows when a personal selling emphasis might fit well with the other marketing elements. Again, these suggestions should be considered only as guidelines, because the development of unique marketing mixes may produce competitive advantages in the marketplace.

An interesting example is Best Buy. Best Buy is the largest consumer electronics retailer in the nation with annual sales in excess of $24 billion. It is, however, beginning to face increased competition from new sources. Wal-Mart, the world's largest

---

**Targeting Market Characteristics and Marketing Communications Strategy**                                     **FIGURE 3.3**

| Business Target Markets → | Personal Selling–Driven Marketing Communications Strategies | Consumer Target Markets → | Advertising–Driven Marketing Communications Strategies |
|---|---|---|---|
| **Characteristics** | | **Characteristics** | |
| • Few Buyers | | • Many Buyers | |
| • Buyers Concentrated Geographically | | • Buyers Dispersed Geographically | |
| • Purchase Information Needs High | | • Purchase Information Needs Low | |
| • Purchases Made in Large Amounts | | • Purchases Made in Small Amounts | |
| • High-Importance Purchases | | • Low-Importance Purchases | |
| • Complex Products Purchased | | • Low-Complexity Products Purchased | |
| • Postpurchase Service Important | | • Postpurchase Service Not Important | |

Personal selling–driven marketing communications strategies are most appropriate for target markets that have characteristics typical of business markets.

| EXHIBIT 3.4 | Marketing Mix Elements and Personal Selling | | |

| Marketing Mix Area | Characteristics | Marketing Mix Area | Characteristics |
|---|---|---|---|
| Product or service | Complex products requiring customer application assistance (computers, pollution control systems, stream turbines) <br><br> Major purchase decisions, such as food items purchased by supermarket chains <br><br> Features and performance of the product requiring personal demonstration and trial by the customer (private aircraft) | Channels | Channel system relatively short and direct to end users <br><br> Product and service training and assistance needed by channel in intermediaries <br><br> Personal selling needed in "pushing" product through channel <br><br> Channel intermediaries available to perform personal selling function for supplier with limited resources and experience (brokers or manufacturers' agents) |
| Price | Final price negotiated between buyer and seller (appliances, automobiles, real estate) <br><br> Selling price or quantity purchased enable an adequate margin to support selling expenses (traditional department store compared with discount house) | | |

retailer with over $250 billion in annual sales, is moving aggressively into high-end consumer electronics. In addition, Dell is also expanding its product mix to include MP3 players and flat-panel TVs. Best Buy's marketing strategy to compete with these giants is to focus more on the personal selling component of its marketing mix. Its salespeople, called "blueshirts," are implementing a CARE Plus sales process to increase sales by connecting more deeply with customers and providing attention, know-how, service, and complete solutions to meet customer needs. This personal selling–driven strategy is intended to differentiate Best Buy's from Wal-Mart, with its low price strategy, and Dell, which has a direct selling Internet model.[14]

## Integrated Marketing Communication

Although marketing communication strategies are typically driven by advertising or personal selling, most firms use a variety of tools in their marketing communication mix. The relative importance of various marketing communication tools in consumer and business markets is shown in the rankings presented in Exhibit 3.5.[15]

The key task facing both business and consumer marketers is deciding how and when to use these tools. **Integrated marketing communication (IMC)** is the increasingly popular term used by many firms to describe their approach. IMC is the strategic integration of multiple marketing communication tools in the most effective and efficient manner. The objective is to use the most cost-effective tool to achieve a desired communication objective and to ensure a consistent message is being communicated to the market.

| Ranking of Marketing Communications Tools | EXHIBIT 3.5 |

| Consumer Markets | Business Markets |
|---|---|
| Television ads | Personal selling |
| Literature, coupons, and point-of-purchase displays | Print ads |
| Print ads | Direct mail |
| Direct mail | Trade shows and exhibits catalogs/directories |
| Radio ads | Literature, coupons, and point-of-purchase displays |
| Catalogs/directories | Public relations |
| Public relations | Dealer and distributor materials |
| Trade shows and exhibits | |

A typical approach is to use some form of advertising to generate company and product awareness and to identify potential customers. These sales leads might then be contacted and qualified by telemarketers. The best prospects are then turned over to the salesforce to receive personal selling attention. This approach uses relatively inexpensive tools (advertising and telemarketing) to communicate with potential customers early in the buying process and saves the more expensive tools (personal selling) for the best prospects later in the buying process.

## Marketing Strategy Summary

Selecting target markets and designing marketing mixes are the key components in marketing strategy development. Marketing strategies must be developed for the target markets served by an SBU and must be consistent with the business unit strategy. One important element of the marketing mix is marketing communications. The critical task is designing a mix that capitalizes on the advantages of each tool. Personal selling has the basic advantage of personal communication and is emphasized in target market situations and marketing mixes in which personal communication is important.

## SALES STRATEGY FRAMEWORK

Corporate, business, and marketing strategies view customers as aggregate markets or market segments. These organizational strategies provide direction and guidance for the sales function, but then sales managers and salespeople must translate these general organizational strategies into specific strategies for individual customers.

A sales strategy is designed to execute an organization's marketing strategy for individual accounts. For example, a marketing strategy consists of selecting a target market and developing a marketing mix. Target markets are typically defined in broad terms, such as the small business market or the university market. Marketing mixes are also described broadly in terms of general product, distribution, price, and marketing communications approaches. All accounts within a target market (e.g., all small businesses or all universities), however, are not the same in terms of size, purchasing procedures, needs, problems, and other factors. The major purpose of a sales strategy is to develop a specific approach for selling to individual accounts within a target market. A sales strategy capitalizes on the important differences among individual accounts or groups of similar accounts.

A firm's sales strategy is important for two basic reasons. First, it has a major impact on a firm's sales and profit performance. Second, it influences many other sales management decisions. Salesforce recruiting, selecting, training, compensation, and performance evaluation are affected by the sales strategies used by a firm as discussed in "Sales Management in the 21st Century: The Importance of Sales Strategy."

### The Importance of Sales Strategy

Jane Hrehocik Clampitt, marketing process manager at DuPont, emphasizes the importance of having a specific sales strategy for different account groups:

*Having an effective sales strategy is so important for a sales organization to be aligned with its business and marketing strategies. The sales strategy provides direction for executing the business and marketing strategies. At DuPont we identify a specific customer interface strategy for each account segment. The customer interface strategy defines how we plan to interact with each customer group. Different customer interface strategies require different selling skills and affect all aspects of sales management. The customer interface strategies determine the types of salespeople to hire, how to develop these individuals and the support systems needed, and how to measure success. Our aim is to maximize the effectiveness, efficiency, and productivity of everyone involved at the customer interface.*

Because personal selling–driven promotion strategies are typical in business marketing, our discussion of sales strategy focuses on organizational (also called industrial or business) customers. Specific customers are referred to as accounts. Thus, a sales strategy must be based on the important and unique aspects of organizational buyer behavior. A framework that integrates organizational buyer behavior and sales strategy is presented in Figure 3.4.

## Sales Strategy Framework    FIGURE 3.4

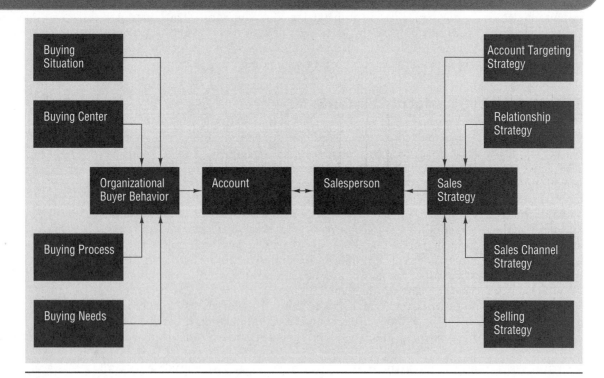

Salesperson interaction with accounts is directed by a sales strategy. The sales strategy, which defines how specific accounts are to be managed and covered, must be based on an understanding of the buying situation, buying center, buying process, and buying needs of the account.

# ORGANIZATIONAL BUYER BEHAVIOR

Organizational buyer behavior refers to the purchasing behavior of organizations. Although there are unique aspects in the buying behavior of any organization, specific types of organizations tend to share similarities in their purchasing procedures (see Exhibit 3.6).[16] Most of our attention is focused on business organizations classified as users or **original equipment manufacturers (OEM)**. However, we provide examples of **resellers, government organizations**, and **institutions** throughout the book.

As indicated in Figure 3.4, the development of sales strategy requires an understanding of organizational buyer behavior. The unique aspects of organizational buyer behavior revolve around the buying situation, buying center, buying process, and buying needs.

## Buying Situation

One key determinant of organizational buyer behavior is the buying situation faced by an account. Three major types are possible, each representing its own problems for the buying firm and each having different strategic implications for the selling firm.

A **new task buying situation**, in which the organization is purchasing a product for the first time, poses the most problems for the buyer. Because the account has little knowledge or experience as a basis for making the purchase decision, it will typically use a lengthy process to collect and evaluate purchase information. The decision-making process in this type of situation is often called **extensive problem solving**.

A **modified rebuy buying situation** exists when the account has previously purchased and used the product. Although the account has information and experience with the product, it will usually want to collect additional information and may make a change when purchasing a replacement product. The decision-making process in this type of situation is often referred to as **limited problem solving**.

| Types of Organizations | | **EXHIBIT 3.6** |
|---|---|---|
| **Major Category** | **Types** | **Example** |
| Business or industrial organizations | Users—purchase products and services to produce other products and services | IBM purchasing facsimile machines from Sharp for their corporate offices |
| | Original equipment manufacturers (OEM)—purchase products to incorporate into products | IBM purchasing microcomputer chips from Intel to incorporate into their personal computers |
| | Resellers—purchase products to sell | Businessland purchasing IBM personal computers to sell to organizations |
| Government organizations | Federal, state, and local government agencies | Virginia State Lottery purchasing IBM personal computers for managers |
| Institutions | Public and private institutions | United Way purchasing IBM personal computers for their offices |

The least complex buying situation is the **straight rebuy buying situation**, wherein the account has considerable experience in using the product and is satisfied with the current purchase arrangements. In this case, the buyer is merely reordering from the current supplier and engaging in **routinized response behavior**.

## Buying Center

One of the most important characteristics of organizational buyer behavior is the involvement of the many individuals from the firm that participate in the purchasing process. The term **buying center** has been used to designate these individuals. The buying center is not a formal designation on the organization chart but rather an informal network of purchasing participants. (However, members of the purchasing department are typically included in most buying centers and are normally represented in the formal organizational structure.) The difficult task facing the selling firm is to identify all the buying center members and to determine the specific role of each.

The possible roles that buying center members might play in a particular purchasing decision are

- *initiators*, who start the organizational purchasing process
- *users*, who use the product to be purchased
- *gatekeepers*, who control the flow of information between buying center members
- *influencers*, who provide input for the purchasing decision
- *deciders*, who make the final purchase decision
- *purchasers*, who implement the purchasing decision

Each buying center role may be performed by more than one individual, and each individual may perform more than one buying center role.

## Buying Process

Organizational buyer behavior can be viewed as a **buying process** consisting of several phases. Although this process has been presented in different ways, the following phases represent a consensus.[17]

Phase 1. Recognition of problem or need
Phase 2. Determination of the characteristics of the item and the quantity needed
Phase 3. Description of the characteristics of the item and quantity needed
Phase 4. Search for and qualification of potential sources
Phase 5. Acquisition and analysis of proposals
Phase 6. Evaluation of proposals and selection of suppliers
Phase 7. Selection of an order routine
Phase 8. Performance feedback and evaluation

These buying phases may be formalized for some organizations and/or for certain purchases. In other situations, this process may only be a rough approximation of what actually occurs. For example, government organizations and institutions tend to have more formal purchasing processes than most business or industrial organizations. Viewing organizational buying as a multiple-phase process is helpful in developing sales strategy. A major objective of any sales strategy is to facilitate an account's movement through this process in a manner that will lead to a purchase of the seller's product.

## Buying Needs

Organizational buying is typically viewed as goal-directed behavior intended to satisfy specific buying needs. Although the organizational purchasing process is made to satisfy organizational needs, the buying center consists of individuals who are also trying to satisfy individual needs throughout the decision process. Exhibit 3.7[18] presents examples of individual and organizational needs that might be important in a purchase situation.

| Personal and Organizational Needs    EXHIBIT 3.7 | |
| --- | --- |
| **Personal Goals** | **Organizational Goals** |
| Want a feeling of power | Control cost in product use situation |
| Seek personal pleasure | Few breakdowns of product |
| Desire job security | Dependable delivery for repeat purchases |
| Want to be well liked | Adequate supply of product |
| Want respect | Cost within budget limit |

Individual needs tend to be career related, whereas organizational needs reflect factors related to the use of the product.

Even though organizational purchasing is often thought to be almost entirely objective, subjective personal needs are often extremely important in the final purchase decision. For example, an organization may want to purchase a computer to satisfy data-processing needs. Although a number of suppliers might be able to provide similar products, some suppliers at lower cost than others, buying center members might select the most well-known brand to reduce purchase risk and protect job security.

We discussed how the influence of buying center members varies at different buying phases in the preceding section. Couple this with the different needs of different buying center members, and the complexity of organization buying behavior is evident. Nevertheless, sales managers must understand this behavior to develop sales strategies that will satisfy the personal and organizational needs of buying center members.

## SALES STRATEGY

Sales managers and salespeople are typically responsible for strategic decisions at the account level. Although the firm's marketing strategy provides basic guidelines—an overall game plan—the battles are won on an account-by-account basis. Without the design and execution of effective sales strategies directed at specific accounts, the marketing strategy cannot be successfully implemented.

The success of Hill-Rom illustrates the importance of developing effective sales strategies. Hill-Rom markets beds and other medical equipment to medical care facilities. The salesforce typically treated all customers about the same, although larger facilities received more attention than smaller facilities. The company performed an extensive customer segmentation analysis and identified two types of customers: key customers and prime customers. These customer groups differed in their buying needs and processes, and not just in size. Hill-Rom found that their current approach provided too much attention to prime customers and not enough to key customers. Based on this analysis, the company developed a specific sales strategy for each customer group. Key customers were assigned multifunctional sales teams under the direction of an account manager. Prime customers were served by territory managers. The results from the new sales strategies are higher sales, more satisfied customers, and lower selling costs.[19]

Our framework suggests four basic sales strategy elements: account targeting strategy, relationship strategy, selling strategy, and sales channel strategy. We consider each of these as a separate, but related, strategic decision area. Sales strategies are ultimately developed for each individual account; however, the strategic decisions are often made by classifying individual accounts into similar categories.

### Account Targeting Strategy

The first element of a sales strategy is defining an account targeting strategy. As mentioned earlier, all accounts within a target market are not the same. Some accounts might not be good prospects because of existing relationships with competitors. Even those that are good prospects or even current customers differ in terms of how much they buy now or might buy in the future, how they want to do business with sales organizations, and other factors. This means that all accounts cannot be effectively or efficiently served in the same way.

An **account targeting strategy** is the classification of accounts within a target market into categories for the purpose of developing strategic approaches for selling to each account or account group. The account targeting strategy provides the foundation for all other elements of a sales strategy. Just as different marketing mixes are developed to serve different target markets, sales organizations need to use different relationship, selling, and sales channel strategies for different account groups.

The account targeting strategy used by IBM for small and medium-sized businesses is illustrative. IBM targets four different types of small and medium-sized business accounts:

1. the largest customers whose business problems need a complex solution
2. the smaller customers that do not need as much attention
3. prospective customers
4. the very smallest customers

Each of these account segments has different needs, and IBM satisfies these needs in different ways.[20]

## Relationship Strategy

As discussed in previous modules, there is a clear trend toward a relationship orientation between buyers and sellers, especially in business markets. However, some accounts want to continue in a transaction mode whereas others want various types of relationships between buyer and seller. A **relationship strategy** is a determination of the type of relationship to be developed with different account groups. A specific relationship strategy is developed for each account group identified by a sales organization's account targeting strategy.

Any number of relationship strategies might be developed, but typically an account targeting strategy defines three to five target groups, each requiring a specific relationship strategy. We illustrate with the general approach established by a large industrial manufacturer. The firm's account targeting strategy identified four different account groups and determined a specific relationship strategy for each group. Exhibit 3.8 presents the characteristics of each relationship strategy.

The relationship strategies range from a transaction relationship based on selling standardized products to a collaborative relationship in which the buyers and sellers work closely together for the benefit of both businesses. In between these extremes are intermediate types of relationships. A solutions relationship emphasizes solving customer problems, and a partnership relationship represents a preferred supplier position over the long term. As a sales organization moves from transaction to collaborative relationships, the time frame becomes longer, the focus changes from buying/selling to creating value, and the products and services offered move from simple and standardized to more complex and customized.

| **EXHIBIT 3.8** | Characteristics of Relationship Strategies | | | |
|---|---|---|---|---|
| | **Transaction Relationsip** | **Solutions Relationship** | **Partnership Relationship** | **Collaborative Relationsip** |
| Goal | Sell Products | ———————————→ | | Add value |
| Time frame | Short | ———————————→ | | Long |
| Offering | Standardized | ———————————→ | | Customized |
| Number of customers | Many | ———————————————→ | | Few |

The different characteristics of the different relationship strategies are further illustrated in Figure 3.5. The move from transaction to collaborative relationships requires a greater commitment between buyer and seller, because they will be working together much more closely. Some buyers and sellers are not willing to make the required commitments. In addition, the selling costs are increased to serve accounts with higher-level relationships. Therefore, sales organizations must consider the sales and costs associated with using different relationship strategies for different account groups. The critical task is balancing the customer's needs with the cost to serve the account.

## Selling Strategy

Successfully executing a specific relationship strategy requires a different selling approach. A **selling strategy** is the planned selling approach for each relationship strategy. Module 2 presented five basic selling approaches: stimulus response, mental states, need satisfaction, problem solving, and consultative. These selling approaches represent different selling strategies that might be used to execute a specific relationship strategy. We illustrate this by continuing the example of the large industrial manufacturer and the relationship strategies presented in Exhibit 3.8 and Figure 3.5.

| Relationship Strategy Selling Costs | FIGURE 3.5 |
| --- | --- |

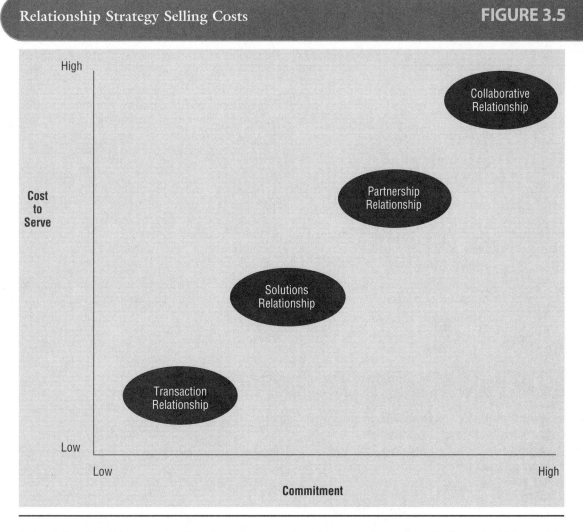

Each relationship strategy represents an increasing commitment between the buyer and seller and a higher cost to serve the customer.

Exhibit 3.9 matches the appropriate selling strategy with the appropriate relationship strategy. As indicated, the stimulus response and mental states approaches typically fit with a transaction relationship strategy. The need satisfaction and problem-solving selling strategies are normally used with a solutions relationship strategy. The consultative approach is most effective with the partnership and collaborative relationship strategies. Sometimes, a collaborative relationship strategy requires a selling strategy that is completely customized to the specific buyer-seller situation. The important point is that achieving the desired type of relationship in a productive manner requires using different selling strategies. Matching selling strategies and relationship strategies is an important sales management task.

## Sales Channel Strategy

Sales channel strategy—ensuring that accounts receive selling effort coverage in an effective and efficient manner—is a necessary component of sales strategy. Various methods are available to provide selling coverage to accounts, including a company salesforce, the Internet, industrial distributors, independent representatives, team selling, telemarketing, and trade shows. Many firms use multiple distribution channels and multiple sales channels for their products. One study found that about 40 percent of sales by U.S. companies come from indirect sales channels, and this is expected to increase to over 60 percent by 2010.[21] However, another study found that salespeople are still the most important means of interacting with customers, followed by the Internet, telephone, e-mail, and fax.[22] Because most of this book is concerned with management of a company field salesforce, our discussion of sales channel strategy focuses on alternatives to the typical company field salesforce.

## The Internet

The Internet is rapidly becoming an important sales channel in selling to organizations. Most companies are not replacing field salesforces but integrating the Internet into a multiple-sales-channel strategy. The focus is using this electronic channel in a way that meets customer needs and reduces selling costs. Consider two examples:

- Cisco Systems has Internet revenues in excess of $9.5 billion annually. But new customers cannot buy directly from Cisco's Internet site. New customers must first work with a dealer to negotiate purchases. Once this initial relationship is established, a customer can go to the Web to research products, place orders, or check the status of orders. This networked business model uses the Internet to handle routine selling and service activities and frees salespeople to focus on more value-adding activities. Cisco estimates that this approach saves $800 million a year and increases salesperson productivity by 15 percent.[23]

- National Semiconductor uses a company salesforce for its largest accounts and a distributor network for the remaining smaller accounts. The company is, however, integrating the Internet as another sales channel for each segment. The objective is to streamline the sales and service process. For the largest accounts, National Semiconductor sets up

**EXHIBIT 3.9**     Matching Selling and Relationship Strategies

| Relationship Strategy | | | |
| --- | --- | --- | --- |
| **Transaction** | **Solutions** | **Partnership** | **Collaborative** |
| Stimulus Response | | | |
| Mental States | | | |
| | Need Satisfaction | | |
| | Problem Solving | | |
| | | Consultative | Consultative |
| | | | Customized |

private extranets for each customer so the customer can access relevant purchasing information. The smaller accounts have access to an open Web site and can use it to determine which distributors to buy from and to coordinate these purchases. The Internet sales channel has allowed National Semiconductor to develop closer relationships with customers and distributors and to reduce selling costs.[24]

These examples illustrate how the Internet is being used as an electronic sales channel by two different companies. These and most other companies are focusing on ways to integrate the Internet into a multiple sales channel strategy that provides value to customers in a cost-effective manner. Thus, the Internet is being blended with field selling effort but also with other sales channels such as industrial distributors, independent representatives, and telemarketing.

## Industrial Distributors

One alternative sales channel is **industrial distributors**—channel middlemen that take title to the goods that they market to end users. These distributors typically employ their own field salesforce and may carry (1) the products of only one manufacturer, (2) related but noncompeting products from different manufacturers, or (3) competing products from different manufacturers. Firms that use industrial distributors normally have a relatively small company salesforce to serve and support the efforts of the distributor.

The use of industrial distributors adds another member to the distribution channel. Although these distributors should not be considered as final customers, they should be treated like customers. Developing positive long-term relationships with distributors is necessary for success. Indeed, the development of a partnership with distributors can be the key to success.

Herman Miller, the furniture manufacturer, has 300 direct salespeople and 240 distributors. Herman Miller salespeople call on customers directly but also work with distributors to make sure customers are satisfied. In large markets, the salespeople are usually the lead on accounts, with the distributors responsible for smaller accounts. Herman Miller also provides the distributors with market information to help them succeed, and the salespeople maintain continuous contact to motivate the distributors to emphasize Herman Miller products.[25]

## Independent Representatives

Firms using personal selling can choose to cover accounts with **independent representatives** (also called *manufacturers' representatives* or just *reps*). Reps are independent sales organizations that sell complementary, but noncompeting, products from different manufacturers. In contrast to industrial distributors, independent representatives do not normally carry inventory or take title to the products they sell. Manufacturers typically develop contractual agreements with several rep organizations. Each rep organization consists of one or more salespeople and is assigned a geographic territory. It is typically compensated on a commission basis for products sold.

Most independent rep agencies are small with an average of six employees, although a few have up to a hundred salespeople and support staff. Independent reps are typically compensated on a commission basis for products sold. There is, however, a trend toward paying larger commissions and even stipends for opening new territories and shifting some compensation toward paying for rep activities rather than just for sales results. Some rep agencies are performing direct mail, telemarketing, newsletter publishing, and Web site design services for clients.[26]

Why would so many manufacturers use reps instead of company salesforces? As indicated in Exhibit 3.10,[27] reps have certain advantages over company salesforces, especially for small firms or for smaller markets served by larger firms. Because reps are paid on a commission basis, selling costs are almost totally variable, whereas a large percentage of the selling costs of a company salesforce are fixed. Thus, at lower sales levels a rep organization is more cost-efficient to use than a company salesforce. However, at some level of

---

**EXHIBIT 3.10**    Advantages of Independent Representatives

Independent sales representatives offer several advantages over company salesforces:

- Reps provide a professional selling capability that is difficult to match with company salespeople.
- Reps offer in-depth knowledge of general markets and individual customers.
- Reps offer established relationships with individual customers.
- The use of reps provides improved cash flow because payments to reps are typically not made until customers have paid for their purchases.
- The use of reps provides predictable sales expenses because most of the selling costs are variable and directly related to sales volume.
- The use of reps can provide greater territory coverage because companies can employ more reps than company salespeople for the same cost.
- Companies can usually penetrate new markets faster by using reps because of the reps' established customer relationships.

---

sales the company salesforce will become more cost-efficient, because reps typically receive higher commission rates than company salespeople (see Figure 3.6).

Marley Cooling Tower capitalizes on the different cost structure between company salesforces and independent reps. Tim Wigger, vice president of sales, manages a company salesforce of 40, plus 70 manufacturers' reps. The company started with only a field salesforce but began adding reps to capitalize on growth outside the original salesperson territories. This approach has been a cost-effective way for Marley to grow in new geographic areas.[28]

Although reps may cost less in many situations, management also has less control over their activities. The basic trade-off is cost versus control. There are two aspects to control. First, because reps are paid a commission on sales, it is difficult to get them to engage in activities not directly related to sales generation. Thus, if servicing of accounts

---

**FIGURE 3.6**    Independent Representatives versus Company Salesforce Costs

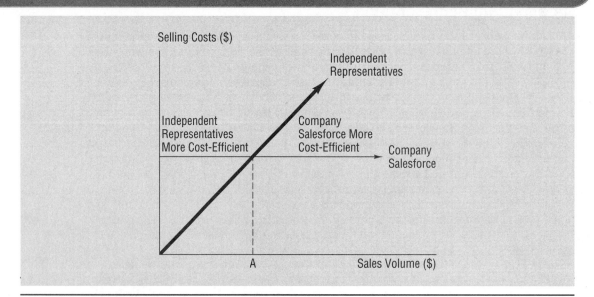

Independent representatives are typically more cost-efficient at lower sales levels, because most of the costs associated with reps are variable. However, at higher sales levels (beyond point A) a company salesforce becomes more cost-efficient.

is important, reps may not perform these activities as well as a company salesforce. Second, the typical rep represents an average of 10 manufacturers or principals. Each manufacturer's products will therefore receive 10 percent of the rep's time if it is divided equally. Usually, however, some products receive more attention than others. The biggest complaints that manufacturers seem to have with reps is that they do not spend enough time with their products and thus do not generate sufficient sales. The use of reps limits the amount of control that management has over the time spent selling their products. The relationship with manufacturer's representative organizations can also produce some complex situations as indicated in "An Ethical Dilemma."

### AN ETHICAL DILEMMA

You are national sales manager for Specialty Chemicals. The company serves manufacturers of specialty chemicals. Most of your customers are in Michigan, Illinois, and Indiana. These customers are served by a company salesforce. Other customers in adjoining states are the responsibility of Thompson & Associates, a manufacturer's representative agency. Thompson has done a good job in building your business in this area. You think it might be time to hire company salespeople for these areas. When you indicate to Mr. Thompson that you do not think you will renew the contract with his agency, he gets very mad. He talks about all of the hard work his salespeople did to sell your products and now that business is good you are taking it away from him. What would you do? Why?

## Team Selling

Our earlier discussion of organizational buyer behavior presented the concepts of buying centers and buying situations. If we move to the selling side of the exchange relationship, we find analogous concepts. As discussed in Module 1, firms often employ multiple-person sales teams to deal with the multiple-person buying centers of their accounts. Figure 3.7[29] illustrates the basic relationships between sales teams and buying centers. A company salesperson typically coordinates the activities of the sales team, whereas the purchasing agent typically coordinates the activities of the buying center. Both the sales team and buying center can consist of multiple individuals from different functional areas. Each of these individuals can play one or more roles in the exchange process.

The use of **team selling** is increasing in many firms. Developing successful relationships with accounts often requires the participation of many individuals from the selling firm. One study found that team selling was important at 42 percent of the responding companies. The importance varied by industry, however. Team selling was most important to firms in the petroleum, chemical, industrial machinery, and electronics industries and less important to those in the food and beverage, retail, and wholesale industries.[30] Another study of global sales leaders indicated that such companies as Sony, Xerox, Hewlett-Packard, Siemens, 3M, and NEC were involved extensively in team selling. Customers like team selling, because they think their needs are better met.[31]

## Telemarketing

An increasingly important sales channel is **telemarketing** (also called *telesales*), which consists of using the telephone as a means for customer contact, to perform some of or all the activities required to develop and maintain account relationships. This includes both outbound telemarketing (the seller calls the account) and inbound telemarketing (the account calls the seller).

## FIGURE 3.7

Team Selling and Buying Centers

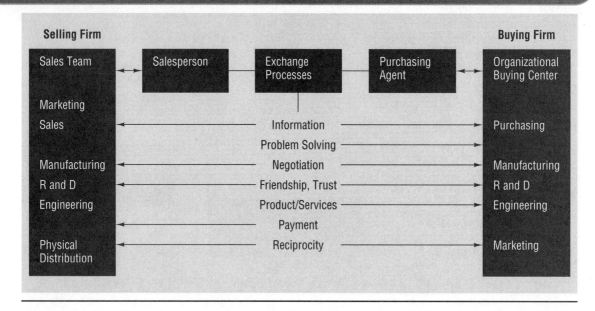

The salesperson coordinates the activities of a sales team to interact with the members of an account's buying center. The size, composition, and activities of the sales team depend on the buying situation faced by the seller.

Firms typically use telemarketing to replace field selling for specific accounts or integrate telemarketing with field selling to the same accounts (see Figure 3.8). The major reason for replacing field selling with telemarketing at specific accounts is the low cost of telemarketing selling. Telemarketing salespeople are able to serve a large number of smaller accounts. This lowers the selling costs to the smaller accounts and frees the field salesforce to concentrate on the larger accounts. Sometimes telemarketing can be used effectively to serve all accounts. For example, SecureWorks once used a field salesforce to bring its Internet security services to distributors and resellers. The company changed to salespeople selling directly to end users over the phone. Results of the change have been spectacular, with the number of clients going from 50 to 850 and annual sales from $700,00 to over $8.5 million.[32]

Telemarketing is also being integrated with other sales channels. For example, Shachihata Inc., sells pre-inked rubber stamps through independent reps. The company created a customer development department consisting of 10 telemarketers. The telemarketers take leads and generate appointments for the independent reps. Once an appointment is made, the telemarketer faxes a profile sheet of the customer to the appropriate rep. The rep later returns it with information on the results of the sales call. The integration of independent reps and telemarketers has increased appointments by more than 400 percent and reduced selling costs by about 60 percent.[33]

The development of telemarketing salesforces to serve some accounts or to support field selling operations can be difficult. One of the keys to success appears to be consistent communication with the field salesforce throughout all stages of telemarketing development. Field salespeople must be assured that the telemarketing operations will help them improve their performance. Specific attention must also be directed toward developing appropriate compensation programs for both salesforces and devising training programs that provide the necessary knowledge and skills for the telemarketing and field salesforces to be able to work effectively together.

## Trade Shows

The final sales channel to be discussed here, **trade shows,** is typically an industry-sponsored event in which companies use a booth to display products and services to potential and

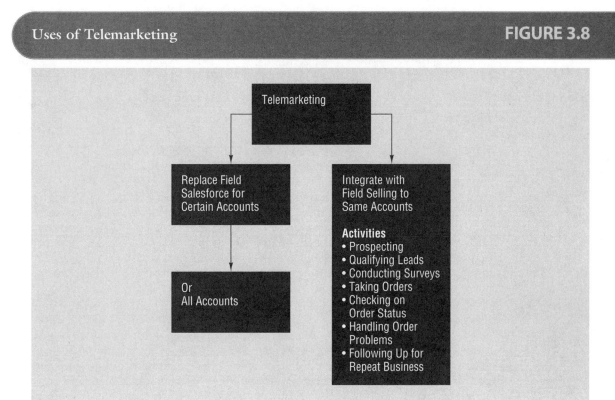

**Uses of Telemarketing**                                                          **FIGURE 3.8**

Telemarketing is typically used either to replace field selling or be integrated with field selling by performing specific activities.

existing customers. Because a particular trade show is held only once a year and lasts only a few days, trade shows should be viewed as supplemental methods for account coverage, not to be used by themselves but integrated with other sales channels.

Statistics show that trade shows are popular. Company budgets for trade shows have nearly doubled in recent years. About 1.5 million companies exhibited at 4,500 U.S. trade shows attended by 102 million people in 1999. This is expected to increase to nearly 6,000 trade shows and 125 million attendees in 2008.[34]

Trade shows are used to achieve both selling and nonselling objectives. Relevant selling objectives are to test new products, to close sales, and to introduce new products. Nonselling objectives include servicing current customers, gathering competitive information, identifying new prospects, and enhancing corporate image. Successful trade shows tend to be those where firms exhibit a large number of products to a large number of attendees, where specific written objectives for the trade show are established, and where attendees match the firm's target market.

The potential value of trade shows can be illustrated through several examples. Express Personnel Services spent $50,000 to exhibit at the Society of Human Resource Managers Conference and generated about 400 sales leads and an increase in sales of $1.2 million. Azanda Network Devices garnered three new customers and $3 million to $5 million in extra sales from a $70,000 investment at the NetWorld-Interprop Conference. Orion International gained 125 new clients and $245,000 in new sales from its exhibit at the National Manufacturers Association Conference.[35]

Developing an effective sales channel strategy is a challenging task. Sales managers must determine the right mix of sales channel alternatives to meet the needs of all their customers in a cost-effective manner. Once a sales channel strategy is created, sales managers are faced with managing multiple channels and the channel conflict that emerges. **Channel conflict** occurs when the interests of different channels are not consistent. Typical examples of channel conflict include the introduction of an Internet sales channel that takes sales away from distributors or independent reps, determining which accounts are served by the field salesforce and which accounts are served by a distributor, or taking accounts from field salespeople and turning them over to telemarketers. There are often no easy answers to channel conflict, but sales managers must balance the needs of each channel with the needs of the sales organization and its customers.

## SUMMARY

1. **Define the strategy levels for multibusiness, multiproduct firms**. Multibusiness, multiproduct firms must make strategic decisions at the corporate, business, marketing, and sales levels. Corporate strategy decisions determine the basic scope and direction for the corporate entity through formulating the corporate mission statement, defining strategic business units, setting strategic business unit objectives, and determining corporate growth orientation. Business strategy decisions determine how each business unit plans to compete effectively within its industry. Marketing strategies consist of the selection of target markets and the development of marketing mixes for each product market. Personal selling is an important component of the marketing communications mix portion and business of marketing strategies and a key element in sales strategies.

2. **Discuss how corporate and business strategy decisions affect the sales function**. Corporate strategy decisions provide direction for strategy development at all organizational levels. The corporate mission statement, definition of strategic business units, determination of strategic business unit objectives, and establishment of the corporate growth orientation provide guidelines within which sales managers and salespeople must operate. Changes in corporate strategy typically lead to changes in sales management and personal selling activities. Business strategy decisions determine how each strategic business unit intends to compete. Different business strategies place different demands on the sales organization.

3. **List the advantages and disadvantages of personal selling as a marketing communications tool**. Personal selling is the only tool that involves personal communication between buyer and seller. As such, personal selling has the advantage of being able to tailor the message to the specific needs of each customer and to deliver complicated messages. The major disadvantage of personal selling is the high cost to reach individual buyers.

4. **Specify the situations in which personal selling is typically emphasized in a marketing strategy**. Marketing strategies tend to be either personal selling driven or advertising driven. Personal selling is normally emphasized in business markets where there are relatively few buyers, usually in concentrated locations, who make important purchases of complex products and require a great deal of information and service. Personal selling is also typically emphasized in marketing mixes for complex expensive products that are distributed through direct channels or through indirect channels by using a "push" strategy and when the price affords sufficient margin to support the high costs associated with personal selling.

5. **Describe ways that personal selling, advertising, and other tools can be blended into effective integrated marketing communications strategies**. Effective strategies typically consist of a mixture of personal selling, advertising, and other tools. Firms often use advertising to generate company and brand awareness and to identify potential customers. Personal selling is then used to turn these prospects into customers of the firm's products or services. Other tools are normally used to supplement the advertising and personal selling efforts.

6. **Discuss the important concepts behind organizational buyer behavior**. The key concepts behind organizational buyer behavior are buying situation, buying center, buying

process, and buying needs. Buying situations can be characterized as new task, modified rebuy, or straight rebuy. The type of buying situation affects all other aspects of organizational buyer behavior. The buying center consists of all the individuals from a firm involved in a particular buying decision. These individuals may come from different functional areas and may play the role of initiators, users, gatekeepers, influencers, deciders, and/or buyers. Organizational purchasing should be viewed as a buying process with multiple phases. Members of the buying center may be involved at different phases of the buying process. Organizational purchases are made to satisfy specific buying needs, which may be both organizational and personal. These concepts are highly interrelated and interact to produce complex organizational purchasing phenomena.

7. **Define an account targeting strategy**. An account targeting strategy is the classification of accounts within a target market into categories for the purpose of developing strategic approaches for selling to each account or account group.

8. **Explain the different types of relationship strategies**. A sales organization might use any number of different relationship strategies to serve targeted accounts. Transaction, solutions, partnership, and collaborative relationship strategies are examples used by some sales organizations.

9. **Discuss the importance of different selling strategies**. A selling strategy is the planned selling approach for each relationship strategy. Selling strategies might include stimulus response, mental states, need satisfaction, problem-solving, consultative, or a completely customized strategy. Different selling strategies are needed to successfully execute different relationship strategies.

10. **Describe sales channel strategies**. A sales channel strategy consists of decisions as to how to provide selling effort coverage to accounts. The sales channel strategy depends on the firm's marketing strategy. If indirect distribution is used, then industrial distributors become the main focus of selling effort coverage. Firms might decide to employ independent representatives instead of having a company salesforce. The concept of team selling is analogous to the buying center concept. Depending on whether the seller faces a new task selling situation, a modified resell situation, or a routine resell situation, different individuals will be included in the sales team. Multilevel selling and major account selling are types of team selling strategies. Telemarketing is a sales channel that can be used to replace or support field selling operations. Finally, trade shows can be used to achieve specific objectives and supplement the other sales channels.

## UNDERSTANDING SALES MANAGEMENT TERMS

| | |
|---|---|
| corporate strategy | user |
| business strategy | original equipment manufacturer |
| strategic business unit (SBU) | (OEM) |
| marketing strategy | reseller |
| corporate mission statement | government organization |
| business unit portfolio | institution |
| generic business strategies | new task buying situation |
| low-cost strategy | extensive problem solving |
| differentiation strategy | modified rebuy buying situation |
| niche strategy | limited problem solving |
| customer relationship management | straight rebuy buying situation |
| (CRM) | routinized response behavior |
| target market | buying center |
| marketing mix | buying process |
| business marketing | buying needs |
| integrated marketing communication | account targeting strategy |
| (IMC) | relationship strategy |

selling strategy                          team selling
sales channel strategy                    telemarketing
industrial distributors                   trade shows
independent representatives               channel conflict

## DEVELOPING SALES MANAGEMENT KNOWLEDGE

1. How does the corporate mission statement affect personal selling and sales management activities?

2. How can sales promotion and publicity be used to supplement a personal selling–driven strategy?

3. Why is personal selling typically emphasized in business markets and advertising emphasized in consumer markets?

4. Why do most firms use both personal selling and advertising in their strategies?

5. How would sales management activities differ for an SBU following a differentiation strategy versus an SBU using a low-cost strategy?

6. Discuss how the buying situation affects the buying center, the buying process, and buying needs.

7. How is the management of relationships with industrial distributors different from the management of relationships with end-user customers?

8. How can trade shows be used to supplement other sales channels?

9. How might telemarketing be used when accounts are covered by distributors?

10. What are the most important organizational buyer behavior trends, and how might these trends affect sales strategies in the future?

## BUILDING SALES MANAGEMENT SKILLS

1. Visit the library or use the Internet to find the annual report or similar information about a company of your choice. Try to choose a firm with whom you might like to work after graduation. Use the information in the annual report to describe the firm's corporate strategy, marketing strategy, and sales function.

2. You are the sales manager for WorldPub, a textbook publishing company. You believe it would be a good idea to get involved in the Internet to help move your company's line of college business textbooks. Discuss your strategy for using the Internet and other sales channels to sell textbooks.

3. Protech Athletics Manufacturing currently markets a line of sporting goods equipment through independent sales representatives. The company has grown considerably since its inception seven years ago. Recently, Protech has become frustrated with its independent reps. It believes its products are not getting the attention they deserve. Protech is wondering if there is something it can do to help motivate the reps. However, given its recent disappointment with the reps, Protech is entertaining the idea of developing its own salesforce. What do you suggest Protech do and why? What are the advantages and disadvantages associated with your solution?

**ROLE PLAY**

4. **Situation:**   Read the Ethical Dilemma on page 69.

   **Characters:**   National sales manager for Specialty Chemicals; Mr. Thompson, President of Thompson & Associates

   **Scene:**   *Location*—National sales manager's office at Specialty Chemicals. *Action*—Role play meeting between the national sales manager for Specialty Chemicals and Mr. Thompson concerning the future relationship between the two companies to arrive at a decision.

# MAKING SALES MANAGEMENT DECISIONS

## Case 3.1: Pronto Retail Centers

### Background

Pronto Retail Centers is a well-established company with 125 outlets in the northeastern United States. Each outlet is a combination convenience store, car wash, and Pronto-Lube oil change center. Of the 125 stores, 31 are company-owned with the remaining stores leased to independent dealers in a quasi-franchising arrangement. The independent dealers agree to buy gasoline and motor oil from Pronto's designated distributors. They also agree to uphold uniformity and facilities appearance standards as set by Pronto. The independent dealers are encouraged to buy their convenience store merchandise from Pronto's designated distributors, but they are not required to do so. Lease payments are collected from independent dealers when gasoline deliveries are made.

### Current Situation

In the past 12 months, Pronto's growth rate has slowed considerably. This has been a major concern to Pronto's upper management, including John Rickles, vice president for sales. Rickles has analyzed the declining growth rate and found that sales volume at company-owned stores is growing at a very acceptable 12 percent on an annualized basis. In contrast, stores run by independent dealers are lagging behind with an annual growth rate of only 2 percent. Rickles believes the independent category is under-performing for three basic reasons. First, the independent stores are generally not kept as clean and professional looking as the company-owned stores. Second, many of the larger independent operators have begun buying a larger share of their convenience store merchandise from low-cost distributors other than Pronto's designated distributors. This hurts sales volume results since Pronto's retail operation gets rebates from their designated distributors, which counts as sales volume in the Pronto financial system. Third, Pronto has suffered volume losses from closed outlets. Competition had intensified, and turnover among dealers was becoming more commonplace. It was taking Pronto an average of 60 days to find new dealers when existing dealers decided to leave the business. When a dealer operation closed, Pronto rarely converted it to a company-owned store, as their aggressive growth strategy at the corporate level left precious little capital for acquisition of existing outlets.

John Rickles had called his five regional managers into his New York headquarters office to discuss the problem with declining sales volume and possible remedies to the problem. Given that the corporate strategy would continue to be to build market share and sales volume, Rickles outlined the following five-point plan:

1. Each salesperson would continue to supervise company-owned stores and independent dealers.
2. Salespeople would be given specific objectives for facilities appearance and percentage of sales of convenience store merchandise purchases from Pronto's designated distributors.
3. Salespeople would be given mandates that no retail outlet would remain closed for more than 30 days.
4. Sales volume objectives for salespeople would remain in place. Current year volume objectives would not change.
5. Regional sales managers' annual objectives would be revised to be consistent with salespeople's new objectives.

The regional managers saw the need for the revised strategy, but raised several concerns. They felt that the corporate strategy focused on building market share, but that the sales organization was expected to both build and hold market share. They complained that the new-dealer team, a corporate group, should be adding new dealers at a faster rate, and that part of the volume short-fall was due to poor performance of the new dealer team, not the salesforce. They also pointed out that Pronto salespeople were paid on a straight salary basis, primarily because they had previously functioned more as managers of multiple retail outlets than as pure salespeople. The discussion became heated, and finally Mary McCarthy spoke for the regional managers: "Look, John, we know that corporate strategy can shift, and we know we have to adapt when that happens. But this drop in sales volume is partly the fault of the corporate new-dealer team. We don't see them having to change their ways. And we are really concerned that without some incentive pay, it will be hard to redirect our salespeople." Rickles, having heard enough at this point, replied, "Tell your salespeople that their incentive is that if they succeed, they get to keep their jobs!" With that, the meeting quickly came to a conclusion.

### Questions

1. Is it reasonable to charge Pronto's salesforce with simultaneously building and holding market share?
2. What are the pros and cons of John Rickles' five-point plan?

3. Since the meeting with the regional managers ended on a sour note, what should Rickles do now? What should the regional managers do?

---

**Situation:**    Read Case 3.1.

**Characters:**   John Rickles, Vice President of Sales; five regional managers

**Scene:**        *Location*—Conference room at Pronto Headquarters. *Action*—Role play meeting among John Rickles and the five regional managers to discuss the five-point plan and to decide on a strategy to increase sales at independent stores.

**ROLE PLAY**

---

## Case 3.2: National Communications Manufacturing

### Background

National Communications Manufacturing (NCM) is a Minneapolis-based manufacturer of consumer communications devices, most notably portable two-way radios commonly called walkie-talkies. In recent years, these devices have exploded in popularity as prices dropped to affordable levels. This is due to advancing technology and low-cost production outside the United States. Although NCM continues to manufacture a few of its own products, most production is outsourced to manufacturers in Taiwan.

A key element in the NCM success story is the growth of dominant retail chains such as Wal-Mart, Target, and Best Buy. NCM uses major account teams to serve these and other large discounters, which accounts for 70 percent of NCM's annual sales. The remaining 30 percent of NCM's sales come from smaller retail accounts that buy either from NCM's manufacturers' reps or directly from NCM's Web site.

### Current Situation

Ann Culligan, NCM's national sales manager, is working on two major isuses. First, she is fighting a losing battle to keep NCM's direct cost of sales at 5 percent of total sales. The 5 percent target has been part of NCM's sales culture for more than 20 years, reflecting a belief that a low-cost operation translates into a more competitive position in the marketplace. Over the past few years, Ann's sales organization had reduced costs in various ways.

E-mail, instead of long-distance phone calls, staying in budget motels, cutting overnight travel to a minimum, and Saturday night stay-overs were just a few of the measures taken to stay within the 5 percent guideline. In spite of diligent efforts, cost of sales was running at 7 percent for the major account sales teams. Commissions paid to the independent reps had remained fixed for several years at 4½ percent.

The second issue currently demanding Ann's attention ironically stemmed from an NCM cost-cutting measure that was implemented 12 months ago. In an attempt to reduce manufacturers' representative costs, NCM had established a Web site as an alternative channel for smaller retail customers. The reps had protested vigorously, but NCM insisted that selling on the Internet was an essential part of a contemporary sales strategy. Not all NCM products were available on the Web, a fact that did little to appease the disgruntled reps. Cost of sales on the Web site was a modest 2 percent of sales. Sales volume on the Web amounted to 3 percent of NCM's total sales during the past year, but current projections were for volume to increase to 5 percent of the total this year, and perhaps as much as 10 percent the following year. Some of the stronger reps were threatening to leave NCM in favor of a major competitor, which offered its reps a partial commission on all Web sales.

As Ann pondered the situation, she began to wonder if she could hit the 5 percent cost-of-sales target this year. Ninety percent of the cost of her major account teams was compensation-related—salaries and incentive pay. Good people were hard to find, and Ann had found that NCM had to pay the going rate or else NCM's top performers would look for new opportunities. Ann still regretted the recent loss of Byron Schuster, a major account manager, to a competitor who offered a better pay package. Sales volume at Byron's former account had dropped 10 percent since his departure.

Ann didn't like to think about changing her major account team strategy, but she wondered if she could move some of her large retail chain accounts to the manufacturers' rep organization. After all, rep commissions ran only 4½ percent, and essentially there were no other direct sales costs associated with the reps. As she headed home after a long day at the office, Ann thought that the next morning she would try to build a case with the CEO of NCM to revise the 5 percent cost-of-sales target to reflect reality. If the answer is no, Ann thought she just might explore the idea of consolidating her major account teams and handing over selected large retail accounts to some of the more capable rep firms. She hated the idea of laying people off, but, she told herself, it may be necessary in this case.

## Questions

1. Should Ann request a revision of the 5 percent cost-of-sales target? If so, what sort of information would she need to convince her CEO?
2. What factors should Ann consider as she contemplates a change in major account sales strategy, especially a change that assigns independent reps to some major accounts?
3. How would you assess NCM's alternative sales channel on the Web? Can you recommend any changes to minimize conflict with the independent reps?

**ROLE PLAY**

**Situation:**    Read Case 3.2.

**Characters:**    Ann Culligan, NCM national sales manager; CEO of NCM; President of Manufacturers' rep agency

**Scene 1:**    *Location*—Office of NCM CEO. *Action*—Role play meeting between Ann Culligan and NCM CEO to discuss 5 percent cost-of-sales target and to arrive at a decision.

**Scene 2:**    *Location*—Ann Culligan's office *Action*—Role play meeting between Ann Culligan and president of manufacturers' rep agency concerning the practice of selling over the Internet by NCM to arrive at a decision.

## STRATEGY AND SALES ORGANIZATION STRUCTURE: IBM

IBM has been in business for over 90 years, operates around the world, and has about 325,000 employees. The company expanded from computer hardware into the financing, software, and consulting businesses. It competes with the likes of Hewlett-Packard in hardware, Accenture in consulting services, and Microsoft in software. Sam Palmisano rose through the sales ranks to take over as CEO. His goal is to generate double-digit earnings growth at IBM by creating "a new era at IBM."

The cornerstone of this growth plan is a new strategy called business-on-demand. Customers can purchase technology solutions to their IT problems on a pay-as-you-go basis. Similar to utilities, companies pay only for what they use. This allows them the flexibility to adjust their computing power up or down, based on marketplace conditions. Several large companies, such as J.P. Morgan Chase and American Express, have responded favorably to this new strategy by signing multiyear, multibillion-dollar deals.

Implementing the new strategy successfully requires several major changes in the IBM sales organization of about 35,000. One of the key changes is in the structure of the IBM sales organization. IBM salespeople typically focused on selling specific products to assigned customers. The salespeople now work in teams to sell complete solutions consisting of both products and services. The teams are organized according to customer size, industry, and location. Salespeople are part of a salesforce that serves three main customer groups: large, integrated accounts; clusters of aligned accounts; or small and medium-sized accounts. This type of structure requires salespeople to be industry experts with product and technical support provided by other members of the team.

IBM is also trying to get more from its sales organization by having salespeople spend more time in front of customers in an effective way. Meetings between salespeople and sales managers are limited to one 30-minute meeting each Monday. No other meetings are required. The meetings focus on coaching and solving customer problems. This frees up more time for IBM salespeople to sell.

The increased selling time is more effective, because a seven-step sales process was been designed based on best practices throughout the company. All salespeople follow this process, and progress is reported and tracked on one common information system. This allows sales management to track sales progress with customers around the world and more easily make comparisons over time and across areas.

These are big changes for IBM. The company had become very bureaucratic and hierarchical, and was slow to respond to customer needs and marketplace changes. The new sales organization structure promotes teamwork and focuses on solving customer problems with complete solutions. Because everyone follows the same basic sales process, it is easier for IBM to monitor how well the new strategy is being implemented.

---

**Sources:** Erin Strout, "Blue Skies Ahead?" *Sales & Marketing Management* (March 2003): 25–29; Spencer E. Ante, "The New Blue," *Business Week* (March 17, 2003): 80–88; Daniel Eisenberg, "There's a New Way to Think @ Big Blue," *Time* (January 20, 2003): 49–52.

Module 3 discussed the close relationships among corporate, business, marketing, and sales strategies. The strategic levels must be consistent and integrated

## Objectives

After completing this module, you should be able to

1 Define the concepts of specialization, centralization, span of control versus management levels, and line versus staff positions.

2 Describe the ways salesforces might be specialized.

3 Evaluate the advantages and disadvantages of sales organization structures.

4 Name the important considerations in organizing major account management programs.

5 Explain how to determine the appropriate sales organization structure for a given selling situation.

6 Discuss salesforce deployment.

7 Explain three analytical approaches for determining allocation of selling effort.

8 Describe three methods for calculating salesforce size.

9 Explain the importance of sales territories and list the steps in the territory design process.

10 Discuss the important "people" considerations in salesforce deployment.

to be effective. Strategic changes at one organizational level typically require strategic changes at other organizational levels.

The development of effective strategies is one thing, successfully implementing them another. In one sense, the remainder of this book is concerned with the development and management of a sales organization to implement organizational strategies successfully. This module begins the journey into successful implementation by investigating the key decisions required in sales organization structure and salesforce deployment.

The IBM example in the opening vignette illustrates the close link between organizational strategy and sales organization structure and salesforce deployment. The business-on-demand strategy requires that salespeople understand customer needs and can sell all of IBM's products and services to meet these needs. Putting salespeople in teams and organizing them according to industry, customer size, and location provides the needed customer focus along with product and technical capabilities. IBM is also getting more effective selling time from its existing salespeople by limiting meetings and implementing a common sales process. These sales organization changes are necessary to implement IBM's new organizational strategy.

## SALES ORGANIZATION CONCEPTS

The basic problem in sales organization structure can be presented in simple terms. The corporate, business, marketing, and sales strategies developed by a firm prescribe specific activities that must be performed by salespeople for these strategies to be successful. Sales managers are also needed to recruit, select, train, motivate, supervise, evaluate, and control salespeople. In essence, the firm has salespeople and sales managers who must engage in a variety of activities for the firm to perform successfully. A sales organization structure must be developed to help salespeople and sales managers perform the required activities effectively and efficiently. This structure provides a framework for sales organization operations by indicating what specific activities are performed by whom in the sales organization. The sales organization structure is the vehicle through which strategic plans are translated into selling operations in the marketplace.

The important role of a sales organization structure for a firm has been described as follows:

> The role of organization in sales has been compared to that of the skeleton in the human body; it provides a framework within which normal functions must take place. There is, however, a degree of uniformity in the human skeleton that does not characterize the sales organization. Each firm has its own objectives and problems, and the structure of the sales organization reflects this diversity.[1]

Developing a sales organization structure is difficult. Many different types of structures might be used, and many variations are possible within each basic type. Often the resultant structure is complex, with many boxes and arrows. The basic concepts involved are specialization, centralization, span of control versus management levels, and line versus staff positions.[2]

## Specialization

Our earlier discussion suggested that a sales organization structure must ensure that all required selling and management activities are performed. In the simplest case, each salesperson could perform all selling tasks, and each sales manager could perform all management activities. Most sales organizations, however, are too complex for this structure and require instead some degree of **specialization**, in which certain individuals concentrate on performing some of the required activities to the exclusion of other tasks. Thus, certain salespeople might sell only certain products or call on certain customers. Some sales managers might concentrate on training, others on planning. The basic idea behind specialization is that, by concentrating on a limited number of activities, individuals can become experts on those tasks, leading to better performance for the entire organization.

**Salesforce Specialization Continuum** FIGURE 4.1

**Generalists**
All selling activities and all products to all customers

Some specialization of selling activities, products, and/or customers

**Specialists**
Certain selling activities for certain products to certain customers

A broad range of alternatives exists for specializing salesforce activities.

A useful way to view salesforce specialization is from the perspective of the continuum presented in Figure 4.1. At one extreme, salespeople act as generalists, performing all selling activities for all the company's products to all types of customers. Moving toward the right of the continuum, salespeople begin to specialize by performing only certain selling tasks, selling only certain types of products, or calling on only specific types of accounts.

## Centralization

An important characteristic of the management structure within a sales organization is its degree of **centralization**—that is, the degree to which important decisions and tasks are performed at higher levels in the management hierarchy. A centralized structure is one in which authority and responsibility are placed at higher management levels. An organization becomes more decentralized as tasks become the responsibility of lower-level managers. Centralization is a relative concept in that no organization is totally centralized or totally decentralized. Organizations typically centralize some activities and decentralize others. However, most organizations tend to have a centralized or decentralized orientation.

The trends from transactions to relationships, from individuals to teams, and from management to leadership are producing a more decentralized orientation in many sales organizations. Salespeople and other sales team members who have contact with customers must be able to respond to customer needs in a timely manner. They must be empowered to make decisions quickly. A decentralized structure facilitates decision making in the field and encourages the development of relationships with customers. This approach can produce difficult situations as indicated in "An Ethical Dilemma."

### AN ETHICAL DILEMMA

Universal Internet Services recently redesigned its sales organization. One objective was to decentralization. This was accomplished by eliminating two layers of sales management and increasing the span of control for field sales managers. Salespeople were also given more authority in making decisions needed to serve assigned accounts and were given an overall budget that could be spent as deemed appropriate by the salesperson. District manager Mary Swenson noticed that soon after these changes were made, one of her poorest performers had suddenly increased sales dramatically. The salesperson, Fred Williams, had apparently landed three new, large accounts. Mary was delighted about this development, until she began to hear rumors that Fred had bought these accounts by giving lavish gifts to key decision makers at each account. Universal had strict guidelines about giving gifts. Mary did not want to violate the recent empowerment of salespeople, but she was concerned about Fred's situation. What should Mary do? Why?

## Span of Control versus Management Levels

**Span of control** refers to the number of individuals who report to each sales manager. The larger the span of control, the more subordinates a sales manager must supervise. **Management levels** define the number of different hierarchical levels of sales management within the organization. Typically, span of control is inversely related to the number of sales management levels. This relationship is illustrated in Figure 4.2.

**FIGURE 4.2**                                    Span of Control versus Management Levels

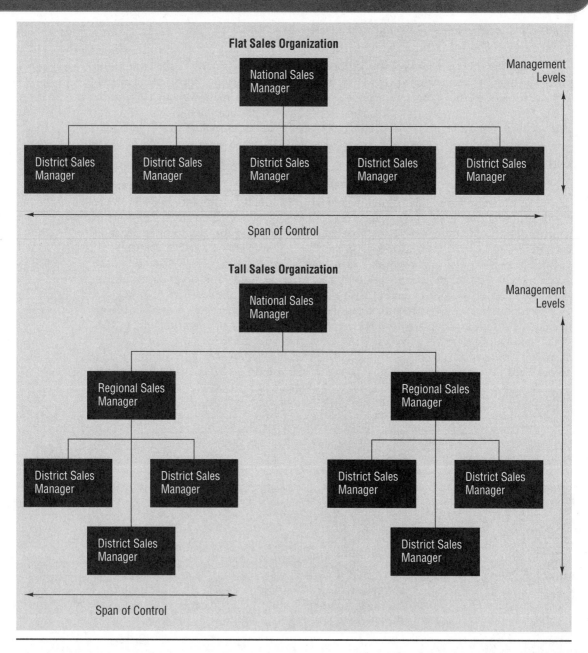

The flat sales organization has only two sales management levels, giving the national sales manager a span of control of 5. The tall sales organization has three sales management levels, giving the national sales manager a span of control of only 2.

In the flat sales organization structure, there are relatively few sales management levels, with each sales manager having a relatively large span of control. Conversely, in the tall structure, there are more sales management levels and smaller spans of control. Flat organization structures tend to be used to achieve decentralization, whereas tall structures are more appropriate for centralized organizations. The span of control also tends to increase at lower sales management levels. Thus, as one moves down the organization chart from national sales manager to regional sales manager to district sales manager, the number of individuals to be supervised directly increases.

## Line versus Staff Positions

Sales management positions can be differentiated as to line or staff positions. **Line sales management** positions are part of the direct management hierarchy within the sales organization. Line sales managers have direct responsibility for a certain number of subordinates and report directly to management at the next highest level in the sales organization. These managers are directly involved in the sales-generating activities of the firm and may perform any number of sales management activities. **Staff sales management** positions, however, are not in the direct chain of command in the sales organization structure. Instead, those in staff positions do not directly manage people, but they are responsible for certain functions (e.g., recruiting and selecting, training) and are not directly involved in sales-generating activities. Staff sales management positions are more specialized than line sales management positions.

A comparison of line and staff sales management positions is presented in Figure 4.3. The regional and district sales managers all operate in line positions. The district sales managers directly manage the field salesforce and report to a specific regional sales manager. The regional sales managers manage the district sales managers and report to the national sales manager. Two staff positions are represented in the figure. These training managers are located at both the national and regional levels and are responsible for sales training programs at each level.

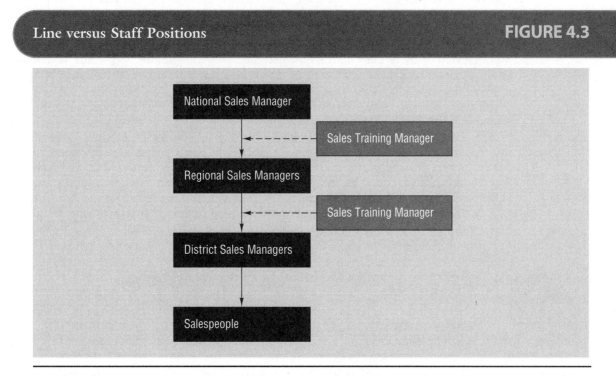

**Line versus Staff Positions**    **FIGURE 4.3**

The national, regional, and district sales managers occupy line positions, whereas the sales training managers represent staff positions.

The use of staff positions results in more specialization of sales management activities. Staff managers specialize in certain sales management activities.

In sum, designing the sales organization is an extremely important and complex task. Decisions concerning the appropriate specialization, centralization, span of control versus management levels, and line versus staff positions are difficult. Although these decisions should be based on the specifics of each selling situation, several trends appear to be emerging. Many sales organizations are moving to some type of specialization, usually a structure that allows salespeople to concentrate on specific types of customers. The downsizing and restructuring of entire companies have affected the sales function. Sales management levels have been eliminated and replaced by sales organization structures that are flatter and that increase the span of control exercised by the remaining sales managers. This restructuring has influenced the trend toward more decentralized orientations and has resulted in the elimination of some staff positions. For example, some sales organizations have outsourced the sales training function to sales training firms, thereby either eliminating or greatly reducing the number of sales training staff positions.

## SELLING SITUATION CONTINGENCIES

Determining the appropriate type of sales organization structure is as difficult as it is important. There is no one best way to organize a salesforce. The appropriate organization structure depends or is contingent on the characteristics of the selling situation. As a selling situation changes, the type of sales organization structure may also need to change. The IBM reorganization provides a good illustration of the way one firm altered its sales organization in response to changes in organizational strategies.

One key decision in sales organization design relates to specialization. Two basic questions must be addressed:

1. Should the salesforce be specialized?
2. If the salesforce should be specialized, what type of specialization is most appropriate?

The decision on specialization hinges on the relative importance to the firm of selling skill versus selling effort. Thus, if sales management wants to emphasize the amount of selling contact, a generalized salesforce should be used. If sales management wants to focus on specific skills within each selling contact, then a specialized salesforce should be used. Obviously, there must be some balance between selling effort and selling skill in all situations. But sales management can skew this balance toward selling effort or selling skill by employing a generalized or specialized salesforce.

Some guidelines for sales organization structure and selling situation factors are presented in Exhibit 4.1.[3] This exhibit suggests that a specialized structure is best when there is a high level of environmental uncertainty, when salespeople and sales managers must perform creative and nonroutine activities, and when adaptability is critical to achieving performance objectives. Centralization is most appropriate when environmental uncertainty is low, sales organization activities are routine and repetitive, and the performance emphasis is on effectiveness.

Two of the most important factors in determining the appropriate type of specialization are the similarity of customer needs and the complexity of products offered by the firm. Figure 4.4[4] illustrates how these factors can be used to suggest the appropriate

| **EXHIBIT 4.1** | Selling Situation Factors and Organizational Structure | | |
| --- | --- | --- | --- |
| **Organization Structure** | **Environmental Characteristics** | **Task Performance** | **Performance Objective** |
| Specialization | High environmental uncertainty | Nonroutine | Adaptiveness |
| Centralization | Low environmental uncertainty | Repetitive | Effectiveness |

**Customer and Product Determinants of Salesforce Specialization**    **FIGURE 4.4**

Analysis of the similarity of customer needs and the complexity of a firm's product offering can provide general guidelines for determining the appropriate type of salesforce specialization.

type of specialization. For example, when the firm has a simple product offering but customers have different needs, a market-specialized salesforce is recommended. If, however, customers have similar needs and the firm sells a complex range of products, then a product-specialized salesforce is more appropriate.

Decisions concerning centralization, span of control versus management levels, and line versus staff positions require analysis of similar selling situation factors. Decisions in these areas must be consistent with the specialization decision. For example, decentralized organization structures with few management levels, large spans of control, and the use of staff positions may be consistent with a specialized salesforce in some selling situations but not in others. The appropriate sales organization structure depends on the specific characteristics of a firm's selling situation.

## SALES ORGANIZATION STRUCTURES

Designing the sales organization structure requires integration of the desired degree of specialization, centralization, span of control, management levels, line positions, and staff positions. Obviously, there are a tremendous number of ways a sales organization might be structured. Our objective is to review several of the basic and most often used ways and to illustrate some variations in these basic structures.

To provide continuity to this discussion, each type of sales organization is discussed from the perspective of the ABC Company. The ABC Company markets office equipment (e.g., printers, furniture) and office supplies (e.g., paper, pencils) to commercial and government accounts. The firm employs 200 salespeople who operate throughout the United States. The salespeople perform various activities that can be characterized as being related either to sales generation or account servicing. Examples of sales organization structures that the ABC Company might use are presented and discussed.

### Geographic Sales Organization

Many salesforces emphasize **geographic specialization.** This is the least specialized and most generalized type of salesforce. Salespeople are typically assigned a geographic area and are responsible for all selling activities to all accounts within the assigned area. There is no attempt to specialize by product, market, or function. An example of a geographic sales organization for the ABC Company is presented in Figure 4.5. Again, note that this type of organization provides no salesforce specialization except by geographic

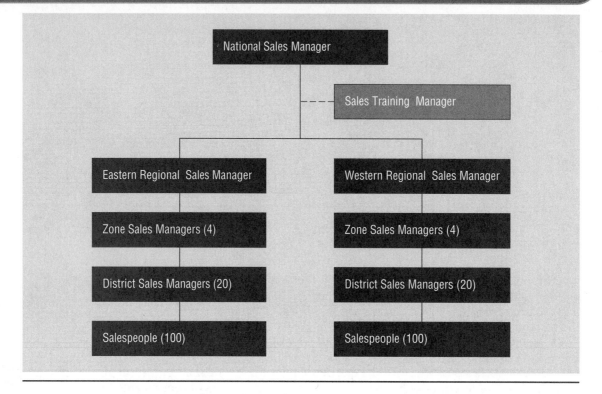

FIGURE 4.5                                                    Geographic Sales Organization

This geographic sales organization structure has four sales management levels, small spans of control, and a staff position at the national level.

area. Because of the lack of specialization, there is no duplication of effort. All geographic areas and accounts are served by only one salesperson.

The structure in this example is a rather tall one and thus somewhat centralized. There are four levels of line sales management with relatively small spans of control, indicated in parentheses: national sales manager (2), regional sales managers (4), zone sales managers (5), and district sales managers (5). Note the sales management specialization in the sales training staff position. Because this staff position is located at the national sales manager level, training activities tend to be centralized.

## Product Sales Organization

**Product specialization** has been popular in recent years, but it seems to be declining in importance, at least in certain industries. Salesforces specializing by product assign salespeople selling responsibility for specific products or product lines. The objective is for salespeople to become experts in the assigned product categories.

An example of a product sales organization for the ABC Company is presented in Figure 4.6. This organization structure indicates two levels of product specialization. There are two separate salesforces: One salesforce specializes in selling office equipment, and the other specializes in selling office supplies. Each of the specialized salesforces performs all selling activities for all types of accounts. The separate salesforces are each organized geographically. Thus, there will be duplication in the coverage of geographic areas, with both office equipment and office supplies salespeople operating in the same areas. In some cases, the salespeople may call on the same accounts.

The example structure in Figure 4.6 is flat and decentralized, especially when compared with the example presented in Figure 4.5. There are only three line management

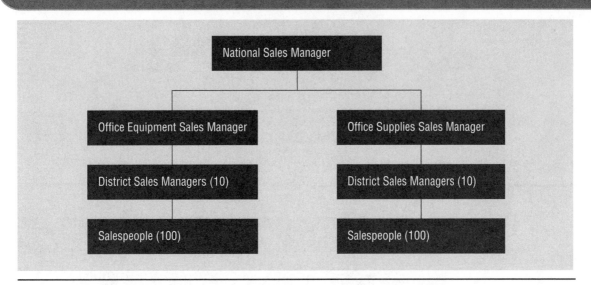

**Product Sales Organization**    FIGURE 4.6

This product sales organization structure has three sales management levels, large spans of control, and no staff positions.

levels with wide spans of control: national sales manager (2), product sales managers (10), and district sales managers (10). This structure has no staff positions and thus no management specialization beyond product specialization. The office equipment and office supplies salesforces are organized in exactly the same manner.

## Market Sales Organization

An increasingly important type of specialization is **market specialization**. Salespeople are assigned specific types of customers and are required to satisfy all needs of these customers. The new sales organization structure for IBM is an example of market specialization, because salespeople specialize in serving one specific industry and customer type. The basic objective of market specialization is to ensure that salespeople understand how customers use and purchase their products. Salespeople should then be able to direct their efforts to satisfy customer needs better. There is a clear trend toward market specializations by many sales organizations.[5]

The market sales organization shown for the ABC Company in Figure 4.7 focuses on account types. Separate salesforces have been organized for commercial and government accounts. Salespeople perform all selling activities for all products but only for certain accounts. This arrangement avoids duplication of sales effort, because only one salesperson will ever call on a given account. Several salespeople may, however, operate in the same geographic area.

The example in Figure 4.7 presents some interesting variations in sales management organization. The commercial accounts salesforce is much more centralized than the government accounts salesforce. This centralization is due to more line management levels, shorter spans of control, and a specialized sales training staff position. This example structure illustrates the important point that the specialized salesforces within a sales organization do not have to be structured in the same manner.

## Functional Sales Organization

The final type of specialization is **functional specialization**. Most selling situations require a number of selling activities, so there may be efficiencies in having salespeople specialize in performing certain of these required activities. As already discussed in

FIGURE 4.7                                              Market Sales Organization

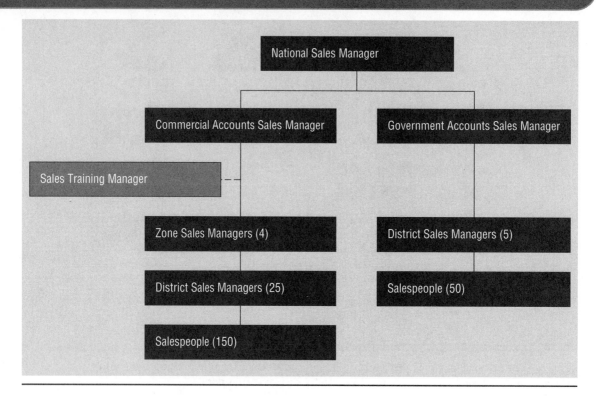

This market sales organization structure organizes its commercial accounts salesforce differently from its government accounts salesforce. The commercial accounts salesforce has three sales management levels, small spans of control, and a staff position. The government accounts salesforce has two sales management levels, large spans of control, and no staff positions.

Module 3, many firms are using a telemarketing salesforce to generate leads, qualify prospects, monitor shipments, and so forth, while the outside salesforce concentrates on sales-generating activities. These firms are specializing by function.

An example of a functional sales organization for ABC Company is presented in Figure 4.8. In this structure, a field salesforce performs sales-generating activities and a telemarketing salesforce performs account-servicing activities. Although the salesforces will cover the same geographic areas and the same accounts, the use of telemarketing helps to reduce the cost of this duplication of effort. The more routine and repetitive activities will be performed by the inside telemarketing salesforce. The more creative and nonroutine sales-generating activities will be performed by the outside field salesforce.

The field salesforce is more centralized than the telemarketing salesforce, but both salesforces tend to be decentralized. The cost-effectiveness of telemarketing is illustrated by the need for only two management levels and three managers to supervise 40 salespeople. This example does not include any staff positions for sales management specialization.

## Major Account Organization

Many firms receive a large percentage of their total sales from relatively few accounts. These large-volume accounts are obviously extremely important and must be considered when designing a sales organization. The term *major account* is used to refer to large, important accounts that should receive special attention from the sales organization. Some firms use the terms *key account* or *strategic account* instead. We use the term *major account* to refer to all large, important accounts in this text. One approach for serving major accounts is presented in "Sales Management in the 21st Century: Organizing Major Accounts."

## Functional Sales Organization                                              **FIGURE 4.8**

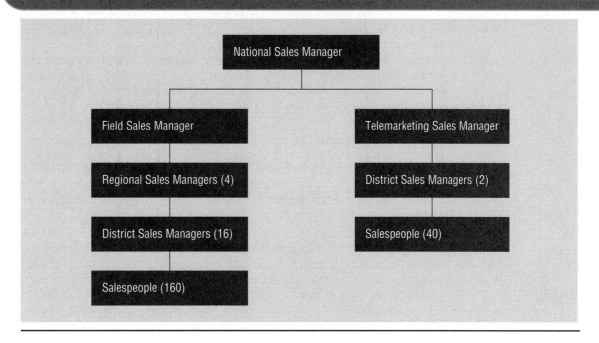

This functional sales organization structure organizes its field salesforce differently from its telemarketing salesforce. The field salesforce has three sales management levels with small spans of control, and the telemarketing salesforce has two sales management levels with large spans of control. Neither salesforce uses staff positions.

A **major account organization** represents a type of market specialization based on account size and complexity. Two types of major account organizations are of particular importance. **National account management (NAM)** focuses on meeting the needs of specific accounts with multiple locations throughout a large region or entire country. For example, the distribution company Unisource has a formal national account management program for major accounts that have many locations nationwide. Major accounts from the printing, publishing, retail grocery, manufacturing, and food processing industries are provided special services, pricing, and delivery schedules. These major accounts have a single contact point within Unisource and the same contract for all their locations.[6]

### SALES MANAGEMENT IN THE 21ST CENTURY

### Organizing Major Accounts

Bob LaMontagne, director of sales excellence for Brown-Forman Corporation, discusses his company's perspective for serving major accounts:

*Brown-Forman is a package consumer goods company in the beverage business. Large retail chains are considered major accounts, because they require special attention and have high potential for product exposure and sales. A major account sales manager is assigned to each retail chain* *major account to provide a single point of contact for the customer. This manager is responsible for working with a team of Brown-Forman colleagues to meet the high standards that major accounts expect and demand. Major account sales managers must be savvy front-line sales managers, but also able to interface effectively with senior buyers, category management specialists, advertising and promotion agencies, and individuals in marketing, packaging, and manufacturing.*

**Global account management (GAM),** by contrast, serves the needs of major customers with locations around the world. Typically, a global account manager will be located at the customer's headquarters. This manager directs the activities of account representatives in that customer's other locations worldwide. Often, a global account management team is assigned to each customer. This team might consist of product specialists, applications specialists, sales support specialists, and others.[7]

Major account organization has become increasingly important in both domestic and international markets. Although major account programs differ considerably across firms, all firms must determine how to identify their own major accounts and how to organize for effective coverage of them.

## Identifying Major Accounts

All large accounts do not qualify as major accounts. As illustrated in Figure 4.9,[8] a major account should be of sufficient size and complexity to warrant special attention from the sales organization. An account can be considered complex under the following circumstances:[9]

- Its purchasing function is centralized.
- Top management heavily influences its purchasing decisions.
- It has multisite purchasing influences.
- Its purchasing process is complex and diffuse.
- It requires special price concessions.
- It requires special services.
- It purchases customized products.

## Organizing for Major Account Coverage

Accounts that are not both large and complex are typically served adequately through the basic sales organization structure, but those identified as major accounts pose problems for organization design that might be handled in a variety of ways. The basic options are shown in Figure 4.10.[10] In one option, major accounts, although identified, are assigned to salespeople, as are other accounts. This approach may provide some special attention to these accounts but is not a formal major account management program.

**FIGURE 4.9**                                        Identifying Major Accounts

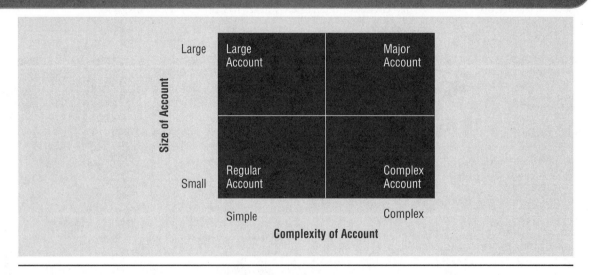

Major accounts are both large and complex. They are extremely important to the firm and require specialized attention.

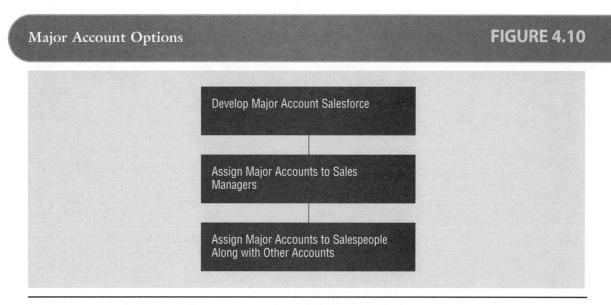

**Major Account Options**    FIGURE 4.10

Once identified, major accounts can be served in three basic ways. The development of a major account salesforce is the most comprehensive approach and is being used increasingly often for customers in domestic and international markets.

Many firms have found that formal major account management programs can strengthen account relationships and improve communications between buyers and sellers. These formal programs are designed in several ways. One approach is to assign major accounts to sales executives, who are responsible for coordinating all activities with each assigned account. This major account responsibility is typically in addition to the executives' normal management activities.

An increasingly popular approach is to establish a separate major account salesforce. This approach is a type of market specialization in which salespeople specialize by type of account based on size and complexity. Each salesperson is typically assigned one or more major accounts and is responsible for coordinating all seller activities to serve the assigned accounts. In other cases, formal sales teams are created to serve specific major accounts. Research indicates that the effectiveness of the major account salesforce depends on the esprit de corps of those serving the major account, access to sales and marketing resources, the number of activities performed with the major account, and top management involvement. Interestingly, the formalization of the major account salesforce approach was not related to effectiveness.[11]

## COMPARING SALES ORGANIZATION STRUCTURES

The sales organization structures described in the preceding section represent the basic types of salesforce specialization and some examples of the variations possible. A premise of this module is that no one best way exists to structure a sales organization. The appropriate structure for a given sales organization depends on the characteristics of the selling situation. Some structures are better in some selling situations than in others. Exhibit 4.2 summarizes much of what has been discussed previously by directly comparing the advantages and disadvantages of each basic sales organization structure.

As is evident from this exhibit, the strengths of one structure are weaknesses in other structures. For example, the lack of geographic and customer duplication is an advantage of a geographic structure but a disadvantage of the product and market structures. Because of this situation, many firms use **hybrid sales organization** structures that incorporate several of the basic structural types. The objective of these hybrid structures is to capitalize on the advantages of each type while minimizing the disadvantages.

An example of a hybrid sales organizational structure is presented in Figure 4.11. This structure is extremely complex in that it includes elements of geographic,

**EXHIBIT 4.2** Comparison of Sales Organization Structures

| Organization Structure | Advantages | Disadvantages |
|---|---|---|
| Geographic | • Low cost<br>• No geographic duplication<br>• No customer duplication<br>• Fewer management levels | • Limited specialization<br>• Lack of management control over product or customer emphasis |
| Product | • Salespeople become experts in product attributes and applications<br>• Management control over selling effort allocated to products | • High cost<br>• Geographic duplication<br>• Customer duplication |
| Market | • Salespeople develop better understanding of unique customer needs<br>• Management control over selling effort allocated to different markets | • High cost<br>• Geographic duplication |
| Functional | • Efficiency in performing selling activities | • Geographic duplication<br>• Customer duplication<br>• Need for coordination |

**FIGURE 4.11** Hybrid Sales Organization Structure

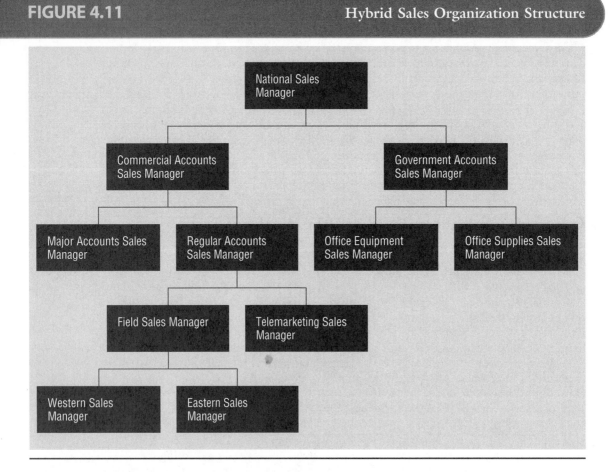

This complex sales organization structure incorporates market, product, functional, and geographic specialization.

product, market, function, and major account organizations. Although Figure 4.11 represents only one possible hybrid structure, it does illustrate how the different structure types might be combined into one overall sales organization structure. The example also illustrates the complex nature of the task of determining sales organization structure. As noted before, the task is an extremely important one; sales management must develop the appropriate sales organization structure for its particular selling situation to ensure the successful implementation of organizational and account strategies. This task becomes increasingly more difficult as firms operate globally.

## SALESFORCE DEPLOYMENT

The important sales management decisions involved in allocating selling effort, determining salesforce size, and designing territories are often referred to as **salesforce deployment.** These decisions are closely related to the sales organization structure decisions. Changes in structure often require adjustments in all three areas of salesforce deployment—selling effort allocation, salesforce size determination, and territory design.

Salesforce deployment decisions can be viewed as providing answers to three interrelated questions.

**1.** How much selling effort is needed to cover accounts and prospects adequately so that sales and profit objectives will be achieved?
**2.** How many salespeople are required to provide the desired amount of selling effort?
**3.** How should territories be designed to ensure proper coverage of accounts and to provide each salesperson with a reasonable opportunity for success?

The interrelatedness of these decisions is illustrated in Figure 4.12. Decisions in one salesforce deployment area affect decisions in other areas. For example, the decision on allocation of selling effort provides input for determining salesforce size, which provides input for territory design.

Despite the importance of salesforce deployment and the need to address the deployment decisions in an interrelated manner, many sales organizations use simplified analytical methods and consider each deployment decision in isolation—an approach not likely to result in the best deployment decisions. Even such simplified approaches, however, can

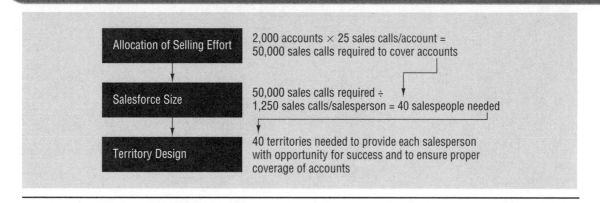

**Interrelatedness of Salesforce Deployment Decisions**      **FIGURE 4.12**

Determining how much selling effort should be allocated to various accounts provides a basis for calculating the number of salespeople required to produce the desired amount of selling effort. The salesforce size decision then determines the number of territories that must be designed. Thus, decisions in one deployment area affect decisions in other deployment areas.

typically identify deployment changes that will increase sales and profits. The basic objectives of and approaches for determining selling effort allocation, salesforce size, and territory design are discussed separately in the remainder of this module.

## Allocation of Selling Effort

The allocation of selling effort is one of the most important deployment decisions, because the salesforce size and territory decisions are based on this allocation decision. Regardless of the method of account coverage, determining how much selling effort to allocate to individual accounts is an important decision strategically speaking, because selling effort is a major determinant of account sales and a major element of account selling costs.

Although decisions on the allocation of selling effort are difficult, several analytical tools are available to help. The three basic analytical approaches are single factor models, portfolio models, and decision models. These three are compared in Figure 4.13[12] and discussed in detail throughout the remainder of this section.

### Single Factor Models

Easy to develop and use, **single factor models** do not, however, provide a very comprehensive analysis of accounts. The typical procedure is to classify all accounts on one factor, such as market potential, and then to assign all accounts in the same category the same number of sales calls. An example of using a single factor model for sales call allocation is presented in Exhibit 4.3.

Although single factor models have limitations, they do provide sales managers with a systematic approach for determining selling effort allocation. Sales managers are likely to make better allocation decisions by using single factor models than when relying totally

| FIGURE 4.13 | Analytical Approaches to Allocation of Selling Effort |

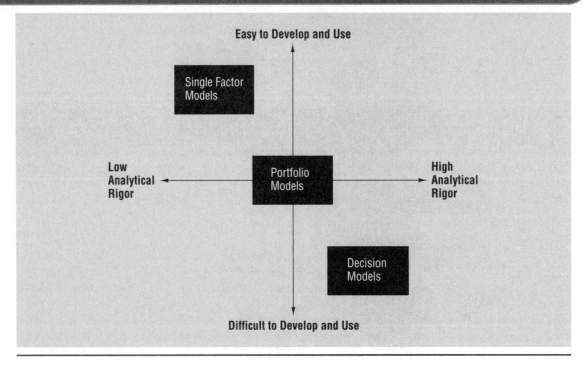

The single factor, portfolio, and decision model approaches for performing a deployment analysis differ in terms of analytical rigor and in ease of development and use. Typically, the more rigorous the approach, the more difficult it is to develop and use.

| Examples of Single Factor Model | EXHIBIT 4.3 |
| --- | --- |

The single factor model was applied to evaluate the market potential of each account and then classify all accounts into A, B, C, and D market potential categories. The average number of sales calls to an account in each market potential category was calculated and evaluated. Based on this analysis, changes in the account effort allocation strategy were made. A summary of the results follows:

| Market Potential Categories | Average Sales Calls to an Account Last Year | Average Sales Calls to an Account Next Year |
| --- | --- | --- |
| A | 25 | 32 |
| B | 23 | 24 |
| C | 20 | 16 |
| D | 16 | 8 |

on judgment and intuition. Because of their ease of development and usage, single factor models are probably the most widely used analytical approach for making these allocation decisions.

## Portfolio Models

A more comprehensive analysis of accounts is provided by **portfolio models,** but they are somewhat more difficult to develop and use than single factor models. In a portfolio model, each account served by a firm is considered as part of an overall portfolio of accounts. Thus, accounts within the portfolio represent different situations and receive different levels of selling effort attention. The typical approach is to classify all accounts in the portfolio into categories of similar attractiveness for receiving sales call investment. Then, selling effort is allocated so that the more attractive accounts receive more selling effort. The typical attractiveness segments and basic effort allocation strategies are presented in Figure 4.14.[13]

Account attractiveness is a function of account opportunity and competitive position for each account. *Account opportunity* is defined as an account's need for and ability to purchase the firm's products (e.g., grocery products, computer products, financial services). *Competitive position* is defined as the strength of the relationship between the firm and an account. As indicated in Figure 4.14, accounts are more attractive the higher the account opportunity and the stronger the competitive positions.

Using portfolio models to develop an account effort allocation strategy requires that account opportunity and competitive position be measured for each account. Based on these measurements, accounts can be classified into the attractiveness segments. The portfolio model differs from the single factor model in that many factors are normally measured to assess account opportunity and competitive position. The exact number and types of factors depend on a firm's specific selling situation. Thus, the portfolio approach provides a comprehensive account analysis that can be adapted to the specific selling situation faced by any firm.

Portfolio models can be valuable tools for helping sales managers improve their account effort allocation strategy. They are relatively easy to develop and use (although more difficult than single factor models) and provide a more comprehensive analysis than single factor models.

## Decision Models

The most rigorous and comprehensive method for determining an account effort allocation strategy is by means of a **decision model.** Because of their complexity, decision models are somewhat difficult to develop and use. However, today's computer hardware and software make decision models much easier to use than before. Research results have consistently supported the value of decision models in improving effort allocation and salesforce productivity.[14]

## FIGURE 4.14 — Portfolio Model Segments and Strategies

**Competitive Position**

|  | Strong | Weak |
|---|---|---|
| **High** | **SEGMENT 1**<br><br>**Attractiveness:**<br><br>Accounts are very attractive because they offer high opportunity, and sales organization has strong competitive position.<br><br>**Selling Effort Strategy:**<br><br>Accounts should receive a heavy investment of selling effort to take advantage of opportunity and maintain/improve competitive position. | **SEGMENT 2**<br><br>**Attractiveness:**<br><br>Accounts are potentially attractive due to high opportunity, but sales organization currently has weak competitive position.<br><br>**Selling Effort Strategy:**<br><br>Additional analysis should be performed to identify accounts where sales organization's competitive position can be strengthened. These accounts should receive heavy investment of selling effort, while other accounts receive minimal investment. |
| **Low** | **SEGMENT 3**<br><br>**Attractiveness:**<br><br>Accounts are moderately attractive due to sales organization's strong competitive position. However, future opportunity is limited.<br><br>**Selling Effort Strategy:**<br><br>Accounts should receive a selling effort investment sufficient to maintain current competitive position. | **SEGMENT 4**<br><br>**Attractiveness:**<br><br>Accounts are very unattractive; they offer low opportunity, and sales organization has weak competitive position.<br><br>**Selling Effort Strategy:**<br><br>Accounts should receive minimal investment of selling effort. Less costly forms of marketing (for example, telephone sales calls, direct mail) should replace personal selling efforts on a selective basis, or the account coverage should be eliminated entirely. |

*Account Opportunity* (vertical axis label)

Accounts are classified into attractiveness categories based on evaluations of account opportunity and competitive position. The selling effort strategies are based on the concept that the more attractive an account, the more selling effort it should receive.

Although the mathematical formulations of decision models can be complex, the basic concept is simple—to allocate sales calls to accounts that promise the highest sales return from the sales calls. The objective is to achieve the highest level of sales for any given number of sales calls and to continue increasing sales calls until their marginal costs equal their marginal returns. Thus, decision models calculate the optimal allocation of sales calls in terms of sales or profit maximization.

# Salesforce Size

Research results have consistently shown that many firms could improve their performance by changing the size of their salesforce. In some situations, the salesforce should be increased. In other situations, firms are employing too many salespeople and could improve performance by reducing the size of their salesforce. Determining the appropriate salesforce size requires an understanding of several key considerations as well as a familiarity with the analytical approaches that might be used.

## Key Considerations

The size of a firm's salesforce determines the total amount of selling effort that is available to call on accounts and prospects. The decision on salesforce size is analogous to the decision on advertising budget. Whereas the advertising budget establishes the total amount that the firm has to spend on advertising communications, the salesforce size determines the total amount of personal selling effort that is available. Because each salesperson can make only a certain number of sales calls during any period, the number of salespeople times the number of sales calls per salesperson defines the total available selling effort. For example, a firm with 100 salespeople who each make 500 sales calls per year has a total selling effort of 50,000 sales calls. If the salesforce is increased to 110 salespeople, then total selling effort is increased to 55,000 sales calls. Key considerations in determining salesforce size are productivity, turnover, and organizational strategy.

### Productivity

In general terms, *productivity* is defined as a ratio between outputs and inputs. One way the **sales productivity** of a salesforce is calculated is the ratio of sales generated to selling effort used. Thus, productivity is an important consideration for all deployment decisions. However, selling effort is often expressed in terms of number of salespeople. This suggests that the critical consideration is the *relationship* between selling effort and sales, not just the total amount of selling effort or the total level of sales. For example, sales per salesperson is an important sales productivity measure.

Sales will generally increase with the addition of salespeople, but not in a linear manner. With some exceptions, costs tend to increase directly with salesforce size. This produces the basic relationship presented in Figure 4.15. In early stages, the addition of salespeople increases sales considerably more than the selling costs. However, as salespeople continue to be added, sales increases tend to decline until a point is reached when the costs to add a salesperson are more than the revenues that salesperson can generate. In fact, the profit maximization point is when the marginal costs of adding a salesperson are equal to the marginal profits generated by that salesperson. It typically becomes more difficult to maintain high sales productivity levels at larger salesforce sizes. This makes it imperative that management consider the relationship between sales and costs when making decisions on salesforce size.

### Turnover

Salesforce turnover is extremely costly. Because some turnover is going to occur for all firms, it should always be considered when determining salesforce size. Once the appropriate salesforce size is determined—that is, one sufficient for salespeople to call on all the firm's accounts and prospects in a productive manner—this figure should be adjusted to reflect expected turnover. If an increase or maintenance of current salesforce size is desired, excess salespeople should be in the recruiting-selecting-training pipeline. If a decrease is desired, turnover might be all that is necessary to accomplish it. For example, a grocery products marketer that found that its salesforce should be reduced from 34 to 32 salespeople achieved the two-salesperson reduction through scheduled retirements in the near future instead of firing two salespeople.

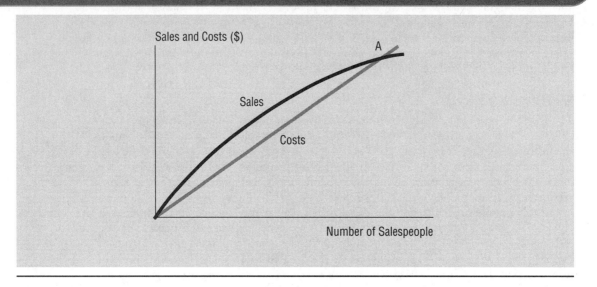

**FIGURE 4.15**          Sales and Cost Relationships

Although costs tend to increase in a linear manner with the addition of salespeople, the associated sales increases are typically nonlinear. In general, the increases in sales tend to decrease as more salespeople are added. A point (A) is reached when the sales from adding a salesperson are not sufficient to cover the additional costs.

### Organizational Strategy

Salesforce size decisions must also be consistent with the firm's organizational strategy. Companies that focus on serving current customers and achieving limited growth during slow economic times might reduce salesforce size as a way to lower costs. In contrast, companies trying to gain market share, capture new customers, and take advantage of market opportunities are likely to increase salesforce size. In fact, increasing salesforce size at the right time can provide a firm with a competitive advantage. For example, when Rilston Electrical Components sensed that economic conditions were improving, it added three salespeople to its salesforce of eight. Because it responded to opportunities before its competitors did, the company was able to increase market share and grow sales by 25 percent.[15]

The pharmaceutical industry provides an interesting example. Most pharmaceutical companies find sales calls to doctors a more effective way to increase prescriptions than consumer advertising. Thus, the number of pharmaceutical salespeople has tripled to over 90,000 in the past decade. Typical is Merck. It has added 1,500 salespeople, bringing its salesforce to about 7,000. The increased number of salespeople has increased drug sales, but there are problems. Sales organization costs are up significantly. Many doctors feel bombarded by pharmaceutical salespeople and have refused to see them or have severely limited their access. This has lowered sales productivity as the number of meetings with a doctor for an average pharmaceutical salesperson has dropped from 808 per year to around 529 per year. Although the drug companies are aware of these problems, individual companies are reluctant to reduce their salesforce size, because this would give their competitors an advantage.[16]

### Analytical Tools

The need to consider sales, costs, productivity, and turnover makes salesforce size a difficult decision. Fortunately, some analytical tools are available to help management process relevant information and evaluate salesforce size alternatives more fully. Before describing these analytical tools, we want to make it clear that there are several types of salesforce size decisions (see Figure 4.16). The most straightforward situation is when

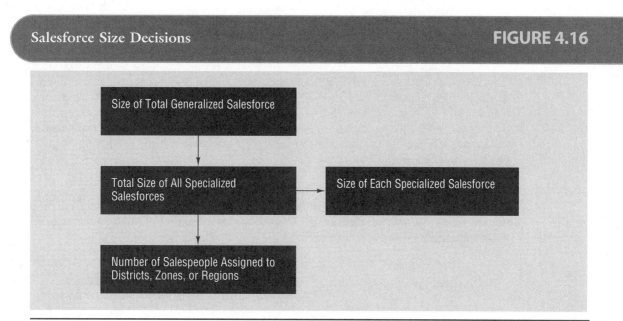

**Salesforce Size Decisions**    **FIGURE 4.16**

Depending on the sales organization structure of a firm, sales managers may be faced with several different types of salesforce size decisions. Each requires the same basic concepts and analytical methods.

a firm has one generalized salesforce. However, as discussed earlier, many firms employ multiple specialized salesforces, in which case both the total number of salespeople employed by the firm and the size of each individual salesforce are important. Both generalized and specialized salesforces are normally organized into geographic districts, zones, regions, and so on. The number of salespeople to assign to each district, zone, region, and so on is a type of salesforce size decision.

These decisions are similar conceptually and can be addressed by the same analytical tools, provided that the type of salesforce size decision being addressed is specified. Unless stated otherwise, you can assume the situation of one generalized salesforce in the following discussion.

### Breakdown Approach

A relatively simple approach for calculating salesforce size, the **breakdown approach** assumes that an accurate sales forecast is available. This forecast is then "broken down" to determine the number of salespeople needed to generate the forecasted level of sales. The basic formula is

$$\text{Salesforce size} = \text{Forecasted sales/Average sales per salesperson}$$

Assume that a firm forecasts sales of $50 million for next year. If salespeople generate an average of $2 million in annual sales, then the firm needs 25 salespeople to achieve the $50 million sales forecast:

$$\text{Salesforce size} = \$50{,}000{,}000/\$2{,}000{,}000 = 25 \text{ salespeople}$$

The basic advantage of the breakdown method is its ease of development. The approach is straightforward, and the mathematical calculations are simple. However, the approach is conceptually weak. The concept underlying the calculations is that sales determine the number of salespeople needed. This puts the cart before the horse, because the number of salespeople employed by a firm is an important determinant of firm sales. A sales forecast should be based on a given salesforce size. The addition of salespeople should increase the forecast, and the elimination of salespeople should decrease it.

Despite this weakness, the breakdown method is probably the one most often used for determining salesforce size. It is best suited for relatively stable selling environments in which sales change in slow and predictable ways and no major strategic changes are planned and for organizations that use commission compensation plans and keep their fixed costs low. However, in many selling situations the costs of having too many or too few salespeople are high. More rigorous analytical tools are recommended for calculating salesforce size in these situations.

### Workload Approach

The first step in the **workload approach** is to determine how much selling effort is needed to cover the firm's market adequately. Then the number of salespeople required to provide this amount of selling effort is calculated. The basic formula is

$$\text{Number of salespeople} = \frac{\text{Total selling effort needed}}{\text{Average selling effort per salesperson}}$$

For example, if a firm determines that 37,500 sales calls are needed in its market area and a salesperson can make an average of 500 annual sales calls, then 75 salespeople are needed to provide the desired level of selling effort:

$$\text{Number of salespeople} = 37,500/500 = 75 \text{ salespeople}$$

The key factor in the workload approach is the total amount of selling effort needed. Several workload methods can be used, depending on whether single factor, portfolio, or decision models were used for determining the allocation of effort to accounts. Each workload method offers a way to calculate how many sales calls to make to all accounts and prospects during any time period. When the sales call allocation strategies are summed across all accounts and prospects, the total amount of selling effort for a time period is determined. Thus, the workload approach integrates the salesforce size decision with account effort allocation strategies.

The workload approach is also relatively simple, although its simplicity depends on the specific method used to determine total selling effort needs. The approach is conceptually sound, because salesforce size is based on selling effort needs established by account effort allocation decisions. Note, however, that we have presented the workload approach in a simplified manner here by considering only selling effort. A more realistic presentation would incorporate nonselling time considerations (e.g., travel time, planning time) in the analysis. Although incorporating these considerations does not change the basic workload concept, it does make the calculations more complex and cumbersome.

The workload approach is suited for all types of selling situations. Sales organizations can adapt the basic approach to their specific situation through the method used to calculate total selling effort. The most sophisticated firms can use decision models for this purpose, whereas other firms might use portfolio models or single factor approaches.

### Incremental Approach

The most rigorous approach for calculating salesforce size is the **incremental approach**. Its basic concept is to compare the marginal profit contribution with the marginal selling costs for each incremental salesperson. An example of these calculations is provided in Exhibit 4.4. At 100 salespeople, marginal profits exceed marginal costs by $10,000. This relationship continues until salesforce size reaches 102. At 102 salespeople, the marginal profit equals marginal cost, and total profits are maximized.

| | Incremental Approach | **EXHIBIT 4.4** |
|---|---|---|
| **Number of Salespeople** | **Marginal Salesperson Profit Contribution** | **Marginal Salesperson Cost** |
| 100 | $85,000 | $75,000 |
| 101 | $80,000 | $75,000 |
| 102 | $75,000 | $75,000 |
| 103 | $70,000 | $75,000 |

If the firm added one more salesperson, total profits would be reduced, because marginal costs would exceed marginal profits by $5,000. Thus, the optimal salesforce size for this example is 102.

The major advantage of the incremental approach is that it quantifies the important relationships between salesforce size, sales, and costs, making it possible to assess the potential sales and profit impacts of different salesforce sizes. It forces management to view the salesforce size decision as one that affects both the level of sales that can be generated and the costs associated with producing each sales level.

The incremental method is, however, somewhat difficult to develop. Relatively complex response functions must be formulated to predict sales at different salesforce sizes (sales $= f$ [salesforce size]). Developing these response functions requires either historical data or management judgment. Thus, the incremental approach cannot be used for new salesforces where historical data and accurate judgments are not possible.

### Turnover

All the analytical tools incorporate various elements of sales and costs in their calculations. Therefore, they directly address productivity issues but do not directly consider turnover in the salesforce size calculations. When turnover considerations are important, management should adjust the recommended salesforce size produced by any of the analytical methods to reflect expected turnover rates. For example, if an analytical tool recommended a salesforce size of 100 for a firm that experiences 20 percent annual turnover, the effective salesforce size should be adjusted to 120. Recruiting, selecting, and training plans should be based on the 120 salesforce size.

Failure to incorporate anticipated salesforce turnover into salesforce size calculations can be costly. Evidence suggests that many firms may lose as much as 10 percent in sales productivity due to the loss in sales from vacant territories or low initial sales when a new salesperson is assigned to a territory. Thus, the sooner that sales managers can replace salespeople and get them productive in their territories, the less loss in sales within the territory.

### Outsourcing the Salesforce

The salesforce size decisions we have been discussing apply directly to an ongoing company salesforce. However, there may be situations where a company needs salespeople quickly, for short periods of time, for smaller customers, or for other reasons, but does not want to hire additional salespeople. An attractive option is to outsource the salesforce. A growing number of companies can provide salespeople to a firm on a contract basis. These salespeople only represent the firm and customers are typically not aware that these are contracted salespeople. Contracts can vary as to length, customer assignment, and other relevant factors. This gives the client firm a great deal of flexibility.

The situation at GE Medical Systems is illustrative. Salespeople at GE Medical Systems called on hospitals with 100 or more beds in major metropolitan areas. This left the market for smaller hospitals in rural areas to competitors. GE decided it needed pursue these smaller markets, but did not want to hire additional salespeople or to have existing salespeople take time away from their large customers. So, GE contracted with a firm to provide seven salespeople experienced in capital equipment sales to serve the smaller markets. The salespeople were hired, trained on GE products, and in the field within three months. These contracted reps grew annual GE sales in the smaller markets to $260 million within five years. The results were so spectacular that GE has renewed the outsourcing contract and continues to use the contracted salespeople.[17]

## Designing Territories

As discussed earlier, the size of a salesforce determines the total amount of selling effort that a firm has available to generate sales from accounts and prospects. The effective use of this selling effort often requires that sales **territories** be developed and each salesperson be assigned to a specific territory. A territory consists of whatever specific accounts are assigned to a specific salesperson. The overall objective is to ensure that all accounts are assigned salesperson responsibility and that each salesperson can adequately cover the assigned accounts. Although territories are often defined by geographic area (e.g., the Oklahoma territory, the Tennessee territory), the key components of a territory are the accounts within the specified geographic area.

The territory can be viewed as the work unit for a salesperson. The salesperson is largely responsible for the selling activities performed and the performance achieved in a territory. Salesperson compensation and success are normally a direct function of territory performance; thus, the design of territories is extremely important to the individual salespeople of a firm as well as to management. An example of trying to balance company and salesperson needs is presented in "Sales Management in the 21st Century: Designing Sales Territories."

### Territory Considerations

The critical territory considerations are illustrated in Exhibit 4.5.[18] In this example, Andy and Sally are salespeople for a consumer durable goods manufacturer. They have each been assigned a geographic territory consisting of several trading areas. The exhibit compares the percentage of their time currently spent in each trading area with the percentages recommended from a decision model analysis. A review of the information provided in the exhibit highlights territory design problems from the perspective of the firm and of each salesperson.

The current territory design does not provide proper selling coverage of the trading areas. The decision model analysis suggests that the trading areas in Andy's territory should require only 36 percent of his time, yet he is spending all his time there. Clearly, the firm is wasting expensive selling effort in Andy's territory. The situation in Sally's territory is just the opposite. Proper coverage of Sally's trading areas should require more than two salespeople, yet Sally has sole responsibility for these trading areas. In this situation the firm is losing sales opportunities because of a lack of selling attention.

---

SALES MANAGEMENT IN THE 21ST CENTURY

**Designing Sales Territories**

Bob LaMontagne, director of sales excellence for Brown-Forman Corporation, discusses the important factors in designing effective sales territories:

*Each of our salespeople is responsible for a territory defined by geographic area and assigned accounts. By law, we sell to distributors (wholesalers) who in turn sell to retail stores. Therefore, the critical driver for our territory design is the number of distributors included in a geographic area. We always start with a state. Since each state has specific laws that govern it, it is a big decision to give more than one state to a sales representative. Large states such as New York, California, and Texas are subdivided into smaller trading areas and assigned to salespeople.*

| | Trading Area[a] | Present Effort (%)[b] | Recommended Effort (%)[b] |
|---|---|---|---|
| **Andy** | 1 | 10 | 4 |
| | 2 | 60 | 20 |
| | 3 | 15 | 7 |
| | 4 | 5 | 2 |
| | 5 | 10 | 3 |
| **Total** | | 100 | 36 |
| **Sally** | 6 | 18 | 81 |
| | 7 | 7 | 21 |
| | 8 | 5 | 11 |
| | 9 | 35 | 35 |
| | 10 | 5 | 11 |
| | 11 | 30 | 77 |
| **Total** | | 100 | 236 |

**Territory Design Example** **EXHIBIT 4.5**

[a]Each territory is made of up several trading areas.
[b]The percentage of salesperson time spent in the trading area (100% = 1 salesperson). Thus, the deployment analysis suggests that Andy's territory requires only 0.36 salespeople, whereas Sally's territory needs 2.36 salespeople for proper coverage.

From the firm's perspective, the design of Andy's and Sally's territories limits sales and profit performance. Sales performance in Sally's territory is much lower than it might be if more selling attention were given to her trading areas. Profit performance is low in Andy's territory because too much selling effort is being expended in his trading areas. The firm is not achieving the level of sales and profits that might be achieved if the territories were designed to provide more productive market coverage. Thus, one key consideration in territory design is the productive deployment of selling effort within each territory.

From the perspective of Andy and Sally, the poor territory design affects their level of motivation. Andy is frustrated. He spends much of his time making sales calls in trading areas where little potential exists for generating additional sales. Andy's motivational level is low, and he may consider resigning from the company. By contrast, Sally's territory has so much sales potential that she can limit her sales calls to the largest accounts or the easiest sales. She is not motivated to develop the potential of her territory but can merely "skim the cream" from the best accounts. The situations facing Andy and Sally illustrate how territory design might affect salesperson motivation, morale, and even turnover. These potential effects are important considerations when designing territories.

Recent research results support the example. Studies of sales managers in several countries found positive relationships between satisfaction with territory design and salesperson performance. These results are confirmed in a study of salespeople. The study concluded that salespeople who are satisfied with the design of their sales territory worked harder, performed better, and were more satisfied with their job. This research provides strong evidence for the impact of sales territory design on the attitudes, behavior, and performance of salespeople.[19]

## Procedure for Designing Territories

A general procedure for designing territories is presented in Figure 4.17. Each step in the procedure can be performed manually or by using computer models. The procedure is illustrated manually by using Andy's and Sally's territories as an example application. The basic problem is to organize the 11 trading areas into three territories that provide proper market coverage of accounts in each territory and equal performance opportunities for each

## FIGURE 4.17                    Territory Design Procedure

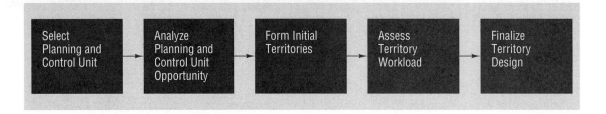

Designing territories requires a multiple-stage approach. Although most territory design approaches follow the stages presented in this figure, the methods used at each stage differ considerably, depending on the analytical tools used.

salesperson. Three territories are developed because the decision model results presented in Exhibit 4.5 indicate that two salespeople cannot adequately cover these trading areas. The data needed to design the sales territories are presented in Exhibit 4.6.

### Select Planning and Control Unit

The first step in territory design is to select the **planning and control unit** that will be used in the analysis—that is, some entity that is smaller than a territory. The total market area served by a firm is divided into these planning and control units, then they are analyzed and grouped together to form territories.

Examples of potential planning and control units are illustrated in Figure 4.18. In general, management should use the smallest unit feasible. However, data are often not available for small planning and control units, and the computational task becomes more complex as more units are included in the analysis. The selection of the appropriate planning and control unit therefore represents a trade-off between what is desired and what is possible under the given data or computational conditions. In our example, trading areas have been selected as the planning and control unit.

### Analyze Opportunity of Planning and Control Unit

First, determine the amount of opportunity available from each planning and control unit. Specific methods for performing these calculations will be covered in the appendix to Module 4. However, the most often used measure of opportunity is *market potential*. The market potentials for the 11 trading areas in our example are provided in Exhibit 4.6. Everything else being equal, the higher the market potential, the more opportunity is available.

## EXHIBIT 4.6    Territory Design Data

| Trading Area | Market Potential | Number of Sales Calls |
|:---:|:---:|:---:|
| 1 | $250,000 | 25 |
| 2 | $700,000 | 100 |
| 3 | $350,000 | 35 |
| 4 | $150,000 | 15 |
| 5 | $200,000 | 20 |
| 6 | $2,000,000 | 175 |
| 7 | $750,000 | 65 |
| 8 | $500,000 | 50 |
| 9 | $1,000,000 | 100 |
| 10 | $500,000 | 50 |
| 11 | $1,750,000 | 175 |

## Potential Planning and Control Units   FIGURE 4.18

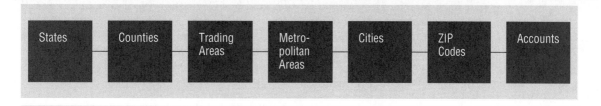

Planning and control units represent the unit of analysis for territory design. Accounts are the preferred planning and control unit. However, often it is not possible to use them as such, in which case a more aggregate type of planning and control unit is used.

## Form Initial Territories

Once planning and control units have been selected and opportunity evaluated, initial territories can be designed. The objective is to group the planning and control units into territories that are as equal as possible in opportunity. This step may take several iterations, as there are probably a number of feasible territory designs. It is also unlikely that any design will achieve complete equality of opportunity. The best approach is to design several territory arrangements and evaluate each alternative. Each alternative must be feasible in that planning and control units grouped together are contiguous. This can be a cumbersome task when done manually but is much more efficient when computer modeling approaches are used.

Two alternative territory designs for our example are presented and evaluated in Exhibit 4.7. Although the first design is feasible, the territories are markedly unequal in opportunity. However, a few adjustments produce reasonably equal territories.

### Initial Territory Design   EXHIBIT 4.7

| | Alternative 1 | | Alternative 2 | |
| --- | --- | --- | --- | --- |
| | Trading Area | Market Potential | Trading Area | Market Potential |
| **Territory 1** | 1 | $   250,000 | 1 | $   250,000 |
| | 2 | 700,000 | 2 | 700,000 |
| | 3 | 350,000 | 5 | 200,000 |
| | 4 | 150,000 | 8 | 500,000 |
| | 5 | 200,000 | 9 | 1,000,000 |
| | | $1,650,000 | | $2,650,000 |
| **Territory 2** | 6 | $2,000,000 | 6 | $2,000,000 |
| | 7 | 750,000 | 7 | 750,000 |
| | 8 | 500,000 | | $2,750,000 |
| | | $3,250,000 | | |
| **Territory 3** | 9 | $1,000,000 | 3 | $   350,000 |
| | 10 | 500,000 | 4 | 150,000 |
| | 11 | 1,750,000 | 10 | 500,000 |
| | | $3,250,000 | 11 | 1,750,000 |
| | | | | $2,750,000 |

## Assess Territory Workloads

The preceding step produces territories of nearly equal opportunity. It may, however, take more work to realize this opportunity in some territories than in others. Therefore, the workload of each territory should be evaluated by (1) the number of sales calls required to cover the accounts in the territory, (2) the amount of travel time in the territory, (3) the total number of accounts, and (4) any other factors that measure the amount of work required by a salesperson assigned to the territory. In our example, workload for each trading area and territory is evaluated by the number of sales calls required. This information is presented in Exhibit 4.8.

## Finalize Territory Design

The final step is to adjust the initial territories to achieve equal workloads for each salesperson. The objective is to achieve the best possible balance between equal opportunity and equal workload for each territory. Typically, both of these objectives cannot be completely achieved, so management must decide on the best trade-offs for its situation. Any inequalities in the final territories can be addressed when quotas are established as discussed in Module 10.

Achieving workload and opportunity balance for our example is illustrated in Exhibit 4.9. The equal opportunity territories resulted in somewhat unequal workloads (see Exhibit 4.8). The final territory design moved trading area 7 to territory 1 and trading area 2 to territory 2. This produces territories that are reasonably equal in both opportunity and workload.

Performing territory design analyses manually is difficult and time consuming. Fortunately, advances in computer hardware and software make it possible to consider multiple factors and rapidly evaluate many alternatives when designing territories.

## Assigning Salespeople to Territories

Once territories have been designed, salespeople must be assigned to them. Salespeople are not equal in abilities and will perform differently with different types of accounts or prospects. Some sales managers consider their salespeople to be either farmers or hunters. *Farmers* are effective with existing accounts but do not perform well in establishing business with new accounts. *Hunters* excel in establishing new accounts but do not fully

---

**EXHIBIT 4.8**   Workload Evaluations

| | Trading Area | Sales Calls |
|---|:---:|:---:|
| **Territory 1** | 1 | 25 |
| | 2 | 100 |
| | 5 | 20 |
| | 8 | 50 |
| | 9 | 100 |
| | | 295 |
| **Territory 2** | 6 | 175 |
| | 7 | 65 |
| | | 240 |
| **Territory 3** | 3 | 35 |
| | 4 | 15 |
| | 10 | 50 |
| | 11 | 175 |
| | | 275 |

| | Trading Area | Market Potential | Sales Calls |
|---|---|---|---|
| **Final Territory Design** | | | **EXHIBIT 4.9** |
| **Territory 1** | 1 | $250,000 | 25 |
| | 5 | 200,000 | 20 |
| | 7 | 750,000 | 65 |
| | 8 | 500,000 | 50 |
| | 9 | 1,000,000 | 100 |
| | | $2,700,000 | 260 |
| **Territory 2** | 2 | $700,000 | 100 |
| | 6 | 2,000,000 | 175 |
| | | $2,700,000 | 275 |
| **Territory 3** | 3 | $350,000 | 35 |
| | 4 | 150,000 | 15 |
| | 10 | 500,000 | 50 |
| | 11 | 1,750,000 | 175 |
| | | $2,750,000 | 275 |

develop existing accounts. Based on these categories, farmers should be assigned to territories that contain many ongoing account relationships, and hunters should be assigned to territories in new or less-developed market areas.

## Using Technology

We have taken you through the territory design process manually so that you understand what is involved in each step. Many sales organizations still perform this process manually using maps, grease pencils, and calculators. There are, however, several software programs that automate the process. Most of these programs make it easy to design potential territories, print maps, and compare opportunity and workload. Then, changes can be made easily and new maps and comparisons produced quickly. This allows sales managers to evaluate many possible territory designs and to assess the impact of territory design changes easily. Examples of available software include Sales Territory Configurator (www.rochestergroup.com), Tactician® (www.tactician.com), and TerrAlign (www.terralign.com).

## "PEOPLE" CONSIDERATIONS

Our discussion of salesforce deployment decisions has, to this point, focused entirely on analytical approaches. This analytical orientation emphasizes objective sales and cost considerations in evaluating different allocations of sales calls to accounts, different salesforce sizes, different territory designs, and different assignments of salespeople to territories. Although such analytical approaches are valuable and should be used by sales managers, final deployment decisions should also be based on "people" considerations. These "people" considerations can produce some problems as presented in "An Ethical Dilemma."

Statistics are numbers, whereas sales managers, salespeople, and customers are people. Analysis of statistical data provides useful but incomplete information for deployment decisions. Models are only representations of reality, and no matter how complex, no model can incorporate all the people factors that are important in any salesforce deployment decision. Accordingly, while using the appropriate analytical approaches, sales managers should temper the analytical results with people considerations before making final deployment decisions.

AN ETHICAL DILEMMA

Business is booming at Lunsford Electronics. The economy is growing and new electronic products are being introduced on a regular basis. The company has decided to add one salesperson to each district. The southeastern district manager, Terry Bearden, will now have 10 salespeople to cover all accounts and prospects in the district. He has spent days examining alternative sales territory designs and thinks one option is best for the company and fair to all salespeople. However, he is considering another option that would give Cathy Swift a better territory and Fred Mangold a poorer one. Terry has always liked Cathy and thinks the better territory will help improve her sales. Fred has been a star performer for years and doesn't mind telling everyone how much money he makes. Terry thinks Fred will still perform well in the new territory and maybe this will eliminate some of his "bragging." Which territory design should Terry decide to use? Why?

What are the important people considerations in salesforce deployment? The most important ones concern personal relationships between salespeople and customers and between salespeople and the sales organization. Consider the allocation of selling effort to accounts. The analytical approaches for making this decision produce a recommended number of sales calls to each account based on some assessment of expected sales and costs for different sales call levels. Although these approaches may incorporate a number of factors in developing the recommended sales call levels, there is no way that any analytical approach can use the detailed knowledge that a salesperson has about the unique needs of individual accounts. Therefore, an analytical approach may suggest that sales calls should be increased or decreased to a specific account, whereas the salesperson serving this account may know that the account will react adversely to any changes in sales call coverage. In this situation, a sales manager would be wise to ignore the analytical recommendation and not change sales call coverage to the account, because of the existing relationship between the salesperson and customer.

Salesforce size decisions also require consideration of people issues. A decision to reduce the size of a salesforce means that some salespeople will have to be removed from the salesforce. How this reduction is accomplished can affect the relationship between salespeople and the sales organization. Achieving this reduction through attrition or offering salespeople other positions is typically a better approach than merely firing salespeople.

Increasing salesforce size means that the new salespeople must be assigned to territories. Consequently, some accounts will find themselves being served by new salespeople. These changes in assignment can have a devastating effect on the existing customer-salesperson relationship. Not only should that relationship be considered but also the issue of fairness in taking accounts from one salesperson and assigning them to another. The situation can be a delicate one, requiring careful judgment as to how these people considerations should be balanced against analytical results.

In sum, sales managers should integrate the results from salesforce deployment analysis with people considerations before implementing changes in sales call allocation, salesforce size, or territory design. A good rule of thumb is to make salesforce deployment changes that are likely to have the least disruptive effect on existing personal relationships.

## SUMMARY

1. **Define the concepts of specialization, centralization, span of control versus management levels, and line versus staff positions.** *Specialization* refers to the division of labor such that salespeople or sales managers concentrate on performing certain activities to the exclusion of others. *Centralization* refers to where in the organization decision-making responsibility exists. Centralized organizations locate decision-making responsibility at higher organizational levels than decentralized organizations. Any sales organization structure can be evaluated in terms of the types and degrees of specialization and centralization afforded by the structure. Sales management organization design also requires decisions concerning the number of management levels, spans of control, and line versus staff positions. In general, more *management levels* result in smaller *spans of control* and more *staff positions* result in more sales management specialization.

2. **Describe the ways salesforces might be specialized.** A critical decision in designing the sales organization is determining whether the salesforce should be specialized and, if so, the appropriate type of specialization. The basic types of salesforce specialization are geographic, product, market (including major account organization), and functional. The appropriate type of specialization depends on the characteristics of the selling situation. Important selling situation characteristics include the similarity of customer needs, the complexity of the firm's product offering, the market environment, and the professionalism of the salesforce. Specific criteria of importance are affordability and payout, credibility and coverage, and flexibility. The use of different types and levels of specialization typically requires the establishment of separate salesforces.

3. **Evaluate the advantages and disadvantages of sales organization structures.** Because each type of sales organization structure has certain advantages and disadvantages, many firms use hybrid structures that combine the features of several types. Usually, the strengths of one structure are weaknesses in other structures.

4. **Name the important considerations in organizing major account management programs.** Identifying major accounts (which should be both large and complex) and organizing for coverage of them are the important considerations in major account management.

5. **Explain how to determine the appropriate sales organization structure for a given selling situation.** There is no one best way to structure a sales organization. The appropriate way to organize a salesforce and sales management depends on certain characteristics of a particular selling situation. Also, because the sales organization structure decision is dynamic, it must be adapted to changes in a firm's selling situation that occur over time.

6. **Discuss salesforce deployment.** Salesforce deployment decisions entail allocating selling effort, determining salesforce size, and designing territories. These decisions are highly interrelated and should be addressed in an integrated, sequential manner. Improvements in salesforce deployment can produce substantial increases in sales and profits.

7. **Explain three analytical approaches for determining allocation of selling effort.** Single factor, portfolio, and decision models can be used as analytical tools to determine appropriate selling effort allocations. The approaches differ in terms of analytical rigor and ease of development and use. Sales organizations should use the approach that best fits their particular selling situation.

8. **Describe three methods for calculating salesforce size**. The breakdown method for calculating salesforce size is the easiest to use but the weakest conceptually. It uses the expected level of sales to determine the number of salespeople. The workload approach is sounder conceptually, because it bases the salesforce size decision on the amount of selling effort needed to cover the market appropriately. The incremental method is the best approach, although it is often difficult to develop. It examines the marginal sales and costs associated with different salesforce sizes.

9. **Explain the importance of sales territories from the perspective of the sales organization and from the perspective of the salespeople, and list the steps in the territory design process**. Territories are assignments of accounts to salespeople. Each becomes the work unit for a salesperson, who is largely responsible for the performance of the assigned territory. Poorly designed territories can have adverse effects on the motivation of salespeople. From the perspective of the firm, territory design decisions should ensure that the firm's market area is adequately covered in a productive manner. The first step in the territory design process is to identify planning and control units. Next, the opportunity available from each planning and control unit is determined, initial territories are formed, and the workloads of each potential territory are assessed. The final territory design represents management's judgment concerning the best balance between opportunity and workload.

10. **Discuss the important "people" considerations in salesforce deployment**. Although analytical approaches provide useful input for salesforce deployment decisions, they do not address people considerations adequately. Sales managers should always consider existing relationships between salespeople and customers and between salespeople and the sales organization before making salesforce deployment changes. Many of these people considerations have ethical consequences.

## UNDERSTANDING SALES MANAGEMENT TERMS

| | |
|---|---|
| specialization | global account management (GAM) |
| centralization | hybrid sales organization |
| span of control | salesforce deployment |
| management levels | single factor models |
| line sales management | portfolio models |
| staff sales management | decision models |
| geographic specialization | sales productivity |
| product specialization | breakdown approach |
| market specialization | workload approach |
| functional specialization | incremental approach |
| major account organization | territory |
| national account management (NAM) | planning and control unit |

## DEVELOPING SALES MANAGEMENT KNOWLEDGE

1. Discuss the situational factors that suggest the need for specialization and centralization. Provide a specific example of each factor discussed.

2. Why do you think there is a trend toward more salesforce specialization?

3. What are the advantages and disadvantages of structuring a sales organization for major account management?

4. What are some problems that a firm might face when undertaking a major restructuring of its sales organization?

5. What are the important relationships between span of control, management levels, line positions, staff positions, specialization, and centralization?

6. How are salesforce deployment decisions related to decisions on sales organization structure?

7. How can the incremental method be used to determine the number of salespeople to assign to a sales district?

8. How are salesforce size decisions different for firms with one generalized salesforce versus firms with several specialized salesforces?

9. How can computer modeling assist sales managers in designing territories?

10. Should firms always try to design equal territories? Why or why not?

# BUILDING SALES MANAGEMENT SKILLS

1. Assume that you are the national sales manager for Replica Inc., a manufacturer and marketer of photocopy equipment and supplies. The firm's products are sold both nationally and internationally by a salesforce of 5,000. Replica sells to accounts of various sizes across several industries. Prepare a proposal that illustrates your recommended sales organization structure. Be sure to justify your recommended structure.

2. As an organization, your university has a specified structure. Identify this structure (draw it or obtain a copy of it). How specialized is this structure? What is its degree of centralization? What does the span of control look like and how appropriate is it? How many levels of management exist? Is this enough or too much? What are the relationships between line and staff positions? Are they appropriate? Assuming you would like the university to run as efficiently and effectively as possible, what changes would you recommend making to this structure and why? If no changes are recommended, why not?

3. Using the following information, calculate the total salesforce size necessary by using each of the following approaches: breakdown, workload, and incremental. (Your answers may vary because each piece of information does not apply to the same company.) Be sure to show your work. Also, explain the advantages and disadvantages of each approach. Which approach would you recommend using to determine salesforce size? Why?

   - Sales of $80 million are forecast for next year.
   - Fifteen thousand calls are needed in the market area to be covered.
   - Salespeople generate an average of $2 million in annual sales.
   - A salesperson can make an average of 500 annual sales calls.
   - Marginal salesperson cost is $65,000. With 88 salespeople, the marginal salesperson profit contribution is $75,000. This profit contribution decreases by $5,000 with each additional salesperson added to the base of 88 salespeople. Marginal salesperson cost remains constant.
   - Turnover is 10 percent annually.

4. **Situation:**    Read the Ethical Dilemma on page 81.

   **Characters:**    Mary Swenson, district manager; Fred Williams, salesperson

   **Scene:**    *Location*—Mary Swenson's office. *Action*—Role play a meeting between Mary Swenson and Fred Williams concerning possible excessive gift-giving by Fred Williams to get new accounts.

**ROLE PLAY**

## MAKING SALES MANAGEMENT DECISIONS

### Case 4.1: Protek Packaging, Inc.

#### Background

Protek Packaging, Inc. (PPI) is a national manufacturer of a wide variety of polyethylene and polystyrene packaging products, including food and ice bags; styrofoam egg cartons, meat trays, and food service products; laundry and dry cleaning packaging; trash bags; construction film and plastic shipping pallets. PPI is a strong competitor in all of its product lines. Not an innovative company, PPI leverages its large manufacturing capacity to drive its costs down, which allows the company to sell its products at highly attractive price levels.

PPI operates five regional offices: Atlanta, New York, Chicago, Dallas, and Los Angeles. These offices are located at manufacturing plants that serve each region. PPI is organized by product line, with each product line run by a regional product manager and a regional sales manager. Eight to 10 sales representatives report to each of the five regional sales managers. The product managers and sales managers in each region report to a regional marketing manager. The key products and customers for each product line are shown in Exhibit 4.10.

#### Current Situation

John Lovett, Western Region marketing manager, has called his four sales managers and four product managers to Los Angeles to discuss alternative approaches to organizing the PPI salesforce. Thirty days earlier, Lovett and his managers had hosted a key customer roundtable at the annual meeting of the Plastics Packaging Manufacturers' Association. Lovett was troubled by several themes that emerged from the roundtable. Some of the most influential paper and plastic distributors are disturbed by the fact that PPI sells to grocery chains, garment manufacturers, egg packers/processors, and uniform rental companies on a direct basis. This is puzzling to Lovett, since PPI has always sold through distributors when feasible. Further, distributors are informed before stocking PPI products that if end-users meet certain sales volume requirements and request that they be sold on a direct basis, PPI will sell direct rather than risk losing the business.

Lovett is also concerned that many of the grocery chain buyers and paper and plastic distributors complained about the amount of time it takes for them to see several PPI salespeople. These customers wanted to deal with a single PPI representative, not one from

---

**EXHIBIT 4.10**     PPI Product Lines and Key Customer Types

| Product Line | Key Products | Key Customer Types |
|---|---|---|
| Food Packaging | Produce bags | Grocery chains<br>Food co-ops<br>Paper and plastic distributors |
| | Foam meat trays | Grocery chains<br>Meat and poultry processors<br>Food co-ops<br>Paper and plastic distributors |
| Institutional | Trash bags | Paper and plastic distributors<br>Restaurant wholesalers<br>Janitorial wholesalers |
| | Food service<br>(plastic plates, bowls) | Restaurant wholesalers<br>Grocery store delis<br>Institutional food wholesalers<br>Paper and plastic distributors |
| Agricultural | Egg cartons | Grocery chains<br>Egg packers/processors |
| Garment | Poly bags | Laundries and dry cleaners<br>Uniform rental companies<br>Garment manufacturers<br>Paper and plastic distributors |

each product line. An additional concern was that PPI did not allow aggregation of products across product lines to make it easier for these buyers to achieve the maximum quantity discounts.

To prepare for the meeting, John Lovett asked each product manager/sales manager team to come ready to discuss these issues:

1. Is it time for PPI to reconsider its salesforce organization by product line?
2. What are the advantages and disadvantages of organizing the PPI salesforce by product line?
3. What are the advantages and disadvantages of developing a new sales organization for the Western Region that would organize according to these customer types: (a) grocery chains and food co-ops; (b) distributors, including paper and plastic distributors, restaurant wholesalers, institutional food wholesalers, and janitorial wholesalers; and (c) end users, including meat and poultry processors, grocery store delis, egg packers/processors, laundries and dry cleaners, uniform rental companies, and garment manufacturers?

Assume you are the sales manager for the food packaging product line. Address the preceding questions as if you will attend the upcoming meeting. In addition, outline your thoughts on other alternatives for organizing the salesforce.

| | |
|---|---|
| **Situation:** | Read Case 4.1. |
| **Characters:** | John Lovett, Western Region marketing manager; sales manager for food packing product line; one or more other product/sales managers |
| **Scene 1:** | *Location*—Lovett's office. *Action*—Role play between Lovett and sales manager for food packing product line discussing the advantages and disadvantages of a salesforce organized by product line. |
| **Scene 2:** | *Location*—Meeting room. *Action*—Role play meeting with Lovett and all product/sales managers, discussing the advantages and disadvantages of different alternatives for organizing PPI's salesforce and arriving at a decision. |

**ROLE PLAY**

## Case 4.2: Opti-Tax Consulting
### Background
Opti-Tax Consulting (OTC) is a 20-year-old company, which specializes in providing small businesses with tax and financial management expertise. OTC focuses on businesses that handle significant amounts of cash in their daily operations, such as service stations, bars, coffee shops, and small restaurants. OTC has three sales representatives serving the Lexington, Kentucky, metropolitan market.

Dave Mason, OTC's founder and current president, was the company's first salesperson. When the company grew to the point that Mason had a hard time servicing all of his accounts, he added Steve Tremaine as a sales representative. Mason gave Tremaine 10 of his existing accounts and instructed him to go after potential customers not yet under contract with OTC. Five years later, Donna Armstrong was hired as a sales representative and added in much the same fashion. Mason and Tremaine turned over 10 accounts each to Armstrong, and she was instructed to add new customers not already doing business with OTC. Both Donna Armstrong and Steve Tremaine report directly to Dave Mason. Of OTC's total sales volume, Dave Mason accounts for approximately half. The remainder is split almost equally between Donna Armstrong and Steve Tremaine. Armstrong and Tremaine are paid a percentage of OTC's billings to their clients.

### Current Situation
Mason is planning to enter semi-retirement in another year, and he has brought his son Franklin into the business. Franklin will learn the business over the next several months, then step into a sales role. Dave Mason will continue to function as sales manager and president of the company, but will give up the sales responsibilities for all of his accounts.

Dave Mason is compiling information that will help him decide how to design OTC's sales territories after he gives up his sales responsibilities. He is not comfortable turning over all of his accounts to his son Franklin. Although talented and hard working, Franklin is inexperienced in the financial consulting industry. A recent graduate of the University of Kentucky with a double major in finance and marketing, Franklin's career goal is to become president of OTC, then expand company operations into other markets.

Mason has also been contemplating the sales performance of Donna Armstrong and Steve Tremaine. Both had been solid, dependable performers over the years, but Tremaine had recently slowed down a bit. While his sales volume compared favorably to Armstrong's, Tremaine was selling in a higher potential sales territory. Further, he had a five-year head start on Armstrong in developing new accounts, yet Armstrong had brought in almost as much new business as had Tremaine during the past year. Mason had talked with Tremaine about the lack of sales growth in his territory but had not learned much. Tremaine made no excuses and acknowledged that his sales levels had been relatively stable in recent years. He promised to try harder to bring in new business. Mason suspected that Tremaine was comfortable with his earnings and simply did not want to work a lot harder, even if he could make more money.

After several weeks of analysis, Dave Mason finally had a rough draft of a new territory design policy that would go into effect in 90 days. The key points of the new policy are:

1. Half of Dave Mason's accounts will be split between Steve Tremaine and Donna Armstrong. Dave Mason's remaining accounts will be assigned to Franklin Mason.
2. After one year, sales territories will be redesigned so that the three territories will be comparable in terms of workload and sales potential.
3. For the current year, OTC salespeople will continue to earn a commission based on OTC billings to their clients.
4. After the sales territories are redesigned in a year, the commission rate for existing clients will be reduced, and a higher commission rate will be implemented for new accounts added within the past year.

Dave Mason distributed the draft plan to Donna, Steve, and Franklin. Both Donna and Steve questioned the idea of assigning half of Dave's accounts to Franklin. Steve came right to the point, saying, "Look, Dave, he's your son and he will do just fine with some seasoning. But I think he ought to start with a smaller group of accounts. He'll learn the business a lot faster if he has to build it by adding his own accounts."

Donna and Steve were also concerned that they would have some of Dave's former accounts for a year, and then lose them to Franklin. Franklin remained neutral on these issues, and voiced neither support nor opposition to the draft plan.

**Questions**

1. What are the implications for Donna Armstrong and Steve Tremaine if the draft plan is implemented?
2. What are the implications for OTC's customers if the draft plan is implemented?
3. What are the pros and cons of Mason's draft plan?
4. What changes and additions would you make to the draft plan?

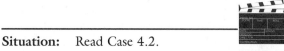

| | |
|---|---|
| **Situation:** | Read Case 4.2. |
| **Characters:** | Dave Mason, president; Franklin Mason, son and salesperson; Steve Tremaine, company's first salesperson; Donna Armstrong, company's second salesperson |
| **Scene 1:** | *Location*—Meeting room. *Action*—Role play discussion among Dave Mason, Franklin Mason, Steve Tremaine, and Donna Armstrong about the draft territory design plan. |
| **Scene 2:** | *Location*—Meeting room. *Action*—Role play discussion among Dave Mason, Franklin Mason, Steve Tremaine, and Donna Armstrong about alternatives to the draft territory design plan and a final territory design decision. |

**ROLE PLAY**

A meteorologist used all the latest technology to predict a bright and sunny day in the mid-80s. It rained most of the day and never got warmer than 70 degrees. The weather forecast missed the mark on this particular occasion, but the meteorologist will continue to make weather forecasts and to work on improving weather forecasting procedures.

Sales managers face a situation similar to that of the meteorologist. The business environment is complex and dynamic, there are a number of forecasting methods available, and often forecasts are incorrect. Nevertheless, sales managers must continue to forecast and to work on improving their forecasting procedures.

Why is forecasting so important to sales managers? In one sense, all sales management decisions are based on some type of forecast. The sales manager decides on a certain action because he or she thinks that it will produce a certain result. This expected result is a **forecast**, even though the sales manager may not have quantified it or may not have used a mathematical forecasting procedure. More specifically, forecasts provide the basis for the following sales management decisions:

1. Determining salesforce size
2. Designing territories
3. Establishing sales quotas and selling budgets
4. Determining sales compensation levels
5. Evaluating salesperson performance
6. Evaluating prospective accounts

## FORECASTING BY SALES MANAGERS

Although top management levels are most concerned with total firm forecasts, sales managers are typically interested in developing and using forecasts for specific areas, such as accounts, territories, districts, regions, and/or zones. For example, a district sales manager would be concerned with the district forecast as well as forecasts for individual territories and accounts within the district. There are, however, different types of forecasts that sales managers might use in different ways, and different approaches and methods might be used to develop these forecasts.

### Types of Forecasts

The term *forecast* is ordinarily used to refer to a prediction for a future period. Although this usage is technically correct, it is too general for managerial value. As illustrated in Figure 4A.1, at least three factors must be defined when referring to a forecast: the product level, the geographic area, and the time period. The figure presents 90 different forecasts that might be made, depending on these factors. Thus, when using the term *forecast*, sales managers should be specific in defining exactly what is being forecast, what geographic area is being targeted, and what period is being forecast.

A useful way for viewing what is being forecast is presented in Exhibit 4A.1. This exhibit suggests that it is important to differentiate between industry and firm levels and to determine whether the prediction is for the best possible

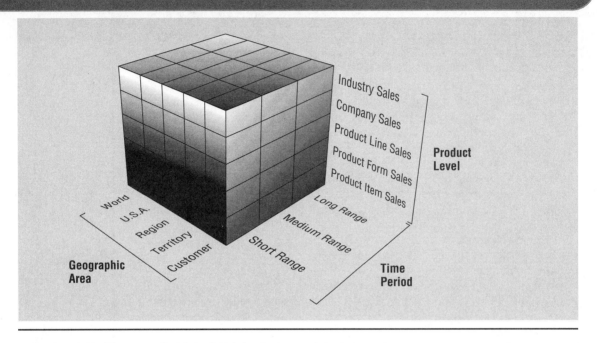

Many different types of forecasts are possible. Every forecast should be defined in terms of geographic area, product level, and time period.

**EXHIBIT 4A.1**     Types of Forecasts

|  | Best Possible Results | Expected Results for Given Strategy |
|---|---|---|
| Industry Level | Market Potential | Market Potential |
| Firm Level | Sales Potential | Sales Potential |

Four different types of forecasts are typically important to sales managers, depending on whether a forecast is needed for the industry or the firm and whether the best possible or expected results are to be forecast.

results or for the expected results given a specific strategy. Four different types of forecasts emerge from this classification scheme:

1. *Market potential*—the best possible level of industry sales in a given geographic area for a specific period
2. *Market forecast*—the expected level of industry sales given a specific industry strategy in a given geographic area for a specific period
3. *Sales potential*—the best possible level of firm sales in a given geographic area for a specific period
4. *Sales forecast*—the expected level of firm sales given a specific strategy in a given geographic area for a specific period

Notice that the geographic area and period are defined for each of these terms and that a true *sales forecast* must include the consideration of a specific strategy. If a firm changes this strategy, the sales forecast should change also.

As an example, assume that you are the district sales manager for a firm that markets microcomputers to organizational buyers. Your district includes Missouri, Kansas, Iowa, and Nebraska. You are preparing forecasts for 2006. You might first try to assess market potential. This market potential forecast would be an estimate of the highest level of microcomputer sales by all brands in your district for 2006. Then, you might try to develop a market forecast, which would be the expected level of industry microcomputer sales in your district for 2006. This forecast would be based on an assumption of the strategies that would be used by all microcomputer firms operating in your district. If you think that new firms are going to enter the industry or that existing firms are going to leave it or change their strategies, your industry forecast will change. Another type of forecast might be a determination of the best possible level of 2006 sales for your firm's microcomputers in the district. This would be a sales potential forecast. Finally, you would probably want to predict a specific level of district sales of your firm's microcomputers given your firm's expected strategy. This would result in a sales forecast that would have to be revised whenever strategic changes were made.

## Uses of Forecasts

Because different types of forecasts convey different information, sales managers use specific types for specific sales management decisions. Forecasts of market potential and sales potential are most often used to identify opportunities and to guide the allocation of selling efforts. Market potential provides an assessment of overall demand opportunity available to all firms in an industry. Sales potential adjusts market potential to reflect industry competition and thus represents a better assessment of demand opportunity for an individual firm. Both of these forecasts of potential can be used by sales managers to determine where selling effort is needed and how selling effort should be distributed. For example, as discussed earlier, designing territories requires an assessment of market potential for all planning and control units. Specific territories are then designed by grouping planning and control units together and evaluating the equality of market potential across the territories.

Market forecasts and sales forecasts are used to predict the expected results from various sales management decisions. For example, once territories are designed, sales managers typically want to forecast expected industry and company sales for each specific sales territory. These forecasts are then used to set sales quotas and selling budgets for specific planning periods.

## Top-Down and Bottom-Up Forecasting Approaches

Forecasting methods can be classified in a variety of ways.[1] Specific examples of two basic approaches are presented in Figure 4A.2. **Top-down approaches** typically consist of different methods for developing company forecasts at the business unit level. Sales managers then break down these company forecasts into zone, region, district, territory, and account forecasts. **Bottom-up approaches**, by contrast, consist of different methods for developing sales forecasts for individual accounts. Sales managers then combine the account forecasts into territory, district, region, zone, and company forecasts. The top-down and bottom-up approaches represent entirely different perspectives for developing forecasts, although some forecasting methods can be used in either approach. However, the focus is on the most popular forecasting methods for each approach.

### Top-Down Approach

Implementing the top-down approach requires the development of company forecasts and their breakdown into zone, region, district, territory, and account levels. Different methods are used to develop company forecasts and break them down to the desired levels.

**FIGURE 4A.2**                                                    Forecasting Approaches

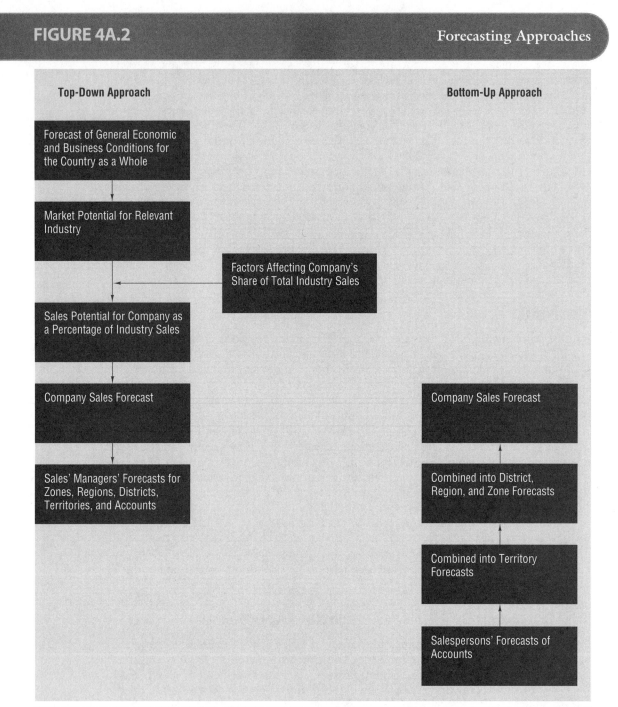

In top-down approaches, company personnel provide aggregate company forecasts that sales managers must break down into zone, region, district, territory, and account forecasts. In bottom-up approaches, account forecasts are combined into territory, district, region, zone, and company forecasts.

### Company Forecasting Methods

Although a variety of methods is available for developing company forecasts, this discussion is limited to three popular time series methods: moving averages, exponential smoothing, and decomposition methods.

**Moving averages** is a relatively simple method that develops a company forecast by calculating the average company sales for previous years. Thus, the company sales forecast for next year is the average of actual company sales for the past three years, past

| | | Moving Averages Example | EXHIBIT 4A.2 |
|---|---|---|---|

**Moving Averages Forecast**

| Year | Actual Sales | Two-Year | Four-Year |
|---|---|---|---|
| 1998 | $ 8,400,000 | | |
| 1999 | 8,820,000 | | |
| 2000 | 8,644,000 | $8,610,000 | |
| 2001 | 8,212,000 | 8,732,000 | |
| 2002 | 8,622,000 | 8,428,000 | $8,520,000 |
| 2003 | 9,484,000 | 8,418,000 | 8,574,000 |
| 2004 | 9,674,000 | 9,054,000 | 8,740,000 |
| 2005 | 10,060,000 | 9,579,000 | 8,998,000 |
| 2006 | | 9,868,000 | 9,460,000 |

where

$$\text{Sales forecast for next year} = \frac{\text{Actual sales for past two or four years}}{\text{Number of years (two or four years)}}$$

six years, or some other number of years. An example of calculating a moving averages company sales forecast for two- and four-year time frames is presented in Exhibit 4A.2. As illustrated in this example, the moving averages method is straightforward and requires simple calculations. Management must, however, determine the appropriate number of years to include in the calculations. In addition, this method weights actual company sales for previous years equally in generating the forecast for the next year. This equal weighting may not be appropriate if company sales vary substantially from year to year or if there are major differences in the business environment between the most recent and past years. Nevertheless, one survey of managers found this to be the most popular technique for short-range and medium-range forecasts in U.S. corporations.[2]

**Exponential smoothing** is a type of moving averages method, except that company sales in the most recent year are weighted differently from company sales in past years.[3] An example of the exponential smoothing method is provided in Exhibit 4A.3. A critical aspect of this method involves determining the appropriate weight ($\alpha$) for this year's company sales. This is typically accomplished by examining different weights for historical sales data to determine which weight would have generated the most accurate sales forecasts in the past. Based on the analysis in Exhibit 4A.3, management should probably use a weight of 0.8 for this year's company sales.

| | | Exponential Smoothing Example | EXHIBIT 4A.3 |
|---|---|---|---|

**Sales Forecast for Next Year**

| Year | Actual Sales | $\alpha = 0.2$ | $\alpha = 0.5$ | $\alpha = 0.8$ |
|---|---|---|---|---|
| 1998 | $ 8,400,000 | | | |
| 1999 | 8,820,000 | $8,400,000 | $8,400,000 | $8,400,000 |
| 2000 | 8,644,000 | 8,484,000 | 8,610,000 | 8,736,000 |
| 2001 | 8,212,000 | 8,516,000 | 8,626,000 | 8,664,000 |
| 2002 | 8,622,000 | 8,456,000 | 8,420,000 | 8,302,000 |
| 2003 | 9,484,000 | 8,488,000 | 8,520,000 | 8,558,000 |
| 2004 | 9,674,000 | 8,686,000 | 9,002,000 | 9,298,000 |
| 2005 | 10,060,000 | 8,882,000 | 9,338,000 | 9,600,000 |
| 2006 | | 9,118,000 | 9,698,000 | 9,968,000 |

where

Sales forecast for next year = ($\alpha$) (actual sales this year) + (1 − $\alpha$) (this year's sales forecast)

**Decomposition methods** involve different procedures that break down previous company sales data into four major components: trend, cycle, seasonal, and erratic events. These components are then reincorporated to produce the sales forecast. An example of a decomposition method is presented in Exhibit 4A.4. Notice that the trend, cycle, and erratic events components are incorporated into the annual forecast but that the seasonal component is used only when forecasting sales for periods of less than a year, such as months or quarters. Decomposition methods are sound conceptually but often require complex statistical approaches for breaking down the company sales data into the trend components. Once this decomposition has been completed, it is relatively easy to reincorporate the components into the development of a company forecast.

### Breakdown Methods

Once sales managers receive a company forecast, they can use different market factor methods to break it down to the desired levels. **Market factor methods** typically involve identifying one or more factors that are related to sales at the zone, region, district, territory, or account levels and using these factors to break down the overall company forecast into forecasts at these levels.

A typical approach is to use the **Buying Power Index (BPI)** supplied by *Sales & Marketing Management*.[4] The BPI is a market factor calculated for different areas in the following manner:

$$BPI = (5I + 2P + 3R) \div 10$$

where

$I$ = Percentage of U.S. disposable personal income in the area

$P$ = Percentage of U.S. population in the area

$R$ = Percentage of U.S. retail sales in the area

---

### EXHIBIT 4A.4     Decomposition Method Example

Assume that various analyses have decomposed previous sales data into the following components:

A 5% growth in sales is predicted due to basic developments in population, capital formation, and technology (trend component). A 10% decrease in sales is expected due to a business recession (cycle component). Increased tensions in the Middle East are expected to reduce sales by an additional 5% (erratic events component). Sales results are reasonably consistent throughout the year except for the fourth quarter, where sales are expected to be 25% higher than the other quarters (seasonal component).

A marketer of consumer products might recombine the different components in the following manner to forecast sales for 2006:

Sales in 2005 were $10,060,000. The trend component suggests that 2006 sales will be $10,563,000 ($10,060,000 × 1.05). However, incorporating the expected business recession represented in the cycle component changes the sales forecast to $9,506,700 ($10,563,000 × 0.90). The annual sales forecast is reduced to $9,031,365 when the erratic events component is introduced ($9,056,700 × 0.95). Quarterly sales forecasts would initially be calculated as $2,257,841 ($9,031,365 ÷ 4). However, incorporating the seasonal component suggests fourth-quarter sales of $2,822,302 ($2,257,841 × 1.25) and sales for the other three quarters of $2,069,688 ($9,031,365 – $2,822,302 ÷ 3).

Performing these calculations for any area produces a BPI for the area. This BPI can be translated as the percentage of U.S. buying power residing in the area: The higher the index, the more buying power in the area. Fortunately, *Sales & Marketing Management* provides these calculations for areas in the United States on an annual basis.

An example of the BPI data provided by *Sales & Marketing Management* is presented in Exhibit 4A.5. BPIs and other data are available for all counties in a state and for the major cities and metropolitan areas. The information in the exhibit suggests that the BPI for the Kansas City metropolitan area is 0.6914; for Jackson County, 0.2557; and for Kansas City, Missouri, 0.1764. This means that 0.6914 percent, 0.2557 percent, and 0.1764 percent of total U.S. buying power resides in the Kansas City metro area, Jackson County, and Kansas City, Missouri, respectively.

Sales managers can use the BPI data to divide the overall company forecast into more disaggregate forecasts. For example, assume that you are the Missouri district sales manager for a marketer of cosmetics. Management has used various methods to forecast total company sales in the United States of $500 million for 2006. The calculations necessary to break down this company forecast into sales forecasts for areas within your district are illustrated in Exhibit 4A.6. Using the appropriate BPIs, you are able to forecast 2006 sales of $3,457,000, $1,278,500, and $882,000 for the Kansas City metro area, Jackson County, and Kansas City, Missouri, respectively.

The BPI is an extremely useful tool for forecasting, because it is readily available and updated on an annual basis. It is most appropriate for often-purchased consumer goods because of the factors used in calculating the index for each area. Marketers of durable consumer goods or industrial products may not find the BPI sufficiently accurate for their needs. In these situations, other market factors must be identified and used. For example, Sherwood Medical uses *total available hospitals* requiring a specific product (based on medical procedures performed at the hospital) as a market factor for forecasting purposes.[5]

Another approach is for a firm to develop a buying power index for its specific situation. For example, a general aviation aircraft marketer developed a buying power index for its products in each county in the United States. The basic formula was

$$\text{Index} = (5I + 3AR + 2P) \div 10$$

where

$$I = \text{Percentage of U.S. disposable income in county}$$
$$AR = \text{Percentage of U.S. aircraft registrations in county}$$
$$P = \text{Percentage of U.S. registered pilots in county}$$

These calculations produced an index for each county that could be translated and used like the BPI. The firm could take U.S. forecasts provided by the industry trade association and convert them to market and sales forecasts for each county by using their calculated indices and market shares.

The use of market factor methods is widespread in the sales management area. Indices such as the BPI or those developed by specific firms and other market factor methods can be extremely valuable forecasting tools for sales managers. These indices and market factors should be continually evaluated and improved. They can be assessed by comparing actual sales in an area to the market factor value for the area. For example, the general aviation aircraft marketer found high correlations between actual aircraft sales in a county and the county indices. This finding provided support for the use of the calculated index as an indirect forecasting tool.

## EXHIBIT 4A.5    Buying Power Index (BPI) Data

| METRO AREA County/City | Total EBI ($000) | Median Household EBI | Effective Buying Income (EBI) Percentage of Households by EBI Group: (A) $10,000 – $19,999 (B) $20,000 – $34,999 (C) $35,000 – $49,999 (D) $50,000 and more | | | | Buying Power Index |
|---|---|---|---|---|---|---|---|
| | | | A | B | C | D | |
| COLUMBIA . . . . . . . . . . . . . . | 1,992,259 | 33,873 | 16.1 | 22.4 | 18.1 | 30.4 | .0516 |
| Boone . . . . . . . . . . . . . . | 1,992,259 | 33,873 | 16.1 | 22.4 | 18.1 | 30.4 | .0516 |
| Columbia. . . . . . . . . . . | 1,241,418 | 29,645 | 18.7 | 21.0 | 15.2 | 28.3 | .0378 |
| Suburban Total . . . . . . . . | 750,841 | 39,208 | 11.7 | 25.0 | 23.2 | 33.9 | .0138 |
| JOPLIN . . . . . . . . . . . | 1,928,856 | 27,823 | 20.2 | 27.1 | 18.7 | 19.2 | .0520 |
| Jasper . . . . . . . . . . . . | 1,270,128 | 27,079 | 20.9 | 26.9 | 18.5 | 18.2 | .0373 |
| Joplin. . . . . . . . . . . | 601,136 | 25,413 | 22.5 | 26.6 | 16.7 | 17.5 | .0225 |
| Newton . . . . . . . . . . . . | 658,728 | 29,348 | 18.7 | 27.6 | 18.8 | 21.4 | .0147 |
| Suburban Total . . . . . . . . | 1,327,720 | 28,931 | 19.1 | 27.4 | 19.5 | 20.1 | .0295 |
| KANSAS CITY . . . . . . . . . . . | 30,987,132 | 40,963 | 12.4 | 20.7 | 19.8 | 38.4 | .6914 |
| Cass . . . . . . . . . . . . . . | 1,163,582 | 39,979 | 13.2 | 22.2 | 22.1 | 35.3 | .0243 |
| Clay . . . . . . . . . . . . . | 2,978,457 | 41,735 | 11.8 | 22.1 | 22.4 | 37.9 | .0748 |
| Clinton . . . . . . . . . . . | 260,091 | 33,954 | 18.0 | 23.2 | 19.2 | 29.3 | .0055 |
| Jackson . . . . . . . . . . . | 11,052,639 | 36,936 | 14.4 | 21.6 | 19.6 | 33.1 | .2557 |
| Blue Springs . . . . . . . . | 860,954 | 51,044 | 7.4 | 14.4 | 21.9 | 51.6 | .0206 |
| Independence. . . . . . . . | 1,919,067 | 37,782 | 15.3 | 22.3 | 21.2 | 32.9 | .0462 |
| Kansas City . . . . . . . . . | 7,482,105 | 35,483 | 14.8 | 21.7 | 19.1 | 31.6 | .1764 |
| Lee's Summit. . . . . . . . | 1,190,035 | 49,815 | 9.1 | 16.3 | 18.9 | 49.8 | .0237 |
| Lafayette. . . . . . . . . . . | 474,375 | 32,757 | 17.1 | 26.2 | 20.3 | 25.9 | .0103 |
| Platte. . . . . . . . . . . . | 1,265,415 | 45,520 | 9.9 | 19.8 | 21.4 | 43.9 | .0256 |
| Ray. . . . . . . . . . . . | 305,948 | 34,906 | 15.7 | 23.5 | 22.4 | 27.5 | .0061 |
| Johnson, Kansas . . . . . . . . | 9,979,906 | 54,758 | 6.8 | 15.7 | 18.3 | 55.5 | .2118 |
| Olathe. . . . . . . . . . . | 1,333,636 | 50,929 | 7.3 | 16.9 | 20.4 | 51.3 | .0321 |
| Overland Park. . . . . . . . | 3,314,864 | 56,241 | 6.8 | 15.5 | 17.3 | 57.2 | .0765 |
| Leavenworth, Kansas . . . . . | 1,162,130 | 43,140 | 10.9 | 19.7 | 21.7 | 40.2 | .0235 |
| Leavenworth. . . . . . . . | 726,671 | 39,967 | 12.1 | 21.5 | 21.6 | 35.4 | .0154 |
| Miami, Kansas. . . . . . . . . | 392,606 | 37,473 | 15.1 | 22.3 | 20.9 | 32.7 | .0081 |
| Wyandotte, Kansas . . . . . . | 1,951,983 | 29,202 | 18.3 | 25.9 | 19.8 | 20.6 | .0457 |
| Kansas City . . . . . . . . . | 1,791,288 | 28,711 | 18.7 | 25.5 | 19.7 | 19.9 | .0419 |
| Suburban Total. . . . . . . . | 19,653,432 | 44,951 | 10.8 | 19.6 | 20.1 | 43.6 | .4256 |
| ST. JOSEPH. . . . . . . . . . . | 1,397,897 | 30,847 | 18.2 | 23.7 | 19.4 | 24.2 | .0349 |
| Andrew . . . . . . . . . . . . | 209,843 | 32,952 | 16.9 | 22.7 | 21.6 | 25.3 | .0045 |
| Buchanan . . . . . . . . . . | 1,188,054 | 30,476 | 18.4 | 23.8 | 19,0 | 24.1 | .0304 |
| St. Joseph . . . . . . . . . | 1,014,905 | 29,567 | 19.0 | 23.4 | 18.7 | 23.0 | .0274 |
| Suburban Total. . . . . . . . | 382,992 | 34,530 | 15.9 | 24.3 | 21.3 | 27.9 | .0075 |

## Bottom-Up Approach

Implementing the bottom-up approach requires various methods to forecast sales to individual accounts and the combination of these account forecasts into territory, district, region, zone, and company forecasts. This section focuses on the survey of buyer

| | Market Factor Calculations | | EXHIBIT 4A.6 |
|---|---|---|---|
| | **Kansas City Metro Area** | **Jackson County** | **Kansas City, Missouri** |
| 2006 company sales forecast | $500,000,000 | $500,000,000 | $500,000,000 |
| BPI | 0.6914% | 0.2557% | 0.1764% |
| 2006 area sales forecast | $ 3,457,000 | $ 1,278,500 | $ 882,000 |

intentions, jury of executive opinion, Delphi, and salesforce composite methods as used in a bottom-up approach.

The **survey of buyer intentions method** is any procedure that asks individual accounts about their purchasing plans for a future period and translates these responses into account forecasts. The intended purchases by accounts might be obtained through mail surveys, telephone surveys, personal interviews, or other approaches. For example, at Dow Chemical's Basic Chemical Division, salespeople provide forecast data based on customers' business plans.[6] Similarly, Hewlett-Packard Company's major customers supply its marketing centers with input concerning future needs.[7] At times, forecasts based on customer intentions may be distorted due to buyers' unwillingness to put much effort into predicting future needs. Moreover, buyers are often unwilling to reveal plans for selling a vendor's product out of fear competitors may retaliate if they find out.[8]

The **jury of executive opinion method** involves any approach in which executives of the firm use their expert knowledge to forecast sales to individual accounts. Separate forecasts might be obtained from managers in different functional areas. These forecasts are then averaged or discussed by the managers until a consensus forecast for each account is reached. Team-based approaches such as this are believed to result in more accurate long-range industry-level forecasts than individually based approaches.[9]

The **Delphi method** is a structured type of jury of executive opinion method. The basic procedure involves selection of a panel of managers from within the firm. Each member of the panel submits anonymous forecasts for each account. These forecasts are summarized into a report that is sent to each panel member. The report presents descriptive statistics concerning the submitted forecasts with reasons for the lowest and highest forecasts. Panel members review this information and then again submit anonymous individual forecasts. The same procedure is repeated until the forecasts for individual accounts converge into a consensus. Because this procedure involves written rather than verbal communication, such negatives as domination, undue conservatism, and argument are eliminated, while team members benefit from one another's input.[10]

The **salesforce composite method** involves various procedures by which salespeople provide forecasts for their assigned accounts, typically on specially designed forms (see Figure 4A.3) or electronically via computer. At Ricoh Corporation, an office products manufacturer, salespeople are asked to provide a three-month rolling forecast for each product and model.[11] Similarly, salespeople at Pfizer Animal Health Care are asked to forecast account sales based on their familiarity with each account's business.[12] Research results suggest that salesperson forecasts can be improved by developing detailed instructions about the forecasting procedures and providing salespeople with detailed information about their accounts and feedback concerning the accuracy of previous forecasts.[13]

## USING DIFFERENT FORECASTING APPROACHES AND METHODS

This discussion of top-down and bottom-up approaches and several forecasting methods is illustrative of the forecasting procedures used by many sales organizations. However, all available forecasting methods have not been introduced, and some sales

## FIGURE 4A.3                                         Quarterly Forecasting Form for Salespeople

| Account | Projected Sales by Product Group for Quarter Beginning 7/5/2006 | | | | | | | Totals |
|---------|--------|--------|--------|--------|--------|--|--|--------|
|         | 364-60 | 364-80 | 28B | 460 | 28 | | | Totals |
| Ace | 1,250 | 960 | 1,400 | 2,100 | 160 | | | 5,870 |
| Sentry | 950 | 1,250 | 1,930 | 470 | 968 | | | 5,568 |
| Cutter | – | 2,110 | – | 960 | 1,750 | | | 4,820 |
| Grossman | – | – | – | – | 364 | | | 364 |
| Paycass | 400 | 1,800 | – | – | 720 | | | 2,920 |
| American | – | – | – | – | 1,230 | | | 1,230 |
| Pro | – | – | – | – | – | | | 700 |
| Totals | 2,600 | 6,820 | 3,330 | 3,530 | 5,192 | | | 21,472 |

This is an example of a form used by a firm to get salespeople to forecast sales for each account and product group.

organizations may use the approaches and methods in different ways than discussed here. For example, some sales organizations use statistical methods, such as regression analysis, to develop sales forecasts for accounts, territories, districts, regions, zones, and/or the company. In the next section, the use of regression procedures for developing sales forecasts as a means for establishing sales quotas is examined.

The actual usage of specific forecasting methods is presented in Exhibit 4A.7. Although this study did not ask respondents their degree of usage of either the survey of buyer intentions approach or the Delphi method, previous research indicates these two approaches are fairly popular.[14] Study results indicate that the bottom-up approaches are more popular than the top-down approaches. Notice the differences that exist in the frequency of usage depending on the forecast period.

Because forecasting is such a difficult task and each approach and method has certain advantages and disadvantages, most firms use multiple forecasting approaches and methods.

## EXHIBIT 4A.7     Usage of Forecasting Methods

| Forecasting Method | Percentage of Firms Using Method by Forecast Period | | | |
|--------------------|---------------------------------|----------------------|-------------------------------|-----------------------------|
|                    | Immediate (less than 1 month) | Short (1–6 months) | Medium (6 months– 1 year) | Long (more than 1 year) |
| **Top-Down** | | | | |
| Moving average | 17.7 | 33.5 | 28.3 | 8.7 |
| Exponential smoothing | 12.9 | 19.6 | 16.8 | 4.2 |
| Decomposition | 0.0 | 6.8 | 11.9 | 9.3 |
| Regression | 13.4 | 25.1 | 25.4 | 16.5 |
| **Bottom-Up** | | | | |
| Jury of executive opinion | 17.5 | 28.9 | 40.1 | 26.2 |
| Salesforce composite | 28.6 | 17.5 | 33.1 | 8.7 |

Then, various approaches are used to combine the results from each method into a final forecast.[15] If different approaches and methods produce similar sales forecasts, sales managers can be more confident in the validity of the forecast. If extremely divergent forecasts are generated from the different approaches and methods, additional analysis is required to determine the reasons for the large differences and to make the adjustments necessary to produce an accurate sales forecast.

Even though firms use multiple forecasting methods, research evidence indicates that several criteria are used to select specific forecasting methods.[16] The most important criterion identified in this study was the accuracy of the forecasting method. Other criteria that were considered in decreasing importance were ease of use, data requirements, cost, and familiarity with methods. These results suggest that the selection of forecasting methods often represents a trade-off between the accuracy of the method and the ease with which it can be implemented. Some of the more accurate forecasting methods are difficult to use and have substantial data requirements. Thus, firms may have to sacrifice some accuracy by selecting methods that they are able to readily implement. This situation is illustrated in Exhibit 4A.7, where some of the more accurate methods (e.g., decomposition) are not used by many firms. Strengths and weaknesses of each forecasting method are found in Exhibit 4A.8.

---

### Strengths and Weaknesses of Forecasting Methods    EXHIBIT 4A.8

| Technique | Strengths | Weaknesses |
|---|---|---|
| Moving averages | Well suited to situations in which sales forecasts are needed for a large number of products | Requires a large amount of historical data |
| | Good for products with fairly stable sales | Adjusts slowly to changes in sales |
| | Smoothes out small random fluctuations | Assigns equal weight to each period, ignoring the fact that more recent periods usually have more impact on future sales |
| | Can compensate to some degree for trend if double moving average model is used | Results cannot be tested statistically |
| Exponential smoothing | Fairly simple to understand and use | Much searching may be needed to find appropriate weight |
| | Provides more weight to recent data points | Poor for medium- and long-term forecasts |
| | Requires little data storage | Erroneous forecasts can result due to large random fluctuations in recent data |
| | Generally accessible software packages are available | |
| | Fairly good accuracy for short-term forecasts | |
| Decomposition method | Simple to understand | Requires a large amount of past data |
| | Included in most computer packages | Does not lend itself to longer-range forecasts |
| | Acknowledges three key factors affecting sales—trend, seasonal, cycles | Does not lend itself to statistical analysis of forecast values (no confidence limits or tests of significance) |
| | Breaks past sales into component parts making it easier to understand the sales pattern | |

*(continued)*

**EXHIBIT 4A.8**     Strengths and Weaknesses of Forecasting Methods—*continued*

| Technique | Strengths | Weaknesses |
|---|---|---|
| Survey of buyer intentions | Forecasts are based on customers' buying plans | Intentions frequently do not culminate in actual purchases |
| | Contacts with customers can also provide feedback about possible problems with the firm's products | Some firms may not be willing to disclose buying intentions, especially if they are not regular customers |
| | Relatively inexpensive if only a few key customers need to be contacted | |
| Jury of executive opinion | Provides input from the firm's key functional areas | May require excessive amounts of executives' time |
| | Executives usually have a solid understanding of broad-based factors and how they affect sales | Executives removed from the marketplace may not understand the firm's sales situation |
| | Can provide fairly quick forecasts | Not well suited to firms with a large number of products |
| | | One or two influential people may dominate the process |
| Delphi method | Eliminates the need for committee or group meetings | Participants are often selected more on their willingness to participate and their accessibility than on their real knowledge or representativeness |
| | Eliminates group decision-making pitfalls, such as specious persuasion or a bandwagon effect | Can take a great deal of time to arrive at a consensus. Process may suffer because of high dropout rate of participants |
| | Participants receive input from other "experts" in an isolated environment | |
| | Allows for voicing of unusual opinions and anonymous mind changing | |
| | Proper facilities (e-mail) enable rapid exchange of ideas | |
| Salesforce composite | Uses input from persons closest to actual markets | Salespeople may underestimate sales when their forecasts are being used to set sales quotas |
| | Provides reasonably detailed forecasts (by product, customer, or territory) | Can take excessive amounts of salespeople's time if done too often |
| | May enhance salesforce morale by letting their input guide decisions | Salespeople often lack the knowledge to evaluate the economic situation and how it might affect future sales |

# Developing the Salesforce

The two modules in Part Three concentrate on the development of a productive salesforce. In Module 5, we review the process of staffing the salesforce through recruitment and selection. Standard recruitment and selection tools such as advertising, job interviews, and tests are discussed. Legal and ethical issues are also raised, and the topic of salesforce socialization is introduced.

Module 6 focuses on the continual development of salespeople through sales training. A model of the sales training process provides a framework for discussing needs assessment; training objectives; alternatives for training; and the design, performance, and evaluation of sales training.

STAFFING THE SALESFORCE:
RECRUITMENT AND SELECTION

## NEW HIRING STRATEGY AT INFORMATION GRAPHICS GROUP ALLOWS THEM TO BRING ABOARD THE BEST

A change in business strategy may impact the approach taken in the recruitment and selection process. Consequently, companies such as Information Graphics have responded by implementing a new hiring strategy that allows them to best meet their needs.

Information Graphics Group, located in Scottsdale, Arizona, had typically performed well when hiring. However, growth opportunities in new markets prompted a change in hiring strategy to add a few rising stars to its salesforce.

Sales applicants at Information Graphics Group were put through a comprehensive selection process. To better understand how sales applicants think, Ron Loback, vice president of sales, decided to change his interviewing format. Rather than the standard interview questions, he asked more "What would you do?" type questions and scenarios. Those who made it through the interview process then spent a full day with two of the company's top salespeople, where they were required to sell them on themselves. Candidates also had to complete presentations and participate in role plays. In addition, candidates were taken to lunch, sometimes with customers, to see how they responded in social situations. Finally, Ron and his top salespeople reviewed the candidates' performance and decided on the "winners."

The approach has paid dividends. According to Loback, "Thanks to our new additions, we're now making big strides in those growing markets—and looking at a huge year ahead."

**Source:** Ron Loback, "Our Revamped Hiring Strategy Brought the Best Salespeople Aboard," *What's Working in Sales Management* 11 (March 29, 2004): 5.

As illustrated in the opening vignette of Information Graphics Group, the recruitment and selection process can be a comprehensive and time-consuming endeavor. However, investing the necessary resources to hire the right people is essential. Recruiting and selecting those best qualified for a position can make the difference between a firm's long-run ultimate success and failure.

Although many factors influence sales performance, sales managers cannot survive without doing a competent job in recruiting and selecting salespeople. The vital and complex nature of the job is summarized by Munson and Spivey:

> The process is complicated by various conflicting factors—the need to select applicants with characteristics related to job success, the difficulty of determining these characteristics, inadequacies inherent in the various selection techniques themselves, and the need to simultaneously insure that the selection process satisfies existing governmental regulations pertaining to discrimination in hiring practices.[1]

Today, the recruitment and selection process must be adjusted to the demographics of an older salesforce with a higher proportion of women and minorities than in the past. The number of Asians, Hispanics, and African-Americans in the United States is projected to continue to grow.[2] Sales managers also face challenges associated with staffing an international salesforce, as well as with

## Objectives

After completing this module, you should be able to

1 Explain the critical role of recruitment and selection in building and maintaining a productive salesforce.

2 Describe how recruitment and selection affect salesforce socialization and performance.

3 Identify the key activities in planning and executing a program for salesforce recruitment and selection.

4 Discuss the legal and ethical considerations in salesforce recruitment and selection.

recruiting and selecting for team selling. Proper staffing of the salesforce is critical given the strong impact of the recruiting process on a firm's performance and profits.[3]

Today's sales manager's role in recruitment and selection is explored in this module. Before examining a basic model of the process, let's discuss further the importance of recruitment and selection.

## IMPORTANCE OF RECRUITMENT AND SELECTION

In most sales organizations, sales managers with direct supervisory responsibilities for salespeople have the primary responsibility for recruitment and selection. They may have the support of top management or coordinate their efforts with human resource personnel or other managers within the firm, but it is the sales manager who generally retains primary recruitment and selection responsibilities. To emphasize the importance of recruitment and selection, consider a few of the problems associated with inadequate implementation:

1. Inadequate sales coverage and lack of customer follow-up
2. Increased training costs to overcome deficiencies
3. More supervisory problems
4. Higher turnover rates
5. Difficulty in establishing enduring relationships with customers
6. Suboptimal total salesforce performance

Clearly, salesforce performance will suffer if recruitment and selection are poorly executed. Other sales management functions become more burdensome when the sales manager is handicapped by a multitude of "bad hires." The full costs of unsuccessful recruitment and selection are probably impossible to estimate. In addition to sales trainee salaries; advertising fees; screening, interviewing, and assessment costs; and employment agency fees, among others, there are hidden costs associated with salesforce turnover, such as the loss of the relationships that salespeople build with their customers over time and increased managerial problems that defy calculation. It is estimated that it costs anywhere from 50 to 150 percent of an employee's salary to replace that person.[4] Federated Insurance estimates that it invests $150,000 in each new recruit before the rep is placed in his or her own territory.[5] For a bad hire, such an investment represents sunk costs that may be nonrecoverable. And in view of studies that tell us that a significant number of salespeople should not be in sales for one reason or another,[6] it is apparent that recruitment and selection are among the most challenging and important responsibilities of sales management.

## INTRODUCTION TO SALESFORCE SOCIALIZATION

**Salesforce socialization** refers to the process by which salespeople acquire the knowledge, skills, and values essential to perform their jobs. The process begins when the sales recruit is first exposed to the organization and may extend for several years. A model of salesforce socialization is shown in Figure 5.1. This model suggests that important job outcomes such as job satisfaction, job involvement and commitment, and performance are directly and indirectly affected by recruitment and selection procedures.

The socialization process is discussed again in subsequent modules. For now, accept the idea that socialization affects salesforce performance and that recruitment and selection procedures play a major role in the socialization process. The two stages of socialization relevant to recruitment and selection are (1) **achieving realism,** which is giving the recruit an accurate portrayal of the job and (2) **achieving congruence,** which is matching the capabilities of the recruit with the needs of the organization. Realism can be achieved by providing accurate job descriptions and perhaps offering a **job preview** through a field visit with a salesperson. Congruence can be achieved through proper screening and selection of candidates who fit the job and the organization. From the candidates' perspective, they are more likely to choose an organization if they perceive

## Proposed Model of Salesforce Socialization    FIGURE 5.1

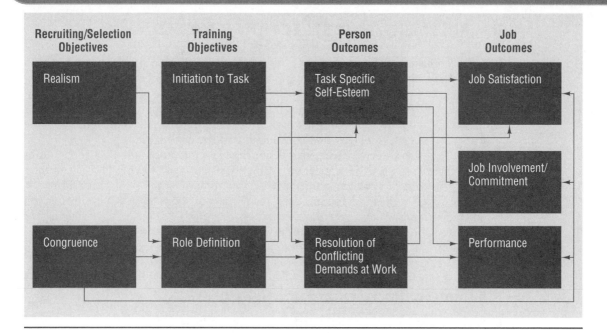

Sales organizations must present accurate portrayals of the sales job (achieving realism) to sales recruits, who must possess skills and needs compatible with the needs and offerings of the organization (achieving congruence). If these objectives of recruiting and selection are met, salesforce socialization is enhanced, and ultimately, salesforce performance, job satisfaction, and job involvement and commitment are improved.

its goals and values to be congruent with theirs.[7] For a closer look at the importance of obtaining congruence at Hershey Chocolate U.S.A., see "Sales Management in the 21st Century: Finding a Fit at Hershey Chocolate U.S.A."

Companies take several approaches to achieve realism and congruence in the recruiting process. For instance, Dictaphone, Inc. gives students an opportunity to view what a career in sales at the company entails by providing a video to college placement centers.

SALES MANAGEMENT IN THE 21ST CENTURY

### Finding a Fit at Hershey Chocolate U.S.A.

Douglas Clopton, former district and region manager for Hershey Chocolate, comments on the importance of congruence.

*Hershey identified 15 traits or dimensions that the company feels individuals should possess in order to be successful sales representatives with Hershey Chocolate U.S.A. A few of these are planning and organizing skills, personal leadership, persuasiveness, initiative, and communication skills. Hershey determines if sales candidates possess these dimensions through extensive questioning and testing of each during the interview process. Having most of these, however, is no guarantee of success. A candidate also must possess what Hershey refers to as motivational fit. This fit occurs when the individual is one who enjoys the selling process. Thus, it is critical for candidates to not only possess certain characteristics, but to enjoy the selling process to be successful at Hershey.*

Companies such as Hershey Chocolate U.S.A., Federated Insurance, and Motorola, Inc., provide candidates with a comprehensive brochure describing the company, its philosophy, and its products.

## RECRUITMENT AND SELECTION PROCESS

Figure 5.2 illustrates the steps in the recruitment and selection process. The first step involves **planning activities**: conducting a job analysis, establishing job qualifications, completing a written job description, setting recruitment and selection objectives, and developing a recruitment and selection strategy. These planning activities are conducted within the overall planning framework of the organization to ensure consistency with the objectives, strategies, resources, and constraints of the organization.

The second step is **recruitment**, which, simply put, is the procedure of locating a sufficient number of prospective job applicants. A number of internal (within the company) and external (outside the company) sources may be used to develop this pool of candidates.

The next step in the model is **selection**, the process of choosing which candidates will be offered the job. Many screening and evaluation methods, including evaluation of resumes and job application forms, interviews, tests, assessment centers, background investigations, and physical exams, are used in this step. A more detailed discussion of each step in the recruitment and selection process follows.

### Planning for Recruitment and Selection

Given the critical nature of recruitment and selection, it would be difficult to overstate the case for careful planning as part of the process. Sales managers are concerned with the current staffing needs of their organizations; but perhaps more important, they are also concerned with future staffing needs, which is what makes planning so essential.

Proper planning provides more time for locating the best recruits. Upper management can be alerted in advance to probable future needs, rather than having to be convinced quickly when the need becomes imminent. Also, training can be planned more effectively when the flow of new trainees into the organization is known. Overall, the main benefit of adequate planning for the recruitment and selection process is that it helps prevent the kind of poor decisions that often prove so expensive both emotionally and financially. The key tasks in planning for recruitment and selection are the following.

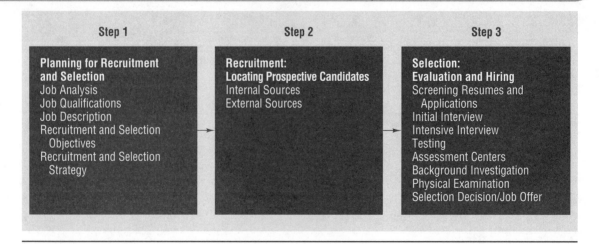

**FIGURE 5.2**                                    Recruiting and Selecting Salespeople

| Step 1 | Step 2 | Step 3 |
| --- | --- | --- |
| **Planning for Recruitment and Selection**<br>Job Analysis<br>Job Qualifications<br>Job Description<br>Recruitment and Selection Objectives<br>Recruitment and Selection Strategy | **Recruitment: Locating Prospective Candidates**<br>Internal Sources<br>External Sources | **Selection: Evaluation and Hiring**<br>Screening Resumes and Applications<br>Initial Interview<br>Intensive Interview<br>Testing<br>Assessment Centers<br>Background Investigation<br>Physical Examination<br>Selection Decision/Job Offer |

Three main steps are involved in recruiting and selecting salespeople: planning, recruiting, and selection.

## Job Analysis

To effectively recruit and select salespeople, sales managers must have a complete understanding of the job for which candidates are sought. Because most sales managers have served as salespeople in their companies before entering management, it is reasonable to think that they would have a good understanding of the sales jobs for which they recruit. However, some have lost touch with changing conditions in the field and thus have an obsolete view of the current sales task to be accomplished.

To ensure an understanding of the sales job, the sales manager may need to conduct, confirm, or update a **job analysis**, which entails an investigation of the tasks, duties, and responsibilities of the job. For example, will the selling tasks include responsibilities for opening new accounts as well as maintaining existing accounts? Will the salesperson be responsible for collecting accounts receivable or completing administrative reports? The job analysis defines the expected behavior of salespeople, indicating which areas of performance will be crucial for success. In most larger companies, the job analysis is completed by human resource managers or other corporate managers, but even then, the sales manager may have input into the job analysis.

## Job Qualifications

The job analysis indicates what the salespeople are supposed to do on the job, whereas **job qualifications** refer to the aptitude, skills, knowledge, personal traits, and willingness to accept occupational conditions necessary to perform the job. For example, when hiring document solutions representatives, Xerox looks for candidates who are college educated; have three years of major account experience; have strong selling and account management skills; have the ability to meet and exceed performance objectives; have excellent communication, teleprospecting, customer service, and presentation skills; and are personal-computer literate with proficiency in MS Office Suite.[8]

Common sales job qualifications address sales experience, educational level, willingness to travel, willingness to relocate, interpersonal skills, communication skills, problem-solving skills, relationship management skills, self-motivation, and ability to work independently. Consistent with our earlier discussion of the diversity of personal selling jobs, there is a corresponding variance in job qualifications for different sales jobs. Therefore, each sales manager should record the pertinent job qualifications for each job in the salesforce. A generic list of job qualifications for all the salespeople in the organization may not be

SALES MANAGEMENT IN THE 21ST CENTURY

### Key Job Qualifications at Hershey Chocolate USA

Douglas Clopton, former region sales manager for Hershey Chocolate U.S.A., comments on key sales job qualifications:

*Selling has evolved from a feature- and benefit-based selling process to a consultative selling process. In the past, sales organizations would attempt to address the customer's needs by providing an arsenal of features in their sales presentation. Today, however, a consumer/customer-focused organization must first uncover their customer's wants, needs, or problems, and then tailor their promotional solutions to best satisfy them. For example, most people don't want to deal with a doctor who* "has all the answers" *even before they discuss their health concerns with him or her. They would rather have the physician thoroughly question and seek out all the symptoms and problems and then write a prescription. The 21st-century sales organization sales reps' first step is to conduct a want/need analysis with the customer, extensively utilizing their questioning skills; then writing a prescription (marketing program) that will serve as the solution to the patient's (customer's) needs. In light of this change, recruiting efforts must be revised to place much greater emphasis on* listening skills *as well as* problem-solving skills. *Recruiting efforts no longer can focus on candidates who can sell, but on individuals who can help their customers buy.*

feasible. Doug Clopton explains key job qualifications necessary for a position in sales at Hershey Chocolate U.S.A. in "Sales Management in the 21st Century: Key Job Qualifications at Hershey Chocolate U.S.A."

For a given sales job within the same company, the qualifications may vary in different selling situations. For example, a multinational company whose salespeople sell the same products to the same types of customers may require different qualifications in different countries. Qualifications considered unimportant, and even discriminatory, in hiring salespeople in the United States, such as social class and religious and ethnic background, are important in hiring overseas.[9] In general, when sending salespeople on international assignments, it is helpful if they are patient, flexible, confident, persistent, motivated, and tolerant of new ways of doing things; have a desire to work abroad; and have a sense of humor.[10]

## Job Description

Based on the job analysis and job qualifications, a written summary of the job, the **job description**, is completed by the sales manager or, in many cases, the human resource manager. Job descriptions for salespeople could contain any or all of the following elements:

1. Job title (e.g., sales trainee, senior sales representative)
2. Duties, tasks, and responsibilities of the salesperson
3. Administrative relationships indicating to whom the salesperson reports
4. Types of products to be sold
5. Customer types
6. Significant job-related demands, such as mental stress, physical strength or stamina requirements, or environmental pressures to be encountered

Job descriptions are an essential document in sales management. Their use in recruitment and selection is only one of their multiple functions. They are used to clarify duties and thereby reduce role ambiguity in the salesforce, to familiarize potential employees with the sales job, to set objectives for salespeople, and eventually, to aid in evaluating performance. A typical job description for a sales representative is shown in Exhibit 5.1.[11]

## Recruitment and Selection Objectives

To be fully operational, recruitment and selection objectives should be specifically stated for a given period. The following general objectives of recruitment and selection could be converted to specific operational objectives in a given firm:

- Determine present and future needs in terms of numbers and types of salespeople (as discussed in Module 4).
- Meet the company's legal and social responsibilities regarding composition of the salesforce.
- Reduce the number of underqualified or overqualified applicants.
- Increase the number of qualified applicants at a specified cost.
- Evaluate the effectiveness of recruiting sources and evaluation techniques.

By setting specific objectives for recruitment and selection, sales managers can channel resources into priority areas and improve organizational and salesforce effectiveness.

## Recruitment and Selection Strategy

After objectives have been set, a **recruitment and selection strategy** can be developed. Formulating this strategy requires the sales manager to consider the scope and timing of recruitment and selection activities as follows:

- When will the recruitment and selection be done?
- How will the job be portrayed?
- How will efforts with intermediaries, such as employment agencies and college placement centers, be optimized?

**EXHIBIT 5.1**

| | |
|---|---|
| **Job Title:** | **Document Solutions Representative, X3336** |
| Department: | Sales/Marketing |
| Requisition Number: | XE00001964 |
| Location: | UT-Salt Lake City |

**Job Description:**

*eXpress* yourself

**Document Solutions Representative—Salt Lake City, Utah**

At Xerox, where business runs on fresh ideas, staying on the crest of digital technology demands originality, creativity, and ingenuity. That's why Xerox recruits exceptional people, whose professional and technical finesse are fueled by imagination. We've created a workplace where inventiveness flourishes, where employees are encouraged to express their vision, their ideas, and their leadership.

The Document Solutions Representative is a full-time salary and commission position that offers excellent compensation, benefits, and career growth opportunities. This is a unique opportunity for the right candidate interested in joining a high potential organization. The territory includes Salt Lake City, Utah.

In this customer satisfaction focused position, you'll be responsible for the development and execution of account strategies using the Xerox Account Management Program (XAMP). Duties include:

- Developing and maintaining key contact relationships with high level representatives of client organizations
- Scheduling and conducting customer appointments throughout an assigned territory
- Developing and presenting detailed written proposals either individually or in collaboration with varied internal partners and specialists
- Performing product demonstrations
- Negotiating close of sale and completing documentation for customer orders
- Coordinating activities with internal partners and specialists to provide customer solutions
- Ensuring resolution of all customer issues by engaging and coordinating with internal resources
- Providing comprehensive solutions to customer document needs
- Providing accurate revenue forecasts

To qualify, you'll need a BS/BA in business, science or liberal arts and a minimum of three years' of major account experience. Strong professional sales and account management skills are a must. The successful candidate will have a consistent record of meeting and exceeding performance objectives and will have excellent customer service, communication, teleprospecting and presentation skills. Strong PC skills and proficiency with the MS Office Suite are also required.

https://xerox.wfrecruiter.com/jobs_details1.asp?Job_id=24062&Page_Id=5619&Published=1

- What type of salespeople will be hired when developing an international salesforce?
- How much time will be allowed for a candidate to accept or reject an offer?
- What are the most likely sources for qualified applicants?

Recruitment and selection are perpetual activities in some sales organizations but in others are conducted only when a vacancy occurs. Most sales organizations could benefit by ongoing recruitment to facilitate selection when the need arises. Some recruit seasonally. For example, large companies often concentrate their efforts to coincide with spring graduation dates on college campuses.

A strategic decision must be made in terms of how the job will be portrayed, particularly in advertisements. Initial descriptions of the job in the media are necessarily limited. Should earnings potential be featured, or perhaps the opportunity for advancement? Or is this job correctly portrayed as ideal for the career salesperson? Consider how the advertisement in Exhibit 5.2[12] portrays the salesperson's job at a pharmaceutical company.

Strategy also involves coordinating recruiting needs and activities with employment agencies and college placement centers. For instance, dates and times for interviewing on campus must be arranged. If an employment agency is to be used, it will need a job description and job qualifications for the position to be filled.

When developing an international salesforce, the sales manager must consider the type of salesperson best suited for selling outside the home country. Options include hiring expatriates, who are salespeople from the firm's home country, hiring host-country nationals, or hiring third-country nationals. Advantages and disadvantages of hiring each type of salesperson are shown in Exhibit 5.3.[13]

Another strategic decision is the length of time a candidate will be given to accept an offer. This time element is important because other recruitment and selection activities may be temporarily suspended until the decision is made. Strategy also involves identifying the sources that look most promising for recruitment. This subject is discussed in detail in the following section.

---

## EXHIBIT 5.2 — Example of an Individual Company's Advertisement to Recruit Salespeople

**An active lifestyle can be enjoyed**

It's our solid dedication, vision, and constant search for answers that allow us to touch millions of people around the world every day. As a major division of Fortune 100 American Home Products Corporation, we help people lead healthier lives through the development of innovative pharmaceutical, vaccine, and nutritional products. We achieve this through our superior research, manufacturing, sales, and marketing capabilities. Enjoy the freedom to develop your own career while having the support of a valuable team. We are recruiting for territories in the New York Metropolitan area, New Jersey, and Connecticut.

**Pharmaceutical Sales Representative**

Great training. And a piece of the business.
As we build on our history of developing successful products and people, you can play an important role in our future, with responsibilities for promotion and sales of pharmaceutical products to physicians, pharmacists, and hospitals. You'll begin by completing a comprehensive training program that prepares you for immediate challenges and development on our career advancement ladder.

A bachelor's degree is required, preferably in a business or life science discipline. Ideally, you also will have a strong record of relevant sales experience. Outstanding communication and presentation skills are also a must. In return, we offer an excellent compensation package that includes bonuses, comprehensive benefits, a company car, and stock options—along with support of members who are among our industry's most accomplished professionals.

Wyeth-Ayerst offers other benefits, including child-care subsidies, educational assistance, and professional development programs. Please forward your resume with salary requirements to **Wyeth-Ayerst. Reference ONNYT-0199, P.O. Box 7886, Philadelphia, PA 19101-7886. Fax in fine mode to: (610) 989-4854.** E mail: **jobs@RAMAIL1.wyeth.com** (ASCII format, no attachments, subject: resume. For more information, visit our Web site at **http://www.ahp.com/wyeth.htm** Principals only.

Equal Opportunity Employer. M/F/D/V

| | Advantages and Disadvantages of Salesperson Types for International Salesforce Development | **EXHIBIT 5.3** |
|---|---|---|

| **Salesperson Type** | **Advantages** | **Disadvantages** |
|---|---|---|
| Expatriates | High product knowledge<br>Good follow-up service<br>Good training for promotion<br>Greater home-country control | Highest maintenance costs<br>High turnover rates<br>High training costs |
| Host-Country Nationals | Easy and inexpensive to hire<br>Significant market knowledge<br>Speak the native language<br>Cultural understanding<br>Quickly penetrate market | Need extensive product training<br>Sales often considered low-esteem position<br>Difficult to instill organization's culture<br>Hard to ensure organizational loyalty |
| Third-Country Nationals | Possible cultural understanding and language skills if from similar region<br>Economical labor force<br>Allows regional sales coverage<br>May allow sales to country in conflict with home country | Nationality unrelated to organization or place of work<br>Low promotion potential<br>Need extensive product and company training<br>Sales often considered low-esteem position<br>Potential difficulty of adapting to new environments<br>Difficult to instill organization's culture<br>Hard to ensure organizational loyalty |

## Recruitment: Locating Prospective Candidates

As Figure 5.2 showed, the next step in recruitment and selection is to locate a pool of prospective job candidates. This step, the actual recruiting, may use a variety of sources. Some of the more popular ones are advertising, employee referrals, online sites and private employment agencies.

### Internal Sources

One of the most popular methods of locating sales recruits is through **employee referral programs**. These programs are relatively quick and inexpensive compared with other recruiting methods, such as advertising, using employment agencies, and visiting college campuses. Referral programs also may be very effective. In a survey of more than 200 sales managers, 47 percent indicated that they found their best salespeople through referrals.[14] Another study found that applicants who are referred by current employees are more likely to receive job offers and become employees than those recruited by other sources.[15] Baystate Financial, for instance, has effectively used salesperson referrals, in part, to nearly triple the size of its salesforce.[16] An employee who furnishes a referral may be paid a "finder's fee." For example, Federated Insurance provides its employees with a $1,500 finders fee for referred applicants who are hired.[17] Existing salespeople are obviously good sources for referral programs because they have a good understanding of the type of person sought for a sales position. Purchasing agents within the company may also be helpful in identifying prospective sales candidates. Employee referral programs can be enhanced by publicly recognizing successful referrals, by regularly providing incentives and promptly rewarding successful referrals, by offering a proactive program that encourages employee participation, and by providing feedback concerning the status of referrals to those making them.[18]

Other internal methods include announcing sales job openings through newsletters, on the company's intranet, in meetings, or on the bulletin board. Internal transfers or promotions may result from announcing an opening on the salesforce. One study found that employees of the firm who transfer to sales positions can be expected to yield more long-run profits than salespeople from any other source.[19]

### External Sources

Although it is a good idea to include internal sources as part of a recruitment and selection program, there may not be enough qualified persons inside the organization to meet the human resource needs of the salesforce. The search then must be expanded to external sources.

### Advertisements

One way to produce a large pool of applicants in a short time is by advertising. On a cost-per-applicant basis, advertising is generally inexpensive. However, a large number of the applicants may not be qualified for the job, even when the ads carefully spell out job qualifications. As a result, advertising usually requires extensive screening procedures to identify a reasonable number of prospective candidates. Exhibit 5.4[20] offers sound advice on how to use print ads to recruit salespeople.

Advertisements in trade publications can attract those already in a specified field. In the case of trade magazines, lead time to place an advertisement in the next issue is longer than with newspapers—typically six to eight weeks. Other specialty publications are nationally distributed employment listings, such as the one published by *The Wall Street Journal*.

### Online

The Internet provides a potentially effective and relatively inexpensive way to recruit. Companies can list job openings on bulletin boards or in job banks such as Monster (http://monster.com) or career builder.com (http://www.careerbuilder.com). Candidates seeking a position can reply to an ad online. Newspapers, such as *The New York Times,* have added Web versions of their classified sections. Furthermore, many companies are using their Web site to advertise job openings and allow candidates to apply online. A company Web site should provide ample information about the position and the company, make it easy to apply, and give the candidate a favorable impression overall.[21] Since Web recruiting

---

**EXHIBIT 5.4**   **Using Print Advertising to Recruit Salespeople**

The sales recruiting ads you run depend on the job, the speed needed to fill it, availability of the applicant, and competition. Here are some tips for maximizing advertising effectiveness:

- Use business publications to recruit those with business experience.
- Use display ads in the business pages for sales management and top selling posts.
- Use classified newspaper advertising when speed is important.
- Advertise on Sunday when running a classified ad.
- Use the ad as a sales tool to motivate candidates to reply.
- Focus on prospective candidates' needs and interests rather than on company characteristics.
- Emphasize the unique aspects of the job.
- Do not exaggerate earnings estimates. This may cause distrust.
- Add restrictions (e.g., bachelor's degree) to avoid being flooded with unqualified applicants.
- Provide a telephone number where the reader can call on Sunday, if possible.
- Add art (e.g., a border) to copy for greater visibility.
- Use a box number to screen telephone calls and surprise visits. However, many employed people will not answer box number ads.
- Provide a fax number.
- Answer inquiries immediately before they cool off.

The ad in Exhibit 5.2 attempts to use many of these suggestions.

can produce a tremendous number of resumes, it may be helpful to use an automated tracking system, such as PeopleClick (www.peopleclick.com), to identify the applicants who are most appropriate for the position.[22]

Recruiting online offers several benefits. For one, it has the potential for fast turnaround. While a week may pass by the time an ad appears in the Sunday paper and the first applications are received, an opening can be posted online and applications received as early as the same day. There is also a cost savings. Posting a position on a national job Web site costs from $100 to $300 for 30 days, whereas a single local Sunday newspaper ad may run $1,000 or more.[23] Finally, given a poll showing that 96 percent of all job seekers use the Internet, having a presence there appears critical. Nevertheless, this method should not be used exclusively since portions of the population may be excluded. Not all demographics use the Internet on an equally proportional basis.[24] As such, strictly relying on online sources to recruit may result in violating antidiscrimination laws.[25]

### Private Employment Agencies

A commonly used source is the **private employment agency.** The fee charged by the agency may be paid by the employer or the job seeker, as established by contract before the agency begins work for either party. Fees vary but typically amount to 15 to 20 percent of the first-year earnings of the person hired through the agency. The higher the caliber of salesperson being sought, the greater the probability the employer will pay the fee.

Many agencies, such as Relocate.com (http://www.relocate.com), findasalesagent.com (http://findasalesagent.com), and IndustrySalesPros (http://www.industrysalespros.com), specialize in the placement of salespeople. Such agencies can be extremely useful in national searches, particularly if the sales manager is seeking high-quality, experienced salespeople. This is true because high-performing salespeople are usually employed but may contact an agency just to see if a better opportunity has arisen.

Employment agencies usually work from a job description furnished by the sales manager and can be instructed to screen candidates based on specific job qualifications. The professionalism of private employment agencies varies widely, but there are enough good agencies that a sales manager should not tolerate an agency that cannot refer qualified candidates.

Employment agencies that specialize in part-timers are sometimes used when a need arises to hire part-time salespeople to support or supplant the full-time salesforce. In most cases, part-time salespeople are not eligible for fringe benefits, so the cost of sales coverage can be reduced by using them. However, when considering using temporaries internationally, keep in mind that many western European countries restrict or even ban their use.[26]

### Colleges and Universities

A popular source for sales recruits, especially for large companies with extensive training programs, are colleges and universities. College students usually can be hired at lower salaries than experienced salespeople, yet they have already demonstrated their learning abilities. Companies seeking future managers often look here for sales recruits.

Campus placement centers can be helpful in providing resumes of applicants, arranging interviews, and providing facilities for screening interviews. Some campus placement centers now offer videoconferencing systems that allow corporate recruiters to interview students from the home office.[27] College campuses are also common sites for career conferences in which multiple companies participate in trade show fashion to familiarize students with sales job opportunities. Most placement centers also provide access to alumni in addition to the current student body. In some instances, contacts with faculty members may provide sales recruits.

Another campus recruiting method is to offer sales internships, which allow both the company and the student an opportunity to see whether a match exists. The internship as a recruiting vehicle is gaining popularity. Northwestern Mutual Financial Network's internship program is designed to develop college students personally and professionally. Approximately 72 percent of the student interns participating each year eventually become full-time agents.[28] Likewise, Vector Marketing, Xerox, and Hershey Chocolate U.S.A. all offer sales internships in hopes of developing future reps for the company. Mutual of Omaha has even gone as far as sponsoring a university's selling program to enable closer contact with students in hopes of recruiting them.[29]

On the international scene, college campuses are gaining in popularity as a source of sales recruits. College students in foreign countries are beginning to see United States–based firms as viable alternatives to home-country firms.

### Career Fairs

Several employers are brought together in one location for recruiting purposes by **career fairs**. Candidates visit the booths of employers they are interested in, or companies request a meeting with a candidate based on a favorable reaction to the candidate's resume. Career fairs are best conducted in the evening hours so that currently employed salespeople can attend. However, virtual career fairs on the Internet circumvent this problem. Companies can participate in online career fairs hosted by companies such as jobweb (http://www.jobweb.com). Employers' banner ads are grouped in common areas. When candidates click on a banner, they are treated to company information, position descriptions, and links to the companies' Web sites.

### Professional Societies

Another worthwhile source of sales recruits is **professional societies**. A primary reason sales executives join professional organizations is to establish a network of colleagues who have common interests. Organizations such as Sales and Marketing Executives International meet regularly and provide the opportunity to establish contacts with professional sales executives, who may provide the names of prospective salespeople. Some professional organizations publish newsletters or operate a placement service, which could also be used in recruiting.

### Computer Rosters

Locating prospective salespeople through **computerized matchmaking** services is becoming a more important recruiting method each day. Computer technology is being used by an increasing number of college placement centers and employment agencies. For instance, at Central Missouri State University, employers can post job vacancies directly to the career services Web site, which is accessible by all students. Independent computer recruiting services are also widely available. For example, Wonderlic Inc. (http://www.wonderlic.com), offers sales managers an automated application service that allows them to screen applicants before taking a phone call or handling a resume or application. Applicants call a special toll-free phone number included in the firm's recruiting ad, or are sent to a designated Web site and respond to questions related to the job. Wonderlic forwards the completed applications to the client company the next day for their review.

Resume-search services such as CIRS (http://www.cirssearch.com) are also useful for finding qualified candidates. These services sort through thousands of resumes they have on file looking for candidates who match the specific qualifications a firm desires. They generally guarantee qualified candidates and charge only when a match is made.

Recruiting software, such as iResumix, is available to help manage the recruitment process. This application allows for automating much of the recruiting process from posting the position online, to screening and contacting candidates, to scheduling interviews and assigning in-house interviewing responsibilities such as prescreening.[30]

## Selection: Evaluation and Hiring

The third step in the recruitment and selection model shown in Figure 5.2 is selection. As part of the selection process, various tools are used to evaluate the job candidate in terms of job qualifications and to provide a relative ranking compared with other candidates. In this section, commonly used evaluation tools are presented and some of the key issues in salesforce selection are discussed.

## Screening Resumes and Applications

The pool of prospective salespeople generated in the recruiting phase often must be drastically reduced before engaging in time-consuming expensive evaluation procedures such as personal interviews. Initially, sales recruits may be screened based on a review of a resume or an application form.

In analyzing resumes, sales managers check job qualifications (e.g., education or sales experience requirements), the degree of career progress by the applicant, and the frequency of job change. Depending on the format and extensiveness of the resume, it may be possible to examine salary history and requirements, travel or relocation restrictions, and reasons for past job changes. Also, valuable clues about the recruit may be gathered from the appearance and completeness of the resume.

New technology makes it possible to screen resumes electronically. Screening software helps select the best applicants by screening for certain words or phrases, thus eliminating the need to examine every single resume received.[31] Using companies such as Taleo (http://www.recruitsoft.com) and Hire.com (http://www.hire.com), businesses also can define e-mail questionnaires that are mailed out to determine candidates' experience and skills. Returned responses are automatically tracked and profiled prior to being entered into the firm's HR database. This process is considered by some to offer improved identification matching over many keyword search screening alternatives.[32] Caution, however, should be exercised when using screening software. If the screening criteria are not carefully chosen, groups of people from various protected categories may be eliminated.[33]

A **job application form** can be designed to gather all pertinent information and exclude unnecessary information. There are three additional advantages of application forms as a selection tool. First, the application form can be designed to meet antidiscriminatory legal requirements, whereas resumes often contain such information. For example, if some applicants note age, sex, race, color, religion, or national origin on their resumes and others do not, a legal question as to whether this information was used in the selection process might arise. A second advantage of application forms is that the comparison of multiple candidates is facilitated because the information on each candidate is presented in the same sequence. This is not the case with personalized resumes. Finally, job applications are usually filled out in handwriting, so the sales manager can observe the attention to detail and neatness of the candidate. In some sales jobs, these factors may be important for success.

## Interviews

Interviews of assorted types are an integral part of the selection process. Because interpersonal communications and relationships are a fundamental part of sales jobs, it is only natural for sales managers to weigh interview results heavily in the selection process.

Although sales managers agree that interviews are important in selecting salespeople, there is less agreement on how structured the interviews should be and how they should be conducted. For example, some sales managers favor unstructured interviews, which encourage the candidates to talk freely about themselves. Others favor a more structured approach in which particular answers are sought, in a particular sequence, from each candidate.

### Initial Interviews

Interviews are usually designed to get an in-depth look at the candidate. In some cases, however, they merely serve as a screening mechanism to support or replace a review of resumes or application forms. These **initial interviews** are typified by the on-campus interviews conducted by most sales recruiters. They are brief, lasting less than an hour. The recruiter clarifies questions about job qualifications and makes a preliminary judgment about whether a match exists between the applicant and the company. Such interviews may also be conducted one-on-one over the telephone or through teleconferencing or videoconferencing if there is a need to involve multiple parties.[34]

A promising time-saving technique for initially interviewing candidates involves them responding to a series of questions on the Internet or over the telephone. Gallup, Inc., helps firms identify recurring patterns of thoughts, feelings, and behaviors exhibited by top performers. Gallup's Selection Research Instrument System then helps to identify new employees who exhibit success factors similar to the organization's top performers. Assessment results are then delivered online to managers responsible for making hiring decisions.[35] These interviews alleviate some of the costs involved in conducting a personal interview.

Computer-assisted interviewing is an emerging device that also can be used for screening candidates. For example, Nike used it to hire 250 retail salespeople for its Niketown outlet in Las Vegas. After seeing an ad in the newspaper and responding to eight questions over the phone, applicants who were not screened out were invited to the store for a computer-assisted interview, followed by a personal interview. As part of the computer interview, applicants viewed a video showing three scenarios for helping a customer and were asked to pick the best one. The computer flagged applicants' strengths, weaknesses, and areas that needed further probing. Although Nike used on-site computer-assisted interviewing, the Internet now provides another venue for this option, allowing greater flexibility for both employers and prospective employees.[36]

During this phase of selection, sales managers should be careful to give the candidate an accurate picture of the job and not oversell it. Candidates who are totally "sold" on the job during the first interview only to be rejected later suffer unnecessary trauma.

### Intensive Interviews

One or more **intensive interviews** may be conducted to get an in-depth look at the candidate. Often, this involves multiple sequential interviews by several executives or several managers at the company's facilities. The interview process at Federated Insurance, for example, involves eight interviews.[37] Another variation on the theme, used less often, is to interview several job candidates simultaneously in a group setting.

When a candidate is to be interviewed in succession by several managers, planning and coordination are required to achieve more depth and to avoid redundancy. Otherwise, each interviewer might concentrate on the more interesting dimensions of a candidate and some important areas may be neglected. An interviewing guide such as the one in Exhibit 5.5[38] could be used with multiple interviewers, each of whom would delve into one or more of the seven categories of information about the candidate. Some evidence suggests that structured interviews are more accurate at predicting a candidate's success than unstructured interviews.[39]

Given the emphasis placed today on developing enduring customer relationships, it is important to hire salespeople who value honesty and integrity, characteristics necessary for developing such relationships. Exhibit 5.6 outlines some sample questions (along with potential responses) geared toward gathering information on past behaviors that illustrate whether a candidate's own ethical values are compatible with those of the organization. Most interview situations would require using only two or three such questions.

The "rightness" or "wrongness" of the answers is up to the interviewer's judgment. As such it's important to train interviewers to follow up with more questions to pin down behavior and the thinking behind the behavior as well as to ask for additional examples. Interviewers then meet so that multiple interpretations of the answers can be obtained and discussed. The interviewers would then agree on a rating for the candidate's level of integrity.[40]

Interviews, like any other single selection tool, may fail to predict adequately applicants' future success on the job.[41] **Interviewer bias**, or allowing personal opinions, attitudes, and beliefs to influence judgments about a candidate, can be a particularly acute problem with some interviewers. Sales managers, like other human beings, tend to have preferences in candidates' appearances and personalities—and any number of other subjective feelings that may be irrelevant for a given interview situation.

Research confirms the subjective nature of interviewing, concluding that different interviewers will rate the same applicant differently unless there is a commonly accepted stereotype of the ideal applicant.[42] For instance, research suggests that race bias is a potential concern.[43] Sales managers must not let bias interfere with the hiring decision.

### Testing

To overcome the pitfalls of subjectivity and a potential lack of critical analysis of job candidates, many firms use tests as part of the selection process. Selection tests may be designed to measure intelligence, aptitudes, personality, and other interpersonal factors.

## Meeting the Candidate

At the outset, act friendly but avoid prolonged small talk—interviewing time costs money.

- Introduce yourself by using your name and title.
- Mention casually that you will make notes. (You don't mind if I make notes, do you?)
- Assure the candidate that all information will be treated in confidence.

### Questions:
- Ask questions in a conversational tone. Make them both concise and clear.
- Avoid loaded and negative questions. Ask open-ended questions that will force complete answers: "Why do you say that?" (Who, what, where, when, how?)
- Don't ask direct questions that can be answered "yes" or "no."

### Analyzing:
- Attempt to determine the candidate's goals. Try to draw the candidate out, but let him or her do most of the talking. Don't sell—interview.
- Try to avoid snap judgments.

## Interviewer Instructions

You will find two columns of questions on the following pages. The left-hand column contains questions to ask yourself about the candidate. The right-hand column suggests questions to ask the candidate. During the interview it is suggested that you continually ask yourself, What is this person telling me about himself or herself? What kind of person is he or she?" In other parts of the interview, you can cover education, previous experience, and other matters relating to specific qualifications.

### Ask Yourself

**I. Attitude**
- Can compete without irritation?
- Can bounce back easily?
- Can balance interest of both company and self?
- What is important to him or her?
- Is he or she loyal?
- Takes pride in doing a good job?
- Is he or she a cooperative team player?

**II. Motivation**
- Is settled in choice of work?
- Works from necessity, or choice?
- Makes day-to-day and long-range plans?
- Uses some leisure for self-improvement?
- Is willing to work for what he or she wants in face of opposition?

**III. Initiative**
- Is he or she a self-starter?
- Completes own tasks?
- Follows through on assigned tasks?
- Works in assigned manner without leaving own trademark?
- Can work independently?

### Ask the Candidate

1. Ever lose in competition? Feelings?
2. Ever uncertain about providing for your family?
3. How can the American way of business be improved?
4. Do you think that you've made a success of life to date?
5. Who was your best boss? Describe the person.
6. How do you handle customer complaints?

1. How does your spouse (or other) feel about a selling career?
2. When and how did you first develop an interest in selling?
3. What mortgages, debts, etc., press you now?
4. How will this job help you get what you want?
5. What obstacles are most likely to trip you up?

1. How (or why) did you get (or want) into sales?
2. Do you prefer to work alone or with others?
3. What do you like most and, like least about selling?
4. Which supervisors let you work alone? How did you feel about this?
5. When have you felt like giving up on a task? Tell me about it.

*(continued)*

**EXHIBIT 5.5    Interview Guide (*continued*)**

**Ask Yourself**

**IV. Stability**
- Is he or she excitable or even-tempered?
- Impatient or understanding?
- Uses words that show strong feelings?
- Is candidate poised or impulsive; controlled or erratic?
- Will he or she broaden or flatten under pressure?
- Is candidate enthusiastic about job?

**V. Planning**
- Ability to plan and follow through? Or will depend on supervisor for planning?
- Ability to coordinate work of others?
- Ability to think of ways of improving methods?
- Ability to fit into company methods?
- Will he or she see the whole job or get caught up in details?

**VI. Insight**
- Realistic in appraising self?
- Desire for self-improvement?
- Interested in problems of others?
- Interested in reaction of others to self?
- Will he or she take constructive action on weaknesses?
- How does he or she take criticism?

**VII. Social Skills**
- Is he or she a leader or follower?
- Interested in new ways of dealing with people?
- Can get along best with what types of people?
- Will wear well over the long term?
- Can make friends easily?

**Ask the Candidate**

1. What things disturb you most?
2. How do you get along with customers (people) you dislike?
3. What buyers' actions irritate you?
4. What were your most unpleasant sales (work) experiences?
5. Most pleasant sales (work) experiences?
6. What do you most admire about your friends?
7. What things do some customers do that are irritating to other people?

1. What part of your work (selling) do you like best? like least?
2. What part is the most difficult for you?
3. Give me an idea of how you spend a typical day.
4. Where do you want to be five years from today?
5. If you were manager, how would you run your present job?
6. What are the differences between planned and unplanned work?

1. Tell me about your strengths and weaknesses.
2. Are your weaknesses important enough to do something about them? Why or why not?
3. How do you feel about those weaknesses?
4. How would you size up your last employer?
5. Most useful criticism received? From whom? Tell me about it. Most useless?
6. How do you handle fault finders?

1. What do you like to do in your spare time?
2. Have you ever organized a group? Tell me about it.
3. What methods are effective in dealing with people? What methods are ineffective?
4. What kind of customers (people) do you get along with best?
5. Do you prefer making new friends or keeping old ones? Why?
6. How would you go about making a friend? Developing a customer?
7. What must a person do to be liked by others?

Historically, the use of such tests has been controversial. In the late 1960s, it appeared that testing would slowly disappear from the employment scene under legal and social pressure related to the lack of validity and possible discriminatory nature of some testing procedures. Instead, selection tests have changed, and perhaps managers have learned more about how to use them as a legitimate part of the selection process. Therefore, they are still used today.

Those who have had success with tests suggest they are useful for identifying candidates' strengths and weaknesses, as well as for revealing candidates who possess key personality traits associated with successful salespeople.[44] For example, the trait

**Interviewing for Integrity    EXHIBIT 5.6**

1. **"We are often confronted with the dilemma of having to choose between what is right and what is best for the company. Give at least two examples of situations in which you faced this dilemma and how you handled them."**

**Good answer:** Once, we discovered a technical defect in a product after it had been shipped and used by a client. The client did not notice the defect. We debated whether to tell the client and admit we had made a stupid error, or just let things go because the client seemed to be using the product with no problem. We decided to tell the client and replace the product at no cost.

**Questionable answer:** We discovered that our sales clerks were making errors in charging for certain combinations of products and that the errors were almost always in favor of the company. In no way were the clerks encouraged or trained to make these errors. We also learned that, with training, the errors could be eliminated, but the training would be fairly expensive. I decided not to institute the training.

2. **"Have you ever observed someone stretching the rules at work? What did you do about it?"**

**Good answer:** One of my fellow executives took a company car to use for a weekend vacation. I spoke to him, and he agreed that it was not right and that he would not do it again.

**Questionable answer:** Everybody stretches the rules sometimes.

3. **"Have you ever had to bend the rules or exaggerate a little bit when trying to make a sale?"**

**Good answer:** My experience is that when salespeople misrepresent products and services, customers buy less from them. Having credibility with customers brings in better long-term sales. For example, when I was selling servers, we had a proprietary server and operating system. The client asked me why my machine was really worth the higher cost. I listed the advantages and disadvantages, which indicated for him that the cheaper solution would work. I lost that sale but came back to win a much larger sale six months later.

**Questionable answer:** Sometimes when selling to a doctor, the doctor will state that he's heard that one of my products is effective against a certain disease. I listen and nod my head and say, "Interesting." I don't correct him even though I know that the drug is not recommended for that purpose. I'm not saying that it does work the way he thinks it does; I'm just not disagreeing with the doctor. You can't give advice to physicians.

4. **"We've all done things that we regretted. Can you give me an example that falls into this category for you? How would you handle it differently today?"**

**Good answer:** When I first took over my job, I let seven people go without a whole lot of knowledge about their skills and contributions. Later I found that three of them were actually outstanding employees who should not have been let go. My jumping to conclusions hurt them and the company's operations. It took us several years to replace their knowledge of our equipment.

**Questionable answer:** I've never regretted anything about business. It's a game. I play the game to win.

5. **"There are two philosophies about regulations and policies. One is that they are to be followed to the letter; the other is that they are just guidelines. What is your opinion?"**

**Good answer:** Regulations and policies are made for important reasons. A regulation seems to me to be stronger, and I feel that I follow all regulations, such as getting reports in at a certain time and accounting for expenses in a certain way. Policies are a little bit more indefinite. They express more of a guideline and a philosophy. There are circumstances when you fall into the "gray area" when applying a policy. When I have had questions, I've checked with my boss.

**Questionable answer:** In order to get things done, you can't be held back by old-fashioned policies of your organization. You have to know what's right and do the right thing. You have to have good ethics and make decisions based on those ethics. You may have to bend the rules sometimes.

**Source:** William C. Byham, "Can You Interview for Integrity?" *Across the Board* (March/April 2004): 1–5.

"conscientiousness" appears to be a valid predictor of sales performance.[45] Sales Success Profile (http://www.doubleeaglecomm.com/salesprofile.htm), a 50-question, multiple-choice test, measures salespeople's strengths and weaknesses in 13 critical areas, including the ability to approach, involve, and build rapport; the ability to identify a buyer's needs and motivations; skill at overcoming objections; and time management.[46] The StrengthsFinder test developed by Gallup International Research & Education Center can be used to identify "competition" and "achiever" strengths, both found to contribute to salesperson drive and performance.[47] Valid tests measuring certain personality traits, sales skills, or strengths may be used to supplement other salesforce selection tools.

Those who remain reluctant to use tests ask three questions: (1) Can selection tests really predict future job performance? (2) Can tests give an accurate, job-related profile of the candidate? (3) What are the legal liabilities arising from testing? In addressing the first question, one must admit it is sometimes difficult to correlate performance on a test at a given point in time with job performance at a later date. For example, how can sales managers account for performance variations caused primarily by changes in the uncontrollable environment, as might be the case in an unpredictable economic setting?

Question 2 really is concerned with whether the tests measure the appropriate factors in an accurate fashion. The precise measurement of complex behavioral variables such as motivation is difficult at best, so it is likely that some tests do not really measure what they purport to measure.

Answers to question 3 depend largely on the complete answers to questions 1 and 2. The capsule response to the third question is that unless test results can be validated as a meaningful indicator of performance, there is a strong possibility that the sales manager is in a legally precarious position.

Suggestions to improve the usefulness to sales managers of tests as selection tools follow.[48]

1. Do not attempt to construct tests for the purpose of selecting salespeople. Leave this job to the testing experts and human resource specialists.
2. If psychological tests are used, be sure the standards of the American Psychological Association have been met.
3. Use tests that have been based on a job analysis for the particular job in question.
4. Select a test that minimizes the applicant's ability to anticipate desired responses.
5. Use tests as part of the selection process, but do not base the hiring decision solely on test results.

Tests can be useful selection tools if these suggestions are followed. In particular, tests can identify areas worthy of further scrutiny if they are administered and interpreted before a final round of intensive interviewing. For example, prospective candidates who enter the career section of Northwestern Mutual Financial Network's Web site to apply online complete a self-employment screening test that examines their characteristics and style as they relate to specific entrepreneurial opportunities. That information is forwarded to an office selected by the candidate prior to further interviewing.[49] Likewise, Federated Insurance requires applicants to take a written personality test as part of the application process.[50]

Sales managers may use commercial testing services in selecting salespeople. For example, Wonderlic Inc., (http://www.wonderlic.com) offers a computer-scored test called the Comprehensive Personality Profile that assesses personality from a job compatibility perspective.[51] This extensively validated test can be used to analyze candidates' strengths and weaknesses related to a position in sales, and may be administered by paper, personal computer, telephone, or online. Companies such as GM Parts, for instance, test job candidates' sales skills utilizing online assessment and testing services provided by the HR Chally Group (http://www.chally.com).[52]

Tests may also be used to assess a candidate's honesty and integrity. Standardized tests designed for this purpose include the Reid Report (www.pearsonreidlondonhours.com/index.html) and the CareerEthic Inventory (www.careerethic.com).[53]

Tests may prove useful for selecting among local candidates when operating in a foreign country. For example, when United States–based Caliper wanted to hire salespeople for its operations in the Czech Republic, it successfully translated and administered to Czech candidates the same examination it gives to American candidates to assess such qualities as ego drive, empathy, and leadership.[54]

## Assessment Centers

An **assessment center** offers a set of well-defined procedures for using techniques such as group discussion, business game simulations, presentations, and role-playing exercises for the purpose of employee selection or development. The participant's performance is evaluated by a group of assessors, usually members of management within the firm. Although somewhat expensive because of the high cost of managerial time to conduct the assessments, such centers are being used more often in the selection of salespeople.

An interesting report on the use of an assessment center to select salespeople comes from the life insurance industry, well known for its continual need for new salespeople. Traditional selection methods used in this industry apparently leave something to be desired because turnover rates are among the highest for salespeople. An assessment-center approach was used by one life insurance firm to select salespeople based on exercises simulating various sales skills, such as prospecting, time management, and sales presentation skills. Results of the study indicated that this program was superior to traditional methods of selecting salespeople in the insurance industry in terms of predicting which salespeople would survive and which would drop out within six months of being hired.[55]

## Background Investigation

Job candidates who have favorably emerged from resume and application screening, interviewing, testing, and perhaps an assessment center may next become the subject of a **background investigation.** This may be as perfunctory as a reference check or comprehensive if the situation warrants it. For instance, Federated Insurance checks each sales applicant's driver's record and credit history, and conducts 10 reference checks.[56] In conducting background investigations, it is advisable to request job-related information only and to obtain a written release from the candidate before proceeding with the investigation.

If a reference check is conducted, two points should be kept in mind. First, persons listed as references are biased in favor of the job applicant. As one sales manager puts it, "Even the losers have three good references—so I don't bother checking them." Second, persons serving as references may not be candid or may not provide the desired information. This reluctance may stem from a personal concern (i.e., Will I lose a friend or be sued if I tell the truth?) or from a company policy limiting the discussion of past employees.

Despite these and other limitations, a reference check can help verify the true identity of a person and possibly confirm his or her employment history. Learning that an applicant or employee lied on the application form can also be used as a defense in a hiring or firing discrimination suit.[57] With personal misrepresentation and resume fraud being very real possibilities, a reference check is recommended.[58] Exhibit 5.7[59] provides techniques for getting valid information in a background check.

## Physical Examination

Requiring the job candidate to pass a physical examination is often a formal condition of employment. In many instances, the insurance carrier of the employing firm requires a physical examination of all incoming employees. The objective is to discover any physical problem that may inhibit job performance.

In recent years, drug and communicable disease testing has made this phase of selection controversial. Although the courts will undoubtedly have a major role in determining the legality of testing in these areas in the future, the current rules, at least in the case of drug testing of potential employees, are fairly simple. A company can test for drug use if the applicant is informed of the test before taking it, if the results are kept confidential,

**EXHIBIT 5.7** How to Get Valid Information in a Background Check

The HR Chally Group's experience shows that many employers never really check references, or else they do it hastily and it becomes little more than a rubber stamp. Here are 10 techniques to make the background check a useful and productive tool in aiding the selection process.

While it is often difficult to get references to cooperate because of cautious internal policies or other legal concerns, many will comment orally or off the record, but not in writing.

1. **Be wary of first-party references.**
   Good sales candidates are not going to name references who will describe them negatively. Such first-party references are not as valuable as the candidate's past customers, who will probably be more candid. These references can indicate how loyal and satisfied the customers were with the candidate, which is a good indication of a prospective employee's past performance.

2. **Radial search referrals might be used.**
   The radial search for referrals is a method of reference checking that requires getting additional references from the first-party references. Such "second generation" references will not be carefully selected to present only a positive impression.

   **Remember:** Ask references to help you out; don't ask them just to criticize. Ask them to highlight strengths and let them build up the salesperson, and see how high they are willing to go.

3. **Use an interview background check.**
   This will show whether or not the salesperson is likely to change in terms of work performance. In other words, what degree of reliability do the references suggest? What "odds" do they give for the person's future success?

4. **Use the critical incident technique.**
   Determine the one trait or incident for which the candidate is best remembered. Could this be described as primarily good, bad, or neutral? Does it indicate an individual who is results oriented or service oriented?

5. **Pick out problem areas.**
   Determine the candidate's customers who were the most difficult to handle, and those problems that were the toughest to solve. Even first-party references may reveal difficulties that can be indicative of future sales performance. Find out if the candidate eventually overcame the difficulties.

6. **Obtain a numerical scale reference rating.**
   Keep in mind that 70 points on a 100 point scale is "passing" to most people; 50 points would be "failing." Reference rating scales are often easier for people to deal with. For example, references generally do not like to say negative things, but they may be willing to call a person an "85" instead of flatly saying "average."

7. **Identify an individual's best job.**
   Notice whether or not the reference needs to think excessively about identifying an Individual's best job. This may suggest that the individual's behavior was consistent, but not necessarily exceptional.

8. **Check for idiosyncrasies.**
   Did the candidate have any outstanding idiosyncrasies? If so, did they help or hinder job performance?

9. **Check financial and personal habits.**
   Credit difficulties and any indication of alcoholism or gambling are clearly negative indicators for future success. A strong interest in betting, even associated with a measure of success, is frequently associated with long-term problems in sales.

10. **Get customer opinion.**
    Has the candidate kept regular customers? How loyal are customers to the candidate personally as opposed to the product or the company? Why? Was the candidate seen as efficient, dependable, and genuinely interested in the customers?

and if the need for drug testing is reasonably related to potential job functions.[60] If a drug testing program is in place, all applicants should be required to be tested.[61]

## Selection Decision and Job Offer

When making the selection decision, the sales manager must evaluate candidates' qualifications relative to characteristics considered most important for the job. A decision must be made about whether a candidate's strength in one characteristic can compensate for a weakness in another characteristic, whether a characteristic is so important a weakness in it cannot be tolerated, or whether the candidate must meet certain minimum levels to be successful.[62] At times, the sales manager may face a dilemma, similar to that found in "An Ethical Dilemma."

AN ETHICAL DILEMMA

You are the district sales manager for an electronics manufacturing company and are responsible for all the recruitment and selection decisions in your district. The company's national sales manager has asked you to interview his son for a sales position that has just opened up in your district. Coincidentally, he mentions that a regional sales manager position (which you desire very much) is about to open up. On interviewing the national sales manager's son, along with several other candidates, you find that he is not the best qualified for the position. What do you do? Explain.

After evaluating the available candidates, the sales manager may be ready to offer a job to one or more candidates. Some candidates may be "put on hold" until the top candidates have made their decisions. Another possibility is that the sales manager may decide to extend the search and begin the recruitment and selection process all over again.

In communicating with those offered jobs, it is now appropriate for the sales manager to "sell" the prospective salesperson on joining the firm. In reality, top salespeople are hard to find, and the competition for them is intense. Therefore, a sales manager should enthusiastically pursue the candidate once the offer is extended. As always, an accurate portrayal of the job is a must.

In addition to standard enticements, such as salary, performance bonuses, company car, and fringe benefits, certain extra incentives are sometimes offered to prospective salespeople. Bonuses for relocation are one type of incentive, especially with today's sentiment for less mobile lifestyles. Another is the **market bonus** paid on hiring to salespeople having highly sought-after skills and qualifications. This one-time payment recognizes an existing imbalance in supply and demand in a given labor market. Using a market bonus could be a reasonable alternative if the supply-demand imbalance is thought to be temporary because the bonus is a one-time payment and not a permanent addition to base compensation. For instance, IBM once offered some high-tech sales reps who were in high demand as much as $50,000 to join its organization.[63]

The offer of employment should be written but can be initially extended in verbal form. Any final contingencies, such as passing a physical examination, should be detailed in the offer letter. Candidates not receiving a job offer should be notified in a prompt, courteous manner. A specific reason for not hiring a candidate need not be given. A simple statement that an individual who better suits the needs of the company has been hired is sufficient.

# LEGAL AND ETHICAL CONSIDERATIONS IN RECRUITMENT AND SELECTION

## Key Legislation

The possibility of illegal discrimination permeates the recruitment and selection process, and a basic understanding of pertinent legislation can be beneficial to the sales manager. Some of the most important legislation is summarized in Exhibit 5.8.[64] The legislative acts featured in Exhibit 5.8 are federal laws applicable to all firms engaged in interstate commerce. Companies not engaging in interstate commerce are often subject to state and local laws that are similar to these federal laws.

---

**EXHIBIT 5.8** Legislation Affecting Recruitment and Selection

| Legislative Act | Purpose |
| --- | --- |
| Fifth and Fourteenth Amendments to the U.S. Constitution | Provides equal protection standards to prevent irrational or unreasonable selection methods. |
| Equal Pay Act (1963) | Requires that men and women be paid the same amount for performing similar job duties. |
| Civil Rights Act (1964) | Prohibits discrimination based on age, race, color, religion, sex, or national origin. |
| Age Discrimination in Employment Act (1967) | Prohibits discrimination against people of ages 40 to 70. |
| Fair Employment Opportunity Act (1972) | Founded the Equal Employment Opportunity Commission to ensure compliance with the Civil Rights Act. |
| Rehabilitation Act (1973) | Requires affirmative action to hire and promote handicapped persons if the firm employs 50 or more employees and is seeking a federal contract in excess of $50,000. |
| Vietnam Veterans Readjustment Act (1974) | Requires affirmative action to hire Vietnam veterans and disabled veterans of any war. Applicable to firms holding federal contracts in excess of $10,000. |
| Americans with Disabilities Act (1990) | Prohibits discrimination against qualified disabled people in all areas of employment. Prohibits the use of employment tests, qualification standards, and selection criteria that tend to screen out individuals with disabilities unless the standard is job related or consistent with business necessity. |
| Civil Rights Act (1991) | Prohibits employers from adjusting scores of, using different cutoff scores for, or otherwise altering the results of employment-related tests on the basis of race, color, religion, sex, or national origin. |
| Amendment to Fair Credit Reporting Act (1997) | When seeking background information from a reporting service company, employers must inform job applicants or employees in writing that a report on them will be procured and must obtain their signature authorizing the move. |

## Guidelines for Sales Managers

The legislation reviewed in Exhibit 5.8 is supported by various executive orders and guidelines that make it clear that sales managers, along with other hiring officials in a firm, have legal responsibilities of grave importance in the recruitment and selection process. In step 1 of the process, planning for recruitment and selection, sales managers must take care to analyze the job to be filled in an open-minded way, attempting to overcome any personal mental biases. For example, in the 1980s, many sales organizations overcame biases against women in sales positions. These organizations are practically unanimous in reporting that women have performed as well as, and in some cases better than, their male counterparts.

Job descriptions and job qualifications should be accurate and based on a thoughtful job analysis. The planning stage may also require that the sales manager consider fair employment legislation and affirmative action requirements before setting recruitment and selection objectives.

In step 2 of the process, recruitment, the sources that serve as intermediaries in the search for prospective candidates should be informed of the firm's legal position. The firm must be careful to avoid sources that limit its hiring from protected classes.[65] It is also crucial that advertising and other communications be devoid of potentially discriminatory content. For example, companies that advertise for "young, self-motivated salesmen" may be inviting an inquiry from the Equal Employment Opportunity Commission on the basis of age and gender discrimination.

Finally, all selection tools must be related to job performance. Munson and Spivey summarize legal advice for selection by stating, "At each step in the selection process, it would be advisable to be as objective, quantitative, and consistent as possible, especially because present federal guidelines are concerned with all procedures suggesting employment discrimination.[66] Such advice should be considered, particularly when facing a situation similar to one found in "An Ethical Dilemma."

### AN ETHICAL DILEMMA

Sales manager John Brown was interviewing several candidates for a sales position with the XYZ company. After interviewing, testing, and assessing several candidates, two clearly stood out above the rest, one male and the other female. Although the male was slightly more qualified, John suspected that his male customers might enjoy the "looks" of the female and thus be more willing to give XYZ their business. What should John do? Explain.

To more fully appreciate the sensitivity necessary in these matters, consider the following list of potentially troublesome information often found on employment applications.[67]

- Age or date of birth
- Length of time at present address
- Height and/or weight
- Marital status
- Ages of children
- Occupation of spouse
- Relatives already employed by the firm
- Person to notify in case of an emergency
- Type of military discharge

These topics leave the employer open to charges of discrimination, as would a request for a photograph of the applicant, a birth certificate, or a copy of military discharge papers.

Further questions to avoid are those concerning the original name of the applicant, race or color, religion (including holidays observed), nationality or birthplace of the applicant, arrests, home ownership, bankruptcy or garnishments, disabilities, handicaps and health problems, and memberships in organizations that may suggest race, religion, color, or ancestral origin of the applicant.

## Ethical Issues

Two ethical issues of particular importance are (1) how the job to be filled is represented and (2) how interviews are conducted. **Misrepresentation** of the job does not always extend into the legal domain. For example, earnings potential may be stated in terms of what the top producer earns, not expected first-year earnings of the average salesperson. Or perhaps the opportunities for promotion are somewhat overstated but no completely false statements are used. As simple as it may sound, the best policy is a truthful policy if the sales manager wants to match the applicant to the job and avoid later problems from those recruited under false pretenses.

Some ethical issues also arise in interviewing, especially regarding the **stress interview.** This technique is designed to put job candidates under extreme, unexpected, psychological duress for the purpose of seeing how they react. A common tactic for stress interviewing in the sales field is to demand an impromptu sales presentation for a convenient item such as a ballpoint pen or an ashtray. Such requests may seem unreasonable to a professional salesperson who is accustomed to planning a presentation before delivering it. Another stress interviewing tactic is to ridicule the responses of the job candidates or to repeatedly interrupt the candidates' responses to questions before they have an adequate opportunity to provide a complete response.

Sales managers who use stress interviewing justify its use by pointing out that salespeople must be able to think on their feet and react quickly to unanticipated questions from customers. Although this is true, there would seem to be better ways of assessing a candidate's skills. The stress interview may create an unfavorable image of the company, and it may alienate some of the better candidates.[68] It appears to be a risky, and ethically questionable, approach.

## SUMMARY

1. **Explain the critical role of recruitment and selection in building and maintaining a productive salesforce**. Recruitment and selection of salespeople can be an expensive process, characterized by uncertainty and complicated by legal considerations. If the procedures are not properly conducted, a multitude of managerial problems can arise, the worst of which being that salesforce performance is suboptimal. The sales manager is the key person in the recruitment and selection process, although other managers in the hiring firm may share responsibilities for staffing the salesforce.

2. **Describe how recruitment and selection affect salesforce socialization and performance**. Socialization, the process by which salespeople adjust to their jobs, begins when the recruit is first contacted by the hiring firm. Two stages of socialization should be accomplished during recruitment and selection: achieving realism and achieving congruence. Realism means giving the recruit an accurate portrayal of the job. Congruence refers to the matching process that should occur between the needs of the organization and the capabilities of the recruit. If realism and congruence can be accomplished, future job satisfaction, involvement, commitment, and performance should be improved. These relationships are shown in a model of the socialization process in Figure 5.1.

3. **Identify the key activities in planning and executing a program for salesforce recruitment and selection**. Figure 5.2 depicts a model of the recruitment and selection

process. There are three steps in the process: planning, recruitment, and selection. *Planning* consists of conducting a job analysis, determining job qualifications, writing a job description, setting objectives, and formulating a strategy. *Recruitment* involves locating prospective job candidates from one or more sources within or outside the hiring firm. The third step, *selection*, entails an evaluation of the candidates culminating in a hiring decision. Major methods of evaluating candidates include resume and job-application analysis, interviews, tests, assessment centers, background investigations, and physical examinations.

4. **Discuss the legal and ethical considerations in salesforce recruitment and selection.** Every step of the recruitment and selection process has the potential to discriminate illegally against some job candidates. Federal laws and guidelines provide the basic antidiscriminatory framework, and state and local statutes may also be applicable. The most important legislation that applies are the Civil Rights Act and the Fair Employment Opportunity Act. Two primary ethical concerns are (1) misrepresentation of the job to be filled and (2) using stress interviews in the selection stage.

## UNDERSTANDING SALES MANAGEMENT TERMS

salesforce socialization
achieving realism
achieving congruence
job preview
planning activities
recruitment
selection
job analysis
job qualifications
job description
recruitment and selection strategy
employee referral programs
private employment agency

career fairs
professional societies
computerized matchmaking
job application form
initial interviews
intensive interviews
interviewer bias
assessment center
background investigation
market bonus
misrepresentation
stress interview

## DEVELOPING SALES MANAGEMENT KNOWLEDGE

1. What are some of the problems associated with improperly executed recruitment and selection activities?

2. To enhance salesforce socialization, recruitment and selection should ensure realism and congruence. How can this be accomplished?

3. Refer to "Sales Management in the 21st Century: Finding a Fit at Hershey Chocolate U.S.A." What are important factors for achieving congruence at Hershey?

4. Describe the relationship between conducting a job analysis, determining job qualifications, and completing a written job description.

5. Refer to "Sales Management in the 21st Century: Key Job Qualifications at Hershey Chocolate U.S.A." What is the relationship between job qualifications and a company's personal selling approach?

6. What are the advantages of using employee referral programs to recruit salespeople? Can you identify some disadvantages?

7. How can private employment agencies assist in the recruitment and selection of salespeople? Who pays the fee charged by such agencies, the hiring company or the job candidate?

8. What can be learned about a job candidate from analyzing a job application that cannot be learned from the candidate's resume?

9. Summarize the primary legislation designed to prohibit illegal discrimination in the recruitment and selection process.

10. What is stress interviewing? How do some sales managers justify using stress interviews?

## BUILDING SALES MANAGEMENT SKILLS

1. Find three advertisements for sales positions (one from a newspaper, one from a trade magazine, and one from the Internet). After examining each ad, list the job qualifications for the position being advertised. Then, develop a job description based on the ad's contents. Finally, using Exhibit 5.4 as a guide, provide your suggestions for improving each ad.

2. Find job qualifications and a position description for a sales position at a company of your choice. Design a series of questions that you could use as a guide to interview a candidate for this position. Now, find a classmate who also has found job qualifications and a position description for a sales position, and swap information. Using your interview guide, take turns interviewing each other. (The information you swapped with your classmate serves as a guide for the interviewee.) Record your interview on audiotape or videotape. Finally, listen to or view your tape and write a critique of your interview, explaining what went well and what did not.

3. The Web is filled with many sites that could be beneficial in the recruitment and selection process. One site that has been designed to make getting around in cyberspace easier for human resource development professionals is WorkIndex (**http://www.workindex.com**). Access this site, then go to the "keyword search" line and type in "recruitment." This will provide you with several sites that could be useful in the recruitment and selection process. Explore some of these sites, and then choose three that you believe would be helpful to a sales manager involved in recruitment and selection. First, provide each site address. Second, provide a description of each site. Finally, explain how each site or the information it contains could be useful in the recruitment and selection process.

4. Due to the high costs associated with turnover, it is critical that companies do a good job in the recruitment and selection process. The HR Chally Group has devised a method to help estimate the costs of turnover. Access the Chally Group's turnover cost calculator at **http://www.chally.com/turnover_cost_calculator.htm.** Given the following information, calculate the annual turnover cost for the salesforce:

- The company employs 100 salespeople.
- Annual turnover is 10 percent.
- Average annual compensation is $50,000.
- Average tax and benefit cost as a percent of salary is $12,500.
- Average number of candidates interviewed per opening is 10.
- Average number of candidates assessed per opening is three.

5. The Claron Corporation's main competitor, Brighton Company, just filed for bankruptcy, presenting a potential opportunity for an increase in customers and revenue at Claron. As a result, several of Brighton's salespeople have contacted George Wills, Claron's vice president of sales, inquiring about employment with Claron. Currently Wills has no openings on his 10-person salesforce. However, he does not want to dismiss the Brighton reps, some of whom are top performers that might be able to enhance Brighton's revenue stream that has been falling for the past year.

After speaking to his CEO about adding a position to his salesforce, Wills was given permission to do so as long as the new salesperson made more of his salary in commissions than base salary. Wills, however, would like to add three of Brighton's salespeople. Currently there are four salespeople on Wills' staff that outperform the

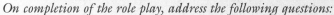

other six, who are approximately equal in talent. Yet, Wills is hard pressed to identify a clear laggard whom he would dismiss in favor of the competition's salespeople. Wills is also concerned that he could disrupt the team chemistry he has worked hard to build the past two years by firing some of his current salespeople and hiring those from Brighton. However, he does not know if he can pass up this opportunity to upgrade his salesforce.

How should Wills approach this dilemma? Should he hire the new reps and deal with the ramifications of letting two of his people go, or can he afford to pass on the new reps altogether?[69]

6. This exercise consists of a series of different role plays involving two characters, a sales manager and a candidate seeking a sales position. Find another classmate to assume one of the roles. Role play the following situations:

   1. The sales manager misrepresents the job in an interview.
   2. The sales manager employs a stress interview.
   3. The sales manager opens him/herself up to charges of discrimination during an Interview.

**ROLE PLAY**

*On completion of the role play, address the following questions:*
   1. What are the dangers of misrepresenting the position during an interview?
   2. What are the pros and cons of using a stress interview?
   3. How can you avoid possible discrimination charges as a result of interviewing?

7. **Situation:**    Read the Ethical Dilemma on page 149.

   **Characters:**   District sales manager; National sales manager

   **Scene:**       *Location*—National sales manager's office. *Action*—Having completed the interview process, the district sales manager explains to the national sales manager who will be hired and why.

**ROLE PLAY**

# MAKING SALES MANAGEMENT DECISIONS

## Case 5.1: Sweet-Treats, Inc.

### Background

Sweet-Treats, Inc., one of the leading manufacturers and marketers of chocolate and cocoa products, has several plants in the United States. Its products can be divided into two major categories: confectionery products, which include several brands of candy bars and assorted candy treats, and grocery products, such as cocoa, syrup, and baking chips. In the United States, Sweet-Treats' products are distributed by a network of strategically located warehouses, with volume customers receiving direct shipment from the manufacturing plants. The method of shipment and warehousing is determined by customer location and quantity ordered.

Sweet-Treats uses a field sales organization to sell products to retailers and wholesalers nationwide. Its overriding goals are to distribute a high-quality product and to provide optimum consumer value. To ensure that these goals are met, the company hires salespeople who possess outstanding planning and organizing skills, have the ability to lead, are persuasive, show initiative, and possess strong communication skills, including the ability to write, speak, and listen.

At Sweet-Treats, salespeople represent the company and carry its image. A crucial responsibility, this calls for salespeople to be consummate professionals. Major responsibilities of the salesperson include selling and maintaining distribution of all products, ensuring the salability of all Sweet-Treat items in an assigned territory, implementing promotional programs, introducing new items, and presenting proper merchandising techniques to both headquarter and retail accounts. In addition, salespeople must act as "sales consultants" to customers. This involves maintaining good customer rapport while developing accounts in an assigned territory. Salespeople work with their sales managers and team members to achieve specific sales and merchandising objectives.

### Current Situation

Sweet-Treats' Kansas City district sales manager, Rob Gum, recently lost one of his top-performing salespeople, Arlene Oellermann, who left for a sudden career change. Although other salespeople in his district are covering Arlene's accounts, Rob fears that leaving Arlene's position unfilled for long will create stress for these salespeople and may affect the quality of service they provide to their accounts as well as to Arlene's.

Rob is presently undergoing an intensive search to locate Arlene's replacement. He placed a classified ad in the local newspaper, the *Kansas City Star*. In addition, he contacted the career placement offices of local colleges and universities to see whether they had any leads on potential candidates. Through these efforts, Rob received several resumes. After examining the resumes, Rob decided to interview two candidates. What follows are excerpts from those interviews:

Excerpts from an interview with Christine Pirrone who is currently a sales rep with an industrial products company in the Kansas City area and who has three years of sales experience.

*Rob:* Why did you get into sales?
*Christine:* I chose sales as a career for several reasons. First, I like dealing with other people and helping them to solve their problems. I view sales as a way to accomplish this. Second, sales provides me with a certain level of independence. I am self-motivated so I like being able to get things accomplished without being closely supervised. Third, there is decent money to be made in sales. I might as well get my share of the pie.
*Rob:* In general, how do you get things accomplished?
*Christine:* Simple, planning. I set certain goals for each day. Then I plan how I will achieve them. Planning helps me to stay organized, and I feel that by being organized I am able to accomplish many things.
*Rob:* This position requires some degree of travel. How do you feel about that?
*Christine:* Currently I travel quite extensively. I enjoy the travel, so it would not bother me.
*Rob:* Have you ever organized a group?
*Christine:* Yes. When I was a junior in college I started a new organization on campus, the Entrepreneurship Club. I was the organization's president for two years. When I graduated we had more than 40 members. I was very proud! I am currently a member of several civic groups, although I did not organize any of these.

Excerpts from an interview with Joe Stein who is from Minnesota, but just received his B.S.B.A. from a local university with a 3.8 (4.0 scale) G.P.A. His major was marketing.

*Rob:* Why do you want a career in sales?
*Joe:* I think sales is a very flexible job. You basically manage your own time, and I like the idea of this. Also, it is more exciting than sitting

behind a desk. You get to meet and interact with people. Also, I understand that there is a fair amount of money to be made in sales.

*Rob:* In general, how do you get things accomplished?

*Joe:* I've found that the best way to get things done is to jump right in and tackle them. Take the bull by the horns, so to speak. Procrastinating only makes things worse.

*Rob:* This position requires some degree of travel. How do you feel about that?

*Joe:* I traveled a lot with the track team in college. I also travel back to Minnesota quite frequently to visit family and friends. I don't think the travel will bother me.

*Rob:* Have you ever organized a group?

*Joe:* In college, we worked in several groups. Sometimes I was the group leader, but I always tried to carry my load. I was also a member of the American Marketing Association.

Rob decided that additional searching at this point might not prove worthwhile. With his salespeople getting restless, he decided he would make a decision between Christine and Joe and make one an offer.

## Questions

1. Based on the information you have about Christine and Joe, how do they rate relative to Sweet-Treats' job qualifications?
2. Who should Rob hire and why? Explain.
3. How could Rob improve his recruiting and selecting process? Explain.
4. What key concepts of salesforce socialization are related to this situation? Explain.

**ROLE PLAY**

| | |
|---|---|
| **Situation:** | Read Case 5.1. |
| **Characters:** | Rob Gum, sales manager; Christine Pirrone, sales candidate; Joe Stein, sales candidate; Candice Cane, regional sales manager |
| **Scene 1:** | *Location*—Rob's office. *Action*—Rob interviews Christine. |
| **Scene 2:** | *Location*—Rob's office. *Action*—Rob interviews Joe. |
| **Scene 3:** | *Location*—Local restaurant over lunch. *Action*—Rob discusses the merits and potential fit of each candidate with Candice. |
| **Scene 4:** | *Location*—Rob's office. *Action*—Rob makes a job offer via a phone call to either Christine or Joe. |

## Case 5.2: Titan Industries

### Background

Titan Industries manufactures and markets industrial equipment throughout the United States. In 2004, Titan did more than $2 billion in sales and appeared to be in an upward growth trend. The company has grown considerably since its inception in 1964. Founder and CEO Carman Pulte is proud of the progress the company has achieved over the years, despite considerable aggressive competition. He attributes much of Titan's success to his management team, most of whom have been with him since the company's founding.

David Winston had been vice president of sales and marketing at Titan since 1968. Two months ago, he retired and was replaced by Duane Blankenship. Blankenship had been in product design and engineering at Titan since 1979. Well-educated, articulate, and likable, Blankenship was believed to be the best candidate for the position.

Blankenship, a very methodical individual, set as his first task an assessment of the marketing program. One of the main things concerning him was the composition of the salesforce. In particular, he was concerned about two items. First, the salesforce was aging, with the average age being 51. Several salespeople were nearing retirement. Only a small percentage were in their twenties or thirties. Second, he noticed that the salesforce did not include any minorities or women. Blankenship scheduled a meeting to discuss these issues with Titan's national sales manager, Tommy Angotti.

Angotti loves his job. He has been with Titan for nearly 25 years. He began as a salesperson and worked his way up to national sales manager. Surprisingly, many of his salespeople have been with the company for 20 years or more. Angotti takes pride in the accomplishments of his salesforce. He believes they have been instrumental in Titan's growth over the years.

### Current Situation

At their scheduled meeting, Blankenship explained to Angotti his ideas concerning the composition of the salesforce. The following are excerpts from their meeting:

*Angotti:* I realize we will have several salespeople soon retiring, but could you explain why it is necessary to hire women and minorities to replace these individuals?

*Blankenship:* Many of the companies we sell equipment to are now being closely monitored and regulated by federal and state governments. Several companies in our industry have recently come under attack from the Equal Employment Opportunity Commission. The commission is putting pressure on these companies to hire women and minorities. It is only a matter of time before they take aim at us. We need to get women and minorities into the salesforce so that they can eventually work their way up into management positions.

*Angotti:* I can't imagine a woman going into the field trying to sell a large piece of industrial equipment. How seriously do you think a woman will be taken in this business? Not very, I can assure you. Our customers want to speak to someone who really understands how this equipment operates.

*Blankenship:* Women can learn to sell our equipment. Just because they may not operate it doesn't mean they can't understand how it works. As a matter of fact, a few months ago a woman was involved in selling us a piece of manufacturing equipment for our operations. She did an outstanding job.

*Angotti:* Maybe so. However, when we hire a replacement, we try to find the best person for the job. As a result, I believe we currently have some of the best salespeople in the business.

*Blankenship:* Unfortunately, that person always seems to be a white male. There are plenty of intelligent and motivated women and minorities graduating from business schools today who are capable of performing the job. Regardless of governmental threats, it is still the right thing to do, and the profitable one. I would like to see us take a leadership role in this area in our industry and begin to make an effort to hire women and minorities.

Angotti was not convinced. He was very concerned that minorities, and women in particular, would not be positively accepted by buyers. The industrial equipment business is largely male dominated. This, in turn, could have a negative impact on sales. Moreover, given that much of his salesforce was composed of "old-timers," he was concerned about how hiring these groups might affect salesforce morale.

Turnover in the salesforce was relatively low. Thus, specific hiring procedures were not well developed. Angotti decided he would recruit women and minorities to appease Blankenship but would develop an entrance test that would be difficult for women and minorities to pass. This way he could actively recruit women and minorities but tell Blankenship they did not qualify because they did not pass the entrance test. Angotti was only a few years from retirement and was unwilling to change his current practices at this juncture, particularly in light of the success his salesforce had experienced over the years.

## Questions

1. Should Blankenship be concerned about the present composition of the salesforce? Explain.
2. How do you evaluate Angotti's method for dealing with the salesforce composition issue?
3. What steps could be taken to effectively bring about a salesforce comprised of more women and minorities?

**ROLE PLAY**

| | |
|---|---|
| **Situation:** | Read Case 5.2. |
| **Characters:** | Duane Blankenship, vice president of sales and marketing; Tommy Angotti, national sales manager |
| **Scene 1:** | *Location*—Blankenship's office. *Action*—Role play the interview between Angotti and Blankenship. |
| **Scene 2:** | *Location*—Angotti's office. *Action*—Blankenship gets a copy of the selection test, figures out what Angotti is up to, and decides to confront him. |

## SALES TRAINING AT UPS: FROM SELLING RATES TO SELLING SOLUTIONS

As UPS shifted its business model, the need arose to alter its sales strategy as well, from a transaction-based to a solutions-based approach. No longer would salespeople simply be taking orders in the shipping department. The new focus required them to call on corporate-level executives. In part, this entailed calling on customer service managers to learn how they interact with their customers and how they answer customer queries. It also called for salespeople to discuss the financial impact of transportation decisions with financial executives. This strategic change required new skills, a new vocabulary, and a new mind-set.

To meet these needs, UPS created a special salesforce. This salesforce worked in teams alongside the traditional salesforce to offer solutions to high-opportunity accounts. Having found success with the solutions-based sales approach, UPS decided to train the entire salesforce in this new approach. In doing so, they created a sales training program called e-Commerce University.

The training program is designed to accomplish three objectives: 1) provide salespeople with the competencies necessary to have a conversational comfort level with varied technology offerings; 2) provide an understanding of what the technology can do for customers; and 3) integrate the technological understanding into UPS' sales methodology and strategy.

Every week UPS sends 40 to 50 people to its corporate office in Atlanta to attend e-Commerce University. This costs more than bringing the program to its salespeople, but UPS believes it provides salespeople with a sense that the company values them and engenders their loyalty to the company, as well as creates a sense of camaraderie. Divided into two groups, students listen to lectures and presentations, participate in discussions and roundtables, work in teams, and role play for nine to ten hours each day. For instance, during the online tools course students learn XML and HTML. Students participate in role plays to exercise their knowledge and vocabulary in the new technology employed by UPS, such as their flat-file billing system (storing bills on a hard drive). Students also outline how they will apply what they learn to one of their accounts and then hold a discussion about this with classmates at the end of the week.

On completing the training, students fill out surveys assessing the training's relevance and effectiveness. Six weeks later, students are asked to complete a Web-based survey asking qualitative and quantitative questions about the usefulness of the training with regard to customer acquisition and retention. Responses to surveys thus far indicate that the training does have an impact on students' sales process. According to Laura Bostic, an e-Commerce University graduate, "I just feel more empowered. When you can start talking the language with customers and talk about process improvement, it puts UPS in a different light. We're not just salespeople—we've become consultants, supply-chain solution consultants." The training program has been a success and is credited for increasing sales performance by up to 7 percent.

### Objectives

After completing this module, you should be able to

1. Understand the role of sales training in salesforce socialization.

2. Explain the importance of sales training and the sales manager's role in sales training.

3. Describe the sales training process as a series of six interrelated steps.

4. Discuss six methods for assessing sales training needs and identify typical sales training needs.

5. Name some typical objectives of sales training programs, and explain how setting objectives for sales training is beneficial to sales managers.

6. Identify the key issues in evaluating sales training alternatives.

7. Identify key ethical and legal issues in sales training.

**Source:** Heather Johnson, "Postmarked for Growth," *Training* 40 (September 2003): 20–22; John Beystehner, "Playing a Brand New Game," *Sales & Marketing Management* 155 (November 2003): 72. All rights in the article are owned by United Parcel Service of America, Inc. © 2003. All rights reserved.

As the opening vignette illustrates, companies often believe that sales training is necessary to successfully implement their strategy. UPS realizes the important role its salespeople play in the success of the company and is willing to invest considerable time and money in developing them. Training can be used to achieve a number of objectives and fulfill various needs. As at e-Commerce University, various methods may be used to accomplish sales training. Another important point illustrated in the vignette is that training must be evaluated to ensure its effectiveness.

Today's salespeople must be prepared to meet the demands of value-conscious customers. Salespeople must do their part by providing solutions to problems and meeting service requirements expected to satisfy customer needs. Proper training can prepare salespeople to meet these challenges.

In this module several training issues and methods are discussed. First, the role of sales training in salesforce socialization is examined. Then the importance of sales training is considered and management of the sales training process is discussed.

## ROLE OF SALES TRAINING IN SALESFORCE SOCIALIZATION

Recall from Module 5 that salesforce *socialization* refers to the process by which salespeople acquire the knowledge, skills, and values essential to perform their jobs. Training plays a key role in this process. Newly hired salespeople usually receive a company orientation designed to familiarize them with company history, policies, facilities, procedures, and key people with whom salespeople interact. Some firms go well beyond a perfunctory company orientation in an effort to enhance salesforce socialization. By referring to Figure 5.1 in Module 5, you can see how sales training can affect salesforce socialization. During initial sales training, it is hoped that each salesforce member will experience a positive **initiation to task**—the degree to which a sales trainee feels competent and accepted as a working partner—and satisfactory **role definition**—an understanding of what tasks are to be performed, what the priorities of the tasks are, and how time should be allocated among the tasks.[1]

The need for socialization as part of the training process is supported by expected indirect linkages between socialization and beneficial job outcomes. As suggested in Figure 5.1, trainees who have been properly recruited and trained tend to be more confident on the job and have fewer problems with job conflicts, leading to higher job satisfaction, involvement, commitment, and performance.

The positive relationships between salespeople's job-related attitudes and perceptions and their commitment to their companies have been supported in empirical studies. For example, a study of 102 salespeople in the food industry found that "among approaches within a company's control, programs aimed at minimizing new salespeople's role ambiguity and improving their satisfaction are most likely to be most effective in building commitment to the company."[2] Another study of 120 manufacturers' salespeople found a positive relationship between job satisfaction and salespeople's commitment to the organization.[3] In addition, a study of 301 industrial salespeople found that when salespeople believe the company is taking certain actions to support the salesforce and reduce the difficulties associated with a sales position, they are more committed to and satisfied with the job.[4] These studies reinforce the importance of sales managers taking an active role in socializing their salespeople to maximize overall salesforce productivity.

Newly hired salespeople should be extremely interested in learning about their jobs, peers, and supervisors. A basic orientation may be insufficient to provide all the information they desire, so more extensive socialization may be indicated. At Federated Insurance, trainees participate in a two-week seminar that introduces them to the company's products, the corporate mission, the Federated business plan, functions and departments within the company, and many of the support people with whom they will work.[5]

The need for salesforce socialization is especially likely to extend past the initial training period. This is particularly true if salesforce members have limited personal contact with peers, managers, and other company personnel.

## SALES TRAINING AS A CRUCIAL INVESTMENT

A comprehensive review of sales management research concludes that whom one recruits is important but it is probably not as important in determining salesforce performance as what sales managers do with the recruits—and to the recruits—after they have been hired.[6]

The importance of sales training in achieving the highest levels of sales performance is shown in *Sales & Marketing Management*'s annual survey of the best salesforces in the United States. The accounts of sales successes for the top salesforces often reveal that the winning salesforces had to adapt to changes in marketing and sales strategies. This obviously requires some degree of salesforce training or retraining. A survey of sales executives finds that 80 percent of respondents claim that training is a key aspect of their business.[7] Some research, in fact, indicates a positive relationship between training expenditures and a firm's share price.[8] One toothbrush manufacturer, for example, credits sales training conducted by Ansir International for a $30-million increase in sales in the first two years after implementing the training.[9] Deluxe Corporation, a financial and check printing company, credits its sales training with improving its client retention rate from 85 percent to 95 percent in less than two years.[10]

Most organizations need sales training of some type, perhaps because of inadequacies of current training programs and/or because new salespeople have joined the organization. Thus, an ongoing need exists to conduct sales training to improve salesforce performance. It should be stressed that the need for sales training is continual, if for no other reason than that the sales environment is constantly changing.

Companies view training as an important means for protecting their investments in their salesforces.[11] U.S. companies spend approximately $7.8 billion annually to provide salespeople with training and devote several hours per year to the average salesperson.[12] Average training costs per salesperson per year can run from over $3,400 to more than $9,000 depending on the industry, company size, and experience of the salesperson.[13] As research shows, this training generally pays off in terms of improvement in salesforce productivity.[14] Exhibit 6.1[15] shows the time invested in sales training as related to its value to the organization.

---

**Investment in Sales Training     EXHIBIT 6.1**

**Sales training received each year:**

| | |
|---|---|
| Less than 8 hours | 18.3%* |
| 1–5 days a year | 46.8% |
| 6–10 days a year | 19.5% |
| 11–15 days a year | 7.9% |
| More than 15 days a year | 7.5% |

**Sales training received by new employees:**

| | |
|---|---|
| Less than 8 hours | 5.9% |
| 1–5 days a year | 31.0% |
| 6–10 days a year | 18.5% |
| 11–15 days a year | 14.3% |
| More than 15 days a year | 30.3% |

**Value of training to the organization:**

| | |
|---|---|
| Extremely valuable | 29.5% |
| Very valuable | 47.0% |
| Somewhat valuable | 18.3% |
| Not very valuable | 4.8% |
| Not valuable at all | 0.4% |

* Percent of respondents indicating each choice.

One aspect of the investment in sales training is the amount of time required of the sales manager. Usually, sales managers are involved not only in the "big picture" of planning but also in the time-consuming details of implementing training, such as the following:[16]

- Arranging for salespeople to work with key personnel in various departments in the firm to familiarize them with the functions of those departments
- Selecting literature, sales aids, software, and materials for study
- Enrolling salespeople in professional workshops or training programs
- Accompanying salespeople in the field to critique their sales behavior and reinforce other training
- Conducting periodic training meetings and professional training conferences

Sales training is indeed expensive, and sales managers should take special care to see that time and money are wisely spent. With these thoughts in mind, let's examine a model for the judicious analysis, planning, and implementation of a sales training program.

## MANAGING THE SALES TRAINING PROCESS

The sales training process is depicted as six interrelated steps in Figure 6.1[17]: assess training needs, set training objectives, evaluate training alternatives, design the sales training program, perform sales training, and conduct follow-up and evaluation.

### Assess Training Needs

The purpose of sales training **needs assessment** is to compare the specific performance-related skills, attitudes, perceptions, and behaviors required for salesforce success with the state of readiness of the salesforce. Such an assessment usually reveals a need for changing or reinforcing one or more determinants of salesforce performance.

All too often, the need for sales training becomes apparent only after a decline in salesforce performance is revealed by decreasing sales volume, rising expenses, or perhaps low morale. Sales training for correcting such problems is sometimes necessary, but the preferred role of sales training is to prevent problems and improve salesforce productivity on a proactive, not reactive, basis.

Needs assessment requires that sales managers consider the training appropriate for both *sales trainees* and regular salespeople. A sales trainee is an entry-level salesperson who is learning the company's products, services, and policies in preparation for a regular sales assignment. For example, entry-level salespeople may need basic training in

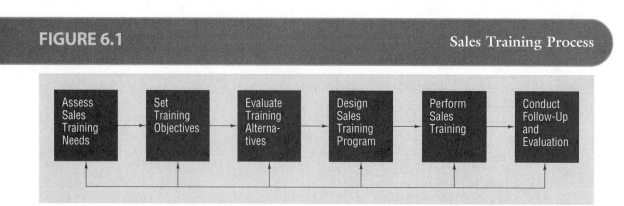

**FIGURE 6.1** Sales Training Process

Assess Sales Training Needs → Set Training Objectives → Evaluate Training Alternatives → Design Sales Training Program → Perform Sales Training → Conduct Follow-Up and Evaluation

The sales training process is performed in six steps, beginning with an assessment of training needs. The process is continual, with the follow-up and evaluation step providing feedback that may alter the other steps in future sales training activities.

sales techniques, whereas experienced salespeople could benefit from training in advanced sales techniques. In addition, the training needs of selling teams must be considered.

## Methods of Needs Assessment

Proactive approaches to determining sales training needs include a salesforce audit, performance testing, observation, a salesforce survey, a customer survey, and a job analysis. Needs assessment can be conducted in-house or by companies such as Wilson Learning Corporation (http://www.wilsonlearning.com).

### Salesforce Audit

A **salesforce audit** is "a systematic, diagnostic, prescriptive tool which can be employed on a periodic basis to identify and address sales department problems and to prevent or reduce the impact of future problems."[18] The salesforce audit (discussed fully in Module 9) includes an appraisal of all salesforce activities and the environment in which the salesforce operates. In the sales training area, the audit examines such questions as these:

- Is the training program adequate in light of objectives and resources?
- Does the training program need revision?
- Is an ongoing training program available for senior salespeople?
- Does the training program positively contribute to the socialization of sales trainees?

To be effective, a salesforce audit should be conducted annually. More frequent audits may be warranted in some situations, but the comprehensive nature of an audit requires a considerable time and money investment. As a result, other periodic assessments of sales training are suggested.

### Performance Testing

Some firms use **performance testing** to help determine training needs. This method specifies the evaluation of particular tasks or skills of the salesforce. For example, salespeople may be given periodic examinations on product knowledge to check retention rates and uncover areas for retraining. Salespeople may be asked to exhibit particular sales techniques, such as demonstrating the product or using the telephone to set up sales appointments while the sales trainer evaluates their performance. Sales managers may even want to administer a recently developed measure of selling skills; this new measure assesses salespeople's interpersonal, salesmanship, and technical skills.[19]

### Observation

First-level sales managers spend a considerable amount of time in the field working with salespeople. They also may have direct responsibility for some accounts, acting as a salesperson or as a member of a sales team. Through these field selling activities, sales managers often **observe** the need for particular sales training. In some instances, the training need is addressed instantaneously by critiquing the salesperson's performance after the sales call has been completed. In other situations, frequent observation of particularly deficient or outstanding sales behavior may suggest future training topics.

### Salesforce Survey

The salesforce may be surveyed in an attempt to isolate sales training needs. The **salesforce survey** may be completed as an independent activity or combined with other sales management activities such as field visits or even included as part of the routine salesforce reporting procedures. The weekly reports submitted by many salespeople to their sales managers often have sections dealing with problems to be solved and areas in which managerial assistance is requested. For example, a faltering, new product introduction may signal the need for more product training, additional sales technique sharpening, or perhaps training needs specific to an individual salesperson. Canon USA, for example, identifies the best practices of its salespeople to determine necessary proficiencies around which training can be designed.[20]

By surveying the salesforce, the task of assessing training needs may become more complex than if sales management alone determines training needs. To ignore the salesforce in this step of the training process, however, could be a serious sin of omission. For example, when implementing a CRM strategy, Storage Tek, a network computing storage company, found resistance from its salesforce. It used phone interviews to survey the salesforce to determine everyone's computer capability and efficiency to assess where deficiencies existed. Storage Tek then enlisted the help of a training company to design and deliver a program to fit its salespeople's needs.[21] If sales managers and their salespeople should disagree on training needs, it is far better to discover this disagreement and resolve it before designing and delivering specific sales training programs.

### Customer Survey

Intended to define customer expectations, a **customer survey** helps determine how competitive the salesforce is compared with other salesforces in the industry. If personal selling is prominent in the firm's marketing strategy, some sort of customer survey to help determine sales training needs is highly recommended. For example, upon surveying its customers, Paxar, a supplier of labels to retailers and apparel manufacturers, learned that its salespeople were miscommunicating with customers and were failing to understand their market needs.[22] Online services such as QuestionPro.com (http://questionpro.com) make it easy to design, deliver, and analyze Web-based customer surveys.[23] Sometimes information gathered from a customer survey may have ethical implications as seen in "An Ethical Dilemma."

---

AN ETHICAL DILEMMA

Your salespeople have been reaching or exceeding their sales goals for the year, and your region is on pace to set a new company sales record, putting you in line for a big bonus. When conducting a recent customer survey to use as input for developing a training program, you discover that some customers are upset about promises salespeople are making but not fulfilling. Is this cause for alarm? What should you do and when?

---

### Job Analysis

The **job analysis**, defined in Module 5, is an investigation of the task, duties, and responsibilities of the sales job. In a well-run sales organization, a job analysis will be part of the recruitment and selection process and then will continue to be used in sales training and other managerial functions. For instance, NBC bases its hiring and training goals for sales teams on a competency model it developed that describes characteristics of its ideal salespeople in 12 areas, including team orientation and communication skills.[24] Because the job analysis defines expected behavior for salespeople, it is a logical tool to be used in assessing training needs. Because sales jobs may vary within the same salesforce, job analyses may also help in determining individualized sales training needs or the needs of different groups of salespeople.

## Typical Sales Training Needs

As the preceding discussion implies, the need for sales training varies over time and across organizations. However, the need for salesforce training on certain topics is widespread. A discussion of some of the more popular sales training topics follows.

### Sales Techniques

There is a universal, ongoing need for training on "how to sell." Research has indicated that salespeople sometimes sell despite themselves; that is, many salespeople do not competently execute fundamental **sales techniques**.[25] Common mistakes identified in this research include the following:

- Ineffective listening and questioning
- Failure to build rapport and trust
- Poor job of prospecting for new accounts
- Lack of preplanning of sales calls
- Reluctance to make cold calls (without an appointment)
- Lack of sales strategies for different accounts
- Failure to match call frequency with account potential
- Spending too much time with old customers
- Overcontrolling the sales call
- Failure to respond to customers' needs with related benefits
- Giving benefits before clarifying customers' needs
- Ineffective handling of negative attitudes
- Failure to effectively confirm the sale

This rather lengthy list of common shortcomings is remarkable in that proper training could erase these problems entirely. In fact, most formal sales training programs spend considerable time on sales techniques. One study of sales executives found that nearly 79 percent indicate that employees receive training in sales skills.[26]

As mentioned previously, the basic nature of sales techniques training is changing, and more emphasis is being placed on developing trusting, enduring relationships with customers. Salespeople are receiving more training on listening and questioning skills so that they may be more effective in learning the customer's needs. Limited research supports the idea that effective listening skills are positively associated with sales performance and work satisfaction.[27] Furthermore, high-pressure sales techniques are declining in popularity and are being replaced with sales techniques based on need satisfaction, problem solving, and partnership forming with the customer's best interests as the focus.[28] Companies such as Motorola and Owens Corning teach their salespeople how to provide solutions to customer problems to facilitate the development of lasting relationships with customers.[29] A study of more than 1,000 salespeople, customers, support staff, and sales managers found that today's salesperson must learn to perform like a "mini-CEO," focusing on issues such as the customer's strategic objectives.[30] Exhibit 6.2[31] points out seven competencies that this research suggests today's successful salesperson must master along with a method for assessing these competencies. To learn how ADP trains its salespeople to build relationships, see "Sales Management in the 21st Century: Training for Relationship Building at ADP."

---

### Competencies of Successful Salespeople    EXHIBIT 6.2

Below each competency are questions that can be used to assess it. Ask salespeople to respond to each question using the following scale to indicate how often they use each behavior: 1—never, or not at all; 2—seldom or to a small extent; 3—sometimes or to a moderate extent; 4—usually or to a great extent; 5—almost always. When finished, calculate the total score for each competency by adding the responses to each question for a particular competency and then adding each competency score together to get a total score. The average score is 63. A score above average indicates the salesperson is using the competencies better than the typical business-to-business salesperson, whereas a score below average may signal a need for improvement.

**Competency 1**
**Aligning customer/supplier strategic objectives** by identifying new opportunities and applications that add value to the customer organization and enhance the value of the relationship with my organization.
  1. I gather information to understand customers' business strategies and view of market opportunities.
  2. I stay up-to-date with new developments and innovations in customers' markets.
  3. I keep current with emerging trends and initiatives of customers' competitors.

*(continued)*

**EXHIBIT 6.2    Competencies of Successful Salespeople (*Continued*)**

**Competency 2**
**Listening beyond product needs** by identifying business process improvement potential and opportunities to add value to my organization and our customers.
  4. I keep the customer regularly updated with information and changes that might be important.
  5. I suggest ways I can bring added value to our customers.
  6. I help customers think differently about their future needs.

**Competency 3**
**Understanding the financial impact of decisions** on the customer's organization and on my organization by quantifying and communicating the value of the relationship.
  7. I look actively for ways to contribute to the customer's profitability.
  8. I search actively for more cost-effective ways to serve customers.
  9. I focus on the financial consequences of approaches to meeting customer needs.

**Competency 4**
**Orchestrating organizational resources** by identifying key contributors; communicating relevant information; and building collaborative, customer-focused relationships.
  10. I communicate customer needs, suggestions, and concerns to appropriate resources in my organization.
  11. I work cooperatively with people in other parts of the customer organization who can be useful sources of ongoing information, resources, and support.
  12. I ensure that my product, sales, and service units work together to deliver value.

**Competency 5**
**Consultative problem solving** to create new solutions, customized products and services, and paradigm changes while being willing and able to work outside the norm when necessary.
  13. I anticipate possible problems and invite discussion about how they can be overcome.
  14. I determine the cause of a problem and identify constraints before recommending a solution.
  15. I propose innovative solutions that go beyond the immediate application of the product or service.

**Competency 6**
**Establishing a vision of a committed customer/supplier relationship** by identifying value-adding products, processes, and services.
  16. I create a relationship that supports the goals and values of both organizations.
  17. I develop relationships that recognize the needs of all contributing functions in both organizations.
  18. I communicate objectives for the relationship that are achievable and challenge the creativity of both organizations.

**Competency 7**
**Engaging in self-appraisal and continuous learning** by securing feedback from customers, colleagues, and managers.
  19. I demonstrate an understanding of what is working, what is not working, and how I can do things differently.
  20. I stay up-to-date in my field of expertise.
  21. I ask for and welcome feedback to assess my performance and the degree to which I am meeting expectations.

**Source:** Dr. Bernard L. Rosenbaum, "Do You Have the Skills for 21st Century Selling? Rate Yourself With This Exercise" *American Salesman* 45 (July 2000): 24–30. Reprinted by kind permission of the author.

### Product Knowledge

Salespeople must have thorough **product knowledge**, including its benefits, applications, competitive strengths, and limitations. Product knowledge may need updating in the event of new product development, product modification, product deletions, or the development of new applications for the product.

### Training for Relationship Building at ADP

Jason Karem, sales manager at ADP, comments on training for relationship building:

*To be successful in any sales job you have to work hard, be able to build rapport with everyone you talk to, and follow through on every expectation you set. But there is one key ingredient that separates the great salespeople from the good ones: The ability to build relationships. Building relationships allows you to work smarter by allowing your territory to work for you all the time—even while you are on vacation. Therefore, training on how to build business partnerships with individuals and influence centers in one's territory is key with every salesperson at ADP. Some of the specifics we focus on are how to truly understand the business of the person with whom we are trying to build a relationship. For instance, for salespeople to be successful at ADP, they must understand the business of some of our critical customers, CPAs, and bankers. Therefore, we constantly train associates about CPA's and banker's needs, what they actually do on a daily basis, and how we can help them fulfill their business goals. This not only builds trust with our partners, but also builds credibility with them for future sales opportunities. Periodically we will bring CPAs or bankers into one of our meetings to determine first hand their expectations. We ask them how we can better serve them and their firm. If an ADP sales associate can build solid, credible relationships with key business partners, their sales only will go one way—up.*

Generally speaking, product knowledge is one of the most commonly covered topics in sales training programs. As expected, the more complex the product or service, the higher the likelihood that detailed knowledge about the offering will be stressed in the training program.

Although it is an essential requirement, adequate product knowledge will not necessarily lead to sales success. Studies have shown that product knowledge levels of high-performing salespeople are not significantly different from those of moderate performers.[32] Having product knowledge is not enough—the salesperson must know the customer and have the necessary sales skills to apply the knowledge of the product to the customer's situation.

### Customer Knowledge

Sales training may include information relating to customers' needs, buying motives, buying procedures, and personalities (i.e., **customer knowledge**). As explained in the opening vignette, salespeople at UPS had to learn how to communicate with executives and better understand their needs. Faced with situational and individual differences among customers, some firms use classification methods to categorize buyers according to personality and the buying situation. An example of different types of buyers and suggested sales training topics is presented in Exhibit 6.3.[33]

As minority populations increase and companies expand their global selling efforts, training programs must address multicultural differences and business protocol in subcultures and foreign countries. For instance, female Hispanic business owners generally take longer to make decisions.[34] Such information can be useful in determining the selling cycle. Gift-giving, for example, is a sensitive area internationally because well-intentioned expressions of goodwill can backfire and instead become personal insults to a prospective customer. It is important that salespeople are trained in intercultural communication to improve their chances of developing international buyer–seller relationships.[35] Insights for understanding foreign customers are provided in Exhibit 6.4.[36]

### Competitive Knowledge

Salespeople must know competitive offerings in terms of strengths and weaknesses to plan sales strategy and sales presentations effectively and to be able to respond effectively to customer questions and objections. This area is extremely important for salespeople who

---

### EXHIBIT 6.3    Sales Training for Different Types of Buyers

| Kind of Buyer | Sales Training Topic |
|---|---|
| 1. Hard Bargainer (a difficult person to deal with) | 1. Teach psychologically oriented sales strategies (e.g., transactional analysis). <br> 2. Teach sales *negotiation* strategies (e.g., the use of different bases of power). <br> 3. Teach listening skills and the benefits of listening to the prospect. <br> 4. Emphasize how to handle objections. <br> 5. Emphasize *competitive* product knowledge. |
| 2. Sales Job Facilitator (attempts to make the sales transaction go smoothly) | 1. Teach importance of a *quid pro quo*. <br> 2. Communicate advantages of having a satisfied customer base. <br> 3. Show how customers can assist salespeople (e.g., by pooling orders, providing leads). |
| 3. Straight Shooter (behaves with integrity and propriety) | 1. Teach importance of selling the "substance" of the product offering and not just the "sizzle." <br> 2. Teach straightforward techniques for handling objections (e.g., a direct denial approach). |
| 4. Socializer (enjoys personal interaction with salespeople) | 1. Communicate company policy information about giving gifts and entertaining and socializing with customers. <br> 2. Discuss ethical and legal implications of transacting business. <br> 3. Emphasize importance of salespeople maintaining an appropriate balance between socializing with customers and performing job responsibilities. |
| 5. Persuader (attempts to "market" his or her company) | 1. Communicate importance of qualifying prospects. <br> 2. Teach techniques for qualifying customers. |
| 6. Considerate (shows compassion for salesperson) | 1. Communicate importance of obtaining market information from customers. <br> 2. Teach importance of a *quid pro quo*. |

are new to the industry because the competitor's salespeople may have years of experience and be quite knowledgeable. Furthermore, customers may exploit a salesperson's lack of **competitive knowledge** to negotiate terms of sale that may be costly to the selling firm. For example, salespeople who are not familiar with a competitor's price structure may unnecessarily reduce their own price to make a sale, thereby sacrificing more revenue and profits than they should have.

---

### EXHIBIT 6.4    Understanding Foreign Customers

Many selling skills that are successful in the United States will also work in other countries. However, one must be aware of cultural variations that can make the difference between closing a deal and losing a customer. Here is some advice for conducting business in certain countries around the world.

**Arab Countries:**
- Don't use your left hand to hold, offer, or receive materials because Arabs use their left hands to touch toilet paper. If you must use your left hand to write, apologize for doing so.
- When first meeting someone, avoid giving a gift as it might be interpreted as a bribe.

**China:**
- Don't refuse tea during a business discussion. Always drink it, even if you're offered a dozen cups a day.
- Printed materials presented to Chinese business leaders should be in black and white because colors have great significance for the Chinese.
- Never begin to eat or drink before your host does in China.
- Deliver presentations in a visually neutral way.
- Present gifts privately and do not make a big issue of it.

**France:**
- Don't schedule a breakfast meeting—the French tend not to meet until after 10 A.M.

**Germany:**
- Don't address a business associate by his or her first name, even if you have known each other for years. Always wait for an invitation to do so.
- Breakfast meetings are unheard of here also.
- Provide detail and lots of supporting documentation during presentations.

**Latin America:**
- People here don't take the clock too seriously—scheduling more than two appointments in the same day can prove disastrous.
- People like to stand close to one another and touch during conversation.
- Give gifts after establishing a relationship and during social encounters, rather than in the course of business.

**Japan:**
- Don't bring up business on the golf course—always wait for your host to take the initiative.
- Don't cross your legs in Japan—showing the bottom of the foot is insulting.
- Deliver presentations in a visually neutral way.
- Avoid giving gifts wrapped with bows (considered unattractive) and ribbons (colors have different meanings). Do not open a gift in front of a Japanese counterpart or expect them to do so.

**Mexico:**
- Don't send a bouquet of red or yellow flowers as a gift—Mexicans associate those colors with evil spirits and death. Instead, send a box of premium chocolates.

**Miscellaneous:**
- The thumbs-up gesture is considered offensive in the Middle East, rude in Australia, and a sign of "OK" in France.
- It is rude to cross your arms while facing someone in Turkey.
- In the Middle East don't ask, "How's the family?"—it is considered too personal. Also, don't show the bottom of your foot.

## Time and Territory Management

The quest for an optimal balance between salesforce output and salesforce expenditures is a perennial objective for most sales managers. Therefore, training in **time and territory management (TTM)**, is often included in formal sales training programs. Essentially, the purpose of TTM training is to teach salespeople how to use time and efforts for maximum work efficiency.

TTM training is important for all sales organizations but especially for those in declining, stagnant, or highly competitive industries. In such situations, salespeople are often overworked, and there comes a point when working harder to improve results is not realistic. Such circumstances call for "working smarter, not harder," an idea that is receiving considerable discussion in sales management circles.[37]

Efforts to make more efficient use of time and increase salesperson productivity have been bolstered by salesforce automation. Salesforce automation (e.g., cellular phones, faxes, portable computers, databases, the Internet, personal digital assistants, and electronic data interchange) can boost productivity by as much as 20 to 40 percent.[38] To do so, salespeople often need training in computer and software applications. Furthermore, as electronic data interchange (a method for transferring information electronically between selling firms and buying firms) and CRM technology become more prominent, the need for computer literacy in the salesforce will increase.[39] Studies indicate that proper training in salesforce automation is necessary for it to be effective.[40]

Perhaps time and territory management could be improved by training salespeople in **self-management**. Self-management refers to an individual's effort to control certain aspects of his or her decision making and behavior, and as such employs strategies that assist individuals in structuring the environment and facilitating behaviors necessary to achieve performance standards. Recent research suggests that salespeople trained in self-management increase both short- and long-term performance.[41]

## Set Training Objectives

Having assessed the needs for sales training, the sales manager moves to the next step in the sales training process shown in Figure 6.1: setting specific **sales training objectives**. Because training needs vary from one sales organization to the next, so do the objectives. In general, however, one or more of the following are included.

1. Increase sales or profits.
2. Create positive attitudes and improve salesforce morale.
3. Assist in salesforce socialization.
4. Reduce role conflict and ambiguity.
5. Introduce new products, markets, and promotional programs.
6. Develop salespeople for future management positions.
7. Ensure awareness of ethical and legal responsibilities.
8. Teach administrative procedures (e.g., expense accounts, call reports).
9. Ensure competence in the use of sales and sales support tools, such as CRM technology.
10. Minimize salesforce turnover rate.
11. Prepare new salespeople for assignment to a sales territory.
12. Improve teamwork and cooperative efforts.

These objectives are interrelated. For example, if salespeople gain competence in the use of a new sales tool, sales and profit may improve, salesforce morale may be positively affected, and other beneficial outcomes may occur. By setting objectives for sales training, the manager avoids the wasteful practice of training simply for training's sake. Furthermore, objectives force the sales manager to define the reasonable expectations of sales training rather than to view training as a quick-fix panacea for all the problems faced by the salesforce. Additional benefits of setting objectives for sales training are as follows:[42]

- Written objectives become a good communications vehicle to inform the salesforce and other interested parties about upcoming training.
- Top management is responsive to well-written, specific objectives and may be more willing to provide budget support for the training.
- Specific training objectives provide a standard for measuring the effectiveness of training.
- By setting objectives, the sales manager finds it easier to prioritize various training needs, and the proper sequence of training becomes more apparent.

## Evaluate Training Alternatives

In the third step of the sales training process, the sales manager considers various approaches for accomplishing the objectives of training. Certainly, many more alternatives exist today than in the past, thanks to such technologies as computer-assisted instruction, video conferencing, and the Internet. The number of sales training professionals for hire also seems to be increasing, or perhaps such trainers are just doing a better job of promoting their services. Even a casual examination of a typical shopping mall bookstore will reveal a number of titles related to building sales skills, along with audio- and videotapes/disks on the subject. Some associations are even offering training courses to help improve the skills of salespeople in their industry. For example, a course cosponsored by the Safety Equipment Manufacturers Agents Association allows distributor reps, manufacturer reps, and independent manufacturer reps to attend a weeklong course on the topic of safety.[43]

Critiquing all these alternatives is a monumental job, so it is recommended that fairly stringent criteria, including cost, location of the training, flexibility of prepackaged materials, opportunity for reinforcement training, and time required to implement an alternative, be established for preliminary screening.

The evaluation of alternatives for training inevitably leads to three key questions. First, who will conduct the training? An answer to this question will require the consideration of internal (within the company) and external (outside the company) trainers. The second question deals with location for the training. Sales training may be conducted in the field, in the office, at a central training location, at hotels and conference centers, or at other locations. The third question is which method (or methods) and media are best suited for conducting the training?

## Selecting Sales Trainers

In general, companies rely most heavily on their own personnel to conduct sales training. In this endeavor, the sales manager is the most important **sales trainer**. Senior salespeople are also often involved as trainers. For example, beer brewing company Molson Canada uses both managers and experienced salespeople to conduct formal training sessions three or four days a year.[44] In larger companies, a full-time sales trainer is often available.

Why are internal sources used so often in sales training? First, and perhaps most important, sales managers and senior salespeople are intimately aware of job requirements and can communicate in very specific terms to the sales trainee. However, outside consultants may be only superficially informed about a specific sales job and often offer generic sales training packages. Second, sales managers are the logical source for training to be conducted in the field, where valuable learning can occur with each sales call. It is extremely difficult to turn field training over to external trainers. Finally, using internal trainers simplifies control and coordination tasks. It is easier to control the content of the program, coordinate training for maximum impact, and provide continuity for the program when it is the sales manager who does the training or who designates other company personnel to do the training.

At some point, a sales manager's effectiveness may be improved by using external trainers. Internal resources, including time, expertise, facilities, and personnel, may be insufficient to accomplish the objectives of the sales training program. Also, outside trainers might be looked to for new ideas and methods. Large training firms such as Forum (http://www.forum.com), Sales Performance International (www.SPISales.com), and U.S. Learning Inc. (http://www. uslearning.com) often customize their generic programs for use within specific companies. Others, such as Wilson Learning Corporation, deliver training programs via the Web that include interactive stories, tutorials, interactive questions, online exercises, role plays, games, summaries, and post-tests.[45] Exhibit 6.5[46] outlines attributes to consider when shopping for an outside training program.

## Selecting Sales Training Locations

Most sales training is conducted in home, regional, or field offices of the sales organization. Manufacturing plants are also popular training sites, and some firms use noncompany sites such as hotels or conference centers to conduct training.

Central training facilities are another possibility, used extensively by Noxell Corporation, Xerox, IBM, General Electric, Armstrong World Industries, and scores of other large firms. One of the largest training facilities in the country is Xerox Document University, located on the banks of the Potomac River in Leesburg, Virginia. At this facility, trainees stay in dormlike confines while being indoctrinated into the company.

As video broadcasting and teleconferencing become more prevalent, many firms are enjoying some of the benefits of a centralized training facility without incurring the

---

**EXHIBIT 6.5**    Choosing an Outside Training Program

Several training organizations, such as the Covey Leadership Center, the Center for Creative Leadership, Decker Communications, and the American Society of Training and Development, provide their input on what makes a useful training program.

1. The program should make it easy to master content by lessening the participant's struggle to learn new skills and knowledge and change old work habits. Content and delivery must consider the skill level, education level, and learning style of participants.
2. The program should anticipate and deal with obstacles to long-term behavior modification. It should motivate participants to drop old habits, adopt new skills, and desire continued training.
3. The program's content should be limited to what has been shown to help participants most on the job.
4. The program's development and delivery should stay within the constraints of time, money, logistics, and repeatability. Only technology that enhances training should be used.
5. Participants should be actively involved in the program to preserve the excitement that comes from self-development.
6. The trainer must clearly understand the program's objectives, as well as the concepts, behaviors, and attitudes to be acquired by participants.
7. When appropriate, the program should accommodate group dynamics and promote a sense of group membership and shared purpose.

---

travel costs and lost time to transport the salesforce to and from training. Field offices arrange for video hook-up, either in-house or at video-equipped conference hotels, and trainees across the country share simultaneously in training emanating from a central location.

### Selecting Sales Training Methods

A variety of methods can be selected to fit the training situation. Indeed, the use of multiple methods is encouraged over the course of a training program to help maintain trainee attention and enhance learning. There are four categories of training methods: classroom/conference, on-the-job, behavioral simulations, and absorption.

### Classroom/Conference Training

The **classroom** or **conference** setting features lectures, demonstrations, and group discussion with expert trainers serving as instructors. This method is often used for training on basic product knowledge, new product introductions, administrative procedures, and legal and ethical issues in personal selling. At Cullinet Software, for instance, trainees spend six to seven months in the classroom learning product knowledge and sales methodologies.[47] The format often resembles a college classroom, with regularly scheduled examinations and overnight homework assignments. In addition to using internal facilities and personnel, some companies send their salespeople to seminars sponsored by the American Management Association, American Marketing Association, Sales and Marketing Executives International, and local colleges and universities. These organizations offer training on practically any phase of selling and sales management.

### On-the-Job Training

In the final analysis, salespeople can be taught only so much about selling without actually experiencing it. Consequently, **on-the-job training (OJT)** is extremely important and is the most prevalent method of training salespeople.[48] OJT puts the trainee into actual work circumstances under the observant (it is hoped) eye of a supportive **mentor** or sales manager. Other OJT methods approximate a "sink or swim" philosophy and often produce disastrous results when the trainee is overwhelmed with unfamiliar job requirements.

Mentors have different objectives from company to company, but they usually strive to make the new hires feel at home in their jobs, relay information about the corporate culture, and be available for discussion and advice on topics of concern to the trainee. Coworker mentoring is popular among salesforces, and in some companies, the sales manager serves as the mentor. For instance, at Ecolab, a provider of commercial cleaning products, sales managers accompany reps on sales calls to coach them and to help them develop monthly improvement plans.[49] The mentoring concept is yet another way that companies are striving to improve salesforce socialization, especially the role definition and initiation-to-task steps explained earlier in this module.

Other than working with a senior salesperson or a mentor, common OJT assignments include the trainee's filling in for a vacationing salesperson, working with a sales manager who acts as a "coach," and job rotation. When senior salespeople act as mentors, they too are undergoing continual training as their ideas and methods are reassessed, and sometimes refined, with each trainee. The sales manager's role as coach is discussed in Module 7 on supervision and leadership of the salesforce. **Job rotation**, the exposure of the sales trainee to different jobs, may involve stints as a customer service representative, a distribution clerk, or perhaps in other sales positions. Job rotation is often used to groom salespeople for management positions.

## Behavioral Simulations

Methods that focus on behavioral learning by means of business games and simulations, case studies, and role playing—where trainees portray a specified role in a staged situation—are called **behavioral simulations**. They focus on defining desirable behavior or in correcting behavioral mistakes, in part by allowing salespeople to experience the consequences of their actions.

Games may come in a variety of forms. For instance, Bax Global, a California-based transportation and logistics company, uses a board game called Apples and Oranges to help its sales reps better understand how executive-level decision makers think by having them run a mock manufacturing company over a simulated three-year period. During six-hour training sessions, reps are divided into teams of four or five. As players progress along the board, they must make decisions regarding productivity changes, resource allocation, and cash flow management. The game helps reps better understand where Bax Global's services can add value for a customer.[50] At International Paper, college sales recruits play Zodiak, a board game that teaches them how their actions impact a company's finances.[51]

An example of a computer-based simulation is one offered by the Brooks Group called the Impact Selling Simulator. This is an off-the-shelf CD-ROM simulation that uses real-world scenarios to help salespeople learn to understand customer problems, develop their questioning skills, and improve customer relationships, among other things.[52] Such simulations provide the advantage of reaching large populations at once via the Internet, company intranet, or CD-ROM.

Along with OJT, **role playing** is extremely popular for teaching sales techniques. Typically, one trainee plays the role of the salesperson and another trainee acts as the buyer. The role playing is videotaped or performed live for a group of observers who then critique the performance. This can be an extremely effective means of teaching personal selling, without the risk of a poor performance in the presence of a real customer. It is most effective when promptly critiqued with emphasis on the positive points of the performance as well as suggestions for improvement. A good way to maximize the benefits of the critique is to have the person who has played the role of the salesperson offer opinions first and then solicit opinions from observers. After role playing, the "salesperson" is usually modest about his or her performance, and the comments from observers may bolster this individual's self-confidence. In turn, future performance may be improved.[53] An alternative format involves using role play software, such as Dialog Coach, that uses artificial intelligence, voice recognition, and video to provide virtual, customized client interaction. Ecolab, a provider of commercial cleaning products, has used the software to help improve its salespeople's close ratio by approximately 13 percent.[54] While role playing offers the opportunity for a positive learning experience, this may not always be the case as seen in "An Ethical Dilemma."

### Absorption Training

As the name implies, **absorption training** involves furnishing trainees or salespeople with materials that they peruse (or "absorb") without opportunity for immediate feedback and questioning. Product manuals, direction-laden memoranda, and sales bulletins are used in absorption training. Federated Insurance, for example, maintains a substantial library of audio- and videotapes, books, workbooks, and self-study material for employees to use.[55] This method is most useful as a supplement to update salesforce knowledge, reinforce previous training, or introduce basic materials to be covered in more detail at a later date.

One time-effective method of absorption training involves furnishing the salesforce with CDs or audiocassettes so that driving time can be used as training time. At Omni Oral Pharmaceuticals, in addition to instructor-led training, salespeople are given a CD filled with audio tips to listen to while driving between sales calls.[56]

### Selecting Sales Training Media

Communications and computer technology have expanded the range of **sales training media** dramatically in the past decade. Sales trainers warn against the tendency to be overly impressed with the glamorous aspects of such training media, but they agree that it is advisable to evaluate new media continually to see whether they should be incorporated into the sales training program. Among other things, electronic media typically allow trainees to learn at their own pace in a risk-free environment. The most promising new media are found at the communications/computer technology interface and are often referred to as e-learning media.

The Internet offers opportunities to cost-effectively train the salesforce across different times and locations without taking salespeople out of the field. One study found that 48 percent of the companies surveyed go online to train salespeople.[57] Companies such as WebEx (http://www.webex.com) and Raindance (http://www.raindance.com) provide Web and telephone conferencing services. Using the Web trainers can display slides, whiteboard visual concepts, introduce real-time interaction, share desktop applications, and lead a Web tour.[58] Cisco used the Web to deliver a tutorial to 2,000 of its salespeople in conference rooms located in Asia, Europe, and the United States, saving the company over $530,000 in training expenditures.[59] It also offered training on the Web via video-on-demand. Trainees could use the Web to access 10 half-day training course videos. Personal digital assistants are likewise being used to deliver sales training. At Monsanto, trainers push e-mail reminders to the field salesforce, which is equipped with Palm handhelds.[60]

Another emerging technology, desktop personal computer videoconferencing, allows sales managers and salespeople to see each other and trade information via their personal computers. Similarly, audiographics connects the instructor simultaneously with several sites via computer displays and audio link.[61] Or sales managers may want to set up an online chat room to train salespeople interactively at remote locations.[62] These technologies can be used to simultaneously train salespeople dispersed in several remote locations.

Satellite television offers another viable training alternative. For instance, RE/MAX uses its satellite network to conduct sales training in more than 1,400 commercial offices throughout the United States.[63]

An example of how video technology can improve sales training comes from Frito-Lay. Frito-Lay's Priority One video series involves its CEO and senior vice president of field operations role playing a Frito-Lay salesperson and a store owner, respectively, in a variety of situations. Each month, the 15-minute videos are distributed to reps who get together with their district managers to view them. The videos suggest one new tactic that reps should try that month.[64]

Sales training software is increasingly available for a few hundred dollars per program or less. Programs cover time and territory management, sales analysis, and the entire sales process. For example, the Brooks Group offers CD-ROM titles such as "How to Build Instant Trust and Rapport" and "The Magic of Asking Questions."[65] An alternative is to custom-build a training module using a program such as RoboDemo eLearning Edition. This program helps managers without technical assistance to develop interactive training sessions that can be posted on the Internet, an intranet, or burned onto a CD.[66] Figure 6.2[67] summarizes results from a study indicating usage of various methods and media used to train salespeople.

## Design the Sales Training Program

The fourth step in the sales training process is a culmination of, and condensation of, the first three steps shown in Figure 6.1. Working toward selected objectives based on needs assessment and having evaluated training alternatives, the sales manager now commits resources to the training to be accomplished. At this point in the process, sales managers may have to seek budget approval from upper management.

In this step of designing the training program, the necessary responses to what, when, where, and how questions are finalized. Training is scheduled, travel arrangements made, media selected, speakers hired, and countless other details arranged. Certainly this can be the most tedious part of the sales training process, but attention to detail is necessary to ensure successful implementation of the process.

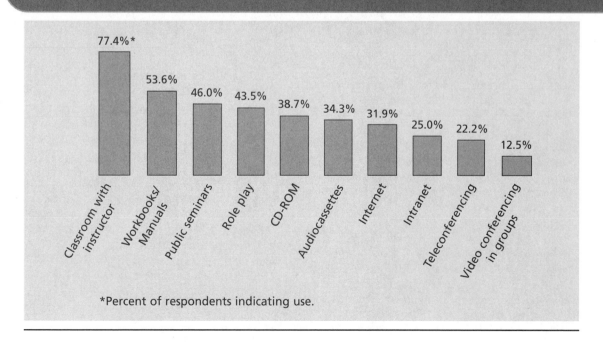

**Methods and Media Used to Train Salespeople**     **FIGURE 6.2**

77.4%* — Classroom with instructor
53.6% — Workbooks/Manuals
46.0% — Public seminars
43.5% — Role play
38.7% — CD-ROM
34.3% — Audiocassettes
31.9% — Internet
25.0% — Intranet
22.2% — Teleconferencing
12.5% — Video conferencing in groups

*Percent of respondents indicating use.

## Perform Sales Training

The fifth step in the process, actually performing the training, may take only a fraction of the time required by the previous steps. This is particularly true in better sales training programs. As the training is being conducted, the sales manager's primary responsibility is to monitor the progress of the trainees and to ensure adequate presentation of the training topics. In particular, sales managers should assess the clarity of training materials. It is also recommended that some assessment of the trainees' continuing motivation to learn be made. Feedback from the trainees might be solicited on everything from the effectiveness of external trainers to the adequacy of the physical training site. For an analysis of the performance of sales training at ADP, see "Sales Management in the 21st Century: Performing Sales Training at ADP."

## Conduct Follow-Up and Evaluation

It is always difficult to measure the effectiveness of sales training. This is a long-standing problem, due in some cases to a lack of clearly stated sales training objectives. Even with clearly stated objectives, however, it is hard to determine which future performance variations are a result of sales training. Other factors, such as motivation, role perceptions, and environmental factors, may affect performance more or less than training in different situations.

Although scientific precision cannot be hoped for, a reasonable attempt must nevertheless be made to assess whether current training expenditures are worthwhile and whether future modification is warranted. Evaluations can be made before, during, and after the training occurs.[68] For example, the pretraining evaluation might include an examination for sales trainees to assess their level of knowledge, corroborate or deny the need for training, and further define the objectives of the training. As suggested earlier, training can be evaluated while it is being conducted, and adjustments may be made at

---

### Performing Sales Training at ADP

Jason Karem, sales manager at ADP, comments on the performance of sales training:

*From the time one is hired for a sales position at Automatic Data Processing (ADP), he or she is constantly trained not only on individual selling skills, buy also on ADP's product set. In fact, ADP places so much energy and resources on new sales associates that it takes two years before that individual associate is profitable for ADP. A majority of ADP's training prior to attending our corporate office for two weeks is made up of computer-based training (CBT), webinars, and role plays with sales managers. One of the most important training tools offered by ADP initially, which becomes even more valuable through a sales associate's career, is a Web site totally dedicated to any topic an associate might uncover in the field. From specific ideas for how to get in the door with a prospect to going through a quick training module on a specific product or solution, the information is right at one's fingertips. After the initial training takes place, associates are trained two to three times each month on specific product and selling skills. In most of these sessions, sales representatives actually facilitate the training themselves. This accomplishes a couple things. First, the associate giving the training becomes very knowledgeable on the topic and becomes a "champion" for the product or selling skill. Secondly, it really helps each associate with preparation and presentation skills, both of which will help him or her in the field. Even more important to a salesperson's success in any company, however, is the desire to continuously learn and improve. Most of this comes from self-study and is done outside of the normal 8 A.M. to 5 P.M. selling time. Quite honestly, what makes a salesperson successful is not what they do between 8–5, it is what they do before 8 and after 5.*

any point in the delivery of training. Post-training evaluations might include reactions or critiques of the trainees, "final examinations," retention examinations at later dates, observations by sales managers as they work in the field with salespeople, customer feedback, new business growth, and an examination of actual performance indicators such as sales volume. At Motorola, Inc., the effectiveness of sales training is determined by measuring customer satisfaction, along with salespeople's ability to affect customer values.[69] Dell measures the strength of its customer relationships as a means of assessing its sales training, as does Dr Pepper/Seven Up, which also gauges volume, distribution, and display.[70] Trainee reactions, however, can serve as an important measure of training effectiveness given research indicating that trainees who are satisfied with their training are more likely to retain and use what they learned, resulting in greater selling effectiveness, improved customer relations, and a stronger commitment to the organization.[71] Exhibit 6.6[72] summarizes the sales training evaluation practices of 129 companies.

Despite the inherent difficulty in relating subsequent sales performance to previously conducted sales training, the effectiveness of sales training is increasingly being measured in dollars and cents. This return-on-investment approach seeks to define training effectiveness in terms of incremental sales volume from existing accounts or volume generated by new accounts. As mentioned, at Dr Pepper/Seven Up training, in part, is evaluated based on its impact on increasing sales growth.

It is also important to reinforce the training in subsequent weeks. According to a study of over 6,000 sales professionals, participants in sales training remember only half of what they learn within five weeks of the training. Post-training implementation and reinforcement are critical to enhanced behavior change. Reinforcement should be integrated with the sales organization's daily work.[72] Molson Canada, for instance, reinforces its training

| Sales Training Evaluation Practices Ranked by Importance and Frequency | | | | **EXHIBIT 6.6** | |
|---|---|---|---|---|---|
| | **Mean Importance*** | | | **Frequency of Use Percentage** | |
| **Source** | **All Companies** | **Service Companies** | **Manufacturing Companies** | **Often  Sometimes  Never** | |
| **Reaction Measures** | | | | | |
| Trainee feedback | 3.42 | 3.39 | 3.39 | 86 | 14 | 0 |
| Supervisor's feedback | 3.15 | 3.14 | 3.12 | 68 | 24 | 8 |
| Training staff comments | 2.95 | 2.92 | 2.85 | 93 | 7 | 0 |
| **Learning Measures** | | | | | |
| Performance tests | 3.10 | 3.31 | 2.85 | 63 | 29 | 8 |
| Pretraining versus post-training measurements | 2.72 | 2.71 | 2.56 | 31 | 51 | 18 |
| **Behavior Measures** | | | | | |
| Supervisory appraisal | 3.38 | 3.50 | 3.29 | 64 | 26 | 10 |
| Self-appraisal | 3.25 | 3.37 | 3.10 | 61 | 30 | 9 |
| Customer appraisal | 3.17 | 3.42 | 2.78 | 41 | 35 | 23 |
| Subordinate appraisal | 2.73 | 2.93 | 2.37 | 32 | 45 | 23 |
| Coworker appraisal | 2.52 | 2.63 | 2.33 | 33 | 45 | 22 |
| **Result Measures** | | | | | |
| Bottom line measurement | 3.20 | 3.34 | 2.94 | 40 | 46 | 14 |

*Mean importance is based on a 1 to 5 scale, with 5 indicating the most importance.

**EXHIBIT 6.7** Methods for Reinforcing New Sales Skills Ranked by Importance

| Method | Percent Indicating as Effective |
|---|---|
| Sharing sales methods and language with the sales team | 49 |
| Coaching by the sales manager | 46 |
| Follow-up training classes | 43 |
| Clear statement of management expectations | 39 |
| Incentive compensation for new sales behaviors | 36 |
| Technology reinforcement and support | 33 |
| Coaching by outside specialists | 30 |
| Participation in a community Web site based on the training | 11 |

Source: Gail Johnson, "Forget Me Not," *Training* 41 (March 2004): 12.

through frequent informal coaching sessions with its salespeople.[73] Exhibit 6.7[74] shows results of a study identifying the most effective methods to reinforce new sales skills.

A reasonable approach to sales training is to ensure that it is not prohibitively expensive by carefully assessing training needs, setting objectives, and evaluating training alternatives before designing the training program and performing the training. Furthermore, the sales training process is incomplete without evaluation and follow-up.

## ETHICAL AND LEGAL ISSUES

Ethical and legal issues are being included in sales training programs more often than in the past. One catalyst for this change has been product liability litigation that has awarded multimillion-dollar judgments to plaintiffs who have suffered as a result of unsafe products. Research has found that salespeople face a number of ethical and legal dilemmas on the job and that salespeople want more direction from their managers on how to handle such dilemmas.[75] Exhibit 6.8[76] lists situations or practices that some salespeople find to be ethically troubling and would like to see addressed by a company policy.

Training in the legal area is extremely difficult because laws are sometimes confusing and subject to multiple interpretations. Training salespeople in ethics is even more difficult because ethical issues are often gray, not black or white. Companies that address ethics and legal issues in their sales training programs usually rely on straightforward guidelines that avoid complexity. Salespeople should be provided with the company's code of ethics and informed of the organization's policies concerning ethical behavior. Furthermore, by providing salespeople with potentially troubling ethical scenarios, having them respond, and then explaining how a similar situation could be handled, it may be possible to lessen salespeople's concerns about such situations. Salespeople are given basic training on applicable legal dimensions and advised simply to tell the truth and seek management assistance should problems arise. For instance, at Owens Corning, a lawyer speaks to salespeople about legal and ethical issues.[77] Another possibility includes role playing, in which trainees learn to develop consistently legal interactive scripts.[78] These guidelines may sound simplistic, but such training can greatly reduce salesperson conflict on the job, help develop profitable long-term relationships with customers, and reduce the liability of the salesperson and the organization.

The legal framework for personal selling is extensive. Some of the key components of this framework are antitrust legislation, contract law, local ordinances governing sales practices, and guidelines issued by the Federal Trade Commission dealing with unfair trade practices. A partial listing of important legal reminders that should be included in a sales training program is shown in Exhibit 6.9. Salespeople must be made aware of changes in the legal environment as soon as they occur.

| Ethically Troubling Situations and Practices Salespeople Would Like Addressed by Company Policy* | EXHIBIT 6.8 |
| --- | --- |

1. Making statements to an existing purchaser that exaggerate the seriousness of his or her problem to obtain a bigger order or other concessions.
2. Soliciting low-priority or low-volume business that the salesperson's firm will not deliver or service in an economic slowdown or periods of resource shortages.
3. Allowing personalities—liking one purchaser and disliking another—to affect price, delivery, and other decisions regarding the terms of sale.
4. Seeking information from purchasers on competitors' quotations for the purpose of submitting another quotation.
5. Having less competitive prices or other terms for buyers who use your firm as the sole source of supply than for firms for which you are one of two or more suppliers.
6. Giving physical gifts such as free sales promotion prizes or "purchase-volume incentive bonuses" to a purchaser.
7. Providing free trips, free luncheons or dinners, or other free entertainment to a purchaser.
8. Using the firm's economic power to obtain premium prices or other concessions from buyers.
9. Gaining information about competitors by asking purchasers.
10. Giving preferential treatment to purchasers whom higher levels of the firm's own management prefer or recommend.
11. Giving preferential treatment to customers who are also good suppliers.
12. Attempting to reach and influence other departments (e.g., engineering) directly rather than going through the purchasing department when such avoidance of the purchasing department increases the likelihood of a sale.

*Ranked from most to least troubling in a survey of industrial salespeople.

| Legal Reminders for Salespeople | EXHIBIT 6.9 |
| --- | --- |

1. Use factual data rather than general statements of praise during the sales presentation. Avoid misrepresentation.
2. Thoroughly educate customers before the sale on the product's specifications, capabilities, and limitations. Remind customers to read all warnings.
3. Do not overstep authority because the salesperson's actions can be binding to the selling firm.
4. Avoid discussing these topics with competitors: prices, profit margins, discounts, terms of sale, bids or intent to bid, sales territories or markets to be served, and rejection or termination of customers.
5. Do not use one product as bait for selling another product.
6. Do not try to force the customer to buy only from your organization.
7. Offer the same price and support to all buyers who purchase under the same set of circumstances.
8. Do not tamper with a competitor's product.
9. Do not disparage a competitor's product, business conduct, or financial condition without specific evidence of your contentions.
10. Avoid promises that will be difficult or impossible to honor.

## SUMMARY

1. **Understand the role of sales training in salesforce socialization**. Newly hired salespeople usually receive a company orientation designed to familiarize them with company history, policies, facilities, procedures, and key individuals with whom they will interact. During initial sales training, it is hoped that each salesforce member will experience a positive initiation to task and satisfactory role definition.

2. **Explain the importance of sales training and the sales manager's role in sales training**. Most organizations have a continual need for sales training as a result of changing business conditions, the influx of new salespeople into the organization, and the need to reinforce previous training. Sizable investments in training are likely in larger companies. The sales manager has the overall responsibility for training the salesforce, although other people may also conduct sales training.

3. **Describe the sales training process as a series of six interrelated steps**. Figure 6.1 presents the sales training process in six steps: assess sales training needs, set training objectives, evaluate training alternatives, design the sales training program, perform sales training, and conduct follow-up and evaluation. The time spent to perform sales training may be only a fraction of the time spent to complete the other steps in the process, especially in well-run sales organizations.

4. **Discuss six methods for assessing sales training needs and identify typical sales training needs**. Sales managers may assess needs through a salesforce audit, performance testing, observation, a salesforce survey, a customer survey, or a job analysis. It is recommended that salesforce training needs be assessed in a proactive fashion; that is, needs should be assessed before performance problems occur rather than after problems occur. Typical sales training needs include product, customer, and competitive knowledge; sales techniques; and time and territory management.

5. **Name some typical objectives of sales training programs, and explain how setting objectives for sales training is beneficial to sales managers**. The objectives of sales training vary over time and across organizations, but they often include preparing sales trainees for assignment to a sales territory, improving a particular dimension of performance, aiding in the socialization process, or improving salesforce morale and motivation. By setting objectives, the sales manager can prioritize training, allocate resources consistent with priorities, communicate the purpose of the training to interested parties, and perhaps gain top management support for sales training.

6. **Identify the key issues in evaluating sales training alternatives**. Evaluation of alternatives is a search for an optimal balance between cost and effectiveness. One key issue is the selection of trainers, whether from outside the company (external) or inside the company (internal). Another is the potential location or locations for training. Still another important factor is the method or methods to use for various topics. Sales training methods include classroom/conference training, on-the-job training, behavioral simulations, and absorption training. The sales manager must also consider whether to use various sales training media, such as printed material, audio- and videotape and CDs, and computer-assisted instruction.

7. **Identify key ethical and legal issues in sales training**. Because of increasing product liability litigation, legal and ethical issues are being incorporated into salesforce training. Exhibits 6.8 and 6.9 point out several issues that should be covered in sales training. Lectures and role playing provide useful means for training in this area.

## UNDERSTANDING SALES MANAGEMENT TERMS

| | |
|---|---|
| initiation to task | time and territory management (TTM) |
| role definition | self-management |
| needs assessment | sales training objectives |
| salesforce audit | sales trainer |
| performance testing | classroom/conference training |
| observation | on-the-job training (OJT) |
| salesforce survey | mentor |
| customer survey | job rotation |
| job analysis | behavioral simulations |
| sales techniques | role playing |
| product knowledge | absorption training |
| customer knowledge | sales training media |
| competitive knowledge | |

## DEVELOPING SALES MANAGEMENT KNOWLEDGE

1. How is sales training related to recruiting and selecting salespeople? How can sales training contribute to salesforce socialization?

2. Why is it important to invest in sales training?

3. What are six methods of assessing sales training needs? Can each of these methods be used in either a proactive or reactive approach to determining training needs?

4. Refer to "Sales Management in the 21st Century: Training for Relationship Building at ADP." How can training salespeople in relationship building help a company?

5. How is the process of setting objectives for sales training beneficial to sales managers?

6. When the sales manager is evaluating sales training alternatives, what four areas should he or she consider?

7. Discuss four methods for delivering sales training.

8. Refer to "Sales Management in the 21st Century: Performing Sales Training at ADP." What are the benefits of using sales reps to facilitate sales training?

9. What is the purpose of the follow-up and evaluation step in the sales training process? When should evaluation take place?

10. What are some of the important ethical and legal considerations that might be included in a sales training program?

## BUILDING SALES MANAGEMENT SKILLS

1. There is a universal ongoing need for training on "how to sell." For instance, knowing how to listen effectively is an extremely important skill that contributes to the success of salespeople. Find several articles on listening. Use this information to design a training program to improve salespeople's listening skills. Assume that you will conduct the training session. Determine what you will teach, along with the methods and media you will use. Also, decide how you will assess whether the training was successful. If possible, conduct your training program on a small group such as your fraternity, sorority, student American Marketing Association chapter, or any other student group.

2. As the sales manager for ABC company, you have decided that as part of your training program you would like to use role playing to achieve three objectives: (1) teach salespeople how to set appointments with prospects properly via the phone, (2) teach salespeople how to approach prospects and build rapport, and (3) teach salespeople how to question prospects effectively. Design three role plays (one of each objective) to achieve

**ROLE PLAY**

these goals. Then, have a classmate play the salesperson and you play the buyer and act out each role play. On completing each role play, critique the salesperson's performance, being sure to emphasize the positive points and to make suggestions for improvements. Consider soliciting self-assessment feedback from the salesperson before making your own critique.

3. Access SalesPro Online Training at **http://4moresales.com.** Address the following questions:

   3a. What types of sales training needs does this company address with its online training?

   3b. What are some potentially important training needs that are not addressed?

   3c. Examine the example of a SalesPro Seminar: "Effective Selling to Different Personality Types." What are the advantages and disadvantages of using this type of online training?

   3d. What does it cost to use this training?

4. The Web contains various sales training Web sites. For instance, by accessing **http://dir.yahoo.com**/business_and_economy/business_to_business/training_and_ development/sales one can find a number of such sites. Search the Web to find a company that offers sales training. Briefly explain the types of training the company offers, the methods and media they use to deliver the training, and the pros and cons of using the company to train the salesforce.

5. As a sales manager, you would like to teach your salespeople how to handle different buyer types. Using Exhibit 6.3 as a guide, for each buyer type explain the methods and media you would use to prepare your salespeople to deal with that buyer type.

**ROLE PLAY**

6. **Situation:**     Read the Ethical Dilemma on page 174.

   **Characters:**     Joe Smith, national sales manager; Jill Horner, sales trainee

   **Scene:**     *Location*—Company training room. *Action*—Joe acts out an alternative method for handling Jill's poor role play performance.

7. As a sales manager, you would like to survey your salesforce to determine their sales techniques training needs. Develop a series of questions for a short salesforce survey to determine their training needs with regard to sales techniques.

# MAKING SALES MANAGEMENT DECISIONS

## Case 6.1: Solutions Software, Inc.

### Background

Solutions Software, Inc., develops and markets software through office and computer software retailers throughout the United States. Established in 1982, the company has been successful competing against larger companies because it offers a quality product at an affordable price. Moreover, it has a reputation of providing a high level of service through a knowledgeable and efficient salesforce.

On entering the salesforce, reps are given formal training at the company's headquarters in St. Louis, Missouri. There they are taught various sales techniques, product knowledge, and competitive knowledge. In addition, they learn about company policies and the company's code of ethics. Each of the company's four regional sales managers is responsible for any additional training, to occur as each deems necessary. Regional sales managers typically have attempted, at a minimum, to keep their salespeople up to speed on product knowledge.

### Current Situation

More than one-third of the way into the fiscal year, sales in the Midwest region at Solutions Software are running about 10 percent behind last year. Regional sales manager Clara Halter is concerned. National sales manager Ken Raft has been pushing Clara hard since last year when her region's sales came in just under the yearly sales target. This year, Clara is determined to exceed her goal. If she does not, she fears she might not be around to make an attempt again next year.

Clara has been the Midwest regional sales manager for four years, having formerly been a salesperson with Solutions for six years. During her tenure as sales manager, she has yet to conduct any formal training beyond keeping her salespeople abreast of new products. Now, she thinks, might be the time for some additional training. Perhaps this would provide her salespeople with the tools they need to increase their sales.

First, Clara thinks, she must decide what the training should include. She recalls that salespeople's initial training did not address time and territory management or customer knowledge. Perhaps her salespeople are not using their time as efficiently and effectively as they should be. She figures that salespeople could always use some additional training in this area. Furthermore, she surmises that her salespeople might benefit from understanding different buyer types along with techniques for handling each. Finally, Clara believes that her salespeople might gain from brushing up on some sales techniques. Clara believes that

because building relationships is such an important part of the business, salespeople could use some additional training on how to build rapport and trust, as well as effectively listen and question.

Having determined what she wants her salespeople to learn, Clara sets out to decide on the methods that will be most suitable for teaching her salespeople. She decides that she will develop a two-page handout on time and territory management to deliver to salespeople during their training session. They can review these materials at their leisure and use the information to make them more efficient. With regard to customer knowledge, Clara thinks she will design a series of role playing exercises involving different customer types. Salespeople will form teams of two. One salesperson will play the role of a specific type of buyer and the other salesperson will attempt to identify and appropriately sell to this buyer type. Salespeople will then critique the performance. Finally, Clara believes that the best way for salespeople to improve their selling skills is for her to lecture on the topics of rapport and trust building, and listening and questioning.

Next, Clara has to decide when and where to hold the training. As far as she is concerned, it cannot be soon enough. She decides to hold a two-day training seminar in sunny Orlando, Florida, at the beginning of next month. She thinks this change in scenery might be conducive to learning. She sends a company memo via e-mail to all her salespeople explaining the program and the date.

On completion of the sales training, Clara feels more upbeat. Surely, she thinks this will help her salespeople pick up the pace. Only time will tell.

### Questions

1. Assess the sales training processes used by Clara Halter. What would you do differently if you were she? (That is, how could the process be improved?)
2. Do you think this program will improve sales? Explain.
3. Do you think that salespeople will find this program useful? Explain.

## Case 6.2: Compusystems, Inc.

### Background

Beth Barnes joined Compusystems, Inc., 18 months ago. She was interested in working for a progressive company with growth potential. Compusystems, Inc., appeared to be such a company. The company sold a variety of business computing systems. Beth was assigned to sell computerized cash register systems.

The salesforce was taught to practice adaptive selling in which salespeople learned how to probe for customer needs and respond to customer wants. This method of selling has proven to be very successful for the company. In fact, the company credits its move in market position from number five to number three in the last three years to its implementation of adaptive selling and its salesforce's ability to build strong customer relationships.

### Current Situation

Beth was running behind as usual. She had a major presentation scheduled with a well-qualified prospect that could bring a substantial payoff to both her and her company. As a result, she had to cancel her first scheduled appointment of the day so that she could finish preparing her presentation for this prospect. This was not the first time she had to cancel an appointment. Just last week she canceled an appointment because she realized she would be unable to make it to the client's firm before it closed. She had failed to budget enough time into her schedule to allow her to travel from one appointment to the next.

Beth arrived at Handyman Hardware five minutes late. Luckily for Beth the owner of Handyman, Joshua Jones, had been on an important conference call that ran a little longer than anticipated. Jones was hoping to purchase a new cash register system that could track his inventory. He was concerned about inventory loss, particularly in terms of pilferage and the possibility of employees inaccurately (both on purpose and otherwise) ringing up sales. Moreover, he hoped to implement a system that would allow him to track sales better, while at the same time expedite the check-out process. Currently, he is using fairly antiquated equipment that does not provide him with the ability to scan merchandise or systematically track inventory and sales.

After introducing herself and her company, Beth got right down to business. She went into a 30-minute presentation explaining the CR2000, a cash register system she believed would be appropriate for Jones' store. What follows are excerpts from her meeting with Jones:

*Beth:* Although we sell several systems, Mr. Jones, I believe the CR2000 cash registers would be good for you. They are relatively inexpensive, provide a more rapid system for checking out customers, and are superior to what you now have.

*Jones:* As I mentioned earlier, I want a system that provides me with the ability to track inventory and total sales. Does this system do that?

*Beth:* No, it doesn't. We sell systems that can monitor inventory, but they are more expensive. You presently have some type of system for tracking inventory, don't you?

*Jones:* Yes, but it is time-consuming and I have always been concerned about its accuracy.

*Beth:* We could provide you with an inventory tracking system. But, in your case, it may not be worth the extra cost.

*Jones:* I'd really be interested in a system that is quicker than my present system and can track sales and inventory. I would also like to begin using bar codes, rather than individually pricing each item.

*Beth:* We carry the CR2500. This system would provide you with the ability to do these things. However, this system runs quite a bit more.

*Jones:* Will this system allow me to monitor sales hourly?

*Beth:* I believe it will. This is a fairly new system. It's an update of an earlier model. Some changes were made, and I'm not sure exactly what has been changed.

*Jones:* Can the system break out sales by department?

*Beth:* The older version of this system could. I am sure the new version can also. If you would like, Mr. Jones, I can write you a proposal for installing the CR2500. When I finish the proposal we can meet again to further discuss the CR2500.

### Questions

1. With regard to Beth, what sales training needs can you identify?
2. If you were Beth's sales manager and you discovered that several of your salespeople had training needs similar to those of Beth, what methods would you suggest for training the salesforce to improve in deficient areas?
3. What are the effects of sales training on salesforce motivation and morale?

**ROLE PLAY**

| | |
|---|---|
| **Situation:** | Read Case 6.2. |
| **Characters:** | Beth Barnes, sales rep; Joshua Jones, store owner; Donna Karin, Beth's sales manager |
| **Scene 1:** | (optional) *Location*—Handyman Hardware. *Action*—Beth is making her presentation to Joshua Jones as her sales manager Donna Karin observes. |
| **Scene 2:** | *Location*—Outside Handyman Hardware following Beth's meeting with Jones. *Action*—Donna coaches Beth regarding her sales presentation (for more detail on coaching see Module 7). |

# Directing the Salesforce

This part contains two modules dealing with the direction of the activities of the salesforce. Module 7 presents a model of sales management leadership. Contemporary views of sales leadership are discussed, along with important leadership functions such as coaching. The critical role of ethics in leadership is investigated, and coverage is provided on dealing with problems such as sexual harassment, conflicts of interest, and disruptive salespeople.

Module 8 deals with motivating the salesforce to work hard on the right activities over a sustained period of time. Reward systems, with an emphasis on financial and nonfinancial compensation are discussed. Special issues related to team compensation and compensating a global salesforce are presented. Guidelines for motivating and rewarding salespeople are offered.

## SALES LEADERSHIP: SAP AMERICA

SAP America is the leader in enterprise application software, with annual sales in excess of $2.8 billion. Bill McDermott became CEO of SAP America in 2002. He had spent 17 years in sales and sales management at Xerox and served as executive vice president of worldwide sales and operations at Siebel Systems. His leadership at SAP has produced overall growth of about 14 percent in a flat market. What key leadership activities are responsible for this type of growth?

One is the development and buy-in by employees of mission and vision statements. Every SAP America employee is given a pocket-sized booklet entitled "Words of Honor: SAP America. Vision. Mission. Values." In it, for example, employees can read that the company's mission is "to build a trusted partnership with each customer by delivering business solutions that create value and superior customer advantage." Employees refer to this booklet on a regular basis as a reminder of the values and commitment of the company.

The mission and vision statements have translated into a customer-centric corporate culture. Bill McDermott reinforces this culture in several ways. He has developed specific sales strategies for each customer group and aligned the sales organization structure to implement these strategies and serve customers more effectively. He and the executive vice president of sales spend a great deal of time with customers, sometimes accompanying salespeople on sales calls. In fact, McDermott often tells customers to call him directly if they need anything and he will take care of it.

Much of McDermott's time is also spent with employees. He hires the best talent and communicates with them often to build the best possible team. One approach he uses is to hold regular, company-wide, town hall–style meetings in which remote employees join via video link. He also e-mails employees on their birthdays and anniversaries, and uses several ways to acknowledge special effort. For example, when one salesperson spent a great deal of time closing an important deal, McDermott sent the rep's husband a gift basket thanking him for his patience while his wife was working long hours.

SAP America is building a network of partners to sell a new product that integrates disparate business applications to smaller customers. This will require changes in the SAP America salesforce. However, the basic mission, vision, and customer-centric culture at SAP America will not change. In fact, the commitment to the company's basic values makes it easier to implement new strategies for the sales organization.

**Source:** Jennifer Gilbert, "Face Time," *Sales & Marketing Management* (June 2004): 30–34.

The opening vignette highlights the leadership activities of Bill McDermott, CEO of SAP America. This is an unusual situation—most CEOs are not as directly involved with customers and employees as Bill McDermott. However, many of the same leadership activities are the responsibility of various sales management positions in other companies. Sales managers are involved in activities that can be classified into the categories of leadership, management, and supervision. Exhibit 7.1 presents a general description of each category for three levels within a sales organization.[1]

## Objectives

After completing this module, you should be able to

1 Distinguish between salesforce leadership, management, and supervision.

2 Explain how the LMX model and leadership style approaches contribute to contemporary sales leadership.

3 List the six components of a sales leadership model.

4 Discuss five bases of power that affect leadership.

5 Explain five influence strategies used in leadership.

6 Discuss issues related to coaching the salesforce, holding integrative meetings, and practicing ethical management.

7 Identify some of the problems encountered in leading and supervising a salesforce.

**EXHIBIT 7.1    Sales Organization Positions and Activities**

| | Leadership | Management | Supervision |
|---|---|---|---|
| **Senior Sales Leadership** | Influencing the entire sales organization or a large subunit by creating a vision, values, culture, direction, alignment, and change, and by energizing action | Planning, implementation, and control of sales management process for entire sales organization or large subunit | Working with sales administrative personnel on day-to-day basis |
| **Field Sales Managers** | Influencing assigned salespeople by creating a climate that inspires salespeople | Planning, implementation, and control of sales management process within assigned sales unit | Working with salespeople on day-to-day basis |
| **Salespeople** | Influencing customers, sales team members, others in the company, and channel partners | Planning, implementation, and control of sales activities within assigned territory | Working with sales assistants on day-to-day basis |

Senior sales leadership includes all positions within a sales organization that have direct responsibility for other sales executives or field sales managers. Typical senior sales leadership titles are chief sales executive, national sales manager, or regional sales manager. Field sales managers have direct responsibility for an assigned group of salespeople and normally include titles like district sales manager or sales manager. The major distinguishing characteristic between senior sales leadership and field sales managers is that salespeople report directly to field sales managers but not to senior sales leaders. Notice that Exhibit 7.1 also includes salespeople. Salespeople are often involved in leadership, management, and sometimes supervision activities.

Although the terms *leadership*, *management*, and *supervision* are often used interchangeably, we think it is important to differentiate among them. **Sales leadership** includes activities that influence others to achieve common goals for the collective good of the sales organization and the company. The leadership activities of senior sales leaders are directed at the entire sales organization or large subunits, and focus on creating the appropriate direction, environment, and alignment within the sales organization. Field sales manager leadership activities emphasize creating the right climate to inspire their assigned salespeople to achieve high levels of performance. Salespeople, in contrast, are engaged in self-leadership and sometimes play a leadership role with customers, others in the sales organization and company, and with channel partners.

**Sales management** activities are those related to the planning, implementation, and control of the sales management process, as presented in Figure 1.1. Senior sales leaders address the broader aspects of the sales management process, while field sales managers are more involved in implementing the process with their assigned salespeople. For example, senior sales leaders typically establish the recruiting and selection process for the sales organization, while field sales managers implement the process by actually recruiting, interviewing, evaluating, and often hiring salespeople. The management activities of salespeople are more focused on the planning, implementation, and control of sales activities within their assigned territory.

**Sales supervision** refers to working with subordinates on a day-to-day basis. Senior sales leadership and salespeople are normally not as involved with supervision as field sales managers. Sales supervision is an extremely important component of the field sales manager position, because field sales managers spend a great deal of time working with assigned salespeople on a day-to-day basis.

This module focuses primarily on sales leadership and secondarily on sales supervision. Because sales leadership activities are becoming increasingly important for all positions within a sales organization, an emphasis on leadership is warranted. Sales supervision is also critical for field sales managers, so it is addressed as well. Sales management activities are the major focus of this book and are covered in detail in the other modules in the text.

## CONTEMPORARY VIEWS OF SALES LEADERSHIP

Sales researchers have advanced two general views of sales leadership: leadership style and the Leader-Member Exchange (LMX) model. Each of these views provides a general perspective on sales leadership.

### Leadership Style

A **leadership style** is the general orientation toward leadership activities. Two basic leadership styles have been examined by sales researchers: transactional and transformational. A **transactional leadership style** is characterized as a contingent reward or contingent punishment orientation.[2] Sales leaders exhibiting a transactional leadership style focus on getting subordinates to perform desired behaviors and achieve high performance levels by providing rewards and punishments. A **transformational leadership style**, in contrast, is represented by an orientation toward inspiring subordinates to engage in desired behaviors and perform at high levels. Specific aspects of a transformational leadership style include articulating a vision, providing an appropriate model, fostering the acceptance of group goals, having high performance expectations, giving individual support, and providing intellectual stimulation.[3]

Although transactional and transformational are the two basic leadership styles, there are individual styles within each category. For example, one categorization suggests visionary, coaching, affiliative, and democratic as transformational styles, and pace setting and commanding as transaction approaches. This research indicates that effective leaders employ multiple leadership styles, depending on the situation. Thus, sales managers might have a general transactional or transformational leadership style, but adapt to each situation by using an appropriate leadership style.[4]

### Leader-Member Exchange Model

Instead of emphasizing general leadership styles, the **Leader-Member Exchange (LMX) model** focuses on the relationships in each salesperson–sales manager dyad. LMX proposes that sales managers interact uniquely with individual salespeople rather than employing a specific leadership style for each situation. Studies have shown that reciprocal trust between sales managers and salespeople has a positive effect on the salesperson–sales manager relationship. This research indicates a positive relationship between trust and job satisfaction, satisfaction with the manager, a positive psychological climate, a willingness to change, goal commitment, performance, and a negative relationship with role conflict.[5]

One appealing aspect of the LMX model is that many sales organizations are reorienting their sales processes toward more long-term, trust-based relationships with customers. Salespeople and sales managers in these companies are learning the benefits of building trust in customer relationships and are likely to be motivated to engage in trust-building in the salesperson–sales manager dyad. By developing quality working relationships with salespeople, sales managers may be able to foster more adaptive selling behaviors by salespeople as a way to develop customer relationships.[6]

## A LEADERSHIP MODEL FOR SALES MANAGEMENT

The LMX model and leadership styles approaches capture some of the key thoughts in contemporary sales leadership: Build a strong, trust-based relationship with individual salespeople. Be an active stimulus for change, and work with salespeople and others to accomplish the mission. Expect salespeople to take an active role in managing themselves. To pull these and other leadership approaches together, we now offer a leadership model for sales management.

Figure 7.1 shows the model with six components:

1. *Power*—of the salesperson, salespeople, or other party with whom the sales manager is interacting
2. *Power*—of the sales manager
3. *Situation*—including time constraints, nature of the task, organizational history, and group norms
4. *Needs*—of the salesperson, salespeople, or other people with whom the sales manager is interacting
5. *Goals and objectives*—of the individuals and the organization
6. *Leadership skills*—anticipation, diagnostic, selection and matching, and communications

**FIGURE 7.1**                    A Leadership Model for Sales Management

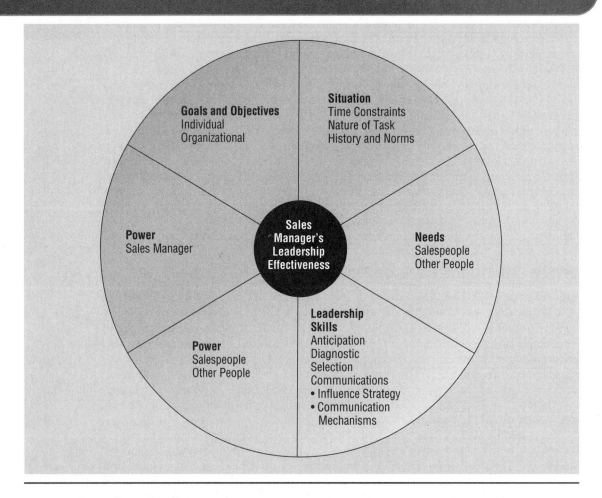

A sales manager's leadership effectiveness is a function of six factors: the power of the salesperson and other people, the power of the sales manager, the situation, human needs, individual and organizational goals and objectives, and the leadership skills of the sales manager.

## Power and Leadership

In most job-related interpersonal situations, sales managers and the parties with whom they interact hold power in some form or another. As the model in Figure 7.1 suggests, the possession and use of this power will have a major impact on the quality of leadership achieved by a sales manager. To simplify discussion, the sales manager–salesperson relationship is emphasized, but keep in mind that sales managers must use their leadership skills in dealing with other personnel in the firm, as well as outside parties such as employment agencies, external trainers, customers, and suppliers.

The power held by an individual in an interpersonal relationship can be of one or more of the following five types.[7] For each type, a sample comment from a salesperson recognizing the sales manager's power is shown in parentheses.[8]

1. **Expert power**—based on the belief that a person has valuable knowledge or skills in a given area. ("I respect her knowledge and good judgment because she is well trained and experienced.")

2. **Referent power**—based on the attractiveness of one party to another. It may arise from friendship, role modeling, or perceived similarity of personal background or viewpoints. ("I like him personally and regard him as a friend.")

3. **Legitimate power**—associated with the right to be a leader, usually as a result of designated organizational roles. ("She has a legitimate right, considering her position as sales manager, to expect that her suggestions will be followed.")

4. **Reward power**—stems from the ability of one party to reward the other party for a designated action. ("He is in a good position to recommend promotions or permit special privileges for me.")

5. **Coercive power**—based on a belief that one party can remove rewards and provide punishment to affect behavior. ("She can apply pressure to enforce her suggestions if they are not carried out fully and properly.")

It should be stressed that it is the various individuals' perceptions of power, rather than a necessarily objective assessment of where the power lies, that will determine the effects of power in interpersonal relationships. For example, a newly appointed district sales manager may perceive the legitimate power associated with being a manager to be extremely high, whereas the salespeople may not share this perception. Such differences in perceptions regarding the nature and balance of power are often at the root of the problems that challenge sales managers.

Many sales managers have been accused of relying too much on reward and coercive power. This is disturbing for three reasons. First, coercive actions are likely to create strife in the salesforce and may encourage turnover among high-performing salespeople who have other employment opportunities. Second, as salespeople move through the career cycle, they tend to self-regulate the reward system. Senior salespeople are often seeking rewards that cannot be dispensed and controlled by sales managers, such as a sense of accomplishment on the job. As a result, rewards lose some of their impact. Third, research has demonstrated that other power bases (expert and referent) are positively related to salespeople's satisfaction with supervision and with sales managers.[9] Thus, it is recommended that sales managers who wish to become effective leaders develop referent and expert power bases.

At times, salespeople have more power in a situation than the sales manager. For example, senior salespeople may be extremely knowledgeable and therefore have dominant expert power over a relatively inexperienced sales manager. Or a sales manager with strong self-esteem needs may be intent on winning a popularity contest with the salesforce, which could give salespeople a strong referent power base. When a sales manager senses that the salesperson is more powerful in one of these dimensions, there is a strong tendency to rely on legitimate, coercive, or reward power to gain control of the situation. Again, it is suggested that these three power bases be used sparingly, however, and that the sales manager work instead toward developing more expert and referent power.

This recommendation is getting results in progressive sales organizations. For example, since being promoted to national sales manager for Century Maintenance Supply,

Theresa Cullens has used a personal approach to leadership to bring about double-digit sales increases. One of her coworkers at Century explains, "She doesn't direct her team from a throne, she gets down in the trenches with you."[10]

The concepts of teamwork and employee participation in management decision making are often used and are largely incompatible with the heavy-handed use of coercive and legitimate power. Sales managers interested in developing an effective power base might consider the advice given in Exhibit 7.2 by Robert Dilenschneider, former president and CEO of Hill and Knowlton, a global public relations firm.[11]

One additional point on sales managers' use of power is that a combination of power bases may be used in a given situation. For example, it might be a sales manager's referent and expert power that allow him or her to conduct a highly effective leadership function, such as an annual sales meeting. Previous research that focused on food brokers suggests that the use of combinations of power bases more accurately reflects reality than does the exclusive use of one power base in a given situation.[12]

## Situational Factors

Scores of studies have tried to uncover what makes an effective leader. One popular category of this research is called the **trait approach**, which attempts to determine the personality traits of an effective leader. To date, trait research, however, has not been enlightening. The **behavior approach**, which seeks to catalog behaviors associated with effective leadership, has likewise failed to identify what makes an effective leader. As the behavior and trait studies continue to be inconclusive, it has become increasingly apparent that the *situation* could have a strong impact on leadership. The model in Figure 7.1 of a **contingency approach** to leadership recognizes the importance of the interaction between situational factors and other factors. Situational contingency factors include the firm's market orientation; sales organization culture; company policies and procedures; the importance of the issue requiring attention; the time available to react; and the power, resources, and interdependencies of the parties involved.[13] When time is at a premium, crisis management is called for, which requires totally different leadership behaviors than usual. For example, a sales manager might rely on legitimate power, or even coercive power, to get immediate, undisputed support of the salesforce if time is constrained.

Certainly the nature of the task is an important part of the situation. Many sales organizations have had a tough time during the recent economic slump. However, there are signs of a recovery and sales managers need to make some changes. Take Mohawk Ltd as an example. The company had sales decrease from $14 million to $13 million in 2003, but expected sales to increase to $16.5 million in 2004 as the economy improved. Suzanne Bakiewicz, vice president of sales and marketing, is continuing a focus on productivity and profitability. However, she has redesigned sales territories and is having more sales meetings to keep her sales teamed geared up for a large increase in sales growth next year.[14]

---

**EXHIBIT 7.2** How Sales Managers Can Develop Power

The former president of Hill and Knowlton, a global public relations firm, offers sales managers several suggestions for developing their power bases:

- Decide on overall objectives.
- Listen to your sales team's wants, needs, and dreams.
- Align the sales team with the firm's corporate culture.
- Meet key customers and industry leaders.
- Make appearances at image-enhancing events.
- Secure support of upper management for sales management programs and activities.
- Use one-on-one meetings to motivate salespeople.
- Develop an information management system to minimize the flow of irrelevant information.

## Needs and Wants of Salespeople

Continuing the discussion of the model shown in Figure 7.1, it should be stressed that leadership is an interactive process requiring one or more individuals to assume the role of followers or constituents. If coercive power-based behavior is cast aside, the needs and wants of salespeople must be given due consideration to ensure a supporting constituency for effective sales management leadership. Obviously the needs and wants of salespeople cannot be met on a carte blanche basis. Furthermore, a sales manager cannot become overly sensitive to the point of paranoia or managerial paralysis brought on by the fear that necessary actions will alienate the salesforce. But on balance, the needs and wants of salespeople must be constantly weighed as an important determinant of leadership behavior.

In assessing the needs and wants of salespeople, it is important to consider each salesperson as a unique individual. Although it is true that individual salespeople are typically part of a work group (i.e., the salesforce), sales managers should attempt to tailor their actions to individual salespeople when feasible. A study of retail and insurance salespeople provides support for these ideas, concluding that sales managers' supervisory behaviors are related to sales performance and that sales managers should manage salespeople individually in terms of supervisory behaviors.[15]

## Goals and Objectives

If salespeople's needs and wants are consistent with the organization's goals and objectives, leadership is an easier task for sales managers. To this end, some companies hold extensive training and development sessions on "life planning" for their salespeople. In these sessions, salespeople define their short- and long-term personal goals. In subsequent sessions, company management attempts to show how the salespeople's personal goal achievement can also assist in organizational goal achievement.

One firm that uses life planning is Combustion Engineering, a large industrial company. Combustion Engineering conducts these sessions on college campuses such as MIT with the assistance of industrial psychologists. The sessions are taken seriously. Company management believes that such goal clarification is beneficial not only to the personal development of their employees, but also because it helps produce a supportive constituency for the leaders of the firm.

## Leadership Skills

As previously suggested, no one has been able to identify the exact personality traits or leadership behaviors that make an effective sales management leader. Likewise, there is no magic combination of skills that ensures effective leadership. Next, several skill areas that may be related to effective leadership are reviewed; keep in mind, however, that possession of a particular skill is no more important than knowing when to use it. The skill areas covered include anticipation and seeking feedback, diagnostic skills, selection and matching, and communication skills. See how sales manager Sabrina Rogers uses various skills to lead her salesforce in "Sales Management in the 21st Century: Leading the Salesforce at Federated Mutual Insurance."

### Anticipation and Seeking Feedback

The business press is full of examples of leadership crises that could have been avoided by **anticipation** of a potential problem. Consider the case of Frontier Corporation, a telecommunications company based in Rochester, New York, whose goal is to be as familiar to businesses and consumers as AT&T, MCI, and Sprint. With revenues sliding, the fifth largest telecommunications company in the United States decided to revamp its misguided sales compensation plan that paid salespeople against the total revenue they generated in a new account over a three-month period. With proper anticipation, management at Frontier might have foreseen that this system provided reps with little

### Leading the Salesforce at Federated Mutual Insurance

Sabrina Rogers, district marketing manager for Federated Mutual Insurance, discusses her leadership approach.

*Leadership in today's salesforce requires a definite and positive approach to each team member. My approach remains consistent. First, Federated has established a business plan that clearly defines the [company's] expectations of each sales representative. The business plan helps guide each individual to take* *responsibility for their own results and, therefore, contributes to the company's success. It is my responsibility to ensure that my reps understand the business plan. Secondly, I strive to provide timely and accurate feedback to each individual regarding the sales approach and sales techniques. I reinforce positive behaviors while providing and monitoring alternatives to poor habits. Finally, as a leader, I provide an example of how to attain goals and overall success while promoting core values and a good work ethic. It is imperative that sales representatives understand that I will work for them and with them.*

reason to further customer relationships beyond the third month. The new plan rewards reps for increasing business in a one-year period and provides them roughly 3 percent of the total revenue in the account each month after that period. Salespeople have embraced the new system because they find that it is easier to sell additional products to a current customer than it is to open a new account.[16]

The Frontier case illustrates how even the best-run companies can benefit from better anticipation of problems to avert leadership crises. It is unfair to expect unerring clairvoyance of sales managers, but it is reasonable to expect that responsible leaders will try to extend their vision into the future. One way they can do this is to **seek feedback** from customers, salespeople, and other important sources regularly. Feedback can be gathered regularly through field visits, salesforce audits, and conscientious reviews of routine call reports submitted by salespeople. The idea of sales managers spending more time in the field, whether or not they are accompanied by salespeople, is increasingly being advocated.

One option is for the sales manager to actually spend time in the field in the role of the salesperson. Some sales managers have actual sales responsibilities; others visit the field as temporary salespeople. While in the sales role, the manager can assess sales support, customer service, availability of required information, job stress, workload factors, and other variables of interest. For example, at Cort Furniture Rental in Capital Heights, Maryland, sales managers may spend two or more days a month accompanying each salesperson on calls.[17]

### Diagnostic Skills

Effective leaders must be able to determine the specific nature of the problem or opportunity to be addressed. Although this sounds simple, it is often difficult to distinguish between the real problem and the more visible symptoms of the problem. Earlier it was noted that sales managers have relied too heavily on reward and coercive power to direct their salesforces. A primary reason for this is a recurring tendency to attack easily identified symptoms of problems, not the core problems that need resolution. Reward and coercive power are also expedient ways to exercise control, and they suit the manager who likes to react without deliberation when faced with a problem.

For example, a sales manager may react to sluggish sales volume results by automatically assuming the problem is motivation. What follows from this hasty conclusion is a heavy dose of newly structured rewards, or just the opposite: a strong shot of coercion. Perhaps motivation is not the underlying problem; perhaps other determinants of performance are actually the source of the problem. But a lack of **diagnostic skills** (discussed further in Module 10) has led the sales manager to attack the easiest target, the symptom of the problem, rather than fully examine the root cause of the problem. As we all know from our experiences with the common cold, treating the symptoms will not solve the problem permanently.

Bob Murphy, vice president of sales for Optimus Solutions, knows that diagnosing and fixing the right problem can be very effective. The company had a sales rep who was not performing well and the company considered letting her go. Murphy decided to identify the cause of her poor performance. He determined that she lacked the confidence to sell without lowering the product price. He worked with her to increase her confidence, improve her selling approach, and eliminate her price-lowering tendencies. This work paid off: The salesperson increased sales by 50 percent and is now a high performer.[18]

## Selection and Matching

As already mentioned, no specific inventory of skills exists for effective leadership. Rather, there is a range of behaviors that should be matched to a particular situation. For example, aspersions have been cast on the use of coercive power in sales management, but its use may be entirely appropriate in some situations. In the case of a problem employee whose insubordination is creating morale problems for the remainder of the salesforce, for example, a "shape up or ship out" ultimatum may be the best response.

The importance of *selecting* appropriate leadership responses to *match* the situation is highlighted in the research dealing with salespeople's concerns as they move through career stages. A study of one company's salespeople found entry-level salespeople to be unhappy with their sales managers and the aspects of the sales jobs over which the manager had considerable control.[19] For example, they did not perceive their sales managers to be open and supportive, and they believed they had little opportunity to make important decisions. More experienced salespeople in this company held positive perceptions toward their sales managers and toward aspects of their jobs heavily influenced by management. Obviously, either a change in managerial behavior toward the discontented entry-level salespeople was called for in this case, or the company's recruitment and selection methods should have been changed. Either way, being able to match managerial actions to the situation, rather than responding within a narrowly defined range of behaviors, would be a big advantage to effective leadership.

## Communication

Recall the definition of leadership from the beginning of this module. At the heart of the definition is the phrase "the use of influence through communication processes." In this section, various influence strategies and communications mechanisms involved in leadership and supervision are discussed. Effective leaders deliver clear, timely information through appropriate media or interpersonal communications. By contrast, the best plans and intentions can be destroyed by faulty communication. All too often, sales operations are damaged by premature leakage of information, inconsistent and conflicting communication, tardy messages, or poorly conceived strategies for influencing the salesforce.

### Influence Strategies

Because sales managers have power from different sources to use in dealing with salespeople, peers, and superiors, they have the opportunity to devise different **influence strategies** according to situational demands. Influence strategies can be based on threats, promises, persuasion, relationships, and manipulation.[20] All are appropriate at some time with some salespeople but not necessarily with superiors or peers.

### *Threats*

In a strategy based on **threats**, a manager might specify a desired behavior and the punishment that will follow if the behavior is not achieved. "If you do not call on your accounts at least once a week, you will lose your job," is an example. Because threats are used only in cases of noncompliance to operational guidelines, their use requires a monitoring system to see whether the threatened person is engaging in the desired behavior. This can be time-consuming and annoying for the manager. Threats should be viewed as a last resort, but they should not be eliminated as a viable influence strategy. Research has indicated that salespeople, contrary to common wisdom, do not appear to react unfavorably to appropriate punishment and that managers "need to overcome their own reluctance in meting out punishment."[21]

### Promises

Sales managers can use reward power as a basis for developing influence strategies based on promises. Research has indicated that promises produce better compliance than threats.[22] This would seem to be especially true for well-educated mobile employees, which many professional salespeople are. Furthermore, influence strategies based on promises as opposed to threats help foster positive feelings among salespeople and boost salesforce morale.

### Persuasion

An influence strategy based on **persuasion** can work without the use of reward or coercive power. Because persuasive messages must be rational and reasonable, however, expert and referent power bases are necessary to make them effective. Persuasion implies that the target of influence must first change his or her attitudes and intentions to produce a subsequent change in behavior. For example, a sales manager might persuade the salesforce to submit weekly activity reports by first convincing them of the importance of the reports in the company's marketing information system.

Sales managers are almost always former salespeople and therefore are comfortable with influence through persuasion. Generally speaking, persuasion is preferred to threats and promises, but it does require more time and skill.

### Relationships

Two types of **relationships** can affect influence processes. The first type is based on referent power. It builds on personal friendships, or feelings of trust, admiration, or respect. In short, one party is willing to do what the other party desires, simply because the former likes the latter. In a salesforce setting, these kinds of relationships are consistent with the notion of the salesforce as a cooperative team.

To develop relationships based on referent power, sales managers can take several actions. First, they should recognize that, generally speaking, they will be better liked by others if they can cope effectively with their own job pressures. Being calm and pleasant under pressure will bring a sales manager more power than caving in to the pressure, which might result in temper tantrums and impulsive reactions. Second, sales managers can take a genuine interest in the people with whom they interact and can learn to show that interest through conversation and other means of communication. Another suggestion is to initiate reciprocation with other parties by being the first to offer information or to provide a service.[23] For example, a sales manager might provide a production manager with a timely sales forecast on a voluntary basis to help schedule future manufacturing processes. In turn, this may lead the production manager to reciprocate with valuable information for the sales manager at some future date.

In the second type of relationship, one party has legitimate power over the other party by virtue of position in the organizational hierarchy. Sales managers have legitimate power in dealing with salespeople. As a result, they can influence salespeople in many situations without the use of threats, promises, or persuasion.

### Manipulation

Unlike the other influence strategies, **manipulation** does not involve direct communications with the target of influence. Rather, circumstances are controlled to influence behavior. For example, a salesperson lacking self-confidence might be assigned to work on a temporary assignment with a confident senior salesperson. In team selling, the sales manager might control the group dynamics within teams by carefully selecting compatible personality types to compose the teams. Manipulation might also involve "office politics" and the use of third parties to influence others. For example, a sales manager might use the backing of his or her superior in dealing with peers on the job.

## Communication Mechanisms

A critical part of using communication in leadership processes is knowing how to use appropriate **communication mechanisms** effectively. In today's productivity-driven environment, sales managers are using every conceivable device to improve the efficiency of their communication with the salesforce. Cell phones, pagers, fax machines, voice mail, e-mail, Internet, company intranet, satellite, and companywide video networks are some of the more popular tools being used to speed communication to salesforces in far-flung locations. The key is to use the communication mechanisms most appropriate to the sales organization. For example, Carole Levin, sales manager for Taconic, has found that a monthly conference call is an effective way for her and her 11 salespeople, scattered throughout the United States, to communicate on a regular basis. She solicits ideas from reps and publishes an agenda to keep the calls on track. The first 30 minutes of the call focus on the agenda and the remaining 30 minutes are used for discussion and feedback. Levin e-mails a call summary to everyone.[24]

All communication with the salesforce must be carefully planned to ensure accuracy and clarity. And remember, although the latest developments offer exciting features, the simple spoken word between a sales manager and a salesperson is still of prime importance in effective leadership. In fact, research suggests that more frequent and informal communication between a sales manager and salespeople is likely to result in better job performance and greater job satisfaction.[25]

## SELECTED LEADERSHIP FUNCTIONS

In this section, three particularly important leadership functions of sales management are discussed: coaching the salesforce, planning and conducting integrative sales meetings, and striving for ethical (or moral) leadership behavior.

## Coaching

In the **coaching** role, a sales manager concentrates on continuous development of salespeople through supervisory feedback and role modeling.[26] The importance of coaching is illustrated in this passage:

> To many a sales manager, a seller either has or hasn't got what it takes to sell. This attitude reduces sales management to a problem of finding the right seller. The difficulty with that approach is that seller turnover rates are often horrendous, leaving many territories poorly covered or not covered at all. . . . Sales managers should be in the field with their low producers, and their new sellers, as much as possible. Like good athletic coaches, they should constantly remind the sellers of the fundamentals, constantly encourage, and constantly praise good performance.[27]

Although coaching may entail the sales manager's interactions with a group of salespeople, its most crucial activities are those conducted with individual salespeople. Coaching sessions may take place in the office or during the sales manager's field visits with salespeople. In the field, such sessions often take the form of "curbstone conferences" immediately before or after each sales call.

Because salespeople often have considerable latitude to plan and execute work activities, coaching is extremely important for most sales managers. Furthermore, the boundary-role demands of sales jobs and the frequent geographic isolation of salespeople from other company personnel add to the significance of coaching activities.

The essence of coaching is providing guidance and feedback as close as possible to the occurrence of an appropriate event related to developing salespeople's skills, attitudes, or behaviors. For example, at Pfizer Inc., sales managers accompany salespeople in the field once a month. After every field ride, sales managers provide salespeople with a coaching guide that analyzes their performance in categories such as work ethic, technical knowledge, and sales skills. Managers provide suggestions for improvement along with positive feedback.[28] By ensuring a close link between the coaching session and the appropriate event (e.g., a sales call), the sales manager is using the principle of *recency* to assist the developmental, or learning, process. Essentially this principle holds that learning is facilitated when it is immediately applied. By making a practice of holding coaching sessions before and after each sales call, sales managers are also using *repetition,* another powerful learning tool.

In addition to using repetition and recency to facilitate learning, sales managers should consider the type of feedback they offer to salespeople during coaching sessions. Feedback can be described as either outcome feedback or as cognitive feedback.[29] **Outcome feedback** is information about whether a desired outcome is achieved. By contrast, **cognitive feedback** is information about how and why the desired outcome is achieved. Post-sales call coaching focusing on outcome feedback might feature such comments as, "Your response to the question on pricing was totally inadequate," whereas cognitive feedback might focus on why the pricing question was poorly handled, how a better response could have been made, and how the proper handling of the question could have facilitated the desired outcome for the sales call.

Researchers have suggested that cognitive feedback can be helpful to salespeople and that positive outcome feedback serves an informational and motivational function and can enhance salespeople's job performance and job satisfaction.[30] The importance of cognitive feedback is reaffirmed in several of the points in Exhibit 7.3.[31]

Successful coaching occurs in an environment of trust and respect between the sales manager and salesperson. By demonstrating honesty, reliability, and competency and by

---

**EXHIBIT 7.3     Coaching Suggestions**

1. Take a "we" approach instead of a "you" approach. Instead of telling the salesperson, "You should do it this way next time," say, "On the next call, we can do it this way."
2. Address only one or two problems at a time. Prioritize problems to be attacked, and deal with the most important ones first.
3. Instead of criticizing salespeople during coaching, help them improve by giving how-to advice. Repeatedly tell them what you like about their performance.
4. Ask questions to maximize the salesperson's active involvement in the coaching process.
5. Recognize differences in salespeople and coach accordingly. Although salespeople should work together as a team, direct some efforts toward meeting individual needs.
6. Coordinate coaching with more formal sales training. Coaching is valuable, but it cannot replace formal sales training. Train regularly to enhance skills, then reinforce with coaching.
7. Encourage continual growth and improvement of salespeople. Use team or one-on-one sessions to evaluate progress and celebrate accomplishments.
8. Insist that salespeople evaluate themselves. Self-evaluation helps develop salespeople into critical thinkers regarding their work habits and performance.
9. Reach concrete agreements about what corrective action is to be taken after each coaching session. Failure to agree on corrective action may lead to the salesperson's withdrawal from the developmental aspects of coaching.
10. Keep records of coaching sessions specifying corrective action to be taken, objectives of the coaching session, and a timetable for accomplishing the objective. Follow up to ensure objectives are accomplished.

listening to salespeople's needs, sales managers can earn the trust and respect of sales-people and enhance their own chances of being a successful coach.[32] One study suggested that sales managers also can enhance salespeople's trust in them by being good role models.[33] As coaches, sales managers must be role models that set positive examples through their behavior. This is crucial because salespeople will emulate the work habits, positive attitudes, and goals of their managers.[34] See how Steve Randazzo at KV Pharmaceutical Company (ETHEX Division), uses collaboration and coaching to help his salespeople achieve their goals in "Sales Management in the 21st Century: Collaboration and Coaching at KV Pharmaceutical Company (ETHEX Division)."

---

SALES MANAGEMENT IN THE 21ST CENTURY

### Collaboration and Coaching at KV Pharmaceutical Company (ETHEX Division)

Steve Randazzo, vice president of sales for KV Pharmaceutical Company, shares his strategy for using collaboration and coaching to help his salespeople achieve their goals:

*We believe that our salespeople are also our customers. Therefore, we listen closely to their needs and then work with them to develop strategies to best serve their accounts. I sit down with salespeople, and together we analyze their current product mix and relationship development strategy for each account. We then determine a strategy for developing a product mix and cultivating relationships that will grow each account to achieve desired sales goals. Besides helping salespeople with strategy, we use coaching to help salespeople improve their sales presentations. After a sales call, I will conduct a post-call analysis. First, salespeople provide a self-critique of the call. Then I give my analysis, letting the salespeople know what they did well or not so well and offering suggestions for improving future calls. Although salespeople are still held fully accountable for reaching their goals, we believe that they will be in a better position to achieve them if we can provide them with direction for doing so.*

---

## Planning and Conducting Integrative Sales Meetings

One of the best opportunities for sales managers to demonstrate leadership ability comes when they plan and execute an **integrative meeting,** one in which several sales and sales management functions are achieved. Although multiple objectives are accomplished at such meetings, their overall purpose is to unite the salesforce in the quest for common objectives, a key part of the leadership model discussed earlier in this module. Such meetings may combine training, strategic planning, motivational programs, recognition of outstanding sales performance, and recreation and entertainment for the attendees. In large sales organizations, the entire salesforce may attend a major integrative sales meeting each year to review the past year's performance and unite for the upcoming year. According to John Mackenzie, a meeting consultant for Coca-Cola, DuPont, and General Foods, such events allow "psychic bonding" among salespeople; that is, salespeople can share common experiences and feel more like team members than isolated employees.[35] Sales managers can use integrative meetings to ensure that salespeople gain a better understanding of their important revenue production role. Mackenzie also stresses that such meetings provide an excellent means for sales managers to reinforce their own visibility, reputation, and image with top management and the salesforce.

As is true with all leadership functions, the needs and wants of the salesforce should be given some consideration in the planning and execution of integrative meetings. Some suggestions from salespeople are given in Exhibit 7.4.[36]

Planning and conducting an integrative sales meeting involves creative, sometimes glamorous, activities, such as selecting a theme for the meeting, arranging for the appearance of professional entertainers, or even assisting in the production of special

| EXHIBIT 7.4 | Suggestions from Salespeople on Conducting Meetings |
|---|---|

1. Keep technical presentations succinct, and use visual aids and breakout discussion groups to maintain salespeople's interest.
2. Keep salespeople informed of corporate strategy and their role in it.
3. Minimize operations reviews unless they are directly related to sales. Use a combination of face-to-face exchanges and written handouts to introduce key people in advertising and customer service.
4. Set a humane schedule. Overscheduling can deter learning. Allow time for salespeople to share experiences so they learn from each other.
5. Let salespeople know what's planned. Be sure they are briefed on the purpose and content of the meeting. Distribute a written agenda.
6. Ask salespeople for their ideas on topics, speakers, and preferred recreational activities, if applicable.
7. Generate excitement with contests. Reward effort and results so that all participants can enjoy the chance to win.

films and other audiovisual materials. For example, Latitude Communications, an online conferencing provider, developed the theme "Fire Up" for its national sales meeting. The meeting began with a volcano erupting with smoke and sound effects and a performance from a fire dancer, and included among other things the vice president of marketing performing a rap song about company sales. To foster teamwork and keep with the meeting's theme, salespeople were taken offsite to participate in exercises used to train firefighters, such as a simulated rescue from a five-story tower, a fire-victim carrying race, the passing of water buckets, and extinguishing a fire with authentic firefighting equipment.[37] However, the ultimate success of all meetings depends on the planning and execution of rather detailed activities, such as communicating with all parties before the meeting, checking site arrangements, preparing materials for the meeting, arranging for audiovisual support, and ensuring that all supplies are on hand when the meeting begins. To increase the effectiveness of a major meeting, sales managers would be well served to heed the advice given in Exhibit 7.5.[38]

Increasingly, communication technology allows off-site meeting participants to join in meetings. This is often an attractive option for salesforces that are geographically dispersed. Computer networks, groupwork software such as Lotus Notes, Web meetings, and videoconferencing can replace some face-to-face meetings without any loss in meeting effectiveness. The cost is often lower as well. For instance, Web conferencing, which may run $100 per participant per month, allows participants to talk on the phone while sharing information on the Web, provides online facilities that enable participants to ask questions, and includes tools that can be used to poll attendees.[39] Nonetheless, face-to-face meetings remain a crucial sales leadership activity.

## Meeting Ethical and Moral Responsibilities

In recent years, increased attention has been paid to the subject of ethical responsibilities of business leaders. As pointed out in a prize-winning *Harvard Business Review* article, "Most business decisions involve some degree of ethical judgment; few can be taken solely on the basis of arithmetic."[40] In previous modules, ethical concerns have been highlighted to stress their importance in practically every sales management function. In this section, three approaches to management ethics are discussed: **immoral management**, **amoral management**, and **moral management**. The key points distinguishing these three approaches are shown in Exhibit 7.6.[41] The author of the material shown in the exhibit contends that most managers fit into the amoral category and that the number of moral managers roughly equals the number of immoral managers.[42]

| Sales Manager's Meeting Review List | EXHIBIT 7.5 |

**Before your meeting**
1. Distribute meeting notice/agenda.
2. Plan and prepare the meeting content, both words and visuals, in terms of the needs of your audience.
3. Rehearse.
4. Check out room and equipment.

**At the start of the meeting**
1. Review the agenda.
2. Review meeting objectives.
3. Explain what role the participants will have in the meeting.

**During the meeting (encouraging participation)**
1. Ask open-end questions . . . that is, questions that can't be answered with yes or no.
2. Ask one or two participants to bring specific relevant information to share at the meeting.
3. Reinforce statements that are on target with meeting objectives.
4. When questions are asked of you, redirect them to the group or to the questioner.
5. Use examples from your own personal experience to encourage the group to think along similar lines.

**During the meeting (maintaining control)**
1. Ignore off-target remarks. Do not reinforce.

2. Ask questions specifically related to the task at hand.
3. Restate relevant points of the agenda when the discussion veers from objectives.
4. When one person is dominating the discussion, tactfully, but firmly, ask him or her to allow others to speak.
5. Ask the group's opinion about whether a certain subject is on target or not with the agenda.

**At the end of the meeting**
1. Summarize.
2. State conclusions and relate to original meeting objectives.
3. Outline actions to be taken as a result of the meeting (who is expected to do what and by when).

**Cautions**
1. Encourage, don't resent, questions.
2. Be a facilitator and not a monopolizer of discussion.
3. A little humor is welcome at most any meeting, but don't attempt to be a constant comic.
4. Don't put anybody down in public. If you have a problem participant, take him or her aside at a break and ask for cooperation.
5. Coming unprepared is worse than not coming.

As you review the information in Exhibit 7.6, examples of immoral management may come to mind easily, whereas examples of amoral and moral management are probably harder to recall. This is partially a function of what types of business practices have been deemed most topical by the business and popular press. However, the press coverage could also indicate a deep concern throughout society about ethics in management.

Before discussing the features of moral, or ethical, sales management, some examples of seemingly immoral management (as described in Exhibit 7.6) might be helpful.

- Over a seven-year period, TAP Pharmaceutical Products Inc., provided free samples of the prostate cancer drug Lupron to physicians who in turn sought reimbursement from Medicaid and Medicare. These illegal actions cost patients nearly $145 million. TAP has agreed to pay $875 million to settle criminal and civil charges. Six TAP sales managers have been indicted on charges of fraud.[43]

- Pre-Paid Legal Services paid $1.5 million in 2001 to settle numerous suits from customers claiming that it overstated the amount of legal coverage it offered. Apparently salespeople were told to inform customers that Pre-Paid would cover all of a person's legal needs, when in reality this was not true.[44]

- Salespeople at a New York-based Internet company that sold advertising campaigns to some of the world's largest companies were encouraged to do whatever it took to get the deal, which usually involved lying. According to a former company sales rep, "If you didn't lie you were fired."[45]

- Some executives at Enron, WorldCom, Adelphia Communications, and IMClone Systems have been indicted on charges of fraud. At Enron, for example, traders sold energy that did not exist.[46]

- A sales consultant in Scottsdale, Arizona, asked the president of a company to let one top salesperson go because he was constantly cheating on his expense reports. He was using company expenses to pay for his "dates" with call girls. While the president agreed he should be fired, he failed to do so, fearing that he would lose clients.[47]

- In a survey of 316 sales and marketing executives, 47 percent suspect that their salespeople have lied on a sales call and only 16.5 percent have never heard their salespeople make an unrealistic promise to a customer.[48]

These examples are in sharp contrast to moral management as described in Exhibit 7.6. Corporate training can help sensitize managers to ethical issues and may be able to convert amoral, and even immoral, managers to the moral school of thought.

---

**EXHIBIT 7.6     Approaches to Management Ethics**

| Organizational Characteristics | | Immoral Management | Amoral Management | Moral Management |
|---|---|---|---|---|
| | Ethical Norms | Management decisions, actions, and behavior imply a positive and active opposition to what is moral (ethical). Decisions are discordant with accepted ethical principles. An active negation of what is moral is implied. | Management is neither moral nor immoral, but decisions lie outside the sphere to which moral judgments apply. Management activity is outside or beyond the moral order of a particular code. May imply a lack of ethical perception and moral awareness. | Management activity conforms to a standard of ethical, or right, behavior. Management activity conforms to accepted professional standards of conduct. Ethical leadership is common on the part of management. |
| | Motives | Selfish. Management cares only about its or the company's gains. | Well-intentioned but selfish in the sense that impact on others is not considered. | Good. Management wants to succeed but only within the confines of sound ethical precepts (fairness, justice, due process). |
| | Goals | Profitability and organizational success at any price. | Profitability. Other goals are not considered. | Profitability within the confines of legal obedience and ethical standards. |
| | Orientation toward Law | Legal standards are barriers that management must overcome to accomplish what it wants. | Law is the ethical guide, preferably the letter of the law. The central question is what we can do legally. | Obedience toward letter and spirit of the law. Law is a minimal ethical behavior. Prefer to operate well above what law mandates. |
| | Strategy | Exploit opportunities for corporate gain. Cut corners when it appears useful. | Give managers free rein. Personal ethics may apply but only if managers choose. Respond to legal mandates if caught and required to do so. | Live by sound ethical standards. Assume leadership position when ethical dilemmas arise. Enlightened self-interest. |

| Code of Ethics for Professional Salespeople | **EXHIBIT 7.7** |
| --- | --- |

*As a certified professional salesperson, I pledge to the following people and organizations:*

**The Customer.** In all customer relationships, I pledge to

- Maintain honesty and integrity in my relationships with customers and prospective customers.

- Accurately represent my product or service to place the customer or prospective customer in a position to make a decision consistent with the principle of mutuality of benefit and profit to the buyer and seller.

- Keep abreast of all pertinent information that would assist my customers in achieving their goals as they relate to my product(s) or service(s).

**The Company.** In relationships with my employer, coworkers, and other parties whom I represent, I will

- Use their resources that are at my disposal for legitimate business purposes only.

- Respect and protect proprietary and confidential information entrusted to me by my company.

**The Competition.** Regarding those with whom I compete in the marketplace, I promise to

- Obtain competitive information only through legal and ethical methods.

- Portray my competitors and their products and services only in a manner that is honest and truthful and that reflects accurate information that can or has been substantiated.

Tighter financial controls and closer supervision of sales activities may help achieve ethical sales management practices. Bribery, for example, is hard to commit when sales expenditures are closely monitored. Many sales organizations are adopting a **code of ethics**. One survey found that 84 percent of the companies surveyed have a code of conduct and 45 percent have an ethics office.[49] Associations also develop ethical codes and urge members to adhere to standards of ethical business behavior. An example of such a code is shown in Exhibit 7.7.[50]

Certainly, the development of a code of ethics is a positive action, although it is probably not enough to ensure ethical management. Sales managers must be willing to evaluate their own behavior and ask themselves if they consistently act in an ethical manner in dealing with their coworkers, employees, customers, and other parties.[51] This process of self-evaluation could be very revealing, as suggested in a study of how sales managers react to unethical sales behavior.[52] The study concluded that sales managers would be more likely to use harsher disciplinary measures if the salesperson were male instead of female or a poor performer rather than a top performer and if negative consequences (e.g., losing a major account) were to follow the unethical action by the salesperson. In an ideal world, sales managers would react to unethical sales behavior without regard for individual characteristics of the salesperson involved or the consequences of the unethical act.

In examining their own behavior and that of the salesforce, sales managers should be aware of three particularly relevant types of unethical acts, as shown in Exhibit 7.8.[53] The first type of unethical act is termed a **nonrole act**. This type of act (e.g., cheating on an expense account) would not relate to a sales manager's or a salesperson's specific job role but rather is a calculated attempt to gain something at the expense of the company. A **role failure act** involves a failure to perform job responsibilities. For example, a sales manager may do a superficial job on a salesperson's performance appraisal. The third type of unethical act is the **role distortion act** (e.g., committing bribery), which may put the individual at risk, presumably to benefit the company and the individual's own job objectives.

Researchers suggest that it is most likely that a given organization will concentrate attention on nonrole acts by implementing financial controls and employee monitoring systems. Interestingly, these researchers conclude that role distortion and role failure

**EXHIBIT 7.8** Types of Morally Questionable Managerial Acts

| Type | Direct Effect | Examples |
|------|---------------|----------|
| Nonrole | Against the firm | • Expense account cheating<br>• Embezzlement<br>• Stealing supplies |
| Role failure | Against the firm | • Superficial performance appraisal<br>• Not confronting expense account cheating<br>• Palming off a poor performer with inflated praise |
| Role distortion | For the firm | • Bribery<br>• Price fixing<br>• Manipulation of suppliers |

acts seldom receive systematic attention in most organizations.[54] Perhaps these findings offer direction to sales managers who are determined to manage their salesforce according to principles of moral, or ethical, conduct.

Those interested in achieving moral management will undoubtedly face some challenges because competitive pressures and the premium placed on expedient action often encourage unethical behavior. As one observer puts it,

> The central nature of selling—a negotiation between buyer and seller—is inherently a laboratory of ethical scenarios. Sales managers likewise face many ethical issues stemming from the discretion they must exercise in adjusting resources for variations in territories, salesperson ability, competitor strength, and social, political, and regulatory climates in the various markets served.[55]

For a long-term horizon for success, we urge you to use a framework for moral, ethical management as described in the last column of Exhibit 7.6 and to embrace, when available, codes of ethics, policies on ethical behavior, training to sensitize salespeople and their managers to ethical issues, and legal instruction. Those who become sales managers will have the added responsibility of providing ethical leadership by setting an example.

## PROBLEMS IN LEADERSHIP

Any managerial position involving the direct supervision of employees will require periodic handling of personnel management problems. As indicated earlier, personnel problems can be minimized through proper recruitment and selection, training, motivation and compensation, and the establishment of clearly stated salesforce plans, policies, and procedures.

Examples of the problems that sales managers may have to deal with include conflicts of interest, chemical abuse and dependency, salespeople who will not conform to guidelines, salespeople whose employment must be terminated, and sexual harassment.

### Conflicts of Interest

Because salespeople assume a boundary-role position, they cannot help but encounter **conflicts of interest**. Such conflicts are part of the job, and problem-solving skills are often tested. In some cases, meeting customer demands could violate company policy. In an even more serious vein, the salesperson could have a vested interest or ownership in a customer's business, or even in a competitor's business. The use of confidential information for individual profit, as in the case of Wall Street insider trading, is also an example of serious—in fact, criminal—conflict of interest. At times, sales managers may be asked to put the company's interest ahead of customers' interests, as seen in "An Ethical Dilemma." Many companies require that employees periodically sign an agreement not to engage in specified situations that may represent conflicting interests.

---

AN ETHICAL DILEMMA

You recently received a promotion to district sales manager. You are eager to show your leadership ability and ready to implement a strategy to make your company successful. Your boss has come to you to explain a new selling strategy that he would like to see you implement. It involves having your salespeople be a little more aggressive with their customers. Essentially, he would like them to oversell their customers. For instance, a salesperson should attempt to convince a customer that he needs an $8,000 copier, even if a $4,000 copier would satisfy his needs. Your boss explains that customers will still be receiving what they need, albeit perhaps a little more, and the company will reap greater profits, resulting in larger bonuses for you. What would you do and why?

---

## Chemical Abuse and Dependency

Salespeople may be no more susceptible to chemical dependency than any other occupational group, nor is there any hard evidence that chemical abuse and dependency are worse among their ranks now than in the past. However, these problems do exist. Chemically dependent employees comprise approximately 10 percent of the workforce. Compared to their peers, these employees are more likely to be late to work, absent, have on-the-job accidents, and file workers' compensation claims. Moreover, they function at only two-thirds of their potential. Estimates indicate that drug abuse in the workplace costs employees more than $100 billion annually.[56] Awareness of this problem is increasing, and sales managers are taking a more active role in identifying individuals with problems and in assisting rehabilitative efforts. This is particularly important given workers' compensation suits and the potential liability for the company and/or individual in the case of employees' misuse of alcohol.[57]

Sales managers have historically played a key role as counselors to salespeople with chemical dependency problems. In today's environment, sales managers might be well advised to leave the counseling to professionals. Many companies have assistance programs to help employees deal with emotional distress, alcoholism, and drug dependency. Such programs take sales managers out of the role of counselor, allowing them to focus on other aspects of their job for which they are better equipped.[58]

## Problem Salespeople: A Disruptive Influence

Sales managers must be able to deal effectively with problem salespeople. In most cases, problems can be remedied by identifying the behavior or attitude to be corrected, then encouraging a change through motivation, supervision, and further training and development. Several caricatures of problem salespeople and the recommended sales management actions are shown in Exhibit 7.9.[59]

Perhaps the most infamous of the "problem salespeople" is the nonconforming "maverick" who breaks all the rules in the quest for sales results. Although mavericks often are high achievers, their flouting of the rules can be disruptive to sales managers and can adversely affect the remainder of the salesforce. A maverick who fails to produce will not survive in most sales organizations, but a rule-breaker who can produce often thrives as the center of attention.

| | Behavior | Nonverbal Signals | Motivated by | Strengths | Problems | How to Manage | Growth Programs |
|---|---|---|---|---|---|---|---|
| Grandstand George | Aggressive | Exuberant | Big awards | Great closer | Overpowering at times | Clip his wings | Team-building program |
| Fearful Fred | Low enthusiasm | Scared | Support | Honesty | Low sales volume | Set/support activity goals | Dale Carnegie course |
| Slumped Sally | Burned out | Depressed | Coaching | Past success experience | Pessimistic attitide | Focus on future goals | Positive attitude programs |
| Excited Eddie | High enthusiasm | Wired | Exotic incentives | Opening new territories | Poor follow-up | Supply new challenges; monitor carefully | Relaxation training |
| Disorganized Debbie | Inconsistent | Frustrated | Meaning | Good team player | Unfinished business | Prioritize; assign specific tasks, deadlines | Time/territory management |
| Perfectionist Pete | Overcontrolled | Rigid | Control | Detail oriented | Lack of flexibility | Relax pressure; reward growth | Stress management |
| Worried Walter | Low enthusiasm | Hesitant | Stability | Amiable, understanding | Tendency to start rumors | Build self-confidence | Self-esteem program |

**EXHIBIT 7.9**     Examples of Problem Salespeople and Remedies

In terms of organizational commitment and job involvement, mavericks are often very enthusiastic about their selling jobs (high involvement) but are not bound to their organizations (low commitment). This high–low combination in terms of involvement and commitment produces a salesperson type sometimes called a **lone wolf**.[60] In some sales environments, for example, if the company sold through independent sales contractors, so-called lone wolves would not present substantial problems. In others, especially when team efforts are required, they would represent a sales management challenge.

Salespeople who are highly committed to the organization but who do not strongly identify with their selling roles might be called **corporate citizens**. They, too, may represent supervisory problems for sales managers, particularly if aggressive sales growth objectives are in place.

Most sales managers would prefer to have a high proportion of salespeople who are both highly committed to the organization and highly involved in their selling jobs. Such salespeople have been called **institutional stars**, and they are the primary targets of retention and reward programs.

Continuing the involvement/commitment typology, salespeople who are low on both dimensions would represent another problem category for sales managers. These salespeople have been referred to as **apathetics** and may be candidates for termination of employment if they cannot be resurrected.

## Termination of Employment

In some cases, problems cannot be overcome, and it is necessary to terminate the employment of a salesperson. When performance consistently fails to meet standards and coaching, training, and retraining are unsuccessful, termination or reassignment may be the only remaining alternatives. Also, a salesperson's insubordination or lack of effort may damage the overall effectiveness or morale of the salesforce, in which case termination could be justified.

The current environment dictates that sales managers pay close attention to the legal ramifications of terminating a salesperson's employment. A permanent record of performance appraisals, conditions of employment, and any deviations from expected performance or behavior should be carefully maintained throughout the salesperson's term of employment. Attempts to correct performance deficiencies should be noted and filed when they occur.

Before firing the salesperson, the sales manager should carefully review all relevant company policies to ensure his or her own adherence to appropriate guidelines. Finally, the actual communication of termination should be written, and any verbal communication of the termination should be witnessed by a third party. At all times, sales managers should respect the dignity of the person whose employment is being terminated while firmly communicating the termination notice.

## Sexual Harassment

In 1980, the Equal Employment Opportunity Commission (EEOC) formally addressed a long-standing workplace problem by issuing guidelines for minimizing **sexual harassment**.[61] Defining this term is not an easy matter, but EEOC guidelines indicate that sexual harassment could include lewd remarks, physical and visual actions, and sexual innuendos. Companies are expected to have guidelines for dealing with this offense, including a written policy prohibiting all forms of sexual harassment, training on this policy, and a method for responding to sexual harassment complaints.[62]

Since the establishment of EEOC guidelines, there have been numerous instances of reported sexual harassment, most often with a woman being the target of the harassment. A survey of 200 sales professionals revealed that 63 percent of the female respondents had been sexually harassed, compared with 9 percent of the men surveyed. Almost three-fourths (74 percent) of the women said that sexual harassment was most likely to occur during job-related travel.[63] Charges filed with the EEOC have increased by nearly 5,000 from 1992 to 2001 going from 10,532 to 15,475. Benefits resulting from these charges have increased from $12.7 million to $53.0 million.[64]

Policies and procedures for dealing with sexual harassment should be developed for the entire company, and sales managers must strive to implement them in a conscientious manner. Furthermore, sales managers must become familiar with EEOC guidelines so that they can serve as role models and communicate clearly to their salespeople the important issues involved in sexual harassment. The job of protecting salespeople from sexual harassment is complicated by the fact that salespeople work with customers away from the office and in social situations.

It is important to take action immediately if a sexual harassment problem comes to light. Employers may be legally accountable, for example, if they ignore sexual harassment of their salespeople by customers or others in the workplace. In a landmark case by the Supreme Court, Burlington Industries was held liable for sexual harassment in a suit filed by a former employee who claimed that her sales manager constantly harassed her. The sales manager reportedly advised her to "loosen up" in the office and told her that he could make her life very hard or very easy at Burlington.[65] As illustrated in "An Ethical Dilemma," similar situations may occur among salespeople.

The examples of conflicts of interest, chemical dependency, rule-breaking salespeople, the need to terminate employment of unsatisfactory salespeople, and sexual harassment are offered here to remind you of the complex human issues of managing a salesforce. Realities dictate that sales managers be able to confront and handle personnel problems as adeptly as strategic sales management issues to be effective leaders of their salesforces.

### AN ETHICAL DILEMMA

It has recently come to your attention that your star salesperson, Bob Smith, has been making sexual innuendos to some of the female salespeople on your salesforce. You have known Bob and his family for more than five years, and during this period, he never struck you as the type of guy who would do this. He has been an outstanding performer for you, being your top salesperson each year. You are afraid that if you falsely accuse Bob of these actions, you might damage your relationship with him, hurt his family, and possibly drive him off. You would hate to lose Bob. Perhaps these women are just overly sensitive. What should you do and why?

## SUMMARY

1. **Distinguish between salesforce leadership, management, and supervision.** As noted in Exhibit 7.1, senior sales leaders, field sales managers, and salespeople can all be involved in leadership, management, and supervision activities. **Sales leadership** includes all activities performed by those in a sales organization to influence others to achieve common goals for the collective good of the sales organization and company. The leadership activities of senior sales leaders are directed at the entire sales organization or large subunits, while field sales manager leadership activities emphasize creating the right climate to inspire their assigned salespeople. Salespeople, in contrast, are engaged in self-leadership and sometimes play a leadership role with customers, others in the sales organization and company, and with channel partners. **Sales management** activities are those related to the planning, implementation, and control of the sales management process. Senior sales leaders address the broader aspects of the sales management process, while field sales managers are more involved in implementing the process with their assigned salespeople. The management activities of salespeople are more focused on the planning, implementation, and control of sales activities within their assigned territory. **Sales supervision** refers to working with subordinates on a day-to-day basis. Senior sales leadership and salespeople are normally not as involved with supervision activities as are field sales managers.

2. **Explain how the LMX model and leadership style approaches contribute to contemporary sales leadership.** These views of sales leadership offer several important thoughts for today's sales managers. The Leader–Member Exchange (LMX) model encourages sales managers and salespeople to build a relationship on mutual trust. Transformational leadership recognizes the necessity and importance of change in most sales organizations.

3. **List the six components of a sales leadership model.** A model for sales leadership, shown in Figure 7.1, identifies six components: power of the sales manager, power of salespeople, situational factors, needs of salespeople and other parties, goals and objectives, and leadership skills.

4. **Discuss five bases of power that affect leadership.** Five power bases are coercive, reward, legitimate, referent, and expert. Coercive power is associated with punishment and is the opposite of reward power. Legitimate power stems from the individual's position in the organizational hierarchy. Referent power is held by one person when another person wants to maintain a relationship with that person. Expert power is attributed to the possession of information. A sales manager and those with whom he or she interacts may use one or more power bases in a given situation.

5. **Explain five influence strategies used in leadership.** Influence strategies used by sales managers could be based on threats, promises, persuasion, relationships, or manipulation. Unlike the other four strategies, manipulation does not involve face-to-face interactions with the target of influence. Threats use coercive power, whereas promises stem from the reward power base. Persuasion uses expert and referent power. Legitimate and referent power are used when influence strategy is based on interpersonal relationships.

6. **Discuss issues related to coaching the salesforce, holding integrative meetings, and practicing ethical management.** Coaching involves the continual development of the salesforce. A most critical part of coaching is one-on-one sessions with a salesperson. Coaching relies on the learning principles of recency and repetition and is often conducted in the field before and after sales calls. Integrative meetings accomplish multiple sales management functions. Sales managers are involved in creative aspects of planning integrative meetings, but paying attention to detail is the key to successful meetings. Meeting ethical responsibilities is not necessarily easy but is essential to long-term success in a sales career.

7. **Identify some of the problems encountered in leading and supervising a salesforce.** Some of the problems encountered in salesforce management are conflicts of interest; chemical abuse and dependency; disruptive, rule-breaking salespeople; salespeople whose employment must be terminated; and sexual harassment.

## UNDERSTANDING SALES MANAGEMENT TERMS

| | |
|---|---|
| sales leadership | persuasion |
| sales management | relationships |
| sales supervision | manipulation |
| leadership style | communication mechanisms |
| transactional leadership style | coaching |
| transformational leadership | outcome feedback |
| Leader–Member Exchange (LMX) model | cognitive feedback |
| | integrative meeting |
| expert power | immoral management |
| referent power | amoral management |
| legitimate power | moral management |
| reward power | code of ethics |
| coercive power | nonrole act |
| trait approach | role failure act |
| behavior approach | role distortion act |
| contingency approach | conflicts of interest |
| anticipation | lone wolf |
| seek feedback | corporate citizens |
| diagnostic skills | institutional stars |
| influence strategies | apathetics |
| threats | sexual harassment |
| promises | |

## DEVELOPING SALES MANAGEMENT KNOWLEDGE

1. Explain why the following views of leadership are relevant for sales organizations: Leader–Member Exchange (LMX) model and transformational leadership.

2. Briefly describe the six components of the sales leadership model shown in Figure 7.1.

3. Describe five types of power that affect leadership. What are the problems associated with overreliance on reward and coercive power?

4. How does the contingency approach to leadership differ from the trait approach and the behavior approach?

5. What are four categories of skills that could be useful in leadership?

6. Describe five influence strategies, including the power bases related to each strategy.

7. What is the difference between outcome feedback and cognitive feedback? Which is most important in coaching?

8. Sales managers may learn a lot about their organizations and salespeople simply by spending time observing activities in the office or in the field and talking with the people involved. To maximize their own learning while simultaneously providing leadership, which power bases would be especially important?

9. Refer to "Sales Management in the 21st Century: Leading the Salesforce at Federated Mutual Insurance." Explain Sabrina Rogers' approach to leadership in your own words.

10. Refer to "Sales Management in the 21st Century: Collaboration and Coaching at KV Pharmaceutical Company." How does Steve Randazzo use collaboration and coaching to help its salespeople succeed?

## BUILDING SALES MANAGEMENT SKILLS

1. Sid Cox has been a steady contributor as an automotive parts representative with Premier Auto Parts for the past five years. Conscientious and hardworking, he has always been willing to pull his weight and then some. Customers and coworkers find that his cheerful and pleasant demeanor make him a joy to be around. Over the past month, his sales manager, Randy Ross, has noticed a significant change in Sid's behavior. Sid appears to be worn down, less than enthusiastic, and reluctant to make as many sales calls as he has in the past. His positive, upbeat demeanor seems to have been replaced with a more pessimistic attitude about things. His generally steady sales results have been on the decline. If you were Randy Ross, what would you do? Explain.

2. Choose an individual who is considered to be (or to have been) a great leader (e.g., Lee Iacocca, J.F.K.). Use library resources, the Internet, and so on, to examine this individual to determine what makes (or made) this person such a good leader. In your analysis, explain this leader's traits or characteristics and the leadership skills that contributed to his or her success. Also, attempt to identify and explain the sources of power generally used by this leader. Finally, explain what you learned about this leader that you could use to help you become a more successful leader.

3. Each month *Sales & Marketing Management* describes a real-life, sales-related problem and asks, "What Should You Do?" Readers are asked to submit their responses and the most noteworthy appear in the following month's issue. This feature can be accessed online at: **http://www.salesandmarketing.com**. Access this address. Go to the section titled "current issue" and click on "What Should You Do?". Study the situation described and the answers given by two real-life working professionals. Write a short paper that answers the following: (1) Describe in your own words the situation that has transpired. (2) What would you do and why?

4. **Situation:**     Sales manager Lisa Lefton is accompanying sales rep Sherry Shorten on a sales call to a local grocery store, Price Chopper. Sherry is attempting to gain shelf space for a new flavor of Lipton bottled tea.

   **Characters:**     Lisa Lefton, sales manager; Sherry Shorten, sales representative; Jim Hopson, store manager

   **Scene 1:**     *Location*—Price Chopper grocery store. *Action*—Sherry attempts to convince Jim Hopson to give her shelf space for a new flavor of Lipton bottled tea. She is very unenthusiastic. Furthermore, she is having trouble overcoming objections, particularly Jim's concern about the need for a new flavor and the space desired. Lisa observes the sales call.

**Scene 2:**    *Location*—in Sherry's car on the way to their next sales call. *Action*— Lisa coaches Sherry regarding her visit with Jim Hopson.

5. **Situation:**    Read the Ethical Dilemma on page 205.

   **Characters:**    District sales manager; district sales manager's boss

   **Scene:**    *Location*—District sales manager's office. *Action*—Having heard the boss's new strategy for selling copiers, the district sales manager provides his/her response by providing pros and cons of the proposed strategy. The boss, in turn, reacts.

6. **Situation:**    Read the Ethical Dilemma on page 208.

   **Characters:**    Bob Smith, salesperson; Bob Smith's sales manager

   **Scene:**    *Location*—Sales manager's office. *Action*—Bob Smith's sales manager confronts Bob Smith concerning his alleged sexual innuendos. Bob Smith reacts to his sales manager's comments (however he desires, depending upon his guilt or innocence and the approach taken by Bob Smith).

7. Access the center for creative leadership at **http://www.ccl.org.** Examine the contents of the Web site. What types of resources are available to sales managers to help them become better leaders (explain at least two of these). Be sure to explain how the resources could be utilized by sales managers.

# MAKING SALES MANAGEMENT DECISIONS

## Case 7.1: Tasti-Fresh Bakery Products

### Background

Tasti-Fresh Bakery Products has been very successful at selling breads, rolls, and other bakery products to small- and medium-sized retailers throughout the Midwest. It has built its reputation on quality products, strong service, honesty, and integrity. The company credits much of its success to its salespeople, who provide the main link between it and its customers. The ability of Tasti-Fresh's salespeople to build strong customer relationships has helped keep the company profitable despite increasing competition.

### Current Situation

Tasti-Fresh district sales manager Laurel Brown recently received the following letter from one of the company's biggest customers.

February 22, 2005
3242 Grand Avenue
St. Louis, MO 63441

Ms. Laurel Brown
District Sales Manager
Tasti-Fresh Bakery Products
1675 Main
St. Charles, MO 63301

Dear Laurel:

We have always been pleased with your company's products and service. The sales rep who calls on us, Curt Stanford, has gone out of his way to ensure our satisfaction. Lately, however, I have noticed some changes in Curt's behavior. Normally I would not complain, but the treatment we have been getting recently is dramatically different from that to which we are accustomed, and I am concerned about Curt.

Over the past couple of months, I have noticed a dramatic shift in Curt's behavior. Usually steady and dependable, his behavior has become erratic. He has been late, or not shown up at all, for some of his scheduled appointments. Curt also has failed to follow through on several occasions. Sometimes he visits us and he is so enthusiastic it is almost unbearable, whereas on other visits he appears very tired and worn down. I suspect and fear that he may be on drugs.

As I said earlier, over the years we have been happy with your products and service. However, if this type of behavior persists, we will be forced to look for another supplier. We simply cannot afford to jeopardize our business.

Sincerely,

*Janice Miller*

Janice Miller
Purchasing Agent, Flanders Groceries, Inc.

Laurel was perplexed. Curt is one of her top performers. He has worked for the company for four years and has been salesperson of the year the past two years. She had not noticed a change in Curt. Then again, she has not had much direct contact with Curt lately because she has been concentrating her efforts on three newly hired sales reps. She wonders if she should confront Curt or simply ignore it. He is making the company a lot of money, and she has not heard any other complaints. If she confronts him, he might quit. Perhaps Janice is simply exaggerating and is really upset about something else. Maybe Janice needs to be confronted. Ignoring her may result in the loss of a big customer.

### Questions

1. Should Laurel confront Curt? If not, why? If so, how should she handle the situation?
2. Should Laurel speak to Janice? Why or why not? If so, what should she say to her?
3. If Curt is taking drugs, what do you recommend that Laurel do? How can she prevent problems like this in the future?

| | |
|---|---|
| **Situation:** | Read Case 7.1. |
| **Characters:** | Laurel Brown, district sales manager; Janice Miller, purchasing agent; Curt Stanford, sales representative |
| **Scene 1:** | *Location*—Laurel's office. *Action*—Laurel has called a meeting with Curt Stanford to confront him regarding the issue brought to her attention by Laurel Brown. |
| **Scene 2:** | *Location*—Tasti-Fresh Bakery Products. *Action*—After speaking to Curt, Laurel decides to visit Janice Miller at Tasti-Fresh to discuss the situation with her. |

**ROLE PLAY**

## Case 7.2: Global Enterprise

### Background

Rock Madd was a drill sergeant in the U.S. Marine Corps for five years before joining Global Enterprise seven years ago as a sales representative. In the Corps, he had been through some tough times and was always willing to face a challenge. A disciplined man, he rapidly became one of the company's best salespeople. However, his goal was to move into sales management. Because of his strong determination and hard work, he was eventually promoted to district sales manager where he replaced Lucille Fagan, who recently retired.

Lucille had done an outstanding job with the district. Her district's sales figures were consistently among the top in the company. She was well liked and respected by her salespeople. Lucille practiced good management skills and was adept at planning, organizing, controlling, and leading. Although she always took the ultimate responsibility for planning, she often consulted salespeople when she thought their ideas might be helpful. When it came to organizing, her goal was to motivate her salespeople to work as a team. As a result, she was able to get salespeople to help each other when the needs arose. She had control over her salespeople, but it was primarily through self-control. By setting realistic and individual-specific goals, she was able to motivate her salespeople not only to commit to those goals but also to supervise their own efforts effectively. Finally, Lucille had a real knack for leadership. She had the ability to get salespeople to realize their true potential and then help them achieve it. It was her contention that a leader should develop people, and she did. In fact, over the years, her salespeople were consistently promoted into management positions.

Rock took a different approach to managing, primarily as a result of his military background. He was a hard-working individual who demanded respect from those around him. He wanted to make sure those he supervised knew he was the boss. His attitude toward planning was that he made the plans and others carried them out. He did not need or seek input from others. He ran a tight organization, calling all the shots. When it came to control, he liked to scrutinize his salespeople closely, making sure they were doing what they were supposed to do.

### Current Situation

On Monday afternoon, Rock completed a sales call with Electra Aveshon, a three-year veteran at Global Enterprise. Although not the most outstanding salesperson in the district, Electra was a good performer. She credited much of her success to Lucille who had helped bring her along. It was Electra's opinion that Lucille could have easily let her go after her rocky start but instead invested the time in coaching her to become a better salesperson. After the call, Rock indicated that he would like to meet with Electra on Friday to discuss the sales call. He

had some other business he had to attend to right away, so they could not meet that afternoon. She agreed and an appointment was scheduled for Friday afternoon.

After finishing her appointments Friday morning, Electra met with Rock as scheduled. Following are excerpts from their meeting:

*Rock:* I was disappointed with your sales call on Monday. It surprised me to see a veteran such as yourself perform so sloppily. You should be ashamed.

*Electra:* I realize I didn't make the sale. But for the first visit, I felt I made progress in beginning to establish trust and build a relationship.

*Rock:* You spent too much time attempting to build rapport. You wasted valuable time that could be spent calling on other prospects or servicing current customers.

*Electra:* I always spend a little more time building rapport. I think it pays off in the long run.

*Rock:* Your handling of objections was poor. Your response to the question on pricing was totally inadequate. Your response to the question on delivery time was likewise inept. You need to work on handling objections.

*Electra:* My responses may not have been perfect, but I did not sense the prospect was unsure about what I was saying or had a problem with my responses.

*Rock:* And where did you learn to close? You need to drive the sale home. You played it a little too soft. I expect to see some real improvement on our next outing. If you can't do any better than this, maybe I'll have to find someone who can.

That evening after work Electra met with a few of her colleagues for some drinks and dinner. The following conversation ensued:

*Electra:* I'm sick of Madd bossing us around like we are a bunch of his soldiers. This isn't the army. We deserve to be treated with a little more respect.

*Andrew:* I hear you. The other day Madd went with me on a sales call. All I heard was what a horrible job I was doing. It was as if nothing I did on my call was right.

*Colette:* Madd always has something to say, and it's usually negative. He doesn't have any problem telling me what's wrong, but he never offers any advice on how to improve.

*Matt:* Come on, you guys. Give the guy a break. He's just doing what he thinks is right. He's trying to impress upper management by showing them he has everything under control down here. Once he sees this hard-guy stuff doesn't work, he'll loosen up.

*Andrew:* Yeah, if half the salesforce doesn't quit first. I don't like working for a guy like him. Why should I bust my tail to make him look good? I won't put up with it for long. I've heard some of the others (salespeople) talking and they aren't happy either. Morale really seems to be down.

*Colette:* Maybe Matt's right. Perhaps soon, Madd will loosen up a bit.

*Electra:* I don't know, Colette. It's been eight months now. Once a sergeant, always a sergeant.

## Questions

1. How would you characterize Rock's management style? How would you assess his sales management performance thus far?
2. What suggestions can you provide to Rock regarding coaching?
3. What would you recommend Rock do differently?

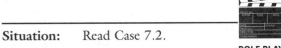

**ROLE PLAY**

| | |
|---|---|
| **Situation:** | Read Case 7.2. |
| **Characters:** | Rock Madd, district sales manager; Electra Aveshon, sales rep; Andrew, sales rep; Colette, sales rep; Matt, sales rep |
| **Scene 1:** | *Location*—Madd's office. *Action*—Role play the meeting between Rock and Electra. |
| **Scene 2:** | *Location*—A local bar and grill. *Action*—Role play the conversation between Electra, Andrew, Colette, and Matt. |
| **Scene 3:** | *Location*—Madd's office on Monday morning. *Action*—Electra, Andrew, Collette, and Matt decide to confront Rock about his management style, letting him know their concerns about how he manages. |

## MOTIVATING AND REWARDING: DRIVING PRODUCT MIX SALES AT FEDEX

Faced with two important problems, shipping and logistics giant FedEx determined that it needed a new compensation plan for its sales organization. First, field salespeople and sales managers were complaining about how confusing and unpredictable the pay program was. According to Mark Jennings, director of sales planning and sales variable compensation programs for FedEx, "We had tweaked our plan so many times that it became almost impossible for the salespeople to understand. We were constantly hearing complaints that the plan wasn't paying out in a timely manner, and the unpredictability on commissions and bonuses was frustrating for the salesforce." Second, due to mergers and new product rollouts, FedEx's 5,000-member salesforce needed a new pay plan that would motivate them to grow the overall business, as well as grow a diverse product line (three products as opposed to one).

To solve the second problem, the company developed and implemented a linked compensation design. Under this system, salespeople have to reach specific targets on each of the three product lines to achieve the highest bonuses and commissions. Previously, a salesperson's commission and bonuses would be determined by an average of sales across three lines. This resulted in the highest bonuses and commissions being paid without target sales levels being reached within each product line.

In turn, the new compensation plan and communication about it helped solve the first problem. To clear up confusion regarding the compensation system, Jennings conducted a survey of the salesforce to determine how salespeople would like to receive information about compensation plan changes. Having determined they wanted to learn about changes from their managers, Jennings trained managers on the new program and provided them with PowerPoint presentations to explain the plan to their salespeople. According to Jennings, "The adoption and comprehension of the new program was dramatically improved because of the delivery method." Salespeople are now clear what targets need to be reached for each product in order to get the largest payout.

The new compensation system appears to be a huge success. Jennings claims that he rarely hears any questions or complaints about the system anymore. "The pay plan is now almost self-explanatory and the predictability of the program has become a motivator for our salesforce. We now have a better focus on selling product mix, and people are actually motivated by the plan, rather than frustrated by it."

---

**Source:** Andy Cohen, "Extreme Makeovers," *Sales & Marketing Management* 156 (May 2004): 36–43.

### Objectives

After completing this module, you should be able to

1 Explain the key components of motivation: intensity, persistence, and direction.

2 Explain the difference between compensation rewards and noncompensation rewards.

3 Describe the primary financial and nonfinancial compensation rewards available to salespeople.

4 Describe salary, commission, and combination pay plans in terms of their advantages and disadvantages.

5 Explain the fundamental concepts in sales-expense reimbursement.

6 Discuss issues associated with sales contests, equal pay for equal work, team compensation, global compensation, and changing a reward system.

7 List the guidelines for motivating and rewarding salespeople.

The opening vignette introduces several important points regarding salesforce motivation and reward system management. First, it illustrates the importance of implementing an appropriate compensation system to properly motivate salespeople to achieve desired company goals. Second, it suggests that the compensation system should be devoid of confusion. Finally, the vignette demonstrates that companies may need to change compensation systems as circumstances dictate.

A salesforce reward system, because of its impact on motivation and job satisfaction, is one of the most important determinants of short- and long-term sales

| EXHIBIT 8.1 | Average Costs of Financial Compensation for Salespeople in 2003 | | |
| --- | --- | --- | --- |
| | **Base Salary** | **Bonus Plus Commissions** | **Total Compensation** |
| Executive | $95,170 | $49,483 | $144,653 |
| Top performer | $87,342 | $66,075 | $153,417 |
| Mid-level performer | $58,546 | $33,791 | $92,337 |
| Low-level performer | $44,289 | $19,486 | $63,775 |
| Average of all reps | $70,588 | $40,547 | $111,135 |

performance. This module examines the sales manager's role in motivating the salesforce through the use of reward systems. We first define motivation and explain some key concepts in reward system management. In the next section of this module, the characteristics of an effective reward system along with the reward preferences of salespeople in general are discussed. The following section concentrates on financial rewards, such as salaries, commissions, and bonuses. As seen in Exhibit 8.1, expenditures for financial rewards are quite substantial, often being the largest component of the sales organization's budget.[1] Expense reimbursement is also covered.

Nonfinancial rewards, such as opportunities for growth, recognition, and promotion, are reviewed. Current issues in reward system management, such as the use of sales contests, equal pay for equal work, team compensation, global compensation, and changing reward systems, are presented. This module concludes with summary guidelines for managing salesforce reward systems.

## MOTIVATION AND REWARD SYSTEMS

Defining **motivation** has been a tedious job for psychologists, sales management researchers, and sales managers. After decades of study, the most commonly used definitions of motivation include three dimensions—intensity, persistence, and direction.[2] **Intensity** refers to the amount of mental and physical effort put forth by the salesperson. **Persistence** describes the salesperson's choice to expend effort over time, especially when faced with adverse conditions. **Direction** implies that salespeople choose where their efforts will be spent among various job activities.[3]

Because salespeople are often faced with a diverse set of selling and nonselling job responsibilities, their choice of which activities warrant action is just as important as how hard they work or how well they persist in their efforts. The motivation task is incomplete unless salespeople's efforts are channeled in directions consistent with the overall strategic role of the salesforce within the firm. These ideas are supported in two studies of salespeople: one in the direct selling industry and the other of a national manufacturer's salesforce.[4] Both studies indicate that higher levels of effort, or intensity, are not necessarily associated with higher levels of performance.

Motivation is an unobservable phenomenon, and the terms *intensity, persistence,* and *direction* are concepts that help managers explain what they expect from their salespeople. It is important to note that although sales managers can observe salespeople's behavior, they can only infer their motivation. Indeed, it is the personal, unobservable nature of motivation that makes it such a difficult area to study.

Motivation can also be viewed as intrinsic or extrinsic. If salespeople find their job to be inherently rewarding, they are **intrinsically motivated**. If they are motivated by the rewards provided by others, such as pay and formal recognition, they are **extrinsically motivated**. Although a salesperson's overall motivation could be a function of both intrinsic and extrinsic motivation, some will have strong preferences for extrinsic rewards, such as pay and formal recognition awards, whereas others will seek intrinsic rewards, such as interesting, challenging work.[5]

**Reward system management** involves the selection and use of organizational rewards to direct salespeople's behavior toward the attainment of organizational objectives. An organizational reward could be anything from a $5,000 pay raise to a compliment for a job well done.

Organizational rewards can be classified as compensation and noncompensation rewards. **Compensation rewards** are those that are given in return for acceptable performance or effort. Compensation rewards can include nonfinancial compensation, such as recognition and opportunities for growth and promotion.

**Noncompensation rewards** include factors related to the work situation and well- being of each salesperson. Sales jobs that are interesting and challenging can increase salespeople's motivation, as can allowing salespeople some control over their own activities. Sales managers can also improve salesforce motivation by providing performance-enhancing feedback to salespeople. Other examples of noncompensation rewards are (1) providing adequate resources so that salespeople can accomplish their jobs and (2) practicing a supportive sales management leadership style. In this module, the focus is on compensation rewards, including financial and nonfinancial compensation.

## OPTIMAL SALESFORCE REWARD SYSTEM

The optimal reward system balances the needs of the organization, its salespeople, and its customers against one another. From the organization's perspective, the reward system should help accomplish the following results:

1. Provide an acceptable ratio of costs and salesforce output in volume, profit, or other objectives.

2. Encourage specific activities consistent with the firm's overall, marketing, and salesforce objectives and strategies. For example, the firm may use the reward system to encourage the selling of particular products or to promote teamwork in the salesforce.

3. Attract and retain competent salespeople, thereby enhancing long-term customer relationships.

4. Allow the kind of adjustments that facilitate administration of the reward system. A clearly stated, reasonably flexible plan assists in the administration of the plan.

From the perspective of the salesperson, reward systems are expected to meet a somewhat different set of criteria than from the sales manager's perspective. As indicated in the previous module, salespeople expect to be treated equitably, with rewards comparable to those of others in the organization doing a similar job—and to the rewards of competitors' salespeople. Most salespeople prefer some stability in the reward system, but they simultaneously want incentive rewards for superior performance. Because the most productive salespeople have the best opportunities to leave the firm for more attractive work situations, the preferences of the salesforce regarding compensation must be given due consideration. Exhibit 8.2[6] shows the most popular incentives based on a survey of sales executives.

In recent years, the needs of the customer have become more important than the needs of the salesforce in determining the structure of reward systems in sales organizations.

| Most Popular Incentives    EXHIBIT 8.2 |  |
| --- | --- |
| **Incentive** | **Executives Indicating as Most Popular** |
| Cash | 58% |
| Plaques/rewards | 30% |
| Recognition dinners | 26% |
| Leisure trips/travel | 26% |
| Merchandise/gifts | 24% |

Companies such as IBM, Eastman Kodak, and Xerox tie compensation to customer satisfaction. In fact, research shows that 93 percent of technology companies tie compensation to customer satisfaction and loyalty.[7] Some automobile dealers have tried to reduce customer dissatisfaction stemming from high-pressure sales techniques by paying their salespeople a salary instead of a commission based on sales volume. Others adjust the salesperson's commission based on customer satisfaction with the salesperson's handling of the sale. Research indicates that salespeople are more customer oriented when customer satisfaction incentives are used.[8]

Meeting the needs of customers, salespeople, and the sales organization simultaneously is indeed a challenging task. As you might suspect, compromise between sometimes divergent interests becomes essential for managing most salesforce reward systems. As noted by Greenberg and Greenberg, "A salesforce is comprised of individual human beings with broadly varying needs, points of view, and psychological characteristics who cannot be infallibly categorized, measured, and punched out to formula."[9]

## TYPES OF SALESFORCE REWARDS

For discussion purposes, the countless number of specific rewards available to salespeople are classified into six categories, as shown in Exhibit 8.3: pay, promotion, sense of accomplishment, personal growth opportunities, recognition, and job security.[10] Each of these reward categories is discussed in the next two sections of this module. The financial compensation section focuses on pay, and the nonfinancial compensation section on the other rewards shown in Exhibit 8.3. Keep in mind that reward preferences may differ internationally. For example, one study found that Japanese salespeople prefer being a member of a successful team with shared goals and values over receiving financial rewards.[11]

## FINANCIAL COMPENSATION

In many sales organizations, financial compensation is composed of current spendable income, deferred income or retirement pay, and various insurance plans that may provide income when needed. The discussion here is limited to the current spendable income because it is the most controllable, and arguably most important, dimension of a salesforce reward system. The other components of financial compensation tend to be dictated more by overall company policy rather than by sales managers.

**Current spendable income** includes money provided in the short term (weekly, monthly, and annually) that allows salespeople to pay for desired goods and services. It includes salaries, commissions, and bonuses. Bonus compensation may include noncash income equivalents, such as merchandise and free-travel awards. A comprehensive study of salesforce financial compensation practices found salaries, commissions, and bonuses to be used widely to pay salespeople. The study concluded that financial compensation plans including a salary and one or more incentives (commission and/or bonus) are the most popular.[12] However, the chosen compensation system often depends on the organization's strategy, competitive offerings, and products or services sold.[13]

**EXHIBIT 8.3** Salesforce Rewards

Pay
Promotion
Sense of Accomplishment
Personal Growth Opportunities
Recognition
Job Security

The three basic types of salesforce financial compensation plans are straight salary, straight commission, and a salary plus incentive, with the incentive being a commission and/or a bonus. A discussion of each type follows (summarized in Exhibit 8.4).

## Straight Salary

Paying salespeople a **straight salary** (exclusively by a salary) is uncommon. Such plans are well suited for paying sales support personnel and sales trainees.

Sales support personnel, including missionaries and detailers, are involved in situations in which it is difficult to determine who really makes the sale. Because missionaries and detailers are concerned primarily with dissemination of information rather than direct solicitation of orders, a salary can equitably compensate for effort. Compensation based on sales results might not be fair.

Salaries are also appropriate for sales trainees, who are involved in learning about the job rather than producing on the job. In most cases, a firm cannot recruit sales trainees on a college campus without the lure of a salary to be paid at least until training is completed.

### Advantages of Salary Plans

One advantage of using salary plans is that they are the simplest ones to administer, with adjustments usually occurring only once a year. Because salaries are fixed costs, **planned earnings** for the salesforce are easy to project, which facilitates the salesforce budgeting process. The fixed nature of planned earnings with salary plans may also facilitate recruitment and selection. For example, some recruits may be more likely to join the sales organization when their first-year earnings can be articulated clearly in salary terms rather than less certain commission terms.

Salaries can provide control over salespeople's activities, and reassigning salespeople and changing sales territories is less a problem with salary plans than with other financial compensation plans. There is general agreement that salesforce loyalty to the company may be greater with salary plans and that there is less chance that high-pressure, non-customer-oriented sales techniques will be used. Salary plans also make it easier to encourage teamwork and customer service.

**Summary of Financial Compensation Plans**    **EXHIBIT 8.4**

| Type of Plan | Advantages | Disadvantages | Common Uses |
|---|---|---|---|
| Salary | Simple to administer; planned earnings facilitates budgeting and recruiting; customer loyalty enhanced; more control of nonselling activities | No financial incentive to improve performance; pay often based on seniority, not merit; salaries may be a burden to new firms or to those in declining industries | Sales trainees; sales support |
| Commission | Income linked to results; strong financial incentive to improve results; costs reduced during slow sales periods; less operating capital required | Difficult to build loyalty of salesforce to company; less control of nonselling activities | Real estate; insurance; wholesaling; securities; automobiles |
| Combination | Flexibility allows frequent reward of desired behavior; may attract high-potential but unproven recruits | Complex to administer; may encourage crisis-oriented objectives | Widely used—most popular type of financial pay plan |

Salaries are also used when substantial developmental work is required to open a new sales territory or introduce new products to the marketplace. Presumably, the income stability guaranteed by a salary allows the salesperson to concentrate on job activities rather than worry about how much the next paycheck will be. In general, salary plans allow more control over salesforce activities, especially nonselling activities.

### Disadvantages of Salary Plans

The most serious shortcoming of straight-salary plans is that they offer little financial incentive to perform past a merely acceptable level. As a result, the least productive members of the salesforce are, in effect, the most rewarded salespeople. Conversely, the most productive salespeople are likely to think salary plans are inequitable. As such, it may be difficult to attract high-performing salespeople.

Differences in salary levels among salespeople are often a function of seniority on the job instead of true merit. Even so, the constraints under which many salary plans operate may cause **salary compression**, or a narrow range of salaries in the salesforce. Thus sales trainees may be earning close to what experienced salespeople earn, which could cause perceptions of inequity among experienced salespeople, leading to diminished motivation.

Salaries represent fixed overhead in a sales operation. If the market is declining or stagnating, the financial burden of the firm is greater with salary plans than with a variable expense such as commissions based on sales.

## Straight Commission

Unlike straight-salary plans, commission-only plans (or **straight commission**) offer strong financial incentives to maximize performance. However, they also limit control of the salesforce. Some industries—real estate, insurance, automobiles, and securities—traditionally have paid salespeople by straight commission. In these industries, the primary responsibility of salespeople is simply to close sales; nonselling activities are less important to the employer than in some other industries.

Manufacturers' representatives, who represent multiple manufacturers, are also paid by commission. Wholesalers, many of whom founded their businesses with limited working capital, also traditionally pay their salesforce by commission.

The huge direct-sales industry, including such companies as Mary Kay Cosmetics, Tupperware, and Avon, also pays by straight commission. The large number of salespeople working for these organizations makes salary payments impractical from an overhead and administrative standpoint.

### Commission Plan Variations

There are several factors to be considered in developing a commission-only plan:

1. **Commission base**—volume or profitability
2. **Commission rate**—constant, progressive, regressive, or a combination
3. **Commission splits**—between two or more salespeople or between salespeople and the employer
4. **Commission payout event**—when the order is confirmed, shipped, billed, paid for, or some combination of these events

Commissions may be paid according to sales volume or some measure of profitability, such as gross margin, contribution margin, or in rare cases, net income. Recently, there has been more experimentation with profitability-oriented commission plans in an effort to improve salesforce productivity. For instance, at technology services provider Technical Concepts Inc., the sales compensation plan was revised to heavily reward for profitable business in order to increase the overall profitability of the salesforce.[14] Despite the gradual adoption of profitability-based commission plans by various companies, the most popular commission base appears to be sales volume.

Commission rates vary widely, and determining the appropriate rate is a weighty managerial task. The commission rate, or percentage paid to the salesperson, may be a **constant**

**rate** over the pay period, which is an easy plan for the salespeople to understand and provides incentive for them to produce more sales or profits (because pay is linked directly to performance). A **progressive rate** increases as salespeople reach prespecified targets. This provides an even stronger incentive to the salesperson, but it may result in overselling and higher selling costs. A **regressive rate** declines at some predetermined point. Regressive rates might be appropriate when the first order is hard to secure but reorders are virtually automatic. Such is the case for many manufacturer salespeople who sell to distributors and retailers.

Some circumstances might warrant a combination of a constant rate with either a progressive or regressive rate. For example, assume that a manufacturer has limited production capacity. The manufacturer wants to use capacity fully (i.e., sell out) but not oversell, because service problems would hamper future marketing plans. In such a case, the commission rate might be fixed, or perhaps progressive up to the point at which capacity is almost fully used, then regressive to the point of full use.

When salespeople are paid on straight commission, the question of splitting commissions is of primary concern. To illustrate this point, consider a company with centralized purchasing, such as Delta Airlines. Delta may buy from a sales representative in Atlanta, where its headquarters are located, and have the product shipped to various hubs across the country. The salespeople in the hub cities are expected to provide local follow-up and be sure the product is performing satisfactorily. Which salespeople will receive how much commission? Procedures for splitting commissions are best established before such a question is asked.

No general rules exist for splitting commissions; rather, company-specific rules must be spelled out to avoid serious disputes. A company selling to Delta Airlines in the situation just described might decide to pay the salesperson who calls on the Atlanta headquarters 50 percent of the total commission and split the remaining 50 percent among the salespeople who serve the hub cities. The details of how commissions are split depend entirely on each company's situation.

Another issue in structuring straight-commission plans is when to pay the commission. The actual payment may be at any time interval, although monthly and quarterly payments are most common. The question of when the commission is earned is probably just as important as when it is paid. The largest proportion of companies operating on the basis of sales-volume commissions declare the commission earned at the time the customer is billed for the order, rather than when the order is confirmed, shipped, or paid for.

Salesforce automation has made it easier to keep track of complicated commission systems. For instance, AccountPro offers a software application called Sales Commission that enables companies to rapidly design, process, and communicate sophisticated commission programs. By communicating sales credit, performance, and earnings information, the software allows sales managers and salespeople to keep abreast of their compensation status.[15]

## Advantages of Commission Plans

One advantage of straight-commission plans is that salespeople's income is linked directly to desired results and therefore may be perceived as more equitable than salary plans. In the right circumstances, a strong financial incentive can provide superior results, and commission plans provide such an incentive. Thus, such plans are likely to attract competent results-oriented salespeople and eliminate incompetent reps.

From a cost-control perspective, commissions offer further advantages. Because commissions are a variable cost, operating costs are minimized during slack selling periods. Also, working capital requirements are lessened with commission-only pay plans. Before choosing a straight-commission plan, however, the disadvantages of such plans should be considered.

## Disadvantages of Commission Plans

Perhaps the most serious shortcoming of straight-commission plans is that they contribute little to company loyalty, which may mean other problems in controlling the activities of the salesforce, particularly nonselling and administrative activities. A lack of commitment may lead commission salespeople to leave the company if business conditions worsen or sales drop. Or, salespeople may neglect cultivating potentially profitable long-run customers in favor of easy sales. Another potential problem can arise if commissions are not limited by an earnings cap, in that salespeople may earn more than their managers. Not only do managers resent this outcome, but the salespeople may not respond to direction from those they exceed in earnings.

## Performance Bonuses

The third dimension of current spendable income is the **performance bonus**, either group or individual. Both types are prevalent, and some bonus plans combine them. Bonuses are typically used to direct effort toward relatively short-term objectives, such as introducing new products, adding new accounts, or reducing accounts receivable. They may be offered in the form of cash or income equivalents, such as merchandise or free travel. At Northcoast Duplicating, a dealer of duplicating equipment, top-performing salespeople's bonuses come in the way of "bid bucks" for meeting and exceeding quotas. Once a quarter, the company holds an auction in which salespeople can bid on anything from flashlights to golf bags with their bid bucks. They have even included a "Let's Make a Deal" component to the auction to allow salespeople to trade their items for mystery gifts.[16] Although commissions or salary may be the financial-compensation base, bonuses are used strictly in a supplementary fashion.

### Advantages of Performance Bonuses

One advantage of the performance bonus is that the organization can direct emphasis to what it considers important in the sales area. In addition, sales emphasis can be changed from period to period. Bonuses are particularly useful for tying rewards to accomplishment of objectives.[17]

### Disadvantages of Performance Bonuses

One problem with the performance bonus is that it may be difficult to determine a formula for calculating bonus achievement if the objective is expressed in subjective terms (e.g., account servicing). Further, if salespeople do not fully support the established objective, they may not exert additional effort to accomplish the goal.[18]

## Combination Plans (Salary plus Incentive)

The limitations of straight-salary and straight-commission plans have led to increasing use of plans that feature some combination of salary, commission, and bonus—in other words, **salary plus incentive**. Combination pay plans usually feature salary as the major source of salesperson income. Salary-plus-bonus and salary-plus-commission-plus-bonus plans are popular.

When properly conceived, combination plans offer a balance of incentive, control, and enough flexibility to reward important salesforce activities. The most difficult part of structuring combination plans is determining the **financial compensation mix**, or the relative amounts to be paid in salary, commission, and bonus. Exhibit 8.5 enumerates a number of factors related to determining the appropriate ratio of salary to total financial compensation.[19]

As indicated in Exhibit 8.5, the compensation mix should be tilted more heavily toward the salary component when individual salespeople have limited control over their own performance. When well-established companies rely heavily on advertising to sell their products in highly competitive markets, the salesforce has less direct control over job outcomes. Then a salary emphasis is logical. Furthermore, if the provision of customer service is crucial as contrasted with maximizing short-term sales volume or if team selling is used, a compensation mix favoring the salary dimension is appropriate. As suggested in Exhibit 8.5, conditions contrary to those favorable to a high salary-to-total-compensation ratio would dictate an emphasis on commissions in the compensation mix.

| Condition | Proportion of Salary to Total Pay Should Be | |
|---|---|---|
| | **Lower** | **Higher** |
| 1. Importance of salesperson's personal skills in making sales | Considerable | Slight |
| 2. Reputation of salesperson's company | Little known | Well known |
| 3. Company's reliance on advertising and other sales promotion activities | Little | Much |
| 4. Competitive advantage of product in terms of price, quality, and so forth | Little | Much |
| 5. Importance of providing customer service | Slight | Considerable |
| 6. Significance of total sales volume as a primary selling objective | Greater | Lesser |
| 7. Incidence of technical or team selling | Little | Much |
| 8. Importance of factors beyond the control of salesperson that influence sales | Slight | Considerable |

**EXHIBIT 8.5** Conditions That Influence the Proportion of Salary to Total Pay for Salespeople

### Advantages of Combination Plans

The primary advantage of combination pay plans is their flexibility. Sales behavior can be rewarded frequently, and specific behaviors can be reinforced or stimulated quickly. For example, bonuses or additional commissions could be easily added to a salary base to encourage such activities as selling excess inventory, maximizing the sales of highly seasonal products, introducing new products, or obtaining new customers. For example, when Management Recruiters International wanted to boost its business one December after having a record-breaking November, it offered the office's nine salespeople a $5,000 bonus to split among themselves if they did two-thirds of the business that they had done in November. Each salesperson's share of the bonus, however, was based on their contribution to sales.[20]

Combination plans can also be used to advantage when the skill levels of the salesforce vary, assuming that the sales manager can accurately place salespeople into various skill-level categories and then formulate the proper combination for each category.[21] In effect, this is done with sales trainees, regular salespeople, and senior salespeople in some companies, with each category of salespeople having a different combination of salary and incentive compensation.

Combination pay plans are attractive to high-potential but unproven candidates for sales jobs. College students nearing graduation, for example, might be attracted by the security of a salary and the opportunity for additional earnings from incentive-pay components.

### Disadvantages of Combination Plans

As compared with straight-salary and straight-commission plans, combination plans are more complex and difficult to administer. Their flexibility sometimes leads to frequent changes in compensation practices to achieve short-term objectives. Although flexibility is desirable, each change requires careful communication with the salesforce and precise coordination with long-term sales, marketing, and corporate objectives. A common criticism of combination plans is that they tend to produce too many salesforce objectives, many of which are of the crisis resolution "fire-fighting" variety. Should this occur, more important long-term progress can be impeded. Furthermore, mediocre salespeople are eliminated less rapidly than they would be under a straight commission plan.

# NONFINANCIAL COMPENSATION

As indicated early in this module, compensation for effort and performance may include nonfinancial rewards. Examples of **nonfinancial compensation** include career advancement through promotion, a sense of accomplishment on the job, opportunities for personal growth, recognition of achievement, and job security. Sometimes, nonfinancial rewards are coupled with financial rewards—for example, a promotion into sales management usually results in a pay increase—so one salesperson might view these rewards as primarily financial, whereas another might view them from a nonfinancial perspective. The value of nonfinancial compensation is illustrated by the considerable number of salespeople who knowingly take cuts in financial compensation to become sales managers. The prevalence of other nonfinancial rewards in salesforce reward systems also attests to their important role.

## Opportunity for Promotion

**Opportunity for promotion** is a highly valued reward among salespeople. Among younger salespeople, it often eclipses pay as the most valued reward.[22] Given the increasing number of young to middle-aged people in the workforce, the opportunities for promotion may be limited severely in nongrowth industries. (Growth industries, such as financial services and direct sales, offer reasonably good opportunities for advancement through promotion.) Because opportunities for promotion are not easily varied in the short run, the importance of matching recruits to the job and its rewards is again emphasized.

It should be noted that a promotion need not involve a move from sales into management. Some career paths may extend from sales into management, whereas others progress along a career salesperson path.

## Sense of Accomplishment

Unlike some rewards, a **sense of accomplishment** cannot be delivered to the salesperson from the organization. Because a sense of accomplishment emanates from the salesperson's psyche, all the organization can do is facilitate the process by which it develops. Although organizations cannot administer sense-of-accomplishment rewards as they would pay increases, promotions, or formal recognition rewards, the converse is not true—they do have the ability to withhold this reward, to deprive individuals of feeling a sense of accomplishment. Of course, no organization chooses this result; it stems from poor management practice.

Several steps can be taken to facilitate a sense of accomplishment in the salesforce. First, ensure that the salesforce members understand the critical role they fulfill in revenue production and other key activities within the company. Second, personalize the causes and effects of salesperson performance. This means that each salesperson should understand the link between effort and performance and between performance and rewards. Third, strongly consider the practice of management by objectives or goal setting as a standard management practice. Finally, reinforce feelings of worthwhile accomplishment in communication with the salesforce.

## Opportunity for Personal Growth

**Opportunities for personal growth** are routinely offered to salespeople. For example, college tuition reimbursement programs are common, as are seminars and workshops on such topics as physical fitness, stress reduction, and personal financial planning. Interestingly, many sales job candidates think the major reward available from well-known companies is the opportunity for personal growth. This is particularly true of entrepreneurially oriented college students who hope to "learn then earn" in their own business. In a parallel development, many companies showcase their training program during recruitment and selection as an opportunity for personal growth through the acquisition of universally valuable selling skills.

## Recognition

**Recognition**, both informal and formal, is an integral part of most salesforce reward systems. Informal recognition refers to "nice job" accolades and similar kudos usually delivered in private conversation or correspondence between a sales manager and a salesperson. Informal recognition is easy to administer, costs nothing or practically nothing, and can reinforce desirable behavior immediately after it occurs.

Formal recognition programs have long been popular in sales organizations. The insurance industry has the Million Dollar Roundtable, and "100%" clubs for those who exceed 100 percent of their sales quota are common. The ultimate recognition for Xerox's sales elite is to be named a member of the President's Club.

Formal recognition programs are typically based on group competition or individual accomplishments representing improved performance. Formal recognition may also be associated with monetary, merchandise, or travel awards but is distinguished from other rewards by two characteristics. First, formal recognition implies public recognition for accomplishment in the presence of peers and superiors in the organization. Second, it includes a symbolic award of lasting psychological value, such as jewelry or a plaque. Sound advice for conducting formal recognition programs is offered in Exhibit 8.6. For example, at Talx Corporation, a provider of outsourced human resources, salespeople with the highest sales, the most quarterly revenue, and the highest percentage of quota receive plaques, in addition to money to put toward a trip of their choosing.[23]

As formal recognition, programs often feature lavish awards banquets and ceremonies to culminate the program and set the stage for future recognition programs. Because lavish expenditures for any salesforce activity ultimately must be well justified in this era of emphasis on productivity improvement, it is evident that many companies believe that money spent on recognition is a good investment. For more on recognition programs, see "Sales Management in the 21st Century: Recognition and Incentive Programs at Federated Mutual Insurance."

## Job Security

**Job security**, although valued highly by salespeople nearing retirement age, is the least-valued reward among those shown in Exhibit 8.3. High-performing salespeople may sense they have job security, if not with their present employer then with the industry in general.

With the current wave of mergers, acquisitions, and general downsizing of corporations, it is becoming more difficult to offer job security as a reward. In the past, job security was easier to assure, at least as long as performance contingencies were met. Another factor that will make it difficult to offer job security with a given company is the lack of unionization of salespeople in most fields.

---

**Guidelines for Formal Programs**   **EXHIBIT 8.6**

Formal recognition programs have a better chance of success if sales managers

1. Remember that recognition programs should produce results well beyond the expected and that the program should make sense from a return-on-investment perspective.
2. Publicize the program before it is implemented. Build momentum for the program while it is under way with additional communiqués, and reinforce the accomplishments of the winners with postprogram communications both inside and outside the company.
3. Ensure that the celebration for winners is well conceived and executed. Consider the possibility of having customers and teammates join in with brief congratulatory testimonials or thanks.
4. Arrange for individual salespeople or sales teams to acknowledge the support of others who helped them win the award—as is the case with the Grammy Awards, for example. This builds the teamwork orientation.
5. Strive for fairness in structuring recognition programs so that winners are clearly superior performers, not those with less difficult performance goals.

SALES MANAGEMENT IN THE 21ST CENTURY

**Recognition and Incentive Programs at Federated Mutual Insurance**

Sabrina Rogers, district marketing manager for Federated Mutual Insurance, discusses how the company uses recognition and incentive programs.

*Federated Mutual Insurance has multiple incentive programs designed to drive and ensure activity, results, and success for individuals who follow our business plan. The incentive plans are designed to provide consistent recognition for the top performing salespeople. At the beginning of the year, standards are set for these awards, including Federated's most sought-after award—President's*

*Council. Salespeople receiving this coveted award are praised for outstanding performance, which can lead to district recognition and national accomplishment. Federated's sales reps have long used the combination of knowledge, energy, and passion to achieve astonishing results, as well as receive one of the industry's best incentive packages. Future success is dependant on monitoring each sales representative to ensure outstanding results through adherence to our business plan, motivation, and a good work ethic. Our celebration of this success keeps our reps focused, resulting in a winning combination for our clients, reps, and the company.*

## SALES EXPENSES

Most sales organizations provide full reimbursement to their salespeople for legitimate **sales expenses** incurred while on the job. As shown in Exhibit 8.7, typical reimbursable expenses include travel, lodging, meals, entertainment of customers, telephone, and personal entertainment.[24] Selling expenses are a substantial amount in most companies, and may average more than $1,000 a month for an experienced salesperson.[25] Given the magnitude of sales expenses, it is easy to understand why most companies impose tight controls to ensure judicious spending by the salesforce.

Controls used in the sales expense reimbursement process include (1) a definition of which expenses are reimbursable, (2) the establishment of expense budgets, (3) the use of allowances for certain expenditures, and (4) documentation of expenses to be reimbursed.

Covered expenses vary from company to company, so it is important for each company to designate which expenses are reimbursable and which are not. For example, some firms reimburse their salespeople for personal entertainment, such as the cost of movies and reading material while traveling, and others do not.

---

**EXHIBIT 8.7     Typical Reimbursable Expense Items**

Automobile (company-leased)
Automobile (company-owned)
Mileage allowance
Other travel reimbursement
Lodging
Telephone
Entertainment
Product samples
Local promotions
Office and/or clerical
Car phone
Home photocopier
Home fax machine
Laptop PC

*Expense budgets* may be used to maintain expenses as a specified percentage of over-all sales volume or profit. Expenditures are compared regularly to the budgeted amount, and expenditure patterns may change in response to budgetary pressures.

Allowances for automobile expenses, lodging, and meal costs are sometimes used to control expenditures. For example, one common practice is to reimburse personal auto-mobile use on the job at a cents-per-mile allowance. Many firms use a per-diem allowance for meals and lodging.

Because of more stringent tax laws, extensive documentation in the form of receipts and other information concerning the what, when, who, and why of the expenditure has become standard procedure. Salespeople whose companies do not reimburse expenses must also provide such documentation to deduct sales expenses in calculating their income taxes. A typical form for documenting sales expenses is shown in Exhibit 8.8.[26]

The job of reporting and tracking sales expenses has become less burdensome and more cost efficient for companies that use expense-report software and Web-based programs. For example, Concur Technologies' Concur Expense Service makes it easier for salespeople to file expense reports and for sales managers to process the reports and analyze expenditures. This Web-based application allows salespeople to generate and submit reports anytime from anywhere. The system, which integrates with a company's back office systems, allows data to be automatically imported from a company's corporate card, increasing accuracy and productivity, and decreasing exposure to mistakes or fraud.[27] With this program, sales managers can easily audit salespeople's expenditures,

Sales Expense Report Form    EXHIBIT 8.8

focus on expenses in a particular area, and compare selling costs with selling budgets. It is also possible to track expenditures with particular hotels or rental car companies, which may enable the sales organization to negotiate more favorable rates.

The area of expense reimbursement is the cause of some ethical and legal concern in sales organizations. Certainly **expense account padding**, in which a salesperson seeks reimbursement for ineligible or fictional expenses, is not unknown. There are countless ways for an unscrupulous salesperson to misappropriate company funds. Tactics include overstating expenses, seeking reimbursement for personal expenses, inventing purchases, and filing the same expenses on separate expense reports.[28] A common ploy of expense account "padders" is to entertain friends rather than customers, then seek reimbursement for customer entertainment. Another tactic is to eat a $5 meal and report that it costs $20, since most companies do not require receipts for expenses less than $25. Others simply add a certain percentage to every expense report they file. One survey shows that 49 percent of sales executives believe expense reports are padded by at least $50 per month by one or more of their reps.[29] "An Ethical Dilemma" illustrates such a situation.

AN ETHICAL DILEMMA

You have been Sherry Smith's sales manager for more than six years. Her dedication to the company, her sales team, and her customers is beyond reproach. For the past two years, she has been named salesperson of the year at your company. Besides being an outstanding performer, she is a genuinely nice person with a great personality. Looking over Sherry's latest expense report, you noticed that she had meal expenses for her and a customer last Thursday. However, you recall making a call to this customer on that very day to follow up with some information he had requested and being informed that he was out of town. Your company has very strict policies regarding business expenses. What should you do? Explain.

Tight financial controls, requirements for documentation of expenditures, an anonymous tip program, and periodic visits by highly trained financial auditors help deter expense account abuse. Although it may sound extreme, many companies have a simple policy regarding misappropriation of company funds—the minimum sanction is termination of employment, and criminal charges are a distinct possibility.

## ADDITIONAL ISSUES IN MANAGING SALESFORCE REWARD SYSTEMS

In addition to the managerial issues raised thus far, five other areas of salesforce reward systems have received considerable attention: sales contests, equal pay for equal work, team compensation, global considerations, and changing an existing reward system.

### Sales Contests

**Sales contests** are temporary programs that offer financial and/or nonfinancial rewards for accomplishing specified, usually short-term, objectives. Popular incentives, as indicated by the extent to which they are awarded to salespeople, include merchandise, gift certificates, cash, electronics, and travel.[30] Contests may involve group competition among salespeople, individual competition whereby each salesperson competes against past performance standards or new goals, or a combination of group and individual competition. Sales contests can be instituted without altering the basic financial compensation plan.

Despite the widespread use of sales contests and the sizable expenditures for them, very little is known about their true effects. In fact, many contests are held to correct bad planning and poor sales performance, and others are held with the belief that contests must have positive effects, despite the difficulty in pinpointing these effects. There is always a concern about whether sales contests have any lasting value or simply boost short-term sales. If contests merely pull sales from a future period into the contest period, little is gained—and the expenses of running contests can be substantial.

To optimize the use of sales contests, the following guidelines are recommended.[31]

1. Minimize potential motivation and morale problems by allowing multiple winners. Salespeople should compete against individual goals and be declared winners if those goals are met. To increase motivation, base the amount of reward on relative rank achieved so that those ranking higher receive larger amounts.

2. Recognize that contests will concentrate efforts in specific areas, often at the temporary neglect of other areas. Plan accordingly.

3. Consider the positive effects of including nonselling personnel in sales contests.

4. Use variety as a basic element of sales contests. Vary timing, duration, themes, and rewards.

5. Ensure that sales contest objectives are clear, realistically attainable, and quantifiable to allow performance assessment.

Contests can be implemented to achieve a variety of objectives. For instance, when NBC wanted to stimulate local ad sales for its coverage of the Olympics in Athens it sponsored a three-week sales contest at Mediacom Communications Corp entitled "Go For the Gold." Salespeople earned points by signing deals with new clients or expanding agreements with existing advertisers that bought ads for NBC Cable's coverage of the Olympics. Trips to New York or Los Angeles were awarded to three gold prize winners, while 10 silver prize winners each won a trip to the Cable Television Advertising Bureau conference in Chicago. Bronze prize winners received NBC premiums.[32]

Companies such as Sales Driver (http://www.salesdriver.com) have made it easier to implement sales contests. This company provides a Web-based application that allows managers to develop a contest tailored to their needs in as little as 20 to 30 minutes. Salespeople view contest details and receive contest updates via the Web. Sales managers can monitor individual and group sales results and make updates to the contest at any time. Salespeople are awarded DriverDollars based on their performance during the contest period. This currency can be used to redeem rewards from the Sales Driver catalog that contains 1,200 different rewards. Salespeople can choose from top brand-name housewares, electronics, luxury goods, sports, travel, and more.[33]

It is hard to design a sales contest that will maximally motivate every member of the salesforce. One study found that salesperson contest design preferences for goal type, number of winners, contest duration, and award value may vary by individual, supervisory, and sales setting characteristics.[34] It is even more difficult to measure precisely the effectiveness of most sales contests. One survey found that the most difficult challenge involved in running a contest was measuring results, followed by administering the program.[35] Even so, sales contests will doubtlessly continue to be a commonly used tool. By following the five guidelines previously mentioned, sales managers can improve the odds of making justifiable investments in sales contests. For more on sales contests, see "Sales Management in the 21st Century: Use of Sales Contests at Allied Office Products."

## Equal Pay

In addition to the motivational aspects of equity in financial compensation systems, there is a legal responsibility to ensure that salespeople are paid on an equitable basis. The Equal Pay Act, mentioned in Module 5, requires that equal pay be given for jobs requiring the same skills, efforts, responsibilities, and working conditions. Furthermore, research shows that rewarding salespeople fairly leads to increased motivation and improved job performance.[36]

### Use of Sales Contests at Allied Office Products

Marty Zucker, division vice president/general manager at Allied Office Products, Long Island, New York, discusses how the company uses sales contests to increase revenues and margins while motivating their salesforce.

*Allied Office Products promotes five main product lines: office supplies, furniture, coffee and other refreshments, printing, and promotional products. Sales contests are run at both the national and divisional levels to promote different product groups within our "onesolution" selling strategy. Each contest is unique. Take for instance our coffee contest. This is a contest that is run on a national level from October through September each year. The rules are simple: The salesperson who sells the most Keurig Coffee systems, as well as the most individual "K Cups,"* *wins a new BMW. The car is presented at the Allied national sales meeting each October. Another contest that we run is known as the President's Council, in which sales representatives compete against quotas. Each year all sales representatives who exceed both their sales and gross margin budgets by 10 percent and attain a specific gross profit dollar threshold are treated (along with their significant others) to a first-class trip to Rose Hall in Jamaica. We also conduct divisional-level sales contests. We recently held a contest in which teams competed for prizes and recognition for most new accounts opened and most new accounts that were regenerated from our "lost account" list. Our most recent new account contest generated a significant amount of new accounts and gave our sales team a huge morale boost. We believe that sales contests are an important tool in sales management in the 21st century.*

Sad to say, some sales managers attempt to pay female salespeople less than males because they think women's family responsibilities will cause them to leave the salesforce, or they think women will be less willing to travel or relocate than male salespeople. Studies show gaps still exist between men and women's pay, 10 percent of which is accounted for by outright discrimination against women.[37] The dangers of such thinking are not limited to legal ramifications, but the Equal Pay Act of 1963 does provide a strong reminder for those who consider paying one group of people less than another.

## Team Compensation

Most salespeople are still paid based on their individual performance. As mentioned throughout this textbook, however, teamwork in selling and team selling are growing in importance. As a result, many sales organizations are adjusting their compensation plans to recognize team performance. This represents a real challenge to sales managers for several reasons. Existing reward systems for individual salespeople typically are not easy to adapt to team selling situations.[38] Salespeople who are accustomed to earning commissions based on their individual efforts may not respond enthusiastically to team-based compensation. They may be concerned that rewards for high performers might be diminished by lower-performing team members. Furthermore, it is difficult to determine an individual salesperson's contribution to overall team performance.

Given these challenges, it is easy to see that experimentation is often required to find the right compensation plan for sales teams. At HomeBanc, a mortgage lender, salespeople with different levels of experience often work as a team. In this case, commissions are split based on experience. For instance, the experienced salesperson might receive 57 percent of the commission, versus 43 percent for the less-experienced salesperson. Plans are reviewed every six months and revised based on an individual's performance on the team.[39] In many cases, discussion among team members determines how incentive pay is distributed.[40]

There are no easy answers for structuring team pay. In general, it is a good idea to reward both individual and team performance. As one expert says, "Team pay does not mean that all team members must be measured and paid alike!"[41] Some research shows that compensation packages that reward individual and team performance are more effective than pay equality (each team member receives the same pay) and pay equity (each member is compensated according to individual performance) approaches to team compensation. Compensation packages in which team members' pay rates rise relative to their individual performance after the team as a whole reaches a certain target, or where pay rates for each rise according to their individual performance only after every member of the team hits an established target, are more effective at keeping high performers motivated and encouraging them to teach and share information with less-talented performers.[42] One sales manager, for example, encouraged team collaboration by mandating that none of his reps could place in the top three of company sales contests unless he or she also placed in the top six of their sales collaboration schemes. Salespeople who placed in the top three in both categories received a weekend at a West Coast Ritz-Carlton. As a result, both gross sales and individual performance improved.[43] In most cases, the majority of compensation will be in salary form, but bonuses and commissions also play an important role in team compensation.

Team recognition rewards are also important because they can build excitement and motivation and lead to higher performance levels. At Ultimus, a business management software firm, support technicians and salespeople work in teams to serve clients. When a customer problem arises, both are notified. If they solve the problem by a deadline, the team is recognized in the form of a memo to the entire company that details how the problem was fixed and congratulates them on a job well done.[44]

## Global Considerations

Global compensation issues are receiving more attention. In many cases, sales representation in other countries is secured through a distributor or sales agent. These situations are not so complex from a compensation management point of view because commissions or discounts from list price provide the income basis for the sellers. The compensation of native salespeople is more difficult. In many countries, political or cultural factors may have a strong influence on salesforce pay practices. For example, salespeople in the United States are less often paid by straight salary than their counterparts in any other part of the world.[45] It has been suggested that this practice is linked to cultural norms; for example, in the United States, we prize individualism, whereas in many other cultures, collectivism is valued. Furthermore, what motivates salespeople can vary from country to country. A survey of nearly 41,000 salespeople in nine countries found that only salespeople in the United States, United Kingdom, and Singapore choose money as their number-one motivator. Salespeople in Australia, Canada, Chile, New Zealand, Norway, and Sweden are more motivated by the opportunity to use their talent.[46] Additionally, in many countries fringe benefits play a significant role. Liberal expense accounts and nontaxable fringe benefits are preferred to income subject to high taxes in some countries.[47] Also, in some countries statutory increases are required for compensation decisions.[48]

The compensation of expatriate salespeople presents a different set of problems.[49] Often, the company is in the position of offering additional incentives to encourage salespeople to take assignments abroad. This pattern is changing somewhat as awareness increases that overseas assignments can enhance career opportunities. Furthermore, as companies cultivate "global" employees who welcome the opportunity to experience new cultures and take advantage of learning opportunities, companies are scaling back the once-lucrative incentives for foreign-based employment.[50] Nonetheless, arriving at equitable pay for salespeople deployed around the world requires knowledge of living costs, taxes, and other factors that are not typically dealt with by sales managers. In fact, sales managers often rely on human resource professionals to assist in global compensation planning. These professionals point out that expatriates should not lose or gain in

---

**EXHIBIT 8.9     DOs AND DON'Ts of Global Compensation**

- Do involve reps from key countries
- Do allow local managers to decide the mix between base and incentive pay
- Do use consistent performance measures (results paid for) and emphasis on each measure
- Do allow local countries flexibility in implementation
- Do use consistent communication and training themes worldwide
- Don't design the plan centrally and dictate to local countries
- Don't create a similar framework for jobs with different responsibilities
- Don't require consistency on every performance measure within the incentive plan
- Don't assume cultural differences can be managed through the incentive plan
- Don't proceed without the support of senior sales executives worldwide

---

spending power as a result of an international assignment. They also point out the importance of tying a deployment plan to the sales growth strategy and specifying the particulars of the job before addressing compensation issues.[51] Exhibit 8.9[52] provides a list of "dos and don'ts" for developing global compensation that comes from experience gained by IBM when it revamped its global compensation scheme.

## Changing the Reward System

The need to change the salesforce reward system for a given company may arise periodically as companies strive for improved performance and productivity. Changes in sales compensation are often made to bring the salesforce more in line with a shift in strategy or to maximize corporate resources. If the current plan is confusing, offers little choice, fails to drive organizational cultural initiatives, or results in unhappy salespeople, it likewise may be time for a change. When Dive Rite, a seller of diving equipment to independent retailers, found that it was not getting the incremental gains that it desired, it decided to change its salesforce compensation system. Thus, it rearranged its bonus structure to improve motivation. It switched from rewarding the one rep who shipped the most goods, to paying out extra cash on sales orders. No longer did reps have to worry that their bonus was in jeopardy if, for example, the manufacturer did not ship on time. The change has created a happier salesforce, one that is now meeting its weekly and monthly goals.[53] Reward systems should be closely monitored and should be changed when conditions warrant. A situation similar to the one in "An Ethical Dilemma" may warrant consideration.

Minor adjustments in reward systems can be made relatively painlessly, and sometimes even pleasurably, for all concerned parties. For example, the sales manager might plan three sales contests this year instead of the customary two, or could announce a cash bonus instead of a trip to Acapulco for those who make quota.

---

AN ETHICAL DILEMMA

You have been hired by a copier supply company to replace their sales manager. Although it is a small company, its salesforce has always performed well, allowing it to hold its own against much larger competitors. The former sales manager had a unique way of motivating his salesforce. Each year all salespeople were rank ordered, and the bottom three performers were fired, despite having performed very profitably for the company. Will you change this system? Why or why not?

However, making major changes in reward systems can be traumatic for salespeople and management alike if not properly handled. Any major change in financial compensation practices is likely to produce a widespread fear among the salesforce that their earnings will decline. Because many changes are precipitated by poor financial performance by the company or inequitable earnings among salesforce members, this fear is often justified for at least part of the salesforce.

To implement a new or modified reward system, sales managers must, in effect, sell the plan to the salesforce. To do this, the details of the plan must be clearly communicated well in advance of its implementation. Feedback from the salesforce should be encouraged and questions promptly addressed. Reasons for the change should be discussed openly, and any expected changes in job activities should be detailed.

It is recommended that, if possible, major changes be implemented to coincide with the beginning of a new fiscal year or planning period. It is also preferable to institute changes during favorable business conditions, rather than during recessionary periods.

The dynamic nature of marketing and sales environments dictates that sales managers constantly monitor their reward systems. It is not unreasonable to think that major changes could occur every few years or even more frequently.

# GUIDELINES FOR MOTIVATING AND REWARDING SALESPEOPLE

Sales managers should realize that practically everything they do will influence salesforce motivation one way or another. The people they recruit, the plans and policies they institute, the training they provide, and the way they communicate with and supervise salespeople are among the more important factors. In addition, sales managers should realize that environmental factors beyond their control may also influence salesforce motivation. Like other managerial functions, motivating salespeople requires a prioritized, calculated approach rather than a futile attempt to address all motivational needs simultaneously. If for no other reason, the complexity of human nature and changing needs of salesforce members will prohibit the construction of motivational programs that run smoothly without periodic adjustment. Guidelines for motivating salespeople are as follows:

1. Recruit and select salespeople whose personal motives match the requirements and rewards of the job.
2. Attempt to incorporate the individual needs of salespeople into motivational programs.
3. Provide adequate job information and ensure proper skill development for the salesforce.
4. Use job design and redesign as motivational tools.
5. Concentrate on building the self-esteem of salespeople.
6. Take a proactive approach to seeking out motivational problems and sources of frustration in the salesforce.

## Recruitment and Selection

The importance of matching the abilities and needs of sales recruits to the requirements and rewards of the job cannot be overstated. This is especially critical for sales managers who have little opportunity to alter job dimensions and reward structures. Investing more time in recruitment and selection to ensure a good match is likely to pay off later in terms of fewer motivational and other managerial problems.

## Incorporation of Individual Needs

At the outset of this module, motivation was described as a complex personal process. At the heart of the complexity of motivation is the concept of individual needs. Although there is considerable pressure and, in many cases, sound economic rationale for supporting mass approaches to salesforce motivation, there may also be opportunities to incorporate individual needs into motivational programs. When possible, individual consideration should be taken into account when motivating and rewarding salespeople. For instance, some companies, such as broadband equipment manufacturer Netopia, have turned to online incentive programs, such as InnergE (http://www.hinda.com/technology/InnergE.html), to meet the diverse needs of its resellers when attempting to motivate them. Resellers participating in the program log on to InnergE, where they can redeem points earned by selling Netopia products for rewards from a catalog of more than 2,000 items ranging from digital cameras and DVD players to travel certificates.[54]

## Information and Skills

Salespeople must have high skill levels and be well equipped with the right information to do their jobs well. If sales managers train their people properly and give them the right information, salespeople can see how their efforts lead to the desired results. If salespeople's understanding of how their efforts produce results is consistent with that of the sales manager, reasonable goals can be set that allow performance worthy of rewards. Providing adequate information to the salesforce also enhances salesforce socialization (discussed in earlier modules), thereby reducing role conflict and role ambiguity.

## Job Design

Given the nature of sales jobs, one would expect good opportunities to stimulate intrinsic motivation without major changes in the job. Sales jobs allow the use of a wide range of skills and abilities; boredom is thus not a typical problem. And given the unique contributions of personal selling to the organization, as discussed in Module 2, salespeople can readily see that their jobs are critical to the organization's success. Most salespeople have considerable latitude in determining work priorities and thus experience more freedom on the job than do many other employees. Finally, feedback from sales managers or through self-monitoring is readily available. In many ways, the motivational task is easier for sales managers than for other managers. The sales job itself can be a powerful motivator.

## Building Self-Esteem

Sales managers increase salesforce motivation by building salespeople's self-esteem. Positive reinforcement for good performance should be standard procedure. This may be done with formal or informal communications or recognition programs designed to spotlight good performance. When performance is less than satisfactory, it should not be overlooked but addressed in a constructive manner.

## Proactive Approach

Sales managers should be committed to uncovering potential problems in motivation and eliminating them before they develop. For example, if some members of the salesforce perceive a lack of opportunity for promotion into management and are demotivated as a result, the sales manager might take additional steps to clearly define the guidelines for promotion into management and review the performance of management hopefuls in light of these guidelines. If promotion opportunities are indeed limited, the matching function of recruitment and selection again shows its importance.

## SUMMARY

1. **Explain the key components of motivation: intensity, persistence, and direction**. A variety of ways exist to define motivation. Our definition includes the qualities of intensity, persistence, and direction. Intensity is the amount of mental and physical effort the salesperson is willing to expend on a specific activity. Persistence is a choice to expend effort over time, especially in the face of adversity. Direction implies that, to some extent, salespeople choose the activities on which effort is expended.

2. **Explain the difference between compensation rewards and noncompensation rewards**. Compensation rewards are those given by the organization in return for the salesperson's efforts and performance. They may include both financial and nonfinancial rewards. Noncompensation rewards are related to job design and work environment. The opportunity to be involved in meaningful interesting work is an example of a noncompensation reward. The provision of adequate resources to do the job and a supportive management system are other examples. The focus in this module has been on the management of compensation rewards.

3. **Describe the primary financial and nonfinancial compensation rewards available to salespeople**. As shown in Exhibit 8.3, six major rewards are available to salespeople: pay (or financial compensation), opportunity for promotion, a sense of accomplishment, personal growth opportunities, recognition, and job security (the last five being nonfinancial). Pay is usually current spendable income generated by salary, commissions, and bonuses.

4. **Describe salary, commission, and combination pay plans in terms of their advantages and disadvantages**. Straight-salary plans and straight-commission plans represent the two extremes in financial compensation for salespeople. Straight salary offers maximum control over salesforce activities but does not provide added incentive for exceptional performance. The opposite is true for straight-commission plans. The limitations of both plans have made combination plans the most popular with sales organizations. Although such plans can become too complex for easy administration, when properly conceived, they offer a balance of control and incentive.

5. **Explain the fundamental concepts in sales-expense reimbursement**. Job-related expenses incurred by salespeople are reimbursed by a large majority of sales organizations. Sales expenses are usually substantial, averaging 20 to 30 percent of total financial compensation paid to salespeople. Companies use budgets, allowances, and documentation requirements to control sales expenses.

6. **Discuss issues associated with sales contests, equal pay for equal work, team compensation, global compensation, and changing a reward system**. Sales contests are used widely to achieve short-term results, but little is known about their true effects. The Equal Pay Act of 1963 reinforces an ethically desirable behavior—paying those who do equal work an equal amount of money. Companies that are new to team selling may find it difficult to move from individual-based compensation to team-based compensation. It is a challenge to determine how much of each team member's pay should be based on individual performance and how much on team performance. In most team selling situations, salary is the major compensation component, although bonuses, commissions, and other team rewards can have a positive influence on motivation. Global compensation may be dependent on different cultures and other business environment factors in varying locations around the world. Sales managers often rely heavily on human resource professionals to structure global compensation plans. Changing a reward system is a delicate procedure, requiring careful communication to the salesforce, who must "buy" the new system much like a customer would buy a product.

7. **List the guidelines for motivating and rewarding salespeople**. Six managerial guidelines for motivating salespeople are as follows: First, match the recruit to the requirements and rewards of the job. Second, incorporate individual needs into motivational programs when feasible. Third, provide salespeople with adequate information and ensure proper skill development to facilitate job performance. Fourth, cultivate salespeople's self-esteem. Fifth, take a proactive approach to uncovering motivational problems. Sixth, try to eliminate problems before they become serious.

## UNDERSTANDING SALES MANAGEMENT TERMS

| | |
|---|---|
| motivation | commission payout event |
| intensity | constant rate |
| persistence | progressive rate |
| direction | regressive rate |
| intrinsic motivation | performance bonus |
| extrinsic motivation | salary plus incentive |
| reward system management | financial compensation mix |
| compensation rewards | nonfinancial compensation |
| noncompensation rewards | opportunity for promotion |
| current spendable income | sense of accomplishment |
| straight salary | opportunities for personal growth |
| planned earnings | recognition |
| salary compression | job security |
| straight commission | sales expenses |
| commission base | expense account padding |
| commission rate | sales contests |
| commission splits | |

## DEVELOPING SALES MANAGEMENT KNOWLEDGE

1. Identify and explain the three key dimensions of motivation.

2. Distinguish between compensation rewards and noncompensation rewards.

3. Describe an optimal salesforce reward system.

4. What are the nonfinancial compensation rewards discussed in this module? What suggestions can you make for administering recognition rewards?

5. Evaluate straight-salary, straight-commission, and combination pay plans in terms of their advantages and disadvantages. When should each be used?

6. Refer to "Sales Management in the 21st Century: Recognition and Incentive Programs at Federated Mutual Insurance." How does Federated Mutual Insurance Company use recognition and incentive programs to motivate its salespeople?

7. What concerns should a sales manager have regarding the use of sales contests?

8. Refer to "Sales Management in the 21st Century: Use of Sales Contests at Allied Office Products". At what levels in the organization does Allied hold sales contests? What are some of the goals that Allied is trying to achieve with their contests? What types of incentives do they offer?

9. What challenges do sales managers face when using team-based compensation? What guidelines can sales managers follow when using team-based compensation?

10. Discuss several guidelines to improve the effectiveness of salesforce motivation and reward system management.

## BUILDING SALES MANAGEMENT SKILLS

1. Assume you have been hired as the national sales manager for a newly formed electronics distributor. Your salesforce will sell directly to electronics retailers. Although the company is not widely known, it will use little other than the salesforce to promote its products in a highly competitive market. Thus, salespeople's skills are very important. Salespeople will be responsible for providing complete customer service, including handling damage claims, helping with merchandising, providing advice, and following up after the sale to ensure the customer is completely satisfied. Devise a reward system for your salesforce, being sure to address the type of financial compensation plan you will use and why, as well as the types of nonfinancial compensation you will provide. What role will recruitment and selection play in this process? Explain.

2. Most student organizations are looking for ways to raise funds. Choose a student (or any other) organization and determine a fundraising activity that involves some form of personal selling (e.g., a raffle). Then, devise a sales contest that would be appropriate for achieving predetermined fundraising objectives. Explain your fundraiser, its objectives, the contest, and the rationale behind the contest's incentives.

3. This exercise is designed to expose you to differences in compensation and motivation across salespeople and companies. Interview three salespeople (in person or via telephone or the Internet) from three companies. Provide a brief report for each salesperson indicating gender, age, experience, company, industry, compensation method, financial and nonfinancial compensation rewards, and what each believes motivates him or her to perform. Then write a summary paragraph that points to similarities and differences among the three and why these might exist. Finally, of the three, whose compensation plan would interest you the most and why?

4. It is important to consider cost of living differences if a company has salespeople who will be located in several different places. Assume that you will pay salespeople a base salary of $35,000 based on the cost of living in St. Louis, Missouri. Access the Career Journal by *The Wall Street Journal* at **http://www.careerjournal.com/salaryhiring/index.html**. Now click on the "Salary Calculator" located in the "Salary and hiring info" section and use the calculator to determine what an equivalent base salary of $35,000 would be in the following places (You will need to access the international Salary Calculator in the pull down window at the bottom of the page to calculate the international locations):

| | |
|---|---|
| Washington, DC _____ | Jacksonville, FL _____ |
| San Diego, CA | Seattle, WA |
| Houston, TX _____ | Syracuse, NY _____ |
| Chicago, IL | Paris, France |
| London, England _____ | Athens, Greece _____ |

5. Nick Pirrone, VP of sales and marketing for Steeltime, Inc., recently invested over $250,000 in a customer relationship management (CRM) system. He has a problem, however. His 10 salespeople either do not know how to use the system or simply do not want to use it. The CRM system was to be used to move prospects through Steeltime's sales cycle more efficiently and improve the level of customer satisfaction. When the system was introduced seven months ago, the sales and marketing staff embarked on extensive training to learn the system. Given this, Pirrone feels that his

salespeople have the knowledge to use the system, but that they are simply ignoring his wishes and choosing not to do so. How can Pirrone convince his salespeople that the CRM system can actually benefit them? How can he motivate them to start using the system?[55]

**ROLE PLAY**

6. **Situation:**    Read the Ethical Dilemma on page 228.

   **Characters:**    Sherry Smith, salesperson; Sherry's sales manager

   **Scene:**    *Location*—Sales manager's office. *Action*—Sherry's sales manager confronts her regarding meal expenses that he believes Sherry falsified on her expense report.

# MAKING SALES MANAGEMENT DECISIONS

## Case 8.1: Stalwart Industrial Products[56]

### Background

Stalwart Industrial Products manufactures and sells a wide variety of industrial tools to various resellers and end users. Founded in 1935, the company prides itself on producing high-quality, durable tools. The company's salesforce has always been an integral part of its success. Sales reps at Stalwart work hard and are rewarded accordingly.

### Current Situation

Stalwart's national sales manager, Tom Beesman, has enjoyed a great deal of success with his salesforce. Since being promoted to his position three years ago, things have gone relatively smoothly, until now. "When it rains, it pours," Tom thinks to himself as he sits at his desk and contemplates two issues confronting him. For starters, one of his star salespeople, Charlie Davidson, seems to be slowing down at a time when his help is desperately needed. Second, the company has added a new Web page, and the reps are upset.

Charlie Davidson has worked for Stalwart for almost three years. His first year he generated $850,000 in revenues, hitting 112 percent of quota. He followed this by racking up sales of $1.29 million, for 119 percent of quota. He accomplished this by prospecting and meeting with customers 14 hours a day during the week, and completing reports and writing proposals on the weekends. At this pace, Davidson looked as if he would exceed quota again this year—that is, until he had his first child two months ago. Currently, he's down to 50 to 60 hours per week, and his sales reflect this.

Beesman is worried. Stalwart currently is undertaking an ambitious growth program. Next month alone, it plans to introduce four new products. Beesman had hoped to make Davidson a member of the management team. In casual conversation with Davidson, however, Beesman discovered that Davidson was not interested in becoming a manager at Stalwart because the big money is in sales. Davidson is still earning a hefty paycheck despite working fewer hours. To be successful, Beesman realizes that he needs to get back the energetic, hard-charging Davidson he hired, but he is not sure how.

In the meantime, the salesforce, including Davidson, is upset. As part of its aggressive growth strategy, the company began accepting orders through its Web site. While customers are happy about this, the salesforce is not. Although salespeople earn commissions on current customers who order through the Web site, they do not receive commissions on any new Web customers in their territories. The company's president, Thurston Howell III,

views the Web site as an additional "rep." However, salespeople see it as competition. Consequently, productivity and morale are down. Beesman is caught in the middle. He needs to find a solution to please both his salesforce and Howell.

### Questions

1. How do you suggest that Beesman handle Davidson?
2. Assess the situation regarding Stalwart's use of the Web. What would you suggest that Beesman do to please both Howell and his salesforce?

| | |
|---|---|
| **Situation:** | Read Case 8.1. |
| **Characters:** | Tom Beesman, national sales manager; Charlie Davidson, star sales representative |
| **Scene 1:** | *Location*—Tom Beesman's office. *Action*—Beesman has called a meeting with Charlie Davidson to discuss with him the company's plans to introduce four new products next month. He discusses with Charlie how important he is to launching the products and confronts him about his drop in production. |
| **Scene 2:** | *Location*—In the car on the way to a sales call. *Action*—Beesman tries to convince Davidson of the merits of the company's new Web-based order system. In doing so, he makes some suggestions for improving the current commission system. Beesman would like to convince Davidson to sell the rest of the salesforce on the Web-based order system and accompanying new commission system. |
| **Scene 3:** | *Location*—A local restaurant for lunch. *Action*—Beesman is meeting with Charlie to discuss the possibility of Charlie moving into sales management. He wants to convince him that it would be a good move for him. Charlie, naturally, explains his side of the story. |

**ROLE PLAY**

## Case 8.2: Floor-Shine Cleaning Products

### Background

Floor-Shine Cleaning Products has been manufacturing and selling household floor cleaning products for more than 60 years. The company offers several brands that can be used to clean a variety of floor surfaces. It stands behind all its products with a "customer satisfaction guarantee." Any consumer who is not fully satisfied with the floor cleaner on applying it properly may return it to the place of purchase and receive a refund or have the product replaced with another of equal value.

Floor-Shine's products are distributed in a variety of outlets, ranging from small grocery and convenience stores to huge discounters such as Wal-Mart and Home Depot. Each customer is highly valued regardless of size. According to the company's founder, Arthur Worthington, "Every customer should be treated as if they are our only customer." For this reason, the company takes pride in establishing long-term customer relationships. In fact, several of the company's current customers have been distributing its products since the company was founded. The company's salesforce was built around this idea and to this day is well noted for its commitment to building strong and satisfying customer relationships.

## Current Situation

Vince Coleman, Floor-Shine's national sales manager, recently asked regional sales manager Bob Herman to coordinate a special fourth-quarter sales push to achieve projected year-end sales goals. Herman, a committed sales manager, was confident he could develop a program that would succeed. He thought a sales contest would be an excellent way to boost fourth-quarter sales in his region. By developing a contest, he could avoid altering the current compensation package, which he believed to be satisfactory to his salespeople.

Herman has 100 salespeople in his region, about 20 percent of whom are women. The region is divided into five districts, each comprised of 20 salespeople. Rather than have all 100 salespeople compete against each other, Herman decided to have five winners, one for each district. Salespeople within each district would compete against each other, and the salesperson with the highest number of sales during the contest period would be declared the winner.

Herman recently heard about a new approach being taken by some companies to motivate their salespeople. Contest winners were awarded a trip to a fantasy baseball camp. Award winners spent a week with baseball legends who taught and coached them. The award proved to be a highly successful motivator. Herman liked this idea and decided to offer this trip to each district winner as the prize for winning the sales contest. Herman

contacted the company's marketing communications group to ask them to design a set of promotional materials to be distributed to each sales-person. He then visited each district explaining the contest rules to its salespeople. At the same time, he delivered pep talks. "Each of you has an equal chance at victory. Now is the time to seize the moment and go for the gold!"

After all the preplanning was completed, the contest finally went into effect. Most salespeople realized that they could increase their sales either by selling more to current customers or by finding new accounts. One method for increasing sales to current customers was to help them in merchandising so that they could sell more product. This seemed to work well for many salespeople. However, several concentrated on their large customers at the expense of their smaller accounts. The larger customers had much more potential and the input-to-output ratio with these customers had a much higher payoff. Several salespeople's obsession with their larger accounts got in the way of providing their smaller customers with the service they had come to expect. Some customers even threatened to take their business elsewhere. In fact, Ray's Groceries, a small but long-standing customer, was so upset with the decline in service that it dropped Floor-Shine as a supplier.

Numerous salespeople got wise to the idea that they could increase their sales by loading their customers with product toward the end of the contest period. Some salespeople asked customers to purchase and take delivery of their next scheduled order early. Others offered customers special incentives if they agreed to order more product than usual. One salesperson went so far as to offer a small kickback.

In an attempt to gain new customers, some salespeople took on customers that were poor credit risks. For instance, salesman Larry Lynn knew a medium-sized hardware store in his territory was in financial trouble, so much so that the store had lost its paint supplier because of its inability to pay. Larry figured he could enhance his sales during the contest period by taking the customer's order. If the customer was unable to pay, it would not show up until after the contest was over, and Larry would already have these sales added to his total for the period.

About one-third of the way into the contest, Dan Tate, a sales rep in District 3, was able to land a new major account, which meant a tremendous increase in sales for him. At that point, the other salespeople in his district seemed to lose enthusiasm for the contest. As Saul Weber put it, "I don't stand a prayer of winning the contest now. The only way I would have a chance is to land a similar account. Given my present territory, that is impossible. Doug has this contest wrapped up. He might as well grab his mitt and pack his bags—he's heading for fantasy baseball camp."As the contest was drawing to a close, Herman noticed that sales had not increased nearly as much as he had anticipated. Moreover, most of the women in the salesforce did not significantly increase their sales figures. In fact, they were about the same as usual. Herman knew Coleman would want a full assessment of the contest on its completion. As he sat at his desk, he began to think about what went wrong.

## Questions

1. How would you evaluate this contest? What are its pros and cons?
2. How could this contest be designed to have a better chance of success?

**ROLE PLAY**

**Situation:**    Read Case 8.2.

**Characters:**    Vince Coleman, national sales manager; Bob Herman, regional sales manager; Larry Lynn, salesperson

**Scene 1:**    *Location*—Bob Herman's office. *Action*—Herman got word of Larry Lynn's tactic of taking on customers with questionable credit risk during the contest period. He is meeting with Larry to discuss these tactics.

**Scene 2:**    *Location*—Vince Coleman's office. *Action*—Vince Coleman is meeting with Bob Herman to get a recap of his sales contest. Herman explains the pros and cons of the contest. Coleman then provides some advice for developing a sales contest in the future.

# Determining Salesforce Effectiveness and Performance

The two modules in Part Five focus on determining salesforce effectiveness and performance. Module 9 addresses the evaluation of sales organization effectiveness. Methods for analyzing sales, costs, profitability, and productivity at different sales organization levels are reviewed. Module 10 addresses the evaluation of salespeople's individual performance and job satisfaction. Ways of determining the appropriate performance criteria and methods of evaluation, and of using the evaluations to improve salesperson performance and job satisfaction, are discussed.

## EVALUATING THE EFFECTIVENESS OF THE ORGANIZATION

# INCREASING PRODUCTIVITY AND EVALUATING EFFECTIVENESS AT SOLCORP

Solcorp, a subsidiary of EDS, provides software solutions and services for the life insurance and wealth management industries. Solcorp found itself in need of a more fluid and centralized system that would enable its salesforce to deliver enterprise software to top-tier global financial services. Most of the tasks associated with forecasting and reporting were done manually, while Microsoft Excel spreadsheets were being used to track account activities, manage territories, and generally guide performance. Furthermore, since sales data was dispersed over several databases, it was difficult to gather real-time reports showing accurate current performance and historical trends.

In an attempt to improve the company's salesforce productivity, as well as enhance its ability to evaluate salesforce effectiveness, Blair Goulet, senior vice president of global sales and marketing at Solcorp, turned to Salesnet, a salesforce automation provider. Salesnet was able to provide a CRM solution that offered real-time access to critical sales data. The solution also supported the proven best practices that Goulet and his team have defined in selling to enterprise-class accounts like Great-West Life Assurance Company and Citigroup.

Salesnet worked collaboratively with Goulet to initiate training of sales, sales support, and executive management. Solcorp's Excel spreadsheets were imported into the Salesnet application, and its proprietary sales processes were incorporated into the system. Solcorp's global sales organization was trained and fully using Salesnet within 60 days of start-up.

There have been several positive results. Solcorp now has real-time access to global sales information and is able to predict business with a higher degree of accuracy. Workflow and process management capabilities allow Solcorp consistency of operations. Salesnet also allows Solcorp a centralized location for reporting, forecasting, and managing global sales activities. Finally, Salesnet makes it easier to track and manage territories, accounts, and opportunities. As such, this system not only helps track salesforce effectiveness, but also helps improve it.

**Source:** Salesnet, http://web.salesnet.com/main.asp?urh=us_custpage_solcorp. Accessed 7/16/04.

## Objectives

After completing this module, you should be able to

1 Differentiate between sales organization effectiveness and salesperson performance.

2 Define a sales organization audit and discuss how it should be conducted.

3 Define benchmarking and discuss how it should be conducted.

4 Describe how to perform different types of sales analysis for different organizational levels and types of sales.

5 Describe how to perform a cost analysis for a sales organization.

6 Describe how to perform an income statement analysis, activity-based costing, and return on assets managed to assess sales organization profitability.

7 Describe how to perform a productivity analysis for a sales organization.

Assessing the success of a sales organization is difficult because so many factors must be considered. For example, the success of the sales organization must be differentiated from the success of individual salespeople[1] (see Figure 9.1).[2] Whereas sales organization effectiveness is a function of how well the sales organization achieved its goals and objectives overall, salesperson performance is a function of how well each salesperson performed in his or her particular situation. Thus, salesperson performance contributes to, but does not completely determine, sales organization effectiveness.

As indicated by the Solcorp example in the opening vignette, sales organization effectiveness must be evaluated to determine means for improving performance and productivity. The focus is on the overall sales organization as well as the levels within the sales organization (territories, districts, regions, and zones). The results of such evaluations are normally general strategic or policy changes. However,

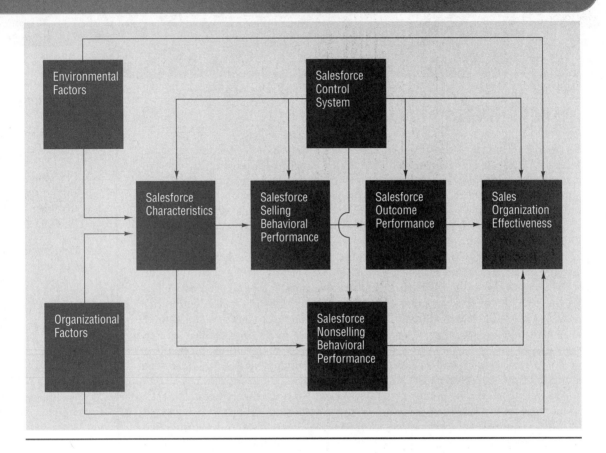

FIGURE 9.1

Sales Organization Effectiveness

analyzing and improving salesperson performance is typically paramount to improving sales organization effectiveness.

Evaluations of salesperson performance are confined to the individuals, not the sales organization or sales organization levels. The results of these evaluations are typically tactical. In other words, they lead a sales manager to take specific actions to improve the performance of an individual salesperson. Generally, different actions are warranted for different salespeople, depending on the areas that need improvement.

Evidence for the difference between sales organization effectiveness and salesperson performance is provided in a study of 144 sales organizations in the United States. A comparison of the more-effective and less-effective sales organizations indicated that those that were more effective had achieved much better results in many areas, compared with their less-effective counterparts. For example, the more-effective sales organizations generated much higher sales per salesperson ($3,988,000 versus $1,755,000) and much lower selling expenses as a percentage of sales (13 percent versus 18 percent) than the less-effective sales organizations. The salespeople in the more-effective organizations also outperformed salespeople in the less-effective ones in several areas. However, the differences in salesperson performance were not sufficient to completely explain the differences in sales organization effectiveness. Thus, sales organization effectiveness is the result of salesperson performance as well as many other factors (e.g., sales organization structure and deployment and sales management performance).[3]

This module addresses the evaluation of sales organization effectiveness, and Module 10 addresses the evaluation of salesperson performance. This module begins with a discussion of a sales organization audit, examines benchmarking, then describes more specific analyses of sales, costs, profits, and productivity to determine sales organization effectiveness.

## SALES ORGANIZATION AUDIT

Although the term *audit* is most often used in reference to financial audits performed by accounting firms, the audit concept has been extended to business functions in recent years. In Module 6, a **sales organization audit** was described as a comprehensive, systematic, diagnostic, and prescriptive tool.[4] The purpose of a sales organization audit is

> to assess the adequacy of a firm's sales management process and to provide direction for improved performance and prescription for needed changes. It is a tool that should be used by all firms whether or not they are achieving their goals.

This type of audit is the most comprehensive approach for evaluating sales organization effectiveness.

A framework for performing a sales organization audit is presented in Figure 9.2.[5] As indicated in the figure, the audit addresses four major areas: sales organization

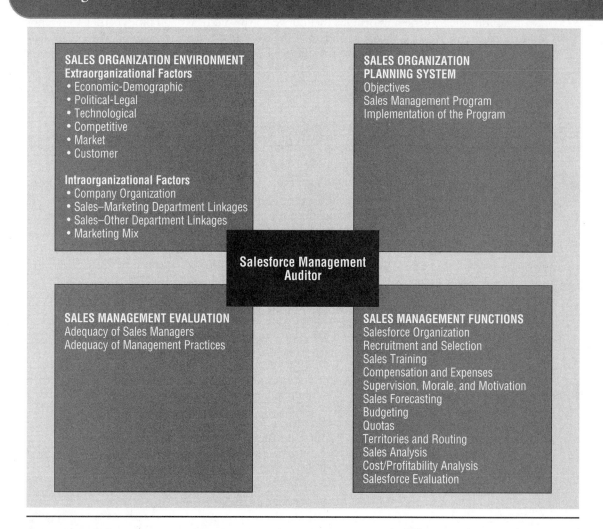

**Sales Organization Audit Framework**                                    **FIGURE 9.2**

**SALES ORGANIZATION ENVIRONMENT**
**Extraorganizational Factors**
• Economic-Demographic
• Political-Legal
• Technological
• Competitive
• Market
• Customer

**Intraorganizational Factors**
• Company Organization
• Sales–Marketing Department Linkages
• Sales–Other Department Linkages
• Marketing Mix

**SALES ORGANIZATION PLANNING SYSTEM**
Objectives
Sales Management Program
Implementation of the Program

**Salesforce Management Auditor**

**SALES MANAGEMENT EVALUATION**
Adequacy of Sales Managers
Adequacy of Management Practices

**SALES MANAGEMENT FUNCTIONS**
Salesforce Organization
Recruitment and Selection
Sales Training
Compensation and Expenses
Supervision, Morale, and Motivation
Sales Forecasting
Budgeting
Quotas
Territories and Routing
Sales Analysis
Cost/Profitability Analysis
Salesforce Evaluation

The sales organization audit is the most comprehensive evaluation of sales organization effectiveness. The audit typically provides assessments of the sales organization environment, sales management evaluation, sales organization planning system, and sales management functions.

**Source:** Alan J. Dubinsky and Richard W. Hansen, "The Sales Force Management Audit." Copyright © 1981, by The Regents of the University of California. Reprinted from the *California Management Review,* Vol. 24, No. 2. By permission of The Regents.

environment, sales management evaluation, sales organization planning system, and sales management functions. The purpose of the audit is to investigate, systematically and comprehensively, each of these areas to identify existing or potential problems, determine their causes, and take the necessary corrective action. For example, after having an agency conduct an audit, Guinness was able to redesign its salesforce to improve its structure and clarity. This resulted in a more motivated, focused, efficient, and subsequently higher-performing sales organization.[6]

The sales organization audit should be performed regularly, not just when problems are evident. One of the major values of an audit is its generation of diagnostic information that can help management correct problems in early stages or eliminate potential problems before they become serious. Because auditing should be objective, it should be conducted by someone from outside the sales organization. This could be someone from another functional area within the firm or an outside consulting firm.

Although outsiders should conduct the audit, members of the sales organization should be active participants in it. Sales managers and salespeople provide much of the information collected. Exhibit 9.1 presents sample questions that should be addressed in a sales organization audit.[7] Answers typically come from members of the sales organization and from company records.

Although obviously an expensive and time-consuming process, the sales organization audit usually generates benefits that outweigh the monetary and time costs. This is especially true when audits are conducted regularly because the chances of identifying and correcting potential problems before they become troublesome increase with the regularity of the auditing process.

---

**EXHIBIT 9.1** Sample Questions from a Sales Organization Audit

**IV. Sales Management Functions**

**A. Salesforce Organization**
1. How is our salesforce organized (by product, by customer, by territory)?
2. Is this type of organization appropriate, given the current intraorganizational and extraorganizational conditions?
3. Does this type of organization adequately service the needs of our customers?

**B. Recruitment and Selection**
1. How many salespeople do we have?
2. Is this number adequate in light of our objectives and resources?
3. Are we serving our customers adequately with this number of salespeople?
4. How is our salesforce size determined?
5. What is our turnover rate? What have we done to try to change it?
6. Do we have adequate sources from which to obtain recruits? Have we overlooked some possible sources?
7. Do we have a job description for each of our sales jobs? Is each job description current?
8. Have we enumerated the necessary sales job qualifications? Have they been recently updated? Are they predictive of sales success?
9. Are our selection screening procedures financially feasible and appropriate?
10. Do we use a battery of psychological tests in our selection process? Are the tests valid and reliable?
11. Do our recruitment and selection procedures satisfy employment opportunity guidelines?

**C. Sales Training**
1. How is our sales training program developed? Does it meet the needs of management and sales personnel?
2. Do we establish training objectives before developing and implementing the training program?
3. Is the training program adequate in light of our objectives and resources?
4. What kinds of training do we currently provide our salespeople?

    5. Does the training program need revising? What areas of the training program should be improved or deemphasized?
    6. What methods do we use to evaluate the effectiveness of our training program?
    7. Can we afford to train internally or should we use external sources for training?
    8. Do we have an ongoing training program for senior salespeople? Is it adequate?

**D. Compensation and Expenses**
    1. Does our sales compensation plan meet our objectives in light of our financial resources?
    2. Is the compensation plan fair, flexible, economical, and easy to understand and administer?
    3. What is the level of compensation, the type of plan, and the frequency of payment?
    4. Are the salespeople and management satisfied with the compensation plan?
    5. Does the compensation plan ensure that the salespeople perform the necessary sales job activities?
    6. Does the compensation plan attract and retain enough quality sales performers?
    7. Does the sales expense plan meet our objectives in light of our financial resources?
    8. Is the expense plan fair, flexible, and easy to administer? Does it allow for geographical, customer, and/or product differences?
    9. Does the expense plan ensure that the necessary sales job activities are performed?
   10. Can we easily audit the expenses incurred by our sales personnel?

**Source:** Alan J. Dubinsky and Richard W. Hansen, "The Sales Force Management Audit." Copyright © 1981, by The Regents of the University of California. Reprinted from the *California Management Review,* Vol. 24, No. 2. By permission of The Regents.

# BENCHMARKING

Although the sales audit can help identify areas in the sales organization that need improvement, an increasingly popular technique for improving sales organization effectiveness is **benchmarking.** Benchmarking is an ongoing measurement and analysis process that compares an organization's current operating practices with the "best practices" used by world-class organizations. It is a tool for evaluating current business practices and finding a way to do them better, more quickly, and less expensively to better meet customer needs.[8] Using benchmarking, Norwest, the nation's largest mortgage company, was able to consolidate its sales brochures and direct mail campaigns resulting in savings of more than $1.4 million. It also increased sales by 102 percent using sales road maps. Rank Xerox, the British unit of Xerox, used benchmarking to increase country unit sales from 152 percent to 328 percent and improve new revenue by $200 million.[9] A research study of more than 1,600 U.S. and Canadian organizations found that those companies willing to learn from the best practices of others are more successful at improving customer satisfaction than those that are more reluctant. Perhaps this explains why such firms as IBM, AT&T, DuPont, GM, Intel, Sprint, Motorola, and Xerox use benchmarking.[10]

    Figure 9.3 outlines steps in the benchmarking process.[11] A pivotal part of this process is identifying the company or salesforce to benchmark. A literature search and personal contacts are means for identifying companies that perform the process in an exceptional manner. Winning an industry award, being recognized for functional excellence, and receiving a national quality award are three indicators of excellence.[12] Eastman Chemical Company and IBM have used the Malcolm Baldrige National Quality Award criteria as bases on which to evaluate their salesforce, map processes leading to desired results, and focus efforts on continuously improving these processes.[13] Those processes that have the greatest impact on salesforce productivity should be benchmarked. Companies such as Best Practices, LLC (http://www.best-in-class.com), the Benchmarking Network (http://www.benchmarkingnetwork.com), and American Productivity and Quality Center (http://www.apqc.org) provide useful Web sites for initiating a benchmarking program.[14]

**FIGURE 9.3** Benchmarking Process

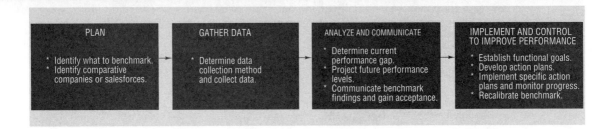

A benchmarking study should provide several outputs. First, it should provide a measure that compares performance for the benchmarked process relative to the organization studied. Second, it should identify the organization's performance gap relative to benchmarked performance levels. Third, it should identify best practices and facilitators that produced the results observed during the study. Finally, the study should determine performance goals for the process studied and identify areas in which action can be taken to improve performance.[15] Exhibit 9.2 provides some keys to successful benchmarking.[16] To see how benchmarking can be used to improve sales organization performance, see "Sales Management in the 21st Century: Using Benchmarking to Succeed."

**EXHIBIT 9.2** Keys to Successful Benchmarking

- Clearly identify critical activities that will improve quality or service or reduce cost.
- Properly prepare and benchmark *only one activity at a time*.
- Make sure that you thoroughly understand your own process first.
- Create a "seek, desire, and listen" environment by choosing curious and knowledgeable people for your benchmark team.
- Verify that your benchmark partner company is the best in its class, and clearly understand your partner's process.
- Provide adequate resources, not only financial, but also knowledgeable personnel.
- Be diligent in selecting the correct partner—do not use a company that may not provide advantages to you.
- Implement the benchmarking action plan.

SALES MANAGEMENT IN THE 21ST CENTURY

**Using Benchmarking to Succeed**

Andre Wickham, corporate regional sales manager, Southeastern United States for Hormel Foods Corporation, comments on his company's use of benchmarking:

*The marketplace today is fast-paced and constantly changing. As a result, sales organizations are continuously challenged to develop a structure that will allow them to effectively meet customer needs and fully penetrate all competitive market segments.*

*At Hormel, we use benchmarking to help us achieve this goal. With benchmarking, we gauge our practices against the "best practices" of others in the marketplace. In recent years, this activity has become an important part of the strategic planning process. This evaluation helps us to assess our current and future course, which may range anywhere from no change to a major overhaul. Importantly, however, this practice allows us to clearly understand our strengths, weaknesses, opportunities, and threats.*

## SALES ORGANIZATION EFFECTIVENESS EVALUATIONS

There is no one summary measure of sales organization effectiveness. Sales organizations have multiple goals and objectives, and thus, multiple factors must be assessed. As illustrated in Figure 9.4, four types of analyses are typically necessary to develop a comprehensive evaluation of any sales organization. Conducting analyses in each of these areas is a complex task for two reasons. First, many types of analyses can be performed to evaluate sales, cost, profitability, and productivity results. For example, a sales analysis might focus on total sales, sales of specific products, sales to specific customers, or other types of sales and might include sales comparisons to sales quotas, to previous periods, to sales of competitors, or other types of analyses. Second, separate sales analyses need to be performed for the different levels in the sales organization. Thus, a typical evaluation would include separate sales analyses for sales zones, regions, districts, and territories.

Many sales organizations focus on sales analysis.[17] The results from one study on methods used to measure salesforce effectiveness are presented in Exhibit 9.3.[18] Customer satisfaction is also heavily relied upon to determine sales organization effectiveness. This involves surveying customers to determine their level of satisfaction with the company's products, service, and salespeople, among other things. Determining the level of customer satisfaction has become easier due to the Internet. Companies such as Apogee Analytics, LLC (http://www.apogeeanalytics.com) and NetReflector (http://www.netreflector.com) will create and administer Web-based customer satisfaction surveys for firms.[19] Now we discuss how sales, cost, profitability, and productivity analyses can be conducted to evaluate sales organization effectiveness.

### Sales Analysis

Because the basic purpose of a sales organization is to generate sales, **sales analysis** is an obvious and important element of evaluating sales organization effectiveness. The difficulty, however, is in determining exactly what should be analyzed. One key consideration is in defining what is meant by a *sale*. Definitions include a placed order, a shipped order, and a paid order. Defining a sale by when an order is shipped is probably most common. Regardless of the definition used, the sales organization must be consistent and develop an information system to track sales based on whatever sales definition is used.

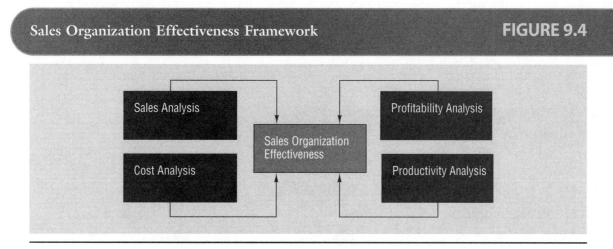

Sales Organization Effectiveness Framework        **FIGURE 9.4**

Evaluating sales organization effectiveness requires analyses of sales, cost, profitability, and productivity. Each type of analysis can be performed in several ways, should be performed at different sales organization levels, and will produce unique evaluative and diagnostic information for sales managers.

**EXHIBIT 9.3**   Methods Used to Measure Salesforce Effectiveness

|  | **Percent Using** |
|---|---|
| Sales results versus goal | 79 |
| Customer satisfaction | 59 |
| Profit versus goal | 49 |
| Sales manager feedback | 45 |
| Market share | 39 |
| Cost of sales | 37 |
| Sales employee feedback | 28 |
| Return on investment of sales resources | 21 |
| Other | 9 |

Another consideration is whether to focus on *sales dollars* or *sales units*. This can be extremely important during times when prices increase or when salespeople have substantial latitude in negotiating selling prices. The sales information in Exhibit 9.4 illustrates how different conclusions may result from analyses of sales dollars or sales units. If just sales dollars are analyzed, all regions in the exhibit would appear to be generating substantial sales growth. However, when sales units are introduced, the dollar sales growth for all regions in 2003 can be attributed almost entirely to price increases, because units sold increased only minimally during this period. The situation is somewhat different in 2004, because all regions increased the number of units sold. However, sales volume for region 2 is relatively flat, even though units sold increased. This could be caused either by selling more lower-priced products or by using larger price concessions than the other regions. In either case, analysis of sales dollars or sales units provides different evaluative information, so it is often useful to include both dollars and units in a sales analysis.

Given a definition of sales and a decision concerning sales dollars versus units, many types of sales evaluations can be performed. Several alternative evaluations are presented in Figure 9.5. The critical decision areas are the organizational level of analysis, the type of sales, and the type of analysis.

### Organizational Level of Analysis

Sales analyses should be performed for all levels in the sales organization for two basic reasons. First, sales managers at each level need sales analyses at their level and the next level below for evaluation and control purposes. For example, a regional sales manager should have sales analyses for all regions as well as for all districts within his or her region. This makes it possible to assess the sales effectiveness of the region and to determine the sales contribution of each district.

**EXHIBIT 9.4**   Sales Dollars versus Sales Units

|  | **2002** | | **2003** | | **2004** | |
|---|---|---|---|---|---|---|
|  | **Sales Dollars** | **Sales Units** | **Sales Dollars** | **Sales Units** | **Sales Dollars** | **Sales Units** |
| Region 1 | $50,000,000 | 500,000 | $55,000,000 | 510,000 | $62,000,000 | 575,000 |
| Region 2 | $55,000,000 | 550,000 | $60,000,000 | 560,000 | $62,000,000 | 600,000 |
| Region 3 | $45,000,000 | 450,000 | $50,000,000 | 460,000 | $56,000,000 | 520,000 |
| Region 4 | $60,000,000 | 600,000 | $65,000,000 | 610,000 | $73,000,000 | 720,000 |

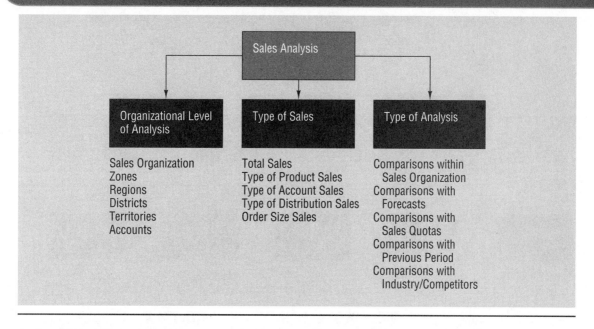

Sales Analysis Framework        **FIGURE 9.5**

A sales analysis can be performed at a number of organization levels and for many types of sales and can use several types of analysis.

Second, a useful way to identify problem areas in achieving sales effectiveness is to perform a **hierarchical sales analysis**, which consists of evaluating sales results throughout the sales organization from a top-down perspective. Essentially, the analysis begins with total sales for the sales organization and proceeds through each successively lower level in the sales organization. The emphasis is on identifying potential problem areas at each level and then using analyses at lower levels to pinpoint the specific problems. An example of a hierarchical sales analysis is presented in Figure 9.6.

In this example, sales for region 3 appear to be much lower than those for the other regions, so the analysis proceeds to investigate the sales for all the districts in region 3. Low sales are identified for district 4; then district 4 sales are analyzed by territory. The results of this analysis suggest potential sales problems within territory 5. Additional analyses would be performed to determine why sales are so low for territory 5 and to take corrective action to increase sales from this territory. The hierarchical approach to sales analysis provides an efficient way to conduct a sales analysis and to identify major areas of sales problems.

## Type of Sales

The analysis in Figure 9.6 addresses only total firm sales at each organizational level. It is usually desirable to evaluate several types of sales, such as by the following categories:

- product type or specific products
- account type or specific accounts
- type of distribution method
- order size

The hierarchical analysis in Figure 9.6 could have included sales by product type, account type, or other type of sales at each level. Or once the potential sales problem in territory 5 has been isolated, analysis of different types of sales could be performed to define the sales problem more fully. An example analysis is presented

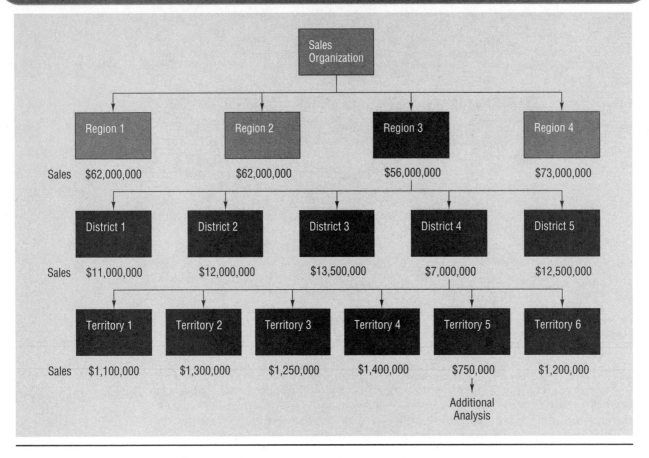

**FIGURE 9.6**                          Example of Hierarchical Sales Analysis

This multistage analysis proceeds from one sales organization level to the next by identifying the major deviations and investigating them in more detail at the next lower level. In the present example, region 3 has the lowest sales, so all districts in region 3 are examined. District 4 has poor sales results, so all the territories in district 4 are examined. Additional analysis is indicated for territory 5.

in Figure 9.7. This example suggests especially low sales volume for product type A and account type B. Additional analyses within these product and account types would be needed to determine why sales are low in these areas and what needs to be done to improve sales effectiveness.

The analysis of different types of sales at different organizational levels increases management's ability to detect and define problem areas in sales performance. However, incorporating different sales types into the analysis complicates the evaluation process and requires an information system capable of providing sales data concerning the desired breakdowns.

## Type of Analysis

The discussion to this point has focused on the actual sales results for different organizational levels and types of sales. However, the use of actual sales results limits the analysis to comparisons across organizational levels or sales types. These within-organization comparisons provide some useful information but are insufficient for a comprehensive evaluation of sales effectiveness. Several additional types of analysis are recommended and presented in Exhibit 9.5.

Comparing actual sales results with sales forecasts and quotas is extremely revealing. A *sales forecast* represents an expected level of firm sales for defined products, markets, and

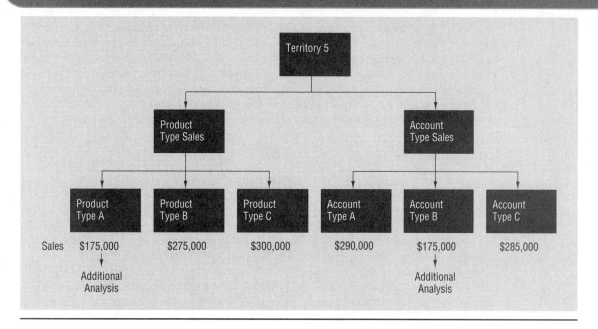

**Example of Type-of-Sales Analysis**                                                   **FIGURE 9.7**

This is a continuation of the hierarchical sales analysis presented in Figure 9.6. Sales in territory 5 are analyzed by product type and account type. The analysis suggests poor sales results for product type A and account type B.

time periods and for a specified strategy. Based on this definition, a sales forecast provides a basis for establishing specific *sales quotas* and reasonable sales objectives for a territory, district, region, or zone (methods for establishing sales quotas are discussed in Module 10). An **effectiveness index** can be computed by dividing actual sales results by the sales quota and multiplying by 100. As illustrated in Exhibit 9.5, sales results in excess of quota will have index values greater than 100, and results lower than quota will have index values less than 100. The sales effectiveness index makes it easy to compare directly the sales effectiveness of different organizational levels and different types of sales.

Another type of useful analysis is the comparison of actual results to previous periods. As illustrated in Exhibit 9.5, this type of analysis can be used to determine sales growth rates for different organizational levels and for different sales types. Incorporating sales data for many periods makes it possible to assess long-term sales trends.

A final type of analysis to be considered is a comparison of actual sales results to those achieved by competitors. This type of analysis can again be performed at different organizational levels and for different types of sales. If the comparison is extended to

**Types of Analysis Examples    EXHIBIT 9.5**

|  | District 1 | District 2 | District 3 | District 4 | District 5 |
|---|---|---|---|---|---|
| Sales | $11,000,000 | $12,000,000 | $13,000,000 | $7,000,000 | $12,000,000 |
| Sales quota | $11,250,000 | $11,500,000 | $12,750,000 | $10,000,000 | $11,000,000 |
| Effectiveness index | 98 | 104 | 102 | 70 | 109 |
| Sales last year | $10,700,000 | $11,000,000 | $12,250,000 | $6,800,000 | $10,350,000 |
| Sales growth | 3% | 9% | 6% | 3% | 16% |
| Industry sales | $42,000,000 | $42,000,000 | $45,000,000 | $40,000,000 | $45,000,000 |
| Market share | 26% | 29% | 29% | 18% | 27% |

overall industry sales, various types of market share can be calculated. Examples of these comparisons are presented in Exhibit 9.5.

Sales analysis is the approach used most often for evaluating sales organization effectiveness. Sales data are typically more readily available than other data types, and sales results are extremely important to sales organizations. However, developing a sales analysis approach that will produce the desired evaluative information is a complex undertaking. Sales data must be available for different organizational levels and for different types of sales. Valid sales forecasts are needed to establish sales quotas for evaluating sales effectiveness in achieving sales objectives. In addition, industry and competitor sales information is also useful. Regardless of the comprehensiveness of the sales analysis, sales organizations need to perform additional analyses to evaluate sales organization effectiveness adequately.

## Cost Analysis

A second major element in the evaluation of sales organization effectiveness is **cost analysis**. The emphasis here is on assessing the costs incurred by the sales organization to generate the achieved levels of sales. The general approach is to compare the costs incurred with planned costs as defined by selling budgets.

Corporate resources earmarked for personal selling expenses for a designated period represent the total **selling budget**. The key sales management budgeting task is to determine the best way to allocate these sales resources throughout the sales organization and across the different selling activities. The budgeting process is intended to instill cost consciousness and profit awareness throughout the organization, and it is necessary for establishing benchmarks for evaluating selling costs.

Selling budgets are developed at all levels of the sales organization and for all key expenditure categories. Our discussion focuses on the major selling expense categories and methods for establishing specific expenditure levels within the budget.

Firms differ considerably in how they define their selling expense categories. Nevertheless, all sales organizations should plan expenditures carefully for the major selling and sales management activities and for the different levels in the sales organization structure. The selling budget addresses controllable expenses, not uncontrollable ones. Typical selling budget expense categories are presented in Exhibit 9.6.

**EXHIBIT 9.6** Selling Expense Categories in Budget

| Classification | Actual 2004 | Original 2005 Budget | April Revision | July Revision | October Revision |
|---|---|---|---|---|---|
| Compensation expenses | | | | | |
|   Salaries | | | | | |
|   Commissions | | | | | |
|   Bonuses | | | | | |
|     Total | | | | | |
| Travel expenses | | | | | |
|   Lodging | | | | | |
|   Food | | | | | |
|   Transportation | | | | | |
|   Miscellaneous | | | | | |
|     Total | | | | | |
| Administrative expenses | | | | | |
|   Recruiting | | | | | |
|   Training | | | | | |
|   Meetings | | | | | |
|   Sales offices | | | | | |
|     Total | | | | | |

Both the total expenditures for each of these categories and sales management budget responsibility must be determined. Sales management budget responsibility depends on the degree of centralization or decentralization in the sales organization. In general, more centralized sales organizations will place budget responsibility at higher sales management levels. For example, if salesforce recruitment and selection take place at the regional level, then the regional sales managers will have responsibility for this budget category. Typically, the sales management activity occurs at all management levels. For example, training activities might be performed at national, zone, regional, and district levels. In this case, the budgeting process must address how much to spend on overall training and how to allocate training expenditures to the organizational levels.

The basic objective in budgeting for each category is to determine the lowest expenditure level necessary to *achieve the sales quotas*. Notice that we did not say the lowest possible expenditure level. Sales managers might cut costs and improve profitability in the short run, but if expenditures for training, travel, and so forth are too low, long-run sales and profits will be sacrificed. However, if expenses can be reduced by more effective or more efficient spending, these productivity improvements can produce increased profitability in the long run. Achieving productivity improvements has been one of the most demanding tasks facing sales managers in recent years because increases in field selling costs and extremely competitive markets have put tremendous pressure on firm profitability.

Determining expenditure levels for each selling expense category is extremely difficult. Although there is no perfect way to arrive at these expenditure levels, two approaches warrant attention: the percentage of sales method and the objective and task method.[20]

Probably the most often used, the **percentage of sales method** calculates an expenditure level for each category by multiplying an expenditure percentage times forecasted sales. The effectiveness of the percentage of sales method depends on the accuracy of sales forecasts and the appropriateness of the expenditure percentages. If the sales forecasts are not accurate, the selling budgets will be incorrect, regardless of the expenditure percentages used. If sales forecasts are accurate, the key is determining the expenditure percentages. This percentage may be derived from historical spending patterns or industry averages. Sales management should adjust the percentage up or down to reflect the unique aspects of their sales organization.

The **objective and task method** takes an entirely different approach. In its most basic form, it is a type of zero-based budgeting. In essence, each sales manager prepares a separate budget request that stipulates the objectives to be achieved, the tasks required to achieve these objectives, and the costs associated with performing the necessary tasks. These requests are reviewed, and through an iterative process, selling budgets are approved. Many variations of the objective and task method are used by different sales organizations.

In reality, the process of establishing a selling budget is an involved one that typically incorporates various types of analysis, many meetings, and much political maneuvering. However, the process has been streamlined in many firms through the use of computer modeling to rapidly evaluate alternative selling budgets.

After a budget has been determined, cost analysis can be performed. Examples of two types of cost analysis are presented in Exhibit 9.7. The first analysis calculates the variance between actual costs and budgeted costs for the regions in a sales organization. Regions with the largest variation, especially when actual costs far exceed budgeted costs, should be highlighted for further analysis. Large variations are not necessarily bad, but the reasons for the variations should be determined. For example, the ultimate purpose of selling costs is to generate sales. Therefore, the objective is not necessarily to minimize selling costs but to ensure that a specified relationship between sales and selling costs is maintained. Evaluate one sales manager's method for determining budgeted costs in "An Ethical Dilemma."

One way to evaluate this relationship is to calculate the selling costs as a percentage of sales achieved. Translating actual selling costs into percentages of sales achieved provides a means for assessing whether the cost–sales relationship has been maintained, even though the actual costs may exceed the absolute level in the selling budget. This situation is illustrated by region 4 in Exhibit 9.7.

**EXHIBIT 9.7** Cost Analysis Examples

| | Compensation Costs | | | Training Costs | | |
|---|---|---|---|---|---|---|
| | **Actual Cost** | **Budgeted Cost** | **Variance** | **Actual Cost** | **Budgeted Cost** | **Variance** |
| Region 1 | $3,660,000 | $3,600,000 | +$ 60,000 | $ 985,000 | $1,030,000 | –$ 45,000 |
| Region 2 | $3,500,000 | $3,700,000 | –$200,000 | $2,110,000 | $2,040,000 | +$ 70,000 |
| Region 3 | $3,150,000 | $3,400,000 | –$250,000 | $ 830,000 | $1,060,000 | –$230,000 |
| Region 4 | $4,200,000 | $3,900,000 | +$300,000 | $2,340,000 | $2,160,000 | +$180,000 |

| | Compensation Costs | | Training Costs | |
|---|---|---|---|---|
| | **Actual % Sales** | **Budgeted % Sales** | **Actual % Sales** | **Budgeted % Sales** |
| Region 1 | 6.1 | 6 | 2.9 | 3 |
| Region 2 | 5.8 | 6 | 3.1 | 3 |
| Region 3 | 5.4 | 6 | 2.6 | 3 |
| Region 4 | 6.0 | 6 | 3.1 | 3 |

AN ETHICAL DILEMMA

At the Alpha company, a contest is held each year among sales regions. Salespeople in the region deemed to be the most effective, based in large part on a cost analysis, receive a weekend trip to an exotic island. As manager of the southeastern region, Kathy has finished as runner-up in the contest the past three years. She thinks her salespeople are long overdue. This year Kathy is considering setting budgeted costs higher than she actually anticipates so that her year-end costs will look significantly lower than budgeted. What do you think Kathy should do? Why?

Sales and cost analyses are the two most direct approaches for evaluating sales organization effectiveness. Profitability and productivity analyses extend the evaluation by assessing relationships between sales and costs. These analyses can be quite complex but may provide very useful information.

## Profitability Analysis

Sales and cost data can be combined in various ways to produce evaluations of sales organization profitability for different organizational levels of different types of sales. This section covers three types of **profitability analysis**: income statement analysis, activity-based costing, and return on assets managed analysis.

### Income Statement Analysis

The different levels in a sales organization and different types of sales can be considered as separate businesses.[21] Consequently, income statements can be developed for profitability analysis. One of the major difficulties in **income statement analysis** is that some costs are shared between organizational levels or sales types.

Two approaches for dealing with the shared costs are illustrated in Exhibit 9.8. The **full cost approach** attempts to allocate the shared costs to individual units based on

| | Full Cost versus Contribution Approaches | **EXHIBIT 9.8** |
|---|---|---|

| **Full Cost Approach** | **Contribution Approach** |
|---|---|
| Sales | Sales |
| Minus: Cost of goods sold | Minus: Cost of goods sold |
| Gross margin | Gross margin |
| Minus: Direct selling expenses | Minus: Direct selling expenses |
| Minus: Allocated portion of shared expenses | Profit contribution |
| Net profit | |

some type of cost allocation procedure. This results in a net profit figure for each unit. The **contribution approach** is different in that only direct costs are included in the profitability analysis; the indirect or shared costs are not included. The net contribution calculated from this approach represents the *profit contribution* of the unit being analyzed. This profit contribution must be sufficient to cover indirect costs and other overhead and to provide the net profit for the firm.

An example that incorporates both approaches is presented in Exhibit 9.9. This example uses the direct approach for assessing sales region profitability and the contribution approach for evaluating the districts within this region. Notice that the profitability calculations for each district include only district sales, cost of goods sold, and district direct selling expenses. A *profit contribution* is generated for each district. The profitability calculations for the region include district selling expenses, region direct selling expenses that have not been allocated to the districts, and an allocated portion of shared zone costs. This produces a net profit figure for a profitability evaluation of the region.

Although either approach might be used, there seems to be a trend toward the contribution approach, probably because of the difficulty in arriving at a satisfactory procedure for allocating the shared costs. Different cost allocation methods produce different results. Thus, many firms feel more comfortable with the contribution approach because it eliminates the need for cost allocation judgments and is viewed as more objective. For a look at how Hormel Foods focuses on selling costs to achieve profitable sales, see "Sales Management in the 21st Century: Focus on Profits at Hormel."

| | Profitability Analysis Example | | **EXHIBIT 9.9** |
|---|---|---|---|

| | **Full Cost Approach** | **Contribution Approach** | | |
|---|---|---|---|---|
| | **Region** | **District 1** | **District 2** | **District 3** |
| Sales | $300,000,000 | $180,000,000 | $70,000,000 | $50,000,000 |
| Cost of goods sold | 255,000,000 | 168,500,000 | 58,500,000 | 28,000,000 |
| Gross margin | 45,000,000 | 11,500,000 | 11,500,000 | 22,000,000 |
| District selling expenses | 11,000,000 | 5,000,000 | 3,500,000 | 2,500,000 |
| Region direct selling expenses | 10,000,000 | — | — | — |
| Profit contribution | 24,000,000 | 6,500,000 | 8,000,000 | 19,500,000 |
| Allocated portion of shared zone costs | 16,000,000 | | | |
| Net profit | 8,000,000 | | | |

**Focus on Profits at Hormel**

Andre Wickham, corporate regional sales manager, Southeastern United States for Hormel Foods Corporation, comments on his company's focus on profitable selling:

*In today's sales environment, simply making the sale is not enough. We are fully invested in making profitable sales that mutually benefit our company and our customers. Our sales organization's ability to achieve desired profit targets is often manifested in two ways: by controlling our selling costs and by improving our product mix. Our sales organiza-*

*tion is accountable for managing controllable expenses such as travel, entertainment, and product samples. This may appear to be a small matter, but we find that our people make better sales (business) decisions when this type of accountability is placed at their level. Further, we believe that by selling our customers a balanced mix of products, our sales organization will benefit with stronger sales volume sold as well as higher profit contributions. When these tasks are effectively accomplished the objectives of the customer and our company are met in a very efficient manner.*

## Activity-Based Costing

Perhaps a more accountable method for allocating costs is **activity-based costing** (ABC). ABC allocates costs to individual units on the basis of how the units actually expend or cause these costs. Costs are accumulated and then allocated to the units by the appropriate drivers, factors that drive costs up or down.[22]

Exhibit 9.10 illustrates how the profitability picture changed for a building supplies company that switched to ABC to assess distribution channel profitability.[23] Notice that with ABC, selling expenses are no longer allocated to each channel based on a percentage of that channel's sales revenues. Instead, costs associated with each activity used to generate sales for a specific channel are allocated to that channel. With ABC, a clearer picture of operating profits per channel emerges. In particular, the original equipment manufacturer channel appears to be much more profitable than the firm's prior accounting system indicates.

ABC places greater emphasis on more accurately defining unit profitability by tracing activities and their associated costs directly to a specific unit. For example, using ABC analysis, the Doig Corporation was able to lower costs by identifying which tasks added value and which ones did not. For instance, it identified which customers could be served just as well by phone, saving both reps and the company time and money.[24] As such, ABC helps foster an understanding of resource expenditures, how customer value is created, and where money is being made or lost.[25]

## Return on Assets Managed Analysis

The income statement approach to profitability assessment produces net profit or profit contribution in dollars or expressed as a percentage of sales. Although necessary and valuable, the income statement approach is incomplete because it does not incorporate any evaluation of the investment in assets required to generate the net profit or profit contribution.

The calculation of **return on assets managed (ROAM)** can extend the income statement analysis to include asset investment considerations. The formula for calculating ROAM is

$$\text{ROAM} = \text{Profit contribution as percentage of sales} \times \text{Asset turnover rate}$$

$$= (\text{Profit contribution/Sales}) \times (\text{Sales/Assets managed})$$

| Activity-Based Costing Example | | | | EXHIBIT 9.10 |

**Profits by Commercial Distribution Channel (Old System)**

| | Contract | Industrial Suppliers | Government | OEM | Total Commercial |
|---|---|---|---|---|---|
| Annual sales (in thousands of dollars) | $79,434 | $25,110 | $422 | $9,200 | $114,166 |
| Gross margin | 34% | 41% | 23% | 27% | 35% |
| Gross profit | $27,375 | $10,284 | $136 | $2,461 | $ 40,256 |
| SG&A allowance[a] (in thousands of dollars) | $19,746 | $ 6,242 | $105 | $2,287 | $ 31,814 |
| Operating profit (in thousands of dollars) | $ 7,629 | $ 4,042 | $ 31 | $ 174 | $ 11,876 |
| Operating margin | 10% | 16% | 7% | 2% | 10% |
| Invested capital allowance[b] (in thousands of dollars) | $33,609 | $10,624 | $179 | $3,893 | $ 48,305 |
| Return on investment | 23% | 38% | 17% | 4% | 25% |

[a]SG&A allowance for each channel is 25 percent of that channel's revenues.
[b]Invested capital allowance for each channel is 42 percent of that channel's revenues.

**Profits by Commercial Distribution Channel (New System: ABC)**

| | Contract | Industrial Suppliers | Government | OEM | Total Commercial |
|---|---|---|---|---|---|
| Gross profit (from previous table) | $27,375 | $10,284 | $136 | $2,461 | $ 40,256 |
| Selling expenses[c] (all in thousands of dollars) | | | | | |
| Commission | $ 4,682 | $ 1,344 | $ 12 | $ 372 | $ 6,410 |
| Advertising | 132 | 38 | 0 | 2 | 172 |
| Catalog | 504 | 160 | 0 | 0 | 664 |
| Co-op advertising | 416 | 120 | 0 | 0 | 536 |
| Sales promotion | 394 | 114 | 0 | 2 | 510 |
| Warranty | 64 | 22 | 0 | 4 | 90 |
| Sales administration | 5,696 | 1,714 | 20 | 351 | 7,781 |
| Cash discount | 892 | 252 | 12 | 114 | 1,270 |
| Total | $12,780 | $ 3,764 | $ 44 | $ 845 | $ 17,433 |
| G&A (in thousands of dollars) | $ 6,740 | $ 2,131 | $ 36 | $ 781 | $ 9,688 |
| Operating profit (in thousands of dollars) | $ 7,855 | $ 4,389 | $ 56 | $ 835 | $ 13,135 |
| Operating margin | 10% | 17% | 13% | 9% | 12% |
| Invested capital[c] | $33,154 | $10,974 | $184 | $2,748 | $ 47,060 |
| Return on investment | 24% | 40% | 30% | 30% | 28% |

[c]Selling expenses and invested capital estimated under an activity-based system.

Profit contribution can be either a net profit figure from a direct approach or profit contribution from a contribution approach. Assets managed typically include inventory, accounts receivable, or other assets at each sales organizational level.

An example of ROAM calculations is presented in Exhibit 9.11. The example illustrates ROAM calculations for sales districts within a region. Notice that district 1 and district 2 produce the same ROAM but achieve their results in different ways. District 1 generates a relatively high profit contribution percentage, whereas district 2 operates with a relatively high asset turnover. Both district 3 and district 4 are

**EXHIBIT 9.11**    Return on Assets Managed (ROAM) Example

|  | District 1 | District 2 | District 3 | District 4 |
|---|---|---|---|---|
| Sales | $24,000,000 | $24,000,000 | $24,000,000 | $24,000,000 |
| Cost of goods sold | 12,000,000 | 12,000,000 | 14,000,000 | 14,000,000 |
| Gross margin | 12,000,000 | 12,000,000 | 10,000,000 | 10,000,000 |
| Direct selling expenses | 7,200,000 | 9,600,000 | 5,200,000 | 8,800,000 |
| Profit contribution | 4,800,000 | 2,400,000 | 4,800,000 | 1,200,000 |
| Accounts receivable | 8,000,000 | 4,000,000 | 16,000,000 | 4,000,000 |
| Inventory | 8,000,000 | 4,000,000 | 16,000,000 | 4,000,000 |
| Total assets managed | 16,000,000 | 8,000,000 | 32,000,000 | 8,000,000 |
| Profit contribution percentage | 20% | 10% | 20% | 5% |
| Asset turnover | 1.5 | 3.0 | .75 | 3.0 |
| ROAM | 30% | 30% | 15% | 15% |

achieving poor levels of ROAM but for different reasons. District 3 has an acceptable profit contribution percentage but very low asset turnover ratio. This low asset turnover ratio is the result of both inventory accumulations or problems in payments from accounts. District 4, however, has an acceptable asset turnover ratio but low profit contribution percentage. This low profit contribution percentage may be the result of selling low margin products, negotiating low selling prices, or accruing excessive selling expenses.

As illustrated in the preceding example, ROAM calculations provide an assessment of profitability and useful diagnostic information. ROAM is determined by both profit contribution percentage and asset turnover. If ROAM is low in any area, the profit contribution percentage and asset turnover ratio can be examined to determine the reason. Corrective action (e.g., reduced selling expenses, stricter credit guidelines, lower inventory levels) can then be taken to improve future ROAM performance.

## Productivity Analysis

Although ROAM incorporates elements of productivity by comparing profits and asset investments, additional **productivity analysis** is desirable for thorough evaluation of sales organization effectiveness. Productivity is typically measured in terms of ratios between outputs and inputs. For example, as discussed in Module 4, one often-used measure of salesforce productivity is sales per salesperson. A major advantage of productivity ratios is that they can be compared directly across the entire sales organization and with other sales organizations. This direct comparison is possible because all the ratios are expressed in terms of the same units.

Because the basic job of sales managers is to manage salespeople, the most useful input unit for productivity analysis is the salesperson. Therefore, various types of productivity ratios are calculated on a per-salesperson basis. The specific ratios depend on the characteristics of a particular selling situation but often include important outputs such as sales, expenses, calls, demonstrations, and proposals. An example of a productivity analysis is presented in Exhibit 9.12.

Exhibit 9.12 illustrates how productivity analysis provides a different and useful perspective for evaluating sales organization effectiveness. As the exhibit reveals, absolute values can be misleading. For example, the highest sales districts are not necessarily the most effective. Although profitability analyses would likely detect this also, productivity analysis presents a vivid and precise evaluation by highlighting specific areas of both high and low productivity. Take the information concerning district 2. Although sales per salesperson is reasonable and expenses per salesperson is relatively low, both calls

| | District 1 | District 2 | District 3 | District 4 |
|---|---|---|---|---|
| | | | | Productivity Analysis Example **EXHIBIT 9.12** |
| Sales | $20,000,000 | $24,000,000 | $20,000,000 | $24,000,000 |
| Selling expenses | $ 2,000,000 | $ 2,400,000 | $ 3,000,000 | $ 3,000,000 |
| Sales calls | 9,000 | 7,500 | 8,500 | 10,000 |
| Proposals | 220 | 180 | 260 | 270 |
| Number of salespeople | 20 | 30 | 20 | 30 |
| Sales/salesperson | $ 1,000,000 | $ 800,000 | $ 1,000,000 | $ 800,000 |
| Expenses/salesperson | $ 100,000 | $ 80,000 | $ 150,000 | $ 100,000 |
| Calls/salesperson | 450 | 250 | 425 | 333 |
| Proposals/salesperson | 11 | 6 | 13 | 9 |

per salesperson and proposals per salesperson are much lower than those for the other districts. This may explain why selling expenses are low, but it also suggests that the salespeople in this district may not be covering the district adequately. The high sales may be due to a few large sales to large customers.

In any case, the productivity analysis provides useful evaluative and diagnostic information that is not directly available from the other types of analyses discussed in this module. Sales productivity and profitability are highly interrelated. However, profitability analysis has a financial perspective, whereas productivity analysis is more managerially oriented. Improvements in sales productivity should translate into increases in profitability.

Productivity improvements are obtained in one of two basic ways:

**1.** increasing output with the same level of input
**2.** maintaining the same level of output but using less input

Productivity analysis can help determine which of these basic approaches should be pursued.

## ETHICAL ISSUES

The value of comparing actual expenses with budgeted expenses depends on the accuracy of the expense information provided by salespeople. Although most sales organizations have prepared forms with the expense categories and instructions for salespeople, salespeople often face ethical problems in reporting their expenses. Consider the following situations:

• A salesperson has been on the road for a week and incurs laundry expenses. He knows that if he places the laundry expenses under the miscellaneous expense category in his expense report, he will have to provide receipts. He decides that he can include them under the meals category because receipts are not required for this category as long as he stays under his per-diem allowance.

• A salesperson is trying to get a customer to purchase a new product. He decides to take three individuals from the customer's firm to dinner and a basketball game, even though he knows that he has exceeded his entertainment budget for the month. He thinks about hiding these entertainment expenses in different categories in his expense report.

The decisions that salespeople make in these and similar situations affect the ability of sales managers to evaluate actual and budgeted expenses in an accurate manner. Sales managers themselves, however, may have opportunities to act unethically when evaluating salesforce effectiveness as illustrated in "An Ethical Dilemma."

## CONCLUDING COMMENTS

As is obvious from the discussion in this module, there is no easy way to evaluate the effectiveness of a sales organization. Our recommendation is to perform separate analyses of sales, costs, profitability, and productivity to assess different aspects of sales organization effectiveness. In addition, salesperson performance, which is discussed in the next module, must also be evaluated and considered. Each type of analysis offers a piece of the puzzle. Sales managers must put these pieces together for comprehensive evaluations. The objective underlying each of the analyses is to be able to evaluate effectiveness, identify problem areas, and use this information to improve future sales organization effectiveness.

## SUMMARY

1. **Differentiate between sales organization effectiveness and salesperson performance.** Sales organization effectiveness is a summary evaluation of the overall success of a sales organization in meeting its goals and objectives in total and at different organizational levels. By contrast, salesperson performance is a function of individual salesperson performance in individual situations.

2. **Define a sales organization audit and discuss how it should be conducted.** The most comprehensive type of evaluation is a sales organization audit, which is a systematic assessment of all aspects of a sales organization. The major areas included in the audit are sales organization environment, sales management evaluation, sales organization planning system, and sales management functions. The audit should be conducted regularly by individuals outside the sales organization. It is intended to identify existing or potential problems early so that corrective action can be taken before the problems become serious.

3. **Define benchmarking and discuss how it should be conducted.** Benchmarking is an ongoing measurement and analysis process that compares an organization's current operating practices with the "best practices" used by world-class organizations. It involves identifying the sales organization processes to be benchmarked and whom to benchmark, collecting data on the benchmarked firm, analyzing performance gaps and communicating them to the salesforce, and establishing goals and implementing plans. Its purpose is to improve processes to improve performance.

4. **Describe how to perform different types of sales analysis for different organizational levels and types of sales.** Sales analysis is the most common evaluation approach, but it can be extremely complex. Specific definitions of a sale are required, and both sales dollars and units typically should be considered. A hierarchical approach is suggested as a top-down procedure to address sales results at each level of the sales organization with an emphasis on identifying problem areas. Sales analysis is more useful when sales results are compared with forecasts, quotas, previous time periods, and competitor results.

5. **Describe how to perform a cost analysis for a sales organization.** Cost analysis focuses on the costs incurred to generate sales results. Specific costs can be compared with the planned levels in the selling budget. Areas with large variances require specific attention. Costs can also be evaluated as percentages of sales and compared to comparable industry figures.

6. **Describe how to perform an income statement analysis, activity-based costing, and return on assets managed to assess sales organization profitability.** Profitability analysis combines sales and cost data in various ways. The income statement approach focuses on net profit or profit contributions from the different sales organization levels. Activity-based costing allocates costs to individual units on the basis of how the units actually expend or cause these costs. The return on assets managed approach assesses relationships between profit contributions and the assets used to generate these profit contributions. Residual income analysis combines the return on assets managed concept with sales growth objectives to produce a very useful evaluative tool. The different profitability analyses address different aspects of profitability that are of interest to sales managers.

7. **Describe how to perform a productivity analysis for a sales organization**. Productivity analysis focuses on relationships between outputs and inputs. The most useful input is the number of salespeople, whereas relevant outputs might be sales, expenses, proposals, and so on. The productivity ratios calculated in this manner are versatile because they can be used for comparisons within the sales organization and across other sales organizations. Productivity analysis not only provides useful evaluative information but also provides managerially useful diagnostic information that can suggest ways to improve productivity and increase profitability.

## UNDERSTANDING SALES MANAGEMENT TERMS

| | |
|---|---|
| sales organization audit | objective and task method |
| benchmarking | profitability analysis |
| sales analysis | income statement analysis |
| hierarchical sales analysis | full cost approach |
| effectiveness index | contribution approach |
| cost analysis | activity-based costing (ABC) |
| selling budget | return on assets managed (ROAM) |
| percentage of sales method | productivity analysis |

## DEVELOPING SALES MANAGEMENT KNOWLEDGE

1. Discuss why it is important to differentiate between sales organization effectiveness and salesperson performance.

2. Discuss what is involved in conducting a sales management audit.

3. What is the purpose of benchmarking? Discuss what is involved in benchmarking.

4. Refer to "Sales Management in the 21st Century: Using Benchmarking to Succeed." How can benchmarking be used to improve performance?

5. What is meant by a hierarchical sales analysis? Can a hierarchical approach be used in analyzing costs, profitability, and/or productivity?

6. What is the difference between the full cost and contribution approaches to income statement analysis for a sales organization? Which would you recommend for a sales organization? Why?

7. Refer to "Sales Management in the 21st Century: Focus on Profits at Hormel." How can a company achieve more profitable sales?

8. What are the two basic components of return on assets managed? How is each component calculated, and what does each component tell a sales manager?

9. Identify five different sales organization productivity ratios that you would recommend. Describe how each would be calculated and what information each would provide.

10. Discuss how you think new computer and information technologies will affect the evaluations of sales organization effectiveness in the future.

# BUILDING SALES MANAGEMENT SKILLS

1. Using the following information, conduct a sales analysis to evaluate sales organization effectiveness. Explain your findings.

| | Region 1 ($000) | Region 2 ($000) | Region 3 ($000) | Region 4 ($000) |
|---|---|---|---|---|
| Sales | $ 4,050 | $ 4,750 | $ 4,250 | $ 2,500 |
| Sales quota | $ 4,125 | $ 4,250 | $ 4,075 | $ 3,900 |
| Sales last year | $ 3,925 | $ 4,375 | $ 4,000 | $ 2,425 |
| Industry sales | $11,500 | $12,500 | $13,500 | $10,500 |

2. Sales and cost data can be combined in various ways to produce evaluations of sales organization profitability for different organizational levels or different types of sales. Three types of profitability analysis are useful for evaluating effectiveness: activity-based costing, income statement analysis, and return on assets managed analysis. Examining Exhibit 9.10, point out differences in operating profits by commercial distribution channel between the company's old and new (ABC) system, and explain why they differ. What would the ABC system lead you to believe regarding the effectiveness of each channel? Using the information in Exhibit 9.10 and the following information, conduct an income statement analysis and return on assets managed analysis. Explain the results of your analyses.

| | Contract ($000) | Industrial Suppliers ($000) | Government ($000) | OEM ($000) |
|---|---|---|---|---|
| Accounts receivable | $26,578 | $16,840 | $72 | $1,633 |
| Inventory | $26,578 | $16,840 | $73 | $1,634 |

3. Several sites are available on the World Wide Web that provide benchmarking services. One such site is Best Practices, LLC (http://www.best-in-class.com), a research and consulting firm that provides business insight and analysis of how world-class companies achieve exceptional economic and operational performance. Access this site and review its services.

   3a. How can a company such as this be useful to a sales manager attempting to improve the sales organization?

   3b. From the Best Practices home page, click on "Best Practice Database." Next, go to "subject areas," click on "sales and marketing," and finally click on "sales management." You will find several reports (click on a report for an overview). Identify two reports that might be helpful for improving a sales organization's effectiveness and briefly explain how each report's information might be used.

3c. Locate another benchmarking service on the World Wide Web. Identify its address and briefly describe its services. Compare and contrast its services to those of Best Practices, LLC.

4. **Situation:**  Read the Ethical Dilemma on page 258.

   **Characters:**  Kathy, southeastern region manager; Brenda, one of Kathy's top salespeople

   **Scene:**  *Location*—local restaurant for lunch. *Action*—Kathy tells Brenda abouther plan to set higher than usual budgeted selling costs. Brenda is skeptical. The two discuss the pros and cons of doing so and consider other alternatives Kathy might take.

**ROLE PLAY**

5. Using the following information, conduct a productivity analysis.

|  | District 1 | District 2 | District 3 | District 4 |
|---|---|---|---|---|
| Sales | $30,000,000 | $36,000,000 | $30,000,000 | $36,000,000 |
| Selling expenses | $ 3,000,000 | $ 3,600,000 | $ 4,500,000 | $ 4,500,000 |
| Sales calls | 13,500 | 11,250 | 12,750 | 15,000 |
| Proposals | 330 | 270 | 390 | 405 |
| Number of salespeople | 30 | 45 | 30 | 45 |

# MAKING SALES MANAGEMENT DECISIONS

## Case 9.1: Beauty Glow Cosmetics Company

### Background

Beauty Glow Cosmetics Company manufactures and markets a line of cosmetics products to retailers throughout the United States. The salesforce is organized into five regions, each comprised of five districts. A national sales manager oversees the five regional sales managers. Each regional manager is responsible for the effectiveness of his or her region and is compensated accordingly.

### Current Situation

Kate Flower is the regional sales manager for the northern region. The fiscal year just ended, and Kate has compiled data to help her analyze her regions's effectiveness. Although her region has had what she believes to be a very successful year, she wants to analyze each district closely. She hopes to use her analysis to identify and correct problems. Moreover, she needs to complete her analysis for her upcoming meeting with her national sales manager, Calvin Cline.

Market shares for each district were fairly sizable (30 percent, 32 percent, 34 percent, 31 percent, and 28 percent for districts 1 through 5, respectively) at the beginning of the fiscal year. Kate had expected these to remain relatively stable over the past year. The company had anticipated a sales growth of 2 percent. In addition, selling costs were budgeted at 10 percent of sales. If Kate's region did not increase sales by 2 percent and stay within the sales budget, her performance appraisal, and subsequently her compensation, would suffer.

Kate knew her boss would carefully scrutinize her analysis. She hoped to be able to identify any problem areas so that she could develop solutions and implement them in the upcoming year. She was scheduled to meet with Cline in 3 days.

Kate compiled the following information. (Shown at the bottom of the page.)

### Questions

1. What analyses should Kate perform with this data? Perform these analyses.
2. What problems can you identify from your analyses?
3. What solutions do you recommend to solve these problems and improve results in the future?

**ROLE PLAY**

| Situation: | Read Case 9.1. |
|---|---|
| Characters: | Calvin Cline, national sales manager; Kate Flower, regional sales manager |
| Scene: | *Location*—meeting room at Beauty Glow Cosmetics headquarters. *Action*—Kate presents her findings from analyzing the effectiveness of her salesforce. She makes suggestions for solving the problems she has identified. Calvin responds to her analysis. He then asks Kate about the performance of her salespeople and who, if anyone, she thinks the company should let go. |

|  | District 1 ($000) | District 2 ($000) | District 3 ($000) | District 4 ($000) | District 5 ($000) |
|---|---|---|---|---|---|
| Sales | $8,200 | $9,500 | $10,450 | $13,750 | $8,400 |
| Cost of goods sold | 4,920 | 5,510 | 6,479 | 8,250 | 4,620 |
| Compensation | 615 | 810 | 735 | 1,140 | 630 |
| Transportation | 41 | 67 | 42 | 70 | 50 |
| Lodging and meals | 17 | 30 | 16 | 41 | 21 |
| Telephone | 8 | 10 | 12 | 14 | 9 |
| Entertainment | 10 | 8 | 15 | 12 | 12 |
| Training | 80 | 95 | 105 | 125 | 110 |
| District accounts receivable | 1,170 | 1,400 | 1,450 | 2,420 | 1,150 |
| District inventory | 2,000 | 3,500 | 3,200 | 5,250 | 2,500 |
| Number of salespeople | 8 | 9 | 11 | 12 | 10 |
| Sales quota | 8,100 | 9,750 | 10,250 | 14,125 | 3,300 |
| Sales last year | 7,500 | 9,250 | 10,250 | 13,925 | 8,200 |
| Industry sales | 26,452 | 29,689 | 30,736 | 45,834 | 30,000 |

## Case 9.2: Induplicate Copiers, Inc.

### Background

Induplicate Copiers, Inc., manufactures and markets photocopiers. The company operates throughout the United States and is divided into four regions, each consisting of four districts with a district sales manager in charge of each. A regional sales manager is assigned ultimate responsibility for each region. The company manufactures its copiers in San Diego, California, and ships them directly to regional warehouses.

For the most part, salespeople at Induplicate are well qualified and experienced. All its salespeople have a college degree, and several have prior sales experience. The average salesperson tenure at Induplicate is seven years.

### Current Situation

Despite competing with major copier manufacturers such as Xerox and Minolta, Induplicate has done well. It continues to produce some of the most innovative and advanced machines on the market. However, Induplicate's president, Alicia Doubleit, believes that the company can do much better. The following is a conversation she recently had with her national sales manager, Rich Getmore:

*Alicia*: I believe that the key to our growth lies in having a successful salesforce.

*Rich*: Absolutely. We have made great strides over the past three years, consistently increasing our sales volume.

*Alicia*: Sales growth is a must. However, we need to measure up to the performance of our competition in other ways.

*Rich*: What do you mean?

*Alicia*: If we want to reach the top, we have to have a salesforce that performs like those at the top. How convenient and quick is our service? How long does it take from order to delivery and setup?

*Rich*: I suppose we could always improve our service. However, our salespeople are well qualified and do a competent job.

*Alicia*: What about our user training program? Can it be made more convenient for customers? Is it possible to accomplish it more quickly and less expensively without sacrificing the quality of the training?

*Rich*: We seem to be doing okay in this area. There haven't been a lot of complaints that I am aware of, so I assume everything is going well.

*Alicia*: If we are going to be the best, we have to have the best salesforce. Rich, I'm counting on you to lead our salesforce to the top. I can't stress how important it is for us to have a high performing salesforce. I'd like to meet with you in two weeks to discuss your plan for addressing these issues.

*Rich*: Perhaps it's time to take a closer look at our sales organization. I'll do my best.

### Questions

1. How could Rich use benchmarking to address Alicia's concerns?
2. Outline a benchmarking study that could be used to help make Induplicate's salesforce more effective.
3. What else can be done to ensure that Induplicate's salesforce is performing effectively?

**ROLE PLAY**

| | |
|---|---|
| **Situation:** | Read Case 9.2. |
| **Characters:** | Alicia Doubleit, president; Rich Getmore, national sales manager |
| **Scene 1:** | *Location*—Getmore's office. *Action*—Role play the conversation between Alicia and Rich as outlined in the case. |
| **Scene 2:** | *Location*—Alicia's office, two weeks later. *Action*—Rich is meeting with Alicia to discuss his plan for improving the sales organization. He outlines his plan and Alicia provides her thoughts regarding it. |

## EVALUATING SALESPERSON PERFORMANCE AT CITY WHOLESALE

Chip Prince, director of sales and marketing at City Wholesale, a provider of food service products based in Birmingham, Alabama, holds his salespeople accountable for their performance. He will not tolerate excuses for poor performance such as "not enough time" or "tough economy right now." However, he wants to help improve his salespeople's performance. To do so, Prince conducts frequent performance evaluations.

When Prince took over in 2000, sales reps were evaluated annually, and the company's turnover was at 50 percent. "We spent five or six months figuring out what was important to our employees," Prince says. "Almost everyone said they wanted to get quicker feedback." As a result, Prince now evaluates his reps quarterly. In doing so, he focuses on determining what needs to be done to help improve each rep's performance. A key question he asks his reps is "What do you think we're not doing?" He then tries to determine what can be done to improve performance and stipulates what he expects from his reps.

The more frequent evaluations at City Wholesale have improved communications and provided better direction. "People are telling us they now know where they're supposed to go and are more in tune with what they're supposed to be doing," says Prince. Consequently, his reps are performing better. Take for instance Catherine, one of Prince's most improved performers. When Catherine began, she was an average performer who was falling well short of her potential. Her problem stemmed from her inability to focus her sales efforts. During one of their quarterly reviews, Prince asked her, "What do you think we could do better?" Catherine told Prince that she was uncertain about what he expected from her and that it would be helpful if he more clearly defined her objectives. Subsequently, Prince clearly outlined her goals and provided her with a specific quota. Catherine increased her sales by 30 to 40 percent after three quarters. According to Prince, "Performance is not going to just happen. Our job is to give guidance."

The improved performance evaluation system at City Wholesale has reaped huge benefits. Turnover has dropped to less than 10 percent and profit margins are up by an average of 15 percent per quarter.

**Source:** Jordana Mishory, "Frequency Matters," *Sales & Marketing Management* 156 (July 2004): 36–38.

Whereas Module 9 focused on evaluating sales organization effectiveness, this module examines the task of evaluating salesperson performance and job satisfaction. Evaluations of sales organization effectiveness concentrate on the overall results achieved by the different units within the sales organization, with special attention given to determining the effectiveness of territories, districts, regions, and zones and identifying strategic changes to improve future effectiveness. These effectiveness assessments examine sales organization units and do not directly evaluate individuals; however, sales managers are responsible for the effectiveness of their assigned units.

The City Wholesale example in the opening vignette illustrates how one firm conducts performance evaluations and how such evaluations might be used. City Wholesale evaluates its salespeople's performance quarterly in an effort to determine

## Objectives

After completing this module, you should be able to

1 Discuss the different purposes of salesperson performance evaluations.

2 Differentiate between an outcome-based and a behavior-based perspective for evaluating and controlling salesperson performance.

3 Describe the different types of criteria necessary for comprehensive evaluations of salesperson performance.

4 Compare the advantages and disadvantages of different methods of salesperson performance evaluation.

5 Explain how salesperson performance information can be used to identify problems, determine their causes, and suggest sales management actions to solve them.

6 Discuss the measurement and importance of salesperson job satisfaction.

salespeople's problems, improve communication, and provide direction. To evaluate salesperson performance, sales managers must understand why and how performance evaluations are conducted, as well as how to use information gained from these evaluations.

The purpose of this module is to investigate the key issues involved in evaluating and controlling the performance and job satisfaction of salespeople. The purposes of salesperson performance evaluations are discussed initially. Then, the performance evaluation procedures currently used by sales organizations are examined. This is followed by a comprehensive assessment of salesperson performance evaluation. The assessment addresses the criteria to be used in evaluating salespeople, the methods for evaluating salespeople against these criteria, and the outcomes of salesperson performance evaluations. The module concludes by discussing the importance and measurement of salesperson job satisfaction and relationships between salesperson performance and job satisfaction.

# PURPOSES OF SALESPERSON PERFORMANCE EVALUATIONS

As the name suggests, the basic objective of salesperson performance evaluations is to determine how well individual salespeople have performed. However, the results of salesperson performance evaluations can be used for many sales management purposes:[1]

1. To ensure that compensation and other reward disbursements are consistent with actual salesperson performance.
2. To identify salespeople who might be promoted.
3. To identify salespeople whose employment should be terminated and to supply evidence to support the need for termination.
4. To determine the specific training and counseling needs of individual salespeople and the overall salesforce.
5. To provide information for effective human resource planning.
6. To identify criteria that can be used to recruit and select salespeople in the future.
7. To advise salespeople of work expectations.
8. To motivate salespeople.
9. To help salespeople set career goals.
10. To relate salesperson performance to sales organization goals.
11. To enhance communications between salesperson and sales manager.
12. To improve salesperson performance.

These diverse purposes affect all aspects of the performance evaluation process. For example, performance evaluations for determining compensation and special rewards should emphasize activities and results related to the salesperson's current job and situation. Performance evaluations for the purpose of identifying salespeople for promotion into sales management positions should focus on criteria related to potential effectiveness as a sales manager and not just current performance as a salesperson. The best salespeople do not always make the best sales managers. Thus, salesperson performance appraisals must be carefully developed and implemented to provide the types of information necessary to accomplish all the desired purposes. For an example of how Allied Office Products uses performance evaluations to determine how to improve salespeople's performance see "Sales Management in the 21st Century: Using Performance Evaluations to Improve Performance at Allied Office Products."

# SALESPERSON PERFORMANCE EVALUATION APPROACHES

Although it is impossible to determine with precision all the performance evaluation approaches used by sales organizations, several studies have produced sufficiently consistent information to warrant some general conclusions.[2]

## Using Performance Evaluations to Improve Performance at Allied Office Products

Marty Zucker, vice president and general manager of the Long Island Division at Allied Office Products, discusses how the company evaluates its salesforce in order to improve revenues and margin performance:

*Allied Office Products is the largest independent office products company in the United States, selling office supplies, furniture, promotion marketing, printing, and beverage services. At Allied Office Products, it is extremely important that we have a well-educated, highly talented, and motivated salesforce.*

*My division, Allied Long Island, is in a very competitive market place. Thus, to compete we must be at the top of our game every day. To do so, we conduct performance evaluations monthly and annually to ensure that valuable assets are being used correctly. Each month, we hold one-on-one meetings with each sales representative to* *discuss their current clients, new prospects, future projects, and strategies for developing and closing accounts. We also discuss our "jackpot" report, which lets us know how much money a client should be spending in each of our offerings. The evaluation takes approximately one hour and lets our management team determine if the sales representative is knowledgeable of our offerings, as well as his or her level of motivation. As for our annual review, we check to determine if the sales rep achieved both sales and margin plans. We examine what accounts were opened, what accounts were lost, and what accounts are good prospects. Furthermore, we scrutinize the outlook for the following year, as well as develop a new budget. By analyzing these reviews, we are able to coach our sales representatives to successful careers. Undoubtedly, conducting performance evaluations will improve your company's health in the 21st century.*

1. Most sales organizations evaluate salesperson performance annually, although many firms conduct evaluations semiannually or quarterly. Relatively few firms evaluate salesperson performance more often than quarterly.

2. Most sales organizations use combinations of input and output criteria that are evaluated by quantitative and qualitative measures. However, emphasis seems to be placed on outputs, with evaluations of sales volume results the most popular.

3. Sales organizations that set performance standards or quotas tend to enlist the aid of salespeople in establishing these objectives. The degree of salesperson input and involvement does, however, appear to vary across firms.

4. Many sales organizations assign weights to different performance objectives and incorporate territory data when establishing these objectives.

5. Most firms use more than one source of information in evaluating salesperson performance. and client and peer feedback are some of the common sources of information.

6. Most salesperson performance evaluations are conducted by the field sales manager who supervises the salesperson. However, some firms involve the manager above the field sales manager in the salesperson performance appraisal.

7. Most sales organizations provide salespeople with a written copy of their performance review and have sales managers discuss the performance evaluation with each salesperson. These discussions typically take place in an office, although sometimes they are conducted in the field.

These results offer a glimpse of current practices in evaluating salesperson performance. Although performance appraisal continues to be primarily a top-down process, changes are taking place in some companies leading to the implementation of a broader-based assessment process. An increasingly popular assessment technique, dubbed **360-degree feedback**, involves performance assessment from multiple raters, including sales managers, internal and external customers, team members, and even salespeople themselves. As part of its 360-degree review, sales managers at Knowledgepoint, a human resources software provider, solicit feedback from coworkers in areas such as rapport with clients, time management, and presentation skills when evaluating salespeople.[3]

Among its many benefits, 360-degree feedback helps managers better understand customer needs, detect barriers to success, assess developmental needs, create job involvement, reduce assessment bias, and improve performance.[4] Because this evaluation method tends to make employees feel valued, they stay with the organization longer.[5] However, when using the process, keep in mind that bias may still exist. Individuals may be less forthright in giving feedback and less accepting of feedback from others if they believe it will have damaging consequences.[6] Furthermore, top salespeople tend to underestimate their performance, while bottom performers overestimate.[7] Also, other ratings and self-ratings tend to differ significantly most of the time.[8] Thus, it may be best to use feedback in conjunction with other appraisal techniques. Exhibit 10.1 provides

**EXHIBIT 10.1    Keys to an Effective 360-Degree Feedback System**

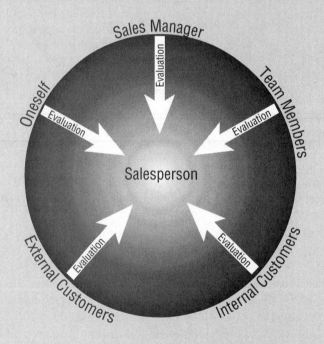

1. Ensure that participants willingly provide honest feedback by distributing the feedback instrument confidentially, aggregating responses by rating source, having rating forms sent directly to the person or group organizing the data, and including feedback from at least three respondents in each rater group (e.g., customers, coworkers, team members). Allow participants some input in selecting raters.
2. Explain to all participants how the data will be used.
3. Ensure that the data sources remain confidential so those being rated do not know specifically who did the rating.
4. Verify that the data are accurate. The assessment tools used to gather the data should be reliable and valid.
5. Ensure that subjects can use the data to improve their performance. Present the feedback from the different groups (perspectives). It should be in a format that is easy to use and interpret. Compare feedback from others with one's own perceptions. Feedback should be linked to development tools and processes.
6. Determine how the system will affect the organization overall and systematically evaluate its effectiveness.
7. Do not rely exclusively on 360-degree feedback. Timely feedback concerning day-to-day performance is important.

keys to implementing an effective 360-degree feedback system.[9] To facilitate this process, some companies use Web sites to distribute and collect multiple evaluations.[10] Companies such as Training Technologies, Inc. (http://www.surveytracker.com) and Cognology (http://www.cognology.biz) use the Internet to conduct 360-degree feedback surveys for companies.[11]

Another evaluation approach that moves away from the traditional top-down appraisal is referred to as **performance management**. This approach involves sales managers and salespeople working together on setting goals, giving feedback, reviewing, and rewarding.[12] With this system, salespeople create their own development plans and assume responsibility for their careers. The sales manager acts as a partner in the process, providing feedback that is timely, specific, regular, solicited, and focused on what is within the salesperson's control to change. Salespeople are compensated on the value of their contributions to the organization's success. To facilitate the review process, sales managers may want to use software applications, such as Performance Now Enterprise Edition, which provide a framework for implementing a comprehensive performance management system.

Performance management ultimately focuses on improving organizational performance by finding new and better ways to satisfy customers.[13] A study of 437 U.S. companies in 58 industries reported that companies following a performance management approach had greater financial and productivity performance relative to other companies in their industry.[14]

A performance management approach is consistent with the principles of **total quality management (TQM)**. TQM incorporates a strong customer orientation, a team-oriented corporate culture, and the use of statistical methods to analyze and improve all business processes including sales management.[15] TQM programs focus on efforts to continuously monitor and improve performance rather than merely evaluating performance over extended periods. This can be accomplished by mapping the processes that lead to desired results and then concentrating effort on improving these processes. As a result, reengineering may occur, resulting in a simpler process with corresponding savings in time and cost and improvements in quality.[16]

One approach for incorporating TQM into the performance evaluation process consists of four stages. In stage one, the sales manager and salesperson discuss the salesperson's evaluation, which is based on feedback from several sources, such as the manager, customers, team members, and oneself. During stage two, the sales manager rates the salesperson relative to predetermined criteria to determine whether he or she is above or below expectations. In stage three, the salesperson's performance is reviewed relative to his or her previous performance evaluation to ascertain accomplishments in performance and areas that need improvement. The final stage focuses on improving the system. During this stage, the sales manager specifies training and resources needed for improvement. The sales manager and salesperson also mutually agree on targets, degree, and type of improvement.[17]

Despite the approach taken, several key decisions concerning the appraisal process must be made. The remainder of this module addresses the key decision areas and alternative methods for developing comprehensive evaluation and control procedures.

## KEY ISSUES IN EVALUATING AND CONTROLLING SALESPERSON PERFORMANCE

A useful way to view different perspectives for evaluating and controlling salesperson performance is presented in Exhibit 10.2.[18] An **outcome-based perspective** focuses on objective measures of results with little monitoring or directing of salesperson behavior by sales managers. By contrast, a **behavior-based perspective** incorporates complex and often subjective assessments of salesperson characteristics and behaviors with considerable monitoring and directing of salesperson behavior by sales managers.[19]

The outcome-based and behavior-based perspectives illustrated in Exhibit 10.2 represent the extreme positions that a sales organization might take concerning salesperson performance evaluation. Although our earlier review of current practice indicates a tendency toward an outcome-based perspective, most sales organizations operate

---

**EXHIBIT 10.2**  Perspectives on Salesperson Performance Evaluation

| Outcome-Based Perspective | Behavior-Based Perspective |
|---|---|
| • Little monitoring of salespeople | • Considerable monitoring of salespeople |
| • Little managerial direction of salespeople | • High levels of managerial direction of salespeople |
| • Straightforward, objective measures of results | • Subjective measures of salesperson characteristics, activities, and strategies |

The perspectives that a sales organization might take toward salesperson performance evaluation and control lie on a continuum. The two extremes are the outcome-based and behavior-based perspectives.

---

somewhere between the two extreme positions. However, emphasis on either perspective can have far-reaching impacts on the salesforce and important implications for sales managers. Several of these key implications are presented in Exhibit 10.3.[20] See how placing too much focus on outcomes may lead to undesirable behavior as illustrated in "An Ethical Dilemma."

On balance, these implications provide strong support for at least some behavior-based evaluations in most selling situations, including internationally. Some research finds a positive relationship between behavior-based control and salesperson outcome performance, and sales organization effectiveness in Australia and Austria.[21] In the absence of any behavior-based measures and limited monitoring and direction from sales management, salespeople are likely to focus on the short-term outcomes that are being evaluated. The process of obtaining the desired outcomes may be neglected, causing some activities that produce short-term results (e.g., selling pressure, unethical activities) to be emphasized and activities related to long-term customer relationships (e.g., customer orientation, post-sale service) to be minimized.

A reasonable conclusion from this discussion is that sales organizations should use both outcome-based and behavior-based measures when evaluating salesperson performance. Research indicates that some firms use a hybrid approach to controlling the salesforce. The hybrid form was found to place considerable emphasis on the following: supervision;

---

**EXHIBIT 10.3**  Outcome-Based versus Behavior-Based Implications

The more behavior-based (versus outcome-based) a salesperson performance evaluation is,

- The more professionally competent, team-oriented, risk averse, planning-oriented, sales support-oriented, and customer-oriented salespeople will be.
- The more intrinsically and recognition-motivated salespeople will be.
- The more committed to the sales organization salespeople will be.
- The more likely salespeople will be to accept authority, participate in decision making, and welcome management performance reviews.
- The less the need for using pay as a control mechanism.
- The more innovative and supportive the culture is likely to be.
- The more inclined salespeople are to sell smarter rather than harder.
- The better salespeople will perform on both selling (e.g., using technical knowledge, making sales presentations) and nonselling (e.g., providing information, controlling expenses ethically) behavioral performance dimensions.
- The better salespeople will perform on outcome (e.g., achieving sales objectives) performance dimensions.
- The better the sales organization will perform on sales organization effectiveness dimensions (e.g., sales volume and growth, profitability, and customer satisfaction).
- The greater salespeople's job satisfaction will be.

AN ETHICAL DILEMMA

It is performance appraisal time again. Dollar sales volume is an important criterion on which salespeople's performance is evaluated. You just found out that your star sales performer is making statements to customers that exaggerate the seriousness of their problem to obtain a bigger order or other concessions. Your yearly bonus is based on how well your salesforce performs. What do you do? Why?

evaluation of attitude, effort, and quantitative results; and complete, accurate paperwork.[22] However, the relative emphasis on outcome-based and behavior-based measures depends on environmental, firm, and salesperson considerations. Limited research finds that behavior-based control is used when the selling environment is uncertain, the salesforce is small, outputs and the cost of measuring them are inadequate, means for measuring behaviors are available, products are less complex, the percentage of routine activities is high, and salespeople are more educated.[23] In addition, when formalization is high, outcome-based control can reduce its negative impact on role ambiguity and organizational commitment.[24] Establishing the desired emphasis should be the initial decision in developing a salesperson performance evaluation and control system. Once this emphasis has been established, the sales organization can then address the specific criteria to be evaluated, the methods of evaluation, and how the performance information will be used. Regardless of the relative emphasis, however, some research suggests that greater control leads to higher levels of salesperson job satisfaction, organizational commitment and job performance, and lower levels of role stress.[25]

## Criteria for Performance Evaluation

The typical salesperson job is multidimensional. Salespeople normally sell multiple products to diverse customers and perform a variety of selling and nonselling activities. Therefore, any comprehensive assessment of salesperson performance must include multiple criteria.

Although the specific criteria depend on the characteristics of a given selling situation and the performance evaluation perspective, the four performance dimensions illustrated in Figure 10.1 should be considered: behavioral and professional development (behavior-based perspective) and results and profitability (outcome-based perspective). Regardless of the specific evaluative criteria chosen, it is important that salespeople know and understand the criteria to achieve desired performance. Moreover, sales managers should explain the rationale underlying the use of specific criteria. They may even want to let salespeople help in determining the evaluation criteria. When salespeople believe that the criteria upon which they are being evaluated is appropriate, they are likely to be more satisfied with their job.[26]

### Behavior

The behavioral dimension consists of criteria related to activities performed by individual salespeople. The emphasis is on evaluating exactly what each salesperson does. These **behavioral criteria** should not only address activities related to short-term sales generation but should also include nonselling activities needed to ensure long-term customer satisfaction and to provide necessary information to the sales organization. Examples of typical behavioral criteria are presented in Exhibit 10.4.[27]

As might be expected, most sales organizations focus on the number of sales calls made as the key behavioral criterion. However, other activities are also important to at least some sales organizations. At Motorola, for instance, customer satisfaction is measured to determine goal achievement.[28] Part of salespeople's compensation at IBM is based on

## FIGURE 10.1    Dimensions of Salesperson Performance Evaluation

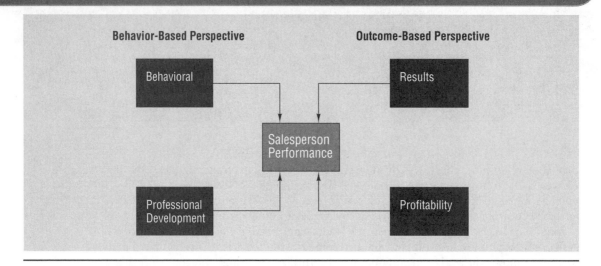

A comprehensive evaluation of salesperson performance should incorporate criteria from these dimensions. Sales organizations using a behavior-based perspective would focus on behavioral and professional development criteria, whereas those using an outcome-based perspective would emphasize results and profitability criteria.

## EXHIBIT 10.4    Behavioral Criteria

| Base | Percentage Reporting Using |
|---|---|
| **Calls** | |
| Number of customer calls | 48 |
| Number of calls per day (or period) | 42 |
| Number of planned calls | 24 |
| Number of calls per account | 23 |
| Number of calls per number of customers— by product class (call frequency ratio) | 18 |
| Average time spent per call | 8 |
| Number of unplanned calls | 7 |
| Planned to unplanned call ratio | 3 |
| | |
| **Ancillary Activities** | |
| Number of required reports turned in | 38 |
| Number of days worked (per period) | 33 |
| Selling time versus nonselling time | 27 |
| Training meetings conducted | 26 |
| Number of customer complaints | 25 |
| Number of formal presentations | 22 |
| Number of quotes | 21 |
| Percentage of goods returned | 17 |
| Number of dealer meetings held | 17 |
| Number of service calls made | 15 |
| Number of formal proposals developed | 15 |
| Advertising displays set up | 13 |
| Number of demonstrations conducted | 12 |
| Dollar amount of overdue accounts collected | 10 |
| Number of letters/phone calls to prospects | 9 |

customer satisfaction. When salespeople's rewards are based on a customer satisfaction rating, salespeople are likely to demonstrate a higher level of customer service activity.[29] This helps to explain research that finds that when buyers rate salespeople highly, they tend to give the salesperson's organization higher performance ratings.[30]

Salespeople have the most control over what they do, so evaluations of their performance should include some assessment of their behaviors. Interestingly, foreign subsidiaries of U.S.–based multinationals appear to rely more heavily than U.S. firms on behavioral criteria for evaluating salesperson performance.[31] This may be because behavior-based systems have been found to be better than compensation at promoting selling techniques among salespeople in other cultures, particularly Europe.[32] As discussed in Exhibit 10.3, the use of behavior-based criteria will also facilitate the development of a professional, customer-oriented, committed, and motivated salesforce.

## Professional Development

Another dimension of considerable importance in evaluating the performance of individual salespeople relates to professional development. **Professional development criteria** assess improvements in certain characteristics of salespeople that are related to successful performance in the sales job. For example, if product knowledge is critical in a particular selling situation, then evaluations of the product knowledge of individual salespeople over various periods should be conducted. Examples of professional development criteria are presented in Exhibit 10.5.[33]

| Professional Development Criteria | EXHIBIT 10.5 |
|---|---|
| **Base** | **Percentage Reporting Using** |
| Communication skills | 88 |
| Product knowledge | 85 |
| Attitude | 82 |
| Selling skills | 79 |
| Initiative and aggressiveness | 76 |
| Appearance and manner | 75 |
| Knowledge of competition | 71 |
| Team player | 67 |
| Enthusiasm | 66 |
| Time management | 63 |
| Judgment | 62 |
| Cooperation | 62 |
| Motivation | 61 |
| Ethical/moral behavior | 59 |
| Planning ability | 58 |
| Pricing knowledge | 55 |
| Report preparation and submission | 54 |
| Creativity | 54 |
| Punctuality | 49 |
| Resourcefulness | 49 |
| Knowledge of company policies | 48 |
| Customer goodwill generation | 41 |
| Self-improvement efforts | 40 |
| Care of company property | 39 |
| Degree of respect from trade and competition | 38 |
| Use of promotional materials | 37 |
| New product ideas | 35 |
| Use of marketing/technical backup teams | 33 |
| Good citizenship | 22 |

Many sales organizations incorporate multiple professional development criteria into their salesperson performance evaluations. This is appropriate, because salespeople have control over the development of personal characteristics related to success in their selling situation. The professional development criteria introduce a long-term perspective into the process of salesperson performance evaluation. Salespeople who are developing professionally are increasing their chances of successful performance over the long run. Although the professional development and behavioral criteria might be combined into one category, we prefer to keep them separate to reflect their different perspectives.

## Results

The results achieved by salespeople are extremely important and should be evaluated. Examples of **results criteria** used in salesperson performance evaluations are listed in Exhibit 10.6.[34]

A potential problem with the use of results criteria in Exhibit 10.6 is that the overall results measures do not reflect the territory situations faced by individual salespeople. The salesperson with the highest level of sales may have the best territory and may not necessarily be the best performer in generating sales. In fact, some research shows that rewards for achieving results have a negative effect on performance and satisfaction because salespeople may view the rewards as arbitrary if the goals are beyond their control.[35] Aside from the impossible task of developing territories that are exactly equal, the only way to address this potential problem is to compare actual results with standards that reflect the unique territory situation faced by each salesperson. These standards are generally called sales quotas.

A **sales quota** represents a reasonable sales objective for a territory, district, region, or zone. Because a sales forecast represents an expected level of firm sales for a defined

## EXHIBIT 10.6   Results Criteria

| Base | Percentage Reporting Using |
| --- | --- |
| **Sales** | |
| Sales volume in dollars | 79 |
| Sales volume to previous year's sales | 76 |
| Sales volume by (versus) dollar quota | 65 |
| Percentage of increase in sales volume | 55 |
| Sales volume by product or product line | 48 |
| Sales volume by customer | 44 |
| Amount of new account sales | 42 |
| Sales volume in units | 35 |
| Sales volume to (versus) market potential | 27 |
| Sales volume by customer type | 22 |
| Sales volume to physical unit quota | 9 |
| Sales volume per order | 7 |
| Sales volume per call | 6 |
| Sales volume by outlet type | 4 |
| Percentage of sales made by telephone or mail | 1 |
| **Market Share** | |
| Market share achieved | 59 |
| Market share per quota | 18 |
| **Accounts** | |
| Number of new accounts | 69 |
| Number of accounts lost | 33 |
| Number of accounts buying the full line | 22 |
| Dollar amount of accounts receivable | 17 |
| Number of accounts (payment is) overdue | 15 |
| Lost account ratio | 6 |

geographic area, time period, and strategy, there should be a close relationship between the sales forecast and the sales quota. Bottom-up and/or top-down approaches might be used to develop sales forecasts that are translated into sales quotas.

One recommended approach for developing a sales forecast is to use statistical methods such as regression.[36] A market response framework to guide this type of approach is presented in Figure 10.2.[37] Depending on the planning and control unit of interest (territory, district, region, or zone), different determinants of market response (e.g., sales, market share) might be important. However, these determinants can be classified as either environmental, organizational, or salesperson factors. Once the determinant and market response factors are identified, their values for each planning and control unit in the previous period must be measured.

Statistical packages can then be used to estimate the parameters of the regression equation. For example, if you are a district sales manager interested in forecasting territory sales, you would identify and measure specific environmental, organizational, and salesperson factors as well as sales for each territory in the previous year. You could then develop a regression model of the following form:

$$\text{Territory sales} = a + (b1)(\text{environmental factor}) + (b2)(\text{organizational factor}) + (b3)(\text{salesperson factor})$$

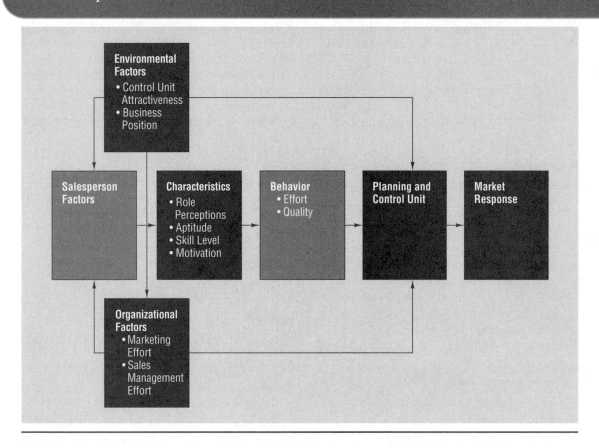

**Market Response Framework**    FIGURE 10.2

These are the types of factors that affect market response for any planning and control unit, whether it be accounts, territories, districts, regions, or zones. Market response might be profits, market share, or some other response, but sales is usually the market response variable of interest to sales managers.

The *a*, *b*1, *b*2, and *b*3 values are the model parameters supplied by the regression procedure to define the relationship between the determinant factors and territory sales.

Although this type of model might be useful, it suffers from two basic weaknesses. First, it incorporates only the independent effects of the determinant variables, yet these variables are highly interrelated. Second, this type of equation is linear, yet the determinant variable relationships are probably nonlinear. These weaknesses can be addressed by performing the linear regression on the logarithms of the actual data, producing a multiplicative power function of the following form:

$$\text{Territory sales} = (a)\,(\text{environmental factor}^{b1})\,(\text{organizational factor}^{b2})\,(\text{salesperson factor}^{b3})$$

This function is nonlinear and incorporates interactions through the multiplication of determinant variables.

A specific example illustrating this type of function is presented in Exhibit 10.7.[38] The environmental factors are *potential* and *concentration*, the salesperson factor is *experience*, and the organizational factor is *span of control*. The data are for three territories and are used in the model to generate sales forecasts for each territory individually. This regression model indicates that the higher the territory potential, account concentration, and level of salesperson experience are, the higher the territory sales will be. The larger the span of control is, the lower the territory sales. The exponents in the model suggest that territory sales are most affected by territory potential and span of control. Thus, the regression model generates a specific sales forecast for each territory, and it also provides information concerning relationships between determinant factors and sales.

The regression forecasting approach develops sales forecasts that explicitly consider the characteristics of a territory or other planning and control unit. Thus, these regression forecasts can be translated directly into sales quotas. For example, the sales forecasts for the three territories in Exhibit 10.7 ($586,000, $238,400, and $173,200) represent expected sales levels given the potential, concentration experience, and span of control evaluations for each territory. Sales management might use these regression sales forecasts as sales quotas for each territory. Alternatively, sales management might adjust the forecasts up or down based on information about the territories not incorporated in the regression model.

---

**EXHIBIT 10.7**    Regression Model Example

Territory sales = (800.82) (potential$^{.53}$) (concentration$^{.03}$) (experience$^{.08}$) (span of control$^{-.55}$)

|  | Territory 1 | Territory 2 | Territory 3 |
|---|---|---|---|
| **Potential** (number of persons employed by firms in customer industry located in territory) | 114,000 | 125,000 | 87,000 |
| **Concentration** (number of persons employed by the large plants in customer industry located in territory) | 94,000 | 52,000 | 12,000 |
| **Experience** (months salesperson has been with company) | 30 | 10 | 20 |
| **Span of control** (number of salespeople supervised by sales manager) | 5 | 8 | 10 |
| **Territory sales forecast** | $586,000 | $238,400 | $173,200 |

Exhibit 10.8 shows results of a survey indicating the relative importance placed on various factors by sales managers when assigning sales quotas.[39] In any case, the territory sales forecasts provide the basis for establishing the territory sales quotas.

The regression approach can be used to develop sales forecasts and establish sales quotas at all sales organization levels.[40] The determinant variables and measures are typically different depending on whether the control unit is a territory, district, region, or zone. Nevertheless, accurate sales forecasts are critical for establishing valid sales quotas at all sales organization levels. To increase the accuracy of sales forecasts and subsequently quotas, they should be developed quarterly, particularly in highly dynamic environments.[41]

Although forecasts provide the basis for developing quotas, they must be adjusted to determine each individual's quota. Research suggests that salesperson performance can be enhanced by assigning more challenging quotas to experienced salespeople who have demonstrated exceptional competence or to novices who quickly exhibit high potential.[42] Likewise, performance may be enhanced by setting fair, consistent, and realistic quotas and by explaining to salespeople the rationale behind the quota assignment.[43]

Web-based applications such as Synygy Quotas, by Synygy, Inc. (http://www.synygy.com), facilitate the quota-setting process. This application provides companies a means for setting corporate sales goals, allocating quotas, communicating them, making field adjustments, tracking changes, and tying quotas to incentive compensation programs. Quota allocation methods are derived from over eight years of industry-leading best practices. Sales managers can use market potential, historical data, revenue, gross margin, profit, or any other measure or combination of measures to set quota.[44]

| Elements Important in Assigning Sales Quotas | | EXHIBIT 10.8 |
|---|---|---|
| **Statement** | **Mean[1,2]** | **Rank** |
| Concentration of businesses within the sales representative's territory is important in determining the amount of quota. | 1.82 | 1 |
| The geographical size of territory is important in determining the amount of quota. | 1.95 | 2 |
| Growth of businesses within the sales representative's territory is important in determining the amount of quota. | 2.11 | 3 |
| Commitment by the sales manager to assisting the sales representative is important in determining the amount of quota. | 2.23 | 4 |
| Complexity of products sold is important in determining the amount of quota. | 2.50 | 5 |
| The sales representative's past sales performance is important in determining the amount of quota. | 2.54 | 6 |
| Extent of product line is important in determining the amount of quota. | 2.59 | 7 |
| The financial support (e.g., compensation) a firm provides sales representatives is important in assigning quota. | 2.76 | 8 |
| The relationship of your product line is important in determining the amount of quota. | 2.82 | 9 |
| The amount of clerical support given to a sales representative is important in determining the amount of quota. | 3.13 | 10 |

[1]The rating scale and weights used to rate the importance of each statement were as follows: 1 = strongly agree; 2 = agree; 3 = neutral; 4 = disagree; and 5 = strongly disagree.
[2]The responses numbered 186.

Although it varies from company to company, some research indicates that a majority of companies require salespeople to achieve 100 percent or more of quota to be considered a strong performer. Over 26 percent of the respondents in this research claimed that achieving 111 percent or more of quota is necessary to be considered a strong performer. However, most companies (72 percent) consider salespeople who make 90 percent or less of quota to be average performers.[45] As seen in Exhibit 10.9, this research also found that sales managers often work closely with salespeople to improve their performance when they fail to achieve quota.[46]

## Profitability

A potential problem with focusing on sales results is that the profitability of sales is not assessed. Salespeople can affect profitability in two basic ways. First, salespeople have an impact on gross profits through the specific products they sell and/or through the prices they negotiate for final sale. Thus, two salespeople could generate the same level of sales dollars and achieve the same sales/sales quota evaluation, but one salesperson could produce more gross profits by selling higher margin products and/or maintaining higher prices in sales negotiations.

Second, salespeople affect net profits by the expenses they incur in generating sales. The selling expenses most under the control of salespeople are travel and entertainment expenses. Therefore, two salespeople could generate the same levels of total sales, the same sales/sales quota performance, and even the same levels of gross profits, but one salesperson could contribute more to net profits through lower travel and entertainment costs. Examples of **profitability criteria** are listed in Exhibit 10.10.[47]

Sales organizations are increasingly incorporating profitability criteria into their salesperson performance evaluations. The most frequently used profitability criterion is net profit dollars. Selling expenditures relative to budget is also heavily emphasized. The need to address profitability criteria is especially important during a slow-growth, competitive environment in which sales growth is so difficult and productivity and profitability so important.

## Comment on Criteria

Conducting a comprehensive evaluation of salesperson performance typically requires consideration of behavioral professional development, results, and profitability criteria. Each set of criteria tells a different story as to how well salespeople have performed and provides different diagnostic information for control purposes. Steve Randazzo of KV Pharmaceutical (ETHEX Division) explains how KV uses various performance criteria to drive relationship development in "Sales Management in the 21st Century: Performance Criteria at KV Pharmaceutical Inc. (ETHEX Division)." Other methods for evaluating salespeople against these criteria are discussed in the following sections.

**EXHIBIT 10.9** Examples of Managerial Actions Resulting from Failure to Achieve Assigned Quota

| | Percentage Agreement | | | | |
|---|---|---|---|---|---|
| **Action to Salesperson** | **Strongly Disagree** | **Disagree** | **Neutral** | **Agree** | **Strongly Agree** |
| Nothing | 12.7 | 38.2 | 18.5 | 25.4 | 5.2 |
| Informal reprimand to do better | 9.2 | 16.1 | 19.0 | 47.1 | 8.6 |
| A stern verbal warning | 10.7 | 30.5 | 23.4 | 29.7 | 5.7 |
| Sales manager works closely with salesperson to improve | 7.6 | 7.0 | 17.4 | 48.8 | 19.2 |
| Formal probation | 12.2 | 34.9 | 24.4 | 22.1 | 6.4 |

| Profitability Criteria   EXHIBIT 10.10 | |
| --- | --- |
| **Base** | **Percentage Reporting Using** |
| **Sales** | |
| Net profit dollars | 69 |
| Gross margin per sales (a percentage of sales) | 34 |
| Return on investment | 33 |
| Net profit as a percent(age) of sales | 32 |
| Margin by product category | 28 |
| Gross margin (in dollars) | 25 |
| Margin by customer type | 18 |
| Net profit per sale | 14 |
| Return on sales cost | 14 |
| Net profit contribution | — |
| **Order(s)** | |
| Number of orders secured | 47 |
| Average size of order secured | 22 |
| Order per call ratio (aka batting average) | 14 |
| Number of orders canceled | 11 |
| Net orders per repeat order | 10 |
| Number of canceled orders per orders booked | 4 |
| **Selling Expense** | |
| Selling expense versus budget | 55 |
| Total expenses | 53 |
| Selling expense to sales | 49 |
| Average cost per call | 12 |
| Selling expense to quota | 12 |
| Expenses by product category | 7 |
| Expenses by customer type | 3 |

**Performance Criteria at KV Pharmaceutical, Inc. (ETHEX Division)**

Steve Randazzo, vice president of sales for KV Pharmaceutical, Inc. (ETHEX Division), discusses how he uses performance criteria to drive relationship development:

*Our salespeople are evaluated on several criteria: industry/product knowledge; promotion of specified and new products; relationship development skills; territory management/work habits; and sales and profitability. While achieving sales and profitability goals are important, it is equally important for our salespeople to be able to develop customer relationships, be creative, and think "outside the box." Good sales numbers might be achieved because we launched a new product, or offered a very competitive price. However, we want to establish relationships with customers that will enable us to withstand turbulent times in the market. For instance, salespeople are evaluated on their ability to get customers to implement promotional programs developed by our marketing department that are designed to help customers move our products. Customers who use these programs are more likely to see us as a partner. Therefore, we evaluate salespeople's ability to build relationships just as seriously as we do their ability to achieve sales and profits. Territory management and work habits are also extremely important to being a successful salesperson. My top producers are always the ones who understand how to work with the corporate office to meet customer needs and work equally hard for the customer plus close for the business.*

## Performance Evaluation Methods

Sales managers can use a number of different methods for measuring the behaviors, professional development, results, and profitability of salespeople. Ideally, the method used should have the following characteristics.[48]

- *Job relatedness:* The performance evaluation method should be designed to meet the needs of each specific sales organization.
- *Reliability:* The measures should be stable over time and exhibit internal consistency.
- *Validity:* The measures should provide accurate assessments of the criteria they are intended to measure.
- *Standardization:* The measurement instruments and evaluation process should be similar throughout the sales organization.
- *Practicality:* Sales managers and salespeople should understand the entire performance appraisal process and should be able to implement it in a reasonable amount of time.
- *Comparability:* The results of the performance evaluation process should make it possible to compare the performance of individual salespeople directly.
- *Discriminability:* The evaluative methods must be capable of detecting differences in the performance of individual salespeople.
- *Usefulness:* The information provided by the performance evaluation must be valuable to sales managers in making various decisions.

Designing methods of salesperson performance evaluation that possess all these characteristics is a difficult task. As indicated in Exhibit 10.11 each evaluative method has certain strengths and weaknesses.[49] No one method provides a perfect evaluation. Therefore, it is important to understand the strengths and weaknesses of each method so that several can be combined to produce the best evaluative procedure for a given sales organization.

### Graphic Rating/Checklist Methods

**Graphic rating/checklist methods** consist of approaches in which salespeople are evaluated by using some type of performance evaluation form. The performance evaluation form contains the criteria to be used in the evaluation as well as some means to provide an assessment of how well each salesperson performed on each criterion. An example of part of such a form is presented in Exhibit 10.12.

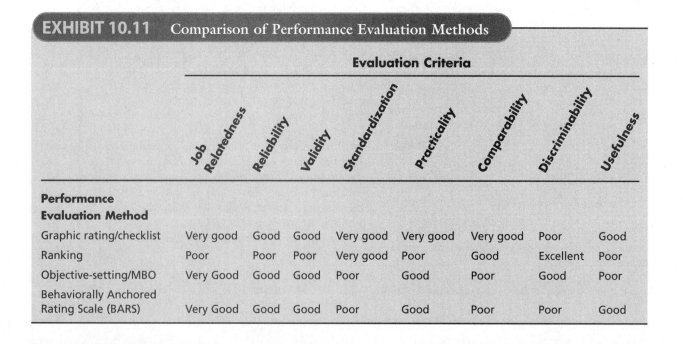

**EXHIBIT 10.11**     Comparison of Performance Evaluation Methods

|  | Evaluation Criteria | | | | | | | |
| --- | --- | --- | --- | --- | --- | --- | --- | --- |
| **Performance Evaluation Method** | Job Relatedness | Reliability | Validity | Standardization | Practicality | Comparability | Discriminability | Usefulness |
| Graphic rating/checklist | Very good | Good | Good | Very good | Very good | Very good | Poor | Good |
| Ranking | Poor | Poor | Poor | Very good | Poor | Good | Excellent | Poor |
| Objective-setting/MBO | Very Good | Good | Good | Poor | Good | Poor | Good | Poor |
| Behaviorally Anchored Rating Scale (BARS) | Very Good | Good | Good | Poor | Good | Poor | Poor | Good |

| Graphic Rating/Checklist Example | **EXHIBIT 10.12** |
| --- | --- |

1. Asks customers for their ideas for promoting business
   Almost Never   1   2   3   4   5   Almost Always   NA
2. Offers customers help in solving their problems
   Almost Never   1   2   3   4   5   Almost Always   NA
3. Is constantly smiling when interacting with customers
   Almost Never   1   2   3   4   5   Almost Always   NA
4. Admits when he/she doesn't know the answer, but promises to find out
   Almost Never   1   2   3   4   5   Almost Always   NA
5. Generates new ways of tackling new or ongoing problems
   Almost Never   1   2   3   4   5   Almost Always   NA
6. Returns customers' calls the same day
   Almost Never   1   2   3   4   5   Almost Always   NA
7. Retains his or her composure in front of customers
   Almost Never   1   2   3   4   5   Almost Always   NA
8. Delivers what he or she promises on time
   Almost Never   1   2   3   4   5   Almost Always   NA

This method is popular in many sales organizations. It is especially useful in evaluating salesperson behavioral and professional development criteria. As part of its assessment process, Eastman Chemical Company asks its customers to evaluate their satisfaction with the company by using a rating scale. As evident from Exhibit 10.13, Eastman's salespeople are responsible for several behavior-based performance factors.[50] Rating methods have

| Eastman Chemical Company Customer Satisfaction Survey | **EXHIBIT 10.13** |
| --- | --- |

| | | Importance<br>5—Definitely Would<br>4—Probably Would<br>3—Uncertain<br>2—Probably Would Not<br>1—Definitely Would Not<br>NA—Not Applicable | Performance<br>5—Outstanding   2—Fair<br>4—Good       1—Poor<br>3—Average<br>NA—Not Applicable | |
| --- | --- | --- | --- | --- |
| **Importance:** | Rate the importance of each statement (your buying criteria) by asking, "Would I place additional business with a supplier who improved performance in this category from 'average' to 'outstanding'?" | | | |
| **Performance:** | Rate Eastman performance and your best "other supplier" on each criteria. | | Eastman | Best Other Supplier |
| ***Product*** | | | | |
| 1. Product Performance: Supplier provides a product that consistently meets your requirements and performance expectations. | | | | |
| 2. Product Mix: Supplier offers a range of products that meets your needs. | | | | |
| 3. Packaging: Supplier has the package type, size, and label to meet your needs. | | | | |
| 4. New Products: Supplier meets your needs through timely introduction of new products. | | | | |
| 5. Product Availability: Supplier meets volume commitments and is also fair and consistent during times of restricted supply. | | | | |
| 6. Product Stewardship: Supplier provides information about the transportation, storage, handling, use, recycling, disposal, and regulation of products and product packaging. | | | | |

*(continued)*

**EXHIBIT 10.13**    Eastman Chemical Company Customer Satisfaction Survey (*Continued*)

| | Importance | Performance | |
|---|---|---|---|
| | | Eastman | Best Other Supplier |
| **Service** | | | |
| 7. Order Entry: Supplier has a user-friendly system to place orders that is flexible and responsive to routine order changes as well as urgent or special requests. | | | |
| 8. Delivery: Supplier consistently delivers the right product on time and in satisfactory condition. | | | |
| 9. Technical Service: Supplier provides timely technical support through training, information, problem solving, and assistance in current and new end-use applications. | | | |
| 10. Sharing Information: Supplier is a resource for product, market, industry, and company information that helps you better understand business issues. | | | |
| 11. New Ideas: Supplier offers new ideas that add value to your business. | | | |
| **Pricing/Business Practices** | | | |
| 12. Pricing Practices: Supplier is consistent with the marketplace in establishing pricing practices. | | | |
| 13. Paperwork: Supplier provides clear and accurate paperwork and business documents that meet your needs. | | | |
| 14. Commitment to total quality management: Supplier exhibits strong commitment to total quality management in all aspects of their business. | | | |
| 15. Responsiveness: Supplier listens and responds to your business needs in a timely manner. | | | |
| **Relationship** | | | |
| 16. Integrity: Supplier is credible, honest, and trustworthy. | | | |
| 17. Dependability: Supplier follows through on agreements. | | | |
| 18. Supplier Contact: Supplier is easy to contact and provides the right amount of interface with the appropriate personnel. | | | |
| 19. Problem Solving: Supplier provides empowered employees to solve your problems. | | | |
| **Supplier Commitment** | | | |
| 20. Industry Commitment: Supplier exhibits a strong commitment to your industry. | | | |
| 21. Regional Commitment: Supplier has the appropriate resources in place in your region to provide products and services needed. | | | |
| 22. Customer Commitment: Supplier is strongly committed to helping your business be successful. | | | |

been developed to evaluate all the important salesperson performance dimensions.[51] There are even employee-appraisal software programs, such as Performance Now!, available to assist in the review process. The program asks users to rate employees by goals, development plans, and competencies.[52]

As evident from Exhibit 10.11, graphic rating/checklist methods possess many desirable characteristics, especially in terms of job relatedness, standardization, practicality, and comparability. The reliability and validity of these methods, however, must be continually assessed and the specific rating scales improved over time.

The major disadvantage of graphic rating/checklist methods is in providing evaluations that discriminate sufficiently among the performances of individual salespeople or among the performances on different criteria for the same salesperson. For example, some sales managers may be very lenient in their evaluations; they may try to play it safe and give all salespeople ratings around the average. In addition, when evaluating an individual salesperson, some sales managers are subject to a *halo effect*, meaning that their evaluations on one criterion affect their ratings on other criteria.

The advantages of graphic rating/checklist methods clearly outweigh the disadvantages. However, care must be taken to minimize potential sales management biases when the evaluation forms are completed, and continuous attention to reliability and validity issues is necessary.

## Ranking Methods

Otherwise similar to graphic rating/checklist methods, **ranking methods** rank all salespeople according to relative performance on each performance criterion rather than evaluating them against a set of performance criteria. Companies such as Ford, General Electric, and Microsoft use ranking methods.[53] Many approaches might be used to obtain the rankings. An example of a ranking approach in which salespeople are compared in pairs concerning relative communication skills is presented in Exhibit 10.14.[54]

Ranking methods provide a standardized approach to evaluation and thus force discrimination as to the performance of individual salespeople on each criterion. The process of ranking forces this discrimination in performance. Despite these advantages, ranking methods have many shortcomings, as indicated in Exhibit 10.11. Of major concern are the constraints on their practicality and usefulness. Ranking all salespeople against each performance criterion can be a complex and cognitively difficult task. The ranking task can be simplified by using paired-comparison approaches like the one presented in Exhibit 10.14. However, the computations required to translate the paired comparisons into overall rankings can be extremely cumbersome.

Even if the evaluative and computative procedures can be simplified, the rankings are of limited usefulness. Rank data reveal only relative ordering and omit any assessment of the differences between ranks. For example, the actual differences in the communication skills of salespeople ranked first, second, and third may be small or large, but there is no

| | Ranking Method Example | **EXHIBIT 10.14** |
|---|---|---|

**Performance Criterion: Communication Skills**

| | Much Better | Slightly Better | Equal | Slightly Better | Much Better | |
|---|---|---|---|---|---|---|
| Jane Haynes | X | ___ | ___ | ___ | ___ | John Evans |
| Ron Castaneda | ___ | X | ___ | ___ | ___ | Jane Haynes |
| Bill Haroldson | ___ | ___ | X | ___ | ___ | Jane Haynes |

way to tell the degree of these differences from the ranked data. In addition, information obtained from graphic rating/checklist methods can always be transformed into rankings, but rankings cannot be translated into graphic rating/checklist form. Despite their limitations, one study of several large companies found forced rankings to be an effective way to identify and reward core competencies.[55] However, given their limitations, it is suggested that ranking methods for salesperson performance evaluations be used as a supplement to other methods.

## Objective-Setting Methods

The most common and comprehensive goal-setting method is **management by objectives (MBO)**. Applied to a salesforce, the typical MBO approach is as follows:[56]

1. mutual setting of well-defined and measurable goals within a specified time period
2. managing activities within the specified time period toward the accomplishment of the stated objectives
3. appraisal of performance against objectives

As with all the performance evaluation methods, MBO and other goal-setting methods have certain strengths and weaknesses (see Exhibit 10.11). Although complete reliance on this or any other goal-setting method is inadvisable, the incorporation of some goal-setting procedures is normally desirable. This is especially true for performance criteria related to quantitative behavioral, professional development, results, and profitability criteria. Absolute measures of these dimensions are often not very meaningful because of extreme differences in the territory situations of individual salespeople. The setting of objectives or quotas provides a means for controlling for territory differences through the establishment of performance benchmarks that incorporate these territory differences.

Quotas can be established for other important results criteria and for specific behavioral, professional development, and profitability criteria. Each type of quota represents a specific objective for a salesperson to achieve during a given period. Actual performance can be compared with the quota objective and a performance index calculated for each criterion being evaluated. The individual performance indices can then be weighted to reflect their relative importance and combined to produce an overall performance index. An example of this procedure is shown in Exhibit 10.15.[57]

---

**EXHIBIT 10.15    Quota Evaluation Example**

| Salesperson | Quota | Weight | Actual Performance | Index | Weighted Performance |
|---|---|---|---|---|---|
| **Laura** | | | | | |
| Sales | 600,000 | 3 | 552,000 | 92 | 276 |
| Gross profits | 150,000 | 6 | 180,000 | 120 | 720 |
| Demonstrations | 200 | 4 | 250 | 125 | 500 |
| Overall performance | | | | | 115 |
| **David** | | | | | |
| Sales | 700,000 | 3 | 710,000 | 101 | 303 |
| Gross profits | 170,000 | 6 | 174,000 | 102 | 612 |
| Demonstrations | 200 | 4 | 200 | 100 | 400 |
| Overall performance | | | | | 101 |
| **Kendra** | | | | | |
| Sales | 550,000 | 3 | 650,000 | 118 | 354 |
| Gross profits | 140,000 | 6 | 100,000 | 71 | 426 |
| Demonstrations | 180 | 4 | 150 | 82 | 332 |
| Overall performance | | | | | 86 |

This example illustrates an evaluation of Kendra, David, and Laura on sales, gross profit, and demonstration quotas. The unequal weights reflect that the firm is placing the most importance on gross profits, followed by demonstrations and then sales. Laura has performed the best overall, but she did not reach her sales quota for this period. David has performed reasonably well on all criteria. Kendra's situation is interesting in that she performed the best on the sales quota but poorly overall due to low performance indices for gross profits and demonstrations. Perhaps she is concentrating too much on short-term sales generation and not concerning herself with the profitability of sales or the number of product demonstrations. In any case, the use of quotas provides an extremely useful method for evaluating salesperson performance and highlighting specific areas in which performance is especially good or especially poor.

### Behaviorally Anchored Rating Scales

The uniqueness of **behaviorally anchored rating scales (BARS)** is due to its focus on trying to link salesperson behaviors with specific results. These behavior–results linkages become the basis for salesperson performance evaluation in this method.

The development of a BARS approach is an iterative process that actively incorporates members of the salesforce.[58] Salespeople are used to identify important performance results and the critical behaviors necessary to achieve those results. The critical behaviors are assigned numbers on a rating scale for each performance result. An example of one such BARS rating scale is presented in Figure 10.3.[59]

The performance result in this example is achieving cooperative relations with sales team members. Seven behaviors have been assigned numbers on a 10-point rating scale to reflect the linkages between engaging in the behavior and achieving the result. This scale can then be used to evaluate individual salespeople. For instance, the example rating of 5 in the figure suggests that the salesperson occasionally supports the sales team on problems encountered in the field and thus achieves only a moderate amount of cooperation with sales team members.

As indicated in Exhibit 10.11, the BARS approach rates high on job relatedness. This is because of the rigorous process used to determine important performance results and critical salesperson behaviors. The results and behaviors identified in this manner are specific to a given selling situation and directly related to the job of the salespeople being evaluated. Research indicates that positive feedback about sales behaviors has a greater impact on salesperson behavior than positive output feedback, perhaps because it gives salespeople direction for improving selling. However, although both have a positive effect on performance, the effect is greater for positive output feedback.[60] The really unique aspect of BARS is the focus on linkages between behaviors and results. No other approach incorporates this perspective.

In sum, the basic methods for evaluating salesperson performance include graphic rating/checklist methods, ranking methods, objective-setting methods, and BARS methods. Each approach has specific strengths and weaknesses that should be considered. Combining different methods into the salesperson performance evaluation process is one way to capitalize on the strengths and minimize the weaknesses inherent in each approach.

## Performance Evaluation Bias

Sales managers must be careful to avoid bias when assessing salespeople. For instance, sales managers tend to give more favorable performance ratings to those with whom they have closer personal relationships and less favorable performance ratings to those with whom they maintain formal role-defined relationships.[61] Similarly, sales managers are more likely to discount internal responsibility while bolstering external explanations when appraising salespeople with whom they work well and are socially compatible. In addition, these salespeople are less likely to receive coercive feedback.[62] Sales managers also tend to rate individuals in more difficult territories higher in ability and performance than those in less difficult territories.[63] Furthermore, supervisors are more likely to

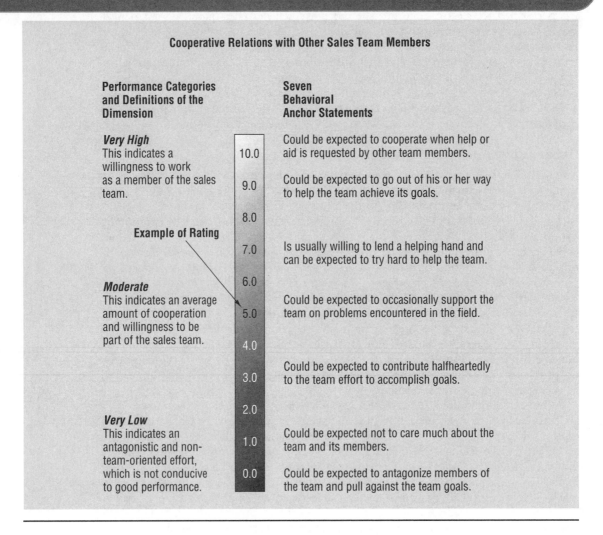

**FIGURE 10.3**                                                                 BARS Scale

**Cooperative Relations with Other Sales Team Members**

| Performance Categories and Definitions of the Dimension | | Seven Behavioral Anchor Statements |
|---|---|---|
| **Very High** This indicates a willingness to work as a member of the sales team. | 10.0 | Could be expected to cooperate when help or aid is requested by other team members. |
| | 9.0 | Could be expected to go out of his or her way to help the team achieve its goals. |
| | 8.0 | |
| **Example of Rating** | 7.0 | Is usually willing to lend a helping hand and can be expected to try hard to help the team. |
| | 6.0 | |
| **Moderate** This indicates an average amount of cooperation and willingness to be part of the sales team. | 5.0 | Could be expected to occasionally support the team on problems encountered in the field. |
| | 4.0 | |
| | 3.0 | Could be expected to contribute halfheartedly to the team effort to accomplish goals. |
| | 2.0 | |
| **Very Low** This indicates an antagonistic and non-team-oriented effort, which is not conducive to good performance. | 1.0 | Could be expected not to care much about the team and its members. |
| | 0.0 | Could be expected to antagonize members of the team and pull against the team goals. |

This scale evaluates a salesperson's cooperation with other sales team members. The example rating of 5 suggests a moderate level of cooperation in which the salesperson gives only occasional support to the sales team.

rate those who are better at impression management (the ability to shape and manage a self-image that positively influences others), which tend to be males, more favorably when using subjective evaluations.[64]

Sales managers must likewise be careful to avoid **outcome bias**. Outcome bias occurs when the outcome of a decision rather than the appropriateness of the decision influences an evaluator's ratings. When sales managers rate the quality of a salesperson's decision, outcome information (e.g., salesperson did or did not make the sale) often influences their ratings across all criteria when the decision is perceived to have been inappropriate. Using the BARS scale to assess behavioral and professional development criteria helps reduce outcome bias.[65]

Performance evaluation bias not only is harmful to the individual being rated but could result in legal action. Personnel actions that discriminate unfairly are unlawful.[66] A performance appraisal system is more likely to withstand a legal challenge if the guidelines in Exhibit 10.16 are adhered to in developing and implementing the system. "An Ethical Dilemma" illustrates potential difficulties a sales manager may face when evaluating salesperson performance.

**Guidelines for Withstanding Discriminatory Appraisal Lawsuits**   **EXHIBIT 10.16**

- Conduct reviews at least once a year, preferably more often.
- Base the appraisal system on a thorough job analysis that identifies the important duties or elements of job performance.
- Base the appraisal system on behaviors or results, not vague or ambiguous salesperson traits or characteristics.
- Observe salespeople performing their work.
- Train performance raters how to use the system, including proper use of the rating forms.
- Use the same rating form, that measures specific criteria, for all salespeople.
- Fill out the rating form *honestly*. Sales managers are asking for trouble if they allow salespeople to think their performances are satisfactory if they are not.
- Address both the salesperson's strengths and weaknesses.
- Carefully document appraisals and their rationale. Both the sales manager and salesperson should sign and date the evaluation after the meeting.
- Develop with the salesperson a plan of action and specific goals for the coming months.
- Bring in a third party for sensitive evaluation meetings.
- Never make reference to a legally protected class of which the salesperson is a member (e.g., racial or religious origin, gender, age).
- Have higher-level managers or human resource managers review appraisals.
- Develop a formal appeal mechanism or system that provides an avenue of appeal to salespeople who are dissatisfied with their evaluations.
- Provide performance counseling, guidance, and/or training to help poor performers improve their performance.

AN ETHICAL DILEMMA

As district manager for the ABC company, you are responsible for evaluating the performance of all eight of your salespeople. Your performance appraisals play a large role in your salespeoples' bonus and promotion opportunities. Your boss has come to you and "suggested" that you look favorably on one of your salespeople, Ann Anderson, during her upcoming performance appraisal. You understand that a sales management position is opening up in another division next month and suspect that Ann may be next in line, particularly if her latest appraisal looks good. Although Ann is a solid performer, she has not exactly been outstanding. Your star sales performer would actually be a good candidate for the position. However, you would hate to lose him. What would you do? Explain.

## Evaluating Team Performance

Sales organizations employing sales teams must also consider how to evaluate them. When designing the appraisal process for teams, sales managers must still consider the criteria on which members will be evaluated and the methods used to evaluate performance. In addition, it is important that sales managers establish a link between team performance and positive outcomes to promote individual and team effort. The process is fostered by allowing team members to participate in developing team goals and objectives.[67] Furthermore, members are more willing to participate when individual goals are linked to team goals.[68] Individual and group assignments necessary for reaching goals should be prioritized to help the team better manage its time.[69]

Generally, the team as a whole should be evaluated, in addition to assessing individual member performance. Team performance can be measured by team members as well as by the sales manager.[70] Exhibit 10.17[71] provides an example of a multidimensional

---

**EXHIBIT 10.17**    Teamwork Effectiveness/Attitude Measurement (TEAM)

### TEAMwork

*(ALWAYS / USUALLY / OFTEN / SOMETIMES / RARELY / NEVER)*

1. Is competitive/wants team to "win."
2. Takes reasonable risks.
3. Has confidence in team members' abilities.
4. Places team success before individual recognition.
5. Contributes "extra effort" to team success/efforts.
6. Implements or supports all team decisions.
7. Shares "credit" with team members.
8. Works well with team.
9. Has personal "chemistry" with other team members.
10. Is resilient; bounces back and regains momentum after setback.
Totals

MAJOR TEAMWORK STRENGTH:

POSITIVE SUGGESTION FOR IMPROVING TEAMWORK:

### TEAM Leadership

*(ALWAYS / USUALLY / OFTEN / SOMETIMES / RARELY / NEVER)*

1. Is assertive, persuasive.
2. Has trust and respect of team members.
3. Sets good example, role model.
4. Is consistent in attitude, actions, behavior.
5. Provides recognition/encouragement to others.
6. Volunteers, takes initiative on assignments.
7. Is willing to assume extra responsibility.
8. Makes effective decisions/uses good judgment.
9. Has high, positive expectations of self and team members.
10. Is firm but fair.
Totals

MAJOR LEADERSHIP STRENGTH:

POSITIVE SUGGESTION FOR IMPROVING LEADERSHIP ROLE:

### TEAM Productivity

*(ALWAYS / USUALLY / OFTEN / SOMETIMES / RARELY / NEVER)*

1. Uses time effectively.
2. Produces quality work.
3. Provides creative ideas and proposals.
4. Is industrious, works at good pace.
5. Meets targets and deadlines.
6. Focuses on high-priority projects.
7. Has discipline and perseverance.
8. Plans and organizes effectively.
9. Produces accurate work.
10. Stays within budget (resources and/or parameters).
Totals

MAJOR PRODUCTIVITY STRENGTH:

POSITIVE SUGGESTION FOR IMPROVING PRODUCTIVITY:

### TEAM Relations

*(ALWAYS / USUALLY / OFTEN / SOMETIMES / RARELY / NEVER)*

1. Is sensitive to needs of others.
2. Is supportive, concerned.
3. Keeps commitments.
4. Has positive attitude.
5. Is pleasant, courteous, tactful.
6. Maintains control, has high threshold of frustration.
7. Levels with others.
8. Cooperates with team members.
9. Is flexible in approach and relationships.
10. Has patience, accepts team members' shortcomings.
Totals

MAJOR RELATIONS STRENGTH:

POSITIVE SUGGESTION FOR IMPROVING RELATIONS WITH TEAM:

### TEAM Communication

*(ALWAYS / USUALLY / OFTEN / SOMETIMES / RARELY / NEVER)*

1. Communicates clearly and specifically.
2. Allows sufficient time for communication.
3. Listens effectively.
4. Keeps others informed, provides feedback.
5. Is concise, to the point.
6. Organizes written and verbal communication.
7. Initiates discussion on important matters.
8. Is open-minded, receptive to others' ideas.
9. Generates or confirms important communication in writing.
10. Responds promptly to requests for information.
Totals

MAJOR COMMUNICATION STRENGTH:

POSITIVE SUGGESTION FOR IMPROVING COMMUNICATION SKILLS:

---

approach team members can use to evaluate teammates' critical skills and behaviors. The measurement allows sales managers to develop a composite performance appraisal, merging each team member's viewpoint. The process helps strengthen teams, enhance morale, and contribute to a healthy working climate.[72] In addition, the team and its members must be evaluated against predetermined performance criteria. Exhibit 10.18 outlines a process for measuring team performance.[73]

Poor team performance is often not the fault of individual team members but of management. A study of 179 companies found top management commitment and support, appropriate use of teams, provision of training, start-up support, cross-team communication, and accountability for team performance to most influence a team's success.[74]

| Steps for Measuring Team Performance | EXHIBIT 10.18 |
| --- | --- |

1. Review the existing organizational measures. Make sure that the measures above and around the team are known to the team and linked to the team's measures.
2. Define team measurement points. Select the best alternatives for identifying starting points for team measurement. Selecting the best alternatives and using them to identify the team's accomplishments provides the basis for all further measurement.
3. Identify individual team member accomplishments that support the team. Identify the results each team member must produce to support the team's results or work process.
4. Weight the accomplishments. The team should discuss and agree upon the relative importance of each accomplishment.
5. Develop team and individual performance measures. Identify the numeric and descriptive yardsticks that will be used to gauge how well results have been achieved.
6. Develop team and individual performance standards. Define how well the team and individuals have to perform to meet expectations.
7. Decide how to track performance. Identify how the team will collect the data for each performance standard and feed this data back to the team.

## Using Performance Information

Using different methods to evaluate the behavior, professional development, results, and profitability of salespeople provides extremely important performance information. The critical sales management task is to use this information to improve the performance of individual salespeople, sales teams, and the overall operations of the sales organization. Initially, it should be used to determine the absolute and relative performance of each salesperson. These determinations then provide the basis for reward disbursements, special recognition, promotions, and so forth.

The second major use of this performance information is to identify potential problems or areas in which salespeople need to improve for better performance in the future. If salespeople are evaluated against multiple criteria, as suggested in this module, useful diagnostic information will be available. The difficulty exists in isolating the specific causes of low performance areas. A framework for performing this analysis is given in Figure 10.4.

The first step in this analysis is to review the performance of each salesperson against each relevant criterion and summarize the results across all salespeople being supervised. The purpose of this step is to determine whether there are common areas of low performance. For example, the situation is different when most salespeople are not meeting their sales quotas than when only one or two salespeople are not meeting their sales quotas.

Once the poor performance areas have been identified, the sales manager must work backward to try to identify the cause of the poor performance. Merely determining that most salespeople did not meet their sales quotas is not sufficient to improve future performance; the sales manager must try to uncover the reason for this poor performance. The basic approach is to try to answer the question, "What factors affect the achievement of this performance dimension?" For instance, in regard to achieving sales quotas, the key question is, "What factors determine whether salespeople achieve their sales quotas?" All the factors identified should be reviewed to isolate the cause of any poor performance. Several factors that might cause poor performance in different areas are presented in Exhibit 10.19.[75]

After identifying the potential causes of poor performance, the sales manager must determine the appropriate action to reduce or eliminate the cause of the problem so that performance will be improved in the future. Examples of potential management actions for specific problems are also presented in Exhibit 10.19.

Consider again poor performance on sales quota achievement. Assume that intense review of this problem reveals that salespeople not meeting sales quotas also do not make many product demonstrations to prospects. This analysis suggests that if salespeople were to make more product demonstrations, they would be able to generate more sales and thus achieve their sales quotas. The sales management task is to determine what management actions will lead to more product demonstrations by salespeople.

**FIGURE 10.4**                    Framework for Using Performance Information

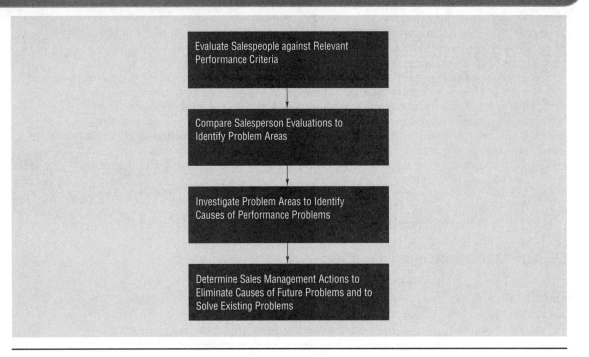

Sales managers need to be able to use the information provided by salesperson performance evaluations in a diagnostic manner. The basic diagnostic approach is to determine problem areas, identify the causes of these problems, and take appropriate action to eliminate the causes and to solve problems that are already present, thus improving future salesperson performance.

**EXHIBIT 10.19**   Sample Problems, Causes, and Management Actions

| Performance Problems | Potential Causes | Sales Management Actions |
| --- | --- | --- |
| Not meeting sales or other results quotas | Sales or other results quotas incorrect; poor account coverage; too few sales calls | Revise sales or other results quotas; revise effort allocation; redesign territories; develop motivational programs; provide closer supervision; increase salesforce size |
| Not meeting behavioral quotas | Behavioral quotas incorrect; too little effort; poor quality of effort | Revise behavioral quotas; develop motivational programs; increase salesforce size; conduct training programs; provide closer supervision |
| Not meeting profitability quotas | Profitability quotas incorrect; low gross margins; high selling expenses | Revise profitability quotas; change compensation; devise incentive programs; provide closer supervision; conduct training programs |
| Not meeting professional development quotas | Professional development quotas incorrect; inadequate training | Revise professional development quotas; conduct training programs; provide closer supervision; develop motivational programs; change hiring practices |

Possible actions include more training on product demonstrations, direct communication with individual salespeople about the need for more product demonstrations, or some combination of these or other management actions.

This discussion highlights the thought processes that sales managers need to use to identify performance problems, isolate the causes of these problems, and determine the appropriate management actions necessary to solve the problems and improve future salesperson performance. Using this approach successfully requires that sales managers have a detailed understanding of the personal selling and sales management processes and relationships. Such an understanding is essential for them to be able to determine the causes of performance problems and identify the appropriate management actions to solve these problems.

Our discussion and examples have emphasized problems affecting many salespeople. The same basic approach can be used for performance problems that are unique to one individual salesperson. In fact, many sales organizations use performance reviews as a means for a sales manager to meet with each salesperson, analyze the salesperson's performance on each criterion, and suggest ways to improve future performance. These performance reviews provide one means for communicating the *performance feedback* that is so important to salespeople. Performance feedback is also an important determinant of salesperson job satisfaction, which is discussed next.

## SALESPERSON JOB SATISFACTION

In addition to evaluating salesperson performance, sales managers should be concerned with the **job satisfaction** of salespeople. Research results have consistently found relationships between salesperson job satisfaction and turnover, absenteeism, motivation, and organizational commitment.[76] Salespeople who are satisfied with their job tend to stay with the firm and work harder than those who are not satisfied.

Other research has investigated relationships between salesperson performance and salesperson satisfaction. This research has produced conflicting findings concerning the direction of the relationship between performance and satisfaction.[77] In other words, it has not been established whether achieving high performance causes salesperson satisfaction or whether salesperson satisfaction determines salesperson performance. However, there is some evidence that salespeople's job satisfaction has a positive effect on customer satisfaction.[78] Thus it is clear, however, that sales managers should be concerned with both the performance and satisfaction of their salespeople. Of importance to sales managers is how salesperson satisfaction might be measured and then how this satisfaction information might be used.

### Measuring Salesperson Job Satisfaction

Because job satisfaction is based on individual perceptions, measures of salesperson satisfaction must be based on data provided by individual salespeople. In addition, there are many different aspects of a salesperson's job, and these different areas should be incorporated into the satisfaction evaluation. Fortunately, a scale for evaluating the job satisfaction of salespeople, termed INDSALES, has been developed, validated, and revised. Portions of the revised scale are presented in Exhibit 10.20.[79,80]

On this scale, salespeople indicate their level of agreement with statements concerning their particular sales job. These statements are designed to measure their satisfaction in seven general areas: satisfaction with the job, fellow workers, supervision, company policy and support, pay, promotion and advancement, and customers. Answers to the specific questions for each area are summed to produce a separate satisfaction score for each job dimension. These individual job dimension scores can then be summed to form an overall salesperson satisfaction score. Sales managers can then view the dimensional or overall satisfaction scores for each salesperson or for specified groups of salespeople.

**EXHIBIT 10.20**    Sample Questions from Revised INDSALES Scale

| Component | Total Number of Items | Sample Items |
|---|---|---|
| The job | 4 | My work gives me a sense of accomplishment.<br>My job is exciting. |
| Fellow workers | 4 | My fellow workers are selfish.<br>My fellow workers are pleasant. |
| Supervision | 4 | My sales manager really tries to get our ideas about things.<br>My sales manager keeps his or her promises. |
| Company policy and support | 4 | Top management really knows its job.<br>Management is progressive. |
| Pay | 4 | My pay is low in comparison with what others get for similar work in other companies.<br>I'm paid fairly compared with other employees in this company. |
| Promotion and advancement | 4 | My opportunities for advancement are limited.<br>I have a good chance for promotion. |
| Customers | 4 | My customers are loyal.<br>My customers are trustworthy. |

## Using Job Satisfaction Information

INDSALES provides extremely useful evaluative and diagnostic information. Because sales managers can evaluate the degree of salesperson satisfaction with specific aspects of the sales job, areas in which satisfaction is low can be investigated further by looking at the individual questions for that dimension. For example, if salespeople tended to express dissatisfaction with the supervision they were receiving, management could investigate the answers to the specific questions designed to evaluate the supervision dimension (see Exhibit 10.20). The sales manager in this example might find that most salespeople responded negatively to the statement, "My sales manager really tries to get our ideas about things." The sales manager could then try to increase salesperson satisfaction by using a more participative management style and trying to incorporate salesperson input into the decision-making process.

One useful approach is to perform separate analyses of salesperson satisfaction for high-performing and low-performing salespeople. Research results suggest that there may be important differences in job satisfaction between high performers and low performers. Not incorporating these differences could lead sales managers to make changes that would tend to reduce the turnover of low performers but not of high performers.[81]

Research has also found an important relationship between salesperson satisfaction and performance feedback. Interestingly, negative output feedback does not lower satisfaction with supervisors, whereas negative behavioral feedback appears to improve satisfaction marginally.[82] This suggests salespeople are open to feedback that helps improve their sales performance. Further support for this finding comes from studies showing that sales managers' leadership and role modeling behaviors positively affect salespeople's job satisfaction.[83] One of the studies, involving 25,000 employees (2,000 of whom were sales professionals), found that 69 percent of employee job satisfaction stems from the leadership skills of managers. The study suggests a sales manager can become a great leader by doing many of the activities involved in performance appraisal: providing feedback on what salespeople need to improve; offering recognition and rewards in a manner that acknowledges individuals and teams; and helping and supporting salespeople in developing their talents and careers.[84] Carefully evaluating salesperson performance and satisfaction, identifying problem areas, and solving these problems is really what sales management is all about.

## SUMMARY

1. **Discuss the different purposes of salesperson performance evaluations**. Performance evaluations can serve many different purposes and should be designed with specific purposes in mind. They may serve to determine appropriate compensation and other reward disbursements, to identify salespeople who should be promoted or fired, to determine training and counseling needs, to provide information for human resource planning to identify criteria for future recruitment and selection of salespeople, to advise salespeople of work expectations, to motivate salespeople, to help salespeople set career goals, to tie indivdual performance to sales organization goals, to enhance communications, and to ultimately improve salesperson performance.

2. **Differentiate between an outcome-based and a behavior-based perspective for evaluating and controlling salesperson performance**. An outcome-based perspective focuses on objective measures of results, with little monitoring or direction of salesperson efforts by sales managers. By contrast, a behavior-based perspective focuses on close supervision of salesperson efforts and subjective measures of salesperson characteristics, activities, and strategies. The perspective taken by a sales organization will affect salespeople and has important implications for sales management.

3. **Describe the different types of criteria necessary for comprehensive evaluations of salesperson performance**. The multifaceted nature of sales jobs requires that performance evaluations incorporate multiple criteria. Although the specific criteria depend on the characteristics of a particular selling situation, comprehensive evaluations of salesperson performance require that four dimensions be addressed: behavioral, professional development, results, and profitability criteria. Addressing each of these areas is necessary to get a complete picture of salesperson performance and to produce the diagnostic information needed to improve future performance.

4. **Compare the advantages and disadvantages of different methods of salesperson performance evaluation**. Sales managers can use four basic methods to evaluate salesperson behaviors, professional development, results, and profitability: graphic rating/checklist methods, ranking methods, objective-setting methods, and behaviorally anchored rating scales (BARS). Each method has certain strengths and weaknesses that must be understood and can be compensated for by using other methods in combination. Special attention should be directed toward developing performance benchmarks or quotas that reflect the unique characteristics of each territory.

5. **Explain how salesperson performance information can be used to identify problems, determine their causes, and suggest sales management actions to solve them**. The suggested approach is to first identify areas of poor performance, then work backward to try to identify the cause by asking, "What factors affect the achievement of this performance dimension?" Finally, the most effective sales management action to remove the cause of the problem and improve future performance must be determined. Examples of possible actions are given in Exhibit 10.19.

6. **Discuss the measurement and importance of salesperson job satisfaction**. Dissatisfied salespeople tend to be absent more, leave the firm more, and work less hard than satisfied salespeople. The INDSALES scale can be used to measure salesperson satisfaction in total and for specific job dimensions. Analysis of the satisfaction with individual job dimensions can be used to determine appropriate action to increase salesperson job satisfaction.

## UNDERSTANDING SALES MANAGEMENT TERMS

| | |
|---|---|
| 360-degree feedback | sales quota |
| performance management | profitability criteria |
| total quality management (TQM) | graphic rating/checklist methods |
| outcome-based perspective | ranking methods |
| behavior-based perspective | management by objectives (MBO) |
| behavioral criteria | behaviorally anchored rating scales (BARS) |
| professional development criteria | outcome bias |
| results criteria | job satisfaction |

## DEVELOPING SALES MANAGEMENT KNOWLEDGE

1. Discuss the different purposes of an evaluation of salesperson performance and how each purpose affects the performance evaluation process.

2. Characterize the salesforce of a firm that uses an outcome-based perspective for evaluating salespeople.

3. Why should sales managers pay more attention to behavioral criteria when evaluating salespeople?

4. Compare and contrast the graphic rating/checklist and ranking methods for evaluating salesperson performance.

5. Refer to "Sales Management in the 21st Century: Performance Criteria at KV Pharmaceutical Company (ETHEX Division)." Discuss the types of performance criteria KV uses and how these drive relationship development.

6. Discuss the importance of using different types of quotas in evaluating and controlling salesperson performance.

7. What is unique about the BARS method for evaluating salesperson performance?

8. Refer to "Sales Management in the 21st Century: Using Performance Evaluations to Improve Performance at Allied Office Products." Identify the outcomes and behaviors assessed when evaluating performance at Allied Office Products.

9. Why should sales managers be concerned with the job satisfaction of salespeople?

10. How can evaluations of salesperson performance and satisfaction be used by sales managers?

## BUILDING SALES MANAGEMENT SKILLS

1. Develop a method that can be used to evaluate salespeople's performance in the following areas: communication skills, attitude, initiative and aggressiveness, appearance and manner, knowledge of competition, enthusiasm, cooperation, and time management. Explain any advantages and/or disadvantages associated with your measurement method.

2. Using the following scale (1 to 5, with 1 = "strongly disagree" and 5 = "strongly agree") and the statements in Exhibit 10.20, interview three salespeople and determine the level of job satisfaction of each. Explain areas of dissatisfaction and offer suggestions for improving satisfaction.

3. Following is an evaluation of salesperson Sally from the XYZ Corporation that was filled out by her sales manager. The company requires all its sales managers to use this form when evaluating salespeople.

The following scale was used: Almost Never    1   2   3   4   5    Almost Always

**Sally's Score**

Asks customers for their ideas for promoting business . . . . . . . . . . . . . . . . 2
Offers customers help in solving their problems . . . . . . . . . . . . . . . . . . . 1
Is constantly smiling when interacting with customers . . . . . . . . . . . . . 4
Admits when she does not know the answer, but promises to find out . . . . 4
Generates new ways of tackling new or ongoing problems . . . . . . . . . . . . 1
Returns customers' calls the same day . . . . . . . . . . . . . . . . . . . . . . . . . 2
Retains her composure in front of customers . . . . . . . . . . . . . . . . . . . . 5
Delivers what she promises on time . . . . . . . . . . . . . . . . . . . . . . . . . . . 1
Remains positive about company in front of customers . . . . . . . . . . . . . 5
Knows the design and specification of company products . . . . . . . . . . . . 4
Knows the applications and functions of company products . . . . . . . . . . 2
Submits reports on time . . . . . . . . . . . . . . . . . . . . . . . . . . . . . . . . . . . 2
Maintains company specified records that are accurate and complete . . . . . 2
Uses expense accounts with integrity . . . . . . . . . . . . . . . . . . . . . . . . . . 3
Uses business gift and promotional allowances responsibly . . . . . . . . . . . 3
Controls costs in other areas of the company (order processing
    and preparation, delivery, etc.) when taking sales orders . . . . . . . . . . . . 3

Identify any problems that you see with Sally and make suggestions for improving her performance. In your analysis, be sure to consider the reasons why Sally may be doing a poor job in some of these areas. How could information like this be used to improve the performance of the sales organization?

4. **Situation:**    Look at the evaluation of Sally from question 3. Identify problems you see with Sally.

    **Characters:**    Brandon, sales manager; Sally, salesperson

    **Scene:**    *Location*—Brandon's office. *Action*—Brandon is discussing Sally's performance evaluation with her. He makes suggestions for improvements. Sally does not take the suggestions well. She becomes upset. She believes that Brandon is biased against her because she is a woman and lets him know this in no uncertain terms. In fact, she threatens to bring a lawsuit against him.

**ROLE PLAY**

5. **Situation:**    Read the Ethical Dilemma on page 293.

    **Characters:**    Ralph, district sales manager; Lisa, district sales manager Ralph's boss

    **Scene:**    *Location*—Ralph's office. *Action*—Lisa is paying a visit to Ralph to solicit his thoughts about Ann Anderson. She is very excited about Ann and makes suggestions about how she might be evaluated. Ralph discusses his thoughts about Ann and suggests who he thinks would make a good candidate for the sales management position opening up next month.

**ROLE PLAY**

6. Use the Internet to search for two performance evaluation software packages. You may want to type "performance evaluation software" or "performance appraisal software" into a search engine such as Google.com. Provide the name of the software package and the company that provides it. Then, list the pros and cons of using each software package to help sales managers evaluate salespeople. Finally, of the two software packages you evaluated, if you were a sales manager, which would you choose to use and why?

# MAKING SALES MANAGEMENT DECISIONS

## Case 10.1: Labels Express

### Background

Sally Stickum has just completed her first year as a district sales manager for Labels Express, a manufacturer and marketer of a wide variety of labels. Before joining Labels Express, Sally was a salesperson for one of Labels' competitors. She was hired partly because of her philosophy on personal selling.

Sally's philosophy on personal selling is simple and consists of three premises. First, to succeed in sales requires the proper attitude. A salesperson should have a positive, forward-looking, nondefeatist, cooperative attitude. Second, a salesperson should be aggressive and show initiative. According to Sally, "Things don't happen until you make them happen." Third, although salespeople should be aggressive, at no time should their behavior be unethical. It is Sally's opinion that honest and ethical behavior leads to long-term, trusting relationships.

### Current Situation

Sally is now in the process of a year-end review. When the year began, she met with each salesperson to explain the criteria on which their performance would be judged. Several quotas were determined for each salesperson, including a sales dollar quota, new account quota, and sales call quota. The relative importance of each was determined by the following weight system: 4 for new accounts, 3 for sales, and 2 for sales calls, with 4 being weighted the highest. Salespeople were also told that their performance would be judged by the number of customer complaints received and by the extent to which they submitted required reports. Finally, salespeople would be judged on their ability to meet customer needs. This includes salespeople's ability to suggest ideas for promoting business, helping customers solve problems, finding answers to customer questions not readily known, returning customers' calls, and delivering what is promised.

Sally had heard about a performance appraisal process dubbed 360-degree feedback that involved getting feedback from multiple sources. She thought that this would be a great way to evaluate her salespeople and decided to implement her plan for using it. She decided that she would have each salesperson give a questionnaire to a customer, a team member, and a member of customer service (with whom salespeople worked very closely) to have them evaluate that salesperson's performance. Each questionnaire contained the following questions: (1) How often did you have contact with this salesperson over the course of the year? (2) Were you able to work closely with this salesperson to satisfy your needs? (3) Overall, how would you evaluate this salesperson's performance? (4) How satisfied are you with this salesperson? The questionnaire was to be signed by the respondent and returned to the salesperson who would submit it to Sally for review. Sally decided that if she saw something that she did not like in the feedback, she would discuss it with the salesperson. Sally thought that evaluating quota achievement would be a fairly straightforward process and that she could easily determine discrepancies and make salespeople aware of their shortcomings.

### Questions

1. Assess Sally's use of 360-degree feedback for performance appraisal. Can you make any suggestions for improving this process?
2. What do you think about the type of feedback Sally is willing to provide her salespeople? How do you suggest performance feedback be handled?
3. What can Sally do to ensure that her salespeople make efforts to improve their performance in the areas she deems important?

**ROLE PLAY**

| | |
|---|---|
| **Situation:** | Read Case 10.1. |
| **Characters:** | Sally Stickum, district sales manager; Nick Pallardy, regional sales manager |
| **Scene:** | *Location*—Nick Pallardy's office. *Action*—Nick is meeting with Sally to review how things have been going for her during her first year. Sally explains her performance review process to Nick. Nick makes some suggestions for improving her appraisal methods and performance feedback. |

## Case 10.2: Oakmaster Furniture Inc.

### Background

Oakmaster Furniture Inc. produces several lines of oak furniture, ranging from traditional to contemporary. The firm has been in business for more than 20 years, serving primarily the western half of the United States. Headquartered in Portland, Oregon, the company employs 360 salespeople. Its salesforce consists of three regions, with four districts in each region. There are three regional sales managers and 12 district sales managers.

About one year ago, Roger Acorn was promoted to district sales manager at Oakmaster. He had been a salesperson with a competing firm for five years before joining the company two years ago. Roger was dissatisfied with the work environment at his previous employer, so when he arrived at Oakmaster, he was eager to take on new challenges with a company he viewed as progressive.

## Current Situation

As Roger reflected on his first year as district sales manager, he was concerned. His district had experienced higher-than-expected turnover among his salesforce during the year, and he was puzzled. In his opinion, Oakmaster offered excellent pay and benefits, a cooperative work environment, a challenging and rewarding job, strong company support, and opportunity for promotion.

Although Roger was very satisfied at Oakmaster, he began to believe that his salespeople might not be as happy. As a salesperson, he had noticed that dissatisfied colleagues' job performance often suffered. However, his salespeople's performance on the whole was not significantly down. Like many salesforces, his salespeople's performances ranged from less than average to outstanding. Nevertheless, he knew the importance of being satisfied. It was job dissatisfaction that led to his departure from his previous job.

In an attempt to measure the level of job satisfaction among his salespeople, Roger administered INDSALES to his salesforce. When the results were tabulated, he was surprised to find several areas in which salespeople expressed dissatisfaction. Salespeople seemed to be dissatisfied with their pay, thinking that it was low in comparison with what others were getting for similar work in other companies. Much to his dismay, Roger's salespeople seemed to be dissatisfied with him. They thought that he did not attempt to solicit their ideas about things and did not live up to his promises. Salespeople also expressed their dissatisfaction with the promotion policy, believing that it was unfair. They did not think that promotion was based on ability.

Although Roger was satisfied with the company's training program, his salespeople were not. Finally, salespeople did not believe they were receiving adequate support from the home office. Although Roger was surprised and disappointed at the level of dissatisfaction among his salespeople, he was glad he took steps to analyze their job satisfaction. He was eager to take steps to bring about greater satisfaction. Roger decided to draw up plans for improving satisfaction and present them to his boss at their meeting scheduled for next week.

## Questions

1. What steps can Roger take to increase the level of satisfaction among his salespeople?
2. Rather than examining overall salesforce job satisfaction, what might be a more useful approach to examining salesforce job satisfaction with INDSALES?
3. What do you perceive the relationship to be between job satisfaction and turnover at Oakmaster?

**ROLE PLAY**

| | |
|---|---|
| **Situation:** | Read Case 10.2. |
| **Characters:** | Roger Acorn, district sales manager; Ben Bark, Roger's boss; Glenda Leaf, member of Roger's salesforce |
| **Scene 1:** | *Location*—Ben's office. *Action*—Roger explains to Ben his plans for improving satisfaction amongst his salespeople. Ben provides his reaction, including his assessment of Roger's method for determining salesforce job satisfaction. |
| **Scene 2:** | *Location*—in the car in route to a sales call. *Action*—Roger is accompanying one of his salespeople, Glenda Leaf, on a sales call. He asks Glenda why his salespeople think he does a poor job soliciting their ideas and following through on promises and how she thinks he could improve in these areas. Glenda provides her thoughts and ideas. |

# CASES

## SMITH & NEPHEW—INNOVEX

At the beginning of March 2000, James Brown, CEO of Smith & Nephew, S.A. (S&N), was in a meeting with Josep Serra, Director of the Medical Division.

Almost six months earlier, on September 29, 1999, they had signed an agency contract with Innovex whereby Innovex employees would promote S&N's moist wound healing (MWH) products Allevyn®, Intrasite® Gel, and Opsite®[1] to primary care centres[2] in Galicia and Asturias (see map in Exhibit 8). It was the first time S&N had used the services of a contract or outsourced sales force in Spain.

Among other things, the contract specified that the agreement would expire on March 29, 2000.

Brown and Serra had to assess the results of their collaboration with Innovex and decide not only what to do in Galicia and Asturias but also, more generally, what their policy should be with respect to the sales personnel who promoted the company's MWH products in the rest of Spain.

### Smith & Nephew, S.A. (S&N)

Smith & Nephew, S.A. (S&N) was the Spanish subsidiary of the Smith & Nephew group (for information on the group, see Exhibit 1).

Founded in Spain in 1963, S&N sold in Spain the healthcare products manufactured by the Smith & Nephew group in various countries, mainly the United Kingdom and the United States, though it also imported products from France, Germany and South Africa, among others.

With annual sales of more than 4,000 million pesetas, the Spanish subsidiary had two commercial divisions: a medical division, and a surgical division. Between them these two sold all of the group's product ranges and families except consumer healthcare products, which were sold almost exclusively in the United Kingdom and some former Commonwealth countries. The company also had an administrative and finance division.

At the beginning of the year 2000, James Brown had been with the Smith & Nephew group for 18 years. He had been appointed CEO of the Spanish subsidiary in 1993. He reported to the Managing Director for Continental Europe, who was responsible for various countries in the north and south of continental Europe. The Managing Director for Continental Europe, in turn, reported to the Group Commercial Director, who was a member of the Group Executive Committee, along with the chief executive, the three presidents of the group's Global Business Units, and other senior executives.

The Spanish subsidiary had been the official supplier of certain healthcare products during the 1992 Barcelona Olympics. It had had ISO 9002 certification for several years and had almost finished computerising its entire sales network.

Since November 1998 S&N had been using the services of a specialized shipping and logistics company, which, under contract, took care of the reception of imported goods, storage, stock control, order preparation, and transport and delivery to the customer's address. Given its small workforce of fewer than 100 people, S&N also outsourced certain other services, such as payroll administration and Social Security paperwork, legal and tax advice, design and execution of advertising materials, organization of sales conventions, etc.

And yet the company had an uneven profit record, and its management faced certain challenges. For example, throughout 1998 and 1999 the pound sterling had steadily appreciated against the peseta, giving rise to a steady increase in the peseta cost of the products sold in Spain, most of which were imported from the United States and the United Kingdom.

Selling prices in the Spanish market for healthcare products were significantly lower than in other European countries. Also, in Spain it was more difficult to raise prices because the Social Security Administration often did its purchasing by a system of open bidding, and because other competitors were less affected by the strength of the dollar and sterling.

### Commercialization of healthcare products in Spain

According to EC directives, before a healthcare product could be commercialized, it first had to obtain the "CE marking" from an authorized body in any EU member country. In addition to this, in Spain the company commercializing the product had to submit, generally to the Ministry of Health or the regional government, a "market

---

Case of the Research Department at IESE.
Prepared by Professor Lluis G. Renart. May 2000.
It is intended to be used as a basis for class discussion rather than to illustrate either effective or ineffective handling of an administrative situation.

introduction report." Once these requirements had been met, the product could be marketed and sold.

However, given the way Social Security operated in Spain, the second key requirement for a product to achieve widespread use was for the product to gain approval from the Social Security Administration as a reimbursable product. Reimbursable products were identified by what was known as the *cupón precinto* or "Social Security coupon."[3] As is explained in greater detail later on, obtaining reimbursable status as certified by the Social Security coupon was critical for sales of a particular product through pharmacies, though not strictly necessary for its use in hospitals.

The Social Security coupon was a rectangle printed on the packaging of each unit of product, with perforated edges to allow it to be detached. On it were printed the initials A.S.S.S. ("Social Security healthcare"), the commercial name of the product, certain data about the product and manufacturer, and the price.

### Healthcare products sold in pharmacies

In the case of drugs and healthcare products sold in pharmacies, patients covered by Social Security had to obtain a prescription from their Social Security physician, who would usually have her office in a primary care centre. They could then take the prescription to any pharmacy to obtain the medicine. At the time of purchase, the patient would have to pay 40 percent of the retail price (except for pensioners and the chronically ill, for whom prescriptions were completely free). Before handing over the product, the pharmacist would cut out the Social Security coupon and staple it to the prescription, so as later to be able to obtain reimbursement of the remaining 60 percent (or 100 percent if sold to a pensioner or chronic patient) from the Social Security Administration.

If a drug or healthcare product was authorized for sale but did not have the Social Security coupon, a patient could still apply to the Social Security Administration's own medical inspection service for reimbursement as an exceptional case, but this was a very laborious procedure with no guarantee of success. The alternative was to pay the full 100 percent of the retail price. In either case use of the product was seriously inhibited, above all if there were alternative healthcare products on the market that had similar therapeutic qualities and were reimbursable.

Given the pressure to contain health spending in the Spanish state budget, it was quite possible for a more modern and more efficient yet more expensive drug or healthcare product not to obtain Social Security approval because an alternative product was available which, while not so advanced from a therapeutic point of view and possibly less efficient, could cover the same need.

### Healthcare products used in hospitals and primary care centres

In hospitals, whether a healthcare product was reimbursable or not had no direct impact on sales (though it did affect them indirectly, as we shall see later). Private hospitals and clinics purchased healthcare products in the normal way, paying the price freely agreed with the manufacturer or distributor.

Hospitals and primary care centres belonging to the Social Security Administration, in contrast, used a system of procurement by public bidding. Usually, an individual hospital or primary care centre, or all of the hospitals and primary care centres in a particular geographical area, would issue an invitation to tender once a year, specifying the quantity and characteristics of the products they wanted to purchase. All of this would be set out in a bidding document, which would also specify the information and other things required of prospective bidders, the bid closing date, the selection criteria, etc.

### Healthcare products for ulcer and wound care

Traditionally, the main wound care products were elastic adhesive bandages, gauzes, and the classic dressings. These constituted what was known as the wet-to-dry method. In the year 2000, wet-to-dry dressings were still commonly used in the management of acute wounds, where it was possible to predict the duration of the healing process. They were products with a low unit value, and so whether they were reimbursable or not was practically irrelevant, as hardly anybody went to the doctor to get a prescription for a roll of plaster.

From the early 80s onward, however, a new method, known as moist wound healing, began to be adopted in the treatment of chronic ulcers.[4] It was found that wounds healed more quickly if they were kept moist and protected from infection, allowing the passage of moisture vapour and maintaining the physiological temperature.

Over the years a variety of products for moist wound healing (MWH) came onto the market, such as polyurethane dressings, hydrocolloids, alginates, hydrocellular dressings, and carbon moist wound dressings.

In Spain, in 1999, the total market for MWH products was worth around 3,200 million pesetas at manufacturer's prices. Of this total, around 1,870 million was sold through pharmacies and around 1,300 to hospitals and clinics. A large proportion of the total MWH market consisted of hydrocolloids.

The main competitors in the MWH product category were C.S. (with a market share of around

35 percent), Danplast (22 percent), and Smith & Nephew (9 percent).[5]

## The medical division of Smith & Nephew, S.A. (S&N)

Under the overall management of Josep Serra, the medical division's sales and marketing activities were carried out by a sales team and a marketing team. In 1999 the division had total sales in the region of 3,000 million pesetas, shared between three product families: wound care (1,000 million); casting and bandaging; and orthosis, rehabilitation and aids for everyday living (2,000 million between these last two families).

Of the 1,000 million pesetas in wound care, around 600 million were wet-to-dry and around 400 million, moist wound healing (MWH) products.

At the beginning of the year 2000, S&N competed in only three categories of MWH products (in various sizes and varieties):

- Intrasite® Gel, a cleansing hydrogel that regenerated the ulcer, debriding and absorptive, sold in packs of five 15g units (see Exhibit 5). It had the Social Security coupon. In 1999, S&N had sold 130 million pesetas of the product and had a market share in this subcategory in the order of 40 percent of sales through pharmacies.

- The Allevyn® range, a controlled absorption hydrocellular dressing (see Exhibit 6). Three sizes of the range had the Social Security coupon. In 1999, S&N had sold 170 million pesetas of the product and had a market share in this subcategory in the order of 50 percent of sales through pharmacies.

- The Opsite® range, a transparent polyurethane dressing (see Exhibit 7). Six sizes of the range had the Social Security coupon. In 1999, S&N had sold 100 million pesetas of the product and had a market share in this subcategory in the order of 90 percent of sales through pharmacies.

These products had various technical advantages that made the healing of an ulcer or wound faster, safer, and less painful.

However, the correct prescription, use and application of MWH products required certain knowledge that only doctors and nurses were likely to have. This meant that patients and their relatives very rarely influenced the type of product used.

Nevertheless, a significant volume of MWH products was sold through pharmacies. It was true that it was always a doctor who prescribed the use of a particular product. But, often, a relative of a housebound chronically ill patient would go to the pharmacy, obtain the product free of charge, and then give it to the nurse who, in the course of a home visit, would apply the dressing.

The management of S&N's medical division estimated that slightly over 50 percent of their MWH products were sold through pharmacies.

Almost all the remainder, just under 50 percent, was used in hospitals and primary care centres belonging to the Social Security Administration.

## S&N medical division's sales and promotional activities

The division's *sales* efforts, strictly speaking (i.e., activities undertaken to generate orders and invoices), were conducted in three channels:

1. Sales to Social Security hospitals and primary care centres were made by bidding in yearly auctions.[6] Products that won a contract would be supplied and billed over the course of the year, and were used either in the hospital or primary care centre itself, or during home visits.

2. Sales to pharmacies were accomplished through pharmaceutical wholesalers or cooperatives, which replenished their stocks at regular intervals without S&N having to make hardly any effort to sell to them.

3. Lastly, the medical division's own sales representatives sold directly to private hospitals and large private clinics, or indirectly, through healthcare product wholesalers/distributors, to other private hospitals and clinics, geriatric homes, and the private practices of doctors and vets.

The division's *promotional* efforts were targeted at doctors and, above all, nurses. The aim was to bring the products to their attention, explain their advantages and how to use them, give the doctors and nurses an opportunity to try them out, and explain to them the differential therapeutic advantages of the company's products compared with older or competing alternatives.

When dealing with healthcare professionals working in the public health system, the sales representatives' mission was also to persuade doctors and nurses to issue favourable reports on S&N's products.

Lastly, an important goal of the promotional effort was to ensure, once a contract had been won and the S&N product was in use in a given healthcare facility, that the product was always at hand for any doctor or nurse who needed it.

As Josep Serra remarked:

> It's a major training and "merchandising" challenge seeing to it that the products we sell are available on every floor, in every consulting room, on every trolley, and that they are used correctly.

### Promotional tasks carried out in the field by the medical division's own sales representatives

The national sales manager supervised two regional sales managers. Between them the two regional sales managers had 18 sales representatives and three commission agents, who did all the sales and promotional work for all the division's products.

This sales team's coverage of the Spanish market as a whole was considered poor, particularly compared with the division's main competitors. It was estimated that it covered almost 100 percent of the hospitals but only 20 percent of the primary care centres. In contrast, Danplast, S.A. was thought to have around 50 sales representatives, and another major competitor, C.S., S.A., more than 40.

S&N's marketing manager estimated that to be able to provide a satisfactory level of promotional and sales service for the medical division's products throughout Spain, they would need about 40 sales representatives. Without that number it would be impossible to visit all the primary care centres.

One of the division's sales representatives nominally covered the area of Galicia. But given the size of the region,[7] in practice he only ever had time to visit hospitals and clinics and healthcare product wholesalers.

In 1999 the medical division's full-time sales representatives had sold an average of 150 million pesetas each, at an average cost per representative of 8.5 million pesetas, including salary, incentives, Social Security, vacations, travelling expenses, etc.

The division's three remaining commission agents (previously it had had five or six of them) had between them sold 150 million pesetas. The agent for the region of Extremadura was a company that had been working with S&N for about eight years. The other two agents were individuals. One covered the islands of Majorca and Ibiza, selling only S&N products. The other covered the island of Menorca, offering a very wide range of products by different companies, exclusively to hospitals. Both had been working with S&N for around 20 years, and in both cases the relationship was considered stable.

The commission agents had agency contracts. They visited only hospitals, that is to say, they did not promote the products to primary care centres. According to Serra, "They go for the guaranteed sales, what I mean is, they try to sell the products for which there's already a demand. They don't make much effort to introduce new products. They're undoubtedly more profitable than having full-time representatives of our own in those territories. That would be too expensive, in the case of Extremadura because its so extensive, and in the other cases because they're islands."

When they made a sale without going through a bidding process, the commission agents would close the deal and pass the order on to S&N, which would serve the goods, invoice the customers, and collect payment. The commission agents were only responsible for collecting debts from private (non-public) customers, and earned a commission of between 7 percent and 10 percent. When there was an auction, the commission agents would gather the necessary information, so that S&N executives could prepare the documentation and put in a bid.

### Other promotional activities carried out by the marketing department: advertising, seminars, "study days"

In addition to the sales and promotional activities carried out by the medical division's sales team, the marketing department, consisting of a marketing manager and two product managers, carried out a number of complementary activities.

These consisted mainly of:

- Advertising the division's products through inserts in medical journals and through special brochures.

- Attending nursing conferences organized by the professional associations of nurses for particular medical specialities. For example, in 1999 S&N had attended four conferences, including one in Bilbao on gerontological nursing. Attending a medium-sized conference could cost S&N around 3 million pesetas. A conference could be attended and sponsored by some 15–20 companies.

- Study days: These were meetings, organized entirely by S&N and generally held in a hotel, with a specific scientific interest provided by a guest speaker. Following the guest speaker's lecture, an S&N product manager would present the company's products for the application in question. The meeting would end with a colloquium and aperitifs.

In 1999, 23 study days had been held, each of which had been attended by around 65 specially invited nurses. The average cost per study day had been around 300,000 pesetas. To make the most of these occasions, it was vital to carry out close personal follow-up.

### Social Security approval for the Allevyn® range and first contacts with Innovex

Up until April 1998, only two of Smith & Nephew, S.A.'s MWH products had the Social Security coupon and were therefore reimbursable: Intrasite® Gel and Opsite®. In fact, hardly any other medical division product had the coupon.

In April 1998, after a long wait, S&N's Allevyn® product was finally granted the right to carry the prized coupon. This was an important development, as Allevyn® was potentially a similarly priced but functionally superior substitute for hydrocolloids, which accounted for a large proportion of the total market for MWH products.

Allevyn® was already sold by bidding to hospitals and primary care centres. Now, with the Social Security coupon, it seemed set to achieve a significant volume of sales through the pharmacy channel. With sales potential to hospitals and primary care centres currently in the order of 1,100 million pesetas, its potential market could therefore be considered to be augmented by a further 1,600 million or so, in the pharmacy channel, despite the fact that only some of the sizes in which the product was sold were reimbursable by Social Security.

As we said earlier, in order to bid in Social Security procurement auctions, a product did not have to be reimbursable. However, doctors and nurses preferred, when starting treatment of a wound or ulcer in hospital, to use products that *were* reimbursable because that made it much easier for the patient to continue the treatment at home, using the same products as in hospital.

Conversely, if a particular product was *not* reimbursable, doctors and nurses were sometimes reluctant to use it, even in hospital, so as not to have to change the patient's prescription on discharge and prescribe a different product that *was* reimbursable and would therefore be free of charge for the patient.

### First fruitless contact with Innovex

In March 1998, with approval of Allevyn® now imminent, the medical division's top executives contacted Innovex, an international company already established in Spain that specialized in providing contract sales teams for the pharmaceutical and medical devices industry (see Exhibit 2 for information on Quintiles Transnational Corporation and its Innovex division).

They were keen to explore the possibility of contracting a team of Innovex sales representatives to reinforce the efforts being made by the medical division's own sales team to promote its MWH products to primary care centres.

Smith & Nephew's Spanish subsidiary had never worked with Innovex previously, nor with any other company that offered this kind of contract sales services. But they knew that it was a fairly common practice among their competitors in the healthcare industry, particularly when launching new products onto the market.

Also, colleagues in the group's United Kingdom offices confirmed that they had worked with Innovex and thought highly of the company. One or two other companies that provided services similar to those of Innovex were contacted for the purpose of comparison.

In the end, however, the idea of working with Innovex was dropped for fear that the necessary level of sales and profitability might not be attained.

### Developments in the period April 1998 to February 1999

Between April and June 1998, sales of Allevyn® rose sharply, only to flatten out again in the following months.

By February 1999, the management of the medical division were concerned that if they did not take decisive action, Allevyn® was in danger of being sidelined, with a share of only 2 or 3 percent of the total MWH market in Spain.

In this situation, they decided that the only course of action was, on the one hand, to intensify and extend the promotional activities aimed at customers already covered by the company's sales team; and on the other, to achieve fuller coverage of primary care centres in the underserved regions of Valencia, Andalusia, Galicia, and Asturias.

The medical division's managers were in a tight spot: there seemed to be a potentially profitable opportunity to promote Allevyn® to primary care centres, but CEO James Brown and his superiors would be reluctant to add to the company's workforce.

### Steps towards an agreement with Innovex

In March 1999 the management of S&N's medical division got back in touch with Innovex to explore the feasibility of contracting a team of medical sales representatives to promote the products of the Opsite®, Intrasite® Gel, and Allevyn® ranges in the regions of Spain hitherto least well covered by the company's own sales staff and commission agents.

In all, they considered the possibility of contracting from Innovex a team of 10 sales representatives and an area manager to serve Galicia [3], Asturias [1], Andalusia [3], and Valencia [3].

Ideally, S&N's management would have preferred to contract a sales team that would devote only 50 percent of its time to promoting S&N's products.

Unfortunately, at that time they were unable to find any other company in the healthcare sector that needed Innovex sales representatives working half-time for precisely the hours that would fit in with S&N's requirements, in the same geographical areas and for the six-month period S&N envisaged.

It was therefore agreed that the sales team contracted from Innovex should devote 100 percent of its time to promoting S&N's MWH products to primary care centres.

In view of the cost this would represent, S&N's management asked Innovex to submit a formal offer for the provision of just two sales representatives to promote S&N's MWH products to primary care centres in Galicia and Asturias. At that time, Arturo, the company's only sales representative in Galicia, only had time to visit the region's hospitals, so the primary care centres were more or less neglected.

If Innovex's offer was accepted, it would be very much an experiment. After six months, they would decide whether the system should be extended to other areas of Spain where the primary care centres were also relatively poorly served, such as Valencia and Andalusia.

S&N's management chose to conduct the trial in Galicia and Asturias because, of all the poorly covered areas, Galicia was the most suitable.

On July 2, 1999, Jesus Polanco, for Innovex, presented the project to the top managers of S&N's medical division (see Exhibit 4 for a summary of his presentation).

On September 29, 1999, after clarifying and discussing certain details without making any substantial changes, James Brown and Jesus Polanco signed the contract for a term of 6 months, i.e., to March 29, 2000. Besides the operational details, the contract included clauses regulating confidentiality, contract termination in the event of noncompliance by either of the parties, etc.

Lastly, S&N undertook not to hire any of the Innovex employees involved in the project, and agreed to pay Innovex compensation equal to a percentage of the employees' base salary if it did. In the case of the sales representatives, the compensation would be equal to 20 percent of 2.8 million pesetas per sales representative per year.

## Execution of the contract

As soon as the contract was signed, Innovex proceeded to select the two sales representatives. S&N gave its approval to the candidates chosen:

- Isabel, the person selected for Galicia, to be based in Vigo, already had some experience of medical sales visits. The S&N products she would have to promote were already known and used in the region, thanks to the hospital work done by Arturo, the local representative, who lived in Corunna. This meant that the new sales representative would have some local support.

- The person chosen for Asturias, Federico, had little experience but the right profile and plenty of enthusiasm. Asturias had the added disadvantage of having been neglected during the previous two years following the death of S&N's previous sales representative, who had not been replaced. Because of this, in Asturias there had not even been the momentary surge in sales registered in other parts of Spain after Allevyn® got the Social Security coupon; and the products Federico would have to promote were practically unknown in the region.

Both the Innovex sales representatives were given two weeks' training. In the first week they had three days' instruction on the products they would be promoting (given by S&N), and one day on sales techniques (given by Innovex). The second week was given over to on-the-job training, accompanied by one of S&N's regional sales managers.

Following this, towards the middle of October 1999, they took up their posts in their respective sales territories and started to visit customers, using a list of primary care centres provided by Innovex and approved by S&N. The centres were ranked on an ABC basis according to their purchasing potential.

The regional sales manager for the central-northern area of S&N's medical division approved the sales routes proposed by Innovex, and after the first week started to accompany the two new representatives on their rounds.

According to the medical division sales manager, "We treated them as if they were our own employees."

It should be said, however, that about two weeks after Isabel, the representative for Galicia, had taken up her post, the marketing department held two study days in Vigo and Corunna, which had already been scheduled from earlier. This gave Isabel a chance to make contacts much more quickly than she could have done without the study days.

In Galicia, Isabel's promotional activities were concentrated in the provinces of Orense (342,000 inhabitants) and Pontevedra (904,000 inhabitants).

Both sales representatives took about three months to adapt to the normal pace of work.

## Evaluation of the results

At the end of February 2000, the director of S&N's medical division, together with his sales manager and marketing manager, analyzed the results on the basis of the data available at the time.

With regard to costs, the average amount billed by Innovex to S&N had been 810,000 pesetas per sales representative per month.

With regard to sales, they had data from the territorial sales analysis (ATV)[8] for the last quarter of 1999, and internal billing data up to January 2000.

Everybody agreed that the results had been very different in the two areas:

In Galicia:

According to the October-December ATV report, the market share of Allevyn®, Intrasite® Gel, and Opsite®, in pesetas, for the whole of Galicia had increased from 3.3 percent to 6.4 percent of the total value of MWH products sold. In Orense and in Pontevedra, the increase had been from 5.4 percent to 12 percent.

The additional sales revenue (on top of the minimal revenue obtained previously in the region) amounted to around 5,133,000 pesetas in four months (October 1999–January 2000 inclusive).[9] The gross margin had been 1,540,000 pesetas, i.e., 30 percent on average.

In Asturias:

The market share of the three products, in the last quarter of 1999, had increased from 0.9 to 2.36 percent of total sales, in pesetas, of all MWH products sold by all companies in Asturias.

The additional sales revenue amounted to only 1,484,000 pesetas. In four months (October 1999–January 2000 inclusive),[10] with a gross margin of 371,000 pesetas (25 percent).

The difference in gross margin was due to the fact that the sales representative in Asturias had sold more products that had a lower gross margin. S&N's sales representatives did not know the gross margin of the products they sold. Only indirectly, through marketing actions, were they encouraged to sell higher gross margin products. Essentially, the difference in gross margin between Galicia and Asturias could be said to be due to chance factors.

In response to the low sales in Asturias, the regional sales manager felt that Federico would have to improve his sales technique, in particular his closing abilities.

## Sales projection

In view of the actual results achieved, the medical division's marketing manager estimated that, if new Innovex sales representatives were introduced in other geographical areas, each one of them could be expected to generate roughly the following sales:

| | | |
|---|---|---|
| Month 1 | 450,000 | pesetas. |
| Month 2 | 900,000 | " |
| Month 3 | 1,650,000 | " |
| Month 4 | 2,225,000 | " |
| Month 5 | 2,700,000 | " |
| Month 6 | 3,000,000 | " |
| Month 7 onward | 3,000,000 | pesetas each month. |

Assuming a gross margin of 30 percent and average Innovex billing steady at 810,000 pesetas per representative per month, breakeven for a representative would be reached in the fifth month (2,700,000 × 30% = 810,000 pesetas of gross margin).

If these sales and margin forecasts were accurate, from month six onward the company would generate new gross income of 90,000 pesetas per month (gross margin less the amount billed by Innovex).

## Other considerations

The following are comments made by the director of the medical division and his sales and marketing managers, during their meeting, as they analyzed the facts and figures:

- "Innovex gives us a chance to try things out, to start working with new people and new regions, with a controlled level of risk. Then we can

decide whether or not we want to actually hire the people once they've proved they can work profitably."

- "You have to remember that Innovex takes over a whole range of management tasks. During the trial period in Galicia and Asturias all we had to do was approve a bill of 1.6 million pesetas each month. And monitor sales as we wanted. Everything else (payroll, checking the expense sheets, mileage, and so on) was taken care of by Innovex."

- "If the Asturias salesman doesn't perform as well as expected, we can ask Innovex to replace him. And it'll be up to them to carry out the selection, hiring, sales training, etc."

- "Before we replace the salesman, though, we need to be sure it's him who's letting us down, rather than the sales potential of the territory itself, or lack of support on our part."

- "I suspect that Innovex doesn't pay its salespeople very highly. Take our sales representative in Galicia, for example. I'm already starting to worry that one of our competitors will notice our sudden gain of market share, realize that this person is worth her salt, or at least has potential, and offer her a permanent job with better pay."

- "Is it feasible to use Innovex sales representatives in the medium and long term? Or do companies just use them for tactical sales drives that never last more than 6 or 9 months?"

## The decision

Given the results of the trial, Brown and Serra now faced a set of alternatives deriving from the possible combinations of three variables:

a) To use salaried sales representatives or to use contract sales representatives employed by Innovex
b) Level of geographical coverage
c) Timing: when would be the best moment to do one thing or another?

For example, without trying to be exhaustive, the three variables could be combined in different ways to generate at least the following possible courses of action:

1. Terminate the contract with Innovex and leave the areas of Galicia and Asturias as they were before, i.e., with a single representative, Arturo, visiting hospitals.

2. Renew the contract with Innovex for another six months, only for Galicia and Asturias, in order to prolong the trial and so obtain more reliable data on sales trends and to verify whether the sales and financial performance could be consolidated.

3. Terminate the contract with Innovex and proceed immediately to hire:
   a. One salaried sales representative for Galicia.
   b. Two salaried sales representatives, one for Galicia and one for Asturias.
   c. Two or three salaried sales representatives for Galicia and one for Asturias, as in the original plan.

And in the rest of Spain:

4. Sign a new agreement with Innovex to establish contract sales representatives in all or some of the regions currently lacking coverage: Valencia (2 or 3 representatives) and Andalusia (2 or 3 representatives). The contract could be for six months or one year. Following that, introduce own salaried sales representatives in all or some of those regions, depending on the level of sales and profitability attained in each one.

5. Directly hire a certain number of salaried sales representatives for those same underserved regions.

Finally, if they decided to hire new salaried sales representatives, they would have to decide whether it was better for the representatives to work in tandem, as Isabel and Arturo had done in Galicia, i.e., with Arturo visiting mainly hospitals and Isabel visiting primary care centres; or whether it would be better to divide up the territory and for each representative to visit both hospitals and primary care centres in the part of the territory assigned to him or her.

Obviously, for each of these options they would have to weigh up the costs and the benefits, both in strictly financial terms and in terms of sales and marketing strategy.

In this latter respect, CEO James Brown was starting to get excited at the thought of the strategic possibilities that would be opened up if he ever reached the position of having a sales team fully deployed throughout Spain.

At the same time, however, he needed to make sure that the Smith & Nephew group's Spanish subsidiary reported a profit, as he personally desired and as the company's year 2000 budget demanded.

The Smith & Nephew group     **EXHIBIT 1**

This global medical device company, headquartered in London, traced its origins back to 1856, when Thomas James Smith founded a pharmacy in Hull in the United Kingdom.[1]

In 1896, the founder brought his nephew Horatio Nelson Smith into the business as a partner, giving rise to the name Smith & Nephew. The company grew rapidly with the addition of products such as elastic adhesive bandages (Elastoplast), plaster casts (Gypsona), and sanitary towels (Lilia), often through acquisitions.

In 1999, the group reported worldwide sales of 1,120 million pounds sterling,[2] with earnings of 171 million pounds[3] before tax and extraordinary income. In that year the group had activities in 90 countries. Geographically, the sales revenues were distributed as follows: 19 percent in the UK, 20 percent in continental Europe, 43 percent in America, and the remaining 18 percent in Africa, Asia, and Oceania.

The main product ranges or families sold worldwide were: orthopaedics and trauma (mainly hip and knee prostheses, and trauma implants, 26 percent of worldwide sales); endoscopy (particularly knee and shoulder arthroscopy, 18 percent); wound management (e.g., Allevyn®, Opsite®, and Intrasite® Gel, 21 percent); orthosis and rehabilitation, casting and bandaging (bandages and plaster casts), and otology (prostheses and instrumentation for microsurgery of the inner ear) (together, 18 percent); and consumer healthcare (17 percent).

In the 1999 Annual Report, Chris O'Donnell, chief executive, declared:

> We are concentrating our strategic investment on the three markets of orthopaedics [implants and trauma procedures], endoscopy, and wound management.

Each of these three Global Business Units was headed by a president.

In these three specialties, or in some of their subspecialties, the Smith & Nephew group held first or second place in the global ranking. In its three priority business units it expected to grow both organically and through acquisitions, whereas growth in its other businesses would be basically organic.

The group invested 4 percent of its sales revenue in research and development. One of its latest developments, precisely in the Wound Management GBU, was Dermagraft, a dressing of human tissue developed through bioengineering processes, which made it possible to heal certain types of chronic ulcers, such as diabetic foot ulcers, in just a few weeks. Although at the beginning of the year 2000 it was already being sold in some countries, Dermagraft was not yet available in Spain.

To summarize, starting from the British parent company, the group had evolved to the point where it had a broad range of ever more high-tech healthcare products that were sold around the globe.

1. In fact, Thomas Southall had founded a pharmacy in Birmingham as early as 1820, and Southalls (Birmingham) Ltd. had been acquired by Smith & Nephew in 1958. So the roots of the company could be said to stretch back even further, to 1820.
2. Equivalent to approximately 1,800 million dollars or euros, or almost 300,000 million pesetas, at the exchange rates prevailing at the beginning of March 2000. On January 1, 1999, the exchange rate of the peseta had been irrevocably fixed at a rate of 166.386 pesetas per euro. At the beginning of 1999, the euro had traded at 1.18 dollars, but over the year had steadily slipped against the dollar until by the end of February 2000 one euro was practically equal to one dollar. Thus, the peseta was quoted at 166 pesetas per dollar, and 267 pesetas per pound sterling. At the beginning of the year 2000 the pound sterling, the Greek drachma, the Swedish krona, and the Danish krone had not joined the euro.
3. Data about the group are taken from the Smith & Nephew plc "1999 Annual Report and Accounts." For more information, go to <http://www.smith-nephew.com>.

**EXHIBIT 2**     The Quintiles Transnational group and its Innovex division

Innovex Spain, S.L. was the Spanish subsidiary of Innovex Inc., which in turn was a division of Quintiles Transnational Corp. Both had their headquarters in North Carolina, United States.[1]

At the end of 1998 the Quintiles group had more than 18,000 employees in 31 countries and that year reported net revenue of 1,188 million dollars. Of this total, 583 million had been generated in the United States and 340 million in the United Kingdom.

The Quintiles group provided full, outsourced research, sales, marketing, healthcare policy consulting and information management services to pharmaceutical, biotechnology, medical devices and healthcare companies throughout the world.

For example, a pharmaceutical laboratory could turn to the Quintiles group to take care of anything from the basic research needed to synthesize a new molecule or active substance (Phase 1), plus any of the intermediate phases of research and development, clinical trials by physicians and hospitals, data compilation, etc., to the management of the new drug approval and registration process (Phase 4). Then, if it wanted, the laboratory could also hire the Quintiles group to do all the marketing and actually bring the product to market.

Innovex Inc. was a division of the Quintiles group that specialized in sales and marketing services for third parties.

In 1998, Innovex Inc. was present in 19 countries and had more than 7,000 sales representatives, sales managers and marketing directors. In that year its sales teams had made an average of almost two million product presentations per month.

Innovex had been present in Spain since 1996, when it had acquired an existing Spanish company that was already active in the business of providing contract sales teams. Subsequently it had extended, or intended to extend, its services to other areas connected with the commercialization of drugs or medical devices, such as marketing and sales strategy consulting, training, communication, resource optimization, etc.

As Jesus Polanco, CEO of Innovex's Spanish subsidiary, pointed out:

> It's not just a matter of "getting people out knocking on doors." In line with the group's general approach, we aim to create value by carefully managing each sales territory, monitoring the costs and results of our actions, collecting and compiling the valuable commercial information generated in each territory, and so on.

See Exhibit 3 for various examples of Innovex's more recent projects in Spain.

At the end of 1999, Innovex's Spanish subsidiary had a team of 152 people. Of these, 17 belonged to the management team, while the remaining 135 made up the sales force that went out "knocking on doors." Seventy-seven of the sales representatives were full-time Innovex employees, with open-ended contracts, while the remaining 58 had temporary contracts linked to a particular job for a client.

1. Data are taken from Quintiles Transnational Corp.'s "Annual Report 1998." For further details, go to <http://www.corporate.quintiles.com> and <http://www.innovexglobal.com>.

> ### Examples of recent projects carried out by Innovex in Spain in the field of contract sales teams
>
> **EXHIBIT 3**

### Zeneca

Before Zeneca merged with Astra to form Astra-Zeneca, it planned to launch two new products in the same year. To do this, Zeneca's sales force required reinforcement in the form of 65 people hired from Innovex for a period of two years to carry out visits to cardiologists, neurologists, psychiatrists, and general practitioners.

The main goal was rapid market share gain to block the entry of competitors.

However, it would have been too expensive to keep the 65 people on for a second phase focused on maintaining the products' market presence.

### Géminis

Géminis was the new generic pharmaceuticals division of Novartis, which marketed out-of-patent products.

As it was a new division, the company did not want to hire extra sales representatives until they had seen what results the new division was capable of achieving. Note that promoting generics requires a different sales approach, both when selling to doctors and when selling to pharmacies.

The task Innovex undertook between 1998 and 2000 initially required a team of 12 promoters, later expanded to 17.

### Pierre Fabre

Pierre Fabre contracted a team of seven "beautician" promoters from Innovex to persuade and educate pharmacists to recommend, for each individual customer, the most appropriate Klorane® product from among a wide range of shampoos and hair creams.

### Cardionetics

At the beginning of the year 2000, Innovex was preparing to set up a "virtual" company, i.e., using only temporary employees, to commercialize in Spain an innovative portable ECG device for monitoring and diagnosing abnormal heart rhythms as a person went about his normal daily activities.

It would be responsible for all the functional areas involved in commercialization, including, among other activities, the deployment of a contract sales team.

**EXHIBIT 4** Summary of the presentation given on July 2, 1999 by Innovex's Jesús Polanco to the top management of Smith & Nephew, A.A.;s medical division

- The plan was to conduct a trial campaign to promote the products Opsite®, Intrasite® Gel, and Allevyn® in the four provinces of Galicia and in Asturias using a team hired from Innovex, whose target contacts would be nurses. If the trial objectives were achieved, the scheme would be extended to other geographical areas.
- The contract would have a term of six months.
- The team contracted from Innovex would consist of two sales representatives, a project manager, and a clerical assistant. The latter two would devote two days a month to the project. The sales representatives would receive five days' training.
- The sales representatives would devote their efforts exclusively to promoting the above mentioned S&N products.
- The fee per sales representative would be 35,102 pesetas per day actually worked, i.e., neither sick leave nor vacations would be billed.

The daily cost given above would include:

- Salary and Social Security.
- Health insurance and accident and third-party cover.
- Monthly food + travel expenses, including the sales representatives' travelling, parking, and telephone expenses up to a maximum of 80,000 pesetas per person per month.
- Vacations.
- All expenses deriving from the vehicles used by Innovex personnel in providing the contracted services.
- Costs of personnel selection by Innovex (in particular the cost of press adverts, costs associated with the selection interview, and the costs of hiring). Innovex would only select people who matched the profile and culture required by S&N.
- All aspects of payroll and associated costs, company cars, and the telephone expenses of the project manager.
- The costs of the administration department.

The following items were not included in the price per day previously given:

- Incentives for the sales representatives.[1]
- Promotions aimed at doctors and customers.
- Promotional materials, samples, etc., which would have to be provided by S&N.
- Trips and field visits by S&N executives.
- Training costs. S&N would be responsible for all training in products, therapeutic areas, and customers.
- Innovex would be responsible for managing the sales team. The two companies would agree on the kind of reporting and information S&N thought necessary in order to monitor the team's activities.

In an appendix, Jesus Polanco's presentation also described:

- The recommended profile for the sales representatives.
- The selection process.
- The functions of the Innovex project manager, who would liaise between the two companies.
- The responsibilities of Innovex's human resources department.
- The responsibilities of Innovex's finance department.

Finally, the presentation included a page stressing the advantages of using a sales team contracted from Innovex as opposed to a company-employed sales team.

1. In the end no incentives were established.

Intrasite® Gel range    **EXHIBIT 5**

# QUEREMOS PONERTELO FACIL

**1** Retirar el protector azul y limpiar la zona de la boquilla del envase con una gasa antiséptica.

**2** Abrir el envase por el extremo de la boquilla.

**3** Apretar suavemente la base del envase para administrar Intrasite®.

| CODIGO S+N | PRESENTACIONES |
|---|---|
| 66000240 | **IntraSite Gel** 5 Unidades de 15 g* |
| 7311 | **IntraSite Gel** 10 Unidades de 15 g |

\* Reembolsable por la S.S.

\* Denotes product is reimbursable by the Spanish Social Security.

**EXHIBIT 6** Allevyn® range

# Apósitos Hidrocelulares de Absorción Controlada

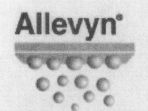

Reembolsables por la Seguridad Social

## Allevyn

| Tamaño | Presentación | C. Nacional |
|---|---|---|
| 10 x 10 cm | 10 Unidades | |
| 10 x 10 cm | 3 Unidades | 483297 * |
| 10 x 20 cm | 10 Unidades | |
| 15 x 15 cm | 10 Unidades | |
| 15 x 15 cm | 3 Unidades | 483305 * |
| 20 x 20 cm | 10 Unidades | |

## Allevyn Adhesive

| Tamaño | Presentación | C. Nacional |
|---|---|---|
| 7,5 x 7,5 cm | 10 Unidades | |
| 12,5 x 12,5 cm | 10 Unidades | |
| 12,5 x 12,5 cm | 3 Unidades | 483313 * |
| 17,5 x 17,5 cm | 10 Unidades | |
| 22,5 x 22,5 cm | 10 Unidades | |

## Allevyn Cavity

| Tamaño | Presentación |
|---|---|
| 5 cm circular | 10 Apósitos |
| 10 cm circular | 5 Apósitos |
| 9 x 2,5 cm | 10 Apósitos |
| 12 x 4 cm | 5 Apósitos |

Reproduction of part of a company brochure.

## Opsite® range

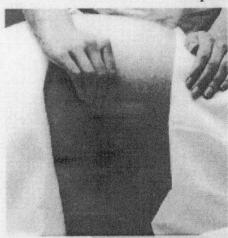

1 Colocación

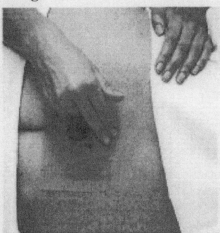

2 Fijación

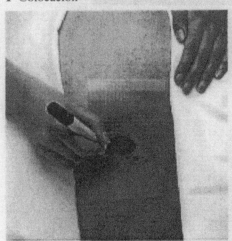

3 Control

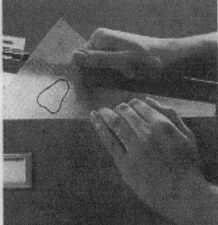

4 Archivo de la lámina cuadriculada

### INDICACIONES

1 Ulceras por decúbito superficiales
2 Prevención de úlceras por decúbito
3 Quemaduras y escaldaduras leves
4 Abrasiones y laceraciones
5 Heridas postoperatorias
6 Protección de la piel periestomal y bajo bolsas de orina de pierna
7 Injertos de piel y zonas donantes
8 Retención de apósitos activos como SCHEROSORBAN*, ALLEVYN*

| PRESENTACIONES | Tamaño Apósito | Presentación | Cod. Nacional |
|---|---|---|---|
| ✳ Reembolsable por la Seguridad Social | 6 cm x 7 cm | 100 apósitos | |
| | 10 cm x 12 cm | 50 apósitos | |
| | 10 cm x 12 cm | 10 apósitos✳ | 471060 |
| | 12 cm x 25 cm | 1 apósito✳ | 477943 |
| | 12 cm x 25 cm | 20 apósitos | |
| | 15 cm x 20 cm | 1 apósito✳ | 477950 |
| | 15 cm x 20 cm | 10 apósitos | |

### MODO DE EMPLEO

La piel debe prepararse de la forma habitual antes de aplicar OPSITE FLEXIGRID, aunque es importante eliminar el exceso de humedad y en caso necesario hay que desengrasar la piel con alcohol. Debe rasurarse cualquier exceso de vello para asegurar una buena adherencia del producto.

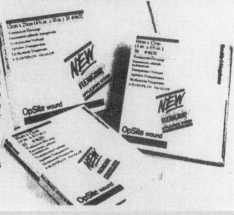

### PRESENTACIÓN

OPSITE FLEXIGRID se presenta en sobres individuales estériles.

* Marca registrada T. J. Smith and Nephew Limited

**EXHIBIT 8** Map of Spain showing autonomous communities

Map of Spain showing autonomous communities

> **Sales representatives' legal status**     **EXHIBIT 9**

### 1. Salaried sales representatives

According to labour legislation in force in Spain in the year 2000, sales representatives who were integrated in a company's workforce had a "labour" contract of employment with that company. In the light of certain court rulings, a worker could be understood to be integrated in a company's workforce when he was unable to organize his professional activity at his own discretion, when his place of work was on the company's premises, and when he was subject to working hours stipulated by the company.

In the event of dismissal, such a sales representative could challenge the company's decision before the labour courts and require them to decide on the "fairness" or "unfairness" of the dismissal. If the dismissal was declared unfair, the company had to pay the worker severance payment or compensation equal to 45 days' salary per year of service up to a maximum of 42 months' salary.

If the company chose to terminate the employment relationship on any of the objective grounds for dismissal specified by the Workers' Statute (Article 52), it had to pay the worker, at the time of notification of termination, compensation equal to 20 days' salary per year of service up to a limit of 12 months' salary. Again in this case, the worker could challenge the dismissal and ask the court to declare it unfair. If in the end the company was unable to demonstrate the existence of objective grounds and the dismissal was declared unfair, the company would have to pay the worker compensation equal to 45 days' salary per year of service up to a maximum of 42 months' salary. Exceptionally, however, if the dismissed worker was hired under the terms of Law 63/1997, which provided for urgent measures to improve the labour market and promote stable employment, the above did not apply. Instead, in such cases, if the dismissal was found to be unfair, the company was obliged to pay compensation equal to 33 days' salary per year of service up to a maximum of 24 months' salary.

### 2. Sales representatives with an agency contract

According to the Agency Contract Law (Law 12/92 of May 27), a company could decide to establish a commercial relationship with a sales agent.

The features that defined a sales agent's commercial relationship with the company were:

- His place of work was not on the company's premises.
- He was not subject to working hours that were set by the company.
- In his professional activities he acted independently and organized his work as he saw fit.
- He could assume the business risk of the activities he performed, but this circumstance was not considered a defining feature of a commercial agency relationship and therefore was not sufficient by itself to prevent the relationship from being declared one of employment.

Any disputes that might arise between the parties in the execution of the commercial agency contract were resolved by the civil courts.

Unless otherwise expressly agreed by the parties, the company was not obliged to pay any compensation upon termination of the contract. Nevertheless, the commercial agent could claim compensation if by his work he had added new customers to the company's customer base. In any case, whether or not this right arose, and in what circumstances, would depend on the specific content of the agreement between the parties.

Given that the relationship was not one of employment, the company was not obliged to pay Social Security contributions for the sales agent.

**EXHIBIT 10** Reproduction of the business cards used. . . .

**. . . by a salaried sales representative employed by Smith & Nephew**

**Ramón Prats**
Sales Representative
Medical Division

Smith & Nephew, S.A.

Fructuós Gelabert, 2 and 4
08970 Sant Joan Despí (Barcelona) Spain
Tel.: 93 373 73 O1*
Fax: 93 373 74 53

# Smith+Nephew

**. . . by a sales representative contracted from Innovex**

**Isabel Fernández**
Sales Representative
Medical Division

"Employee of Innovex, Spain, S.L."

Smith & Nephew, S.A.

Fructuós Gelabert, 2 and 4
08970 Sant Joan Despí (Barcelona) Spain
Tel.: 93 373 73 O1*
Fax: 93 373 74 53
Mobile: 654 918 997

# Smith+Nephew

## PARTNERING STRATEGIES IN A BIOTECH WORLD: THE CASE OF DAIRYLAND SEED COMPANY

The morning sun was shining brightly as Tom Strachota, Chief Executive Officer for Dairyland Seed, drove up Highway 45 in southeast Wisconsin in late February 1999. Because of the snow cover on either side of the road, it was not immediately apparent that these fields were the sites of research plots that have generated some of the most cutting-edge biotechnologies in the seed industry. Tom couldn't help but smile as he reflected on the past few years' accomplishments. He was particularly pleased with the success of their line of soybean varieties tolerant to the DuPont Chemical Company's Sulfonylurea herbicides. Dairyland had pioneered the technology—a credit to Dairyland's long-standing commitment to research and development.

However, a lot had happened in the soybean market since the introduction of the Sulfonylurea Tolerant Soybean (STS) varieties five years ago. Competition in the STS seed market had intensified as competitors developed and promoted their own varieties. While Tom believed Dairyland still enjoyed some advantage in the expanding enhanced trait soybean seed business, other seed companies were making rapid progress in many of the same markets.

The market share growth of Round-Up® tolerant soybean varieties was one of the newest challenges. These new varieties enabled Monsanto, manufacturer of the well-known Round-Up® herbicide, to compete directly with DuPont's STS. Initially, limited amounts of Round-Up® tolerant seeds constrained growth, but Monsanto has taken major steps to ensure greater supplies in each of the past two years. As a result, Round-Up® tolerant seeds captured between 35–40 percent market share in 1998 and projections are that Round-Up® tolerant seeds will command as much as 50 percent of the market this year.

Dairyland had not been caught off guard by the Round-Up® tolerant technology, of course. In fact, Dairyland had acquired a license to develop its own Round-Up® tolerant soybean varieties. Dairyland researchers have been successful in developing several varieties that have faired extremely well in state yield trials and in the marketplace this year.

Combined, Dairyland's STS and Round-Up® tolerant varieties account for over 60 percent of Dairyland's soybean sales. This is remarkable given that STS traits entered the market in 1993, and Round-Up® in 1996. However, the growing importance of these varieties brings with it new challenges for Dairyland. By marketing both STS and Round-Up® tolerant varieties, Dairyland is in a position where Tom must manage business relationships with competitors in the chemical and biotechnology market, namely DuPont and Monsanto. With the market demands for Round-Up® tolerant technology, how closely should he establish his business relationship with Monsanto? He wondered what the impact of partnering with Monsanto might be on his carefully developed alliance with DuPont.

Adding to Tom's new challenges, agricultural chemical and biotechnology companies have chosen to become further committed to the seed industry by acquiring or establishing joint ventures with larger seed firms. Of particular interest to Tom were DuPont's 20 percent ownership position in Pioneer, and Monsanto's recent acquisitions of Asgrow and DEKALB—two major seed companies. These mergers have caused these two major technology suppliers to become more tightly allied with Dairyland's direct competitors. What might this mean to Dairyland's access to future technologies? Success had certainly brought a new set of problems, and positioning was going to be especially important for Dairyland to ensure continuity of its role as a cutting-edge seed producer.

### Company Background

Simon and Andrew Strachota founded the Dairyland Seed Company in 1907. In 1920, Andrew retired, leaving his brother Simon to head the company. When Simon died unexpectedly in 1940, his son Orville left college and returned home to run the company. At 79, Orville Strachota continues to be active in the business and serves as Chairman of Dairyland's Board. However, his three sons, Steve, Tom, and John Strachota have

"Partnering Strategies in the BioTech World: The Case of Dairyland Seed Company" by Mark P. Leach, Luiz Mesquita, and W. David Downey in *Journal of Business and Industrial Marketing*, 2002. Republished with permission of the Publisher, Emerald. Copyright © 2002 MCB UP Ltd.

Dr. Mark P. Leach is Assistant Professor of Marketing, Loyola Marymount University; Mr. Luiz Mesquita is a Doctoral Student of Management, Purdue University; and Dr. W. David Downey is Professor and Director, Center for Agricultural Business, Purdue University.

The authors would like to thank Dairyland Seed for permission to develop this case around issues facing their organization. The generous contributions of information and time by Tom Strachota (CEO), John Froelich (Director of Sales), and the many others at Dairyland Seed are gratefully acknowledged. In addition, they would like to recognize the contributions of Danny Kennedy (Co-Leader for North American Markets, Monsanto Global Seed Group as of February 1999), and Tom Matya (Director of Strategic Marketing, DEKALB Genetics Corporation). Note: This case was prepared as the basis for class discussion rather than to illustrate either effective or ineffective handling of an administrative situation.

managed day-to-day operations of the company for over 10 years.

Dairyland began as Strachota Seeds. The company operated out of the Strachota family's general store in eastern Wisconsin. White Dutch Clover Seed was their primary product. But when the market for White Dutch Clover suddenly dropped off in 1955, Orville shifted to the production of alfalfa seed—a product with rapidly growing demand driven by Wisconsin dairy farmers searching for better forages for their cows. Dairy continued to grow in importance in their region. In 1963, Orville decided to change the name of the company to Dairyland Seed Company to reflect its commitment to the market.

Dairyland continued to respond to challenges and opportunities in the seed industry as they arose. They began to produce and market seed corn on a large scale in 1961. As soybeans began to develop in the United States in the 1960s, Dairyland also added soybean seed to their product line.

Today, Orville Strachota's three sons, Steve (President), Tom (Chief Executive Officer), and John (Vice President) jointly manage Dairyland Seed. The company is privately held, with majority stock owned by the Strachota family. Of the over 800 companies listed by the American Seed Trade Association, Dairyland is the only American family-owned seed company with proprietary research in alfalfa, corn, and soybeans. Dairyland's board of directors, which includes family stockholders and outside directors, meets quarterly to review business strategy and plans.

The company is divided into seven functional operating areas: management, finance, research, production, distribution, marketing, and sales. Dairyland employs approximately 100 people plus seasonal help. Executive management is located at Dairyland's headquarters in West Bend, Wisconsin, while research, sales, and production employees are located throughout the company's market and production area. Dairyland's production/processing plants are in Mt. Hope and West Bend, Wisconsin. In addition, five research stations are located in Otterbein, Indiana; Sloughhouse, California; Gibson City, Illinois; Clinton, Wisconsin; and Gilbert, Iowa.

Dairyland has built its image around new product development and is well known in the upper-Midwest for innovation. Orville Strachota established a commitment to research early in the company's history. Today, over 40 percent of the company's employees work in research and development, making it the largest department in the company. Management believes Dairyland has a competitive advantage in certain markets with its continued commitment to research and development.

## The Marketing Mix at Dairyland
### Product

Dairyland has worked hard to build its image around quality products, its high standards of business ethics, and as a successful family-run business. This message is intentionally promoted in a myriad of ways including a highly visible commitment to research, maintaining a first-class physical plant, demonstrating employee pride in the organization, and the active involvement of Orville and three third-generation principals. Tom Strachota believes the positioning effort over the years has resulted in a positive and consistent image of Dairyland among customers and competitors alike. Tom believes that this image is very important and valuable.

The focus of Dairyland has been on high-yielding genetics rather than on specific traits. This commitment to high-performance genetics is captured in their statement of values:

1. Dairyland has a responsibility to its customers to deliver consistently high-performing products.
2. New traits are of value only if they add to the consistency of performance or bring more profit to the farmer.
3. No single genetic trait is of value by itself.

Tom Strachota puts it this way; "It is better to have high-yielding genetics with no specialty traits, than to have specialty traits with poor genetics." Guided by these values, researchers at Dairyland have developed a product mix that consists of varieties of alfalfa, corn, and soybean seed.

### Alfalfa

Dairyland is especially proud of its success with alfalfa varieties. According to company executives, Dairyland has the world's largest alfalfa breeding program. Dairyland's alfalfa lineup includes several specialty alfalfa varieties from which the farmer can choose to match their particular needs (e.g., varieties suited for wet soil conditions, other varieties for high traffic fields, etc.). Strachota is quick to mention recent successful innovations Dairyland has made in the release of patented Sequential Maturity Alfalfa™ products that provide farmers with more high quality forage.

### Corn

Dairyland's seed corn business has grown steadily since hybrid corn was first introduced into their product line in 1961. Seed corn now plays an important role in their overall strategy. Dairyland currently offers over 40 corn varieties that have been bred to meet the unique needs of the upper-Midwestern states. The company's "Stealth" hybrid corn breeding program (which emphasizes consistency in performance) has been a major emphasis in their rapidly growing research program. Dairyland's current lineup includes both insect resistant (i.e., Bt Hybrids) as well as herbicide tolerant (i.e., Round-Up®) hybrids.

### Soybeans

Dairyland entered the soybean market in the early 70s. In the late 70s, Dairyland purchased an aggressive research program—the oldest private breeding program in the country, according to Dairyland executives. Varieties developed by the Dairyland Soybean Research (DSR) program have performed well in yield trials across the Midwest. Dairyland boasts a series of firsts in introducing varieties tolerant to the soybean cyst nematode, brown stem rot, phytophthora root rot, and iron chlorosis—all significant problems for many soybean producers, especially in specific local market areas that Dairyland refers to as "niche" markets. Dairyland executives believe that despite Dairyland's research and development of alfalfa and corn seed, the company is best known in the Corn Belt for its soybean research and the soybean varieties it has developed for the upper-Midwest market area.

An important part of the DSR effort has focused on introducing herbicide resistance into its high-yielding soybean varieties. This technology involves genetically enhancing a variety of soybeans to be resilient to a specific herbicide. Thus, producers can use herbicides for weed control in their fields without killing their soybean crops. An example of this technology is DuPont's STS. DuPont's Liberty herbicide, which is usually detrimental to soybean plants, can be used to control weeds on STS soybean crops. Another example is Monsanto's Round-Up® Ready technology. Monsanto's Round-Up® herbicide can be used on Round-Up® Ready soybeans. Thus, producers can choose soybean seed that has been engineered with specific traits that allow them to use safer, easier, and more environmentally friendly herbicides.

Dairyland initially began to breed STS seeds in the belief that new technology products would attract new seed corn buyers. They believed that their cutting-edge soybean technology would help them gain access to different customers and create new opportunities for additional, profitable corn sales. Furthermore, the company wanted to increase volume of product sales and revenue, as well as enhance the company's image with the launch of traditionally bred herbicide tolerant soybean seed. This boost in the company's image was expected to create the opportunity to sell high-tech, high-yielding products to the more sophisticated, larger producer.

### Distribution

Dairyland annually provides seed for more than 1 million acres of farmland in the United States, Canada, South America, Europe, and Asia. However, their primary market area is concentrated in the upper-Midwest with a focus on Michigan, Minnesota, Wisconsin, South Dakota, Iowa, northern Illinois, Indiana, and Ohio. The area is highly diverse agriculturally—dairy, hogs, corn, soybeans, and forages are the primary crops. The relative importance of each depends on local soil and climatic factors.

Dairyland pursues two primary forms of distribution to reach its farmer customers. The first is a farmer-dealer network that had evolved to be primarily a direct channel with sales managers calling on farmer "dealers" who may or may not sell seed to other farmers. The second is farm retail stores. This second channel allows Dairyland to reach markets where direct methods are not in place or do not make economic sense.

Dairyland's Director of Sales, John Froelich, heads the sales department and works closely with Tom Strachota. There are two regional managers and 28 district sales managers (DSMs). In addition, there are three assistant district managers working in the largest territories and three part-time district managers in less concentrated areas. DSMs are responsible for sales of all three seed product lines through their farmer-dealer distribution system. Each DSM is responsible for approximately 15 counties in his or her state.

Many seed companies in the Midwest rely heavily on a farmer dealer distribution system. Farmers buy seed at a discount and are authorized to resell seed to other farmers. However, many "farmer-dealers" do not aggressively resell seed. Instead, they become "dealers" primarily to obtain the discounted wholesale price, better credit terms, and special programs, and to have more direct access to their supplier's best/newest varieties and technical assistance.

Dairyland is no exception to this system. Dairyland's farmer distribution system has grown to approximately 4,000 farmer dealers. But approximately 80 percent of these dealers are end users and resell little seed. In fact, Dairyland no longer refers to these customers as "dealers" but merely "partners." In recent years there have been attempts toward attracting more and more large farmers into their "dealer/partner" system. In total, however, the number of dealers has not grown appreciably in recent years.

A second form of distribution is the retail farm supply stores. Dairyland has had relatively good success at reaching the farmer through this distribution channel. The advent of biotechnology has required growers to make increasingly more complex decisions about inputs (seed, chemicals, and fertilizer), and the spectrum of knowledge required has grown prohibitively large. Many farmers favor retailers that can provide more technical advice to growers and maintain superior service standards. As such, a growing percentage of Dairyland's business flows through these intermediaries, and Dairyland is continuing to look for appropriate resale partners with which to license.

### Promotion

Dairyland uses a wide variety of promotional programs to communicate the benefits of its soybean seed to farmers. The Dairyland Soybean Management Guide provides farmers with technical and practical advice on the best soybean production methods. Each year, the company produces a pocket-sized Dairyland seed reference guide and calendar. There is a quarterly newsletter called "The Leader" that communicates a variety of information to the customer. Other promotional efforts include tours of research and production facilities, crop management clinics, field days at Dairyland test plots, and maintenance of "show case" quality facilities.

Most of Dairyland's advertising is direct mail from an extensive database maintained on all dealers and customers. The internal database is supplemented by mailing lists from other sources. In addition, the company includes ads in state farm publications, magazines (especially Soybean Digest), agricultural newspapers, etc. Occasionally DSMs will prepare brief ads or radio announcements for local areas to promote a field day or educational program in that area.

Dealers are offered a wide range of individual and customer incentives intended to promote sales. Traditional caps, jackets, etc. are all available to dealers and their customers. In addition, dealers may work toward larger value gifts (e.g., television sets or trips to Florida are common, and even a car in the case of Dairyland's Stealth seed corn program). District sales managers are also offered sales incentives and bonus awards for achievement in increasing the sales of

Dairyland's three product lines. Individual award programs depend on the specific activities that Dairyland is attempting to promote throughout the year.

### Pricing

Dairyland's seed is priced slightly above the market average in all product lines (see Table 1). "This is a strategy designed to encourage the premium quality image that is the core of our marketing strategy, and to generate margins necessary to support an aggressive research and development program," says Tom Strachota. "We believe farmers are willing to pay a little higher price when we deliver high quality seed, consistent performance, dependability, and cutting-edge technology." Although Dairyland seeds may not be the highest priced alternative in the market, this philosophy generally places Dairyland's average prices at 5–10 percent above the average in market. "The idea is to realize that we can't price like the market leader, but we can deliver the best overall value," Tom argues.

Tom Strachota believes that this premium value strategy is highly successful. Dairyland has enjoyed an increase in its soybean sales for the last five years. This includes an increase in 1997 despite not having Round-Up® Ready soybeans; STS accounted for over one-third of Dairyland's soybean sales in 1997.

## Channel Partners

Chemical companies like DuPont and Monsanto are using seed companies to bring their products to market. The developers of the biotechnology have sought to use a combination of seed production and distribution companies as well as licensing agreements with distributors and small seed companies in order to achieve access to growers with a high level of service. Dairyland has among its channel partners two main providers of biotechnology: DuPont and Monsanto. Among these partners, Dairyland has worked most closely in the past with DuPont. Through this relationship with DuPont, Dairyland has marketed its seed varieties of STS soybeans.

---

| **TABLE 1** Estimated Industry Average Seed Prices for 1998 | | | |
|---|---|---|---|
| | **Alfalfa** | **Corn** | **Soybeans** |
| Average Retail Price—Industry | $189 | $99 | $19.00 |
| Average Retail Price—Dairyland | $193 | $95 | $18.65 |
| Average Discounted Price—Industry | $176 | $78 | $15.20 |

Based on the 1998 price list of Pioneer, Novartis, Mycogen, Dekalb, and Cargill companies.

## DuPont

DuPont began licensing with several larger seed companies over five years ago, giving them the right to sublicense to other smaller seed firms. While Dairyland was one of the first seed companies licensed to produce and sell STS seed, there are now nearly 100 seed companies who have been licensed to sell the STS technology. These companies have developed more than 170 varieties of STS seeds. The more aggressive companies include Dairyland Seeds, Asgrow (recently purchased by Monsanto), Pioneer, Stine Seed, Countrymark and GROWMARK, and Novartis Seed. Even though Asgrow is owned by Monsanto, it still maintains a licensing contract with DuPont.

Discussions between DuPont and Dairyland were opened in the mid-80s. Acquisition of the Sulfonylureas germplasm by Dairyland occurred in the late 80s. DuPont selected Dairyland for its strong reputation in soybean development and its independent research capability. The relationship is not exclusive, however. Other companies received the germplasm and have had the opportunity to develop their own tolerant varieties.

The agreement between Dairyland and DuPont stipulates formation of a "joint-commercialization" team to review the marketing strategies for STS. Dairyland and DuPont agreed that in marketing the product, DuPont would sell herbicides and help farmers understand the benefits of STS, while Dairyland would sell seed and talk about the benefits of STS as they relate to seed selection. The joint marketing strategy was a tremendous success as the salesforces of each company were able to establish mutually supportive professional relationships. As the STS technology represents important market potential for DuPont, Dairyland anticipates continued marketing support. DuPont's efforts have clearly helped position Dairyland as one of the leading developers of Sulfonylurea Tolerant Soybeans.

DuPont has basically maintained their aggressive marketing strategy to promote the use of STS seed varieties in the market through programs that include sizable advertising and incentive programs. They have executed major herbicide launches that include TV in major markets and heavy print media advertising. DuPont sales representatives will support local agricultural chemical dealers and seed companies with educational programs in local markets and support plot tours to demonstrate the new technology. DuPont has elected not to place any premium on the Sulfonylurea herbicides.

DuPont has relied heavily on media campaigns to successfully increase its brand name and product awareness among users. However, they have recently been forced to recognize the rapid growth of Round-Up® technology, and the potential cost savings and ease of the Round-Up® system to the farmer. While most industry experts have predicted the increase of Round-Up® soybeans, almost no one expected acceptance to be as rapid as it developed in the 1997 and 1998 markets (see Table 2).[1]

DuPont has responded by increasing commitment with the seed industry substantially with the recent purchase of 20 percent of Pioneer Hybrid International stock and the holding of two seats on Pioneer's board of directors in 1997. Pioneer and DuPont also have announced the formation of a new joint venture called Optimum whose purpose is to bringing new value-added crops to market, such as high-oil corn, etc. It is clear that DuPont will be working more closely with Pioneer than with any other seed company. However, Dairyland feels that DuPont has not abandoned its STS technology or its initial seed industry partners. DuPont's relationship with other seed companies has remained the same. Time will tell whether DuPont's new relationship with Pioneer will have an impact on other seed industry firms.

In addition, DuPont made a substantial change in its pricing strategy—announcing a 75 percent price cut in August 1997 on its STS-related herbicides. This price reduction was a clear attempt to level the economics of the farmer's decision process in choosing which herbicide resistant technology to embrace. On an average basis, the farmer would pay approximately $28 per acre for Round-Up® tolerant

| Estimated Market Share for STS and Round-Up® Tolerant Soybean Seed Varieties | | | | | TABLE 2 |
|---|---|---|---|---|---|
| | **1996** | **1997** | **1998** | **1999*** | **2000*** |
| STS Varieties | 7% | 8–12% | 10–15% | 15–20% | 20–25% |
| Round-Up Ready | 3% | 18–20% | 35–40% | 45–50% | 50–60% |

*The economic situation faced by producers varies widely by region. This table is based on 1998 University of Wisconsin yield trials on three varieties of Dairyland seed.

seeds (including a $6.50 technology fee). The herbicide would cost about $15 per acre per application. With the new lower price, DuPont claims it can offer the farmer superior protection (longer weed control) for basically the same price. Dairyland believes that its STS seeds outperform most competitors' Round-Up® varieties and so it continues to be committed to the STS technology.

### Monsanto and Round-Up® Ready

Monsanto's Round-Up® Ready technology has been under development for sometime. From its introduction, market growth has been limited only by supply. In 1994 and 1995, Round-Up® tolerant soybeans hit the market with limited quantity and sold out. In 1996, they sold out with a 3 percent market share. In 1997, supplies sold out, this time with approximately 20 percent market share. In

1998 Round-Up® soybeans did not sell out, but did capture nearly 40 percent of the market.

Dairyland did not have Round-Up® technology initially. In fact, Dairyland was not licensed to market Round-Up® soybeans in 1997, but it did enter into an arrangement with Monsanto in 1998. Tom attributes Dairyland's ability to license with Monsanto to Dairyland's commitment to quality, and the recognition that Dairyland receives for being the first to market with STS herbicide-resistant soybeans.

Recently Monsanto has escalated its activity in the seed industry. Through its acquisitions, partnerships, and incentive programs, Monsanto has effectively elevated its position in the seed supply chain (see Figure 1). These acquisitions and partnerships are part of a continuing effort of Monsanto to strengthen its position in the market for new biotechnological products. This is consistent with Monsanto's strategic

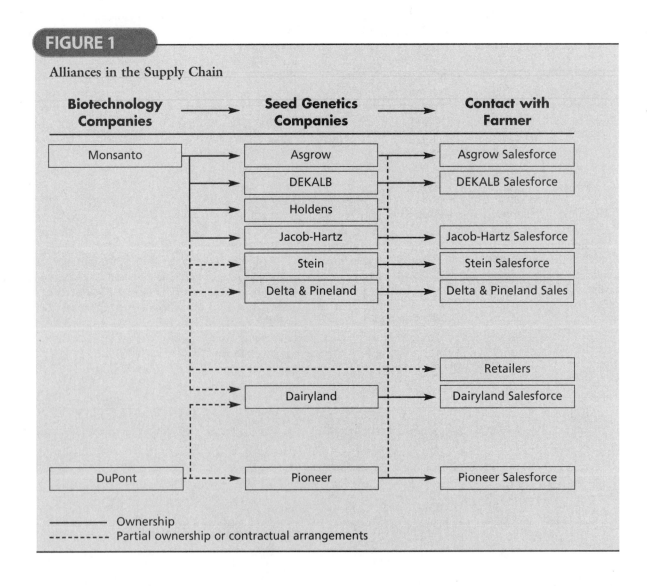

**FIGURE 1**

Alliances in the Supply Chain

vision, "to create cutting-edge environmental solutions in order to assure sustainable growth for our company," says Monsanto's CEO Robert Shapiro (Monsanto Press Release, 1998).[2]

In 1996, Monsanto Company acquired Asgrow Agronomics. Asgrow is a major U.S. soybean seed company with international operations. According to Monsanto's executive vice president, Hendrik A. Verfaillie: "Asgrow's strength in soybeans is particularly important to us as we accelerate the sales of our Round-Up® soybeans and other new soybean products to farmers worldwide. The acquisition of Asgrow Agronomics strengthens our ability to quickly move our innovations into the marketplace" (Monsanto Press Release, 1998). Other examples of recent Monsanto acquisitions and alliances include:

- In December 1997, Monsanto Company, Asgrow Seed Company, and Stine Seed Company announced a collaboration agreement. This research agreement was reportedly designed to further improve and develop soybean genetics and related technologies.
- On December 4, 1998, DEKALB Genetics became a wholly-owned subsidiary of Monsanto.
- Monsanto also bought Holdens in early 1997. Holdens is a major supplier of corn genetics to both large and independent seed companies.
- In June 1998 Monsanto signed an agreement to purchase Cargill's international seed operations in Latin America, Asia, Africa, and parts of Europe. This acquisition includes seed research, production, and testing facilities in 21 countries and distribution systems in 51 countries.

Through these partnerships, Monsanto has acquired a solid distribution network that should facilitate rapid seed product introduction. Also, through gearing research to complement one another, these new alliances will achieve synergies in new product development. Thus, at the same time Dairyland's initial soybean technology partner (i.e., DuPont) has become more tightly allied with one of Dairyland's key competitors (i.e., Pioneer), Monsanto has been managing its relationships with several other Dairyland competitors.

Another way that Monsanto is managing the supply-chain of its Round-Up® Ready technology is through incentive programs. Monsanto has established an incentive structure for seed manufactures, for agricultural retailing, and for growers. For example, growers who use both Round-Up® Ready soybeans and Monsanto's YieldGard Bt corn on a high percentage of acres are given a rebate.

Given the demand for Round-Up® Ready soybeans, Monsanto has been able to charge a technology fee to growers. This fee was originally $5 per 50-pound bag, but was increased to $6 for spring 1999 (the price increase was coupled with a price reduction of Round-Up® Ready herbicide so that the overall cost to a customer was essentially the same).

One incentive that Monsanto provides to seed suppliers is a special handling fee. For suppliers, Monsanto provides 10 percent of this fee back to the supplier (i.e., $0.60). In addition, if a supplier meets certain share-of-business requirements, Monsanto will rebate another 10 percent (i.e., $0.60) to the supplier. These requirements include having 90 percent of herbicide-resistant soybeans sold be Round-Up® Ready soybeans, 85 percent of herbicide-resistant corn be Round-Up® Ready corn, and 90 percent of corn borer insect-protected corn be YieldGard Bt corn. In order to obtain the additional 10 percent, all three share-of-business requirements must be met. Together, these two rebates can more than double the retail profit on a bag of seed.

For any seed company, this program can generate a lot of money. For a firm selling 100,000 bags of soybeans, meeting these requirements would mean receiving $60,000. Likewise, for a firm selling 500,000 units, this means an additional $300,000 in revenue. Given, the relatively low profit margin on a bag of soybeans, this provides substantial incentive for suppliers to sell products with Monsanto technologies.

However, for companies like Dairyland who are allied with other biotechnology channel partners, Monsanto's incentive structure raises several issues. First of all, with such an attractive inducement to sell Round-Up® tolerant soybeans, should Dairyland continue to develop its relationship with DuPont? Furthermore, because this offer will shape decisions made by other genetic companies, a result may be the decrease in the number of companies providing STS technologies. Will DuPont continue to aggressively market STS even when they foresee markets becoming less attainable? Is this an opportunity for Dairyland, or a threat to its position in the market?

Another concern for Dairyland is that not all of Monsanto's business partners operate under the same set of restrictions. Due to prior contractual arrangements, neither Novartis nor Pioneer is required to pay Monsanto the $6.50/bag technology fee. However, each of these firms charges this fee to customers. This raises concerns of the equity of Monsanto business relationships, as this money may provide a source of funds for research and development that is not available to most Round-Up® tolerant soybean suppliers, or allow a significant disparity in dealer or retail pricing.

Danny Kennedy, Co-President of Asgrow Seed, believes Monsanto's success stems from its ability to add value to the farmer by capitalizing on the synergies from its portfolio of companies and technologies representing several sectors in agriculture. He states that Monsanto considers its involvement in agricultural business to be a core part of the overall technology platform. This view is consistent with the strategic actions of Monsanto. Since heading up the company in 1995, Robert Shapiro has spun off the core chemical business to focus on being the "main provider of the agricultural biotechnology . . ." (Monsanto Press Release, 1998).

With regard to herbicide-resistance technology, Monsanto executives see both seed and biotechnology as key ingredients to their long-term strategy. Danny Kennedy realizes that seed is the distribution system by which Monsanto technologies reach the farmer. He believes that seed will drive farmers' decisions in the future, and states that, "farmers will buy seed that is specialized genetically to suit their own feed stock needs, grain market needs, consumer needs, etc." Asgrow and DEKALB have competitive advantages in some regions, however, because small firms can have a strong presence in certain regions and market niches, he believes that Monsanto cannot afford not to license other seed firms with its new technologies. As an example of the commitment of Monsanto to licensing its technology to the broad market (family and small firms), as of February 1999 Monsanto has already agreed to licensing its technology to more than 200 seed firms.

### Other Providers of Herbicide-Tolerant Soybean Technology

Although Dairyland has business partnerships with DuPont and Monsanto, there are several other chemical and biotechnical firms that operate in this market. AgrEvo, is the third player in the herbicide-resistant seed market. AgrEvo's herbicide, Liberty, targets a broad spectrum of broad leaf weeds. The Liberty technology was late to enter the market. Early efforts of AgrEvo to bring its herbicide-resistance technology to the seed market were through Asgrow and Holdens. This strategy has proven to be problematic, especially since Monsanto now owns both. AgrEvo has been licensing its technology to other seed companies, though it has been less successful than Monsanto and DuPont to bring its technology to the market. While pricing of the AgrEvo product is not yet clear, it appears that AgrEvo may choose a premium price strategy rather than a licensing fee as Monsanto has chosen. Liberty is faster-acting than Round-Up® but has about the same kill spectrum for weeds and grasses as Round-Up®.

American Cyanamid has maintained a significant share of the soybean herbicide market with Pursuit®, which is used with nonherbicide-tolerant soybean varieties. Recently, they have cut prices approximately 40 percent so that its use is competitively priced with Round-Up® Ultra and Dupont's Symphony. Thus, American Cyanamid continues to represent a major market challenge for DuPont/STS and Monsanto Round-Up® products. If DuPont is to be successful, it will be necessary to demonstrate a significant advantage over this and other traditional herbicide alternatives. Another relatively new release is Flexstar® by Zeneca, a formulation intended for broadleaf weed control in soybeans.

### Competitive Environment in the Soybean Seed Industry

Dairyland faces a wide range of competitors in their diverse market area (see Table 3). Some competitors are large international companies such as Pioneer, DEKALB, and Novartis Seeds that have broad product lines that parallel Dairyland's. Furthermore, there are a large number of regional and local seed companies who offer all or part of the seed products sold by Dairyland. Some of Dairyland's competitors develop and sell proprietary products, while others sell public varieties that are genetically identical to each other, but carry the producer's own label. Many of these smaller companies are aggressive and have strong loyalties within their own local market areas.

Competition is intense in all three product lines. Pioneer is the clear industry leader in the seed corn market with an estimated market share of about 42 percent. There is no dominant supplier in alfalfa although alfalfa has always been one of Dairyland's strengths. Pioneer has become aggressive in the soybean market with an estimated 14 percent share. Asgrow recently announced that it was the leader in soybean share with 16 percent. Accurate market share information is difficult to obtain and to interpret since many seed companies are privately held and the market is so geographically fractured. Aggregate market share information is also often misleading because it varies dramatically among local market areas. For example, while Dairyland Seed does not have a large market share on a national basis (i.e., less than 2 percent), in some core market areas, their market share may run as high as 30 percent.

Most soybean seed companies are marketing some STS varieties. However, these companies differ basically in their enthusiasm and commitment to the technology. Among the major players, a few of them are worth mentioning. Asgrow has had STS products developed since 1993. Asgrow has not priced their STS varieties at a premium relative to their non-STS varieties. Cenex, a major cooperative in the

| Estimated 1998 National Market Share **TABLE 3** | |
|---|---|
| | **Percent of Soybean Acres** |
| **Farmer Saved Seed** | 32.5% |
| **Public Varieties** | 15.0% |
| **Private Varieties:** | |
| Asgrow (Monsanto) | 16.0% |
| Pioneer | 14.0% |
| DEKALB (Monsanto) | ≅5.0% |
| Novartis | ≅5.0% |
| Stine | ≅5.0% |
| Jacob-Hartz (Monsanto) | <5.0% |
| Cokers (Sandoz) | <5.0% |
| FS (GROWMARK) | <5.0% |
| Mycogen | <5.0% |
| Others | ≅8.0% |
| Total Private | (52.5%) |
| **Total** | 100.0% |

upper-Midwest, has introduced an STS product, and DEKALB has STS products in the market. Other seed companies, such as Stine, have introduced STS varieties but lack breadth in this product line.

A major new player in the STS market is Pioneer. Consistent with Pioneer's general pricing strategy, it is pricing its STS products at a premium relative to its non- STS products. Many in the industry expect the new relationship of DuPont and Pioneer will result in additional introductions of enhanced trait seeds.

John Froelich feels that one of Dairyland's competitive advantages continues to be their lead in the development of STS varieties. While some companies are still working to improve the performance of their STS varieties, Dairyland executives feel that their "commanding lead" allows them to concentrate on introducing enhanced traits into varieties that have already proven to be strong performers. Pursuing this strategy, Dairyland researchers have successfully bred additional traits into the STS product line. New Dairyland varieties have demonstrated resistance to a series of plant diseases, such as white mold, brown stem rot, and phytophtora. Dairyland believes these new traits will be particularly important in "niche" markets where these diseases are problematic.

Dairyland has responded to the growing market demand for Round-Up® Ready soybeans by introducing several new varieties for the '98 and '99 selling seasons. So far, over 30 percent of Dairyland's sales today come from Round-Up® Ready products.

John Froelich expects this trend to continue to the end of the 1999 selling season. Research is currently underway to introduce still more Round-Up® Ready varieties in the future.

Asgrow is expected to continue the aggressive introduction of new soybean varieties. This Monsanto- affiliate is marketing a new "stacked traits" variety—one that has resistance to both STS and Round-Up® herbicides. Monsanto has not given other seed companies the legal right to offer "stacked trait" varieties. On the other hand, DuPont has announced that it will allow companies already licensed to sell (STSs) to develop and market stacked trait soybean varieties. It is unclear what Monsanto's intentions are for the future.

**Dairyland's Customer Focus**

Putting the customer first has always been the core of Dairyland's business philosophy. As Orville Strachota puts it, Dairyland's objective has always been to treat farmers fairly and understand their needs. If you have a good product at a fair price with good service and hold true to your word, you've got a customer and a friend for life.

However, customer buying behavior is changing. On today's large farms, more people influence decisions, and farmers are more business-oriented. Tom Matya, Director of Strategic Marketing for DEKALB Genetics Corporation, finds customers today to be more economically focused, more highly educated in germplasm and herbicides, and less brand loyal than 10 years ago. Although there is still a strong sense of loyalty, he attributes the increase in brand switching by customers today to the rapid acceleration of product innovation, and the leapfrogging of technologies.

Farmers today have been characterized as being value-driven. Farmers must justify the economics of the variety that is being purchased, and understand the mix of products that work together to provide optimal solutions. This may be one reason for the increase in sales through agricultural retailers. Through their ability to provide customers bundled packages and product expertise on everything from seeds to chemicals, agricultural retailers are providing farmers with added value through expertise, convenience, and often through creative discounting.

Farmer customers have a high level of risk aversion. Both John Froelich from Dairyland Seed and Tom Matya from DEKALB agree that farmers will be more inclined to test new technologies themselves before converting large numbers of acres to a new product. However, if the product works, adoption moves quickly.

Similarly, Tom Strachota foresees that farmers will become more focused on high-quality genetics and less driven by new specialty traits until they have been proven in the field. However, the growth of herbicide-tolerant varieties of soybean in general and Round-Up® Ready soybeans in particular, provides evidence that specialty traits are highly desired by today's farmers. At Dairyland, herbicide-tolerant soybeans accounted for 62 percent of total soybean sales in 1998 and are expected to increase to 73 percent in 1999 (see Table 4).[3]

Dairyland has been encouraged by experiences reported by many of their key accounts who have been aggressively testing the STS and Round-Up® Ready seed on their farms. The net result has been an increase in their purchases of Dairyland STS. John Froelich believes that the sales increases further demonstrate that performance continues to be the major factor for many business-minded

farmers. Yet John is quick to recognize that the differences in performance may not be enough for many farmers who simply like the convenience of Round-Up®.

John relates a Monsanto study showing approximately 95 percent of the farmers using the Round-Up® Ready system experienced "satisfaction" with the product. "That is, they got what they thought they would get with their product," John says. "I believe this means these farmers did not expect to have higher yields, but were focusing on a wider span of weed control. On the other hand," John continues, "I believe the initial impact of Round-Up® Ready will be dimmed by performance of the Round-Up® Ready varieties as farmers have more data and experience to really evaluate the results."

Dairyland believes that in many regions the STS varieties will continue to show a performance advantage over the newer Round-Up® tolerant beans. However, they believe their current advantage is temporary and the Round-Up® tolerant beans will soon equal STS varieties in performance. Further, because of all the variables involved, this performance advantage is increasingly difficult to prove. John Froelich expects that most independent seed companies will continue to work with both Monsanto and DuPont in order to cover all the bases. Yet the appeal of Round-Up® Ready soybeans is unmistakable. Many farmers have had much experience with Round-Up® and are very comfortable with its use.

However, some of the economic appeal of the Round-Up® system has been reduced by recent competitive actions. Prices on both DuPont's Synchrony and American Cyanamid's Pursuit have been cut substantially, making purchase decisions less dependent on price. Dairyland believes that much of the customer demand for the Round-Up® system was the up-front cost savings that the system provided for farmer customers. If this was a major

| TABLE 4 | Percentage of Dairyland Soybean Sales | | |
|---|---|---|---|
| **Year** | **STS Sales** | **Round-Up® Sales** | **Conventional Sales** |
| 1993 | <1% | 0% | 99% |
| 1994 | 6% | 0% | 94% |
| 1995 | 31% | 0% | 69% |
| 1996 | 41% | 0% | 59% |
| 1997 | 40% | 1% | 59% |
| 1998 | 41% | 21% | 38% |
| 1999 est. | 41% | 32% | 27% |

purchase motive, the virtual elimination of Round-Up® Ready's cost savings advantage may reduce the demand for Round-Up® tolerant varieties (see Table 5).

A lot has changed in the soybean market in the few years since Dairyland introduced that first line of herbicide-tolerant soybean varieties. The excitement created by the advent of biotechnology has led to a rapidly changing environment where Dairyland's biotechnology suppliers are becoming more closely aligned with its competitors and where soybean seed customers are demanding the inclusion of biotechnological traits in addition to high-yielding genetics. As Tom puzzles over his current situation, and how to best manage his relationships with his technology suppliers and his customers, he is also keenly aware that herbicide tolerance is just the tip of the proverbial biotech iceberg. What will that next market-changing trait be, and when will it be developed? Will he have access to develop varieties with that trait? What types of relationships will he be managing in the future? Tom sits back from his desk and smiles. Yes, there hasn't been a more interesting time to be in the seed industry.

## Dairyland Case Questions

Three alternative product strategies that Tom Strachota might take with Dairyland Seed are:

(a) Attempt to associate more strongly with Monsanto and sell over 90 percent Round-Up® Ready herbicide-resistant seed.

(b) Continue with the status quo and produce both Round-Up® Ready and STS beans letting the market dictate the level of each.

(c) Attempt to associate more strongly with DuPont and focus on STS herbicide-resistant beans.

For EACH of these alternatives answer the following four questions:

1. What are the pros and cons of each strategy?
2. Are there other significantly different strategies that Dairyland should consider?
3. What would you recommend Dairyland do in the immediate future and why?
4. How can Dairyland remain family-owned and a successful seed business in the future?

| | Yield/ acre | Seed costs/acre | Herbicide costs/acre[†] |
|---|---|---|---|
| **Economic Decisions Faced by Customers*    TABLE 5** | | | |
| Dairyland Round-Up® 241 variety | | | Round-Up® Ultra |
| One application of Herbicide | 61 | 29.73** | 35.00 |
| Two applications of Herbicide | | | 5.00[††] |
| Dairyland STS variety | | | Synchrony |
| One application of Herbicide | 61 | 18.63 | 35.00 |
| Two applications of Herbicide | | | 25.00 |
| Dairyland Conventional 256 variety | | | Pursuit |
| One application of Herbicide | 64 | 18.63 | 35.00 |
| Two applications of Herbicide | | | 25.00 |

*The economic situation faced by producers varies widely by region. This table is based on 1998 University of Wisconsin yield trials on three varieties of Dairyland seed.

**Seed costs include seed, and applicable technology fees (i.e., $19.98 + (1.5*$6.50) = $29.73).

[†]Herbicide costs are based on manufacturer suggested application rates and include a $5.00 /acre application fee, and an estimated $10.00 for pre-plant and burn-down.

[††]The warranty for a second application of herbicide for Round-up® customers depends on the producer following specific planting and application guidelines. Dairyland believes many farmers will not meet these requirements.

## BUSINESSLAND COMPUTERS, INC.: WHAT IF WE AUTOMATED OUR SALESFORCE?

Bill Pfaff, Sales Manager for Businessland, was reviewing sales performance and selling expenses from the past fiscal period in preparation of a budget which was due in a couple of weeks. At first glance, Bill was surprised to see that the company's total selling expenses were approaching $300 million. In pursuing initial analysis, he noted two areas in particular that were quite disturbing: First, the average cost of a sales call had been increasing substantially in recent years to where it was near $300 during the previous year. Secondly, nearly 60% of the sales rep's time was spent in non-selling activities. Compounding this was the company's profit trend which last year dropped to an all-time low ending at a loss of $23 million. Bill's thoughts centered upon some of his own company's technology products. He questioned,

> "What if. . . . we were to look toward technology-based solutions. Could Businessland develop new sales systems to bring together data from many sources providing sales reps access to the most up-to-date information? How would the sales reps respond to it; for that matter, how would Businessland's clients respond to it?"

As Bill began to formulate ideas about using technology, he projected that a process could reduce administrative communication tangles so sales professionals would have more time for customers, and improve information accuracy and efficiency for more effective time usage.

> "Maybe we could use our own technology (computers) to provide the salesforce immediate information on order status, pricing, availability of items, electronic mail, spread sheets, account and territory profiles, etc. This would help manage information and improve communications among the sales reps, sales managers, corporate marketing personnel and, most importantly, the customer."

### Background

Businessland was founded in the mid 1980s by Bret Lane and Gerald Parsons. They combined knowledge, skill and the experience of marketing and technology to form a company that sells, services, and supports computer and workstation products from leading manufacturing companies. Today, Businessland is a prominent, privately held company that specializes in building PCs from multiple manufacturers and integrating them into customer environments by using an outside salesforce of 300. In addition, they provide customer training, service, and telephone hotline support.

The personal computer industry is very dynamic and has experienced rapid changes in technology and products that have a relatively short life cycle. By the mid-1980s, hundreds of manufacturers had entered the market and there was a scramble to sell hardware with little attention to applications, systems, or support. There was an industry-wide rush to establish computer stores and retail outlets with the anticipation that personal computers would ultimately be marketed similarly to that of refrigerators. In the latter part of the decade, a large number of those companies ceased to operate either due to failure, mergers, or acquisitions. World sales of personal computers exceeded $150 billion in the mid-1990s up from $12 billion a decade earlier. Similar growth occurred in the US as sales of $6 billion in 1985 exceeded $60 billion in 1995. Sales of personal computers dwarf all other computer markets including mainframes which have plateaued at $50 billion annually.

The companies that did survive discovered the need to emphasize software ahead of hardware and to address user needs. The initial surge for personal computers was limited as most users required education in the applications and selection of both software and hardware. Essentially, it was an evolution. With the development of more sophisticated software and more extensive usage in many different areas of applications, the need for systems and networking became apparent. Thus, a more complex "systems approach" required not only a change in marketing but also a need for service and support. Many of these changes called for greater resources than originally planned. Inventories of equipment and parts were higher than anticipated, the need for knowledge and well-trained personnel increased, and there was an increase in the training of users and in providing after-sale support.

### Sales and Earnings

Adding to Bill's dilemma of rising costs and inefficiency in the selling process, was the realization that Businessland's orders for the last year increased only 1% as compared to a 19% increase five years earlier. In a similar pattern, current year revenues increased only 13.8% compared to a revenue growth of 21.1% the previous year and 42.7% two years earlier. Earnings,

Source: Allen J. Wedell, Colorado State University. This case was prepared for classroom discussion rather than to illustrate either effective or ineffective managerial decisions. Copyright © 1997.

however, decreased to negative $23 million in the last year as compared to a decreasing growth rate of 91.5% in the previous year and 37% two years earlier. Parallel to this, Bill noted that the category of expenses identified as selling, general, and administrative increased nearly 19% during the past year compared to only 9.6% the previous year. It was immediately apparent that revenues were still increasing but at a decreasing rate but that actual orders had almost become stagnet during the past year. By contrast, operating expenses were running wild and if Businessland were to remain competitive, these would have to be brought back under control. Bill began to focus upon alternatives. Revenues and earnings are shown in Figure 1.

### Sales and Marketing Automation

At a recent seminar entitled "Marketing Technology," Bill had been exposed to the concept of Sales and Marketing Automation (SMA) which is a system designed to add efficiency to sales operations. In the words of Steve Husner, a sales rep for Nation's Carriers, "The laptop allows one to follow through with a customer rather than having to get back to them at a later time." It permits a rep to hook right up to a mainframe via a modem and get answers to any question the customer may have right on the spot. SMA also improves salesforce productivity and increases effectiveness by:

- reducing the amount of time a salesperson devotes to administrative tasks such as the preparation of call reports.
- tracking sales leads.
- managing time and territory
- developing proposals and persuasive presentations

Impressed with the opportunities of such a program, Bill began to think about a program that would provide Businessland's salesforce the productivity tools that would increase selling productivity and, at the same time, lower selling costs. Immediately, Bill set up a task group to help him outline the goals and objectives for the project and to identify the resources that would be required—financial, equipment, and support personnel. The group identified three fundamental objectives that would evaluate the effectiveness of such a program:

1. To increase sales productivity and effectiveness by 25%.
2. To increase customer visibility of Businessland's automation solutions through the use of their own products (computers).
3. To increase sales rep job satisfaction, confidence and motivation.

**FIGURE 1**

Businessland Computers, Inc.

### Five-Year Selected Financial Data

| (in thousands) | Year 1 (last fiscal period) | Year 2 | Year 3 | Year 4 | Year 5 |
|---|---|---|---|---|---|
| Net Sales | $1,367,170 | $1,200,628 | $990,119 | $693,828 | $501,053 |
| Gross Profit | 287,550 | 313,645 | 265,868 | 198,956 | 136,475 |
| Selling, General, & Administrative Exp. | 298,076 | 250,762 | 228,673 | 181,364 | 139,435 |
| Restructuring Exp. | 13,635 | — | — | — | — |
| Income (loss) from Operations | (24,161) | 62,884 | 37,195 | 17,592 | (2,959) |
| Income (loss) for IRS | (30,880) | 56,334 | 31,663 | 13,882 | (8,044) |
| Income (loss) before extra-ordinary item | (24,354) | 33,205 | 17,485 | 8,078 | (10,763) |
| **Net Income (loss)** | **(23,297)** | **33,497** | **17,485** | **12,759** | **(2,180)** |

In order to evaluate future sales productivity, the group analyzed the past performance of the salesforce. They identified work patterns falling into the following major categories with time spent as shown:

- Contact with Customers         26%
- Administrative Sales Activities  31%
- Travel and waiting             15%
- Meetings and training          13%
- Office and personal time       15%

Total                            100%

The group estimated the automation costs to run about $7900 per salesperson as shown in Figure 2: The task group thought it would be relatively easy to measure the second and third objectives by randomly surveying both Businessland's clients and the salesforce once the program was initiated. They proposed that clients could be surveyed as to how they perceived sales automation and the impact Businessland had upon their purchasing decisions. Similarly, they thought that reports could be obtained from the salesforce regarding their satisfaction with the implementation and usage of SMA. The group, however, was much more concerned as to how they would measure the productivity of the sales automation and with the determination of the return on investment. Bill was rather clear that he wanted to know the break even point before he would be willing to include the proposal in the budget.

## FIGURE 2

**Estimated SMA Costs**

| | First Year | Second Year |
|---|---|---|
| **Basic:** | | |
| Hardware | $3,500 | |
| Software | 1,000 | $1,500 |
| Supplies | 500 | |
| **Total** | **$5,000** | **$1,500** |
| **Operational:** | | |
| Insurance | $100 | $100 |
| Electronic mail | 150 | 150 |
| Software Upgrade | 100 | 100 |
| Extended Warranty | — | 350 |
| **Total** | **$350** | **$700** |
| **Implementation:** | | |
| Consultant | $300 | |
| Training | 400 | |
| Spare Equipment | 350 | |
| **Total** | **$1,050** | |
| **Overall Total** | **$6,400** | **$2,200** |
| Amount added for management support personnel | $1,500 | $500 |
| **Grand Total** | **$7,900** | **$2,700** |

## ROYAL CORPORATION

As Mary Jones, a third-year sales representative for the Royal Corporation, reviewed her call plans for tomorrow, she thought about her sales strategy. It was only July 1993, but Jones was already well on her way toward completing her best year, financially, with the company. In 1992, she had sold the largest dollar volume of copiers of any sales representative in the northeast and was the tenth most successful rep in the country.

But Jones was not looking forward to her scheduled activities for the next day. In spite of her excellent sales ability, she had not been able to sell the Royal Corporate Copy Center (CCC). This innovative program was highly touted by Royal upper management. Jones was one of the few sales reps in her office who had not sold a CCC in 1992. Although Jones had an excellent working relationship with her sales manager, Tom Stein, she was experiencing a lot of pressure from him of late because he could not understand her inability to sell CCCs. Jones had therefore promised herself to concentrate her efforts on selling CCCs even if it meant sacrificing sales of other products.

Jones had five appointments for the day— 9:00 a.m., Acme Computers; 9:45, Bickford Publishing; 11:45, ABC Electronics; 12:30, CG Advertising; and 2:00 p.m., General Hospital. At Acme, Bickford, and ABC, Jones would develop CCC prospects. She was in various states of information gathering and proposal preparation for each of the accounts. At CG, Jones planned to present examples of work performed by a model 750 color copier. At General Hospital, she would present her final proposal for CCC adoption. Although the focus of her day would be on CCCs, she still needed to call and visit other accounts that she was developing.

Source: Copyright © 1994. This case was prepared at Babson College by Professor H. David Hennessey and Barbara Kalunian, graduate student, as the basis for discussion rather than to illustrate either effective or ineffective sales performance. Names and locations have been disguised.

## Royal Introduces CCC Concept

In 1990, Royal had introduced its Corporate Copy Center facilities management program (CCC). Under this concept, Royal offered to equip, staff, operate, and manage a reproduction operation for its clients, on the clients' premises (see Exhibit 1). After

---

**EXHIBIT 1**

| | |
|---|---|
| *Labor*<br>Secretary (Hrs 3 4.3 Wks)<br>Executive (Hrs 3 4.3 Wks)<br>Supervisor (Hrs 3 4.3 Wks) | CCC provides expert operators and experienced reprographic managers so all labor costs are included in one convenient monthly invoice. |
| *Paid Benefits*<br>Social Security<br>Vacations<br>Sick Leave<br>Pensions<br>Medical Plans | CCC eliminates all "people problems"—your repro staff is on our payroll, and we pay for their benefits. |
| *Recruiting & Training*<br>Advertising Costs<br>Personnel Time<br>Interviewer Time<br>Operator Time<br>Supervisor Time | No more recruiting and training . . . we handle that job, and we cover all related expenses! |
| *Administrative Time*<br>Purchase Orders<br>Filing Work<br>Calling Service People<br>Talking to Sales People | We handle all repro management—you receive a single monthly invoice for your entire repro system (and supplies)! |
| *Waste*<br>Operator Negligence<br>Unauthorized Copies<br>Equipment Malfunction | You only pay for the copies you use . . . |
| *Downtime*<br>Resulting In . . .<br>Vendor Charges<br>Overtime Costs<br>Missed Deadlines | Comprehensive back-up capabilities at your local Royal Reproduction Center—job turnaround times are guaranteed at no extra cost to you! |
| *Price Increases*<br>Labor<br>Materials<br>Overhead<br>Interest | The CCC price includes everything and it's guaranteed for the length of our agreement! |
| *Space Requirements*<br>Inventory<br>File Cabinets<br>Additional Equipment | Equipment and supplies are our responsibility, eliminating the need for anything extra on your part . . . |
| *Chargeback Control*<br>Clients<br>Departments<br>Individuals | At no charge, we maintain a log of all copies made . . . for clients, departments and individuals. |

To see what Royal Corporate Copy Center can do for you—and for your operating budget—take a minute to explore the *true* cost of your *present* system, outlined in the chart above. As you can see, it includes those "hidden" reprographic expenses that *many* organizations fail to consider . . .

The CCC concept is a familiar one, of course . . . many progressive organizations are now utilizing similar arrangements for their food service and data processing programs.

analyzing the needs of the client; Royal selected and installed the appropriate equipment and provided fully trained, Royal employed operators. The CCC equipment also permits microfilming, sorting, collating, binding, covering, and color copying, in addition to high-volume copying.

The major benefits of the program include: reproduction contracted for at a specified price, guaranteed output, tailor-made capabilities, and qualified operators.

As she pulled into the Acme Computers parking lot, she noticed that an unexpected traffic jam had made her ten minutes late for the 9:00 a.m. appointment. This made her uncomfortable as she valued her time, and assumed that her clients appreciated promptness. Jones had acquired the Acme Computers account the prior summer and had dealt personally with Betty White, Director of Printing Services, ever since. She had approached White six months earlier with the idea of purchasing a CCC, but had not pursued the matter further until now because Betty had seemed very unreceptive. For today's call, Jones had worked several hours preparing a detailed study of Acme's present reproduction costs. She was determined to make her efforts pay off.

Jones gave her card to the new receptionist, who buzzed White's office and told her that Jones was waiting. A few minutes later, Betty appeared and led Jones to a corner of the lobby. They always met in the lobby, a situation that Jones found frustrating but it was apparently company policy.

"Good morning, Betty, it's good to see you again. Since I saw you last, I've put together the complete analysis on the CCC that I promised. I know you'll be excited by what you see. As you are aware, the concept of a CCC is not that unusual anymore. You may recall from the first presentation that I prepared for you, the CCC can be a tremendous time and money saver. Could you take a few moments to review the calculations that I have prepared exclusively for Acme Computers?" Betty flipped through the various pages of exhibits that Jones had prepared, but it was obvious that she had little interest in the proposal. "As you can see," Jones continued, "the savings are really significant after the first two years."

"Yes, but the program is more expensive the first two years. But what's worse is that there will be an outsider here doing our printing. I can't say that's an idea I could ever be comfortable with."

Jones realized that she had completely lost the possibility of White's support, but she continued.

"Betty, let me highlight some of the other features and benefits that might interest Acme."

"I'm sorry, Mary, but I have a 10:00 meeting that I really must prepare for. I can't discuss this matter further today."

"Betty, will you be able to go over these figures in more depth a little later?"

"Why don't you leave them with me, I'll look at them when I get the chance," White replied.

Jones left the proposal with White hoping that she would give it serious consideration, but as she pulled out of the driveway to Acme Computers, she could not help but feel that the day had gotten off to a poor start.

The Royal Corporation established the Royal Reproduction Center (RRC) Division in 1956. With 51 offices located in 24 states in the United States, the RRC specializes in high quality quick-turnaround copying, duplicating, and printing on a service basis. In addition to routine reproduction jobs, the RRC is capable of filling various specialized requests including duplicating engineering documents and computer reports, microfilming, color copying, and producing overhead transparencies. In addition, the RRC sales representatives sell the Royal 750 color copier (the only piece of hardware sold through RRCs) and the Royal Corporate Copy Center program (CCC). Although the RRC accepts orders from "walk ins," the majority of the orders are generated by the field representatives who handle certain named accounts which are broken down by geographic territory.

At 9:45 a.m., Jones stopped at Bickford Publishing for her second sales call of the day. She waited in the lobby while Joe Smith, Director of Corporate Services, was paged. Bickford Publishing was one of Jones's best accounts. Last year her commission from sales to Bickford totaled 10 percent of her pay. But her relationship with Joe Smith always seemed to be on unstable ground. She was not sure why, but she had always felt that Smith harbored resentment towards her. However, she decided not to dwell on the matter as long as a steady stream of large orders kept coming in. Jones had been calling on Bickford ever since Tim McCarthy, the sales representative before her, had been transferred. Competition among the RRC sales reps for the Bickford account has been keen. But Stein had decided that Jones's performance warranted a crack at the account, and she had proven that she deserved it by increasing sales 40 percent within six months.

"Good morning, Miss Jones, how are you today?" Smith greeted her. He always referred to her formally as Miss Jones.

"I'm fine, Mr. Smith," Jones replied. "Thank you for seeing me today. I needed to drop by and give you some additional information on the CCC idea that I reviewed with you earlier."

"Miss Jones, to be perfectly honest with you, I reviewed the information that you left with me, and although I think that your CCC is a very nice idea,

I really don't believe it is something that Bickford would be interested in at this particular point in time."

"But Mr. Smith, I didn't even give you any of the particulars. I have a whole set of calculations here indicating that the CCC could save Bickford a considerable amount of time, effort, and money over the next few years."

"I don't mean to be rude, Miss Jones, but I am in a hurry, I really don't care to continue this conversation."

"Before you go, do you think that it might be possible to arrange to present this proposal to Mr. Perry [Tony Perry, V.P. of Corporate Facilities, Joe Smith's immediate supervisor] in the near future? I'm sure that he would be interested in seeing it. We had discussed this idea in passing earlier, and he seemed to feel that it warranted serious consideration."

"Maybe we can talk about that the next time you are here. I'll call you if I need to have something printed. Now I really must go."

As Jones returned to her car, she decided that in spite of what Smith had told her about waiting until next time, she should move ahead to contact Mr. Perry directly. He had seemed genuinely interested in hearing more about the CCC when she had spoken to him earlier, even though she had mentioned it only briefly. She decided that she would return to the office and send Perry a letter requesting an appointment to speak with him.

Although Jones was not yet aware of it, Joe Smith had returned to his desk and immediately began drafting the following memo to be sent to Tony Perry:

To:     Tony Perry, V.P. Corporate Facilities
From:   Joe Smith, Corporate Services
Re:     Royal CCC

Tony:
I spoke at length with Mary Jones of Royal this morning. She presented me with her proposal for the adoption of the CCC program at Bickford Publishing. After reviewing the proposal in detail, I have determined that the program: (a) is not cost effective, (b) has many problem areas that need ironing out, and (c) is inappropriate for our company at this time.

Therefore, in light of the above, my opinion is that this matter does not warrant any serious consideration or further discussion at this point in time.

## Royal 750 Color Copier

The Royal 750 color copier made its debut in 1983 and was originally sold by color copier specialists in the equipment division of Royal. But sales representatives did not want to sell the color copier exclusively and sales managers did not want to manage the color copier specialists. Therefore, the 750 was not a particularly successful product. In 1989, the sales responsibility for the color copier was transferred to the RRC division. Since the RRC sales representatives were already taking orders from customers needing the services of a color copier, it was felt that the reps would be in an advantageous position to determine when current customer requirements would justify the purchase of a 750.

Jones arrived back at her office at 10:45. She checked her mailbox for messages, grabbed a cup of coffee, and returned to her desk to draft the letter to Tony Perry. After making several phone calls setting up appointments for the next week and checking on client satisfaction with some jobs that were delivered that day, she gathered up the materials that she needed for her afternoon sales calls. Finishing her coffee, she noticed the poster announcing a trip for members of the "President's Club." To become a member, a sales representative had to meet 100% of his or her sales budget, sell a 750 color copier, sell a CCC program, and sell a short-term rental. Jones believed that making budget would be difficult but attainable, even though her superior performance in 1992 led to a budget increase of 20% for 1993. She had already sold a color copier and a short-term rental. Therefore, the main thing standing in her way of making the President's Club was the sale of a CCC. Not selling a CCC this year would have even more serious ramifications, she thought. Until recently, Jones had considered herself the prime candidate for the expected opening for a senior sales representative in her office. But Michael Gould, a sales rep who also had three years experience, was enjoying an excellent year. He had sold two color copiers and had just closed a deal on a CCC to a large semiconductor manufacturing firm. Normally everyone in the office celebrated the sale of a CCC. As a fellow sales rep was often heard saying, "it takes the heat off all of us for a while." Jones, however, found it difficult to celebrate Michael's sale. For not only was he the office "Golden Boy" but now, in her opinion, he was also the prime candidate for the senior sales rep position as well. Michael's sale also left Jones as one of the few reps in the office without the sale of a CCC to his or her credit. "It is pretty difficult to get a viable CCC lead," Jones thought, "but I've had one or two this year that should have been closed." Neither the long discussions with her sales manager, nor the numerous inservice training sessions and discussions on how to sell the CCC had helped. "I've just got to sell one of these soon," Jones resolved.

On her way out, she glanced at the clock. It was 11:33. She had just enough time to make her

11:45 appointment with Sam Lawless, operations manager, at ABC Electronics. This was Jones's first appointment at ABC and she was excited about getting a foot in the door there. A friend of hers was an assistant accountant at ABC. She had informed Jones that the company spent more than $15,000 a month on printing services and that they might consider a CCC proposal. Jones knew who the competition was, and although their prices were lower on low-volume orders, Royal could meet or beat their prices for the kind of volume of work for which ABC was contracting. But Jones wasn't enthusiastic about garnering the account for reproduction work. She believed she could sell ABC a CCC.

Jones's friend had mentioned management dissatisfaction with the subcontracting of so much printing. Also, there had been complaints regarding the quality of work. Investment in an in-house print shop had been discussed. Jones had assessed ABC's situation and had noticed a strong parallel with the situation at Star Electronics, a multi-division electronics manufacturing firm that had been sold CCCs for each of their four locations in the area. That sale, which occurred over a year ago, was vital in legitimatizing the potential customers in the Northeast. Jones hoped to sell ABC on the same premise that Fred Myers had sold Star Electronics. Myers had been extremely helpful in reviewing his sales plan with Jones and had given her ideas on points he felt had been instrumental in closing the Star deal. She felt well prepared for this call.

Jones had waited four months to get an appointment with Lawless. He had a reputation for disliking to speak with salespeople, but Jones's friend had passed along to him some CCC literature and he had seemed interested. Finally, after months of being unable to reach him by telephone, or get a response by mail, she had phoned two weeks ago and he had consented to see her. Today she planned to concentrate on how adoption of the CCC program might solve ABC's current reproduction problems. She also planned to ask Lawless to provide her with the necessary information to produce a convincing proposal in favor of CCC. Jones pulled into a visitor parking space and grabbed her briefcase. "This could end up being the one," she thought as she headed for the reception area.

Jones removed a business card from her wallet and handed it to the receptionist. "Mary Jones to see Sam Lawless, I have an appointment," Jones announced.

"I'm sorry," the receptionist replied, "Mr. Lawless is no longer with the company."

Jones tried not to lose her composure, "But I had an appointment to see him today. When did he leave?"

"Last Friday was Mr. Lawless's last day. Mr. Bates is now operations manager."

"May I see Mr. Bates, please?" Jones inquired, knowing in advance, the response.

"Mr. Bates does not see salespeople. He sees no one without an appointment."

"Could you tell him that I had an appointment to see Mr. Lawless? Perhaps he would consider seeing me."

"I can't call him. But I'll leave him a note with your card. Perhaps you can contact him later."

"Thank you, I will." Jones turned and left ABC, obviously shaken. "Back to square one," she thought as she headed back to her car. It was 12:05 p.m.

Jones headed for her next stop, CG Advertising, still upset from the episode at ABC. But she had long since discovered that no successful salesperson can dwell on disappointments. "It interferes with your whole attitude," she reminded herself. Jones arrived at the office park where CG was located. She was on time for her 12:30 appointment.

CG was a large full-service agency. Jones's color copy orders from CG had been increasing at a rapid rate for the past six months, and she had no reason to believe that their needs would decrease in the near future. Therefore she believed the time was ripe to present a case for the purchase of a 750 color copier. Jones had been dealing primarily with Jim Stevens, head of Creative Services. They had a good working relationship, even though on certain occasions Jones had found him to be unusually demanding about quality. But she figured that characteristic seemed to be common in many creative people. She had decided to use his obsession with perfection to work to her advantage.

Jones also knew that money was only a secondary consideration as far as Stevens was concerned. He had seemingly gotten his way on purchases in several other instances, so she planned her approach to him. Jones had outlined a proposal which she was now ready to present to Jim.

"Good morning, Jim, how's the advertising business?"

"It's going pretty well for us here, how's things with you?"

"Great, Jim," Jones lied, "I have an interesting idea to discuss with you. I've been thinking that CG has been ordering large quantities of color copies. I know that you utilize them in the presentations of advertising and marketing plans to clients. I also know that you like to experiment with several different concepts before actually deciding on a final idea. Even though we have exceptionally short turnaround time, it occurred to me that nothing would suit your needs more efficiently and effectively than the presence of one of our Royal 750 color copiers right here in your production room.

That way, each time that you consider a revision one of your artists will be able to compose a rough, and you can run a quick copy and decide virtually immediately if that is the direction in which you want to go, with no need to slow down the creative process at all."

"Well, I don't know; our current situation seems to be working out rather well. I really don't see any reason to change it."

"I'm not sure that you're fully aware of all the things that the 750 color copier is capable of doing," Jones pressed on. "One of the technicians and I have been experimenting with the 750. Even I have discovered some new and interesting capabilities to be applied in your field, Jim. Let me show you some of them."

She reached into her art portfolio and produced a wide variety of samples to show Stevens. "You know that the color copier is great for enlarging and reducing as well as straight duplicating. But look at the different effects we got by experimenting with various sizes and colors. Don't you think that this is an interesting effect?"

"Yes, it really is," Stevens said loosening up slightly.

"But wait," Jones added, "I really have the ultimate to show you." Jones produced a sheet upon which she had constructed a collage from various slides that Stevens had given her for enlarging.

"Those are my slides! Hey, that's great."

"Do you think that a potential client might be impressed by something like this? And the best part is you can whip something like this up in a matter of minutes, if the copier is at your disposal."

"Hey, that's a great idea, Mary, I'd love to be able to fool around with one of those machines. I bet I'd be able to do some really inventive proposals with it."

"I'm sure you would, Jim."

"Do you have a few minutes right now, I'd like to bounce this idea off of Bill Jackson, Head of Purchasing, and see how quickly we can get one in here."

Jones and Stevens went down to Jackson's office. Before they ever spoke, Jones felt that this deal was closed. Jim Stevens always got his own way. Besides, she believed she knew what approach to use with Bill Jackson. She had dealt with him on several other occasions. Jackson had failed to approve a purchase for her the prior fall, on the basis that the purchase could not be justified. He was right on that account. Their present 600 model was handling their reproduction needs sufficiently, but you can't blame a person for trying, she thought. Besides, she hadn't had Stevens in her corner for that one. This was going to be different.

"How's it going, Bill. You've met Mary Jones before, haven't you?"

"Yes, I remember Miss Jones. She's been to see me several times, always trying to sell me something we don't need," he said cynically.

"Well, this time I do have something you need and not only will this purchase save time, but it will save money, too. Let me show you some figures I've worked out regarding how much you can save by purchasing the 750 color copier." Jones showed Jackson that, at their current rate of increased orders of color copies, the 750 would pay for itself in three years. She also stressed the efficiency and ease of operation. But she knew that Jackson was really only interested in the bottom line.

"Well, I must admit, Miss Jones, it does appear to be a cost-effective purchase."

Stevens volunteered, "Not only that, but we can now get our artwork immediately, too. This purchase will make everyone happy."

Jones believed she had the order. "I'll begin the paperwork as soon as I return to the office. May I come by next week to complete the deal?"

"Well, let me see what needs to be done on this end, but I don't foresee a problem," Jackson replied.

"There won't be any problem," Stevens assured Jones.

"Fine, then. I'll call Jim, the first of next week to set up an appointment for delivery."

Jones returned to her car at 1:00. She felt much better having closed the sale on the 750. She had planned enough time to stop for lunch.

During lunch, Jones thought about her time at Royal. She enjoyed her job as a whole. If it weren't for the pressure she was feeling to sell the corporate copy center program, everything would be just about perfect. Jones had been a straight "A" student in college where she majored in marketing. As far back as she could remember, she had always wanted to work in sales. Her father had started out in sales, and enjoyed a very successful and profitable career. He had advanced to sales manager and sales director for a highly successful Fortune 500 company and was proud that his daughter had chosen to pursue a career in sales. Often they would get together, and he would offer suggestions that had proven effective for him when he had worked in the field. When Jones's college placement office had announced that a Royal collegiate recruiter was visiting the campus, Jones had immediately signed up for an interview. She knew several recent graduates that had obtained positions with Royal and were very happy there. They were also doing well financially. She was excited at the idea of working for an industry giant. When she was invited for a second interview, she was ecstatic. Several days later, she received a phone call offering her a position at the regional office. She accepted immediately. Jones attended various pre-training workshops for 6 weeks at her regional office preparing her for her 2-week intensive training period at the Royal Training Headquarters. The training consisted of product training and sales training.

She had excelled there, and graduated from that course at the head of her class. From that point on everything continued smoothly . . . until this problem with selling the CCC.

After a quick sandwich and coffee, Jones left the restaurant at 1:30. She allowed extra time before her 2:00 appointment at General Hospital, located just four blocks from the office, to stop into the office first, check for messages, and check in with her sales manager. She informed Tom Stein that she considered the sale of a 750 to CG almost certain.

"That's great, Mary, I never doubted your ability to sell the color copiers, or repro for that matter. But what are we going to do about our other problem?"

"Tom, I've been following CCC leads all morning. To tell you the truth, I don't feel as though I've made any progress at all. As a matter of fact, I've lost some ground." Jones went on to explain the situation that had developed at ABC Electronics and how she felt when she learned that Sam Lawless was no longer with the company. "I was pretty excited about that prospect, Tom. The news was a little tough to take."

"That's okay. We'll just concentrate on his replacement, now. It might be a setback. But the company's still there, and they still have the same printing needs and problems. Besides, you're going to make your final presentation to General Hospital this afternoon, and you really did your homework for that one." Stein had worked extensively with Jones on the proposal from start to finish. They both knew that it was her best opportunity of the year to sell a CCC.

"I'm leaving right now. Wish me luck."

He did. She filled her briefcase with her personals and CCC demonstration kit that she planned to use for the actual presentation and headed toward the parking lot.

Jones's appointment was with Harry Jameson of General Hospital. As she approached his office, his receptionist announced her. Jameson appeared and led her to the board room for their meeting. Jones was surprised to find three other individuals seated around the table. She was introduced to Bob Goldstein, V.P. of operations, Martha Chambers, director of accounting, and Dr. J. P. Dunwitty, chairman of the board. Jameson explained that whenever an expenditure of this magnitude was being considered, the hospital's executive committee had to make a joint recommendation.

Jones set up her demonstration at the head of the table so that it was easily viewed by everyone and began her proposal. She presented charts verifying the merits of the CCC (Exhibits 2, 3) and also the financial calculations that she had generated based upon the information supplied to her by Jameson.

Forty minutes later, Jones finished her presentation and began fielding questions. The usual concerns were voiced regarding hiring an "outsider" to work within the hospital. But the major concern seemed to revolve around the loss of employment on the part of two present printing press operators. One, John Brown, had been a faithful employee for more than five years. He was married and had a child. There had never been a complaint about John personally, or with regard to the quality or quantity of his work. The second operator was Peter Dunwitty, a recent graduate of a nearby vocational school and nephew of Dr. Dunwitty. Although he had been employed by the hospital for only three months, there was no question about his ability and performance.

In response to this concern, Jones emphasized that the new equipment was more efficient, but different, and did not require the skills of experienced printers like Brown and Dunwitty. She knew, however, that this was always the one point about the adoption of a CCC program that even she had the most difficulty justifying. She suddenly felt rather ill.

---

**EXHIBIT 2    Why Royal Corporate Copy Center?**

- No Hidden Costs
- No Downtime
- No Capital Investment
- No Recruiting or Training
- No People Problems
- No Inventory Problems
- Increased Quality
- Expert Operators—Plus Guaranteed Turnaround Time

- Allows You to Devote Full Time to Your Business
- Departmental Budget Control
- RRC Full Center Support
- Tailor-made System
- Full Write Off
- Guaranteed Cost per Copy
- Short-term Agreement
- Trial Basis

**What Is Royal Corporate Copy Center?   EXHIBIT 3**

*General Hospital Copying Objectives*
1. To lower on-hand inventory of forms
2. To be able to upgrade or relocate equipment if needed
3. To have a competent full-time operator as well as back-up operators
4. To increase productivity
5. To be more cost efficient
6. 89-day trial option period
7. To eliminate downtime
8. To eliminate waste
9. To assure fast turnaround
10. To establish an inventory control system for paper and copier supplies
11. To install an accurate departmental charge-back system
12. To improve copy quality
13. To eliminate queuing time
14. To allow administrative support personnel to devote their full time to General Hospital's daily business
15. To eliminate having to worry about service on machines

*General Hospital Offset vs. Printing*
1. You won't eliminate all your related printing problems such as:
   A. You will still have to keep Savins for short-run lengths.
   B. You will still have waste problems.
   C. You still need plates and printing supplies.
   D. It is messy and complicated.
   E. You must have a dependable operator every day, and someone for vacations.
   F. You will have to vend some printing.
   G. You won't be able to cut down inventory of forms on hand, and you will have to have long-run lengths to be profitable and long turnaround for two-sided copying.
   H. You will be running a copying print shop, but this is still not state of the art.
   I. It is very noisy. You wouldn't be able to put it in this building. You might have to find another location or keep it in the old building.
   J. Only 3 out of about 15 hospitals on the North Shore area have printing presses—those that do have large duplicators that do 100,000 to 200,000 in volume per month besides long-run lengths on presses.
2. You would lose all of the extra benefits the Royal Corporate Copy Center would give you. (See Attached)
3. For the first full year because of expense for press, your cost would be $14,890 higher than Royal Corporate Copy Center, and your estimated price increases over the next two years would not be fixed, thus still costing you more for a less efficient operation.

*Royal Corporate Copy Center Will Satisfy These Objectives in the Following Manner*:
1. By having a high-speed duplicator and professional operator, you will be able to order forms on an as-needed basis. This will lower your present inventory by at least 80%, thus freeing up valuable space for other use.
2. Because of the flexibility that Royal Corporate Copy Center gives you, you have the opportunity to change or upgrade equipment at any time. If relocation of equipment is necessary because of changes in the hospital's structure, this can be done also.
3. Royal Corporate Copy Center will provide a trained, professional operator whose hours will conform to General Hospital's. Regardless of vacation schedules, sickness, or personal absences, a competent operator will report to General Hospital every day. If these operators do not meet with General Hospital's satisfaction, they can be changed within 24 hours' time. Because Royal will supply the operators, you will be relieved of this person as a staff member. Benefits, sick time, and vacation will be taken care of by Royal. You will receive operators for your facility 52 weeks a year.

Royal Corporate Copy Center is the means whereby Royal will equip, staff, operate and manage a reproduction operation for you on your own premises. First, we analyze your needs, then we select and install the appropriate equipment. Secondly, we provide two fully trained Royal employed operators and professional reproduction management. Finally, we schedule all work, and protect you with comprehensive back-up capabilities at our Royal Reproduction Center . . . and you receive just one monthly bill for the entire package.

*(continued)*

**EXHIBIT 3** What Is Royal Corporate Copy Center? (*continued*)

4. Our people will report directly to your supervisor for their assignment the same as any other employee under your supervision. These people will be able to sort incoming jobs as we have discussed or may be used for other work in the copy center at non-peak times. These people would also be available to pick up copying work from various central locations throughout General Hospital at specified times, thus eliminating the need for people to come to the copy center. These people may also be used to operate other various types of equipment that General Hospital has.

5. By having a Royal Corporate Copy Center program at General Hospital and letting Royal take care of all your duplicating needs in a professional manner, your copying costs will become much more cost efficient. We believe that the cost savings alone in the first year could be upwards of 10–15% and would increase as your copy volume grows with you. Your present system does not offer several of the important benefits that Royal Corporate Copy Center offers that now will be included in one fixed cost—in dollars and cents, by not having to pay for these services, this is where the additional 10–15% cost savings per year could come in. We also will give you a fixed reproduction cost so that you can budget more accurately. We will also fix all of your cost for the next three years (that includes supplies, machine, support and operators) if you sign a three-year agreement at the end of the trial period. this will enable you to sve upwards of another 10% per year.

6. We at Royal feel very confident about this program and its success. We, therefore, wish to minimize our customers' risk for installing a new program. We feel we are able to do this by offering a trial option period of up to 89 days. This program works in the following way: General Hospital must sign a trial option pricing addendum and a three-year agreement. This will put into action the following:
   A. $1,050.00 per month credit off the original pricing for the first partial month, the first full month, and the second full month (total of $3,150.00).
   B. At the end of the trial option period General Hospital can elect to:
      a. Remain on the three-year agreement date May 1, 1993.
      b. Execute a 90-day, one-year, or two-year agreement with applicable pricing.
      c. Cancel the agreement date May 1, 1993, without liquidation damages.

7. With Royal Corporate Copy Center you will never experience downtime. Your work will always be done timely. We will back up the machines with a back-up copier running the work there or send it to our closest center to be completed and returned. By being a Royal Corporate Copy Center customer, General Hospital will always receive priority on service. Also, our operators will be able to handle more extensive types of service to the equipment.

8. General Hospital will be charged only for the copies ordered. This will eliminate all of your present waste that is involved with offset.

9. Trained Royal operators should reduce turnaround time on work. These operators will know how to run jobs on the equipment properly and in the fastest way so that productivity will increase and turnaround time will decrease.

10. Royal will order all toner and developer, thus eliminating the need for General Hospital to make large commitments and maintain large inventories. We will order paper also for you on a weekly basis if you so choose.

11. Royal will install an accurate departmental charge-back system, allowing General Hospital to accurately account for all copies. You will receive a copy of this breakdown each month.

12. Royal will provide trained operators, guaranteeing high-quality copies. By using a Xerographic process, you will always have consistently high-quality copies.

13. By providing General Hospital with skilled operators, copying and duplicating requirements will be met in a timely fashion, eliminating the need for General Hospital employees to stand and wait to use other equipment. In essence, General Hospital employees will be free to do General Hospital business; Royal will fulfill the copying and duplicating requirements.

14. Administrative personnel will no longer have to worry about sales people, service problems, obtaining purchase orders, or buying supplies.

15. All machines used will be the responsibility of Royal for service and maintenance.

*General Hospital Cash Flow (One-Year Period) Royal Corporate Copy Center vs. Present System*

| Corporate Copy Center | | Hospital |
|---|---|---|
| Royal 900 | Equipment | Obsolete presses & mimeo |
| $6,500.00 | Supplies and Paper | $42,189.00 |
| Included | Toner and Developer | –0– |
| Included | Labor | $22,496.00 |
| Included | Benefits | $ 2,681.00 |
| Included | Administrative Time | –?– |
| Included | Management Time | –?– |
| Included | CCC Benefits | None |
| Eliminated | Savin 680 Rental | $ 4,534.00 |
| Eliminated | Smaller Savin I Rental | $ 1,080.00 |
| Eliminated | Smaller Savin II Rental | $ 1,320.00 |
| Eliminated | Savin Copying Cost | $ 2,400.00 |
| Eliminated | Vending | $ 7,000.00 |
| | (Forms that could be kept in-house) | |
| Eliminated | Issuing of P.O.s | $    500.00 |
| Eliminated | Expense for Present Building | $ 2,500.00 |
| $80,310.00 | Royal Facilities Management | — |
| ($.029 per copy) | (200,000 copies) | |
| $86,810.00 | TOTAL CASH FLOW | $86,700.00 |

| | Fixed | Price Increases | Est. | |
|---|---|---|---|---|
| $86,810.00 | 0 | 15 months | 5% | $ 91,035.00 |
| $89,414.00 | 3% | 2nd year | 9% | $ 99,228.00 |
| $91,202.00 | 2% | 3rd year | 9% | $108,158.00 |
| $267,426.00 | PROJECTED 3-YEAR COST | | | $298,421.00 |
| $30,995.00 | PROJECTED 3-YEAR SAVINGS | | | None |

*Recommendation*

Royal feels at this time that it would be very beneficial for General Hospital to change from its present reproduction system of two offset presses, mimeograph equipment, several smaller copiers, and a collator to a Royal 900 and a professional operator under the Royal Corporate Copy Center program. Royal feels it would be beneficial for General Hospital to effect this change presently for the following reasons:

1. Professional people would replace a part-time operator (20 hours) and an operator that is on leave (20 hours).
2. State-of-the-art equipment would replace the present presses, which are very old and outdated.
3. The large amount of waste presently experienced would be eliminated.
4. The high maintenance cost for the presses would be eliminated.
5. Hand collating and off-line collating would be eliminated.
6. Poor and inconsistent quality in the copies would be eliminated.
7. The back-up problem would be eliminated.
8. You would have better turnaround and accountability.
9. Some of the smaller copiers, and lower copy volumes on the smaller copiers, would be eliminated.
10. You would receive all other Royal Corporate Copy Center benefits unattainable with your present program.

In the following pages I hope to show you how we will accomplish these goals by installing the Royal Corporate Copy Center at General Hospital.

"Well, Miss Jones, if you'll excuse us for a few minutes, we'd like to reach a decision on this matter," said Jameson.

"There's no need to decide right at this point. You all have copies of my proposal. If you'd like to take a few days to review the figures, I'd be happy to come by then," said Jones, in a last-ditch attempt to gain some additional time.

"I think that we'd like to meet in private for a few minutes right now, if you don't mind," interjected Dunwitty.

"No, that's fine," Jones said as she left the room for the lobby. She sat in a waiting room and drank a cup of coffee. She lit a cigarette, a habit that she seldom engaged in. Five minutes later, the board members called her back in.

"This CCC idea is really sound, Miss Jones," Jameson began. "However, here at General Hospital, we have a very strong commitment to our employees. There really seems to be no good reason to put two fine young men out of work. Yes, I realize that from the figures that you've presented to us, you've indicated a savings of approximately $30,000 over three years. But I would have to question some of the calculations. Under the circumstances, we feel that maintaining sound employee relations has more merit than switching to an unproven program right now. Therefore, we've decided against purchasing a CCC."

Jones was disappointed. But she had been in this situation often enough not to show it. "I'm sorry to hear that, Mr. Jameson, I thought that I had presented a very good argument for participation in the CCC program. Do you think that if your current operators decided to leave, before you filled their positions, you might consider CCC again?"

"I can't make a commitment to that right now. But feel free to stay in touch," Jameson countered.

"I'll still be coming in on a regular basis to meet all your needs for other work not capable of being performed in your print shop," Jones replied.

"Then you'll be the first to know if that situation arises," said Jameson.

"Thank you all for your time. I hope that I was of assistance even though you decided against the purchase. If I may be of help at any point in time, don't hesitate to call," Jones remarked as she headed for the door.

Now, totally disappointed, Jones regretted having scheduled another appointment for that afternoon. She would have liked to call it a day. But she knew she had an opportunity to pick up some repro work and develop a new account. So she knew she couldn't cancel.

Jones stopped by to see Paul Blake, head of staff training at Pierson's, a large department store with locations throughout the state. Jones had made a cold call one afternoon the prior week and had obtained a sizable printing order. Now she wanted to see whether Blake was satisfied with the job, which had been delivered earlier in the day. She also wanted to speak to him about some of the other services available at the RRC. Jones was about to reach into her briefcase for her card to offer to the receptionist when she was startled by a "Hello, Mary" coming from behind her.

"Hello, Paul," Jones responded, surprised and pleased that he had remembered her name. "How are you today?"

"Great! I have to tell you that report that you printed for us is far superior to the work that we have been receiving from some of our other suppliers. I've got another piece that will be ready to go out in about an hour. Can you have someone come by and pick it up then?"

"I'll do better than that. I'll pick it up myself," Jones replied.

"See you then," he responded as he turned and headed back towards his office.

"I'm glad I decided to stop by after all," Jones thought as she pressed the elevator button. She wondered how she could best use the next hour to help salvage the day. When the elevator door opened, out stepped Kevin Fitzgerald, operations manager for Pierson's. Jones had met him several weeks earlier when she had spoken with Ann Leibman, a sales rep for Royal Equipment Division. Leibman had been very close to closing a deal that would involve selling Pierson several "casual" copying machines that they were planning to locate in various offices to use for quick copying. Leibman informed Jones that Tom Stein had presented a CCC proposal to Pierson's six months earlier but the plan was flatly refused. Fitzgerald, she explained, had been sincerely interested in the idea. But the plan involved a larger initial expenditure than Pierson's was willing to make. Now, Leibman explained, there would be a much larger savings involved, since the "casual" machines would not be needed if a CCC were involved. Jones had suggested to Fitzgerald that the CCC proposal be reworked to include the new machines so that a current assessment could be made. He had once again appeared genuinely interested and suggested that Jones retrieve the necessary figures from Jerry Query, Head of Purchasing. Jones had not yet done so. She had phoned Query several times, but he had never responded to her messages.

"Nice to see you again, Mr. Fitzgerald. Ann Leibman introduced us, I'm Mary Jones from Royal."

"Yes, I remember. Have you spoken with Mr. Query, yet?"

"I'm on my way to see him right now," Jones said as she thought that this would be the perfect way to use the hour.

"Fine, get in touch with me when you have the new calculations."

Jones entered the elevator that Fitzgerald had been holding for her as they spoke. She returned to the first floor and consulted the directory. Purchasing was on the third floor. As she walked off the elevator on the third floor, the first thing that she saw was a sign that said, "Salespeople seen by appointment only. Tuesdays and Thursdays, 10 a.m.–12 noon."

"I'm really out of luck," Jones thought, "not only do I not have an appointment, but today's Wednesday. But I'll give it my best shot as long as I'm here."

Jones walked over to the receptionist who was talking to herself as she searched through a large pile of papers on her desk. Although Jones knew she was aware of her presence, the receptionist continued to avoid her.

"This could be a hopeless case," Jones thought. Just then the receptionist looked up and acknowledged her.

"Good afternoon. I'm Mary Jones from Royal. I was just speaking to Mr. Fitzgerald who suggested that I see Mr. Query. I'm not selling anything. I just need to get some figures from him."

"Just a minute," the receptionist replied as she walked towards an office with Query's name on the door.

"Maybe this is not going to be so bad after all," Jones thought.

"Mr. Query will see you for a minute," the receptionist announced as she returned to her desk.

Jones walked into Mr. Query's plushly furnished office. Query was an imposing figure at 6 feet, 4 inches, nearly 300 pounds, and bald. Jones extended her hand, which Query grasped firmly. "What brings you here to see me?" Query inquired.

Jones explained her conversations with Ann Leibman and Kevin Fitzgerald. As she was about to ask her initial series of questions, Query interrupted. "Miss Jones, I frankly don't know what the hell you are doing here!" Query exclaimed. "We settled this issue over six months ago, and now you're bringing it up again. I really don't understand. You people came in with a proposal that was going to cost us more money than we were spending. We know what we're doing. No one is going to come in here and tell us our business."

"Mr. Query," Jones began, trying to remain composed, "the calculations that you were presented with were based upon the equipment that Pierson's was utilizing six months ago. Now that you are contemplating additional purchases, I mentioned to Mr. Fitzgerald that a new comparison should be made. He instructed me to speak with you in order to obtain the information needed to prepare a thorough proposal," Jones tried to explain.

"Fitzgerald! What on earth does Fitzgerald have to do with this? This is none of his damn business. He sat at the same table as I six months ago when we arrived at a decision. Why doesn't he keep his nose out of affairs that don't concern him? We didn't want this program six months ago, we don't want it now!" Query shouted.

"I'm only trying to do my job, Mr. Query. I was not part of the team that presented the proposal six months ago. But from all the information that is available now, I still feel that a CCC would save you money here at Pierson's."

"Don't you understand, Miss Jones? We don't want any outsiders here. You have no control over people that don't work for you. Nothing gets approved around here unless it has my signature on it. That's control. Now I really see no need to waste any more of my time or yours."

"I appreciate your frankness," Jones responded, struggling to find something positive to say.

"Well, that's the kind of man I am, direct and to the point."

"You can say that again," Jones thought. "One other thing before I go, Mr Query. I was noticing the color copies on your desk."

"Yes, I like to send color copies of jobs when getting production estimates. For example, these are of the bogs that we will be using during our fall promotion. I have received several compliments from suppliers who think that by viewing color copies they get a real feel for what I need."

"Well, it just so happens that my division of Royal sells color copiers. At some time it may be more efficient for you to consider a purchase. Let me leave you some literature on the 750 copier which you can review at your leisure." Jones removed a brochure from her briefcase. She attached one of her business cards to it and handed it to Query. As she shook his hand and left the office, Jones noted that she had half an hour before the project of Blake's would be ready for pick-up. She entered the donut shop across the street and as she waited for her coffee, she reviewed her day's activities. She was enthusiastic about the impending color copier sale at CG Advertising, and about the new repro business that she had acquired at Pierson's. But the rest of the day had been discouraging. Not only had she been "shot down" repeatedly, but she'd now have to work extra hard for several days to insure that she would make 100% of budget for the month. "Trying to sell the CCC is even harder than I thought it was," Jones thought.

## MORGANTOWN INC.

In November 1995 Morgantown Inc. merged with Lea-Meadows Industries, a manufacturer of upholstered furniture for living and family rooms. The merger was not planned in a conventional sense. Charlton Bates's father-in-law died suddenly in August 1995, leaving his daughter with controlling interest in the firm. The merger proceeded smoothly, since the two firms were located on adjacent properties and the general consensus was that the two firms would maintain as much autonomy as was economically justified. Moreover, the upholstery line filled a gap in the Morgantown product mix, even though it would retain its own identity and brand names.

The only real issue that continued to plague Bates was merging the selling effort. Morgantown had its own salesforce, but Lea-Meadows Industries relied on sales agents to represent it. The question was straight-forward, in his opinion: "Do we give the upholstery line of chairs and sofas to our salesforce, or do we continue using the sales agents?" Mr. John Bott, Morgantown's sales vice-president, said the line should be given to his sales group; Mr. Martin Moorman, national sales manager of Lea-Meadows Industries, said the upholstery line should remain with sales agents.

### Lea-Meadows Industries

Lea-Meadows Industries is a small manufacturer of upholstered furniture for use in living and family rooms. The firm is over seventy-five years old. The company has some of the finest fabrics and frame construction in the industry, according to trade sources. Net sales in 1995 were $3 million. Total industry sales of 1,500 upholstered furniture manufacturers in 1995 were $4.4 billion. Company sales had increased 15 percent annually over the last five years, and company executives believed this growth rate would continue for the foreseeable future.

Lea-Meadows Industries employed fifteen sales agents to represent its products. These sales agents also represented several manufacturers of noncompeting furniture and home furnishings. Often a sales agent found it necessary to deal with several buyers in a store in order to represent all lines carried. On a typical sales call, a sales agent would first visit buyers. New lines, in addition to any promotions being offered by manufacturers, would be discussed. New orders were sought where and when it was appropriate. A sales agent would then visit a retailer's selling floor to check displays, inspect furniture, and inform sales people on furniture.

Lea-Meadows Industries paid an agent commission of 5 percent of net company sales for these services. Moorman thought sales agents spent 10 to 15 percent of their in-store sales time on Lea-Meadows products.

The company did not attempt to influence the type of retailers that agents contacted. Yet it was implicit in the agency agreement that agents would not sell to discount houses. All agents had established relationships with their retail accounts and worked closely with them. Sales records indicated that agents were calling on furniture and department stores. An estimated 1,000 retail accounts were called on in 1995.

### Morgantown Inc.

Morgantown Inc. is a manufacturer of medium- to high-priced living and dining room wood furniture. The firm was formed in 1902. Net sales in 1995 were $50 million. Total estimated industry sales of wood furniture in 1995 were $7.1 billion at manufacturers' prices.

The company employed 10 full-time sales representatives who called on 1,000 retail accounts in 1986. These individuals performed the same function as sales agents, but were paid a salary plus a small commission. In 1995 the average Morgantown sales representative received an annual salary of $65,000 (plus expenses) and a commission of 0.5 percent on net company sales. Total sales administration costs were $112,500.

The Morgantown salesforce was highly regarded in the industry. The salesmen were known particularly for their knowledge of wood furniture and willingness to work with buyers and retail sales personnel. Despite these points, Bates knew that all retail accounts did not carry the complete Morgantown furniture line. He had therefore instructed John Bott to "push the group a little harder." At present, sales representatives were making ten sales calls per week, with the average sales call running three hours. Remaining time was accounted for by administrative activities and travel. Bates recommended that the call frequency be increased to seven calls per account per year, which was consistent with what he thought was the industry norm.

### Merging the Sales Effort

In separate meetings with Bott and Moorman, Bates was able to piece together a variety of data and perspectives on the question. These meetings also made it clear that Bott and Moorman differed dramatically in their views.

Source: This case is used with the permission of its author, Roger A. Kerin, Edwin L. Cox School of Business, Southern Methodist University, Dallas, Texas.

John Bott had no doubts about assigning the line to the Morgantown salesforce. Among the reasons he gave for this approach were the following. First, Morgantown had developed one of the most well-respected, professional sales groups in the industry. Sales representatives could easily learn the fabric jargon, and they already knew personally many of the buyers who were responsible for upholstered furniture. Second, selling the Lea-Meadows line would require only about 15 percent of present sales call time. Thus he thought the new line would not be a major burden. Third, more control over sales efforts was possible. He noted that Charlton Bates's father-in-law had developed the sales group twenty-five years earlier because of the commitment it engendered and the service "only our own people are able and willing to give." Moreover, our people have the Morgantown "look" and presentation style that is instilled in every person. Fourth, he said it wouldn't look right if we had our representatives and agents calling on the same stores and buyers. He noted that Morgantown and Lea-Meadows Industries overlapped on all their accounts. He said, "We'd be paying a commission on sales to these accounts when we would have gotten them anyway. The difference in commission percentages would not be good for morale."

Martin Moorman advocated keeping sales agents for the Lea-Meadows line. His arguments were as follows. First, all sales agents had established contacts and were highly regarded by store buyers, and most had represented the line in a professional manner for many years. He, too, had a good working relationship with 15 agents. Second, sales agents represented little, if any, cost beyond commissions. Moorman noted, "Agents get paid when we get paid." Third, sales agents were committed to the Lea-Meadows line: "The agents earn a part of their living representing us. They have to service retail accounts to get the repeat business." Fourth, sales agents were calling on buyers not contacted by Morgantown sales representatives. He noted, "If we let Morgantown people handle the line, we might lose these accounts, have to hire more sales personnel, or take away 25 percent of the present selling time given to Morgantown product lines."

As Bates reflected on the meetings, he felt that a broader perspective was necessary beyond the views expressed by Bott and Moorman. One factor was profitability. Existing Morgantown furniture lines typically had gross margins that were 5 percent higher than those for Lea-Meadows upholstered lines. Another factor was the "us and them" references apparent in the meetings with Bott and Moorman. Would merging the sales efforts overcome this, or would it cause more problems? Finally, the idea of increasing the salesforce to incorporate the Lea-Meadows line did not sit well with him. Adding a new salesperson would require restructuring of sales territories, potential loss of commission to existing people, and "a big headache."

## HOSPITAL SUPPLY INTERNATIONAL: RX FOR INCREASED SALES

Hospital Supply International (HSI), an international manufacturer and distributor of hospital supplies, sells a diverse line of high quality patient care products. Over 20 years, HSI built a commanding market share and was known in the industry for its strong salesforce, reliable products, and excellent service.

Profitability, however, had slipped in the last two years as a result of increased competition and new hospital purchasing strategies. For example, many of HSI's largest hospitals had joined buying groups for the purpose of negotiating bulk discounts. HSI's chief competitor, Acme, had developed new products that matched one of HSI's most profitable lines. Reducing price by 40 percent and using a team selling strategy, Acme had taken some of HSI's most profitable hospitals.

The situation was especially challenging for Charles Duffy, 43 years old, who had been recently promoted to sector executive. With direct responsibility for all hospitals on the East Coast, he decided that his first priority was to take a hard look at marketing strategy, and in four weeks he was scheduled to update senior management on his initial thinking. Duffy's predecessor, unable to reverse HSI's decline in market share, was fired.

But while spending time on field visits with some of the salespeople, Duffy observed that they were often unclear about their goals and reasons for making a particular call. During a joint call on New York University Hospital, they met an HSI sales product "specialist" who did not know the sales "generalist" responsible for NYU. Another salesperson got lost while searching for Central Supply in a large suburban hospital. Disturbed by these observations, Duffy had hired

This case developed by Stephen X. Doyle and Kurt Engemann. Reprinted with permission.

a respected consultant to conduct an audit and develop recommendations.

The consultant's recommendations were unexpected, and prompted Duffy to circulate the report along with Exhibits 1 and 2, to several key managers.

The managers gave Duffy their own recommendations the following week.

### Report from Florence Hoover, VP Marketing/Sales

Dear Chuck:

I've studied the consultant's report, and I agree with his assessment of the situation. We don't have a traditional motivation or training problem; the issue is one of sales strategy and organizational structure.

The sales program he recommends would replace broad territorial coverage with in-depth account management, reassign salespeople from 25 to 30 accounts to only 5 major accounts, and change their title to Account Manager. The individual Account Manager would coordinate and supervise HSI's technical specialists and act as the chief liaison to a particular hospital. A telemarketing and direct mail unit would take over the hundreds of smaller community hospitals in the area.

The program seems to offer several key advantages. The account manager would develop a deeper relationship with individual hospitals. He or she would dedicate more time and resources to a particular customer. And, in order to position HSI as the "preferred supplier," the account manager would develop relationships with administration, finance, engineering, central supply, and other areas that were previously outside our reach.

It was our weak penetration of these decision centers, in part, that made Acme's attack possible. We've had close ties with end users for years, but "buying power" is shifting to finance and administration—especially for high-technology items, long-term contracts and large suppliers. Our contact with key hospitals is too limited, too uncoordinated, and too superficial.

These strengthened relationships could also be our way of addressing the threat posed by buying groups and the preferred supplier arrangements offered by competitors. Just last week, 17 of 32 Connecticut hospitals signed up with a new buying group in Hartford. Two others signed exclusive contracts with Acme, enticed by a discount and special services like custom labeling, a simplified ordering procedure, and floor-specific delivery.

---

### EXHIBIT 1

| Transactional Selling | Relationship Selling |
|---|---|
| **Goal** | |
| Sales and satisfied customer | Position of preferred supplier |
| **Essence** | |
| Probing, handling objections, closing | Building trust and intense service |
| **Length of Relationship** | |
| Short; the sales call itself may only be 30 minutes | Long; months, years |
| **Salesforce Goals** | |
| Closed sale | Manage the relationship |
| **Number of Customers Appropriate for each Approach** | |
| Many; 30–200 customers/salesperson | Few; 2 to 5 accounts/account manager |
| **Organizational Level and Size of Selling Team** | |
| Low level, one or two sales people involved | Higher level, team selling |
| **Teamwork Required to Support the Selling Effort Low** | High, often involves mfg., dist., prod. dev. in the selling process |
| **Examples** | |
| Chicago Commodity Exchange | IBM Main Frame |

**Excerpts from Consultant's Interviews in "City Hospital"**   **EXHIBIT 2**

"When you walk into the 'City Hospital,'" according to one of its nurses, "you can tell you're in a small town. We all know each other here; we care about each other. There's a community-mindedness you won't find in large city hospitals."

The hospital itself is three buildings just off the downtown Expressway. Since its founding as a community hospital in 1958, it has served patients primarily from the Central, Southern and Eastern sections of the city and has grown with the community from its original 115 beds to 628 beds and several outpatient clinics in adjoining buildings. Today, it houses more than 2,000 professional staff, 300 affiliated doctors and 1,200 volunteers.

What you notice first, however, is a large volunteer staff—dozens of senior citizens who tend the shops, staff the cafeteria, and offer help and directions—and the seasoned nursing staff, some of whom have been at the hospital for decades.

You also notice the fellowship among the staff. They greet each other with first names. Many seem to know the husbands, wives and children of their co-employees. And just last year, according to one of the nursing directors, the head of physiology lost her husband, a young man in his thirties. "Hundreds of the staff attended the funeral," she recalled, "and the women in the hospital cooked all the food." It was like an old-time gathering, in which a whole town rallied to the side of a family in trouble.

It is this environment—with its emphasis on direct personal contact and responsibility to the local community—that seems to set the tone for "City's" management of suppliers.

**Relations with Suppliers**

When the staff talks about Martin Troy, president of "City Hospital," they speak in reverential tones, as if they were describing a local minister or elder statesman. "Martin has been with the hospital for 30 years," according to one of the unit administrators, "but he's remarkably unpretentious and supportive." As another added, "You can see Martin in the lunchroom and chat with him. He'll ask you how things are going." Speaking with him, one is impressed by the dignity and respect he accords his staff.

"I want the decision making to remain close to the action," he says, "and I think that trust and communication are the basis of our culture. I spend time trying to understand what is going on within the hospital. I make site visits. I meet monthly with senior management. I participate in the committees. I give a presentation at each new employee orientation."

But, despite his involvement, Troy insists on the decentralization of responsibility. "It's not just that I encourage decision making at the lower levels with the organization; I also cannot personally keep track of the technology and the systems. I want those who are closest to patient care to be involved. They know more about how the technology impacts the quality of care."

As one of the nursing directors added, "the administration doesn't get involved in the selection of suppliers; they count on materials management and those of us who actually use the products. They don't have the time—and that's also Martin Troy's style."

Consequently, the primary responsibility falls to the materials management department, which is located on the ground floor and handles everything from printing and vending to the purchase of medical and surgical supplies. Medical and surgical supplies alone account for about $12 million in annual expenditures, and are supervised by a director of materials management, a purchasing manager, two purchasing agents, and three assistants.

According to Kathy Smith, the purchasing agent, "about 90 percent of our re-orders are medical/surgical items. On our main line products, we reorder about once a week. The exceptions include emergency items such as those ordered from the surgical suite, like bi-pass materials." Inventory levels are monitored as part of the materials planning process that tracks level for the various departments. When an item is low, it is red-flagged and an order is generated by computer. Manual checks are also used to supplement this system.

Once an order is generated, Kathy designates someone to initiate the purchase. If the item is on contract, price is not discussed. If not, the price must be negotiated, and at least three suppliers are asked to tender bids.

*(continued)*

**EXHIBIT 2**    Excerpts from Consultant's Interviews in "City Hospital" (*continued*)

In the tender process, there is a balance of power between the purchasing department and the end users. Typically, end users provide input and recommendations relative to patient care and product technology. They may suggest potential suppliers, share insights on past service or check up on new products by calling other hospitals. Purchasing gets involved to manage the transaction, arrange trials, control costs, and handle the ongoing relationship with the suppliers.

Depending on their particular needs, some end users are more involved in the selection and bidding process than others. Barb Donahue, the director of the surgical unit, explained that in her unit "the purchasing agents protect us. We articulate our needs through them, gather information through them, arrange trials, and set up meetings with suppliers." Others, like Rob Jensen, the Unit Administrator in CH, prefer to leave more of the work to purchasing. "They want us to be involved, to offer input and arrange trials, but I'm really short on time. I usually let purchasing take care of everything, make sure that the product is here, keep the reps out of my hair, and see that we have no stock outs."

In either case, because it acts as the liaison to suppliers, the purchasing department—and the negotiating and tendering process—is central to the management of supplies at "City Hospital."

When talking about the bidding process, however, it is clear that the staff considers it more than a convenient arrangement. "I believe in the free market," says John Mills, the director of materials management. "I don't like single suppliers; I don't even like oligopoly. For example, I don't hear from an Abbott sales rep anymore and I wonder how that is affecting our pricing." Florence McGuinness, a hospital vice president, described similar feelings: "I believe in competition among suppliers, and I want competitive bids. You have to remember that we get our funding from public sources—90 percent of our budget—and we have a responsibility to these taxpayers in terms of sound fiscal management." Other staffers insist that the bidding process is the only "ethical" and "fair" way to manage suppliers.

### Budgeting Concerns

The concern with budgets and pricing seem to be driven by a number of factors. Last year, the hospital ran a $1.4 million deficit and was forced into a period of serious fiscal restraint. It was also the first year that the "City" was forced to reduce staff. "As a taxpayer I feel the crunch," says the head of the OR, "and it motivates me to try and save money here. There's a real crisis today in hospital finances."

Suppliers, at times, have aggravated the hospital by ignoring the seriousness of the budget crunch. The director of Materials Management remarked that "suppliers seem to forget the kind of budget pressures we feel here." For example, he recalled that "last year, some suppliers came in asking for a 15% increase in prices. They just aren't listening, and when that happens, we simply won't deal with them."

Among end users in the labs and on surgical floors, financial imperatives are highlighted by a feedback system that forces accountability and budget-consciousness. On a monthly basis, each of the eight directors receives a report that

> tracks expenses against the budget established for that fiscal year. "The key," according to the director of the critical care units, "is to make sure that everything balances. If we're over for some reason—maybe because of employee turnover and training time, unexpected patient volume or changes in supply costs—I have to prepare a formal report that explains why my units are over. It makes us all very budget-conscious."

### Service Criteria

Despite the attention to budgeting, however, the end users are quick to acknowledge that price is only one of the criteria they consider when evaluating suppliers. The director of the critical care units (who's been at "City" for some 30 years), notes that "only inexperienced people buy just on price—they don't have the track record with suppliers. My experience gives me a more global view, and the realization that factors like quality, longevity and service are crucial. Some people become very short-sighted, narrow in their focus. Fortunately, there are others who balance out this view."

In fact, the "City Hospital" seems to have a two-tiered relationship with its suppliers. At the top is an inner circle of companies and reps who are known and trusted by materials management and the end users. Among these qualified candidated, price competition is encouraged. A purchasing agent commented: "We often prefer to go with a more trusted supplier—we'll even pay a premium for it. Price becomes an issue only with parity products, within a group of known, trusted suppliers who then bid for the contract."

Myra Mills, a director of nursing, recalled a recent choice made by her department. "A few months ago we were buying beds. There are many suppliers for these hospital beds and they all have acceptable quality. But one supplier stood out. They were responsive to our nurses in recognizing that it is not a bed that is being sold, but a concept of care. Frequently, particularly with chronic illnesses, patients will develop bedsores. This company provided inservice, products, follow-up about skin care, and information on how to take care of these patients. They put on training programs. Interestingly enough, though their bed product was just equal to what competitors were offering, they got all our business."

Conversely, poor service has led to the rejection of several suppliers in the past. Rita Diaz, a nursing director, described her dissatisfaction with a potential supplier: "Periodically, one of our suppliers goes through the motions of coming in and doing a sales call. They keep on telling us that they want a presence here. But, bottom line, I don't think they are going to develop the trust and responsiveness we require."

Rita recalled a similar experience: "I don't think that Kendall is much of a contender. What happens is that they sell their product through distributors who carry 500 to 600 products and really don't know the types of in-depth information we require. In fact, I find them next to useless. We need service, follow-up and communication. For example, when I buy morphine, I buy it from one or two pharmaceutical companies that have proven to me that they are responsive. I know their people, I know their names, and I know they are there for me."

Finally, the program also promises a more focused use of sales resources, particularly time, which should be reserved for high profit products and high revenue hospitals. Sales and service time would be invested where it is likely to reap the greatest return. Telemarketing and direct mail can effectively handle the smaller accounts in hard-to-reach areas; right now these accounts aren't growing at all because no one is selling or servicing them.

I was impressed by the report. Let's seize the opportunity!

### Report from Edward Sharp, VP Distribution

Chuck:

I took a look at the report, and I can't argue with the fact that the sales effort is in a slump. Even so, his recommendations are a bit too drastic for me.

It worries me, in particular, that we'll take our eye further off the ball—at a time when we need to be playing to our traditional strengths, namely, developing highly profitable, specialized products for the health care system and providing outstanding service. Can we, for example, afford to turn away at this time from investing in our home health care line?

The recommendations are all based on the assumption that we can differentiate ourselves with more coordinated and indepth customer relationships. And he may be right to some extent—hospitals do demand more from their suppliers

today—but I don't agree that differentiated, superior products are less important than a relationship. If we accept his advice, broadening and deepening our relationship with a particular hospital, wouldn't we wind up with the same products to offer? Where, ultimately, is the added value? It seems that we run the risk of investing time and money in relationships—only to find ourselves in a price war with other suppliers of commodity products.

The report suggested that we develop value added services like new packaging, special skids and customized information systems that facilitate the hospital's acquisition and ordering cycle. This seems to make sense on paper, but what about the extra costs? And will these services truly differentiate us? Shouldn't we worry about these sorts of innovations—ones that make our products distinct—rather than change the way we sell them?

Also, if we're worried about relationships with customers, we should remember: the new account "quarterback" will create power struggles within HSI, and drastically change the channels of internal communication. This can't help but further destabilize our relationships with hospitals.

The report asks us to budget $250,000 for sales training, and to be prepared to manage salesforce turnover as high as 40 percent. The process will also escalate our selling costs over the next few years, during which we won't likely see any improvement in revenues. As you know, this comes at a particularly bad time, as we're still trying to absorb a major acquisition, and corporate management is pushing all of its divisions for increased R.O.I. I'm not sure we can absorb the added blows right now.

Times may have changed, but that doesn't mean we should abandon our strategy of developing superior products, and selling them aggressively. Let's get back to the basics!

## Report from Keith Rose, VP Information Systems

Charles:

The consultant may be onto something, but before we proceed let's address the fact that the potential benefits are still soft. His preliminary estimate of a market share increase needs to be solidified. We should work with him to quantify the revenue and cost changes.

I believe the modeling approach he mentions to pinpoint benefits would be a good starting point before we fully commit to organizational changes. I would feel better if we use a model to explore various scenarios to determine if we can pull it off. For example, what happens if more of our products become commodities? A model would help us focus on important issues and clarify our assumptions.

We have much of the data he needs for the model. We can provide the historical data on sales and costs, and Ron Enrico is looking at current costs. It does seem that there will be quite a bit of subjective input needed also. The consultant indicated the need for some workshops to elicit the judgment of knowledgeable participants. This would keep the results consistent with our collective intuition about the future. Hopefully, the results will be robust enough so that changes in our assumptions wouldn't alter our actions drastically.

This model is not a typical MIS project. It will require special talent and a nontraditional approach. Rapid feedback to keep everyone participating is essential. We are ready to work with the consultant to get things going.

If the model works out we should be able to use it as a tool on an ongoing basis, making improvements to it as we learn how it would be useful. There is good linkage to the price discounting project we're working on. Our experience has been that if the development of a model is well managed the return on that investment is outstanding.

## Report from Ron Enrico, VP Manufacturing

Dear Charlie:

In light of the consultant's report, let me just bring to the forefront some of our recent observations and efforts. As you know, manufacturing has been working quite earnestly with R&D to keep a competitive edge to HSI's broad product line. However, despite our efforts, we are slipping on several fronts. My initial feeling is that the consultant's recommendations have some validity and should be explored in depth at our next monthly management team meeting. If we implemented his recommendations, we would not only alter our selling approach, but also manufacturing would be impacted. We need to coordinate.

We expect the foreign competitors to increase the pressure. Gusendwerk has been much more adaptive to newer technology than we have been able to because of our budget constraints. As a result, their higher end items contain features which are easily modified to comply with an individual customer's requests. Our traditional strength in the highly specialized products is eroding because of our inability to provide customized changes as casually as they do. We don't recover our fixed costs if we don't have sufficient volume. The proposed Account Managers may be in a unique position to provide valuable feedback about customer requests, but we need to be be tooled up to handle them. I'm suggesting that if we want to provide in-depth account management, we'd better be prepared to back it up with custom options for our high-technology items. Otherwise, we're out of the ball game.

There are several maintenance and service issues on the hi-tech products which need to be looked at also.

In addition, from what I can determine, Katsuhara is producing substitute products for our low end items at a much lower cost. Their adherence to high quality standards have decreased their cost by drastically limiting waste. They also have an edge on us with their inventory systems, helping to further keep costs down. We can compete, but to do it right the capital expenditures to manufacturing needs to be shifted up to outfit us properly.

Next week, you'll be receiving the first draft of our productivity study. You won't be surprised that our costs are escalating because: demand projections are way off, labor turnover costs are high, and inventory is costly. The recent decrease in sales is having a severe impact on our unit cost, when we can least afford it. Discounting to buying groups needs to be looked at very carefully. I'm not a marketing man but I do know it's easier to sell anything if the cost is low.

We can coordinate with Ed Sharp and Keith Rose to provide the telemarketing customers an automated acquisition process to give them a steady supply of "just in time" goods. We know that hospitals are under a lot of pressure to keep costs down and minimizing their inventory will help. We'll need better coordination to keep our own inventory levels consistent with the new form of selling.

### Report from Dick Trask, Regional Sales Manager

Dear Chuck:

I had just a few thoughts I'd like to add to the consultant's report. In general, I agree: times have changed in the hospital supply business, and we're falling behind. In the old days, we dominated the market with great products. We sold and serviced the hell out of them, and no one tried to attack. If they did attack, the hospitals would let us know, and we'd respond with all types of horsepower and service.

One step above were hard-driving sales managers, and these individuals really built this company—even today, the average length of service is about 17 years. They were taught to cut deals, negotiate price, hire and fire aggressively.

Today, some of them feel like eunuchs. The consultant's report has leaked to the field, and many of them are worried that their days at HSI are numbered. One commented, "What will my job be when they bring in all the new account managers?"

As you know, most of our products are becoming commodities. Acme and others have matched many of our high-end systems, and have attacked us on price. My sales people haven't made any inroads with the new buying groups, and we don't have many relationships outside of end users and purchasing.

Perhaps our problem is that we're not clear on who we are right now. Are we going to become a broad-based distributor that sells thousands of products and makes money doing so? Or are we a company whose profits are driven by a limited number of high-profit products, sold to a limited number of key clients? I'm not sure I have an answer.

### Questions:

1. What do you think about the proposed change in selling strategy for HSI?
2. If you were Duffy, what would you do?
3. How would you implement your plan?

---

## ADAMS BRANDS

Ken Bannister, Ontario Regional Manager for Adams Brands, was faced with the decision of which of three candidates he should hire as the key account supervisor for the Ontario region. This salesperson would be responsible for working with eight major accounts in the Toronto area. Bannister had narrowed the list to the three applicants and began reviewing their files.

### Company

Warner-Lambert, Inc., a large, diversified U.S. multinational, manufactured and marketed a wide range of health care and consumer products. Warner-Lambert Canada Ltd., the largest subsidiary, had annual sales exceeding $200 million. Over one-half of the Canadian sales were generated by Adams Brands, which focused on the confectionery business. The major product lines carried by Adams were:

1. Chewing gum, with brands such as Chiclets, Dentyne, and Trident.
2. Portable breath fresheners including Certs and Clorets.
3. Cough tablets and antacids such as Halls and Rolaids.
4. Several other products, including Blue Diamond Almonds and Sparkies Mini-Fruits.

In these product categories, Adams Brands was usually the market leader or had a substantial market share.

The division was a stable unit for Warner-Lambert Canada, with profits being used for investments throughout the company. Success of the Adams Brands was built on:

1. Quality products.
2. Strong marketing management.
3. Sales force efforts in distribution, display, and merchandising.
4. Excellent customer service.

Adams was organized on a regional basis. The Ontario region, which also included the Atlantic provinces, had 46 sales representatives whose responsibilities were to service individual stores. Five district managers coordinated the activities of the sales representatives. As well, three key account supervisors worked with the large retail chains (e.g.,

Source: This case was prepared by Gordon McDougall, Wilfrid Laurier University, and Douglas Snetsinger, Institute of Market Driven Quality.

supermarkets) in Ontario and the Atlantic area. The key account supervisor in the Toronto area had recently resigned his position and joined one of Adams' major competitors.

## The Market

The confectionery industry comprised six major competitors that manufactured chocolate bars, chewing gum, mints, cough drops, chewy candy, and other products. The 1993 market shares of these six companies are provided in Exhibit 1.[1]

In the past few years, total industry sales in the confectionary category had been flat to marginally declining in unit volume. This sales decline was attributed to the changing age distribution of the population (i.e., fewer young people). As consumers grew older, their consumption of confectionery products tended to decline. While unit sales were flat or declining, dollar sales were increasing at a rate of 10 percent per annum as a result of price increases.

In the confectionery business, it was critical to obtain extensive distribution in as many stores as possible and, within each store, to obtain as much prominent shelf space as possible. Most confectionary products were purchased on impulse. In one study it was found that up to 85 percent of chewing gum and 70 percent of chocolate bar purchases were unplanned. While chocolate bars could be viewed as an indirect competitor to gum and mints, they were direct competitors for retail space and were usually merchandised on the same display. Retailers earned similar margins from all confectionary products (25–86 percent of the retail selling price) and often sought the best-selling brands to generate those revenues. Some industry executives felt that catering to the retailers' needs was even more important than understanding the ultimate consumers' needs.

Adams Brands had always provided store display racks for merchandising all confectionary items, including competitive products and chocolate bars. The advantage of supplying the displays was that the manufacturer could influence the number of prelabeled slots that contained brand logos and the proportion of the display devoted to various product groups such as chewing gum versus chocolate bars. The displays were usually customized to the unique requirements of a retailer, such as the height and width of the display.

Recently, a competitor, Effem, had become more competitive in the design and display of merchandising systems. Effem was regarded as an innovator in the industry, in part because of their limited product line and their new approach to the retail trade. The company had only eight fast-turnover products in their line. Effem had developed their own salesforce, consisting of over 100 part-time merchandising salespeople and 8 full-time sales personnel, and focused on the head offices of "A" accounts. "A" accounts were large retail chains such as 7-Eleven, Beckers, Loblaws, A&P, Food City, Shopper's Drug Mart, K-Mart,

| **EXHIBIT 1** | | Major Competitors in the Confectionery Industry | |
|---|---|---|---|
| **Company** | **Market Share (%)** | **Major Product Lines** | **Major Brands** |
| Adams | 23 | Gum, portable breath fresheners, cough drops | Trident, Chiclets, Dentyne, Certs, Halls |
| Nielsen/Cadbury | 22 | Chocolate bars | Caramilk, Crunchie, Dairy Milk, Crispy Crunch |
| Nestlé Canada | 15 | Chocolate bars | Coffee Crisp, Kit-Kat, Smarties, Turtles |
| Hershey | 14 | Gum, chocolate bars, chewy candy | Glossette, Oh Henry, Reese's Pieces, Lifesavers |
| Effem Foods | 11 | Chocolate bars, chewy candy | Mars, Snickers, M&M's, Skittles |
| Wrigley's | 9 | Gum | Hubba Bubba, Extra, Doublemint |
| Richardson-Vicks | 2 | Cough drops | Vicks |
| Others | 4 | | |

Towers and Zellers. Other than Adams, Effem was one of the few companies that conducted considerable research on racking systems and merchandising.

## The Retail Trade

Within Adams Brands, over two-thirds of confectionary volume flowed through wholesalers. The remaining balance was split between direct sales and drop shipments to retailers. Wholesalers were necessary because, with over 66,000 outlets in food, drug, and variety stores alone, the sales force could not adequately cover a large proportion of the retailers. The percentage of Adams sales through the various channels is provided in Exhibit 2.

The volume of all consumer packaged goods sold in Canada was increasingly dominated by fewer and larger retail chains. This increased retail concentration resulted in retailers becoming more influential in trade promotion decisions, including dictating the size, timing, and number of allowance, distribution, and coop advertising events. The new power of the retailers had not yet been fully wielded against the confectionary business. Confectionery lines were some of the most profitable lines for the retailer. Further, the manufacturers were not as reliant on listings from any given retailers as were other food and household product manufacturers.

The increased size of some retail chains also changed the degree of management sophistication at all levels, including that of the retail buyers—those individuals responsible for deciding what products were carried by the retail stores. At one time, the relationship between manufacturers' sales representatives and retail buyers was largely based on long-term, personal associations. Usually the sales representative had strong social skills, and an important task was to get along well with the buyers. Often when the representatives and buyers met to discuss various promotions or listings, part of the conversation dealt with making plans for dinner or going to a hockey game. The sales representative was the host for these social events.

More recently, a new breed of buyer had been emerging in the retail chains. Typically the new retail managers and buyers had been trained in business schools. They often had product management experience, relied on analytical skills, and used state-of-the-art, computer-supported planning systems. In some instances, the buyer was more sophisticated than the sales representative with respect to analytical approaches to display and inventory management. The buyers frequently requested detailed plan-o-grams with strong analytical support for expected sales, profits and inventory turns. The buyer would also at times become the salesperson. After listening to a sales presentation and giving an initial indication of interest the buyer would attempt to sell space, both on the store floor and in the weekly advertising supplements. For example, the buyer for Shopper's Drug Mart offered a dump bin location in every store in the chain for a week. In some instances, both the buyer and the representative had the authority to conclude such a deal at that meeting. At other times, both had to wait for approval from their respective companies.

The interesting aspect of the key account supervisor's position was that the individual had to feel comfortable dealing with both the old and new schools of retail management. The task for Bannister was to select the right candidate for this position. The salary for the position ranged from

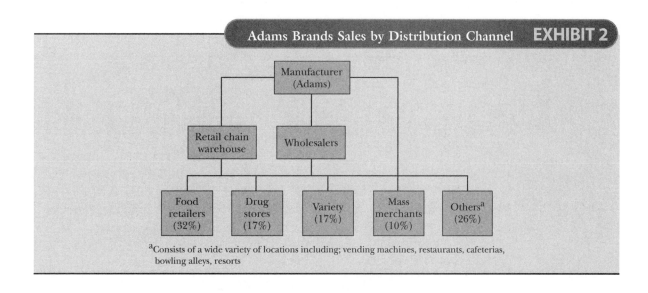

**Adams Brands Sales by Distribution Channel    EXHIBIT 2**

Manufacturer (Adams)

Retail chain warehouse — Wholesalers

Food retailers (32%) — Drug stores (17%) — Variety (17%) — Mass merchants (10%) — Others[a] (26%)

[a]Consists of a wide variety of locations including; vending machines, restaurants, cafeterias, bowling alleys, resorts

$31,000 to $54,200, depending on qualifications and experience. Smith expected that the candidate selected would probably be paid somewhere between $38,000 and $46,000. An expense allowance would also be included in the compensation package.

## The Key Accounts Supervisor

The main responsibility of the key accounts supervisor was to establish and maintain a close working relationship with the buyers of eight A accounts whose head offices were located in the Toronto area. An important task was to make presentations (15 to 30 minutes in length) to the retail buyers of these key accounts every three to six weeks. At these meetings, promotions or deals for up to five brands would be presented. The supervisor was responsible for all Adams brands. The buyer might have to take the promotions to the buying committee, where the final decision would be made. In addition, the representative used these meetings to hear about and inform the buyer of any merchandising problems occurring at the store level.

Midyear reviews were undertaken with each account. These reviews, lasting for one hour, focused on reviewing sales trends and tying them into merchandising programs, listings, service, and new payment terms. Another important and time-consuming responsibility of the key account supervisor was to devise and present plan-o-grams and be involved with the installation of the displays. The key account representative also conducted store checks and spent time on competitive intelligence. Working with the field staff was a further requirement of the position.

Bannister reflected on what he felt were the attributes of the ideal candidate. First, the individual should have selling and merchandising experience in the retail business in order to understand the language and dynamics of the situation. On the merchandising side, the individual would be required to initiate and coordinate the design of customized display systems for individual stores, a task that involved a certain amount of creativity. Second, strong interpersonal skills were needed. The individual had to establish rapport and make effective sales presentations to the buyers. Because of the wide range of buyer sophistication, these skills were particularly important. Bannister made a mental note to recommend that whoever was hired would be sent on the Professional Selling Skills course, a one-week program designed to enhance listening, selling, and presentation skills. Finally, the candidate should possess analytic skills because many of the sales and performance reports (from both manufacturers and retailers) were or would be computerized. Thus, the individual should feel comfortable working with computers. Bannister hoped that he could find a candidate who would be willing to spend a minimum of three years on the job in order to establish a personal relationship with the buyers.

Ideally, the candidate selected would have a blend of all three skills because of the mix of buyers he or she would contact. Bannister felt it was most likely that these characteristics would be found in a business school graduate. He had advertised the job internally (through the company's newsletter) and externally (in the *Toronto Star*). A total of 20 applications were received. After an initial screening, three possible candidates for the position were identified. None were from Warner-Lambert (Exhibit 3).

In early August 1994, Bannister and a member of the personnel department interviewed each of the candidates. After completing the interviews, brief fact sheets were prepared. Bannister began reviewing the sheets prior to making the decision.

---

**EXHIBIT 3**

**Lydia Cohen**

| | |
|---|---|
| Personal: | Born 1963, 168 cm; 64 kg; Single |
| Education: | B.B.A. (1985), Wilfrid Laurier University, Active in Marketing Club and Intramural sports |
| Work: | 1992–94   Rowntree Macintosh Canada, Inc.—District Manager |

Responsible for sales staff of three in Ottawa and Eastern Ontario region. Establish annual sales plan and ensure that district meets its quota.

1985–91   Rowntree Macintosh Canada, Inc.—Confectionary Sales Representative

Responsible for selling a full line of confectionary and grocery products to key accounts in Toronto (1990–91) and Ottawa (1985–89). 1991 Sales Representatives of the Year for highest volume growth.

**Lydia Cohen** *(continued)*

Interests:       Racquet sports

Candidate's      I am interested in working in the Toronto area, and I would look forward to concentrat-
Comments:        ing on the sales task. My best years at Rowntree were in sales in the Toronto region.

Interviewer's    Lydia presents herself very well and has a strong background in confectionary sales. Her
Comments:        record at Rowntree is very good. Rowntree paid for her to take an introductory course in
                 Lotus 1-2-3 in 1991, but she has not had much opportunity to develop her computer
                 skills. She does not seem to be overly ambitious or aggressive. She stated that personal
                 reasons were preeminent in seeking a job in Toronto.

**John Fisher**

Personal:        Born 1967, 190 cm; 88kg; Single

Education:       B.A. (Phys. Ed.) (1992), University of British Columbia

                 While at UBC, played four years of varsity basketball (team captain in 1990–91). Assistant
                 Coach, Senior Basketball, at University Hill High School 1988–92. Developed and ran a
                 two-week summer basketball camp at UBC for three years. Profits from the camp were
                 donated to the Varsity Basketball Fund.

Work:            1987–93    Jacobs Suchard Canada, Inc. (Nabob Foods)

                 Six years' experience (full-time 1992–93, and five years part-time, 1987–92, during school
                 terms and full-time during the summers) in coffee and chocolates distribution and sales;
                 two years on the loading docks, one year driving truck, and three years as a sales repre-
                 sentative. Sales tasks included calling on regular customers, order taking, rack jobbing
                 and customer relations development.

                 1993–94    Scavolini (Professional Basketball)

                 One year after completing studies at UBC, traveled to Western Europe and Northern
                 Africa. Travel was financed by playing professional basketball in the Italian First Division.

Candidate's      I feel the combination of educational preparation, work experience, and my demon-
Comments:        strated ability as a team player and leader make me well suited for this job. I am particu-
                 larly interested in a job, such as sales, that rewards personal initiative.

Interviewer's    A very ambitious and engaging individual with a good record of achievements. Strong
Comments:        management potential is evident, but interest in sales as a career is questionable.
                 Minored in computer science at UBC. Has a standing offer to return to a sales manage-
                 ment position at Nabob.

**Barry Moore**

Personal:        Born 1954, 180 cm; 84 kg; Married with two children

Education:       Business Administration Diploma (1979), Humber College

                 While at school, was active participant in a number of clubs and political organizations.
                 President of the Young Liberals (1978–79).

Work:            1991–94    Barrigans Food Markets—Merchandising Analyst

                 Developed merchandising plans for a wide variety of product categories. Negotiated
                 merchandising programs and trade deals with manufacturers and brokers. Managed a
                 staff of four.

                 1988–91    Dominion Stores Ltd.—Assistant Merchandise Manager

                 Liaison responsibilities between stores and head office merchandise planning.
                 Responsible for execution of merchandising plans for several food categories.

*(continued)*

**EXHIBIT 3**   *(continued)*

**Barry Moore** *(continued)*

1987   Robin Hood Multifoods, Inc.—Assistant Product Manager

Responsible for the analysis and development of promotion planning for Robin Hood Flour.

1982–87   Nestlé Enterprises Ltd.—Carnation Division Sales Representative.

Major responsibilities were developing and maintaining sales and distribution to wholesale and retail accounts.

1979–82   McCain Foods Ltd.—Inventory Analyst

Worked with sales staff and head office planning to ensure the quality and timing of shipments to brokers and stores.

| Activities | Board of Directors, Richview Community Club |
| | Board of Directors, Volunteer Centre of Etobicoke |
| | Past President of Etobicoke Big Brothers |
| | Active in United Way |
| | Yachting—CC 34 Canadian Champion |
| Candidate's Comments: | It would be a great challenge and joy to work with a progressive industry leader such as Adams Brands. |
| Interviewer's Comments: | Very articulate and professionally groomed. Dominated the interview with a variety of anecdotes and humorous stories, some of which were relevant to the job. Likes to read popular books on management, particularly books that champion the bold, gut-feel entrepreneur. He would probably earn more money at Adams if hired. |

## ROMANO PITESTI

Events had come to a head in Tickton-Jones Ltd. and the Marketing Director, Jack Simpson, had called in his Consumer Products Sales Manager, David Courtney, to sort out the problem.

"To come straight to the point, David," said Jack, "I'm about up to here with this sales rep of yours. Romano Pitesti. . . . Am I sick of hearing the guy's name! Everywhere I go, someone bends my ear about him. Last week it was the receptionist complaining about his making personal telephone calls during company time. Yesterday it was the security people about his untidy parking habits. And this morning, the accounts department is abuzz with outrage over his expense returns. Quite frankly, David, these are not isolated instances—he's out of control and I want to know what you intend to do about him, before the whole company is in uproar."

### Background

Tickton-Jones Ltd. was formed two years previously, when Tickton Flexible Products Ltd. acquired Samuel Jones Ltd., a local family-owned company. At the time, Tickton's annual sales were approaching $12 million and they employed 230 people; compared with Jones' $4.5 million and 110 people, respectively. Tickton was well established as a compounder of polyurethane and rubber materials and had its own molding facility for a wide range of industrial components. Jones, after years of steady business as a manufacturer of shoes, ladies' handbags, and travel goods, had recently moved successfully into sports shoes and for the first time had made an impact in the export field.

Source: This case was prepared by Tony Millman, University of Buckingham School of Business, United Kingdom. Reproduced by permission.

Ben Jones was the Chairman and majority owner of Samuel Jones Ltd. He was the grandson of the founder and the last of the Jones family line with an active participation in the business. At age 63, he wanted to sell out and retire to the Channel Islands with his wife, who had a health problem. The remaining two senior Directors were willing to accept early retirement on generous terms.

Ben Jones had been very happy to accept Tickton's offer and was satisfied that the new company would not involve too much upheaval for his employees. He was a paternal Chairman with a strong Protestant work ethic, but in recent years this had softened, and the organization had become somewhat looser in all aspects of its operations.

Not everyone on the Tickton Board had been in favor of the acquisition, largely because it represented a major diversification into consumer products. But the Managing Director had swayed the decision on grounds of too much current dependence on declining customer industries (e.g., motor vehicles, railways, general mechanical engineering). Jones was considered to have good products in growth markets. In the words of Tickton's Managing Director: "An opportunity like this might never pass our way again. Ben Jones assures me that he has a sound labor force and, like our own, they're not strongly unionized. The sports and leisure shoe business looks particularly attractive. Put our expertise in molding technology alongside their distribution network, and it could be one of our main product lines in five years. It's now or never—it would be virtually impossible to find equivalent facilities within

a five-mile radius." Within four weeks, the acquisition was agreed upon.

Due to the departure of Jones's senior Directors, integration of managerial staff provided few problems. Jones's production manager, Bill Thompson, was retained and placed in charge of the Jones site, which was effectively reduced to a manufacturing operation. All nonproduction staff, including the sales manager, David Courtney, were moved to the Tickton site.

However, the absorption of middle-/lower-level administrative staff had not been easy, and there were still cliques of former Jones employees who felt aggrieved. For example, certain secretaries had found themselves reporting to managers of lower status; friction in the sales administration office and accounts office caused internal divisions; and there was growing rivalry among the industrial sales engineers and the consumer sales representatives.

The organization of Tickton-Jones's marketing department is shown in Exhibit 1. From the marketing point of view, Jack Simpson had merely added another arm to his departmental organization—the Consumer Products Groups under David Courtney.

Prior to the acquisition, David Courtney had been very much a field sales manager. He was responsible for the usual sales management tasks of forecasting and budgeting, and spent most of his time dealing with major existing accounts or on the road developing new accounts. David Courtney, Romano Pitesti, and Jim Wells were all paid a salary plus commission. The commission element accounted for 20–25 percent of their annual pay. On joining Tickton-Jones's

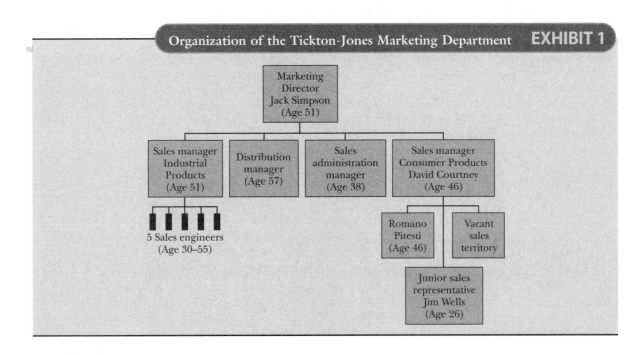

**Organization of the Tickton-Jones Marketing Department**     **EXHIBIT 1**

Marketing Director Jack Simpson (Age 51)

- Sales manager Industrial Products (Age 51)
  - 5 Sales engineers (Age 30–55)
- Distribution manager (Age 57)
- Sales administration manager (Age 38)
- Sales manager Consumer Products David Courtney (Age 46)
  - Romano Pitesti (Age 46)
  - Vacant sales territory
  - Junior sales representative Jim Wells (Age 26)

salary structure they received salary only, though in money terms this did not constitute a loss of total pay.

On the question of company car policy and day-to-day business expenses, there were major differences. Indeed, since at Samuel Jones Ltd. they applied to so few people, there were no formal procedures and Ben Jones signed off on everything, almost without question. In contrast, Tickton had a written document clearly setting out the type of car applicable to particular grades; spending limits for travel and entertainment, and so on. There was also a handbook covering Tickton's general conditions of service, which automatically became the Tickton-Jones handbook.

## Romano Pitesti

To say that Romano Cesare Pitesti was *different* from the industrial sales engineers would be an understatement. While they "toed the line" and had quite similar training and attitudes, Romano "sailed close to the wind."

Romano liked to feel that he was an individualist and repeatedly proved disruptive in formal group situations. Though basically conscientious and hardworking, he operated in bursts of enthusiasm that usually came to nothing but sometimes, through sheer tenacity on his part, brought the company an important order.

He was the master of the instant opinion and often entered into conversation on a range of issues of which he had only cursory knowledge and experience. This led him into a number of embarrassing situations, reflecting his gullability and boyish naiveté.

There were occasions when he could be charming, understanding, and a good listener, especially in female company. And even more so in the presence of Sheila Jones, his previous Chairman's wife! It was well known that she had a soft spot for Romano and had once saved him from serious trouble following an incident involving a secretary after the office Christmas party.

Romano was flamboyant in all things, yet beneath this facade lay a caring and deeply sensitive person. His colleague, Jim Wells, summed him up as "part hero, part villain, and part clown."

From the day he transferred to Tickton-Jones, Romano was regarded as a curiosity and a "figure of fun." The reasons were not hard to find. He dressed impeccably and in the height of fashion. Some would say that he overdid it for a 46-year-old, and he was soon dubbed "The Great Gatsby," "Peter Pan," and "The Aging Lothario."

In his first year with Tickton-Jones, Romano married Wendy Churchill, a 28-year-old set designer with a regional television company. This brought him in contact with numerous television personalities and turned him into a prolific name dropper. The stories he told provided unlimited ammunition for the industrial sales engineers, who cruelly taunted him at every opportunity. But Romano, unperturbed, shrugged off their remarks, usually with some witty return.

Despite all these oddities and eccentricities, Romano's sales performance was exemplary.

## The Meeting with David Courtney

With Jack Simpson's words ringing in his ears, David Courtney summoned Romano to a meeting. Romano insisted that it would upset his call schedule, but after some cajoling agreed to attend the following morning.

David opened the meeting with firm words: Romano, something has to be done about the way you operate in this company. It has been put to me that you are out of control. I'm taking the kicks at the moment and I don't like it! I've got a list of incidents to review with you—and you had better have good answers."

1. *David:* Your time-keeping leaves a lot to be desired, and you've been accused of wasting your own time and other people's. The normal starting time is 8:30 A.M. and not some time after 9:00 A.M. when you can make it!

   *Romano:* That's all very well, but I'm entitled to a little freedom on time. Only yesterday I left home at 6:00 A.M. to visit a customer and didn't return home until late in the evening. How many of those complaining about my time-keeping would be prepared to join me at such times of the day and night without overtime payments?

   *David:* And what about time wasting? You seem to spend a fair amount of time with secretaries and typists.

   *Romano:* No more than anyone else. It's just that other people spread their time over the week and mine's more concentrated. You know how much importance you attach to letter and report writing. Well, they all have to be typed.

2. *David:* That brings me to the time you claim to spend report writing. Taking Fridays off is a favorite for sniping by the industrial sales engineers.

   *Romano:* If you want me to write reports, you have got to allow me time to write them— it's as simple as that.

   *David:* The industrial sales engineers write their reports over their lunch break or between sales calls. Why can't you? There's a rumor circulating the company that you played golf last Friday.

*Romano:* Yes, that right. I played golf with Arthur Dixon—you know, Singleton's Purchasing Manager. I'm pretty close to a regular order from them. I'm playing with Arthur again on the 29th—should I cancel it?

*David:* No, no—I only wish you to make yourself a little more *visible* on Fridays. Not every Friday, just now and then.

3. *David:* Are you aware that you have higher claims for replacement of damaged clothing than anyone in the company? Why?

*Romano:* I can't help it if I wear trendy Italian suits and shoes. That damaged briefcase I claimed last month really was two-tone crocodile skin and cost me $180. I can't visit my customers dressed like those scruffy *Herberts* in the Industrial Group. They wouldn't let me on the premises.

*David:* OK, OK, just try to moderate your claims in future. I'm the poor guy who has to sign them off.

4. *David:* The biggest problem, as always, surrounds your company car. It's like a big orange blotch on the company landscape!

*Romano:* I can't see what you have against my car, David. It's only a Ford Escort 1.3 and bought within the company rules. We have very little flexibility on choice of model. After all, it's my mobile office—I live in it for 15 hours per week.

*David:* Yes, but do you have to choose bright orange and add all those accessories? The industrial sales engineers all have more sober colors such as bottle green and navy blue. Do you really need two large spot lamps with checkered covers, a rear spoiler, and whiplash radio aerial?

*Romano:* I paid for the accessories myself. You could do the same if you wish. Incidentally, there's a nice vivid green in the Ford Sierra right now!

*David:* I can almost bear the color with my sunglasses on—but not when you park your car on the double yellow lines near the reception area.

*Romano:* I knew it! That receptionist has got it in for me. It would be her who complained and not the security people. I only popped in to the switchboard to collect my telephone messages from the overnight answering machine.

*David:* I can accept that as an isolated incident. But your car is so obvious—everywhere you go, it's instantly recognizable. Which leads me to a very serious issue—did you or did you not use your company car to ferry voters to the local Council elections?

*Romano:* Yes, I did. I had my doubts about it and was on the verge of opting out. Then I realized Bill Thompson, the Production Manager, was using his company car for the Labour Party, so I thought, what's good enough for Labour is good enough for the Liberals.

*David:* Perhaps I had better have a word with Bill about the matter. We'll pick this one up later.

5. *Romano:* You've mentioned all these minor irritations, David. Have you ever had cause to question my sales performance? I'm the best salesperson in this company, and you know it! When did I last fail to meet my targets? And have you received any complaints from customers? I was the same at Samuel Jones. Don't forget, we're a rep short at the moment. A few more salespeople like me and we would be a market leader in no time. Who is it who secured the Milan export order?

But at that particular moment there was an interruption. Romano's telephone paging beeper was signaling an incoming call, and he picked up David's telephone. It was Joe Pinkerton, Romano's number two customer, with an urgent query.

Romano sat back in his chair, put his feet on David's wastepaper basket, and entered into a drawn-out conversation. Twenty minutes later he was still engrossed in conversation. David shook his head and decided to abandon the meeting. Romano gave him a wry grin as he left the office.

## MODERN PLASTICS

Institutional sales manager Jim Clayton had spent most of Monday morning planning for the rest of the month. It was early July and Jim knew that an extremely busy time was coming with the preparation of the following year's sales plan.

Since starting his current job less than a month ago, Jim had been involved in learning the

Source: This case was written by Professor Kenneth L. Bernhardt, Georgia State University, Professor Tom Ingram, Colorado State University, and Professor Danny N. Bellenger, Auburn University. Copyright © 1982 the authors.

requirements of the job and making his initial territory visits. Now that he was getting settled, Jim was trying to plan his activities according to priorities. The need for planning had been instilled in him during his college days. As a result of his three years' field sales experience and development of time management skills, he felt prepared for the challenge of the sales manager's job.

While sitting at his desk, Jim recalled a conversation that he had a week ago with Bill Hanson, the former manager, who had been promoted to another division. Bill told him that the sales forecast (annual and monthly) for plastic trash bags in the Southeast region would be due soon as an initial step toward developing the sales plan for the next year. Bill had laughed as he told Jim, "Boy, you ought to have a ball doing the forecast being a rookie sales manager!"

When Jim had asked what Bill meant, he explained by saying that the forecast was often "winged" because the headquarters in New York already knew what they wanted and would change the forecast to meet their figures, particularly if the forecast was for an increase of less than 10 percent. The experienced sales manager could throw numbers together in a short time that would pass as a serious forecast and ultimately be adjusted to fit the plans of headquarters. However, an inexperienced manager would have a difficult time "winging" a credible forecast.

Bill had also told Jim that the other alternative meant gathering mountains of data and putting together a forecast that could be sold to the various levels of Modern Plastics management. This alternative would prove to be time-consuming and could still be changed anywhere along the chain of command before final approval.

Clayton started reviewing pricing and sales volume history (see Exhibit 1). He also looked at the key account performance for the past two and a half years (see Exhibit 2). During the past month Clayton had visited many of the key accounts, and on the average they had indicated that their purchases from Modern would probably increase about 15–20 percent in the coming year.

### Schedule for Preparing the Forecast

Jim had received a memo recently from Robert Baxter, the regional marketing manager, detailing

---

**EXHIBIT 1     Plastic Trash Bags—Sales and Pricing History, 1994–1996**

| | Pricing dollars per case | | | Sales volume in cases | | | Sales volume in dollars | | |
|---|---|---|---|---|---|---|---|---|---|
| | 1994 | 1995 | 1996 | 1994 | 1995 | 1996 | 1994 | 1995 | 1996 |
| January | $6.88 | $ 7.70 | $15.40 | 33,000 | 46,500 | 36,500 | $ 227,000 | $ 358,000 | $ 562,000 |
| February | 6.82 | 7.70 | 14.30 | 32,500 | 52,500 | 23,000 | 221,500 | 404,000 | 329,000 |
| March | 6.90 | 8.39 | 13.48 | 32,000 | 42,000 | 22,000 | 221,000 | 353,000 | 296,500 |
| April | 6.88 | 10.18 | 12.24 | 45,500 | 42,500 | 46,500 | 313,000 | 432,500 | 569,000 |
| May | 6.85 | 12.38 | 11.58 | 49,000 | 41,500 | 45,500 | 335,500 | 514,000 | 527,000 |
| June | 6.85 | 12.65 | 10.31 | 47,500 | 47,000 | 42,000 | 325,500 | 594,500 | 433,000 |
| July | 7.42 | 13.48 | 9.90* | 40,000 | 43,500 | 47,500* | 297,000 | 586,500 | 470,000* |
| August | 6.90 | 13.48 | 10.18 | 48,500 | 63,500 | 43,500 | 334,500 | 856,000 | 443,000 |
| September | 7.70 | 14.30 | 10.31 | 43,000 | 49,000 | 47,500 | 331,000 | 700,500 | 489,500 |
| October | 7.56 | 15.12 | 10.31 | 52,500 | 50,000 | 51,000 | 397,000 | 756,000 | 526,000 |
| November | 7.15 | 15.68 | 10.72 | 62,000 | 61,500 | 47,500 | 443,500 | 964,500 | 509,000 |
| December | 7.42 | 15.43 | 10.59 | 49,000 | 29,000 | 51,000 | 363,500 | 447,500 | 540,000 |
| Total | $7.13 | $12.25 | $11.30 | 534,500 | 568,500 | 503,500 | $3,810,000 | $6,967,000 | $5,694,000 |

*July–December 1996 figures are forecast of sales manager J. A. Clayton and other data comes from historical sales information.

| | | | First Six Months 1996 | 1994 Monthly Average | 1995 Monthly Average | First Half 1996 Monthly Average | First Quarter 1996 Monthly Average |
|---|---|---|---|---|---|---|---|
| **Customer** | **1994** | **1995** | | | | | |
| Transco Paper Company | 125,774 | 134,217 | 44,970 | 10,481 | 11,185 | 7,495 | 5,823 |
| Callaway Paper | 44,509 | 46,049 | 12,114 | 3,709 | 3,837 | 2,019 | 472 |
| Florida Janitorial Supply | 34,746 | 36,609 | 20,076 | 2,896 | 3,051 | 3,346 | 2,359 |
| Jefferson | 30,698 | 34,692 | 25,004 | 2,558 | 2,891 | 4,174 | 1,919 |
| Cobb Paper | 13,259 | 23,343 | 6,414 | 1,105 | 1,945 | 1,069 | 611 |
| Miami Paper | 10,779 | 22,287 | 10,938 | 900 | 1,857 | 1,823 | 745 |
| Milne Surgical Company | 23,399 | 21,930 | — | 1,950 | 1,828 | — | — |
| Graham | 8,792 | 15,331 | 1,691 | 733 | 1,278 | 281 | 267 |
| Crawford Paper | 7,776 | 14,132 | 6,102 | 648 | 1,178 | 1,017 | 1,322 |
| John Steele | 8,634 | 13,277 | 6,663 | 720 | 1,106 | 1,110 | 1,517 |
| Henderson Paper | 9,185 | 8,850 | 2,574 | 765 | 738 | 429 | 275 |
| Durant Surgical | — | 7,766 | 4,356 | — | 647 | 726 | 953 |
| Master Paper | 4,221 | 5,634 | 600 | 352 | 470 | 100 | — |
| D.T.A. | — | — | 2,895 | — | — | 482 | — |
| Crane Paper | 4,520 | 5,524 | 3,400 | 377 | 460 | 566 | 565 |
| Janitorial Service | 3,292 | 5,361 | 2,722 | 274 | 447 | 453 | 117 |
| Georgia Paper | 5,466 | 5,053 | 2,917 | 456 | 421 | 486 | 297 |
| Paper Supplies, Inc. | 5,117 | 5,119 | 1,509 | 426 | 427 | 251 | 97 |
| Southern Supply | 1,649 | 3,932 | 531 | 137 | 328 | 88 | 78 |
| Horizon Hospital Supply | 4,181 | 4,101 | 618 | 348 | 342 | 103 | 206 |
| Total cases | 345,997 | 413,207 | 156,094 | 28,835 | 34,436 | 26,018 | 17,623 |

**EXHIBIT 2** 1996 Key Account Sales History (in cases)

the plans for completing the 1997 forecast. The key dates in the memo began in only three weeks:

| August 1 | Presentation of forecast to regional marketing manager. |
|---|---|
| August 10 | Joint presentation with marketing manager to regional general manager. |
| September 1 | Regional general manager presents forecast to division vice president. |
| September 1– September 30 | Review of forecast by staff of division vice president. |
| October 1 | Review forecast with corporate staff. |
| October 1– October 15 | Revision as necessary. |
| October 15 | Final forecast forwarded to division vice president from regional general manager. |

## Company Background

The plastics division of Modern Chemical Company was founded in 1965 when Modern Chemical purchased Cordco, a small plastics manufacturer with national sales of $15 million. At that time the key products of the plastics division were sandwich bags, plastic tablecloths, trash cans, and plastic-coated clothesline.

Since 1965 the plastics division has grown to a sales level exceeding $200 million with five regional profit centers covering the United States. Each regional center has manufacturing facilities and a regional salesforce. There are four product groups in each region:

1. Food packaging: Styrofoam meat and produce trays; plastic bags for various food products.
2. Egg cartons: Styrofoam egg cartons sold to egg packers and supermarket chains.
3. Institutional: Plastic trash bags and disposable tableware (plates, bowls and so on).
4. Industrial: Plastic packaging for the laundry and dry cleaning market; plastic film for use in pallet overwrap systems.

Each product group is supervised jointly by a product manager and a district sales manager, both of whom report to the regional marketing manager. The sales representatives report directly to the district sales manager but also work closely with the product manager on matters concerning pricing and product specifications.

The five regional general managers report to J. R. Hughes, vice president of the plastics division. Hughes is located in New York. Although Modern Chemical is owned by a multinational oil company, the plastics division has been able to operate in a virtually independent manner since its establishment in 1965. The reasons for this include:

1. Limited knowledge of the plastic industry on the part of the oil company management.
2. Excellent growth by the plastics division has been possible without management supervision from the oil company.
3. Profitability of the plastics division has consistently been higher than that of other divisions of the chemical company.

### The Institutional Trash Bag Market

The institutional trash bag is a polyethylene bag used to collect and transfer refuse to its final disposition point. There are different sizes and colors available to fit the various uses of the bag. For example, a small bag for desk wastebaskets is available as well as a heavier bag for large containers such as a 55-gallon drum. There are 25 sizes in the Modern line with 13 of those sizes being available in 3 colors—white, buff, and clear. Customers typically buy several different items on an order to cover all their needs.

The institutional trash bag is a separate product from the consumer grade trash bag, which is typically sold to homeowners through retail outlets. The institutional trash bag is sold primarily through paper wholesalers, hospital supply companies, and janitorial supply companies to a variety of end users. Since trash bags are used on such a wide scale, the list of end users could include almost any business or institution. The segments include hospitals, hotels, schools, office buildings, transportation facilities, and restaurants.

Based on historical data and a current survey of key wholesalers and end users in the Southeast, the annual market of institutional trash bags in the region was estimated to be 55 million pounds. Translated into cases, the market potential was close to 2 million cases. During the past five years, the market for trash bags has grown at an average rate of 8.9 percent per year. Now a mature product, future market growth is expected to parallel overall growth in the economy. The 1997 real growth in GNP is forecast to be 4.5 percent.

### General Market Conditions

The current market is characterized by a distressing trend. The market is in a position of oversupply with approximately 20 manufacturers competing for the business in the Southeast. Prices have been on the decline for several months but are expected to level out during the last six months of the year.

This problem arose after a record year in 1995 for Modern Plastics. During 1995, supply was very tight due to raw material shortages. Unlike many of its competitors, Modern had only minor problems securing adequate raw material supplies. As a result the competitors were few in 1995, and all who remained in business were prosperous. By early 1996 raw materials were plentiful, and prices began to drop as new competitors tried to buy their way into the market. During the first quarter of 1996 Modern Plastics learned the hard way that a competitive price was a necessity in the current market. Volume fell off drastically in February and March as customers shifted orders to new suppliers when Modern chose to maintain a slightly higher than market price on trash bags.

With the market becoming extremely price competitive and profits declining, the overall quality has dropped to a point of minimum standard. Most suppliers now make a bag "barely good enough to get the job done." This quality level is acceptable to most buyers who do not demand high quality for this type of product.

### Modern Plastics versus Competition

A recent study of Modern versus competition had been conducted by an outside consultant to see how well Modern measured up in several key areas. Each area was weighted according to its importance in the purchase decision, and Modern was compared to its key competitors in each area and on an overall basis. The key factors and their weights are shown below:

|  | Weight |
|---|---|
| 1. Pricing | .50 |
| 2. Quality | .15 |
| 3. Breadth of line | .10 |
| 4. Sales coverage | .10 |
| 5. Packaging | .05 |
| 6. Service | .10 |
| Total | 1.00 |

As shown in Exhibit 3, Modern compared favorably with its key competitors on an overall basis. None of the other suppliers was as strong as Modern in breadth of line nor did any competitor offer as good sales coverage as that provided by Modern. Clayton knew that sales coverage would be even better next year since the Florida and North Carolina territories had grown enough to add two salespeople to the institutional group by January 1, 1997.

Pricing, quality, and packaging seemed to be neither an advantage nor a disadvantage. However, service was a problem area. The main cause for this, Clayton was told, was temporary out-of-stock situations which occurred occasionally primarily due to the wide variety of trash bags offered by Modern.

During the past two years, Modern Plastics had maintained its market share at approximately 27 percent of the market. Some new competitors had entered the market since 1994 while others had left the market (see Exhibit 4[1]). The previous district sales manager, Bill Hanson, had left Clayton some comments regarding the new competitors. These are reproduced in Exhibit 5.

### Developing the Sales Forecast

After a careful study of trade journals, government statistics, and surveys conducted by Modern marketing research personnel, projections for growth potential were formulated by segment and are shown in Exhibit 6.[2] This data was compiled by Bill Hanson just before he had been promoted.

Jim looked back at Baxter's memo giving the time schedule for the forecast and knew he had to get started. As he left the office at 7:15, he wrote himself a large note and pinned it on his wall—"Get Started on the Sales Forecast!"

## Competitive Factors Ratings (by competitor*)  EXHIBIT 3

| Weight | Factor | Modern | National Film | Bonanza | South-eastern | PBI | BAGCO | South-west Bag | Florida Plastics | East Coast Bag Co. |
|---|---|---|---|---|---|---|---|---|---|---|
| .50 | Price | 2 | 3 | 2 | 2 | 2 | 2 | 2 | 2 | 3 |
| .15 | Quality | 3 | 2 | 3 | 4 | 3 | 2 | 3 | 3 | 4 |
| .10 | Breadth | 1 | 2 | 2 | 3 | 3 | 3 | 3 | 3 | 3 |
| .10 | Sales coverage | 1 | 3 | 3 | 3 | 4 | 3 | 3 | 4 | 3 |
| .05 | Packaging | 3 | 3 | 2 | 3 | 3 | 1 | 3 | 3 | 3 |
| .10 | Service | 4 | 3 | 3 | 2 | 2 | 2 | 3 | 4 | 3 |

### Overall Weighted Ranking[†]

| | | | | |
|---|---|---|---|---|
| 1. BAGCO | 2.15 | | 6. Southeastern | 2.55 |
| 2. Modern | 2.20 | | 7. Florida Plastics | 2.60 |
| 3. Bonanza | 2.25 | | 8. National Film | 2.65 |
| 4. Southwest Bag (Tie) | 2.50 | | 9. East Coast Bag Co. | 3.15 |
| 5. PBI (Tie) | 2.50 | | | |

*Ratings on a 1-to-5 scale with 1 being the best rating and 5 the worst.
†The weighted ranking is the sum of each rank times its weight. The lower the number, the better the overall rating.

## EXHIBIT 4     Market Share by Supplier, 1994 and 1996

| Supplier | Percent of Market 1994 | Percent of Market 1996 | Supplier | Percent of Market 1994 | Percent of Market 1996 |
|---|---|---|---|---|---|
| National Film | 11 | 12 | BAGCO | — | 6 |
| Bertram | 16 | 0* | Southwest Bag | — | 2 |
| Bonanza | 11 | 12 | Florida Plastics | — | 4 |
| Southeastern | 5 | 6 | East Coast Bag Co. | — | 4 |
| Bay | 9 | 0* | Miscellaneous and | | |
| Johnson Graham | 8 | 0* | unknown | 8 | 22 |
| PBI | 2 | 5 | Modern | 28 | 27 |
| Lewis | 2 | 0* | | 100 | 100 |

*Out of business in 1996

## EXHIBIT 5     Characteristics of Competitors

| | |
|---|---|
| **National Film** | Broadest product line in the industry. Quality a definite advantage. Good service. Sales coverage adequate, but not an advantage. Not as aggressive as most suppliers on price. Strong competitor. |
| **Bonanza** | Well-established tough competitor. Very aggressive on pricing. Good packaging, quality okay. |
| **Southeastern** | Extremely price competitive in southern Florida. Dominates Miami market. Limited product line. Not a threat outside of Florida. |
| **PBI** | Extremely aggressive on price. Have made inroads into Transco Paper Company. Good service but poor sales coverage. |
| **BAGCO** | New competitor. Very impressive with a high-quality product, excellent service, and strong sales coverage. A real threat, particularly in Florida. |
| **Southwest Bag** | A factor in Louisiana and Mississippi. Their strategy is simple—an acceptable product at a rock bottom price. |
| **Florida Plastics** | Active when market is at a profitable level with price cutting. When market declines to a low profit range, Florida manufactures other types of plastic packaging and stays out of the trash bag market. Poor reputation as a reliable supplier, but can still "spot-sell" at low prices. |
| **East Coast Bag Co.** | Most of their business is from a state bid which began in January 1989 for a two-year period. Not much of a threat to Modern's business in the Southeast as most of their volume is north of Washington, D.C. |

| 1997 Real Growth Projections by Segment | EXHIBIT 6 |
|---|---|
| Total industry | +5.0% |
| Commercial | +5.4% |
|    Restaurant | +6.8% |
|    Hotel/motel | +2.0% |
|    Transportation | +1.9% |
|    Office users | +5.0% |
|    Other | +4.2% |
| Noncommercial | +4.1% |
|    Hospitals | +3.9% |
|    Nursing homes | +4.8% |
|    Colleges/universities | +2.4% |
|    Schools | +7.8% |
|    Employee feeding | +4.3% |
| Other | +3.9% |

## EVALUATING THE SUCCESS OF A SALESFORCE PROMOTIONAL PROGRAM: DENMAN INDUSTRIAL PRODUCTS (A)

# Denman Industrial Products
### Serving our Customers Around the World Since 1936

Internal Memorandum

To:      A.L. Medina
         Sales Manager for South American Operations

From:    K.P. DuJong
         Vice President of Sales

Date:    January 3, 1997

Regarding:  Evaluation of 1996 Sales Promotion Efforts

I will be meeting with other senior management officers and the Board of Directors at the upcoming global company meetings in Toronto on February 3rd. In preparation for those meetings I am asking all twelve regional sales managers to assess the outcomes of the two major sales force targeted promotion campaigns held in the last calendar year. More specifically, I need to know which, if either, of the campaigns directed at our sales force was successful in increasing sales to (or beyond) the targeted levels.

Below, and on the accompanying pages, are data from our M.I.S. department concerning sales levels, territory staffing, and related information for each of the territory offices in the South American division. Please analyze the information and provide me a memo of your conclusions by January 17th.

Concerning two related issues, Denman currently employs a single territory office and sales force for the combined Surinam, Trinidad and Tobago, Guyana, and French Guyana areas. The possibility has been advanced of breaking this territory into one or more separate territories, each with its own office and sales force. Additionally, we do not currently service the country of Chile. As regional sales manager, I would like your assessment of the potential benefits and problems connected with (1) breaking up the combined territory and (2) adding Chile as a new territory with our existing personnel.

Worldwide Headquarters
2344 West Zumont Place  Toronto, Ontario Canada 1Z6 5CT
Telephone: 1-13-676-8819  Internet: emgr.45.f44@wwh.acme.com.can

Source: This case was prepared by Michael R. Luthy, Drake University."

Denman Industrial Products
South American Operations Division
Report Alpha/DT–12-month period ending 12/31/1996
printed 1/2/1997–2:05:47 a.m. G.M.T.
page 1 of 5

| Territory Code | Territory Office | Territory in Square Miles | General Population | Number of Salespeople | Local Currency | Exchange Rate to U.S. Dollar |
|---|---|---|---|---|---|---|
| Paraguay | Asunción | 157,047 | 5,026,699 | 6 | Guaraní | 1,900.000 |
| Colombia | Bogotá | 439,735 | 37,038,240 | 17 | Peso | 894.000 |
| Brazil | Brasilia | 3,286,470 | 160,625,080 | 128 | Real | 0.950 |
| Argentina | Buenos Aires | 1,072,067 | 34,787,129 | 42 | Peso | 0.999 |
| Venezuela | Caracas | 352,143 | 22,421,998 | 14 | Bolivar | 169.790 |
| French Guiana | see Guyana | 35,126 | 150,897 | — | Franc | 5.390 |
| Guyana | Georgetown | 83,000 | 829,059 | 7 | Guyana Dollar | 142.000 |
| Bolivia | La Paz | 424,162 | 8,648,778 | 17 | Boliviano | 4.680 |
| Peru | Lima | 496,222 | 23,825,160 | 19 | Nuevo Sol | 2.224 |
| Uruguay | Montevideo | 68,040 | 3,251,405 | 3 | Peso | 6.410 |
| Surinam | see Guyana | 63,251 | 412,902 | — | Surinam Guilder | 183.120 |
| Trinidad/Tobago | see Guyana | 1,980 | 1,331,387 | — | T & T Dollar | 5.560 |
| Ecuador | Quito | 106,927 | 11,327,838 | 4 | Sucre | 2,572.000 |

page 2 of 5

| Territory Code | Territory Office | Annual Hours by Territory | | | | | | Territory Supervisor |
|---|---|---|---|---|---|---|---|---|
| | | Face-to Face Selling | Phone Selling | Travel | Admin. | Other Non-Selling | Vaca-tion | |
| Paraguay | Asunción | 5,025 | 1,800 | 2,775 | 2,250 | 1,650 | 540 | Carlos Wasmosy |
| Colombia | Bogotá | 14,450 | 5,100 | 7,650 | 6,375 | 4,675 | 1,530 | Ernesto Menem |
| Brazil | Brasilia | 108,800 | 38,400 | 57,600 | 48,000 | 35,200 | 11,520 | Marie Caldera |
| Argentina | Buenos Aires | 36,225 | 12,600 | 18,375 | 15,750 | 11,550 | 3,780 | Luis Lacalle |
| Venezuela | Caracas | 12,075 | 4,200 | 6,125 | 5,250 | 3,850 | 1,260 | Rafael Lozada |
| French Guiana | see Guyana | — | — | — | — | — | — | — |
| Guyana | Georgetown | 5,863 | 2,100 | 3,238 | 2,625 | 1,925 | 630 | Edwardo Tagle |
| Bolivia | La Paz | 14,663 | 5,100 | 7,438 | 6,375 | 4,675 | 1,530 | Gloria Nunez |
| Peru | Lima | 15,913 | 5,700 | 8,788 | 7,125 | 5,225 | 1,710 | Toma Hernandez |
| Uruguay | Montevideo | 2,700 | 900 | 1,200 | 1,125 | 825 | 270 | Jill Rodriguez |
| Surinam | see Guyana | — | — | — | — | — | — | — |
| Trinidad/Tobago | see Guyana | — | — | — | — | — | — | — |
| Ecuador | Quito | 3,300 | 1,200 | 1,900 | 1,500 | 1,100 | 360 | Suzanne Ortega |

Denman Industrial Products
South American Operations Division
Report Alpha/DT–12-month period ending 12/31/1996
printed 1/2/1997–2:05:47 a.m. G.M.T.
page 3 of 5

| Territory Code | Territory Office | Large Accounts (5 calls per quarter) | | Medium Accounts (3 calls per quarter) | | Small Accounts (2 calls per quarter) | |
|---|---|---|---|---|---|---|---|
| | | Number | Avg. Call Duration | Number | Avg. Call Duration | Number | Avg. Call Duration |
| Paraguay | Asuncion | 34 | 150 min. | 114 | 90 min. | 212 | 45 min. |
| Colombia | Bogotá | 142 | 150 min. | 208 | 90 min. | 601 | 45 min. |
| Brazil | Brasilia | 1,102 | 150 min. | 1,785 | 90 min. | 3,595 | 45 min. |
| Argentina | Buenos Aires | 404 | 150 min. | 455 | 90 min. | 1,305 | 45 min. |
| Venezuela | Caracas | 168 | 150 min. | 145 | 90 min. | 177 | 45 min. |
| French Guiana | see Guyana | — | — | — | — | — | — |
| Guyana | Georgetown | 70 | 150 min. | 78 | 90 min. | 159 | 45 min. |
| Bolivia | La Paz | 195 | 150 min. | 225 | 90 min. | 143 | 45 min. |
| Peru | Lima | 180 | 150 min. | 352 | 90 min. | 96 | 45 min. |
| Uruguay | Montevideo | 14 | 150 min. | 22 | 90 min. | 267 | 45 min. |
| Surinam | see Guyana | — | — | — | — | — | — |
| Trinidad/Tobago | see Guyana | — | — | — | — | — | — |
| Ecuador | Quito | 32 | 150 min. | 62 | 90 min. | 97 | 45 min. |

page 4 of 5

| Territory Code | Territory Office | 1996 Annual Sales in U.S. $ | First Promotional Campaign Period (duration = 5 weeks) Target: 6.50% above non-promotional period amount | | |
|---|---|---|---|---|---|
| | | | Large Accounts | Medium Accounts | Small Accounts |
| Paraguay | Asuncion | $4,688,250 | $225,263 | $145,321 | $110,000 |
| Colombia | Bogotá | $14,082,075 | $656,891 | $468,597 | $398,254 |
| Brazil | Brasilia | $110,085,982 | $5,898,214 | $3,258,987 | $2,145,583 |
| Argentina | Buenos Aires | $35,228,981 | $1,458,789 | $1,225,698 | $1,158,743 |
| Venezuela | Caracas | $10,937,520 | $258,974 | $479,855 | $446,983 |
| French Guiana | see Guyana | — | — | — | — |
| Guyana | Georgetown | $5,169,875 | $185,983 | $158,987 | $143,352 |
| Bolivia | La Paz | $12,885,250 | $789,058 | $242,697 | $321,542 |
| Peru | Lima | $14,685,791 | $648,252 | $520,258 | $346,855 |
| Uruguay | Montevideo | $2,544,684 | $92,018 | $72,155 | $108,963 |
| Surinam | see Guyana | — | — | — | — |
| Trinidad/Tobago | see Guyana | — | — | — | — |
| Ecuador | Quito | $3,325,100 | $221,589 | $84,644 | $35,881 |

Denman Industrial Products
South American Operations Division
Report Alpha/DT–12-month period ending 12/31/1996
printed 1/2/1997–2:05:47 a.m. G.M.T.
page 5 of 5

| Territory Code | Territory Office | 1996 Annual Sales in U.S. $ | Second Promotional Campaign Period (duration = 4 weeks) Target: 7.25% above non-promotional period amount | | |
| --- | --- | --- | --- | --- | --- |
| | | | **Large Accounts** | **Medium Accounts** | **Small Accounts** |
| Paraguay | Asuncion | $4,688,250 | $175,325 | $125,869 | $88,795 |
| Colombia | Bogotá | $14,082,075 | $570,025 | $404,255 | $331,699 |
| Brazil | Brasilia | $110,085,982 | $5,340,185 | $2,719,885 | $1,422,302 |
| Argentina | Buenos Aires | $35,228,981 | $1,089,954 | $998,753 | $887,452 |
| Venezuela | Caracas | $10,937,520 | $221,983 | $375,944 | $384,933 |
| French Guiana | see Guyana | — | — | — | — |
| Guyana | Georgetown | $5,169,875 | $152,977 | $131,558 | $163,554 |
| Bolivia | La Paz | $12,885,250 | $701,299 | $216,379 | $296,771 |
| Peru | Lima | $14,685,791 | $554,699 | $468,008 | $226,874 |
| Uruguay | Montevideo | $2,544,684 | $82,044 | $61,588 | $74,611 |
| Surinam | see Guyana | — | — | — | — |
| Trinidad/Tobago | see Guyana | — | — | — | — |
| Ecuador | Quito | $3,325,100 | $202,446 | $73,499 | $29,811 |

*Notes to report:*

1. Sales representatives work a typical 50 week year of approximately 45 hours per week.
2. For analysis purposes, dollar amounts, time assessments, etc., do not include territory managers. These individual's activities and performance are evaluated under other criteria and with other systems.
3. Sales of Denman products are not subject to seasonal and cyclical variations.
4. Vacation hours taken by sales representatives are sufficiently spread out to have no significant effect on the maintenance of existing accounts.

**EVALUATING THE SUCCESS OF A SALESFORCE PROMOTIONAL PROGRAM:
DENMAN INDUSTRIAL PRODUCTS (B)**

# Denman Industrial Products
Serving our Customers Around the World Since 1936

Internal Memorandum

To:    A.L. Medina
        Sales Manager for South American Operations

From:   K.P. DuJong
        Vice President of Sales

Date:    January 21, 1997

Regarding: Further Evaluation of 1996 Sales Promotion Efforts

I have completed reading your analysis of the South American Division's sales performance for 1996 and the effectiveness of the two major annual salesforce promotional programs (memo dated January 17, 1997). Additional information in the form of the accompanying exception report has been generated. I would like your assessment of whether information in that report affects the conclusions you stated in your memo.

Also, the policy concerning the "reward" for each of the promotional programs we have run company-wide over the last three years has been to award one trip for two people, all expenses paid, anywhere in the world for one week for the leading sales representative in each of the twelve regions Denman operates in. It has been suggested that this policy be altered to a "smaller" award for the top sales representative in each sales territory. For the South American Division, this would have the effect of increasing the number of awards substantially. I would like your comments on this issue and how you believe sales representative behavior, motivation, etc. will be affected by January 30th so that I can review them prior to the global company meetings.

Worldwide Headquarters
2344 West Zumont Place  Toronto, Ontario Canada 1Z6 5CT
Telephone: 1-13-676-8819  Internet: emgr.45.f44@wwh.acme.com.can

Source: This case was prepared by Michael R. Luthy, Drake University."

Denman Industrial Products
South American Operations Division
Report Beta/LR–12-month period ending 12/31/1996
printed 1/20/1997–4:14:47 a.m. G.M.T.
page 1 of 3

| | | **Sales Exception Report/Large Accounts** | | | | | |
| --- | --- | --- | --- | --- | --- | --- | --- |
| | | **First Promotional Campaign 1996** | | | **Second Promotional Campaign 1996** | | |
| **Territory Code** | **Territory Office** | **Pre** | **Post** | **Returns** | **Pre** | **Post** | **Returns** |
| Paraguay | Asuncion | | | | | | |
| Colombia | Bogotá | | | | | | |
| Brazil | Brasilia | | | | (–) | (–) | (+) |
| Argentina | Buenos Aires | | | | | | |
| Venezuela | Caracas | | | | | | |
| French Guiana | see Guyana | | | | | | |
| Guyana | Georgetown | (+) | (+) | (–) | | | |
| Bolivia | La Paz | | | | | (–) | (+) |
| Peru | Lima | | | | | | |
| Uruguay | Montevideo | | | | | | |
| Surinam | see Guyana | | | | | | |
| Trinidad/Tobago | see Guyana | | | | | | |
| Ecuador | Quito | | | | (–) | (+) | |

Denman Industrial Products
South American Operations Division
Report Beta/LR–12-month period ending 12/31/1996
printed 1/20/1997–4:14:47 a.m. G.M.T.
page 2 of 3

| | | **Sales Exception Report/Medium Accounts** | | | | | |
| --- | --- | --- | --- | --- | --- | --- | --- |
| | | **First Promotional Campaign 1996** | | | **Second Promotional Campaign 1996** | | |
| **Territory Code** | **Territory Office** | **Pre** | **Post** | **Returns** | **Pre** | **Post** | **Returns** |
| Paraguay | Asuncion | | | | | | |
| Colombia | Bogotá | | | | (–) | (–) | (+) |
| Brazil | Brasilia | | | | | | |
| Argentina | Buenos Aires | (–) | | | | | |
| Venezuela | Caracas | | | | (–) | | (+) |
| French Guiana | see Guyana | | | | | | |
| Guyana | Georgetown | (+) | (+) | | | | |
| Bolivia | La Paz | | | | (–) | (+) | |
| Peru | Lima | | | | | | |
| Uruguay | Montevideo | | | | | | |
| Surinam | see Guyana | | | | | | |
| Trinidad/Tobago | see Guyana | | | | | | |
| Ecuador | Quito | | | | | | |

Denman Industrial Products
South American Operations Division
Report Beta/LR–12-month period ending 12/31/1996
printed 1/20/1997–4:14:47 a.m. G.M.T.
page 3 of 3

| | | **Sales Exception Report/Large Accounts** | | | | | |
|---|---|---|---|---|---|---|---|
| | | **First Promotional Campaign 1996** | | | **Second Promotional Campaign 1996** | | |
| **Territory Code** | **Territory Office** | **Pre** | **Post** | **Returns** | **Pre** | **Post** | **Returns** |
| Paraguay | Asuncion | | | | | | |
| Colombia | Bogotá | (–) | (–) | (+) | (–) | (–) | (+) |
| Brazil | Brasilia | | | | | | |
| Argentina | Buenos Aires | (–) | | | | | |
| Venezuela | Caracas | | | | | | |
| French Guiana | see Guyana | | | | | | |
| Guyana | Georgetown | (+) | | | | | |
| Bolivia | La Paz | | | | (–) | (–) | |
| Peru | Lima | | | | | | |
| Uruguay | Montevideo | | | | | | |
| Surinam | see Guyana | | | | | | |
| Trinidad/Tobago | see Guyana | | | | | | |
| Ecuador | Quito | | | | | | |

*Notes to report:*

1. Exception reports identify, by account type and territory, sales levels significantly different from forecasts for equal length periods immediately prior to and following promotional periods.

2. Sales return levels and/or contract cancellations for post-promotional periods are also identified where significantly different from forecasts.

## DURA-PLAST, INC. (A): GLOBAL ACCOUNT MANAGEMENT

Tom Parker, CEO of Dura-plast-Americas, Inc. (DP-A), directs the U.S. subsidiary of a profitable international equipment manufacturer, Kovner DP International (DP International). He is responsible for directing DP-A's long-term growth and welfare, as well as meeting annual sales and profitability targets. As the head of the manufacturer's largest subsidiary, Parker also has been given the task of developing and implementing sales and marketing strategies that will support the entire Dura-plast group's profitability.

It is now January, 1995, and Mr. Parker is sitting in his office at DP-A's Flint, Michigan, headquarters. He is thinking about the efforts his company made and the difficulties it encountered in presenting a successful sales contract to provide Techno Plastics, Inc. with Dura-plast granulator equipment. Techno Plastics, based in France, is a major international plastics producer which had decided to build a plant in the southeastern part of the United States. The sales process was complicated by the need for coordination across DP-A's different country-based subsidiaries and because Techno Plastics was a new customer for DP-A. Parker was pleased to receive reassurance from

Source: *Written by Ryan Oliver under the supervision of Professor Joe Cannon as a basis for classroom discussion. As part of the case development, firm and individual specifics have been disguised.* Copyright © 1996 by the Roberto C. Goizueta Business School of Emory University. No part of this publication may be reproduced, stored in a retrieval system, or transmitted in any form or by any means—electronic, mechanical, photocopying, recording, or otherwise—without the permission of the Goizueta Business School. Reproduced March, 1996.

Techno Plastics that his bid would be successful, but, realizing that more and more plastics manufacturers are setting up global manufacturing operations, Parker wondered if changes were needed to better serve global accounts.

## Granulation Equipment

DP-A and its parent company are in the business of designing, manufacturing, assembling, and selling plastics granulators. A plastics granulator is used to chop plastics waste (bad parts and production rejects) into small granules for closed-loop recycling. Granulators are most commonly used in industrial shops, where excess scrap is fed into the granulator hopper for conversion through rotating knives. The small uniform bits of processing scrap and bad parts which emerge from the granulator, called the "regrind," can then be recycled.

Granulators are specified by their infeed or throat size, throughput and weight, and by the composition and chemical makeup of the plastic waste they can process within an hour. Each is fitted with an infeed hopper designed to handle various plastics dimensions. Granulators positioned next to the plastic manufacturing machine to reclaim plastic scraps immediately are known as beside-the-press (B-T-P) granulators. Other types of granulators are placed in a central location (Central) in the plant and scraps are delivered to them manually or by conveyor or sold as smaller, stand-alone (Automated) units.

The granulators sold range widely in price, feature, and quality/performance tradeoffs. Because granulators can be tailored to the specific production process of the customer, both the analysis and identification of customer requirements and customization costs are figured into the price of the product.

## Thorton Group and Kovner DP International

DP-A is a wholly-owned subsidiary of the Norwegian Thorton Group member, DP International. The group consists of a number of medium-sized engineering companies in the producer-goods industry, each with the developing medium-sized industrial companies in a particular specialty area. The Thorton Group continues to grow through expanded sales and company acquisitions. Its operational structure and tactics support the growth of individual companies operating as important market markers in focused geographic areas. While most subsidiaries hold prominent positions near their customer bases, Thorton Company Headquarters have traditionally been placed close to their representative Norwegian manufacturing plants. Thorton and DP International specifics are provided in Exhibit 1 (Organizational Structure).

DP International follows a typical Thorton company organizational system: it develops and produces its granulation equipment in Norway and conducts sales through its international subsidiaries, thereby manufacturing globally with local market support. DP International invoiced sales totaling $233 and $326 million in 1992 and 1993 with respective earnings of $11 and $47 million. The parent company had a return on capital of over 35% during this period. In 1994, approximately 2700 units were sold in Europe, 2050 in America, and 500 in Asia. There has been substantial improvement in earnings as a result of the strong volume growth. However, DP International, with its high level of sales abroad, has also benefited from a weaker Norwegian krone rate.[1]

DP International's low-noise granulators have primarily been used for granulating plastic waste in connection with the automated manufacture of plastic products. A proprietary design offers technical superiority which has allowed the company to establish a strong global market presence. Its unique, patented reversible knife design is currently produced only in Norway.

In addition to supplying all the cutting chambers to its international subsidiaries, DP International sells a large number of complete machines because of the complexity of the electrical and drive systems. However, because products qualifying as locally made have lower costs due to lower import duties, DP International established an assembly and manufacturing plant in the US and an assembly plant in Germany. These run as autonomous P&L locations, typically assembling, customizing and adding local content to the larger granulators that are sourced

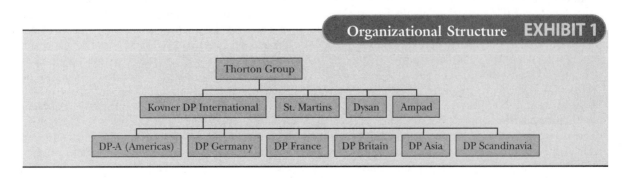

Organizational Structure    **EXHIBIT 1**

from Norway for sale throughout the Americas and Europe. The small to medium-sized machines currently do not qualify as US products under NAFTA content requirements, and as such are not free from import duties.

DP International is planning further decentralization of its manufacturing operations with the establishment of a cutting chamber production facility in the US. This move will lower transportation costs, which currently add 6% or more to the final sale price of DP International units. In addition, it would enable the company to meet in-country product requirements, lessen the risk of international currency fluctuations, and lower tax and tariff duties.

DP International has responded to the cost of maintaining large product lines by developing flexibility in the manufacturing cycle. Increasingly, DP International has been able to customize its products to meet customer requirements, an important factor in DP International's low-cost, high-volume strategy. In fact, during 1992, DP International successfully launched a new product generation based on a modular product system, which brought about a strong volume increase in 1993. In 1994, the US subsidiary, DP-A, developed a US hopper welding cell which allowed for additional, in-house customization of the larger machines.

In order to handle market demand changes and increasing sales, DP International expanded its plant capacity in Norway this past year. When at full capacity, the new plant will allow the organization to expand sales from 5,000 to 7,000 with a substantial increase in its large-capacity machine production facilities.

## Subsidiary Companies

Torger Erlandsen, the managing director of DP International, directs the integration of the international operations. Under his leadership, each of the subsidiary companies retains significant autonomy in both organizational structure and management. As a result, the operational manager in each of the countries functions in an atmosphere that offers a high degree of entrepreneurial freedom. Country managers make their own decisions with respect to sales strategy, pricing, and promotion. Erlandsen believes that granting this leadership independence is the most effective way to maximize the opportunities within the granulation equipment sales' niche marketplace.

While each of the subsidiary companies reports to the Norwegian headquarters, the subsidiary organizations do not have formal ties with each other. In a growing number of cases, however, an order may be generated from an area outside of a subsidiary's direct responsibility; the individual subsidiaries then have the responsibility to coordinate efforts which take into account specification development and

business practice initiatives suitable to that business environment and culture. Final responsibility, however, and authority in decision making is given to the local subsidiary.

However, because of the interrelated nature between international marketing and manufacturing, there have been increasing problems regarding contract specification and pricing issues internationally. Some members of the DP International group, for instance, have begun to wonder if it might be a good idea to set a standard price internationally. With respect to sales strategy, some agree with the DP-A Vice President for Sales, Richard Foster, who argues that confusion in the sales cycle could be limited if the criteria for involvement in the sales relationship were more narrowly defined. His suggestion is for "involvement only when a person can enhance the sales relationship." Others suggest greater or lesser involvement across countries.

Traditionally, most countries have employed Agents[2] to sell and distribute granulators. Agents buy the Dura-plast granulators and then sell them to their own customer base, setting their own price levels. Prices in some cases are higher than DP International has wanted. In this set-up, the agent decides how he wants to sell in the market, and determines his own segmentation, targeting, and positioning, perhaps to the exclusion of some areas of the market. If the market is slumping, the agent argues that the price is too high. However, the manufacturer has limited knowledge of the specific competitors, contract terms, or agent mark-up. In fact, if the agent forgoes the contract, the manufacturer can lose an entire customer base.

One of DP International's new channel strategies is its transition to Manufacturer's Representative (MR)[3] relationships in each of the DP International offices worldwide—thus standardizing part of its selling strategy. This strategy focuses on generating sales through MRs contracts instead of through sales agents. One of the primary benefits of this strategy is to help DP International to protect its current and long-term market position by getting closer to the customer. It is important for DP International to understand where its machines are being sold and to develop brand name loyalty in the market. The global program to take control of the customer has helped to clarify pricing and stabilize production. If the market is slumping, DP International's regional sales managers will be able to intensify the sales efforts or make strategic decisions, such as price reductions.

Each of DP International's subsidiaries handles the MR and other selling issues differently. The following sections provide more detail about DP International's subsidiaries in Germany, France, Britain and North America.

**DP Germany (DPG).**   Germany is a large market that is treated as an individual unit in DP International's international planning exercises. Germany's solo status and competitive advantage stems from its market size, homogeneity, and the location of a manufacturing plant which supplies the rest of Europe. The German market is almost as large as the US market with respect to the total number of customers.

German companies typically bid on a packaged basis. Each offer generally includes pricing and terms regarding auxiliary equipment, start-up and installation, plans, and long-term spare part commitments. Each part of the bid package is important to contract acquisition.

Germany recently changed its sales organization structure by shifting from an agent driven salesforce to one which includes both agents and MRs. Under the direction of a DPG sales manager who controls a group of sales reps and one agent, the country has been divided into territories where representatives are given regional exclusivity. In addition to managing the salesforce, the sales manager develops relationships and bids for larger granulation systems, calling on original equipment manufacturers (OEMs) and the largest potential purchasers.

**DP France (DPF).**   In France, as with the rest of Europe, sales cycles have traditionally been much longer than those in the US. The time from initial inquiry for granulation equipment to delivery averages 12–18 months. As a result, manufacturers and their customers have a longer time to plan and delineate product quote and specifications. Tom Parker suggests that "the introduction of MRs has allowed DP France to manage its customer base more closely." Consequently, DP France has developed sales relationships with several larger firms that have plants throughout France and worldwide. France is currently the smallest DP International European subsidiary. French customers typically expect bids to be presented in the same manner that German customers do—including all details on service, spare parts and support.

**DP Britain (DP-UK).**   The DP International office in Britain still uses an agent system to promote and sell its products. The agent system works because it is a generally accepted practice in the market and because of the limited interaction required in the sales process. Unlike the rest of Europe, distributors in Britain do not have to delineate each of the engineering and sales support requirements in the sales contract. DP-UK is a mid-sized DP International European subsidiary.

**DP-Americas (DP-A).**   DP-A, the biggest company in the DP International Group, faces the challenge of marketing within the quick cycle, volatile US, Canadian, and Mexican marketplaces. Strong in the US and Canada, DP-A has not made significant inroads into the Mexican, Latin American or South American markets as yet, principally because of practically non-existent safety standards, which allow competitors in these developing countries to build machines at a significantly lower cost.

DP-A's operations are led by a board of directors, consisting of Torger Erlandsen, a Norway-based manufacturing expert, and DP-A CEO Tom Parker. While Parker is responsible for day-to-day management of the DP-A activities, major decisions are approved by the board of directors. The board of directors currently meets on a quarterly basis with additional meetings as needed.

DP-A's domestic staff are split into three operational groups. The operations group manages the assembly and small-scale manufacturing operations in Flint, Michigan and a larger manufacturing plant just outside Knoxville, Tennessee, which will come on line in 1998. The Administration and Planning functions, as well as the Sales functions, are centralized in Flint.

The US bidding system is unlike Europe's. In addition to the faster selling cycle (the time from initial inquiry to final sale lasts between 2–8 months), US customers do not require the same amount of specificity and long-term price guarantees as those in Europe. DP-A, for instance, typically bids systems without the inclusion of auxiliary equipment and start-up costs. Start-up tends to be handled in-house and auxiliary equipment purchases are placed as needed. Most equipment installations are designed to be self-service—usually handled easily by in-plant engineers. DP-A does not bid for long-term spare part commitments or with detailed plant location specs either. Primarily because the market does not expect it, but also because the North American market is much more price-driven, bidding is more narrowly focused than in Europe.

DP-A's sales structure primarily relies on a network of Manufacturers Representatives. Each of DP-A's sales managers directs 4–5 MRs, spread out on a regional basis. Sales managers have responsibility for non-contiguous regions, such as a territory covering California, Canada, New England, and Texas. Richard Foster notes that non-contiguous sales areas give DP-A the ability to determine whether sales performance is a result of regional economic downturns or lackluster performance. Rising airline costs may cause DP-A to review this policy.

Currently, DP-A has exclusive, non-compete contracts with 25 MR groups, which in turn employ over 100 sales representatives. The DP-A MRs are located throughout the United States, Canada, and

Mexico. MRs are the dominant distribution channel in the granulation industry because of their ability to cross-sell to the customer. A typical MR represents injection molding, blow molding, extrusion molding, vacuum systems for moving plastic, and drying systems equipment to the companies he or she visits. As such, representatives are a one-stop shop for a company's comprehensive plastic production equipment requirements.

The use of MRs allows DP-A to increase coverage while keeping full-time personnel to a minimum. MRs are not always the only contact with the end-user; however, their expertise and relationship with the buyers, built through the cross-sale of different types of plant equipment provides an effective and efficient sales strategy. MRs do not sell to all DP-A accounts. Larger sales are handled by DP-A's own marketing managers on the basis of leads generated from MRs and DP-A's direct advertising. If a lead generated by an MR generates a sale, the MR still receives the standard commission.

The best MRs generally carry the most effective and best known products because of their ability to close deals with a large group of well-established principals. MR groups have between 2 and 10 salespeople and close total sales in the range of 1 to 15 million dollars annually. Commissions on machines sales are generally 12% for mid-sized machines, 6% for the large-size machines, and 14% for machines under $10,000. If the MR and/or DP-A negotiated price discounts, these are generally split between the MR and DP-A.

MRs do not direct the installation or provide service for DP-A. Installation is not a critical sales factor for the smaller machines, because the machines arrive assembled and ready to run. For the larger central system machines, DP-A typically sends a service technician to the installation sight to check wiring and set-up specifications before the machine is first used. Service is directed from DP-A's central headquarters in Flint, Michigan.

Of DP-A sales, approximately 90% of all machines sold are used for new applications and 10% to replace outdated equipment. DP-A sales managers and MRs sell to a wide variety of individuals and companies on both a transactional and collaborative basis. DP-A classifies its current customers into the following categories.

- **Transactional accounts**, where customers purchase with both price and features in mind. In general, there are no long-term relationship or purchase commitments. Machines sold to these customers generally sell for under $10,000.

- **System accounts** are developed when MRs work with customers to define needs and establish fit.

Granulators sold to customers in this category generally sell for between $10,000 and $50,000. While the service aspect of the sale provides ground for an ongoing relationship, there are no long-term purchase commitments.

- **Key accounts** represent the top 15% of DP-A sales and include large unit volume and annual dollar sales. The DP-A employee acts as a consultant in this relationship; more technologically proficient DP-A managers discuss the company's long-term plans and project goals. Currently, there are no formal long-term purchase commitments. Machines sold to these customers often cost more than $50,000.

### Customers

The plastics industry uses two types of materials—thermoplastics and thermosets—in combination with stabilizers, colorants, flame retardants, and reinforcing agents in the plastic production process. These are then shaped or molded under heat and pressure to a solid state. Thermoplastics can be resoftened to their original condition by heat; however, thermosets cannot. Thermoplastics account for almost 90% of total plastic production and nearly 100% of granulation activity.

In general, thermoplastics output takes the form of pellets, flakes, granules, powders, liquid resins, sheeting, pipe, profile, parts, or film. It can be divided into four production categories:

| Type | Examples | % Total Industry |
|------|----------|------------------|
| Injection molding | Automobile parts, pudding cups | 50 |
| Blow molding | Soda and milk bottles | 12 |
| Extrusion | Trash bags, plastic pipes | 30 |
| Reclaim | Post consumer recycling | 7 |

DP International sells the largest number of its granulators to injection molding companies. Nonetheless, it generates its highest level of profit from equipment utilizing extrusion processing, because the machines in this production category are significantly larger and more complex.

Large injection molding companies include Ford, Chrysler, and GM, as well as consumer product producers such as Black and Decker. Injection molding is a versatile and quick production process, and companies relying upon it have recently taken advantage of improvements in technology to expand productivity.

In 1992 and 1993, this segment's plastic purchases grew by more than 11%.

Blow molding has shown high growth in the last few years because its resulting products are less expensive and easier to design. As new technology makes blow molding more profitable, blow molding firms, which include Coke, Pepsi, Tupperware, and Rubbermaid, have continued to expand their operations.

Extrusion is a popular method of producing large quantities of both uniform and dissimilar material that can be packaged into small units and distributed easily. The demand for plastics used in extrusion grew by over 12% for both 1992 and 1993. Future projections are not so rosy; growth in some segments of the extrusion industry which are expected to drop to less than 1% in 1995, and to contract by 4.4% in 1996, due to excess capacity.

**Granulator Sales.** DP-A offers approximately 30 different models in four primary product groups and one secondary product group through a strategic alliance with an original equipment manufacturer (OEM). The automation product group focuses on small, automated granulators for the injection molding market segment; the B-T-P product group is geared toward mid-size granulators for the injection molding/blow molding market; the central product group concentrates mostly in central reclamation in the extrusion market, while the parts/auxiliary/service product group is directed toward all customers.

The manufacturing process for DP-A equipment is a flexible multi-step process because of the unique design needs of individual clients. Compact machines generally require less customization. These machines come with DP-A's positive feed and rotating knife systems. Specifically, the design in the cutting chamber ensures positive feed of bulky materials and high throughputs. The reversible rotating knives allow the clearance between the cutting edges of the rotating and bed knives and the screen to remain constant. Both contribute to improved efficiency by reducing energy consumption and averting heat buildup.

The heavy-duty models include the positive feed and reversible rotating knife systems, as well as engineering systems capability and special hopper availability. Specialists in the engineering department are able to design a system to fit particular production requirements. As Tom Parker remarked, "the machines are generic but the applications are specific." Some applications require specially designed hoppers for maximum throughput and increased productivity. Energy efficiency remains a common concern in the design and purchase of both heavy-duty or compact machines.

In recent years, large global purchasers are increasingly seeking suppliers which can provide international turn-key solutions and services as opposed to sourcing from multiple suppliers for products and services. Using a single global supplier enhances negotiating power, standardizes spare parts, and allows the customer to build a closer relationship with one supplier. Global customers are asking granulator manufacturers to solve scrap recycling problems rather than simply sell them machines. This move is partly a result of the reduction in engineers at plastic manufacturer's production facilities. One customer commented that his firm wanted to focus its efforts on manufacturing, not on developing an expertise in recycling systems.

The trend is especially prevalent among European multinational firms, which traditionally have expected a high degree of supplier technical support. Additionally, rather than hiring technical expertise, purchasers are now contracting with companies which provide a centralized rather than local engineering focus.

A recent survey of DP-A customers and MRs found that they most value product performance, features, and the ability to customize the application. When asked to determine the most important attribute in the purchase decision, 41.7% of the customers chose quality/overall performance. In contrast, price was the most frequent response given by the MRs (31.4%). DP-A customers seem to view price as more of an order qualifier rather than an order winner. (Exhibit 2 provides a price/attribute comparison of DP-A customers and manufacturer representatives).

DP-A's most recent value-added solutions include its efforts within the injection molding, blow molding and film extrusion market segments of the plastic industry. Specialized niche development includes reclaim for scrap plastic, robot-fed injection molding, hot melt resin reclamation, edge trim film/sheet, post-consumer waste bottle, vinyl siding and central thermoform scrap market segments. The niche markets are highly customized and provide high gross profits with limited competition. In support of these markets, DP-A engineers have worked with the market managers to further develop product engineered systems to meet their customer's application needs. Identification of these opportunities, however, continues to be a challenge.

DP-A's product portfolio overview provides information on each of the company's three major product groupings, the Automated, B-T-P, and Central. Individual components which are critical to application success and compliance include cutting chamber size, horsepower, rate screen, rotor configuration, RPM, and product features such as the tilt-back hopper and clam-shell screen cradle.

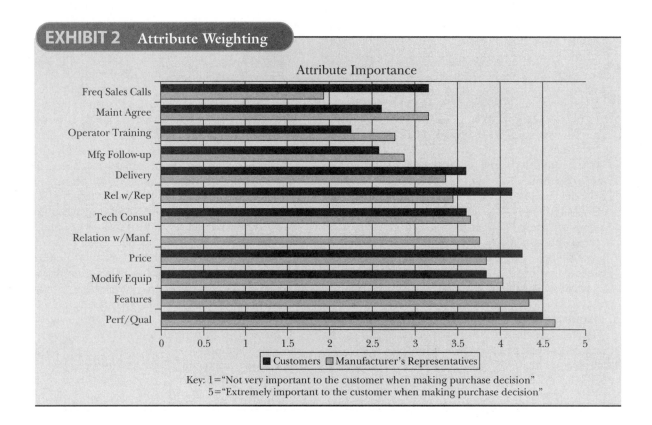

**EXHIBIT 2** Attribute Weighting

Attribute Importance

Key: 1 = "Not very important to the customer when making purchase decision"
5 = "Extremely important to the customer when making purchase decision"

Companies also have the choice of specialized features such as low infeed heights, oversized bearings, integral soundproofing, auger in feed, and conveyor infeed.

DP International is one of the largest producers of granulators worldwide and within the United States, DP-A has grown to be the largest supplier in unit volume of granulation equipment. Serving the entire range of companies in the plastic reclamation process, DP-A's installed customer account base includes over 6000 locations across the United States.

Part of this growth comes from the addition of a new OEM client to the DP-A portfolio. DP-A's strategic alliance with Fields (Powerflow) enables it to purchase and distribute up to 500 B-T-P units a year at a percentage discount. These units are sold under Powerflow's nameplate. DP-A is also considering the expansion of its OEM relationships to other major plastics manufacturers. Both partners benefit through these expanded relationships: DP International can increase market share and the OEMs can service their key accounts with a high quality product.

The key factors in DP-A's 1995 $21 million sales effort include the introduction of new machines, expanded service relationships, and enhanced marketing efforts, combined with further expansion of the OEM alliance with Powerflow.

For Tom Parker, DP-A volume leadership is "not a reason to be complacent." In addition to the company's drive for customer satisfaction and total quality management in the early 1990's, DP-A must now address issues related to account management and market change. Many of DP-A's larger machine segment clients now conduct business on both a domestic and international basis. Sales efforts have required significant synchronization of efforts between subsidiaries. In addition, under the goal of expanding profitability, management is working to raise the dollar volume on individual sales. Focusing on the mid- to large-size machine sales efforts has resulted in a mixed response from the salesforce. The numbers, however, continue to grow, with DP-A projecting dollar bookings of 45% of the US market in 1995.

In the last year, DP-A has posted record profits, with an average profit margin of 9% per sale. Gross profit, operating income, and net income information for 1993 and 1994 are presented in Table 1.

**Competition**

DP-A was one of 15 competitors in the US Market which contributed to the 4500 granulators orders received overall in 1989 totaling $32.7 million and 7000 granulators in 1994 totaling $120 million.

Although DP-A is the newest competitor in the US granulator sales marketplace, it is currently the leader in volume sales, primarily through the OEM relationship with Powerflow. Before the linkage, it

## TABLE 1

| Dura-plast, Inc.* | 1993 | 1994 |
|---|---|---|
| Gross Profit | $5,067,029 | $6,995,259 |
| Operating Income | $294,289 | $1,697,332 |
| Net Income | $167,055 | $959,810 |

*Dura-plast, Inc. Income Statement as of December 31, 1994 and 1993.

was number three in the market, driven by a strong sales push.

DP-A's price position in relation to that of its competitors may hamper unit sales in some market segments. Some of its competitors are large conglomerates which often use granulators as loss-leaders in negotiations to close higher dollar, turn-key system orders. DP-A has traditionally had a poor record in acquiring these orders, which are generally multi-unit contracts.

DP-A credits its success in the market to outperforming competitors by delivering the highest standard of customer service. While it has created the perception of technical design superiority through marketing proprietary concepts such as the "constant flow methodology," DP-A has traditionally viewed itself as the underdog. The company continues to resist complacency: one corporate motto states "we must provide better service than our competitors; as such, our customers are right 98% of the time."

The market leader in dollars sold is the Northway Corporation, which is owned by the Abrahams Group, a division of the German conglomerate Ludwig-Crow. It averages 35% gross margins on granulators, 60% on parts/knives, and 35% on pelletizers. Its profits last year averaged around 10%–14%.

Northway has a product management organizational structure with a vice president of Marketing and a product manager for its B-T-P/Automation, Central/Systems and Pelletizing product groups. Each product manager has an application engineer and clerical support. The company has a vice president of Sales who manages its regional sales managers, parts department and service department. The marketing group prepares their sales quotes and supports the sales group with marketing intelligence and new products. Northway recently acquired a manufacturer of screen changes and pelletizing which seems, at least in the short run, to have negatively affected the company's ability to support its granulator sales. Northway has, however, been able to use its multi-product sales to continue as a dominant force in the Central and System markets.

Northway distribution efforts have been shifted from a 20-man direct salesforce to 2 regional sales managers and 18 manufacturer representative agencies. Perhaps the two regional sales managers currently cannot provide the level of service necessary to meet customer retention requests; at any rate Northway now has the reputation of being hard to deal with and increasingly non-responsive.

Northway historically has had a wider range of products, as compared to DP-A, because of its ability to offer 20 machines in a market where DP-A has 3–4. Consequently DP-A has had to price aggressively to remain competitive, especially on granulator sales that fall into a DP-A market gap. There are times, for example, when customers want machines specified for power requirements and size that lie in between DP-A's offerings. In order to get the sale, DP-A has to bid its larger machine.

Northway currently is not advertising aggressively. In the past, however, it led the market in advertising dollars spent. The parent company, the Abrahams Group, has a cooperative advertising strategy which promotes a comprehensive turn-key organization. This reputation supplements Northway's exceptional brand awareness and solid reputation. Northway also runs a direct mail program to targeted acquisition and retention customers on a quarterly basis.

## TABLE 2

| Competitor | 1989 | | | | 1994 | | | |
|---|---|---|---|---|---|---|---|---|
| | Units | Unit % | Dollars | $ % | Units | Unit % | Dollars | $ % |
| Northway | 1200 | 26% | $18 Million | 28% | 1400 | 20% | $33.5 Mill. | 28% |
| Grindall | 150 | 33% | 16 Million | 25% | 1650 | 23% | 27.5 Mill. | 23% |
| DP-A | 650 | 14% | 8.5 Million | 13% | 2050 | 28% | 30 Million | 25% |
| Fields (Powerflow) | 450 | 10% | 6 Million | 9% | 700 | 10% | 12 Million | 10% |
| Smith & Smith | 400 | 8% | 5 Million | 8% | 600 | 9% | 10 Million | 8% |

DP-A, however, is the leading advertiser in the North American market. It runs full-page color and ¼-page black and white ads in five major publications. It also attends 5–7 trade shows per year in order to exhibit its new products. DP-A has invested heavily in high-tech contemporary literature to complement its quotations.

## Techno Plastics Request for Proposals

Techno Plastics, located outside of Paris, is a multi-national blow molding company that specializes in the production of hardened plastic fuel tank systems for automobiles. Part of its expansion plan includes the development plan, namely, to be the largest producer of fuel tanks globally. To meet its goals, the company decided to open a new fuel tank plant in the US.

DP International has developed a strong relationship with Techno Plastics over the past 12 years and is currently servicing Techno Plastics manufacturing plants in Germany, UK, and France. Despite this relationship, Techno Plastics submitted a request for proposals (RFP) to each of the major granulator producers as part of a plan to supply the plant it was building in Lawrenceville, Georgia. What follows is a summary and timeline of events related to the RFP, which originated in France. (Exhibit 3 provides an overview of organization teams within the DP International and Techno Plastics organizations.)

**August 1994.** DP International's US subsidiary submitted its first quote for Techno Plastics' Georgia granulator services in August of 1994. US executives visiting Europe on a planning trip were introduced to Techno Plastics personnel at a plastics convention. The local French contact for Techno Plastics, Jean Handel, a DP France sales manager, facilitated the introduction. In private, he explained Techno Plastics' strategic importance to DP International, in part due to its annual purchases of $1,000,000 in new equipment, parts and service.

At the plastics convention, the US team members demonstrated several of DP International's latest machines to Techno Plastics and began initial strategy discussions for the upcoming RFP response. Over the next few weeks, Jean Handel followed up with information regarding the US plant's specifications and also provided recommendations with respect to pricing.

With Handel's information, the DP-A bid was developed to mirror the specifications of Techno Plastics' German Plant, currently supplied by DP-G, with slightly higher pricing than the typical US bid. These specifications included a cooling device for regrind and a conveyer system, but did not include

self-cleaning capabilities because these were not currently in place at the newest Techno Plastics plant in Germany.

DP-A proposed to provide a "system to meet Techno Plastics specifications," a standard practice for US bidding. Typical of DP-A's bids to its US customers, the bid not provide specifics regarding each piece of individual equipment, formalized engineering drawings, or spare part commitments.

In addition to the bid, the US sales executives traveled to the Lawrenceville plant to meet with Michel Duval, the plant manager. Scott Millar, DP-A Regional Manager, and Richard Foster presented a sales proposal to Duval and other Techno Plastics staff. Both the presentation and bid were well received.

**September 1994.** At another plastics convention in Paris in late September, US and European staff met in France for a second time with Stefan Sevan, the Techno Plastics engineer responsible for the Lawrenceville, Georgia plant and Technical Director for Techno Plastics' Blow Molding Division. During this meeting, Sevan and his colleague Bill Dubois were led by Jean Handel in a discussion of the technical specification requirements for the new plant. On the basis of that discussion a new DP International product was offered to the Techno Plastics engineers. At the end of the meeting, Sevan requested that DP-A re-submit its quote for equipment and services, based on the new DP International machine and specification modifications.

The need for outside vendor support for the new offering and associated pricing of additional conveyor and blower equipment in the revised quote forced DP-A to delay its bid resubmittal for six weeks. At the end of this period, Sevan contacted DP International's US office regarding the quote. He requested that it be forwarded as soon as possible. Additional problems surfaced, however, when Sevan contacted DP-A again, telling them he had not received the offer. Evidently it had been misdirected by office staff. Neither side admitted to the error.

During this period, Sevan also contacted Peter Olsen, Technical Director for DP International's Norwegian Headquarters team, in an attempt to gain control over the sale. Following the quote's re-transmission and review, Sevan offered a temporary approval to the sale.

Richard Foster and Scott Millar traveled again to the Lawrenceville plant, following the third quote, to meet with Michel Duval. Duval was very pleased with DP-A following rigorous technical discussions.

**January 1995.** Notwithstanding the previous multi-quote issues, DP International seemed well

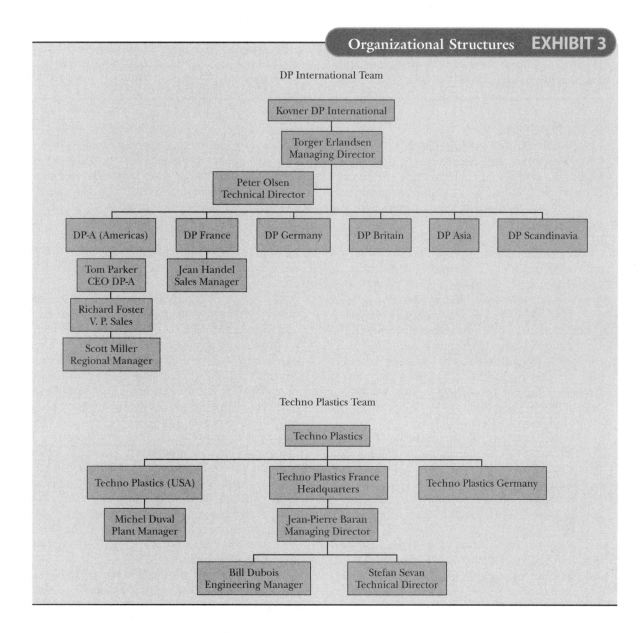

Organizational Structures   **EXHIBIT 3**

positioned to acquire Techno Plastics' granulator business. Then reports from DP International European staff member visiting the Fukuma Plastics's trade show in Germany indicated another problem. The staff member had been informed by Stefan Sevan that the US subsidiary quotation was not adequate. The specifications had been quoted according to proposal requirements (the standard for project conformance), rather than to the current system in use at the Rothenburg, Germany plant. As such, the current bid would not meet all of Techno Plastics' needs.

The bid was re-submitted according to the Rothenburg set-up. However, Sevan contacted the DP International US Headquarters again, claiming that the bid still was not sufficient. Sevan encouraged Tom Parker to cut his price to ensure the

order. DP-A responded by lowering its price, because Parker did not want to jeopardize DP-A's global position with Techno Plastics. To support the relationship, Parker and Richard Foster flew to France to find out more about the French specification expectations.

Caucusing with the French DP International subsidiary in Paris, a US, French, and Norwegian corporate management team reviewed the Techno Plastics case, preparing what they hoped would be the final bid. Although Jean Handel offered to negotiate on behalf of the US subsidiary, his offer was rejected, following what DP-A staff considered to be internal coordination errors and technical misinformation.

After lengthy intercompany caucusing, that DP-A and Techno Plastics executives worked through plant specifications and at least half a dozen new issues developed in response to granulation require-ments at the German plant. During this meeting, DP International offered its final quotation, follow-ing extensive technical discussions with Techno Plastics engineers and management. Both sides were elated with the outcome. Sevan reassured Parker at the meeting saying, "I told you, I've always been a Dura-plast man."

## DURA-PLAST, INC. (B): GLOBAL ACCOUNT MANAGEMENT

It is June, 1995, and Tom Parker, CEO of Dura-plast, Inc. (DP-A), is reconstructing DP-A's han-dling of the Techno Plastics granulation equipment order. He was surprised and extremely disappointed to learn that Techno Plastics had not selected DP-A to supply granulators for their new plant.

The considerable expenditure in human and cap-ital resources, along with meetings in both the US and France to clarify issues related to equipment specification, time frame and bid pricing, were not to be justified by first-year earnings alone. DP-A's efforts were targeted at extending the on-going DP International-Techno Plastics relationship in the US through a comprehensive order for both equipment and service for Techno Plastics' new plant in Lawrenceville, Georgia. The talks and the bid had been well received. It had seemed that the only for-mality left was the paperwork.

However, Torger Erlandsen, managing director of DP International Operations, recently informed Parker that the Lawrenceville plant bid was awarded to Northway, a US-based granulator producer and a major competitor. The news was delivered to Erlandsen by his DP France sales manager, Jean Handel.

To make matters worse, it now seems evident that DP-A sold to the wrong decision maker, and did not offer the right equipment and price pack-age. Technically, there was no problem with the DP International product offering.

It also appears that the final purchase decision was made at the plant level in Lawrenceville by Michel Duval and in France by Stefan Sevan's boss, the Techno Plastics engineer responsible for the Lawrenceville, Georgia plant, Jean-Pierre Baran. DP-A had thought, that the decision would be made by DP-A's main contact, Sevan, and his direct reports. To DP-A's surprise, management in Lawrenceville com-mented that they were more comfortable with Northway, which "seemed more interested in their business and provided comprehensive information and service specifics in its bid." They also stated that, while price was not the order winner, the Northway offer was lower than the DP-A bid.

Re-examination of the bids, however, showed that Northway's slightly less expensive pricing did not include the same specifications as the DP-A offer. As a result, the Northway package, when complete, will actually be more expensive than the DP-A offer.

For Tom Parker, a significant problem with the Techno Plastics bid failure revolves around the issue of marketing coordination. As a group, Dura-plast did not understand who was the key player in charge and who was the key decision maker. While everyone intended to do the right thing, each mem-ber of the DP-A team made mistakes. Parker com-mented, "When Richard and I went to France and met with Stefan Sevan and his people, he assured us we had the order. We were convinced. However, we never really had the order. Sevan may have thought he could give us the order, but he was not the deci-sion maker. It was a nightmare . . . The only solu-tion I see is structured coordination among the DP International groups."

Global accounts are raising new issues for DP International, particularly with respect to pricing, cross-subsidiary coordination, technology and mar-keting strategy. These issues were brought to a head in the Techno Plastics situation. Currently, Dura-plast is trying to price at the local market, in effect, to maximize the profit potential in each subsidiary. However, there are concerns regarding this practice as a long-term policy.

Up to this point, all of Techno Plastics' granulator purchases had been through a DPI subsidiary—it was very loyal to Dura-plast. Now, however, Northway is also threatening DPG and DP-UK because of dispar-ities between European and US pricing. Northway's inroad is a major concern because it threatens other DP International key accounts.

Known for his critical evaluation and analysis, Mr. Parker is committed to supporting the current DP-A and DP International customer bases. He is currently working on a plan to regain the US Techno Plastics account and is outspoken regarding the importance of avoiding similar situations in the future. He is also committed to supporting business expansion through appropriate corporate change and new, viable projects. Mr. Parker wonders what is the best next step for DP-A.

**360-degree feedback** An assessment technique that involves performance assessment from multiple raters.

## A

**absorption training** A method of sales training that involves furnishing trainees or salespeople with materials that they peruse without opportunity for immediate feedback and questioning.

**account targeting strategy** The classification of accounts within a target market into categories for the purpose of developing strategic approaches for selling to each account or account group.

**achieving congruence** The process of matching the capabilities of a sales recruit with the needs of the organization.

**achieving realism** The process of giving a sales recruit an accurate portrayal of the sales job.

**activity-based costing (ABC)** A method that allocates costs to individual units on the basis of how the units actually expend or cause these costs.

**adaptive selling** The ability of a salesperson to alter their sales messages and behaviors during a sales presentation or as they encounter different sales situations and different customers.

**AIDA** An acronym for the various mental states the salesperson must lead their customers through when using mental states selling: attention, interest, desire, and action.

**amoral management** A form of management in which management is neither moral nor immoral, but decisions lie outside the sphere to which moral judgments apply.

**anticipation** The process of sales managers extending their view into the future to determine potential problems.

**apathetics** A salesperson who are low on commitment to the organization and low on involvement in his or her selling job.

**assessment center** Centers that offer a set of well-defined procedures for using techniques such as group discussions, business game simulations, presentations, and role-playing exercises for the purpose of employee selection or development.

## B

**background investigation** A reference check on the job candidate that can help verify the true identity of the person and possibly confirm his or her employment history.

**behavior approach** A category of research trying to uncover what makes an effective leader that seeks to catalog behaviors associated with effective leadership.

**behavioral criteria** A criteria for performance evaluation that emphasizes exactly what each salesperson does.

**behavioral simulations** A method of sales training in which trainees portray specified roles in staged situations.

**behaviorally anchored rating scales (BARS)** A performance evaluation method that links salesperson behaviors with specific results.

**behavior-based perspective** A perspective that incorporates complex and often subjective assessments of salesperson characteristics and behaviors with considerable monitoring and directing of salesperson behavior by sales managers.

**benchmarking** A ongoing measurement and analysis process that compares an organization's current operating practices with the "best practices" used by world-class organizations.

**bottom-up forecasting approaches** A forecasting approach that consists of different methods for developing sales forecasts for individual accounts; these forecasts are then combined by sales managers into territory, district, region, zone, and company forecasts.

**breakdown approach** An approach used for calculating salesforce size that assumes an accurate sales forecast is available, which is then "broken down" to determine the number of salespeople needed to generate the forecasted level of sales.

**business consultant** A role the salesperson plays in consultative selling where he or she uses internal and external (outside the sales organization) sources to become an expert on the customer's business. This role also involves educating customers on the sales firm's products and how these products compare with competitive offerings.

**business marketing** A marketing situation in which business is the target market.

**business strategy** An organizational strategy level that must be developed for each strategic business unit (SBU) in the corporate family, defining how that SBU plans to compete effectively within its industry.

**business unit portfolio** A firm's portfolio of their SBUs.

**buying center** The many individuals from a firm who participate in the purchasing process.

**buying needs** Buying behavior that can be personal and organizational. The organizational purchasing process is meant to satisfy the needs of the organization; however, the buying center

**389**

is made up of individuals who want to satisfy individual needs.

**Buying Power Index (BPI)** A market factor calculated for different areas by the equation $BPI = (5I + 2P + 3R) \div 10$ where I = Percentage of U.S. disposable personal income in the area, P = Percentage of U.S. population in the area, and R = Percentage of U.S. retail sales in the area.

**buying process** Organizational buyer behavior that consists of several phases: Phase 1 is recognition of problem or need; Phase 2 is determination of the characteristics of the item and the quantity needed; Phase 3 is description of the characteristics of the item and quantity needed; Phase 4 is search for and qualification of potential sources; Phase 5 is acquisition and analysis of proposals; Phase 6 is evaluation of proposals and selection of suppliers; Phase 7 is selection of an order routine; Phase 8 is performance feedback and evaluation.

## C

**canned sales presentation** A structured "script" used by salespeople to guide them in making sales.

**centralization** The degree to which important decisions and tasks in an organization are performed at higher levels in the management hierarchy.

**classroom/conference training** Sales training that features lectures, demonstrations, and group discussion with expert trainers serving as instructors.

**coaching** A leadership function in which a sales manager concentrates on continuous development of salespeople through supervisory feedback and role modeling.

**code of ethics** A written code of ethical business behavior that members of an association are urged to adhere to.

**coercive power** Power in an interpersonal relationship that is based on a belief that one party

can remove rewards and provide punishment to affect behavior.

**cognitive feedback** Information about how and why the desired outcome is achieved.

**combination sales job** A sales job in which the salesperson performs multiple types of sales jobs within the framework of a single position.

**commission base** Commission pay based on sales volume or some measure of profitability.

**commission payout event** Commission pay that is given when the order is confirmed, shipped, billed, paid for, or some combination of these events.

**commission rate** Commission pay in which a percentage of the commission earned is paid to the salesperson.

**commission splits** Commission pay that is divided between two or more salespeople or between salespeople and the employer.

**communication mechanisms** Communication leadership processes that include letter and memo writing, report writing, and the use of e-mail.

**compensation rewards** Organizational rewards that are given in return for acceptable performance or effort.

**competitive knowledge** Knowledge of a competitive product's strengths and weaknesses in the market.

**computerized matchmaking** The process of sales recruiters and recruitees using computer technology such as company and career services Web sites and automated application services to screen each other and match up specific qualifications.

**conflicts of interest** Job conflicts that place the salesperson in a position that could violate customer demands to benefit the company, or that could violate company policy to benefit customer demands.

**constant rate** A commission rate in which the salesperson is paid a constant percentage of what he or she sells.

**consultative selling** The process of helping customers reach their strategic goals by using the products, services, and expertise of the sales organization.

**contingency approach** A category of research trying to uncover what makes an effective leader that recognizes the importance of the interaction between situational factors and other factors.

**continued affirmation** An example of stimulus response selling in which a series of questions or statements furnished by the salesperson is designed to condition the prospective buyer to answering "yes" time after time, until, it is hoped, he or she will be inclined to say "yes" to the entire sales proposition.

**contribution approach** An approach to determining an organization's profitability that only uses direct costs, not indirect or shared costs; net contribution is calculated from this approach.

**corporate citizens** A salesperson who is highly committed to the organization, but who do not strongly identify with his or her selling role.

**corporate mission statement** A statement that provides direction for strategy development and execution throughout the organization.

**corporate strategy** An organizational strategy level that consists of decisions that determine the mission, business portfolio, and future growth directions for the entire corporate entity.

**cost analysis** The assessment of costs incurred by the sales organization to generate the achieved levels of sales.

**current spendable income** Money provided in the short term that allows salespeople to pay for desired goods and services.

**customer knowledge** Information relating to customers' needs, buying motives, buying procedures, and personalities.

**customer relationship management (CRM)** A business strategy to select and manage the most valuable customer relationships. It requires a customer-centric business philosophy and culture to support effective marketing, sales, and service processes.

**customer survey** A survey intended to define customer expectations.

## D

**decision models** An analytical approach to the allocation of selling effort in which mathematical formulations are used to achieve the highest level of sales for any given number of sales calls and to continue increasing sales calls until their marginal costs equal their marginal returns.

**decomposition methods** Method for developing company forecasts by breaking down previous company sales data into four major components: trend, cycle, seasonal, and erratic events.

**Delphi method** A structured type of jury of executive opinion method that involves selection of a panel of managers from within the firm who submit anonymous forecasts for each account.

**detailer** A salesperson in the pharmaceutical industry working at the physician level to furnish valuable information regarding the capabilities and limitations of medications in an attempt to get the physician to prescribe their product.

**diagnostic skills** Skills sales managers have to fully examine the root cause of a problem.

**differentiation strategy** A type of generic business strategy. It involves the creation of something perceived industrywide as being unique and provides insulation against competitive rivalry because of brand loyalty and resulting lower sensitivity to price.

**diffusion of innovation** The process whereby new products, services, and ideas are distributed to the members of society.

**direction** Salespeople choose where their efforts will be spent among various job activities.

## E

**economic stimuli** Something that stimulates or incites activity in the economy.

**effectiveness index** A type of sales analysis that can be computed by dividing actual sales results by the sales quota and multiplying by 100.

**ego drive** An indication of the degree of determination a person has to achieve goals and overcome obstacles in striving for success.

**ego strength** The degree to which a person is able to achieve an approximation of inner drives.

**employee referral programs** Interorganizational programs in which existing employees are used as sources for recruiting new salespeople because they have a good understanding of the type of person sought for a sales position.

**enthusiasm** A strong excitement of feeling. Salespeople should have an enthusiastic attitude in a general sense and a special enthusiasm for selling.

**expense account padding** Expense reimbursement in which a salesperson seeks reimbursement for ineligible or fictional expenses.

**expert power** Power in an interpersonal relationship that is based on the belief that a person has valuable knowledge or skills in a given area.

**exponential smoothing** A type of moving averages method that weights company sales in the most recent year differently than company sales in the past years.

**extensive problem solving** The lengthy decision-making process to collect and evaluate purchase information in new task buying situations.

**extrinsically motivated** Motivation occurring when salespeople are rewarded by others.

## F

**financial compensation mix** The relative amounts to be paid in salary, commission, and bonus.

**forecast** A prediction for a future period; forecasts provide the basis for making sales management decisions.

**full cost approach** An approach that deals with shared costs in an organization by allocating the shared costs to individual units based on some type of cost allocation procedure that results in a net profit figure.

**functional specialization** Term used to describe a salesforce in which salespeople specialize in a required number of selling activities.

## G

**generic business strategies** The most popular of classification schemes used in developing a business unit strategy. These generic strategies are low cost, differentiation, or niche.

**geographic specialization** Term used to describe a salesforce whose salespeople are typically assigned a geographic area and are responsible for all selling activities to all accounts within the assigned area.

**global account management (GAM)** A type of major account organization that serves the needs of major customers with locations around the world.

**government organizations** Federal, state, and local government agencies.

**graphic rating/checklist methods** Approaches in which salespeople are evaluated by using some type of performance evaluation form.

## H

**hierarchical sales analysis** A way to identify problem areas in achieving sales effectiveness that consists of evaluating sales results throughout the sales organization from a top-down perspective.

**hybrid sales organization** A sales organization structure that incorporates several of the basic structural types; the objective of a hybrid structure is to capitalize on the advantages of each type while minimizing the disadvantages.

## I

**immoral management** A form of management in which management decisions, actions, and behavior imply a positive and active opposition to what is ethical.

**income statement analysis** A type of profitability analysis that studies the different levels in a sales organization and different types of sales.

**incremental approach** An approach used for calculating salesforce size that compares the marginal profit contribution with the marginal selling costs for each incremental salesperson.

**independent representatives** Independent sales organizations that sell complementary, but noncompeting, products from different manufacturers; also called manufacturers' representatives or reps.

**industrial distributors** Sales channel middlemen who take title to the goods they market to end users.

**influence strategies** A type of communication strategy sales managers can use on their salesforce that can be based on threats, promises, persuasion, relationships, and manipulation.

**initial interviews** Brief interviews used to screen job applicants in order to replace a review of resumes or application forms.

**initiation to task** The degree to which a sales trainee feels competent and accepted as a working partner.

**inside sales** Nonretail salespeople who remain in their employer's place of business while dealing with customers.

**institutional stars** A salesperson who is highly committed to the organization and highly involved in his or her selling job.

**institutions** Public and private organizations.

**integrated marketing communication (IMC)** The strategic integration of multiple marketing communication tools in the most effective and efficient manner.

**integrative meeting** A sales meeting in which several sales and sales management functions are achieved.

**intensity** The amount of mental and physical effort put forth by the salesperson.

**intensive interviews** Interviews conducted to get an in-depth look at a job candidate.

**interpersonal communication skills** Skills that include listening and questioning.

**interviewer bias** Something that occurs when an interviewer allows personal opinions, attitudes, and beliefs influence judgments about a job candidate.

**intrinsically motivated** Motivation occurring when salespeople find their jobs inherently rewarding.

## J

**job analysis** A investigation of the task, duties, and responsibilities of the sales job.

**job analysis** The process of investigating the tasks, duties, and responsibilities of the job.

**job application form** A form job applicants fill out designed to gather all pertinent information and exclude unnecessary information.

**job description** A written summary of the job.

**job involvement** A strong attachment by the salesperson to the job itself.

**job preview** The process of giving a sales recruit an idea of what the sales job constitutes and how the job is performed.

**job qualifications** The aptitude, skills, knowledge, personal traits, and willingness to accept occupational conditions necessary to perform the job.

**job rotation** The exposure of the sales trainee to different jobs.

**job satisfaction** A salesperson's happiness with his or her job.

**job security** Job reward in which the salesperson feels comfortable that his or her job will last.

**jury of executive opinion method** A bottom-up forecasting approach in which the executives of the firm use their expert knowledge to forecast sales to individual accounts.

## L

**Leader–Member Exchange (LMX) model** A sales leadership model that focuses on the salesperson–sales manager dyad as a reciprocal influence process.

**leadership** The use of influence with other people through communication processes to attain specific goals and objectives.

**legitimate power** Power in an interpersonal relationship that is associated with the right to be a leader, usually as a result of designated organizational roles.

**limited problem solving** The decision-making process that occurs in a modified rebuy buying situation that involves collecting additional information and making a change when purchasing a replacement product.

**line sales management** Sales management position that is part of the direct management hierarchy within the sales organization. Line sales managers have direct responsibility for a certain number of subordinates and report directly to management at the next highest level in the sales organization.

**lone wolf** A salesperson who is often enthusiastic about his or her selling job (high involvement), but who is not bound to his or her organization (low commitment).

**long-term ally** A role the salesperson plays in consultative selling where he or she supports the customer, even when an immediate sale is not expected.

**low-cost strategy** A type of generic business strategy. It involves aggressive construction of efficient-scale facilities, vigorous pursuit of cost reductions from experience, tight cost, and overhead control, usually associated with high relative market share.

## M

**major account organization** A type of market specialization based on account size and complexity; an organization that handles major accounts, or large, important accounts.

**major account selling** The development of specific programs to serve a firm's largest and most important accounts.

**management by objectives (MBO)** A performance evaluation method that involves the (1) mutual setting of well-defined and measurable goals within a specified time period, (2) managing activities within the specified time period toward the accomplishment of the stated objectives, and (3) appraisal of performance against objectives.

**management levels** The number of different hierarchical levels of sales management within the organization.

**manipulation** An influence strategy that involves sales managers controlling circumstances to influence the target of influence.

**market bonus** A one-time payment given upon hiring that recognizes an existing imbalance in the supply and demand in a given labor market to entice a sales recruit to join the organization.

**market factor method** Method for breaking down company forecasts that involves identifying one or more factors that are related to sales at the zone, region, district, territory, or account levels and using these factors to break down the overall company forecast into forecasts at these levels.

**market specialization** Term used to describe a salesforce that assigns salespeople specific types of customers and are required to satisfy all needs of these customers.

**marketing mix** A marketing offer designed to appeal to a defined target market.

**marketing strategy** An organizational strategy level that includes the selection of target market segments and the development of a marketing mix to serve each target market.

**mental states selling** An approach to personal selling that assumes that the buying process for most buyers is essentially identical and that buyers can be led through certain mental states, or steps, in the buying process; also called the formula approach.

**mentor** A coach or sales trainer who observes and informs sales trainees on how to improve their sales performances.

**misrepresentation** Something that occurs when incorrect information is given about a job to entice a sales recruit into taking that job.

**missionary salespeople** Salespeople who usually work for a manufacturer but may also be found working for brokers and manufacturing representatives. Sales missionaries are expected to "spread the word" to convert noncustomers to customers.

**modified rebuy buying situation** A situation that exists when an account has previously purchased and used the product.

**moral management** A form of management in which management activity conforms to a standard of ethical, or right, behavior.

**motivation** A measurement of an individual's intensity, persistence, and direction.

**moving averages** Method for developing company forecasts by calculating the average company sales for previous years.

**multilevel selling** A variation of team selling in which the emphasis is to match functional areas between the buying and selling firms.

## N

**national account management (NAM)** A type of major account organization that focuses on meeting the needs of specific accounts with multiple locations throughout a large region or entire country.

**need satisfaction selling** An approach to selling based on the notion that the customer is buying to satisfy a particular need or set of needs.

**needs assessment** A process performed to compare the specific performance-related skills, attitudes, perceptions, and behaviors required for salesforce success with the state of readiness of the salesforce.

**new task buying situation** A situation in which an organization is purchasing a product for the first time.

**niche strategy** A type of generic business strategy. It involves service of a particular target market, with each functional policy developed with this target market in mind. Although market share in the industry might be low, the firm dominates a segment within the industry.

**noncompensation rewards** Organizational rewards that include factors related to the work situation and well-being of each salesperson.

**nonfinancial compensation** Job rewards that include career advancement through promotion, sense of accomplishment on the job, opportunities for personal growth, recognition of achievement, and job security.

**nonrole act** An unethical act that would not related to a sales manager's or a salesperson's specific job role but rather is a calculated attempt to gain something at the expense of the company.

## O

**objective and task method** A type of zero-based budgeting in which each sales manager prepares a separate budget request that stipulates the objectives achieved, the tasks required to achieve these objectives, and the costs associated with performing the necessary tasks.

**observation** The process in which sales managers monitor their salespeople during field selling activities.

**on-the-job training (OJT)** Sales training that puts the trainee into actual work circumstances under the observant eye of a supportive mentor or sales manager.

**opportunities for personal growth** Job reward such as college tuition reimbursement programs and seminars and workshops on such topics as physical fitness, stress reduction, and personal financial planning.

**opportunity for promotion** Job reward in which a salesperson obtains a higher job position on the organizational chain.

**order-getters** Salespeople who actively seek orders, usually in a highly competitive environment.

**order-takers** Salespeople who specialize in maintaining existing business.

**organizational commitment** A psychological bond to an organization or a bond demonstrated through behavior over time.

**original equipment manufacturers (OEM)** Organizations that purchase products to incorporate into products.

**outcome bias** The prejudice that occurs when the outcome of a decision rather than the appropriateness of the decision influences an evaluator's ratings.

**outcome feedback** Information about whether a desired outcome is achieved.

**outcome-based perspective** A perspective that focuses on objective measures of results with little monitoring or directing of salesperson behavior by sales managers.

**P**

**percentage of sales method** A method of cost analysis that calculates an expenditure level for each category by multiplying an expenditure percentage times forecasted sales.

**performance bonus** A type of current spendable income used to direct effort toward relatively short-term objectives.

**performance management** An approach that involves sales managers and salespeople working together on setting goals, giving feedback, reviewing, and rewarding.

**performance testing** A method used to determine sales training needs that specifies the evaluation of particular tasks or skills of the salesforce.

**persistence** The salesperson's choice to expend effort over time, especially when faced with adverse conditions.

**personal selling** Personal communication with an audience through paid personnel of an organization or its agents in such a way that the audience perceives the communicator's organization as being the source of the message.

**persuasion** An influence strategy in which sales managers use expert and referent power to imply that the target of influence must first change his or her attitudes and intentions to produce a subsequent change in behavior.

**pioneers** Salespeople who are constantly involved with either new products, new customers, or both. Their task requires creative selling and the ability to counter the resistance to change that will likely be present in prospective customers.

**planned earnings** An advantage of fixed salaries in which management can predict easily what individuals will be paid.

**planning activities** The first step in the salesperson recruitment and selection process; they include (1) conducting a job analysis, (2) establishing job qualifications, (3) completing a written job description, (4) setting recruitment and selection objectives, and (5) developing a recruitment and selection strategy.

**planning and control unit** The first step in territory design; an entity that is smaller than a territory.

**portfolio models** An analytical approach to the allocation of selling effort where each account served by a firm is considered as part of an overall portfolio of accounts; therefore, accounts within the portfolio represent different situations and receive different levels of selling effort attention.

**private employment agency** An external source for recruiting salespeople in which a fee is charged by the agency that is paid by the employer or the job seeker, as established by contract before the agency begins work for either party.

**problem-solving selling** An extension of need satisfaction selling that goes beyond identifying needs to developing alternative solutions for satisfying these needs.

**product knowledge** Knowledge about a product's benefits, applications, competitive strengths, and limitations.

**product specialization** Term used to describe a salesforce that assigns salespeople selling responsibility for specific products or product lines.

**productivity analysis** A form of analysis that is measured in terms of ratios between outputs and inputs.

**professional development criteria** A criteria for performance evaluation that assesses improvements in certain characteristics of salespeople that are related to successful performance in the sales job.

**professional societies** Professional organizations sales executives join to establish a network of colleagues who have common interests.

**profitability analysis** An analysis that combines sales and cost data to produce a measure of how profitable an organization is.

**profitability criteria** A criteria for performance evaluation that assesses the profitability of sales.

**progressive rate** A commission rate in which the percentage a salesperson is paid increases as he or she reaches prespecified selling targets.

**promises** An influence strategy in which sales managers can use reward power to achieve desired behaviors.

**R**

**ranking methods** Approaches in which salespeople are evaluated according to a relative performance on each performance criterion rather than evaluating them against a set of performance criteria.

**recognition** Job reward that can be informal such as "nice job" accolades, or formal such as group competition or individual accomplishments representing improved performance.

**recruitment** The second step in the salesperson recruitment and selection process; it is the procedure of locating a sufficient number of prospective job applicants.

**recruitment and selection strategy** A plan formulated after the recruitment and selection objective have been set that requires the sales manager to consider the scope and timing of recruitment and selection activities.

**referent power** Power in an interpersonal relationship that is based on the attractiveness of one party to another.

**regressive rate** A commission rate in which the percentage a salesperson is paid declines at some predetermined point.

**relationship strategy** A determination of the type of relationship to be developed with different account groups.

**relationships** An influence strategy containing two types of influence processes: one based on referent power that builds on personal friendships, or feelings of trust, admiration, or respect; the other based on legitimate power over another party by virtue of position in the organizational hierarchy.

**resellers** Organizations that purchase products to sell.

**results criteria** A criteria for performance evaluation that assesses the results achieved by salespeople.

**return on assets managed (ROAM)** A calculation that can extend the income statement analysis to include asset investment considerations.

**revenue producers** Something that brings in revenue or income to a firm or company.

**reward power** Power in an interpersonal relationship that stems from the ability of one party to reward the other party for a designated action.

**reward system management** The selection and use of organizational rewards to direct salespeople's behavior toward the attainment of organizational objectives.

**role definition** A salesperson's understanding of what tasks are to be performed, what the priorities of the tasks are, and how time should be allocated among the tasks.

**role distortion act** An unethical act that may put the individual at risk, presumably to benefit the company and the individual's own job objectives.

**role failure act** An unethical act that involves a failure to perform job responsibilities.

**role playing** A method of sales training in which one trainee plays the role of the salesperson and another trainee acts as the buyer; role playing is videotaped or performed live for a group of observers who then critique the performance.

**routinized response behavior** The process in which a buyer is merely reordering from the current supplier.

## S

**salary compression** A narrow range of salaries in a salesforce.

**salary plus incentive** Payment plans for salespeople that feature some combination of salary, commission, and bonus pay.

**sales analysis** An important element in evaluating sales organization effectiveness in which the organization studies its sales progress.

**sales channel strategy** The process of ensuring that accounts receive selling effort coverage in a effective and efficient manner.

**sales contests** Temporary programs that offer financial and/ or nonfinancial rewards for accomplishing specified, usually short-term, objectives.

**sales expenses** Expenses incurred while on the job that include travel, lodging, meals, entertainment of customers, telephone, and personal entertainment.

**sales organization audit** A comprehensive, systematic, diagnostic, and prescriptive tool used to assess the adequacy of a firm's sales management process and to provide direction for improved performance and prescription for needed changes.

**sales process** A series of interrelated steps beginning with locating qualified prospective customers. From there, the salesperson plans the sales presentation, makes an appointment to see the customer, completes the sale, and performs post-sale activities.

**sales productivity** The ratio of sales generated to selling effort used.

**sales professionalism** A customer-oriented approach that uses truthful, nonmanipulative tactics to satisfy the long-term needs of both the customer and the selling firm.

**sales quota** A reasonable sales objective for a territory, district, region, or zone.

**sales support personnel** A firm's personnel whose primary responsibility is dissemination of information and performance of other activities designed to stimulate sales.

**sales techniques** Fundamental procedures salespeople can follow to make sales.

**sales trainer** A mentor for salespeople in their organization who provides advice and information for improving sales performance.

**sales training media** Communications and computer technology used in the sales training process.

**sales training objectives** Objectives sales managers set during sales training that force the manager to define the reasonable expectations of sales training.

**salesforce audit** A systematic, diagnostic, prescriptive tool that can be employed on a periodic basis to identify and address sales department problems and to prevent or reduce the impact of future problems.

**salesforce composite method** A bottom-up forecasting approach that involves various procedures by which salespeople provide forecasts for their assigned accounts, typically on specially designed forms or electronically via computer.

**salesforce deployment** Important sales management decisions involved in allocating selling effort, determining salesforce size, and designing territories.

**salesforce socialization** The process by which salespeople acquire the knowledge, skills, and values essential to perform their jobs.

**salesforce survey** A survey in which sales managers monitor their salesforce in an attempt to isolate sales training needs.

**seek feedback** One way sales managers can improve anticipation of potential problems by interacting with customers, salespeople, and other important sources regularly.

**selection** The third step in the salesperson recruitment and selection process; it is the process of choosing which candidates will be offered the job.

**self-efficacy** The strong belief that success will occur in the job.

**self-management** An individual's effort to control certain aspects of his or her decision making and behavior.

**selling budget** Corporate resources earmarked for personal selling expenses for a designated period.

**selling strategy** The planned selling approach for each relationship strategy.

**sense of accomplishment** Job reward that emanates from the salesperson's psyche.

**service motivation** A strong desire to provide service to the customer. Service motivation comes from desiring the approval of others.

**sexual harassment** Lewd remarks, physical and visual actions, and sexual innuendos that make individuals feel uncomfortable.

**single factor models** An analytical approach to the allocation of selling effort in which the typical procedure is to classify all accounts on one factor and then to assign all accounts in the same category the same number of sales calls.

**span of control** The number of individuals who report to each sales manager.

**specialization** A concept in which certain individuals in an organ-ization concentrate on performing some of the required activities to the exclusion of other tasks.

**staff sales management** Sales management position that does not directly manage people, but is responsible for certain functions (e.g., recruiting and selecting, training) and are not directly involved in sales-generating activities.

**stimulus response selling** An approach to selling in which the key idea is that various stimuli can elicit predictable responses from customers. Salespeople furnish the stimuli from a repertoire of words and actions designed to produce the desired response.

**straight commission** A form of payment in which salespeople are paid by commission only.

**straight rebuy buying situation** A situation wherein an account has considerable experience in using the product and is satisfied with the current purchase arrangements.

**straight salary** A form of payment in which salespeople are paid one set salary.

**strategic business unit (SBU)** A single product or brand, a line of products, or a mix of related products that meets a common market need or a group of related needs, and the unit's management is responsible for all (or most) of the basic business functions.

**strategic orchestrator** A role the salesperson plays in consultative selling in which he or she arranges the use of the sales organization's resources in an effort to satisfy the customer.

**stress interview** An interview designed to put job candidates under extreme, unexpected, psychological duress for the purpose of seeing how they react.

**supervision** The day-to-day control of the salesforce under routine operating conditions.

**survey of buyer intentions method** A bottom-up forecasting approach that asks indi-vidual accounts about their purchasing plans for a future period and translates these responses into account forecasts.

# T

**target market** A specific market segment to be served.

**task-specific self-esteem** The feeling salespeople have about themselves relating to performing and accomplishing job-related duties; high levels have been linked to improved performance and job satisfaction.

**team selling** The use of multiple-person sales teams in dealing with multiple-person buying centers of their accounts.

**technical support sales-people** Technical specialist who may assist in design and specification processes, installation of equipment, training of the customer's employees, and follow-up service of a technical nature.

**telemarketing** A sales channel that consists of using the telephone as a means for customer contact to perform some of or all the activities required to develop and maintain account relationships; also called telesales.

**territory** A designated area that consists of whatever specific accounts are assigned to a specific salesperson.

**threats** An influence strategy in which a manager might specify a desired behavior and the punishment that will follow if the behavior is not achieved.

**time and territory management (TTM)** Salesperson's training to teach salespeople how to use time and efforts for maximum work efficiency.

**top-down forecasting approaches** A forecasting approach that consists of different methods for developing company forecasts at the business unit level that are then broken down by sales managers into zone, region, district, territory, and account forecasts.

**total quality management (TQM)** An approach that incorporates a strong customer orientation, a team-oriented corporate culture, and the use of statistical methods to analyze and improve all business processes including sales management.

**trade shows** A typically industry-sponsored event in which companies use a booth to display products and services to potential and existing customers.

**trait approach** A category of research trying to uncover what makes an effective leader that attempts to determine the personality traits of an effective leader.

**transformational leadership** A sales leadership model in which the leaders are charismatic, inspirational, and driven by a sense of mission.

## U

**users** Organizations that purchase products and services to produce other products and services.

## W

**workload approach** An approach used for calculating salesforce size that first determines how much selling effort is needed to cover the firm's market adequately and then calculates the number of salespeople required to provide this amount of selling effort.

## Module 1

[1] Henry Canaday, "How Did You Become a Sales Manager?" *Selling Power* (June 2004): 16–17.

[2] Canaday, "How Did You Become a Sales Manager?" 15–16.

[3] Lain Chroust Ehmann, "Secrets of the Sales Giants," *Selling Power* (March 2003): 53.

[4] Henry Canaday, "Are National Accounts Part of Your Company's Sales Strategy?" *Selling Power* (September 2004): 14–15.

[5] Bennett Voyles, "The Will to Survive," *Sales & Marketing Management* (May 2002): 46.

[6] Canaday, "Are National Accounts Part of Your Company's Sales Strategy?" 19.

[7] Karen E. Starr, "CEM Solution Keeps Sales Force in Tune," *Selling Power* (July/August 2001): 21.

[8] Erika Rasmusson, "Best at Customer Loyalty," *Sales & Marketing Management* (July 2000): 76.

[9] Andy Cohen, "Making Salespeople Smarter," *Sales & Marketing Management* (July 2000): 74.

[10] Thomas W. Leigh and Greg W. Marshall, "Research Priorities in Sales Strategy and Performance," *Journal of Personal Selling & Sales Management* (Spring 2001): 83–94; and Thomas N. Ingram, Raymond W. LaForge, and Thomas W. Leigh, "Selling in the New Millennium: A Joint Agenda," *Industrial Marketing Management* 31, no. 6 (October 2002): 559–567.

[11] Michele Marchetti, "Home-Style Selling," *Sales & Marketing Management* (August 1999): 16.

[12] Ken Liebeskind, "Guiding Light," *Selling Power* (March 1999): 15.

[13] Ken Liebeskind, "Service in Overdrive," *Selling Power* (March 1999): 18.

[14] From "Selling Teams: A Conceptual Framework and Research Agenda." Copyright © 1994 by Pi Sigma Epsilon. From *Journal of Personal Selling & Sales Management* 15, no. 1 (Summer 1994): 23. Reprinted with permission of M. E. Sharpe, Inc.

[15] Tricia Campbell, "Getting Top Executives to Sell," *Sales & Marketing Management* (October 1998): 32.

[16] Linda Strnad, "Top of Their Class," *Sales & Marketing Management* (February 2004): 54–56.

[17] Kate Fitzgerald, "An Automation Breakthrough," *Sales and Field Force Automation* (April 1999): 32.

[18] Henry Canaday, "Go Forth—With Care," *Selling Power* (Special Edition 2003): 8–11.

[19] Don Labriola, "Videoconferencing in Action," *Sales and Field Force Automation* (September 1999): 74.

[20] Melinda Ligos, "Point, Click, & Sell," *Sales & Marketing Management* (May 1999): 51.

[21] David W. Cravens, "The Changing Role of the Sales Force," *Marketing Management* (Fall 1995): 54; and Thomas N. Ingram, Raymond W. LaForge, and Thomas W. Leigh, "Selling in the New Millennium: A Joint Agenda," *Industrial Marketing Management* 31 (2002): 559–567.

[22] Adapted from William Keenan, Jr., "The Man in the Mirror," *Sales & Marketing Management* (May 1995): 95.

[23] Gabrielle Birkner, "Wish List," *Sales & Marketing Management* (September 2000): 65–70.

[24] "Top Reasons for Voluntary Turnover," *Sales & Marketing Management* (June 1999): 14.

[25] Tricia Campbell, "Death of a Salesman's Loyalty," *Sales & Marketing Management* (August 1999): 13.

[26] "Sales Execs Need to Lead as Well as Manage," *Selling Power* (May 1999): 103.

[27] "The Right Stuff," *Sales & Marketing Management* (January 1999): 15.

[28] Henry Canaday, "Where Does the Time Go?" *Selling Power* (October 2003): 19.

[29] Adapted from Michael H. Morris, Minet Schindehutte, and Raymond W. LaForge, "Entrepreneurial Marketing: A Construct for Integrating Emerging Entrepreneurship & Marketing Perspectives," *Journal of Marketing Theory and Practice* (Fall 2002): 119.

[30] Michael Weinreb, "Power of the People," *Sales & Marketing Management* (April 2003): 30–35.

[31] "SMM's Best of Sales & Marketing," *Sales & Marketing Management* (September 2001): 32.

[32] Robert J. Kelly, "Tomorrow's Labor Pool," *Sales & Marketing Management* (March 1994): 34.

[33] Chris Sandlund, "There's a New Face to America," *Success* (April 1999): 38.

[34]Ellen Neuborne, "Bridging the Culture Gap," *Sales & Marketing Management* (July 2003): 22.

[35]This section synthesizes information provided in Henry Canaday, "A New Vision of Change," *Selling Power* (July/August 2001): 61–68; Erin Strout, "Fast Forward," *Sales & Marketing Management* (December 2001): 37–43; Andy Cohen, "The Traits of Great Sales Forces," *Sales & Marketing Management* (October 2000): 67–72; Lisa Gschwandtner, "What Makes an Ideal Sales Manager," *Selling Power* (June 2001): 52–59; Bernard L. Rosenbaum, "What You Need for Success in the 21st Century," *Selling* (November 1999): 8–9.

[36]Cohen, "The Traits of Great Sales Forces," 72.

[37]Benson Smith and Tony Rutigliano, "Building a World-Class Salesforce," http://www.destinationcrm.com. Accessed 3/8/02.

[38]Cohen, "The Traits of Great Sales Forces," 70.

[39]Cohen, "The Traits of Great Sales Forces," 69.

[40]Maryann Hammers and Gerhard Gschwandtner, "Tap into the 7 Qualities of the Best Sales Managers," *Selling Power* (May 2004): 60–65.

## Module 2

[1]Marjorie J. Caballero, Roger A. Dickinson, and Dabney Townsend, "Aristotle and Personal Selling," *Journal of Personal Selling & Sales Management* 4 (May 1984): 13.

[2]William T. Kelley, "The Development of Early Thought in Marketing," in *Salesmanship: Selected Readings,* ed. John M. Rathmell (Homewood, IL: Irwin, 1969): 3.

[3]Thomas L. Powers, Warren S. Martin, Hugh Rushing, and Scott Daniels, "Selling before 1900: A Historical Perspective," *Journal of Personal Selling & Sales Management* 7 (November 1987): 5. For additional review of personal selling from 1600 to the present era, see Robert Desman and Terry E. Powell, "Personal Selling: Chicken or Egg," in *Proceedings,* 13th Annual Conference of the Academy of Marketing Science, ed. Jon M. Hawes (Orlando, FL: 1989).

[4]Michael Bell, *The Saleman in the Field* (Geneva: International Labour Office, 1980): 1.

[5]Stanley C. Hollander, "Anti-Salesman Ordinances of the Mid-19th Century," in *Salesmanship: Selected Readings,* ed. John M. Rathmell (Homewood, IL: Irwin, 1969): 9.

[6]*Ibid.,* 10.

[7]Jon M. Hawes, "Leaders in Selling and Sales Management," *Journal of Personal Selling & Sales Management* 5 (November 1985): 60.

[8]Charles W. Hoyt, *Scientific Sales Management* (New Haven, CT: George W. Woolson and Co., 1913): 3.

[9]*Ibid.,* 4.

[10]Edward C. Bursk, "Low-Pressure Selling," *Harvard Business Review* 25 (Winter 1947): 227.

[11]Jon M. Hawes, Anne K. Rich, and Scott Widmier, "Assessing the Development of the Sales Profession," *Journal of Personal Selling & Sales Management* 24 (Winter 2004): 27–38.

[12]Synthesized from Thomas N. Ingram, "Relationship Selling: Moving from Rhetoric to Reality," *Mid-American Journal of Business* 11 (Spring 1996): 5; David W. Cravens, Emin Babakus, Ken Grant, Thomas N. Ingram, and Raymond W. LaForge, "Removing Sales Force Performance Hurdles," *Journal of Business and Industrial Marketing* 9, no. 3 (1994): 19; Eli Jones, Steven P. Brown, Andris A. Zoltners, and Barton A. Weitz, "The Changing Environment of Selling and Sales Management," *Journal of Personal Selling & Sales Management* (forthcoming 2005).

[13]"Best Buy Accelerates Customer Centricity Transformation," press release dated May 3, 2004, from www.bestbuy.com.

[14]Neil Rackham and John DeVincentis, *Rethinking the Sales Force* (New York: McGraw-Hill, 1999): 1–28.

[15]Robert F. Gwinner, "Base Theory in the Formulation of Sales Strategy," *MSU Business Topics* (Autumn 1968): 37.

[16]Ramon A. Avila, Thomas N. Ingram, Raymond W. LaForge, and Michael R. Williams, *The Professional Selling Skills Workbook* (Fort Worth, TX: The Dryden Press, 1996): 20.

[17]Michael Bruce, "How to Get Better Sales Talent Through State-of-the-Art Advertising," *Personal Selling Power* 13 (March 1993): 46–47.

[18]Gina Rollins, "This Thing Will Sell Itself!" *Selling Power* (June 2004): 69–71.

[19]This section on consultative selling is based on Kevin J. Corcoran, Laura K. Petersen, Daniel B. Baitch, and Mark F. Barrett, *High Performance Sales Organizations* (Chicago: Irwin, 1995): 44.

[20]Steve Atlas, "Deliver Quality at Every Step," *Selling Power* (June 2004): 40.

[21]*Ibid.,* 42.

[22]Jon M. Hawes, Kenneth E. Mast, and John E. Swan, "Trust Earning Perceptions of Sellers and Buyers," *Journal of Personal Selling & Sales Management* 9 (Spring 1989): 1.

[23]Interview by the authors with Blake Conrad, sales representative with Centurion Specialty Care.

## Module 2 Appendix

[1]*Occupational Outlook Handbook, 2004–05 ed.* (Washington, D.C.: U.S. Department of Labor, 2004); and U.S. Department of Labor, Bureau of Labor Statistics, "Occupational Employment Projections to 2012," *Monthly Labor Review* (February 2004): Table 21.

[2]Michele Marchetti, "A Sales Pro Tries to Energize HP," *Sales & Marketing Management* (September 1999): 15.

[3]Thomas N. Ingram and Charles H. Schwepker Jr., "Perceptions of Salespeople: Implications for Sales Managers and Sales Trainers," *Journal of Marketing Management* 2 (Fall/Winter 1992–93): 1.

[4]Thomas N. Ingram, "Relationship Selling: Moving from Rhetoric to Reality," *Mid-American Journal of Business* 11 (Spring 1996): 5.

[5]"Here's to the Winners," *Sales & Marketing Management* (July 1999): 66.

[6]Michael J. Swenson, William R. Swinyard, Frederick W. Langrehr, and Scott M. Smith, "The Appeal of Personal Selling as a Career: A Decade Later," *Journal of Personal Selling & Sales Management* 13 (Winter 1993): 51.

[7]*Occupational Outlook Handbook, 2004–05 ed.*

[8]Emin Babakus, David W. Cravens, Ken Grant, Thomas N. Ingram, and Raymond W. LaForge, "Removing Salesforce Performance Hurdles," *Journal of Business and Industrial Marketing* 9, no. 3 (1994): 19.

[9]See Herbert M. Greenberg and Jeanne Greenberg, *What It Takes to Succeed in Sales* (Homewood, IL: Dow-Jones Irwin, 1990).

[10]James M. Comer and Alan J. Dubinsky, *Managing the Successful Sales Force* (Lexington, MA: D.C. Heath and Co., 1985): 5; Steven P. Brown, Thomas W. Leigh, and J. Martin Haygood, "Salesperson Performance and Job Attitudes," in *The Marketing Manager's Handbook*, 3rd ed., eds. Sidney J. Levy, George R. Frerichs, and Howard L. Gordon (Chicago: The Dartnell Corporation, 1994): 107.

[11]Babakus et al., "Removing Salesforce Performance Hurdles," 19; Greg W. Marshall, Daniel J. Goebel, and William C. Moncrief, "Hiring for Success at the Buyer-Seller Interface," *Journal of Business Research* 56 (April 2003): 247–255.

[12]Rosann L. Spiro and Barton A. Weitz, "Adaptive Selling: Conceptualization, Measurement, and Nomological Validity," *Journal of Marketing Research* 27 (February 1990): 61.

[13]Marshall et al., "Hiring for Success," 251.

[14]Kevin J. Corcoran, Laura K. Petersen, Daniel B. Baitch, and Mark F. Barrett, *High Performance Sales Organizations* (Chicago: Irwin Professional Publishing, 1995): 77.

[15]Marshall et al., "Hiring for Success," 251.

[16]Arun Sharma and Rajnandini Pillai, "Customers' Decision-Making Styles and Their Preference for Sales Strategies: Conceptual Examination and an Empirical Study," *Journal of Personal Selling & Sales Management* 16 (Winter 1996): 21.

[17]Victoria D. Bush, Greg Rose, Faye Gilbert, and Thomas N. Ingram, "Managing Culturally Diverse Buyer–Seller Relationships: The Role of Intercultural Disposition and Adaptive Selling Behavior in Developing Intercultural Communication Competence," *Journal of the Academy of Marketing Science* 29, no. 4 (Fall 2001): 391–404.

[18]"And the Surveys Say," *Personal Selling Power* (October 1995): 55.

## Module 3

[1]David W. Cravens, *Strategic Marketing* (Homewood, IL: Irwin, 1994): 30.

[2]Betsy Cummings, "Getting Reps to Live Your Mission," *Sales & Marketing Management* (October 2001): 15.

[3]Cravens, *Strategic Marketing*, 46.

[4]Matt Murray, "GE Says It Will Combine Appliances, Lighting Units," *The Wall Street Journal Online* (August 30, 2002): 1–2.

[5]Robert Schoenberger, "GE Finds Merger Pays Off in Profits," *The Courier-Journal* (September 13, 2003): F1–F2.

[6]Adapted from William Strahle and Rosann L. Spiro, "Linking Market Share Strategies to Salesforce Objectives, Activities, and Compensation Policies," *Journal of Personal Selling & Sales Management* (August 1986): 14–15. Used with permission.

[7]Michael E. Porter, *Competitive Strategy* (New York: The Free Press, 1980): 34.

[8]Adapted from William L. Cron and Michael Levy, "Sales Management Performance Evaluation: A Residual Income Perspective," *Journal of Personal Selling & Sales Management* (August 1987): 58. Used with permission.

[9]Madhubalan Viswanathan and Eric M. Olson, "The Implementation of Business Strategies: Implications for the Sales Function," *Journal of Personal Selling & Sales Management* (Winter 1992): 45.

[10]Bob Thompson, "What Is CRM?" *The Customer Relationship Management Primer*, CRMguru.com (January 2001): 1.

[11]Alex R. Zablah, Danny N. Bellenger, and Wesley J. Johnston, "An Evaluation of Divergent Perspectives on Customer Relationship Management: Towards a Common Understanding of an Emerging Phenomenon," *Industrial Marketing Management* 33 (2004): 475–489.

[12]Darrell K. Rigby, Frederick F. Reichheld, and Phil Schefter, "Avoid the Four Perils of CRM," *Harvard Business Review* (February 2002): 101–110.

[13]David W. Cravens, Gerald E. Hills, and Robert B. Woodruff, *Marketing Management* (Homewood, IL: Irwin, 1987): 546. Reprinted by permission of the McGraw-Hill Companies.

[14]Michael V. Copeland, "Best Buy's Selling Machine," *Business 2.0* (July 2004): 93–102.

[15]Cyndee Miller, "Marketing Industry Report: Who's Spending What on Biz-to-Biz Marketing," *Marketing News* (January 1, 1996): 1, 7; Cyndee Miller, "Marketing Industry Report: Consumer Marketers Spend Most of Their Money on Communications," *Marketing News* (March 11, 1996): 1, 5.

[16]Adapted from Michael D. Hutt and Thomas W. Speh, *Business Marketing Management* (Fort Worth, TX: The Dryden Press, 1995): 18–21.

[17]Michael D. Hutt and Thomas W. Speh, *Business Marketing Management* (Fort Worth, TX: The Dryden Press, 1995): 71.

[18]David W. Cravens, Gerald E. Hills, and Robert B. Woodruff, *Marketing Management,* 161. Reprinted by permission of The McGraw-Hill Companies.

[19]Ernest Waaser, Marshall Dahneke, Michael Pekkarinen, and Michael Weissel, "How You Slice It: Smarter Segmentation for Your Sales Force," *Harvard Business Review* (March 2004): 105–111.

[20]Malcolm Campbell, "The New Sales Force," *Selling Power* (July/August 1999): 51.

[21]"e-market stats," *Sales & Marketing Management* (May 2002): 19.

[22]"Point of Contact," *Sales & Marketing Management* (March 2001): 11.

[23]Reported in Chad Kaydo, "You've Got Sales," *Sales & Marketing Management* (October 1999): 30.

[24]*Ibid.,* 34.

[25]Andy Cohen, "Herman Miller," *Sales & Marketing Management* (July 1999): 60.

[26]Henry Canaday, "Independent Rep's Comp," *Selling Power* (January/February 2001): 79.

[27]Adapted from Harold J. Novick, "The Case for Reps vs. Direct Selling: Can Reps Do It Better?" *Industrial Marketing* (March 1982): 90–98; and "The Use of Sales Reps," *Small Business Report* (December 1986): 72–78.

[28]Tricia Campbell, "Who Needs a Sales Force Anyway?" *Sales & Marketing Management* (February 1999): 13.

[29]Adapted from Michael D. Hutt, Wesley J. Johnston, and John R. Rouchelto, "Selling Centers and Buying Centers: Formulating Strategic Exchange Patterns," *Journal of Personal Selling & Sales Management* (May 1985): 34. Used with permission.

[30]"Team Selling by Industry," *Selling* (January/February 1994): 46.

[31]Thomas N. Ingram, "Relationship Selling: Moving from Rhetoric to Reality," *Mid-American Journal of Business* 11, no. 1 (Spring 1996): 5–13.

[32]Eilene Zimmerman, "Making the Dysfunctional Functional," *Sales & Marketing Management* (September 2004), 30–31.

[33]John F. Yarbrough, "Salvaging a Lousy Year," *Sales & Marketing Management* (July 1996): 72.

[34]Danielle Harris, "The Shows Will Go On," *Sales & Marketing Management* (May 2000): 85.

[35]Deborah L. Vence, "Trade Show Magic," *Marketing News* (November 11, 2002): 4.

## Module 4

[1]Reported in "Structuring the Sales Organization," in *Sales Manager's Handbook,* ed. John P. Steinbrink (Chicago: The Dartnell Corporation, 1989): 90.

[2]See Robert W. Ruekert, Orville C. Walker, Jr., and Kenneth J. Roering, "The Organization of Marketing Activities: A Contingency Theory of Structure and Performance," *Journal of Marketing* (Winter 1985): 13, for a more complete presentation of structural characteristics and relationships. The discussion in this section borrows heavily from this article.

[3]*Ibid.,* 20–21.

[4]From David W. Cravens, *Strategic Marketing,* 7th ed. (New York: McGraw-Hill): 541. Reprinted by permission of The McGraw-Hill Companies.

[5]Christian Homburg, John P. Workman, Jr., and Ove Jensen, "Fundamental Changes in Marketing Organization: The Movement Toward a Customer-Focused Organizational Structure," *Journal of the Academy of Marketing Science* (Fall 2000): 459–478.

[6]Andy Cohen, "Managing," *Sales & Marketing Management* (April 1996): 77.

[7]Charles T. Clark, "Is Your Company Ready for Global Marketing?" *Sales & Marketing Management* (September 1994): 42.

[8]Adapted from Benson P. Shapiro and Rowland T. Moriarity, *National Account Management: Emerging Insights* (Cambridge, MA: Marketing Science Institute, March 1982): 6.

[9]Benson P. Shapiro and Rowland T. Moriarity, *National Account Management: Emerging Insights* (Cambridge, MA: Marketing Science Institute, 1982): 19.

[10]Adapted from Benson P. Shapiro and Rowland T. Moriarity, *Organizing the National Account Force* (Cambridge, MA: Marketing Science Institute, April 1984): 1–37.

[11]John P. Workman, Jr., Christian Homburg, and Ove Jensen, "Intraorganizational Determinants of Key Account Management Effectiveness," *Journal of the Academy of Marketing Science* (Winter 2003): 3–21.

[12]From David W. Cravens and Raymond W. LaForge, "Salesforce Deployment," in *Advances in Business Marketing,* ed. Arch G. Woodside (1990): 76.

[13]Raymond W. LaForge, David W. Cravens, and Clifford E. Young, "Improving Salesforce Productivity," *Business Horizons* (September–October 1985): 54. Copyright 1985 by the Foundation for the School of Business at Indiana University. Reprinted by permission.

[14]See Raymond W. LaForge, David W. Cravens, and Clifford E. Young, "Using Contingency Analysis to Select Effort Allocation Methods," *Journal of Personal Selling & Sales Management* (August 1986): 23, for a summary of productivity improvements from decision model applications.

[15]Andy Cohen, "Profits Down? Time to Add to Your Headcount," *Sales & Marketing Management* (August 2002): 15.

[16]Scott Hensley, "As Drug-Sales Teams Multiply, Doctors Start to Tune Them Out," *The Wall Street Journal Online* (June 12, 2003): 1–4.

[17]Betsy Wiesendanger, "Temp Reps," *Selling Power* (May 2004): 68–71.

[18]LaForge, Cravens, and Young, "Improving Salesforce Productivity," 57.

[19]Ken Grant, David W. Cravens, George S. Low, and William C. Moncrief, "The Role of Satisfaction with Territory Design on the Motivation, Attitudes, and Work Outcomes of Salespeople," *Journal of the Academy of Marketing Science* (Spring 2001): 165–178.

## Module 4 Appendix

[1]For other classification schemes and more detailed discussion of individual forecasting methods, see Harry R. White, *Sales Forecasting: Timesaving and Profit-Making Strategies That Work* (Glenview, IL: Scott, Foresman and Company, 1984): 6; David M. Georgoff and Robert G. Murdick, "Manager's Guide to Forecasting," *Harvard Business Review* (January–February 1986): 113; J. Scott Armstrong, Roderick J. Brodie, and Shelby McIntyre, "Forecasting Methods for Marketing: Review of Empirical Research," *International Journal of Forecasting* 3 (1987): 355.

[2]Nada R. Sanders and Karl B. Manrodt, "Forecasting Practices in U.S. Corporations: Survey Results," *Interfaces* 24 (March–April 1994): 92.

[3]See John T. Mentzer, "Forecasting with Adaptive Extended Exponential Smoothing," *Journal of the Academy of Marketing Science* (Fall 1986): 62, for discussion and examples of different exponential smoothing methods.

[4]See "Survey of Buying Power," *Sales & Marketing Management* (August 13, 1990), for a discussion of the Buying Power Index and for the calculated indices throughout the United States.

[5]Conversation with director of marketing at Sherwood Medical in St. Louis, MO.

[6]William Keenan, Jr., "Numbers Racket," *Sales & Marketing Management* (May 1995): 64.

[7]Joel Bryant and Kim Jensen, "Forecasting Inkjet Printers at Hewlett-Packard Company," *Journal of Business Forecasting* (Summer 1994): 27.

[8]Mark Barash, "Eliciting Accurate Sales Forecasts from Market Experts," *Journal of Business Forecasting* (Fall 1994): 24.

[9]Kenneth B. Kahn and John T. Mentzer, "The Impact of Team-based Forecasting," *Journal of Business Forecasting* (Summer 1994): 18.

[10]Norton Paley, "Welcome to the Fast Lane," *Sales & Marketing Management* (August 1994): 65.

[11]Keenan, "Numbers Racket."

[12]"Keeping Sales in the Loop," *Sales & Marketing Management* (June 1995): 34.

[13]These and other recommendations are available in Robin T. Peterson, "Sales Force Composite Forecasting—An Exploratory Analysis," *Journal of Business Forecasting* (Spring 1989): 23; James E. Cox, Jr., "Approaches for Improving Salespersons' Forecasts," *Industrial Marketing Management* 18 (1989): 307.

[14]Essam Mahmoud, Gillian Rice, and Naresh Malhotra, "Emerging Issues in Sales Forecasting and Decision Support Systems," *Journal of the Academy of Marketing Science* (Fall 1988): 53.

[15]See Benito E. Flores and Edna M. White, "A Framework for the Combination of Forecasts," *Journal of the Academy of Marketing Science* (Fall 1988): 95, for an examination of different combination approaches.

[16]Sanders and Manrodt, "Forecasting Practices in U.S. Corporations."

## Module 5

[1]Michael Munson and W. Austin Spivey, "Salesforce Selection That Meets Federal Regulation and Management Needs," *Industrial Marketing Management* 9 (February 1980): 12.

[2]http://www.census.gov. Accessed 5/14/04.

[3]Rene Darmon, "Where Do the Best Sales Force Profit Producers Come From?" *Journal of Personal Selling & Sales Management* 3 (Summer 1993): 17.

[4]Julia Lawlor, "Highly Classified," *Sales & Marketing Management* (March 1995): 75; Chad Kaydo, "Overturning Turnover," *Sales & Marketing Management* 149 (November 1997): 50.

[5]Presentation by Jim Sodomka, Sabrina Rogers, and Brad Parrack, managers, Federated Insurance, at Central Missouri State University, February 26, 2004.

[6]Herbert Greenberg, Harold Weinstein, and Patrick Sweeney, *How to Hire and Develop Your Next Top Performer: The Five Qualities That Make Salespeople Great* (New York: McGraw-Hill Company, 2001).

[7]Georgia Chao, Anne O'Leary-Kelly, Samantha Wolf, Howard Klein, and Philip Gardner, "Organizational Socialization: Its Content and Consequences," *Journal of Applied Psychology* 79 (October 1994): 730.

[8]Position description taken from http://xerox.wfrecruiter.com/jobs_details1.asp?Job_id=24062&Page_id=5619&Published=1. Accessed 5/17/04.

[9]John S. Hill and Meg Birdseye, "Salesperson Selection in Multinational Corporations: A Study," *Journal of Personal Selling & Sales Management* 9 (Summer 1989): 39.

[10]Erika Rasmusson, "Can Your Reps Sell Overseas? How to Make Sure They Have What It Takes," *Sales & Marketing Management* 150 (February 1998): 110.

[11]Xerox Corporation, https://xerox.wfrecruiter.com/jobs_details1.asp?Job_id=24062&Page_Id=5619&Published=1. Accessed May 2004.

[12]From Michael Bruce "How to Get Better Sales Talent Through State-of-the-Art Advertising" in *Personal Selling Power* 13 (March 1993): 46–47. Reprinted with permission of Personal Selling Power Inc.

[13]Adapted from *Industrial Marketing Management* (March 1995), Vol. 24, 135–144, "Guidelines for Managing an International Sales Force" by Earl Honeycutt and John Ford. Copyright © 1995, with permission from Elsevier.

[14]Lawlor, "Highly Classified."

[15]James A. Breaugh, Leslie A. Greising, James W. Taggart, and Helen Chen, "The Relationship of Recruiting Sources and Pre-Hire Outcomes: Examination of Yield Rations and Application Quality," *Journal of Applied Social Psychology* 33 (November 2003): 2267–2287.

[16]Dave Porter, "Creating a Recruiting Culture," *National Underwriter Life & Health* (March 22, 2004): 17, 39.

[17]Sodomka, Rogers, and Parrack, 2004.

[18]Andy Bargerstock and Hank Engel, "Six Ways to Boost Employee Referral Programs," *HRM Magazine* 39 (December 1994): 72; Kathryn Tyler, "Employees Can Help Recruit New Talent," *HR Magazine* 41 (September 1996): 57.

[19]Darmon, "Where Do the Best Sales Force Profit Producers Come From?"

[20]Bruce, "How to Get Better Sales Talent Through State-of-the-Art Advertising," 46–47; "What's Wrong with Your Recruitment Ads?" *Sales & Marketing Management* (November 1994): 50; and William H. Krause, "Advertising for Agents?" *Agency Sales Magazine* 28 (May 1998): 4–7.

[21]Martha Frase-Blunt, "Make a Good First Impression," *HR Magazine* 49 (April 2004): 80–84.

[22]Watson Wyatt, "Staffing Expense per Hire," *The Controller's Report* (November 2003): 8.

[23]Joe Rudich, "Job Hunting on the Web," *Link-Up* 17 (March/April 2000): 21.

[24]Gillian Flynn, "E-Recruiting Ushers in Legal Dangers," *Workforce* 81 (April 2002): 70–72.

[25]Judith Marshall, "Don't Rely Exclusively on Internet Recruiting," *HR Magazine* 48 (November 2003): 24.

[26]Max Messmer, "Temporary Employees Are Permanent Part of New Europe," *Personnel Journal* 73 (January 1994): 100.

[27]Barb Cole-Gomolski and Tim Ouellette, "Hiring Managers Turn to Video," *Computerworld* 32 (April 1998): 29.

[28]Jessica Feinberg and Erin Strout, "Cheap Sales Help," *Sales & Marketing Management* 155 (March 2003): 50.

[29]Michele Marchetti, "Sales Reps to Go," *Sales & Marketing Management* 151 (January 1999): 14.

[30]James Borck, "Recruiting Systems Control Resume Chaos," *Infoworld* 22 (July 24, 2000): 47–48.

[31]Flynn, "E-Recruiting Ushers in Legal Dangers."

[32]Borck, "Recruiting Systems Control Resume Chaos."

[33]Flynn, "E-Recruiting Ushers in Legal Dangers."

[34]Erin Strout, "Recruiting and Hiring for Less," *Sales & Marketing Management* 154 (May 2002): 61.

[35]http://gallup.com/content/?CI=62. Accessed 5/25/04.

[36]Linda Thornburg, "Computer-Assisted Interviewing Shortens Hiring Cycle," *HR Magazine* 43 (February 1998): 73.

[37]Sodomka, Rogers, and Parrack, 2004.

[38]"Interviewing the Candidate," Sales Consultants International, Inc., Cleveland, Ohio.

[39]Paul Taylor, "Providing Structure to Interviews and Reference Checks," *Workforce* (1999): 7–10.

[40]Taken (with permission) from William C. Byham, "Can You Interview for Integrity?" *Across the Board Magazine* (March/April 2004).

[41]Robert Gatewood and Hubert Feild, *Human Resource Selection* (Fort Worth, TX: The Dryden Press, 1994).

[42]Wesley J. Johnson and Martha C. Cooper, "Industrial Sales Force Selection: Current Knowledge and Needed Research," *Journal of Personal Selling & Sales Management* 1 (Spring–Summer 1981): 49.

[43]Greg W. Marshall, Miriam B. Stamps, and Jesse N. Moore, "Preinterview Biases: The Impact of Race, Physical Attractiveness, and Sales Job Type on Preinterview Impressions of Sales Job Applicants," *Journal of Personal Selling & Sales Management* 18 (Fall 1998): 21.

[44]Ron Panko, "Getting Testy about Sales Screening Tests," *Best's Review—Life-Health Insurance Edition* 98 (December 1997): 67; Michael Santo, "How to Recruit and Retain Top-Level Talent," *Agency Sales Magazine* 28 (May 1998): 39.

[45]Seymour Adler, "Personality Tests for Salesforce Selection: Worth a Fresh Look," *Review of Business* 16 (Summer/Fall 1994): 27.

[46]http://www.doubleeaglecomm.com/salesprofile.htm. Accessed 5/25/04.

[47]Alison Overholt, "A Nice Personality," *Fast Company* (June 2004): 20.

[48]Based on Samual J. Maurice, "Stalking the High-Scoring Salesperson," *Sales & Marketing Management* (October 7, 1985): 63; George B. Salsbury, "Properly Recruit Salespeople to Reduce Training Cost," *Industrial Marketing Management* 11 (April 1982): 143; Richard Kern, "IQ Tests for Salesmen Make a Comeback," *Sales & Marketing Management* (April 1988): 42.

[49]Northwestern Mutual Financial Network, http://www.nmfn.com/tn/careers-fr0-fr. Accessed 5/24/04.

[50]Sodomka, Rogers, and Parrack, 2004.

[51]http://www.wonderlic.com/products/product.asp? prod_id_ = 10. Accessed 5/25/04.

[52]http://www.chally.com/assessment/testimonial.html. Accessed 5/25/04.

[53]Anne Fisher, "How Can We Be Sure We're Not Hiring a Bunch of Shady Liars?" *Fortune* 147 (May 26, 2003): 180–181.

[54]Weld Royal, "From Socialist to Sales Rep," *Sales & Marketing Management* (August 1994): 63.

[55]E. James Randall, Ernest F. Cooke, and Lois Smith, "A Successful Application of the Assessment Center Concept to the Salesperson Selection Process," *Journal of Personal Selling & Sales Management* 5 (May 1985): 53.

[56]Sodomka, Rogers, and Parrack, 2004.

[57]"Background/Reference Checks May Provide Defense to Discrimination Suit," *Fair Employment Practices Guidelines* (December 1, 2003): 4–5.

[58]Anne Fisher, "How Can We Be Sure We're Not Hiring a Bunch of Shady Liars?" *Fortune* 147 (May 26, 2003): 180–181.

[59]*How to Select a Sales Force That Sells*, 3d ed. (Dayton, OH: The HR Chally Group, 1998): 14. Reprinted with kind permission from H. R. Chally Group.

[60]Gatewood and Feild, *Human Resource Selection*.

[61]*Ibid.*

[62]W. E. Patton III and Ronald King, "The Use of Human Judgement Models in Sales Force Selection Decisions," *Journal of Personal Selling & Sales Management* 12 (Spring 1992): 1.

[63]Michele Marchetti, "The New Gold Rush," *Sales & Marketing Management* 150 (September 1998): 42.

[64]Alan J. Dubinsky, Roy D. Howell, Thomas N. Ingram, and Danny N. Bellenger, "Salesforce Socialization." Reprinted from *Journal of Marketing* 50 (October 1986): 203, published by the American Marketing Association; and Mike Delaney, "Background Checks: Five Steps Toward Compliance," *HR Focus* 74 (December 1997): S6.

[65]C. David Shepherd and James Heartfield, "Discrimination Issues in the Selection of Salespeople: A Review and Managerial Suggestions," *Journal of Personal Selling & Sales Management* 11 (Fall 1991): 67.

[66]Munson and Spivey, "Salesforce Selection," 15.

[67]For more discussion of what information should not be sought in a job interview, see John P. Steinbrink, ed., *The Dartnell Sales Manager's Handbook*, 14th ed. (Chicago: The Dartnell Press, 1989): 820; Shepherd and Heartfield, "Discrimination Issues."

[68]Jon M. Hawes, "How to Improve Your College Recruiting Program," *Journal of Personal Selling & Sales Management* 9 (Summer 1989): 51.

[69]Adapted from "What Would You Do?" *Sales & Marketing Management* 154 (March 2002): 64.

## Module 6

[1]Alan J. Dubinsky, Roy D. Howell, Thomas N. Ingram, and Danny N. Bellenger, "Salesforce Socialization," *Journal of Marketing* 50 (October 1986): 195.

[2]Mark W. Johnston, A. Parasuraman, Charles M. Futrell, and William C. Black, "A Longitudinal Assessment of the Impact of Selected Organizational Influences on Salespeople's Organizational Commitment During Early Employment," *Journal of Marketing Research* 27 (August 1990): 341.

[3]Jeffrey K. Sager, "How to Retain Salespeople," *Industrial Marketing Management* 19 (May 1990): 155.

[4]Judy A. Siguaw, Gene Brown, and Robert E. Widing II, "The Influence of the Market Orientation of the Firm on Sales Force Behavior and Attitudes," *Journal of Marketing Research* 31 (February 1994): 106.

[5]"Your Marketing Opportunity: Anticipations, Expectations, and Realizations," brochure by Federated Mutual Insurance Co. (2000).

[6]Gilbert A. Churchill, Jr., Neil M. Ford, Steven W. Hartley, and Orville C. Walker, Jr., "The Determinants of Salesperson Performance: A Meta-Analysis," *Journal of Marketing Research* 22 (May 1985): 117.

[7]Christine Galea and Carl Wiens, "2002 Sales Training Survey," *Sales & Marketing Management* 154 (July 2002): 34–37.

[8]Brandon Hall, "Should Corporate Shareholders Care About Training?" *Training* 41 (May 2004): 16.

[9]Julia Chang, "More Bang for Your Buck," *Sales & Marketing Management* 155 (June 2003): 26.

[10]"Training Managers' Forum," *IOMA's Report on Managing Training & Development* (October 2003): 15.

[11]Christen Heide, *Dartnell's 30th Sales Force Compensation Survey* (Chicago: The Dartnell Corporation, 1999).

[12]Galea and Wiens, "2002 Sales Training Survey"; William Powell, "Train Today, Sell Tomorrow," *T & D* 55 (September 2001): 40–48.

[13]Heide, *Dartnell's 30th Sales Force Compensation Survey.*

[14]Seonaid Farrell and A. Ralph Hakstain, "Improving Salesforce Performance: A Meta-Analytic Investigation of the Effectiveness and Utility of Personnel Selection Procedures and Training Interventions," *Psychology & Marketing* 18 (March 2001): 281–316.

[15]From Galea and Wiens, "2002 Sales Training Survey." Copyright © VNU Business Media Inc. Reprinted by permission.

[16]For an extensive review of how the sales manager might be involved in the details of sales training, see John P. Steinbrink, ed., *The Dartnell Sales Manager's Handbook,* 14th ed. (Chicago: The Dartnell Corporation, 1989): 850.

[17]Galea and Wiens, "2002 Sales Training Survey."

[18]See Alan J. Dubinsky and Richard W. Hansen, "The Sales Force Management Audit," *California Management Review* 24 (Winter 1981): 86.

[19]Joseph O. Rentz, C. David Shepherd, Armen Tashchain, Pratibha A. Dabholkar, and Robert T. Ladd, "A Measure of Selling Skill: Scale Development and Validation," *Journal of Personal Selling & Sales Management* 22 (Winter 2002): 13–21.

[20]"Gallup Study of Sales Force Effectiveness Kicks Up Old Debate About Need for Sales Training," *Lifelong Learning Marketing Report* 8 (September 5, 2003): 1, 3–4.

[21]Erin Strout, Geoffrey Brewer, and Chad Kaydo, "Are Your Salespeople Tech Savvy?" *Sales & Marketing Management* 152 (July 2000): 109.

[22]Betsy Cummings, "Wake Up, Salespeople!" *Sales & Marketing Management* 154 (June 2002): 11.

[23]http://questionpro.com. Accessed 6/3/04.

[24]Chad Kaydo, "Training: A Complete Regimen for Making Your Salespeople Smarter," *Sales & Marketing Management* 150 (December 1998): 33.

[25]See "Study Reveals Needs of Business Marketers," *Marketing News* (March 13, 1989): 6; *Success Factors in Selling* (Stamford, CT: Learning International, 1989); "How Do Salespeople Rate Themselves?" *Sales & Marketing Management* (March 1989): 17; Heide, *Dartnell's 30th Sales Force Compensation Survey.*

[26]Galea and Wiens, "2002 Sales Training Survey."

[27]C. David Shepherd, Stephen B. Castleberry, and Rick E. Ridnour, "Linking Effective Listening with Salesperson Performance: An Exploratory Investigation," *Journal of Business & Industrial Marketing* 12 (Fall 1997): 315.

[28]Jaclyn Fierman, "The Death and Rebirth of the Salesman," *Fortune* (July 25, 1994): 80; David Stamps, "Training for a New Sales Game," *Training* 34 (July 1997): 46.

[29]Sue Melone and Gary Summy, "Sales Training 101: Best Practices for Keeping Pace with Rapid Change in Selling," presentation at the National Conference in Sales Management, April 5, 2002.

[30]Bernard L. Rosenbaum, "Do You Have the Skills for 21st Century Selling? Rate Yourself with This Exercise," *American Salesman* 45 (July 2000): 24–30.

[31]Rosenbaum, "Do You Have the Skills for 21st Century Selling?" Reprinted by kind permission of the author.

[32]Marc Hequet, "Product Knowledge: Knowing What They're Selling May Be the Key to How Well They Sell It," *Training* (February 1988): 18.

[33]Alan J. Dubinsky and Thomas N. Ingram, "A Classification of Industrial Buyers: Implications for Sales Training," *Journal of Personal Selling & Sales Management* 2 (Fall–Winter 1981–1982): 49.

[34]Julia Chang, "Multicultural Selling," *Sales & Marketing Management* 155 (October 2003): 26.

[35]Victoria Davies Bush and Thomas N. Ingram, "Adapting to Diverse Customers: A Training Matrix for International Marketers," *Industrial Marketing Management* 25 (September 1996): 373; Strout, Brewer, and Kaydo, "Are Your Salespeople Tech Savvy?"

[36]From "Global Do's and Don'ts" by Andy Cohen from *Sales & Marketing Management* 148 (June 1996): 72. Reprinted by permission of Reprint Management Services.

[37]Harish Sujan, Barton A. Weitz, and Mita Sujan, "Increasing Sales Productivity by Getting Salespeople to Work Smarter," *Journal of Personal Selling & Sales Management* 8 (August 1988): 9.

[38]Thayer C. Taylor, "Take Your Time," *Sales & Marketing Management* 146 (July 1994): 45.

[39]Ned C. Hill and Michael J. Swenson, "The Impact of Electronic Data Interchange on the Sales Function," *Journal of Personal Selling & Sales Management* 14 (Summer 1994): 80.

[40]Scott A. Inks and Amy J. Morgan, "Technology and the Sales Force: Increasing Acceptance of Sales Force Automation," *Industrial Marketing Management* 30 (June 2001): 463–472; Robert C. Erffmeyer and Dale A. Johnson, "An Exploratory Study of Sales Force Automation Practices: Expectations and Realities," *Journal of Personal Selling & Sales Management* 21 (Spring 2001): 167–175.

[41]Colette A. Frayne and J. Michael Geringer, "Self-Management Training for Improving Job Performance: A Field Experiment Involving Salespeople," *Journal of Applied Psychology* 85 (June 2000): 361–372.

[42]Jared F. Harrison, ed., *The Sales Manager as a Trainer* (Orlando, FL: National Society of Sales Training Executives, 1983): 7.

[43]Craig Lindsay, "Successful Distributor Reps," *Industrial Distribution* 90 (March 2001): S8–S9.

[44]Julia Chang, "What Worked," *Sales & Marketing Management* 155 (July 2003): 29

[45]http://www.wilsonlearning.com. Accessed 6/03/04.

[46]Adapted from Linda Cecere, "Picking the Perfect Training Program," *Sales & Marketing Management* (July 1994): 38.

[47]Julia Chang, "Faker or Deal Maker?" *Sales & Marketing Management* 155 (December 2003): 28–33.

[48]Heide, *Dartnell's 30th Sales Force Compensation Survey.*

[49]Julia Chang, "The Premium Blend," *Sales & Marketing Management* 156 (April 2004): 19.

[50]Julia Chang, "What Worked," *Sales & Marketing Management* 155 (September 2003): 27.

[51]Olivia Thetgyi and Geoffrey Brewer, "The Games Salespeople Play," *Sales & Marketing Management* 152 (January 2002): 74.

[52]http://www.sales-training-management-institute. com/products/digital/simulator.htm. Accessed 6/3/2004.

[53]For guidelines for enhancing role playing, see "Skills," *Personal Selling Power* (January/February 1995): 54. Also see Thomas N. Ingram, "Guidelines for Maximizing Role-Play Activities," in *Proceedings*, National Conference in Sales Management, Dallas, TX, 1990.

[54]Julia Chang, "The Premium Blend" *Sales & Marketing Management* 156 (April 2004): 19; Julia

Chang, "No Instructor Required?" *Sales & Marketing Management* 155 (May 2003): 26.

[55]http://www.federatedinsurance.com/Employment/ training.html. Accessed 6/8/04.

[56]Galea and Wiens, "2002 Sales Training Survey."

[57]*Ibid.*

[58]http://www.raindance.com/rndc/services/services. jsp?it=header and http://www.webex.com/home/ services_trainingcenter.html. Accessed 6/8/04.

[59]Max Smetannikov, "Content Distribution Meets E-Learning," *Interactive Week* 8 (May 2001): 24.

[60]Powell, "Train Today, Sell Tomorrow."

[61]Erffmeyer and Johnson, "The Future of Sales Training."

[62]Carl L. Pritchard, "From Classroom to Chat Room," *Training & Development* 52 (June 1998): 76.

[63]http://www.remax.com/press/2002/07_30.html. Accessed 6/3/04.

[64]Sarah Lorge, "Top of the Charts—Frito-Lay," *Sales & Marketing Management* (July 1998): 38.

[65]http://www.sales-training-management-institute. com/products/digital/simulator.htm. Accessed 6/3/2004.

[66]"E-Train," *Sales & Marketing Management* 155 (October 2003): 26.

[67]Christine Galea and Carl Wiens, "2002 Sales Training Survey," *Sales & Marketing Management* 154 (July 2002): 34–37.

[68]Jon M. Hawes, Stephen P. Huthchens, and William F. Crittenden, "Evaluating Corporate Sales Training Programs," *Training and Development Journal* 36 (November 1982): 44.

[69]Melone and Summy, "Sales Training 101: Best Practices for Keeping Pace with Rapid Change in Selling."

[70]Charles Gottenkieny, "Proper Training Can Result in Positive ROI," *Selling* (August 2003): 9.

[71]Mark P. Leach and Anie H. Liu, "Investigating Interrelationships Among Sales Training Evaluation Methods," *Journal of Personal Selling & Sales Management* 23 (Fall 2003): 327–339.

[72]Robert C. Erffmeyer, K. Randall Russ, and Joseph F. Hair, Jr., "Needs Assessment and Evaluation in Sales-Training Programs," *Journal of Personal Selling & Sales Management* 11 (Winter 1991): 17–30.

[73]Julia Chang, "What Worked," *Sales & Marketing Management* 155 (July 2003): 29.

[74]Gail Johnson, "Forget Me Not," *Training* 41 (March 2004): 12.

[75]Alan J. Dubinsky, Marvin A. Jolson, Ronald E. Michaels, Masaaki Kotabe, and Chae Un Lim, "Ethical Perceptions of Field Sales Personnel: An Empirical Assessment," *Journal of Personal Selling & Sales Management* 12 (Fall 1992): 9; Karl A. Boedecker, Fred W. Morgan, and Jeffrey J. Stoltman, "Legal Dimensions of Salespersons' Statements: A Review and Managerial Suggestions," *Journal of Marketing* 55 (January 1991): 70.

[76]Adapted from Alan J. Dubinsky, Marvin A. Jolson, Ronald E. Michaels, Masaaki Kotabe, and Chae Un Lim, "Ethical Perceptions of Field Sales Personnel: An Empirical Assessment," *Journal of Personal Selling & Sales Management* 12 (Fall 1992): 9–21.

[77]Melone and Summy, "Sales Training 101: Best Practices for Keeping Pace with Rapid Change in Selling."

[78]Boedecker et al., "Legal Dimensions of Salespersons' Statements."

## Module 7

[1]The figure and discussion are adapted from Thomas N. Ingram, Raymond W. LaForge, William B. Locander, Scott B. MacKenzie, and Philip M. Podsakoff, "New Directions for Sales Leadership Research," *Journal of Personal Selling & Sales Management* (Spring 2005—forthcoming).

[2]Bernard M. Bass, *Leadership and Performance Beyond Expectations* (New York: Free Press, 1985).

[3]Philip M. Podsakoff, Scott B. MacKenzie, Robert H. Moorman, and Richard Fetter, "Transformational Leader Behaviors and Their Effects on Followers' Trust in Leader, Satisfaction, and Organizational Citizenship Behaviors," *Leadership Quarterly* (1990): 107–142.

[4]Daniel Goleman, "Leadership That Gets Results," *Harvard Business Review* (March–April 2000): 78–90; Daniel Goleman, Richard Boyatzis, and Annie McKee, *Primal Leadership: Realizing the Power of Emotional Intelligence* (Boston: Harvard Business School Press, 2002).

[5]Rosemary R. Lagace, "An Exploratory Study of Trust between Sales Managers and Salespersons," *Journal of Personal Selling & Sales Management* 11 (Spring 1991): 49; David Strutton, Lou E. Pelton, and James R. Lumpkin, "The Relationship between Psychological Climate and Salesperson–Sales Manager Trust in Sales Organizations," *Journal of Personal Selling & Sales Management* 13 (Fall 1993): 1; Karen E. Flaherty and James M. Pappas, "The Role of Trust in Salesperson–Sales Manager Relationships," *Journal of Personal Selling & Sales Management* 20 (Fall 2000): 271–278; Howard J. Klein and Jay S. Kim, "A Field Study of the Influence of Situational Constraints, Leader–Member Exchange, and Goal Commitment on Performance," *Academy of Management Journal* 41 (February 1998): 88.

[6]Susan K. Delvecchio, "The Quality of Salesperson–Manager Relationship: The Effect of Latitude, Loyalty and Competence," *Journal of Personal Selling & Sales Management* 18 (January 1998): 31–47.

[7]Based on John French, Jr. and Bertram Raven, "The Bases of Social Power," in *Studies in Social Power*, ed. D. Cartwright (Ann Arbor, MI: The University of Michigan Press, 1959).

[8]Paul Busch, "The Sales Manager's Bases of Social Power and Influence upon the Sales Force," *Journal of Marketing* 44 (Summer 1980): 95.

[9]*Ibid.*, 98.

[10]Prescott Tolk, "Supplying Success," *Sales & Marketing Management* 150 (April 1998): 22.

[11]From L.B. Gshwandtner "Personal PR Strategies for Creating Power and Influence" in *Personal Selling Power* (October 1990): 20. Reprinted with permission of Personal Selling Power Inc.

[12]Janet E. Keith, Donald W. Jackson, Jr., and Lawerence A. Crosby, "Effects of Alternative Types of Influence Strategies under Different Channel Dependence Structures," *Journal of Marketing* 54 (July 1990): 30.

[13]Donald W. Jackson, Jr., Stephen S. Tax, and John W. Barnes, "Examining the Salesforce Culture: Managerial Applications and Research Propositions," *Journal of Personal Selling & Sales Management* 14 (Fall 1994): 1.

[14]Michele Marchetti, "Shifting into Growth Mode," *Sales & Marketing Management* (March 2004): 12.

[15]Francis J. Yammarino and Alan J. Dubinsky, "Salesperson Performance and Managerially Controllable Factors: An Investigation of Individual and Work Group Effects," *Journal of Management* 16 (1990): 87.

[16]Michele Marchetti, "Master Motivators," *Sales & Marketing Management* 150 (April 1998): 38.

[17]Elana Harris, "Stars in the Making," *Sales & Marketing Management* 153 (March 2001): 58–61.

[18]Betsy Cummings, "From Good to Great," *Sales & Marketing Management* (December 2001): 53–54.

[19]William L. Cron and John W. Slocum, Jr., "Career Stages Approach to Managing the Sales Force," *Journal of Consumer Marketing* 3 (Fall 1986): 11.

[20]This discussion of influence strategies is largely based on Madeline E. Heilman and Harvey Hornstein, *Managing Human Forces in Organization* (Homewood, IL: Irwin, 1982): 116.

[21]Ajay K. Kohli, "Some Unexplored Supervisory Behaviors and Their Influence on Salespeople's Role Clarity, Specific Self-Esteem, Job Satisfaction, and Motivation," *Journal of Marketing Research* 22 (November 1985): 424.

[22]*Ibid.*, 118.

[23]L. B. Gschwandtner, "How to Influence with Integrity," *Personal Selling Power* (January–February 1990): 40.

[24]Harry Campbell, "Phone Efficiency," *Sales & Marketing Management* (May 2004): 16.

[25]Mark C. Johlke, Dale F. Duhan, Roy D. Howell, and Robert W. Wilkes, "An Integrated Model of Sales Managers' Communication Practices," *Journal of the Academy of Marketing Science* 28 (Spring 2000): 263–277.

[26]Gregory A. Rich, "The Constructs of Sales Coaching: Supervisory Feedback, Role Modeling and Trust," *Journal of Personal Selling & Sales Management* 18 (Winter 1998): 53.

[27]Saul W. Gellerman, "The Tests of a Good Salesperson," *Harvard Business Review* 68 (May–June 1990): 68.

[28]Gabrielle Birkner, "Wish List," *Sales & Marketing Management* 153 (September 2000): 64–70.

[29]Barton A. Weitz, Harish Sujan, and Mita Sujan, "Knowledge, Motivation, and Adaptive Behavior: A Framework for Improving Sales Effectiveness," *Journal of Marketing* 50 (October 1986): 183; Bernard J. Jaworski and Ajay K. Kohli, "Supervisory Feedback: Alternative Types and Their Impact on Salespeople's Performance Satisfaction," *Journal of Marketing Research* 28 (May 1991): 190–201.

[30]*Ibid.*

[31]Compiled from Barry J. Farber, "Sales Managers: Do Yourself a Favor," *Personal Selling Power* (April 1990): 33; "First Train Them, Then Coach Them," *Sales & Marketing Management* (August 1987): 64–65; Stuart R. Levine, "Performance Coaching," *Selling Power* (July/August 1996): 46; and Bill Cates, "A Coach for All Reasons," *Selling Power* (June 1996): 64–65.

[32]Rich, "The Constructs of Sales Coaching."

[33]Gregory A. Rich, "The Sales Manager as a Role Model: Effects on Trust, Job Satisfaction, and Performance of Salespeople," *Journal of the Academy of Marketing Science* 25 (Fall 1997): 319.

[34]Rich, "The Constructs of Sales Coaching."

[35]Elaine Evans, "How to Create Sales Meeting Magic," *Personal Selling Power* (September 1990): 34.

[36]Complied from Rayna Skolnik, "Salespeople Sound Off on Meetings," *Sales & Marketing Management* (November 1987): 108; and Hank Trisler, "Million Dollar Meetings," *Selling Power* (March 1996): 66–67.

[37]Mark McMaster, "Sales Meetings Your Reps Won't Hate," *Sales & Marketing Management* 153 (May 2001): 63–67.

[38]"Six Secrets to Holding a Good Meeting," furnished by 3M Visual Systems Division. Reproduced by permission of and copyrighted by Minnesota Mining and Mfg. Co.

[39]Mark Roberti, "Meet Me on the Web," *Fortune* 144 (Winter 2002): 37.

[40]Sir Adrian Cadbury, "Ethical Managers Make Their Own Rules," *Harvard Business Review* 65 (September–October 1987): 70.

[41]Archie B. Carroll, "In Search of the Moral Manager," *Business Horizons* 30 (March–April 1987): 12. Copyright 1987 by the Foundation for the School of Business at Indiana University. Reprinted by permission.

[42]Carroll, "In Search of the Moral Manager," 7.

[43]*Chemical Market Reporter* 260 (October 8, 2001): 2.

[44]Christopher Palmeri, "On the Defense at Pre-Paid Legal Services," *Business Week Online* (April 25, 2002): N.PAG.

[45]Erin Strout, "To Tell the Truth," *Sales & Marketing Management* 154 (July 2002): 40–47.

[46]"The Charge Sheet: So Far, So Few," *The Economist* 364 (September 14, 2002): 62; Strout, "To Tell the Truth."

[47]Strout, "To Tell the Truth."

[48]*Ibid.*

[49]Michele Marchetti, "Whatever It Takes," *Sales & Marketing Management* 149 (December 1997): 28.

[50]Excerpted from Sales and Marketing Executives International Certified Professional Salesperson Code of Ethics (Cleveland: Sales and Marketing Executives International, 1994). Reprinted by permission of SME International at 800-999-1414.

[51]Michael R. Hyman, Robert Skipper, and Richard Tansey, "Ethical Codes Are Not Enough," *Business Horizons* (March–April 1990): 15.

[52]Joseph A. Bellizzi and Robert E. Hite, "Supervising Unethical Salesforce Behavior," *Journal of Marketing* 53 (April 1989): 36.

[53]Adapted from James A. Waters and Frederick Bird, "Attending to Ethics in Management" from *Journal of Business Ethics* 8 (June 1989): 494. Reprinted with kind permission of Kluwer Academic Publishers and Frederick Bird, author of *Good Management: Business Ethics in Practice* and *The Muted Conscience: Moral Silence and the Practice of Ethics in Business.*

[54]James A. Waters and Frederick Bird, "Attending to Ethics in Management," *Journal of Business Ethics* 8 (June 1989): 493.

[55]Thomas R. Wotruba, "A Comprehensive Framework for the Analysis of Ethical Behavior, with a Focus on Sales Organizations," *Journal of Personal Selling & Sales Management* 10 (Spring 1990): 30.

[56]Michael Prince, "Battling Workplace Drug Use," *Business Insurance* 35 (January 29, 2001): 20.

[57]Judith Spain and Rosemary Ramsey, "Workers' Compensation and Respondeat Superior Liability Legal Cases Involving Salespersons' Misuse of Alcohol," *Journal of Personal Selling & Sales Management* 20 (Fall 2000): 263–269.

[58]Melinda Ligos, "Are Your Reps High?" *Sales & Marketing Management* 149 (October 1997): 80; Andy Cohen, "Getting Personal," *Sales & Marketing Management* (May 1996): 45.

[59]From "How to Manage the 7 Most Difficult (but Promising) Sales Personalities" by Donald J. Moine and Gerhard Gschwandtner in *Personal Selling Power*, 15th Anniversary Issue (1995): 71. Reprinted with permission of Personal Selling Power Inc.

[60]Thomas N. Ingram, Keun S. Lee, and George H. Lucas, Jr., "Commitment and Involvement: Assessing a Salesforce Typology," *Journal of Academy of Marketing Science* 19 (Summer 1991): 187.

[61]Leslie M. Fine, C. David Shepherd, and Susan L. Josephs, "Sexual Harassment in the Sales Force: The Customer Is Not Always Right," *Journal of Personal Selling & Sales Management* 16 (Fall 1994): 15.

[62]Michael Barrier, "Sexual Harassment," *Nation's Business* (December 1998): 14.

[63]Julia Lawlor, "Stepping Over the Line," *Sales & Marketing Management* (October 1995): 91.

[64]http://www.eeoc.gov/stats/harass.html, "Sexual Harassment Charges EEOC & FEPAs Combined: FY 1992–FY 2001." Accessed on 10/7/02.

[65]Barrier, "Sexual Harassment."

## Module 8

[1]From Christine Galea, "2004 Compensation Survey," *Sales & Marketing Management* 156 (May 2004): 28–34.

[2]Orville C. Walker, Jr., Gilbert A. Churchill, Jr., and Neil M. Ford, "Where Do We Go from Here? Selected Conceptual and Empirical Issues Concerning the Motivation and Performance of the Industrial Salesforce," in *Critical Issues in Sales Management: State-of-the-Art and Future Research Needs,* eds. Gerald Albaum and Gilbert A. Churchill, Jr. (Eugene, OR: Division of Research, College of Business Administration, University of Oregon, 1979): 25.

[3]Barton A. Weitz, Harish Sujan, and Mita Sujan, "Knowledge, Motivation, and Adaptive Behavior: A Framework for Improving Selling Effectiveness," *Journal of Marketing* 50 (October 1986): 180.

[4]See Thomas R. Wotruba, "The Effect of Goal-Setting on Performance of Independent Sales Agents in Direct Selling," *Journal of Personal Selling & Sales*

*Management* 9 (Spring 1989): 22; Jeffrey K. Sager and Mark W. Johnston, "Antecedents and Outcomes of Organizational Commitment: A Study of Salespeople," *Journal of Personal Selling & Sales Management* 9 (Spring 1989): 30.

[5]A study of salespeople that illustrates the interrelationship, yet distinctiveness, of intrinsic and extrinsic dimensions of motivation is Thomas N. Ingram, Keu S. Lee, and Steven J. Skinner, "Empirical Assessment of Salesperson Motivation, Commitment, and Job Outcomes," *Journal of Personal Selling & Sales Management* 9 (Fall 1989): 25.

[6]Galea, "The 2004 Compensation Survey."

[7]CyberAtlas staff, "Customer Satisfaction Playing Role in IT Compensation," *eCRM News* (February 4, 2002). Accessed at http://www.ecrmguide.com/news/article/0,3376,10382_967751,00.html on 11/7/02.

[8]Scott Widmier, "The Effects of Incentives and Personality on Salesperson's Customer Orientation," *Industrial Marketing Management* 31 (October 2002): 609–615.

[9]Jeanne Greenberg and Herbert Greenberg, *What It Takes to Succeed in Sales: Selecting and Retaining Top Producers* (Homewood, IL: Dow-Jones Irwin, 1990): 112.

[10]Compiled from two studies: Thomas N. Ingram and Danny N. Bellenger, "Personal and Organizational Variables: Their Relative Effect on Reward Valences of Industrial Salespeople," *Journal of Marketing Research* 20 (May 1983): 198–205; and Neil M. Ford, Gilbert A. Churchill, Jr., and Orville C. Walker, Jr., "Differences in the Attractiveness of Alternative Rewards Among Industrial Salespeople: Additional Evidence," *Journal of Business Research* 13 (April 1985): 123–138. Another study confirmed pay as salespeople's most preferred reward, but did not provide rankings of alternative rewards. This study is: Lawrence B. Chonko, John F. Tanner, and William A. Weeks, "Selling and Sales Management in Action: Reward Preferences of Salespeople," *Journal of Personal Selling & Sales Management* 12 (Summer 1992): 67–75.

[11]Judith A. Ross, "Japan: Does Money Motivate?" *Harvard Business Review* 75 (September–October 1997): 9.

[12]Christen P. Heide, *Dartnell's 30th Sales Force Compensation Survey* (Chicago: The Dartnell Corporation, 1999): 43; see also Bridget McCrea, "Hanging on to Good Sales Reps," *Industrial Distribution* 90 (June 2001): 73–75.

[13]Donald L. Caruth and Gail D. Handlogten-Caruth, "Finding Just the Right Formula," *American Salesman* 49 (June 2004): 6–15.

[14]Andy Cohen, "Battling the Competition's Falling Prices," *Sales & Marketing Management* 155 (March 2003): 12.

[15]http://www.accountprosoftware.com/salescommission.htm. Accessed 6/28/04.

[16]Ellen Neuborne, "Save Your Stars," *Sales & Marketing Management* 155 (March 2003): 36–39.

[17]Donald L. Caruth and Gail D. Handlogten-Caruth, "Compensating Sales Personnel," *American Salesman* 47 (April 2002): 6–15.

[18]*Ibid.*

[19]From "Salesforce Compensation Plans" by Amiya K. Basu, Rajiv Lal, V. Srinivasan and Richard Staelin in *Marketing Science* 4 (Fall 1985): 270. Reprinted by permission of INFORMS.

[20]Betsy Cummings and Erin Strout, "The Perfect Plan," *Sales & Marketing Management* 154 (February 2002): 53.

[21]Ram C. Rao, "Compensating Heterogeneous Salesforces: Some Explicit Solutions," *Marketing Science* 9 (Fall 1990): 319.

[22]See William L. Cron, Alan J. Dubinsky, and Ronald E. Michaels, "The Influence of Career Stages on Components of Salesperson Motivation," *Journal of Marketing* 52 (January 1988): 78; Gilbert A. Churchill, Jr., Neil M. Ford, and Orville C. Walker, Jr., "Personal Characteristics of Salespeople and the Attractiveness of Alternative Rewards," *Journal of Business Research* 7 (June 1979): 25; Ford, Churchill, and Walker, "Differences in the Attractiveness of Alternative Rewards among Industrial Salespeople: Additional Evidence"; Ingram and Bellenger, "Personal and Organizational Variables: Their Relative Effect on Reward Valences of Industrial Salespeople," 198.

[23]Jennifer Gilbert, "What Motivates Me," *Sales & Marketing Management* 155 (February 2003): 30–35.

[24]Heide, *Dartnell's 30th Sales Force Compensation Survey,* 121.

[25]*Ibid.*

[26]Gene Garofalo, *Sales Manager's Desk Book* (Englewood Cliffs, NJ: Prentice-Hall, 1989): 128.

[27]Concur Technologies www.concur.com/solutions/exp/default.htm. Accessed 6/28/04.

[28]Jay Boehmer, "Common T&E Expense Reporting Frauds," *Business Travel News* 20 (August 11, 2003): 68.

[29]"T&E Report," *Sales & Marketing Management* 155 (July 2003): 62.

[30]"Super Sales Manager's Source Book 2002," *Personal Selling Power* 21 (Special Edition 2002): 16.

[31]Andy Cohen, "Why Some Contests Are Losers," *Sales & Marketing Management* (August 1996): 39; Thayer C. Taylor, "Selling with Sales Contests," *Sales & Marketing Management* (June 1995): 35; Andy Cohen, "Motivating the Masses," *Sales & Marketing Management* (January 1996): 30; William H. Murphy and Peter A. Dacin, "Sales Contests: A Research Agenda," *Journal of Personal Selling & Sales Management* 18 (Winter 1998): 1; Melanie Berger, "When Their Ship Comes In: How to Create an Incentive Program That Motivates All of Your Salespeople and Sends More Happy Winners on That Coveted Trip," *Sales & Marketing Management* 149 (April 1997): 60; Ajay Kalra and Mengze Shi, "Designing Optimal Sales Contests: A Theoretical Perspective," *Marketing Science* 20 (Spring 2001): 170–193.

[32]Steve Donohue, "Sales Reps Go for Olympic Gold," *Multichannel News* (May 24, 2004): 22.

[33]SalesDriver, www.salesdriver.com/tour/catalog.asp. Accessed 6/30/04.

[34]William H. Murphy, Peter A. Dacin, and Neil M. Ford, "Sales Contest Effectiveness: An Examination of Sales Contest Design Preferences of Field Sales Forces," *Journal of the Academy of Marketing Science* 32 (Spring 2004): 127–143.

[35]"Super Sales Manager's Source Book 2002."

[36]Sridhar N. Ramaswami and Jagdip Singh, "Antecedents and Consequences of Merit Pay Fairness for Industrial Salespeople," *Journal of Marketing* 67 (October 2003): 46–66.

[37]Aaron Bernstein, "Women's Pay: Why the Gap Remains a Chasm," *Business Week* (June 14, 2004): 58–59.

[38]From a presentation by Ron Burke, Towers Perrin Consulting, at the New Horizons in Personal Selling and Sales Conference, July 14, 1996, Orlando, Florida.

[39]Betsy Cummings, Julia Chang, and Erin Strout, "All for One," *Sales & Marketing Management* 154 (August 2002): 53–54.

[40]"How to Reward Project Teams," *Harvard Management Update* 5 (July 2000): 6–7.

[41]From a presentation by Ron Burke, Towers Perrin Consulting, at the New Horizons in Personal Selling and Sales Conference, July 14, 1996, Orlando, Florida.

[42]Nancy Katz, "Getting the Most Out of Your Team," *Harvard Business Review* 79 (September 2001): 22.

[43]Michael Schrage, "A Lesson in Perversity," *Sales & Marketing Management* 156 (January 2004): 28.

[44]Julia Chang and Erin Strout, "Care Package," *Sales & Marketing Management* 154 (September 2002): 69.

[45]Sonke Albers, Manfred Krafft, and Wilhelm Bielert, "Global Salesforce Management: A Comparison of German and U.S. Practices," in *Emerging Trends in Sales Thought and Practice,* eds. Gerald J. Bauer, Mark S. Bauchalk, Thomas N. Ingram, and Raymond W. LaForge (Westport, CT: Quorum Books, 1998).

[46]John F. Tanner, Jr. and George Dudley, "International Differences—Examining Two Assumptions about Selling," reported in *Baylor Business Review* (Fall 2003): 44–45.

[47]Richard B. Peterson, Nancy K. Napier, and Won Sul-Shim, "Expatriate Management: A Comparison of MNCs Across Four Parent Countries," *Thunderbird International Business Review* 42 (March–April 2000): 145–166.

[48]Al Wright, "Don't Settle for Less: Global Compensation Programs Need Global Compensation Tools," *Employee Benefit Plan Review* 58 (March 2004): 14–18.

[49]Earl D. Honeycutt, Jr., and John B. Ford, "Guidelines for Managing an International Sales Force," *Industrial Marketing Management* (March 1995): 135.

[50]Michele Marchetti, "Paring Expatriate Pay," *Sales & Marketing Management* (January 1996): 28; Timothy Dwyer, "Trends in Global Compensation," *Compensation and Benefits Review* 31 (July/August 1999): 48–52.

[51]Charlene Marmer Solomon, "Global Compensation: Learn the ABCs," *Personnel Journal* (July 1995): 70.

[52]From "Global Gamble" by Michele Marchetti from *Sales & Marketing Management* 148 (July 1996): 64–69. Copyright © VNU Business Media Inc. Reprinted by permission.

[53]Ellen Neuborne, "A Compensation Plan Checkup," *Sales & Marketing Management* 155 (May 2003): 38–41.

[54]Michelle Gillan and Erin Strout, "E-Motivation," *Sales & Marketing Management* 155 (April 2003): 50.

[55]Adapted from Erin Strout, "What Would You Do?" *Sales & Marketing Management* 153 (March 2001): 78.

[56]This case is developed from information in "What Would You Do?" *Sales & Marketing Management* 150 (June 1998): 100–101.

## Module 9

[1]For a more complete discussion of this issue, see Orville C. Walker, Jr., Gilbert A. Churchill, Jr., and Neil M. Ford, "Where Do We Go from Here? Selected Conceptual and Empirical Issues Concerning the Motivation and Performance of the Industrial Salesforce," in *Critical Issues in Sales Management: State-of-the-Art and Future Research Needs*, eds.; Gerald Albaum and Gilbert A. Churchill, Jr. (Eugene, OR: University of Oregon, 1979). Also see David Cravens, Thomas Ingram, Raymond LaForge, and Clifford Young, "Behavior-Based and Outcome-Based Salesforce Control Systems," *Journal of Marketing* 57 (October 1993): 47; Arthur Baldauf, David W. Cravens, and Nigel F. Piercy, "Examining Business Strategy, Sales Management, and Salesperson Antecedents of Sales Organization Effectiveness," *Journal of Personal Selling & Sales Management* 21 (Spring 2001): 109–122; Ken Grant and David W. Cravens, "Examining the Antecedents of Sales Organization Effectiveness: An Australian Study," *European Journal of Marketing* 33 (Issue 9/10): 945–957; Nigel F. Piercy, David W. Cravens, and Neil A. Morgan, "Relationships Between Sales Management Control, Territory Design, Salesforce Performance and Sales Organization Effectiveness," *British Journal of Management* 10 (Issue 2): 95–111; Emin Babakus, David W. Cravens, Ken Grant, Thomas N. Ingram, and Raymond W. LaForge, "Investigating the Relationships Between Sales Management Control, Sales Territory Design, Salesperson Performance, and Sales Organization Effectiveness," *International Journal of Research in Marketing* 13 (Summer 1996): 345–363.

[2]Adapted from David W. Cravens, Thomas N. Ingram, Raymond W. LaForge, and Clifford E. Young, "Behavior-Based and Outcome-Based Salesforce Control Systems," *Journal of Marketing* 57 (October 1993): 47–59. Reprinted by permission of American Marketing Association.

[3]David W. Cravens, Thomas N. Ingram, Raymond W. LaForge, and Clifford E. Young, "Hallmarks of Effective Sales Organizations," *Marketing Management* 1 (March 1992): 56.

[4]Much of the discussion in this section comes from Alan J. Dubinsky and Richard W. Hansen, "The Sales Force Management Audit," *California Management Review* (Winter 1981): 86.

[5]From "The Sales Force Management Audit" by Alan J. Dubinsky and Richard W. Hansen. Copyright © 1981, by The Regents of the University of California. Reprinted from the *California Management Review*, Vol. 24, No. 2. By permission of The Regents.

[6]Meridian's, http://www.meridiansds.com/Case Studies/Testimonials.htm. Accessed 7/21/04.

[7]From Dubinsky and Hansen, "The Sales Force Management Audit."

[8]George Smith, Dorris Ritter, and William Tuggle, "Benchmarking: The Fundamental Question," *Marketing Management* 2 (1993): 43.

[9]Best Practices LLC Web site, http://www.best-in-class.com/site_tools/faq.htm. Accessed 6/17/04.

[10]Stanley Brown, "Don't Innovate—Imitate!" *Sales & Marketing Management* 147 (January 1995): 24.

[11]Adapted from George Smith, Dorris Ritter, and William Tuggle, "Benchmarking: The Fundamental Question" in *Marketing Management* (1993): 43–48. Reprinted by permission of American Marketing Association.

[12]C. Jackson Grayson, "Benchmarking," in *Marketing Encyclopedia*, ed. Jeffrey Heilbrunn (Chicago: American Marketing Association, 1995): 324.

[13]Paulette Kitchen, "Sales Quality," *Sales Manager's Bulletin* 1351 (April 1995): 3.

[14]"Benchmarking Made Easy: Benchmarking Websites," *The Public Manager: The New Bureaucrat* 27 (Summer 1998): 62.

[15]Grayson, "Benchmarking."

[16]"The 'What,' 'Why,' and 'How' of Benchmarking" by Gary Beasley and Joseph Cook from *Agency Sales Magazine* 25 (June 1995): 52–56. Copyright © 1995, Manufacturers' Agents National Association. P.O. Box 3467, Laguna Hills, CA 92654-3467. Phone (949) 859-4040; toll free: (877) 626-2776; fax: (949) 855-2973. E-mail: mana@manaonline.org; Website: http://www.manaonline.org. All rights reserved. Reproduction without permission is strictly prohibited.

[17]Michael Morris, Duane Davis, Jeffrey Allen, Ramon Avila, and Joseph Chapman, "Assessing the Relationships among Performance Measures, Managerial Practices, and Satisfaction When Evaluating the Salesforce: A Replication and Extension," *Journal of Personal Selling & Sales Management* 11 (Summer 1991): 25; Geoffrey Brewer, "Measuring Sales Effectiveness," *Sales & Marketing Management* 152 (October 2000): 136.

[18]From "Measuring Sales Effectiveness" by Geoffrey Brewer from *Sales & Marketing Management* 152 (October 2000): 136. Copyright © VNU Business Media Inc. Reprinted by permission.

[19]Web Survey, http://www.apogeeanalytics.com. Accessed 11/15/02; NetReflector, http://www.netreflector.com. Accessed 6/15/04.

[20]Nigel F. Piercy, "The Marketing Budgeting Process: Marketing Management Implications," *Journal of Marketing* (October 1987): 45.

[21]For a more complete presentation of this concept, see J. S. Schiff, "Evaluate the Sales Force as a Business," *Industrial Marketing Management* 12 (1983): 131.

[22]Thomas Stevenson, Frank Barnes, and Sharon Stevenson, "Activity-Based Costing: An Emerging Tool for Industrial Marketing Decision Makers," *Journal of Business and Industrial Marketing* 8 (1993): 40; William M. Baker, "Understanding Activity-Based Costing," *Industrial Management* 36 (March/April 1994): 28.

[23]Reprinted by permission of *Harvard Business Review*. From "Measure Costs Right: Make the Right Decisions" by Robin Cooper and Robert S. Kaplan, (September/October 1988): 96–103. Copyright © 1988 by the Harvard Business School Publishing Corporation, all rights reserved.

[24]Bridget McCrea, "A-B-C, Easy as 1-2-3," *Industrial Distribution* 92 (October 2003): H1–H4.

[25]Jagdish Sheth and Rajendra Sisodia, "Improving Marketing Productivity," in *Marketing Encyclopedia*, ed. Jeffrey Heilbrunn (Chicago: American Marketing Association, 1995): 217.

## Module 10

[1]Adapted from Jan P. Muczyk and Myron Gable, "Managing Sales Performance through a Comprehensive Performance Appraisal System," *Journal of Personal Selling & Sales Management* (May 1987): 41; Steven Thomas and Robert Bretz, "Research and Practice in Performance Appraisal: Evaluating Employee Performance in America's Largest Companies," *SAM Advanced Management Journal* (Spring 1994): 28. Harry Levinson, "Management by Whose Objectives," *Harvard Business Review* 81 (January 2003): 107–116.

[2]For more complete results, see Donald Jackson, Jr., John Schlacter, and William Wolfe, "Examining the Bases Utilized for Evaluating Salespeople's Performance," *Journal of Personal Selling & Sales Management* 15 (Fall 1995): 57; William Wolfe, John Schlacter, and Donald Jackson, Jr., "Examining How Sales Managers Evaluate Their Salespeople's Performance," *National Conference in Sales Management Proceedings*, ed. Timothy Longfellow, (Normal, IL: Illinois State University, 1995): 75; Michael H. Morris and Sean R. Aten, "Sales Force Performance Appraisal: Contemporary Issues and Practices," in *Progress in Marketing Thought*, eds. L. M. Capella, H. W. Nash, J. M. Starling, and R. D. Taylor (Mississippi State University, MS: Southern Marketing Association, 1990): 413; Michael H. Morris, Duane L. Davis, Jeffrey W. Allen, Ramon A. Avila, and Joseph Chapman, "Assessing the Relationships between Performance Measures, Managerial Practices, and Satisfaction when Evaluating the Salesforce," *Journal of Personal Selling & Sales Management* (Summer 1991).

[3]Betsy Cummings and Erin Strout, "Tell It Like It Is," *Sales & Marketing Management* 153 (August 2001): 59–60.

[4]Robert Hoffman, "Ten Reasons You Should Be Using 360-Degree Feedback," *HR Magazine* 40 (April 1995): 82; Dana Ray, "See the Big Picture," *Personal Selling Power* (October 1995): 3.

[5]Andie Evans, "From Every Angle," *Training* 38 (September 2001): 22.

[6]Clive Fletcher, "Circular Argument," *People Management* 4 (October 1998): 46.

[7]Fernando Jaramillo, Francois A. Carrillat, and William B. Locander, "Starting to Solve the Method Puzzle in Salesperson Self-Report Evaluations," *Journal of Personal Selling & Sales Management* 23 (Fall 2003): 369–377.

[8]Robert W. Eichinger and Michael M. Lombardo, "Knowledge Summary Series: 360-Degree Assessment," *Human Resource Planning* 26 (2003): 34–44.

[9]Adapted from Allan Church, "First-Rate Multirater Feedback," *Training & Development* 49 (August 1995): 42–43; and Scott Wimer and Kenneth M. Nowack, "13 Common Mistakes Using 360-Degree Feedback," *Training & Development* 52 (May 1998): 69–78; Bret J. Becton and Mike Schraeder, "Participant Input into Rater Selection: Potential Effects on the Quality and Acceptance of Ratings in the Context of 360-Degree Feedback," *Public Personnel Management* 33 (Spring 2004): 23–32.

[10]David W. Bracken, Lynn Summers, and John Fleenor, "High-Tech 360," *T & D* 52 (August 1998): 42.

[11]Information obtained from http://www.survey-tracker.com and http://www.cognology.biz. Accessed 7/12/04.

[12]Helen Rheem, "Performance Management: A Progress Report," *Harvard Business Review* (March–April 1995): 11.

[13]William Fitzgerald, "Forget the Form in Performance Appraisals," *HR Magazine* 40 (December 1995): 134.

[14]Rheem, "Performance Management."

[15]David Cravens, Raymond LaForge, Gregory Pickett, and Clifford Young, "Incorporating a Quality Improvement Perspective into Measures of Salesperson Performance," *Journal of Personal Selling & Sales Management* 13 (Winter 1993): 1.

[16]Thomas R. Wotruba, "The Transformation of Industrial Selling: Causes and Consequences," *Industrial Marketing Management* 25 (September 1996): 327.

[17]Khalid A. Aldakhilallah and Diane H. Parente, "Redesigning a Square Peg: Total Quality Management Performance Appraisals," *Total Quality Management* 13 (2002): 39–51. For further discussion on TQM and the salesforce, see Stephen B. Knouse and David Strutton, "Molding a Total Quality Salesforce Through Managing Empowerment, Evaluation, and Reward and Recognition Processes," *Journal of Marketing Theory & Practice* 4 (Summer 1996): 24–35.

[18]Adapted from Erin Anderson and Richard L. Oliver, "Perspectives on Behavior-based versus Outcome-based Salesforce Control Systems," *Journal of Marketing* 51 (October 1987): 86, published by the American Marketing Association.

[19]For a more complete discussion and theoretical rationale for these perspectives, see Erin Anderson and Richard L. Oliver, "Perspectives on Behavior-based versus Outcome-based Salesforce Control Systems," *Journal of Marketing* 51 (October 1987): 76.

[20]David Cravens, Thomas Ingram, Raymond LaForge, and Clifford Young, "Behavior-based and Outcome-based Salesforce Control Systems," *Journal of Marketing* 57 (October 1993): 47–59; and Richard Oliver and Erin Anderson, "An Empirical Test of the Consequences of Behavior- and Outcome-based Sales Control Systems," *Journal of Marketing* 58 (October 1994): 53–67.

[21]Arthur Baldauf, David W. Cravens, and Kegn Grant, "Consequences of Sales Management Control in Field Sales Organizations: A Cross-National Perspective," *International Business Review* 11 (October 2002): 577–609.

[22]Richard Oliver and Erin Anderson, "Behavior- and Outcome-based Sales Control Systems: Evidence and Consequences of Pure-Form and Hybrid Governance," *Journal of Personal Selling & Sales Management* 15 (Fall 1995): 1.

[23]Manfred Krafft, "An Empirical Investigation of the Antecedents of Sales Force Control Systems," *Journal of Marketing* 63 (July 1999): 120–134.

[24]Sanjeev Agarwal, "Impact of Job Formalization and Administrative Controls on Attitudes of Industrial Salespersons," *Industrial Marketing Management* 28 (July 1999): 359–368.

[25]David W. Cravens, Greg W. Marshall, Felicia G. Lassk, and George S. Low, "The Control Factor," *Marketing Management* 13 (January/February 2004): 39–44.

[26]Charles E. Pettijohn, Linda S. Pettijohn, and Albert J. Taylor, "An Exploratory Analysis of Salesperson Perceptions of the Criteria Used in Performance Appraisals, Job Satisfaction, and Organizational Commitment," *Journal of Personal Selling & Sales Management* 20 (Spring 2000): 77–80.

[27]Donald Jackson, Jr., John Schlacter, and William Wolfe, "Examining the Bases Utilized for Evaluating Salespeople's Performance," *Journal of Personal Selling & Sales Management* 15 (Fall 1995): 57–65.

[28]Gary Summy, "Sales Training 101: Best Practices for Keeping Pace with Rapid Change in Selling," presentation at the National Conference in Sales Management, April 5, 2002. Part of salespeople's compensation at IBM is based on customer satisfaction.

[29]Arun Sharma and Dan Sarel, "The Impact of Customer Satisfaction–Based Incentive Systems on Salespeople's Customer Service Response: An Empirical Study," *Journal of Personal Selling & Sales Management* 15 (Summer 1995): 17; Bulent Menguc and A. Tansu Barker, "The Performance Effects of Outcome-Based Incentive Pay Plans on Sales Organizations: A Contextual Analysis," *Journal of Personal Selling & Sales Management* 23 (Fall 2003): 341–358.

[30]Douglas M. Lambert, Arun Sharma, and Michael Levy, "What Information Can Relationship Marketers Obtain from Customer Evaluation of Salespeople?" *Industrial Marketing Management* 26 (March 1997): 177.

[31]John Hill and Arthur Allaway, "How U.S.-based Companies Manage Sales in Foreign Countries," *Industrial Marketing Management* 22 (1993): 7.

[32]Dominique Rouzies and Anne Macquin, "An Exploratory Investigation of the Impact of Culture on Sales Force Management Control Systems in Europe," *Journal of Personal Selling & Sales Management* 23 (Winter 2003): 61–72.

[33]Jackson, Schlacter, and Wolfe, "Examining the Bases Utilized for Evaluating Salespeople's Performance."

[34]*Ibid.*

[35]Goutam Challagalla and Tasaduq Shervani, "Dimensions and Types of Supervisory Control: Effects of Salesperson Performance and Satisfaction," *Journal of Marketing* 60 (January 1996): 89.

[36]For a review and more complete discussion of this approach, see Adrian B. Ryans and Charles B. Weinberg, "Territory Sales Response," *Journal of Marketing Research* (November 1979): 453; Adrian B. Ryans and Charles B. Weinberg, "Territory Sales Response Models: Stability Over Time," *Journal of Marketing Research* (May 1987): 229.

[37]From "A Market Response Model for Sales Management Decision Making" by Raymond LaForge and David Cravens. Copyright © 1981 by Pi Sigma Epsilon. From *Journal of Personal Selling & Sales Management* (Fall/Winter 1981–82): 14. Reprinted with permission of M. E. Sharpe, Inc.

[38]Adapted from Adrian B. Ryans and Charles B. Weinberg, "Territory Sales Response Models: Stability Over Time," *Journal of Marketing Research* (May 1987): 231, published by the American Marketing Association.

[39]From "Selling and Sales Management in Action" by David J. Good and Robert W. Stone. Copyright © 1991 by Pi Sigma Epsilon. From *Journal of Personal Selling & Sales Management,* vol. 11, no. 3 (Summer 1991): 57–60. Reprinted with permission of M. E. Sharpe, Inc.

[40]For specific examples of regression analysis used to establish territory sales quotas, see David W. Cravens, Robert B. Woodruff, and James C. Stamper, "An Analytical Approach for Evaluating Sales Territory Performance," *Journal of Marketing* (January 1972): 31; David W. Cravens and Robert B. Woodruff, "An Approach for Determining Criteria of Sales Performance," *Journal of Applied Psychology* (June 1973): 240.

[41]Erin Strout, "Is Your Pay Plan on Target?" *Sales & Marketing Management* 154 (January 2002): 18.

[42]Jhinuk Chowdhury, "The Motivational Impact of Sales Quotas on Effort," *Journal of Marketing Research* 30 (February 1993): 28.

[43]Charles H. Schwepker, Jr. and David J. Good, "Understanding Sales Quotas: An Exploratory Investigation of Consequences of Failure," *Journal of Business & Industrial Marketing* 19 (2004): 39–48.

[44]http://www.synygy.com/news/press_release.asp?doc_id=6. Accessed 7/12/04.

[45]David J. Good and Charles H. Schwepker, Jr., "Sales Quotas: Critical Interpretations and Implications," *Review of Business* 22 (Spring 2001): 32–36.

[46]*Ibid.*

[47]Jackson, Schlacter, and Wolfe, "Examining the Bases Utilized for Evaluating Salespeople's Performance."

[48]See Mark R. Edwards, W. Theodore Cummings, and John L. Schlacter, "The Paris-Peoria Solution: Innovations in Appraising Regional and International Sales Personnel," *Journal of Personal Selling & Sales Management* (November 1984): 27.

[49]Adapted from Mark R. Edwards, W. Theodore Cummings, and John L. Schlacter, "The Paris-Peoria Solution: Innovations in Appraising Regional and International Sales Personnel," *Journal of Personal Selling & Sales Management* (November 1984): 29. Used with permission.

[50]Eastman Chemical Company, "Checking Customer Value Through Continual Improvement" survey.

[51]For a comprehensive scale for evaluating salesperson performance, see Douglas N. Behrman and William D. Perreault, Jr., "Measuring the Performance of Industrial Salespersons," *Journal of Business Research* 10 (1982): 355.

[52]Jim Meade, "Automated Performance Appraisal," *HR Magazine* 43 (October 1998): 42.

[53]Mark McMaster and Andy Cohen, "Should You Rank Your Salespeople?" *Sales & Marketing Management* 153 (August 2001): 13.

[54]Jan P. Muczyk and Myron Gable, "Managing Sales Performance Through a Comprehensive Performance Appraisal System," *Journal of Personal Selling & Sales Management* (May 1987): 46. Used with permission.

[55]McMaster and Cohen, "Should You Rank Your Salespeople?"

[56]Edwards, Cummings, and Schlacter, "The Paris-Peoria Solution," 30.

[57]Adapted from Mark R. Edwards, W. Theodore Cummings, and John L. Schlacter, "The Paris-Peoria Solution: Innovations in Appraising Regional and International Sales Personnel," *Journal of Personal Selling & Sales Management* (November 1984): 31. Used with permission.

[58]For a more complete discussion of this process, see A. Benton Cocanougher and John M. Ivancevich, "BARS' Performance Rating for Sales Force Personnel," *Journal of Marketing* (July 1978): 87.

[59]A. Benton Cocanougher and John M. Ivancevich, "BARS' Performance Rating for Sales Force Personnel," reprinted from *Journal of Marketing* 42 (July 1978): 91, published by the American Marketing Association.

[60]Bernard Jaworski and Ajay Kohli, "Supervisory Feedback: Alternative Types and Their Impact on Salespeople's Performance and Satisfaction," *Journal of Marketing Research* 28 (May 1991): 190.

[61]Cathy Owens Swift and Constance Campbell, "The Effect of Vertical Exchange Relationships on the Performance Attributions and Subsequent Actions of Sales Managers," *Journal of Personal Selling & Sales Management* 15 (Fall 1995): 45.

[62]Thomas E. DeCarlo and Thomas W. Leigh, "Impact of Salesperson Attraction on Sales Managers' Attributions and Feedback," *Journal of Marketing* 60 (April 1996): 47.

[63]Greg Marshall, John Mowen, and Keith Fabes, "The Impact of Territory Difficulty and Self versus Other Ratings on Managerial Evaluations of Sales Personnel," *Journal of Personal Selling & Sales Management* 12 (Fall 1992): 35.

[64]"Study Shows Appraisals Favor Male Workers," *HR Briefing* (July 1, 2002): 7.

[65]Greg Marshall and John Mowen, "An Experimental Investigation of the Outcome Bias in Salesperson Performance Evaluations," *Journal of Personal Selling & Sales Management* 13 (Summer 1993): 31.

[66]Peter Allan, "Designing and Implementing and Effective Employee Appraisal System," *Review of Business* 16 (Winter 1994): 3.

[67]Robert Trent and Robert Monczka, "Guidelines for Developing Team Performance Appraisal Systems," *NAPM Insights* (July 1994): 30.

[68]Michael Campion and A. Catherine Higgs, "Design Work Teams to Increase Productivity and Satisfaction," *HR Magazine* 40 (October 1995): 101.

[69]Jack Zigon, "Team Performance Measurement," *Journal for Quality & Participation* 21 (May/June 1998): 48–54.

[70]Trent and Monczka, "Guidelines for Developing Team Performance Appraisal Systems."

[71]*Profile Booklet, Teamwork Effectiveness/Attitude Measurement (TEAM)* (New York: Education Research, 1994). Reprinted with permission from Education Research, NY: Tel: 212-661-9280. Fax: 212-953-5899.

[72]*Ibid.*

[73]Taken from Jack Zigon, "Team Performance Measurement," *Compensation and Benefits Review* 29 (January/February 1997): 38–47.

[74]Betsy Wiesendanger, "Making (and Staying on) the Team," *Selling* (April 1996): 46.

[75]Adapted from Peter Allan, "Designing and Implementing and Effective Employee Appraisal System," *Review of Business* 16 (Winter 1994): 3–8; and Minda Zelin, "How to Avoid Lawsuits," *Sales & Marketing Management* (December 1994): 86.

[76]For examples of these studies, see A. Parasuraman and Charles M. Futrell, "Demographics, Job Satisfaction, and Propensity to Leave of Industrial Salesmen," *Journal of Business Research* 11 (1983): 33; Charles M. Futrell and A. Parasuraman, "The Relationship of Satisfaction and Performance to Salesforce Turnover," *Journal of Marketing* (Fall 1984): 33; Steven Brown and Robert Peterson, "Antecedents and Consequences of Salesperson Job Satisfaction: Meta-Analysis and Assessment of Causal Effects," *Journal of Marketing Research* 30 (February 1993): 63; Emin Babakus, David W. Cravens, Mark Johnston, and William C. Moncrief, "Examining the Role of Organizational Variables in the Salesperson Job Satisfaction Model," *Journal of Personal Selling & Sales Management* 16 (Summer 1996): 33; Earl Naumann, Scott M. Widmeier, and Donald W. Jackson, Jr., "Examining the Relationship Between Work Attitude and Propensity to Leave Among Expatriate Salespeople," *Journal of Personal Selling & Sales Management* 20 (Fall 2002): 227–242.

[77]For examples of this research, see Richard P. Bagozzi, "Performance and Satisfaction in an Industrial Sales Force: An Examination of Their Antecedents and Simultaneity," *Journal of Marketing* (Spring 1980): 65; Douglas N. Behrman and William D. Perreault, Jr., "A Role Stress Model of the Performance and Satisfaction of Industrial Salespersons," *Journal of Marketing* (Fall 1984): 9; Steven Brown and Robert Peterson, "The Effect of Effort on Sales Performance and Job Satisfaction," *Journal of Marketing* 58 (April 1994): 70.

[78]Christian Homburg and Ruth M. Stock, "The Link Between Salespeople's Job Satisfaction and Customer Satisfaction in a Business-to-Business Context: A Dyadic Analysis," *Journal of the Academy of Marketing Science* 32 (Spring 2004): 144–158.

[79]For a complete discussion of the scale, see Gilbert A. Churchill, Jr., Neil M. Ford, and Orville C. Walker, Jr., "Measuring the Job Satisfaction of Industrial Salesmen," *Journal of Marketing Research* (August 1974): 254. For validation support, see Charles M. Futrell, "Measurement of Salespeople's Job Satisfaction: Convergent and Discriminant Validity of Corresponding INDSALES and Job Descriptive Index Scales," *Journal of Marketing Research* (November 1979): 594; Rosemary Lagace, Jerry Goolsby, and Jule Gassenheimer, "Scaling and Measurement: A Quasi-Replicative Assessment of a

Revised Version of INDSALES," *Journal of Personal Selling & Sales Management* 13 (Winter 1993): 65. See also Sarath A. Nonis and S. Altan Erdem, "A Refinement of INDSALES to Measure Job Satisfaction of Sales Personnel in General Marketing Settings," *Journal of Marketing Management* 7 (Spring/Summer 1997): 34.

[80]James M. Comer, Karen A. Machleit, and Rosemary R. Lagace, "Psychometric Assessment of a Reduced Version of INDSALES," *Journal of Business Research* 18 (1989): 295–296. Reprinted by permission of Elsevier Science.

[81]Futrell and Parasuraman, "The Relationship of Satisfaction and Performance to Salesforce Turnover."

[82]Jaworski and Kohli, "Supervisory Feedback."

[83]Jeffrey K. Sager, Junsuab Yi, and Charles M. Futrell, "A Model Depicting Salespeople's Perceptions," *Journal of Personal Selling & Sales Management* 18 (Summer 1998): 1; Gregory A. Rich, "The Sales Manager as a Role Model: Effects on Trust, Job Satisfaction, and Performance of Salespeople," *Journal of the Academy of Marketing Science* 25 (Fall 1997): 319; Melissa Campanelli, "What Price Sales Force Satisfaction," *Sales & Marketing Management* (July 1994): 37; Mary E. Shoemaker, "Leadership Practices in Sales Managers Associated with the Self-Efficacy, Role Clarity, and Job Satisfaction of Individual Industrial Salespeople," *Journal of Personal Selling & Sales Management* 19 (Fall 1999): 1–20

[84]Melissa Campanelli, "What Price Sales Force Satisfaction."

## Cases

### Smith & Nephew—Innovex

[1]Allevyn®, Opsite®, and Intrasite® Gel are registered trademarks of T. S. Smith & Nephew Ltd. Innovex™ and Quintiles™ are registered trademarks of Quintiles Transnational Corporation.

[2]Also known as health centres, basic health areas, or, previously, outpatient clinics. They delivered primary care services to the population covered by Spanish Social Security. There were some 3,000 primary care centres in the country as a whole, each tied to a referral hospital. A hospital and the group of primary care centres tied to it made up what was known as a health management area.

[3]Only products classed as "medical accessories" (under Royal Decree Legislative 9/1996 of January 15, which regulates the selection of medical accessories, their financing from Social Security funds or government funds earmarked for healthcare, and the basis on which they may be supplied and dispensed to outpatients) could apply for reimbursement.

[4]Chronic ulcers are ulcers of unpredictable duration. The healing process can easily go on for several months. The most common causes of chronic ulcers are continuous pressure on a particular part of the body (e.g., bedsores) or vascular or circulatory problems. A chronic ulcer can be shallow or deep, and in serious cases can lead to necrosis, gangrene, and may even require amputation of the affected part.

[5]Throughout the case, unless stated otherwise, the market shares of specific products refer to the pharmacies channel, which was monitored by IMS, a market research services company. Market share data for hospitals were difficult to estimate, as they depended on the outcome of the bidding process.

[6]In 1999, S&N had bid in almost 500 auctions.

[7]Galicia has an area of 29,575 km² and is almost square in shape. In 1998 its population was approximately 2,716,000. Asturias is elongated and narrow in shape, with an area of 10,604 km² (approx. $260 \times 50$ km), and in 1998 had 1,060,000 inhabitants.

[8]The company IMS conducted a panel study of pharmaceutical retailers. Usually, it only provided aggregate data for the whole of Spain. The territorial sales analysis *(análisis territorial de ventas, ATV)* was a special service that IMS provided, offering the same data broken down by geographical areas similar in size to postal districts.

[9]606,000 pesetas in October; 1,042,000 in November; 1,779,000 in December 1999; and 1,706,000 in January 2000.

[10]134,000 pesetas in October; 252,000 in November; 528,000 in December 1999; and 570,000 in January 2000.

### Dairyland Seed Company

[1]Estimation by Dairyland executives, based on reports of the American Seed Trade Association. Assuming the development of high-yielding varieties of soybean. Seeds out of the bag (does not include bin seed).

[2]Monsanto press releases are available online at http://www.monsanto.com/monsanto/media.

[3]Dairyland.

### Adams Brands

[1]Company records and industry data.

### Modern Plastics

[1]This information was developed from a field survey conducted by Modern Plastics.

[2]Developed from several trade journals.

## Dura-plast, Inc. (A): Global Account Management

[1]The unit of currency is the Norwegian krone, which is abbreviated NOK. NOK 1 = 100 ore. Note that all figures are in U.S. dollars unless otherwise noted. The assumed exchange rate is 7.00 NOK to $1 U.S.

[2]Agents are generally businesses that contract with original equipment manufacturers to sell their products for a given period of time. Agents take ownership of the products and usually have protected territories.

[3]Manufacturing Representatives have been employed by many original equipment manufacturers because of their knowledge and ties within a particular industry. Manufacturer's Representatives represent multiple, noncompeting manufacturers, and are generally granted exclusive territories. They represent the supplier, but are not usually involved in distribution or installation. MRs do not take possession or ownership of equipment—they only operate as agents on behalf of (usually) multiple principals (i.e., manufacturers).

Bold indicates key terms.